T0181550

Lecture Notes in Computer Science

Lecture Notes in Artificial Intelligence   14267

Founding Editor

Jörg Siekmann

Series Editors

Randy Goebel, *University of Alberta, Edmonton, Canada*
Wolfgang Wahlster, *DFKI, Berlin, Germany*
Zhi-Hua Zhou, *Nanjing University, Nanjing, China*

The series Lecture Notes in Artificial Intelligence (LNAI) was established in 1988 as a topical subseries of LNCS devoted to artificial intelligence.

The series publishes state-of-the-art research results at a high level. As with the LNCS mother series, the mission of the series is to serve the international R & D community by providing an invaluable service, mainly focused on the publication of conference and workshop proceedings and postproceedings.

Huayong Yang · Honghai Liu · Jun Zou ·
Zhouping Yin · Lianqing Liu · Geng Yang ·
Xiaoping Ouyang · Zhiyong Wang
Editors

Intelligent Robotics and Applications

16th International Conference, ICIRA 2023
Hangzhou, China, July 5–7, 2023
Proceedings, Part I

 Springer

Editors
Huayong Yang
Zhejiang University
Hangzhou, China

Jun Zou 🄳
Zhejiang University
Hangzhou, China

Lianqing Liu 🄳
Shenyang Institute of Automation
Shenyang, Liaoning, China

Xiaoping Ouyang 🄳
Zhejiang University
Hangzhou, China

Honghai Liu 🄳
Harbin Institute of Technology
Shenzhen, China

Zhouping Yin
Huazhong University of Science
and Technology
Wuhan, China

Geng Yang 🄳
Zhejiang University
Hangzhou, China

Zhiyong Wang
Harbin Institute of Technology
Shenzhen, China

ISSN 0302-9743   ISSN 1611-3349 (electronic)
Lecture Notes in Artificial Intelligence
ISBN 978-981-99-6482-6   ISBN 978-981-99-6483-3 (eBook)
https://doi.org/10.1007/978-981-99-6483-3

LNCS Sublibrary: SL7 – Artificial Intelligence

Preface

With the theme "Smart Robotics for Sustainable Society", the 16th International Conference on Intelligent Robotics and Applications (ICIRA 2023) was held in Hangzhou, China, July 5–7, 2023, and designed to encourage advancement in the field of robotics, automation, mechatronics, and applications. It aimed to promote top-level research and globalize quality research in general, making discussions and presentations more internationally competitive and focusing on the latest outstanding achievements, future trends, and demands.

ICIRA 2023 was organized and hosted by Zhejiang University, co-hosted by Harbin Institute of Technology, Huazhong University of Science and Technology, Chinese Academy of Sciences, and Shanghai Jiao Tong University, co-organized by State Key Laboratory of Fluid Power and Mechatronic Systems, State Key Laboratory of Robotics and System, State Key Laboratory of Digital Manufacturing Equipment and Technology, State Key Laboratory of Mechanical System and Vibration, State Key Laboratory of Robotics, and School of Mechanical Engineering of Zhejiang University. Also, ICIRA 2023 was technically co-sponsored by Springer. On this occasion, ICIRA 2023 was a successful event after the COVID-19 pandemic. It attracted more than 630 submissions, and the Program Committee undertook a rigorous review process for selecting the most deserving research for publication. The Advisory Committee gave advice for the conference program. Also, they help to organize special sections for ICIRA 2023. Finally, a total of 431 papers were selected for publication in 9 volumes of Springer's Lecture Note in Artificial Intelligence. For the review process, single-blind peer review was used. Each review took around 2–3 weeks, and each submission received at least 2 reviews and 1 meta-review.

In ICIRA 2023, 12 distinguished plenary speakers delivered their outstanding research works in various fields of robotics. Participants gave a total of 214 oral presentations and 197 poster presentations, enjoying this excellent opportunity to share their latest research findings. Here, we would like to express our sincere appreciation to all the authors, participants, and distinguished plenary and keynote speakers. Special thanks are also extended to all members of the Organizing Committee, all reviewers for peer-review, all staffs of the conference affairs group, and all volunteers for their diligent work.

July 2023

Huayong Yang
Honghai Liu
Jun Zou
Zhouping Yin
Lianqing Liu
Geng Yang
Xiaoping Ouyang
Zhiyong Wang

Organization

Conference Chair

Huayong Yang   Zhejiang University, China

Honorary Chairs

Youlun Xiong   Huazhong University of Science and Technology, China

Han Ding   Huazhong University of Science and Technology, China

General Chairs

Honghai Liu   Harbin Institute of Technology, China
Jun Zou   Zhejiang University, China
Zhouping Yin   Huazhong University of Science and Technology, China
Lianqing Liu   Chinese Academy of Sciences, China

Program Chairs

Geng Yang   Zhejiang University, China
Li Jiang   Harbin Institute of Technology, China
Guoying Gu   Shanghai Jiao Tong University, China
Xinyu Wu   Chinese Academy of Sciences, China

Award Committee Chair

Yong Lei   Zhejiang University, China

Publication Chairs

Xiaoping Ouyang   Zhejiang University, China
Zhiyong Wang   Harbin Institute of Technology, China

Regional Chairs

Zhiyong Chen   University of Newcastle, Australia
Naoyuki Kubota   Tokyo Metropolitan University, Japan
Zhaojie Ju   University of Portsmouth, UK
Eric Perreault   Northeastern University, USA
Peter Xu   University of Auckland, New Zealand
Simon Yang   University of Guelph, Canada
Houxiang Zhang   Norwegian University of Science and Technology,
                           Norway
Duanling Li   Beijing University of Posts and
                           Telecommunications, China

Advisory Committee

Jorge Angeles   McGill University, Canada
Tamio Arai   University of Tokyo, Japan
Hegao Cai   Harbin Institute of Technology, China
Tianyou Chai   Northeastern University, China
Jiansheng Dai   King's College London, UK
Zongquan Deng   Harbin Institute of Technology, China
Han Ding   Huazhong University of Science and Technology,
                           China
Xilun Ding   Beihang University, China
Baoyan Duan   Xidian University, China
Xisheng Feng   Shenyang Institute of Automation, Chinese
                           Academy of Sciences, China
Toshio Fukuda   Nagoya University, Japan
Jianda Han   Nankai University, China
Qiang Huang   Beijing Institute of Technology, China
Oussama Khatib   Stanford University, USA
Yinan Lai   National Natural Science Foundation of China,
                           China
Jangmyung Lee   Pusan National University, Korea
Zhongqin Lin   Shanghai Jiao Tong University, China

Contents – Part I

Multimodal Collaborative Perception and Fusion

Vision-Based Human Robot Interaction and Application

Human-Centric Technologies for Seamless Human-Robot Collaboration

A Method for Identifying Knee Joint Stiffness During Human Standing

Gong Cheng[1,2], Yanjiang Huang[1,2], and Xianmin Zhang[1,2(✉)]

[1] School of Mechanical and Automotive Engineering, South China University of Technology, Guangzhou 510640, China
zhangxm@scut.edu.cn
[2] Guangdong Provincial Key Laboratory of Precision Equipment and Manufacturing Technology, South China University of Technology, Guangzhou 510640, China

Abstract. During human-robot interaction, the robot should react according to the change in the human body state. The stiffness is one of the important information. It is closely related to the stability and comfort in human movement. At present, the auxiliary equipment for standing does not consider the change of human joint stiffness. Therefore, this paper proposes a method that can identify the stiffness of the knee joint during human standing. Firstly, the human body structure is simplified to a three-section inverted pendulum model. The kinetic analysis is performed using Lagrange's equation. Then the expression of joint stiffness is solved by joint torque. The angles and angular velocities of the joints of the lower limbs of the human body during standing are measured experimentally. The errors in the measurements are modified by geometric relationships. The stiffness of the human body during standing is derived by substituting them into the derived expressions. The result shows that the method can identify the stiffness of the human knee joint during standing.

Keywords: Standing · Joint stiffness · Three-stage inverted pendulum model · Lagrange's equation

1 Introduction

Standing movement is the key movement of daily activities. However, it's a very difficult task for elderly people with skeletal muscle degeneration and patients with diseases such as stroke and spinal cord injury [1]. The knee joint is the most stressed joint during standing activities [2]. It is also the main joint being assisted [3]. Many researchers have investigated devices to help people with lower limb impairment to stand [2, 4–7]. However, during human-robot interaction, the relevant devices only consider the trajectory and joint torque of the standing process [8, 9], without taking into account the stiffness changes of human joints.

Stiffness is closely related to stability and comfort in human movement [10]. Several authors have identified lower limb joint stiffness by external perturbations combined with statistical system identification, static loading tests and biomechanical models [11–14]. The effect of stiffness on knee motion has also been investigated [15].

H. Yang et al. (Eds.): ICIRA 2023, LNAI 14267, pp. 3–9, 2023.
https://doi.org/10.1007/978-981-99-6483-3_1

The structure of this paper is as follows. Section 2 presents the derivation of the knee joint stiffness. Section 3 shows the discussion of experimental and stiffness results. Section 4 shows the conclusion and future work.

2   Problem Formulation

Generally, the joint stiffness K is obtained from the measurement of the torque τ. The relationship between K and τ can be written as:

$$K = \frac{\partial \tau}{\partial \theta} \tag{1}$$

Therefore, the stiffness can be solved by analyzing the dynamics of human standing.

The human body stands by means of the hip, knee and ankle joints of the lower limbs. Among them, the knee joint is the main joint that receives the force and is also the main part of the auxiliary. Therefore, this paper focuses on solving for the stiffness of the knee joint. These three joints divide the human body into upper body, thighs and lower legs. So the human being is simplified into a three-section inverted pendulum model (see Fig. 1). On the basis of this model, the Lagrange equation is used to calculate the joint torques of human lower limbs.

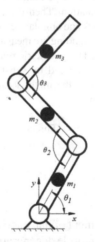

Fig. 1. Three-section inverted pendulum model.

The Lagrangian equation can be written as:

$$\frac{\partial}{\partial t}\left(\frac{\partial L}{\partial \dot{\theta}}\right) - \frac{\partial L}{\partial \theta} = \tau \tag{2}$$

where L means the Lagrangian function. t is the time. θ and $\dot{\theta}$ are the angular and angular velocities of the joints, respectively. τ is the joint torques. The Lagrangian function can be written as:

$$L = \phi_t - \phi_v \tag{3}$$

where ϕ_t means the total potential energy of the system and ϕ_v means the total kinetic energy of the system.

Substitute Eq. (3) into Eq. (2):

$$\frac{\partial}{\partial t}\left(\frac{\partial \phi_t}{\partial \dot{\theta}}\right) - \frac{\partial \phi_t}{\partial \theta} - \frac{\partial}{\partial t}\left(\frac{\partial \phi_v}{\partial \dot{\theta}}\right) + \frac{\partial \phi_v}{\partial \theta} = \tau \qquad (4)$$

The equation relates the joint torque τ to the kinetic energy ϕ_v and potential energy ϕ_t.

The kinetic energy of the system is divided into two parts, which are the translational kinetic energy and the rotational kinetic energy. The translational kinetic energy of each segment of the body ϕ_{vi} can be written as:

$$\phi_{vi} = \frac{1}{2}m_i\left(\left(\frac{\partial x_i}{\partial t}\right)^2 + \left(\frac{\partial y_i}{\partial t}\right)^2\right) \qquad (5)$$

where m_i means the mass of each segment of the body. x_i and y_i are the horizontal and vertical coordinates of the center of mass of each segment of the body in the base coordinate system, respectively.

The kinetic energy of rotation of each segment of the body ϕ_{vr} can be written as:

$$\phi_{vr} = \frac{1}{2}I_1\dot{\theta}_1^2 + \frac{1}{2}I_2(\dot{\theta}_1 - \dot{\theta}_2)^2 + \frac{1}{2}I_3(\dot{\theta}_1 - \dot{\theta}_2 + \dot{\theta}_3)^2 \qquad (6)$$

where I_1, I_2, I_3 are the inertia of the lower legs, thighs and upper limbs. $\dot{\theta}_1, \dot{\theta}_2, \dot{\theta}_3$ are the angular velocities of the ankle, knee and hip joints.

The total kinetic energy of the body ϕ_v is:

$$\phi_v = \phi_{v1} + \phi_{v2} + \phi_{v3} + \phi_{vr} \qquad (7)$$

The potential energy of each segment of the body ϕ_{ti} can be expressed as:

$$\phi_{ti} = m_i g y_i \qquad (8)$$

where g is gravitational acceleration.

The total potential energy of the system ϕ_t can then be obtained as:

$$\phi_t = \phi_{t1} + \phi_{t2} + \phi_{t3} \qquad (9)$$

The joint torque τ can be calculated by substituting the results of Eqs. (7) and (9) into (4). Substituting the torque τ into Eq. (1) yields an expression for the joint stiffness K during standing.

3 Experiment and Analysis

3.1 Experimental Procedure

In this section, the joint angles and joint angular velocities required to calculate the stiffness are measured. The measurement equipment uses an optical 3D motion capture system from NOKOV. The system consists of 8 infrared high-speed cameras. And it can measure the displacement of marker points and the angle of their connecting lines. Figure 2 shows the experimental scene.

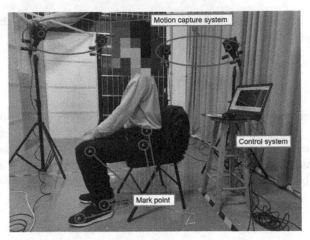

Fig. 2. The experimental scene, including a motion capture system, marker points and control system.

There are 8 subjects in this experiment. Their height is 174 ± 6 cm and their weight is 73.48 ± 7.23 kg. Five marker points are applied to each subject's leg. Among them, three marker points are attached to the rotation centers of hip joint, knee joint and ankle joint respectively. The other two are attached to the front of the waist and feet. The connecting line of five points can form a simple structure of lower limbs. Any three consecutive marker points can form a joint angle. Before the experiment starts, the subject sits quietly in a chair. When the command to start is heard, the subject stands according to their own habits. The measurement is stopped after completing the stand. Each person performs three sets of experiments. During the experiment, the motion capture system captures the angular changes of the subject's three joint angles.

3.2 Modification of Measurement Results

In the experiments, the marker points are attached to the surface of the human body instead of the real joint rotation center. In Fig. 3(a), the red line is the measured lower limb structure and the blue line is the real lower limb structure. The uneven distribution of human leg width can cause some errors in the measurement of joint angles. Therefore, the measurement results need to be modified. All three joints have similar structures so they can be represented by one model (see Fig. 3(b)).

The marker point is at the same level as the real point. And the real joint rotation center line is in the vertical plane. Thus the model can be equated to two right-angle trapezoids. The geometric relationship can be written as:

$$
\begin{cases}
l_{a1}^2 + (d_2 - d_1)^2 = l_{m1}^2 \\
l_{a2}^2 + (d_3 - d_2)^2 = l_{m2}^2 \\
l_{a1}^2 + l_{a2}^2 - 2l_{a1}l_{a2}\cos\theta_a + (d_1 - d_3)^2 = l_{m1}^2 + l_{m2}^2 - 2l_{m1}l_{m2}\cos\theta_m
\end{cases}
\tag{10}
$$

where l_{m1} and l_{m2} are the length measured on the surface of the human body. l_{a1} and l_{a2} are the distance between real points. d_1, d_2, d_3 are the horizontal deviation of the

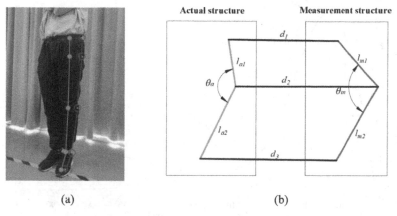

Fig. 3. Comparison of measured points with real points. (a) Comparison of the measured lower limb structure with the real lower limb structure. (b) Structural model of a single joint.

corresponding measurement point from the true point, respectively. θ_a and θ_m are the real joint angle and the measured joint angle, respectively. The relationship allows the conversion of the measured joint angle to the true joint angle. The effect of lower limb width is avoided.

3.3 Experimental Results and Discussion

The angular velocity during standing can be obtained by differencing and filtering the collected angles. The stiffness can be calculated by substituting the angle and angular velocity into the expression. Since different subjects can't stand for the same amount of time, the movement process is used to unify the standing process. The equation for calculating the movement process S can be written as:

$$S = \frac{t}{t_{\max}} \tag{11}$$

where t is the current moment and $t_{\max}$ is the moment of completing the stand.

Theoretically, the joint angle of the lower extremity is almost constant before the person has completely left the chair and after he has finished standing. However, due to slight human jitter and equipment measurement errors, a large error will be introduced into the denominator of Eq. (1), resulting in inaccurate data results. Therefore, it is accurate and appropriate to intercept the part of the subject that is completely off the chair surface until he completes standing. To avoid the effect of height and weight of different subjects, the stiffness of each individual is divided by subject's own height and weight, respectively. The average results after summarizing the results of all subjects are shown in Fig. 4.

The overall trend of stiffness during standing is high on both sides and low in the middle. It means that the joint stiffness is higher when the person is just standing and about to stop standing. Basically, the stiffness data for each subject exhibits such a high

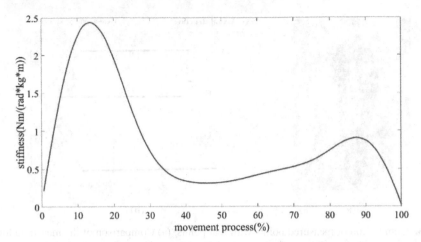

Fig. 4. Average knee stiffness curve during standing

side and low middle, with some variation in the size and occurrence of the higher points at each end.

The reason for this trend in stiffness is that the need for stability is higher when a person is just standing and immediately stopping, so the joint stiffness increases to help stabilize the body. In the middle section, the body is in the rapid stance phase, and the smaller stiffness facilitates the angle change of the joints.

4 Conclusion and Future Work

This paper designs a method to identify the stiffness of the knee joint during human standing. First, the standing motion of the human body is simplified to a three-stage inverted pendulum model. It is used to analyze the dynamics of the human lower limb joints in combination with the Lagrange equation. Then, the expression of stiffness is obtained according to the relationship between joint torque and stiffness. The joint angles and angular velocities during the standing are measured by a motion capture system. And the errors in the measurements are modified by geometric relationships. The stiffness can be calculated by substituting the results into the expression for stiffness. The result shows that the method can identify the stiffness of the knee joint. In the future, the auxiliary standing mechanism will be designed and analyzed according to the stiffness change of knee joint during standing in order to achieve better human-robot interaction. People can get a stable, supple and comfortable assistance based on it.

Acknowledgement. This work was supported in part by the National Natural Science Foundation of China under Grant 52075178 and Grant 52130508; and the Opening Project of Key Laboratory of Safety of Intelligent Robots for State Market Regulation, PR China under Grant GQI-KFKT202201.

References

1. Huo, W., Mohammed, S., Amirat, Y., Kong, K.: Active Impedance Control of a lower limb exoskeleton to assist sit-to-stand movement. In: 2016 IEEE International Conference on Robotics and Automation (ICRA), pp. 3530–3536 (2016)
2. Shepherd, M.K., Rouse, E.J.: Design and characterization of a torque-controllable actuator for knee assistance during sit-to-stand. In: 2016 38th Annual International Conference of the IEEE Engineering in Medicine and Biology Society (EMBC), pp. 2228–2231 (2016)
3. Seko, S., Matthew, R.P., Riemer, R.: Passive knee assistance affects whole-body biomechanics during sit-to-stand. In: 2019 41st Annual International Conference of the IEEE Engineering in Medicine and Biology Society (EMBC), pp. 4440–4444 (2019)
4. Chuy, O., Hirata, Y., Wang, Z., Kosuge, K.: Approach in assisting a sit-to-stand movement using robotic walking support system. In: 2006 IEEE/RSJ International Conference on Intelligent Robots and Systems, pp. 4343–4348 (2006)
5. Furusawa, T., Sawada, T., Fujiki, N., Suzuki, R., Hofer, E.P.: Practical assistive device for sit-to-stand tasks. In: 2017 IEEE 6th Global Conference on Consumer Electronics (GCCE), pp. 1–3 (2017)
6. Kim, S.-W., Song, J., Suh, S., Lee, W., Kang, S.: Design and experiment of a passive sit-to-stand and walking (STSW) assistance device for the elderly. In: 2018 40th Annual International Conference of the IEEE Engineering in Medicine and Biology Society (EMBC), pp. 1781–1784 (2018)
7. Daines, K., Lemaire, E.D., Smith, A., Herbert-Copley, A.: Sit-to-stand and stand to-sit crutch use for lower extremity powered exoskeletons. In: 2017 IEEE International Symposium on Robotics and Intelligent Sensors (IRIS), pp. 358–363 (2017)
8. Kamali, K., Akbari, A.A., Akbarzadeh, A.: Trajectory generation and control of a knee exoskeleton based on dynamic movement primitives for sit-to-stand assistance. Adv. Robot. 30(13), 846–860 (2016)
9. Qureshi, M.H., Masood, Z., Rehman, L., Owais, M., Khan, M.U.: Biomechanical design and control of lower limb exoskeleton for sit-to-stand and stand-to-sit movements. In: 2018 14th IEEE/ASME International Conference on Mechatronic and Embedded Systems and Applications (MESA), pp. 1–6 (2018)
10. Shamaei, K., Cenciarini, M., Adams, A.A., Gregorczyk, K.N., Schiffman, J.M., Dollar, A.M.: Biomechanical effects of stiffness in parallel with the knee joint during walking. IEEE Trans. Biomed. Eng. 62(10), 2389–2401 (2015)
11. Pfeifer, S., Vallery, H., Hardegger, M., Riener, R., Perreault, E.J.: Model-based estimation of knee stiffness. IEEE Trans. Biomed. Eng. 59(9), 2604–2612 (2012)
12. Roy, A., et al.: Measurement of human ankle stiffness using the anklebot. In: 2007 IEEE 10th International Conference on Rehabilitation Robotics, pp. 356–363 (2007)
13. Smidt, G.: Biomechanical analysis of knee flexion and extension. J. Biomech. 6(1), 79–92 (1973)
14. Misgeld, B.J.E., Lüken, M., Riener, R., Leonhardt, S.: Observer-based human knee stiffness estimation. IEEE Trans. Biomed. Eng. 64(5), 1033–1044 (2017)
15. Lahiff, C.-A., Ramakrishnan, T., Kim, S.H., Reed, K.: Knee orthosis with variable stiffness and damping that simulates hemiparetic gait. In: 2016 38th Annual International Conference of the IEEE Engineering in Medicine and Biology Society (EMBC), pp. 2218–2221 (2016)

Motion Control and Simulation Analysis of a Manipulator Based on Computed Torque Control Method

Changqian Feng, Zhengcang Chen[✉], Weiqing Jin, and Wanjin Guo

Key Laboratory of Road Construction Technology and Equipment of MOE, Chang'an University, Middle-Section of Nan'er Huan Road, Xian 710064, China
chenzhc8905@chd.edu.cn

Abstract. The accurate position and motion control of the end-effector for robot execution is an important research direction of robot control. Based on the computed torque model, a Proportional-Integral-Derivative computed torque control (PID-CTC) method is introduced, in order to describe the process of implementing the end position control strategy for the robot manipulator. Compared with the traditional position control method, the computed torque control method can better handle the nonlinear problem when the parameters all known. Compared with the response and tracking performance of the robot manipulator to the two input trajectories, the results show that the PID-CTC control effect has low error and high accuracy, which is an efficient motion control method.

Keywords: Nonlinear control · Dynamic modeling · Robot kinematics

1 Introduction

The robot manipulator is a typical nonlinear and uncertain system, which is the fundamental reason why the robot manipulator motion control problem was complicated [1,2]. With the continuous development and progress of robotics, many classical control theories and control methods are increasingly applied to the robot manipulator motion control, such as the classical proportional-integral-differential control method. [3,4] PID can well solve the robustness problem of common industrial robot manipulators. However, traditional PID controllers are suitable for systems with constant rate of function, when faced with complex time-varying input situations, obvious time-domain deviations occur, and it is difficult for the actual signal to reach the ultimate position of the predetermined signal, and this phenomenon becomes more significant when the signal frequency becomes larger, which is caused by the unmatched properties of such controllers for higher-order inputs [5,6]. In addition, the PID linear control method can only be effective at a certain equity point and its neighborhood for a highly nonlinear

Supported by National Natural Science Foundation of China under Grant No. 52275005 and Natural Science Basic Research Plan in Shaanxi Province of China under Grant No.2022JQ-342 controlled object such as the robot arm, and once the imbalance condition is triggered, the system will diverge or collapse [7]. Moreover, the time lag of the robot arm joint motion will lead to irregular changes of the PID control model error with time, which in turn leads to poor tracking ability of the control model.

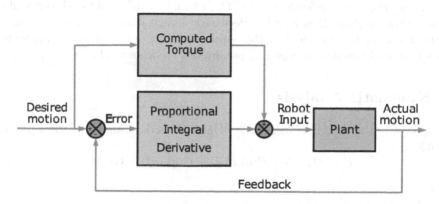

Fig. 1. PID-CTC block diagram. The yellow one above is the CTC module, and the one below is the PID module. (Color figure online)

The computed torque control is a method to achieve precise motion control of a robot while performing a task by applying torque control to the robot end-effector [8]. This control method, shown in Fig. 1, uses the actual motion of the robot as negative feedback, the difference between the desired motion value of the robot and the actual motion value as input to the linear control module, The desired motion value as input to the CTC model. the CTC module and linear control module PID modules are jointly adjusted to precisely control the motion of the robot. This control method achieves improved stability and accuracy of task execution by regulating the required torque of the joints [9,10]. This method protected the mechanical structure of the controlled object from damage and avoiding system overload operation [11,12].

There have been attempts by researchers to combine adaptive control and fuzzy control methods to improve the intelligence of computed torque control methods, Emran [13] showed that design of linear controllers for robot manipulators is very difficult because they are nonlinear and uncertain. To reduce these challenges, nonlinear robust controllers are used for the control of robotic manipulators where the CTC is a powerful nonlinear controller in the presence of partial uncertainty in the dynamic parameters of the system. Muhammad [14] showed that the main advantages of this technique are its potential higher tracking accuracy, lower feedback gain, better suitability for flexible control and lower CTC utilizes the idea of feedback linearization and offers the availability of many linear control techniques. There are also studies that show that the use of newer intelligent algorithms, including deep learning and reinforcement learning, to improve the efficiency and accuracy of Computed Torque Control is a popular trend at present, such as the study by Sangdan et al [15]. S. Kousik et al. [16]

suggest that the real-time nature of robot manipulator control is an important indicator to evaluate the goodness of a robot control model. The authors of the appeal propose that the robotic manipulator is a nonlinear system, and to increase the performance of the robotic manipulator control process, they propose a robust controller(e.g., CTC) to better control the arm motion. This is the reason why this paper references the CTC, which is widely used in the control of robotic manipulators. It is based on feedback linearization and uses a nonlinear feedback control law to calculate the required arm torque. This controller works well when all dynamic and physical parameters are known. [17,18].

2   Kinematic Analysis

The motion of the rigid link arm of the PUMA 560 is determined by the following equation:

$$\Gamma = M(q).\ddot{q} + B(q).(\dot{q}.\dot{q}) + C(q).(\dot{q}^2) + G(q) \tag{1}$$

where:

Γ : vector of torques

$M(q)$: inertia matrix of the robot manipulator

q : position vector

$B(q)$: vector of Coriolis terms

$C(q)$: vector of Centrifugal terms

$G(q)$: vector of gravity terms

The above equation consists of a kinetic equation with an internal nonlinear loop of compensation and an external loop with an external control signal $\dot{q}$ [8]. In PUMA 560, the kinematic equations of the system are reduced to ensure the accuracy of the end-effector by making $q_4 = q_5 = q_6 = 0$. Therefore, $(\dot{q}.\dot{q})$ is the vector of joint velocity products of in the equation, and $(\dot{q}^2)$ is vector of order 2. The element of matrix$M(q)$ in Eq. (1) is:

$$M(q) = \begin{bmatrix} M_{ij(i,j=1...3)} & M_{ij(i=3,j=5)} \\ 0_{3\times3} & M_{ij(i,j=4...6)} \end{bmatrix}_{6\times6} \tag{2}$$

Table 1. Values of the elements in the matrix M

Parameter	Value	Parameter	Value
M_{11}	$I_{m1} + I_1 + I_3 \cdot CC2 + I_7 \cdot SS23 + I_{10} \cdot SC23 + \dots$ $I_{11} \cdot SC2 + I_{21} \cdot SS23 + 2 \cdot [I_5 \cdot C2 \cdot S23 + \dots$ $+ I_{12} \cdot C2 \cdot C23 + I_{15} \cdot SS23 + I_{16} \cdot C2 \cdot S23 + I_{22} \cdot SC23]$	M_{35}	$I_{15} + I_{17}$
M_{12}	$I_4 \cdot S2 + I_8 \cdot C23 + I_9 \cdot C2 + I_{13} \cdot S23 - I_{18} \cdot C23$	M_{44}	$I_{m4} + I_{14}$
M_{13}	$I_8 \cdot C23 + I_{13} \cdot S23 - I_{18} \cdot C23$	M_{55}	$I_{m5} + I_{17}$
M_{22}	$I_{m2} + I_2 + I_6 + 2 \cdot [I_5 \cdot S3 + I_{12} \cdot C2 + I_{15} + I_{16} \cdot S3]$	M_{66}	$I_{m6} + I_{23}$
M_{23}	$I_5 \cdot S3 + I_6 + I_{12} \cdot C3 + I_{16} \cdot S3 + 2 \cdot I_{15}$	M_{31}	M_{13}
M_{33}	$I_{m3} + I_6 + 2 \cdot I_{15}$	M_{32}	M_{23}

The Coriolis force coefficient matrix is calculated as follows:

$$B(q) = \begin{bmatrix} b_{ijk(i,j=1,k=2,3,5;i=2,j=1,k=4;i=3,j=1,k=4)} & b_{ijk(i,j=2,k=5;i=2,j=3,k=5)} \\ b_{ijk(i,j=4,k=2,3,5;i=5,j=1,k=4)} & 0_{3\times10} \end{bmatrix}_{6\times15}$$

$$(3)$$

Table 2. Values of parameters in the coriolis force coefficient matrix B

parameter	Value
b_{112}	$2 \cdot [I_3 \cdot SC2 + I_5 \cdot C223 + I_7 \cdot SC23 I_{12} \cdot S223 + I_{15} \cdot 2 \cdot SC23 + I_{16} \cdot C223 + \cdots$ $+ I_{21} \cdot SC23 + +I_{22} \cdot (1 - 2 \cdot SS23)] + I_{10} \cdot (1 - 2 \cdot SS23) + I_{11} \cdot (1 - 2 \cdot SS2)$
b_{113}	$2 \cdot [I_5 \cdot C2 \cdot C23 + I_7 \cdot SC23 - I_{12} \cdot C2 \cdot S23 + I_{15} \cdot 2 \cdot SC23 + I_{16} \cdot C2 \cdot C23 + \cdots$ $+ I_{21} \cdot SC23 + +I_{22} \cdot (1 - 2 \cdot SS23)] + I_{10} \cdot (1 - 2 \cdot SS23)$
b_{115}	$2 \cdot [-SC23 + I_{15} \cdot SC23 + I_{16} \cdot C2 \cdot C23 + I_{22} \cdot CC23]$
b_{123}	$2 \cdot [-I_8 \cdot S23 + I_{13} \cdot C23 + I_{18} \cdot S23]$
b_{214}	$I_{14} \cdot S23 + I_{19} \cdot S23 + 2 \cdot I_{20} \cdot S23 \cdot (1 - 0.5)$
b_{223}	$2 \cdot [-I_{12} \cdot S3 + I_5 \cdot C3 + I_{16} \cdot C3]$
b_{225}	$2 \cdot [I_{16} \cdot C3 + I_{22}]$
b_{235}	$2 \cdot [I_{16} \cdot C3 + I_{22}]$
b_{314}	$2 \cdot [I_{20} \cdot S23 \cdot (1 - 0 \cdot 5)] + I_{14} \cdot S23 + I_{19} \cdot S23$
b_{412}	$-[I_{14} \cdot S23 + I_{19} \cdot S23 + 2 \cdot I_{20} \cdot S23 \cdot (1 - 0.5)]$
b_{413}	$-2 \cdot [I_{20} \cdot S23 \cdot (1 - 0 \cdot 5)] + I_{14} \cdot S23 + I_{19} \cdot S23$
b_{415}	$-I_{20} \cdot S23 - I_{17} \cdot S23$
b_{514}	$I_{20} \cdot S23 + I_{17} \cdot S23$

Centrifugal force of matrix is:

$$C(q) = \begin{bmatrix} C_{ij(i,j=1,2,3;i\neq j)} & 0_{3\times3} \\ C_{ij(i=5;j=1,2)} & 0_{3\times3} \end{bmatrix}_{6\times6}$$

$$(4)$$

Table 3. The parameters in the centrifugal force matrix C

Parameter	Value	Parameter	Value
C_{12}	$I_4 \cdot C2 - I_8 \cdot S23 - I_9 \cdot S2 + I_{13} \cdot C23 + I_{18} \cdot S23$	C_{13}	$0.5 \cdot b_{123}$
C_{21}	$-0.5 \cdot b_{112}$	C_{23}	$0.5 \cdot b_{223}$
C_{32}	$I_{12} \cdot S3 - I_5 \cdot C3 - I_{16} \cdot C3$	C_{31}	$-0.5 \cdot b_{113}$
C_{51}	$-0.5 \cdot b_{115}$	C_{52}	$-0.5 \cdot b_{225}$

The gravity matrix $G(q)$ is shown as follows:

$$g(q) = [0\ g_2\ g_3\ 0\ g_5\ 0]^T$$

$$(5)$$

$$where: g_2 = g_1 \cdot C2 + g_2 \cdot S23 + g_3 \cdot S2 + g_4 \cdot C23 + g_5 \cdot S23$$

$$g_3 = g_2 \cdot S23 + g_4 \cdot C23 + g_5 \cdot S23 ;\ g_5 = g_5 \cdot S23$$

$$\ddot{q} = M^{-1}(q) \cdot \{\Gamma - [B(q).\dot{q}\dot{q} + C(q).\dot{q}^2 + g(q)]\}$$

$$Let \quad K = \{\Gamma - [B(q).\dot{q}\dot{q} + C(q).\dot{q}^2 + g(q)]\}$$

$$(6)$$

Then (6) can be abbreviated to the following form:

$$\ddot{q} = M^{-1}(q) \cdot K$$

$$(7)$$

The coefficients for the above abbreviations are shown below:

$$Si = sin\,(\theta_i)\,; Ci = cos\,(\theta_i)\,; Cij = cos\,(\theta_i + \theta_j)\,;$$
$$Sijk = sin\,(\theta_i + \theta_j + \theta_k)\,; CCi = cos\,(\theta_i) \cdot cos\,(\theta_i)\,; CSi = cos\,(\theta_i) \cdot sin\,(\theta_i)$$

The data for PUMA560 below are the parameters used in the above calculation [19, 20].

Table 4. Table of inertia constants(N·m)

I_i	Value	I_i	Value	I_i	Value	I_{mi}	Value
1	1.43 ± 0.05	9	$+0.0238 \pm 0.012$	17	$(+0.642 \pm 0.3) \times 10^{-3}$	1	1.14 ± 0.27
2	1.75 ± 0.07	10	-0.0213 ± 0.0022	18	$(+0.431 \pm 0.13) \times 10^{-3}$	2	4.71 ± 0.54
3	1.38 ± 0.05	11	-0.0142 ± 0.0070	19	$(+0.03 \pm 0.14) \times 10^{-2}$	3	0.827 ± 0.093
4	0.69 ± 0.02	12	-0.011 ± 0.0011	20	$(-0.202 \pm 0.8) \times 10^{-3}$	4	0.2 ± 0.016
5	0.372 ± 0.031	13	-0.00379 ± 0.0009	21	$(-0.10 \pm 0.60) \times 10^{-3}$	5	0.179 ± 0.014
6	0.333 ± 0.016	14	$+0.00164 \pm 0.00007$	22	$(-0.58 \pm 0.15) \times 10^{-4}$	6	0.193 ± 0.016
7	$+0.298 \pm 0.029$	15	$+0.00125 \pm 0.0003$	23	$(+0.40 \pm 0.20) \times 10^{-4}$		
8	-0.134 ± 0.014	16	$+0.00124 \pm 0.0003$				

Table 5. Gravity constants (N·m)

g_i	value	g_i	value	g_i	value	g_i	value	g_i	value
1	1.43 ± 0.05	2	1.75 ± 0.07	3	1.38 ± 0.05	4	0.298 ± 0.029	5	-0.134 ± 0.014

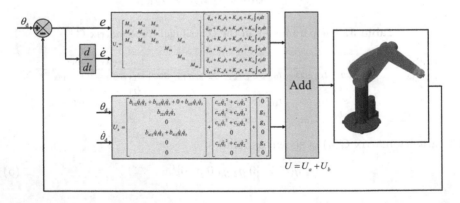

Fig. 2. PID/PD-CTC block diagram. The blue one above is the calculation formula of PID module, and the blue one below is the calculation formula of CTC module. (Color figure online)

3 PID-CTC Model Design

3.1 PID-CTC Model Analysis

As shown in Fig. 2, computed torque control is a nonlinear controller that uses both nonlinear feedback and linear control methods. U_a represents the nonlinear feedback module and U_b represents the linear control module in Fig. 2. In the feedback linearization, a closed-loop linear time-invariant system with guaranteed global asymptotic stability is obtained, which is based on the feedback linearization and uses the nonlinear feedback control law to calculate the desired torque. The computed torque controller works very well when all dynamic and physical parameters are known. Assuming the desired trajectory of the robot manipulator $q_d(t)$, determined by the path planner, and the actual trajectory, the tracking error is defined as: $e(t) = q_d(t) - q_a(t)$.

If instead the linear state space equation is: $\dot{x} = Ax + BU$

Then it can be defined as:

$$\dot{x} = \begin{bmatrix} 0 & I \\ 0 & 0 \end{bmatrix} x + \begin{bmatrix} 0 \\ I \end{bmatrix} U \tag{8}$$

$$where : U = -M^{-1}(q) \cdot N(q, \dot{q}) + M^{-1}(q) \cdot \Gamma \tag{9}$$

By Eqs. (8) and (9), the Brunousky canonical form can be written in terms of the state $x = [e^T, \dot{e}^T]^T$ as:

$$\frac{d}{dx} \begin{bmatrix} e \\ \dot{e} \end{bmatrix} = \begin{bmatrix} 0 & I \\ 0 & 0 \end{bmatrix} \cdot \begin{bmatrix} e \\ \dot{e} \end{bmatrix} + \begin{bmatrix} 0 \\ I \end{bmatrix} U \tag{10}$$

$$U = \ddot{q}_d + M^{-1}(q) \cdot \{N(q, \dot{q}) - \Gamma\} \tag{11}$$

From Eq. (11), it follows that:

$$\Gamma = M(q) \cdot (\ddot{q} - U) + N(\dot{q}, q) \tag{12}$$

This is a nonlinear feedback control law that guarantees the tracking of the desired trajectory. Selection of proportional plus differential integral (PID) feedback to obtain a PID calculated torque controller.

$$\Gamma = M(q) \cdot (\ddot{q} + K_v \dot{e} + K_p e + K_i \int edt) + N(\dot{q}, q)$$

$$where : N(q, \dot{q}) = B(q)\dot{q}\dot{q} + C(q)\dot{q}^2 + g(q) \tag{13}$$

3.2 Simulink Model Building

In Fig. 3, where the yellow part of KP1, KV1, KI1 represent the coefficients of proportional, integral and differential control respectively, and the error is adjusted and changed into different linear control by adjusting its value. In the green module error1 is the difference between the desired value and the actual value, and derror1 is the rate of change of this difference, and these two specific values can be observed in the measurement center.

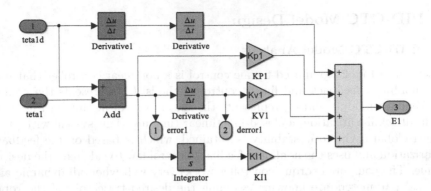

Fig. 3. Simulink module for PID control section.Different simulation results can obtain by changing the value of KP,KV,KI.

The control module in blue is the linear control module of the Fig. 4, The M.matrix in the upper left corner is the mass matrix $M(q)$, and the input of the linear module is U1, At the end, the $N(\dot{q}, q)$ block in the lower right corner is the U2 we need, and the output of the two is the torque we need.

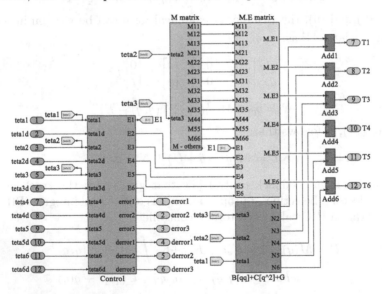

Fig. 4. The entire control section of the simulink module diagram. The blue section is the total module of all PID control sections. (Color figure online)

Figure 5 shows all the blocks simulated in the SUIMULINK/MATLAB environment. the error of the end-effector of the PUMA560 can be adjusted by observing the root mean square error of the RMS block, while finally the nature of all the signals can be observed by measuring the center. Then the properties of all responses are analyzed in the next section.

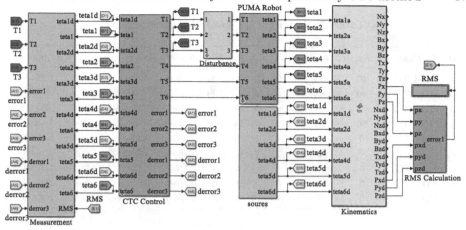

Fig. 5. Block diagram of the Simulink module of the whole part of PID-CTC. The orange part is the module that changes the disturbance. (Color figure online)

4   Results and Analysis

In the following simulations, the optimal parameters are acquired by comparing the steady-state error (SS error) and the root mean square error (RMS error) of PID-CTC and PD-CTC.

Table 6. PID/PD-CTC control of sine signal

NO.	Method	K_{P_1}	K_{I_1}	K_{V_1}	K_{P_2}	K_{I_2}	K_{V_2}	K_{P_3}	K_{I_3}	K_{V_3}	$SSerror^1$	$SSerror^2$	$SSerror^3$	RMSerror
1	PID-CTC	70	40	80	70	40	80	70	40	80	-2.35e-3	-2.35e-3	-2.35e-3	8.23e-4
2	PID-CTC	70	50	80	70	50	80	70	50	80	-2.71e-3	-2.71e-3	-2.71e-3	9.48e-4
3	PID-CTC	70	40	100	70	40	100	70	40	100	-1.70e-3	-1.70e-3	-1.70e-3	5.85e-4
4	PID-CTC	80	40	100	80	40	100	80	40	100	-1.69e-3	-1.69e-3	-1.69e-3	5.89e-4
5	PD-CTC	10	0	8	10	0	8	10	0	8	-1.68e-2	-1.68e-2	-1.68e-2	5.88e-3
6	PD-CTC	20	0	8	20	0	8	20	0	8	-1.13e-2	-1.13e-2	-1.13e-2	3.96e-3
7	PD-CTC	20	0	6	20	0	6	20	0	6	-1.20e-2	-1.20e-2	-1.20e-2	4.18e-3
8	PD-CTC	10	0	2	10	0	2	10	0	2	-2.61e-2	-2.61e-2	-2.61e-2	9.11e-3
9	PD-CTC	8	0	1	8	0	1	8	0	1	-3.41e-2	-3.40e-2	-3.40e-2	1.19e-2

In this simulation, the first, second and third joints are moved from the origin to the final position without external disturbance, and the results of the simulation are implemented in MATLAB/SIMULINK environment. The rows marked in blue in Tables 6 and 7, indicate their best performance, and then the best parameters of the ramp signal response are: KP=2, KV=4, when it is PD-CTC control, by comparing the advantages and disadvantages of SS error and RMS error in the combined graphs and plots. The optimal parameters of the sine signal response are: KP=20, KV=8, when it is PID-CTC control, the optimal parameters of the ramp signal response are: KP=85, KV=40, KI=100, the optimal parameters of the sine signal response are: KP=70, KV=40, KI=100, and then use the derived optimal parameters to further analyze the performance

Table 7. PID/PD-CTC control of ramp signal

NO.	Method	K_{P_1}	K_{I_1}	K_{V_1}	K_{P_2}	K_{I_2}	K_{V_2}	K_{P_3}	K_{I_3}	K_{V_3}	SSerror[1]	SSerror[2]	SSerror[3]	RMSerror
1	PID-CTC	40	40	100	40	40	100	40	40	100	-3.54e-8	-3.54e-8	-3.54e-8	1.22e-8
2	PID-CTC	85	40	100	85	40	100	85	40	100	0	0	0	0
3	PID-CTC	85	40	80	85	40	80	85	40	80	-3.55e-15	-3.55e-15	-3.55e-15	1.21e-15
4	PID-CTC	85	80	100	85	80	100	85	80	100	-4.42e-9	-4.42e-9	-4.42e-9	1.53e-9
5	PD-CTC	1	0	4	1	0	4	1	0	4	9.23e-5	9.23e-5	9.23e-5	3.19e-5
6	PD-CTC	2	0	4	2	0	4	2	0	4	3.78e-8	3.78e-8	3.78e-8	1.10e-8
7	PD-CTC	0.5	0	4	0.5	0	4	0.5	0	4	2.11e-3	2.11e-3	2.11e-3	7.27e-4
8	PD-CTC	2	0	6	2	0	6	2	0	6	6.97e-6	6.97e-6	6.97e-6	2.41e-6
9	PD-CTC	10	0	35	10	0	35	10	0	35	5.66e-6	5.66e-6	5.66e-6	1.95e-6

of PID-CTC, PD-CTC control methods in the absence and presence of disturbances, where the system is tested in the presence of disturbances by means of band-limited white noise that is equal to 0.1 with respect to the sampling time and a signal power of 15. This type of noise is used for the simulation of external disturbances in continuous and hybrid systems.

4.1   Working in the Absence of Disturbance

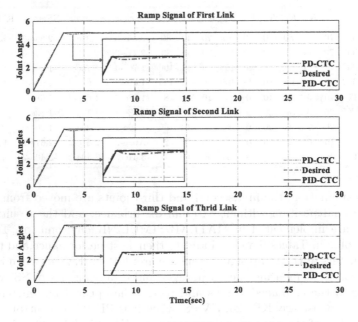

Fig. 6. Performance of input as ramp signal without disturbance. The magnified area is a detailed representation of the response curve.

The above Fig. 6 shows the tracking performance of PD-CTC and PID-CTC for the ramp trajectory without perturbation, and the best agreement between PID-CTC and the ideal trajectory can be observed at the local zoomed-in view. In the above figure, by comparing the sine response trajectory without perturbation in PD and PID-CTC, it is concluded that the average overshoot of PID is 0.54% amount lower than the average overshoot of PD of 0.85%, moreover, the steady-state and RMS errors (SS error = 0 and RMS error = 0) of PID-CTC are much lower than those of PD (SS error and RMS error = 0.00053). The ramp signal reaches the steady state after operating for a period of time, and finally it is concluded that the trajectory coincidence of PID-CTC is more excellent than that of PD-CTC in the case of the input signal being a ramp signal.

4.2   Working in the Disturbance

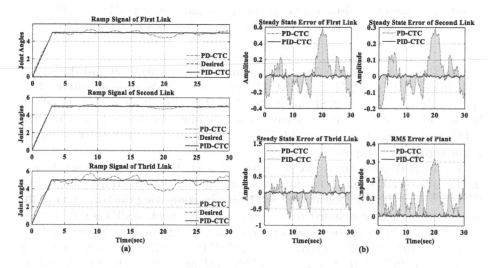

Fig. 7. Presence of disturbance: (a) the performance of PID-CTC and PD-CTC when the input is a ramp signal, (b) Tracking performance of PID-CTC and PD-CTC.

Figure 7(a) shows the tracking performance of PD-CTC and PID-CTC in the case of disturbance of the ramp signal, it can be seen that the fluctuation amplitude of PD-CTC is better than PID-CTC. Through analysis of the Fig. 7, it is concluded that the average overshoot of PID-CTC is 0.87% lower than the average overshoot of PD-CTC is 12.1%. In addition, the steady-state and RMS errors of PID-CTC (ss1=0.0115,ss2=0.0061,ss3=0.0249,RMS error=0.0072) are much lower than those of PD (ss1=-0.1724,ss2=-0.0922,ss3=-0.3739 and RMS error=0.1068) . By observing Fig. 7(b), it can be concluded that the immunity of the PID-CTC is better than that of the PD-CTC, and this performance difference is more obvious especially at the third joint, when the input is a ramp

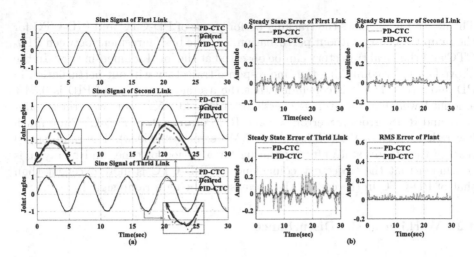

Fig. 8. Presence of disturbances in (a). the performance of PID-CTC and PD-CTC when the input is a sine signal, (b). Tracking performance of PID-CTC and PD-CTC.

signal, the average amplitude of the steady-state error 0.00306 and the amplitude of the RMS 0.012 of the PID-CTC are lower than the average amplitude of the steady-state error 0.2781 of the PD-CTC RMS amplitude 0.2441. Finally it is concluded that the trajectory coincidence and interference resistance of PID-CTC is more excellent than PD-CTC in the presence of interference when the input signal is a ramp signal.

Figure 8(a) shows the trajectory performance in the presence of disturbances in the sine signal, through the images it can be seen that the third joint of PD-CTC has large fluctuations around 8s,17s,21s, by comparing the trajectory of the sine response, it is concluded that the average overshoot of PID is 0.83% lower than 3.23% of PD average overshoot; in addition, the SS and RMS errors of PID-CTC (SS1=0.0088,SS2=0.0031,SS3=0.0267,RMS=0.0072) are much lower than those of PD (SS1=0.0069,SS2=-0.0017,SS3=0.0296,RMS= 0.0076). By observing Fig. 8(b), it can be concluded that the immunity of the PID-CTC is better than that of the PD-CTC, and this performance difference is more obvious especially at the third joint, When the input is a sine signal, the average amplitude of the steady-state error 0.0018 and the amplitude of RMS 0.0085 of PID-CTC are lower than the average amplitude of steady-state error 0.0318 and the amplitude of RMS 0.0196 of PD-CTC, and comparing their images in the presence of disturbances, It can be seen that the PID-CTC is better than the PD-CTC.

5 Conclusion

In this paper, the CTC method was introduced. The robotic manipulator control is divided into two main parts, kinematic and dynamical. The kinetic parameters of the system are highly nonlinear. In order to control the system, a nonlinear control method (CTC) is introduced. The CTC has an effect on certain and partially uncertain systems and is based on feedback linearization and uses a nonlinear feedback control law to calculate the required arm torque. Finally, through simulation verification, it can be seen that the PID-CTC is better than the PD-CTC.CTC works well when the parameters of the dynamic model are accurate. In future work, the CTC method can be improved by adding compensation for the outer loop control to avoid inaccurate control due to insufficient parameters.

References

1. Khan, M.F., et al.: Control strategies for robotic manipulators. In: 2012 International Conference of Robotics and Artificial Intelligence, IEEE (2012)
2. Elsisi, M., et al.: Effective nonlinear model predictive control scheme tuned by improved NN for robotic manipulators. IEEE Access **9**, 64278–64290 (2021)
3. Zhang, D., Wei, B.: A review on model reference adaptive control of robotic manipulators. Annu. Rev. Control. **43**, 188–198 (2017)
4. Kurfess, T.R.: Robotics and Automation Handbook. CRC Press, Boca Raton (2018)
5. Iqbal, J., et al.: Nonlinear control systems-a brief overview of historical and recent advances. Nonlinear Eng. **6**(4), 301–312 (2017)
6. Qin, Y., et al.: A control theoretic approach to ABR video streaming: a fresh look at PID-based rate adaptation. IEEE Trans. Mob. Comput. **19**(11), 2505–2519 (2019)
7. Vaidyanathan, S., Volos, C.: Advances and applications in nonlinear control systems. Springer (2016). https://doi.org/10.1007/978-3-319-30169-3
8. Breazeal, C., et al.: Social Robotics. Springer handbook of robotics: 1935–1972 (2016)
9. AL-Azzawi, S.F., Aziz, M.M.: Strategies of linear feedback control and its classification. TELKOMNIKA (Telecommunication Computing Electronics and Control) **17**(4), 1931–1940 (2019)
10. Kchaou, A., et al.: Second order sliding mode-based MPPT control for photovoltaic applications. Sol. Energy **155**, 758–769 (2017)
11. Nagababu, V., Imran, A.: Artificial neural networks based attitude controlling of longitudinal autopilot for general aviation aircraft. Int. J. Adv. Res. Electrical, Electron. Instrum. Eng. **7**(1) (2018)
12. Toquica, A., et al.: Kinematic modelling of a robotic arm manipulator using Matlab. J. Eng. Appl. Sci. **12**(7) (2017)
13. Emran, B.J., et al.: Robust adaptive control design for quadcopter payload add and drop applications. In: 2015 34th Chinese Control Conference (CCC), IEEE (2015)
14. Islam, R., et al.: Design and comparison of two control strategies for multi-DOF articulated robotic arm manipulator. J. Control Eng. Appl. Inform. **16**(2), 28–39 (2014)
15. Sangdani, M., et al.: Genetic algorithm-based optimal computed torque control of a vision-based tracker robot: simulation and experiment. Eng. Appl. Artif. Intell. **67**, 24–38 (2018)
16. Kousik, S., et al.: Bridging the gap between safety and real-time performance in receding-horizon trajectory design for mobile robots. Int. J. Robot. Res. **39**(12), 1419–1469 (2020)

17. Piltan, F., et al.: Design baseline computed torque controller. Int. J. Eng. **6**(3), 129–141 (2012)
18. Varga, Á., et al.: Experimental and simulation-based performance analysis of a computed torque control (CTC) method running on a double rotor aeromechanical testbed. Electronics **10**(14), 1745 (2021)
19. Armstrong, B., et al.: The explicit dynamic model and inertial parameters of the PUMA 560 arm. Proceedings. In: 1986 IEEE International Conference on Robotics and Automation, IEEE (1986)
20. Corke, P.I., Armstrong-Helouvry, B.: A search for consensus among model parameters reported for the PUMA 560 robot. In: Proceedings of the 1994 IEEE International Conference on Robotics and Automation, IEEE (1994)

Design and Realization of a Multi-DoF Robotic Head for Affective Humanoid Facial Expression Imitation

Jiayan Li[1], Honghao Lv[1], Nan Zhang[1], Haiteng Wu[2], and Geng Yang[1,2(✉)]

[1] State Key Laboratory of Fluid Power and Mechatronic Systems, School of Mechanical Engineering, Zhejiang University, Hangzhou, China
gengyang@zju.edu.cn
[2] Key Laboratory of Intelligent Robot for Operation and Maintenance of Zhejiang Province, Hangzhou Shenhao Technology, Hangzhou, China

Abstract. As the elderly population continues to expand, there is a corresponding rise in the demand for service robotics in home environments, with a particular focus on humanoid service robots. This paper presents the design of a multi-DoF robotic head based on the Facial Action Coding System (FACS). The head comprises 26 servo motors that drive the independent Action Units on the face, enabling the imitation of facial expressions following the FACS theory. Additionally, a camera is embedded in the eye for visual perception and interaction, while a 6-DOF Stewart platform driven by six servo motors is integrated as the neck part, ensuring the head's flexibility of movement. Finite element simulation experiments are conducted to validate the robotic facial expression imitation performance of 6 basic expressions including happy, sad, surprise, fear, anger and disgust. The optimized load parameters of the corresponding action units are obtained through simulation, allowing for effective facial expression imitation. The proposed robotic head with facial expression imitation functionality has potential utility for improving human-robot interaction in homecare scenarios and the service quality of the homecare robots.

Keywords: humanoid robotic head · human-robot interaction · humanoid expression simulation

1 Introduction

The world is suffering from an increasing aging population and labor shortages, especially in China, which has the largest elderly population in the world [1]. The ages over 60 years accounted for 18.7% of total population, while those over 65 years reach 13.5% [2]. As people age, some physical invariance and cognitive impairment may occur, affecting their ability to perform independent social activities [3]. Therefore, the demand for long-term care services increases, which puts significant pressure on the healthcare and social welfare systems. However, the shortage of caregivers and healthcare professionals has made it difficult to meet the growing demand for long-term care services. Furthermore, other service-oriented robots are gradually applied in the service industry such as hospitality, retail, education, companionship and medical rehabilitation.

© The Author(s), under exclusive license to Springer Nature Singapore Pte Ltd. 2023
H. Yang et al. (Eds.): ICIRA 2023, LNAI 14267, pp. 23–32, 2023.
https://doi.org/10.1007/978-981-99-6483-3_3

The use of service-oriented robots can help to address this issue by providing assistance with daily activities and reducing the workload of caregivers. Currently, there already available commercial products like Asimo Robot designed by Honda, which has abilities to make eye contact with humans and to communicate using body language, such as nodding or bowing [4]. The Nao [5] and Pepper Humanoid robot [6], developed by SoftBank Robotics, can be interacted by screen information and body language. Compared to general functional robots, humanoid robots can perform a wider range of actions and behaviors that are more human-like, which makes them more user-friendly for service purposes. One of the key advantages of humanoid robots is their ability to display facial expressions, which further enhances their human-like qualities. Most humanoid robots utilize screens and voice for interaction, providing visual feedback and a user-friendly interface, which can be particularly helpful for tasks that involve complex information or data. Meanwhile, the main limitation of screen-based interactions is that interaction based on traditional peripherals gives the robot more of a tool attribute than a human attribute. They may not be well-suited for all users, particularly those with visual impairments or limited dexterity. In addition, screen-based interfaces may not be intuitive or easy to use for all users and may require some level of training or support.

Thus, it is crucial to expand the way robots interact, like anthropomorphic emotional communication, as facial expressions contain abundant emotion information. While great breakthroughs have been made in humanoid robots at home and abroad, such as the pneumatic driving robotic head SAYA [7, 8], KOBIAN bipedal humanoid robot [9, 10]. Meanwhile, some of the existing expression robotic heads pretend to be more abstract and cartoonish for the purpose of making it easier for the user to identify the expression states. During 1999–2012, WE series humanoid robotic head utilizes rope to drive movable parts for abstract expressions [10–13]. Melvin, compared with a human face, has extremely sparse features without face skin, along with some restrictions on motions [14]. Overall, some robots have fewer degrees of freedom (DoF), as windows to the mind, lack a movable mechanism for the eyeballs and eyelids, which missing emotional information in the interaction. Some other robots do not have vision or lack integration for mounting cameras outside the body.

The objective of this work was to design a multi-DoF robotic head for humanoid facial expression imitation and verified for interaction under service scenarios, as shown in Fig. 1. Compared with the rope driving mechanism, four-bar linkage mechanisms were adopted for the stable and precise expression imitation according to the theory of facial action coding system (FACS) within the limited space of the robotic head. A Stewart platform was utilized to satisfy the demand of the yaw, pitch and roll motion of the head. Furthermore, this work successfully demonstrated the simulations of six humanoid facial expressions under varying conditions of boundary and load, which were validated mechanical structure fits the FACS theory well by visual strain cloud maps.

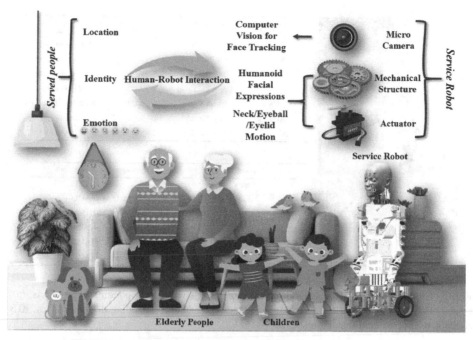

Fig. 1. Service robotic head with humanoid facial expressions.

2 Mechanical Design of Humanoid Expression Robotic Head

2.1 Composition of Robotic Facial Expressions

The humanoid robotic face plays a vital role in improving the barrier-free interaction between humans and robots. To achieve more natural and effective communication, the robot's expression necessitates multiple degrees of freedom. in 1976, The Facial Action Coding System (FACS), a theory of facial muscle division, was proposed by the famous American psychologists Paul Ekman and W. V. Friesen [15–17]. In the theory, Mr. Ekman decomposed the muscle movements which drive human facial expressions into 44 Action Units (AUs). But there is no explicit encoding mapping of facial expressions and AUs until 1984, Mr. Ekman brought forward a new theory—Emotion FACS (EFACS), which delineated the correspondence between 44 different facial muscle movements and expressions. As shown in Fig. 2a. When multiple Action Units act together, the AUs interact and influence each other, forming an expression. Thus, it's of great importance to select reasonable AUs while considering internal space interference and mechanical reliability of the humanoid robotic head, six remarkable facial expressions (happy, sad, surprised, fearful, angry, disgusted) were chosen in dozens of expressions, along with mapping relationship the AUs defined in Fig. 2b and 2c, respectively.

As shown in Fig. 2a, there are a total of 9 independent AUs on the single side of the face, along with 4 DoFs for each eye's rotation in two axes and the movement of the upper and lower eyelids. AUs including AU1, AU2 and AU9 affect face deformation on the specific point, while AU6 affects the surface. AU25 and AU26 are assigned for the

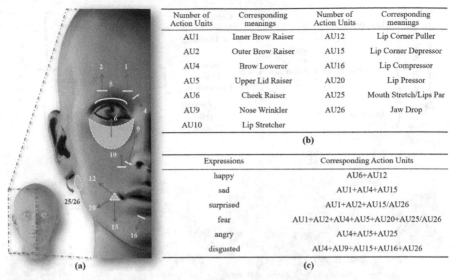

Number of Action Units	Corresponding meanings	Number of Action Units	Corresponding meanings
AU1	Inner Brow Raiser	AU12	Lip Corner Puller
AU2	Outer Brow Raiser	AU15	Lip Corner Depressor
AU4	Brow Lowerer	AU16	Lip Compressor
AU5	Upper Lid Raiser	AU20	Lip Pressor
AU6	Cheek Raiser	AU25	Mouth Stretch/Lips Par
AU9	Nose Wrinkler	AU26	Jaw Drop
AU10	Lip Stretcher		

(b)

Expressions	Corresponding Action Units
happy	AU6+AU12
sad	AU1+AU4+AU15
surprised	AU1+AU2+AU15/AU26
fear	AU1+AU2+AU4+AU5+AU20+AU25/AU26
angry	AU4+AU5+AU25
disgusted	AU4+AU9+AU15+AU16+AU26

(a)   (c)

Fig. 2. Emotion FACS (EFACS) theory and relative AUs with corresponding expressions. (a): Distribution of AUs on the half face; (b): Adopted AUs and corresponding definitions; (c): AUs composition of six common expressions.

rotation of the jaw, spurring the opening and closing of the mouth. AU10 and AU16 were abandoned Considering the limited space and simplifying the design. Therefore, there are 26 independent DoFs distributed throughout the entire face. It is worth noting that the interpretation of these facial expressions may be subjective, as different individuals may perceive the same expression differently.

2.2 Kinematic Model and Mechanism Design

How to Arrange these DoFs into such a narrow space determines the final effect and the ease of assembly. According to the AUs mentioned in Sect. 2.1, humanoid robotic head was mainly divided into four submodules, eyeball-eyelid mechanism, facial expression module, jaw module and neck module. Other components include a photosensitive resin shell, Ecoflex-made human-like silicone face, 26 SG90 servo motors, 6 MG90S servo motors, a Raspberry Pi microcomputer, a micro camera module, 2 PCA9685 servo control boards, a power supply, several ball joint buckle rod assemblies and other parts.

The movement of eyeballs and eyelids conveys a wealth of emotional information. To replicate eye movement as far as possible, alongside the limitation of narrow space in the head, the eyelid servos of both eyes are arranged longitudinally to form a typical planar four-bar linkage mechanism.

In the same way, the motion of facial AUs can be inferred by fitting the crank end trajectory of the linkage mechanism according to the facial model features. Flange bearings were used as rotating shafts. The upper part of Fig. 3 shows distribution of all AUs (AU1 、AU2、AU4、AU5、AU6、AU10、AU12、AU15、AU20) throughout the robotic head. To avoid the over-constrained problem of the mechanism, especially for AUs that are close to each other near the vicinity of the mouth corner, such as the AU12, AU15, and AU20. Hence a mechanism with 2 DoFs was conducted to approximate the motion trajectory of the mouth corner, as shown in the bottom left two pictures of Fig. 3. The lower and upper servos provide approximate 20 degrees and 30 degrees of motion, respectively. This range of motion allows the end joint trajectory to fit the skin contours effectively.

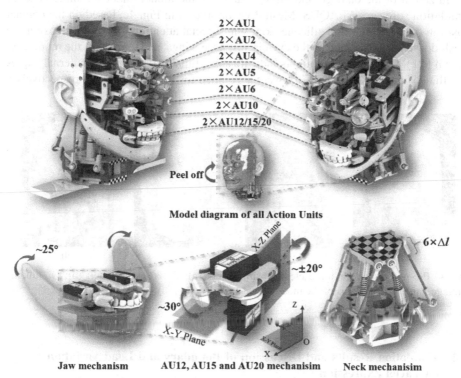

Fig. 3. Model diagram of eyeball-eyelid mechanism, facial expression mechanism, jaw mechanism and neck mechanism.

Besides the eyeball-eyelid mechanism and facial expression mechanism, a jaw mechanism was designed for the ultimate opening-closing angle of 25 degrees, which imitates the natural opening and closing of the mouth. It's also of necessity to change the roll, pitch and yaw states of the neck during the interaction with users. Thus, the bottom right corner of Fig. 3 demonstrates the Composition Stewart mechanism, which utilizes the 6 MG90S servos to adjust the rotation angle individually so as to change the length (Δl) of 6 fixed-length M3 ball head rods, resulting in neck movements such as nodding and shaking to enrich the emotion expression.

3 Experiments and Results

3.1 Pre-Processing of the Simulation for Facial Expression

Silicone face conforming to the skeleton is the key to expressions, thus C4D modeling software was used to model the facial skin for this specific face shape. Figure 4a shows the model of the desired face shape. Figure 4b demonstrates pre-processing including optimization of the damage and missing areas of the model under the finite element simulation software, ABAQUS. Mesh division figures in Fig. 4c, based on the contact position between AUs and silicone skin, with special attention given to increasing the mesh density in areas such as the eye circles, nose wings, and corners of the mouth. As shown in Fig. 4d, yellow highlights indicate suboptimal cells, involving internal angles less than 5° and greater than 170°, were accounted for 1.58% and 0.26% respectively.

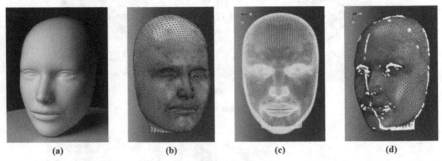

(a)   (b)   (c)   (d)

Fig. 4. Pre-processing for finite element simulation. (a): Facial skin model; (b): Optimizing damaged and missing areas of the model; (c): Mesh division; (d): Mesh quality check.

3.2 Simulation Results and Discussion of Boundary and Load Variation for Facial Expression

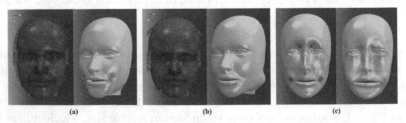

(a)   (b)   (c)

Fig. 5. Pre-processing for finite element simulation. (a): Happy expression with more restrictions; (b): Happy expression with fewer restrictions; (c): Different sad expressions under two restrictions.

The position, magnitude and direction of the displacement load applied to the face has a decisive influence on the rendering effect of each expression. As demonstrated in Fig. 5a and 5b, two happy expressions were applied with constant loads with different restrictions. The former constraints include bridge of nose, temple, junction between the neck and the face, and facial contour. Meanwhile, the control group lacks sufficient facial contour constraints. It's not difficult to figure out that the latter has a large displacement distortion of the cheek under the movement of AU12 mechanism. Similarly, under the same displacement loads of two sad expressions, the difference between two groups is whether boundary restriction of the nose bridge is applied. The comparison between the two is shown in Fig. 5c. Lacking constraints makes the entire face resulting in the longitudinal elongation and distortion under the movement of AU15 mechanism. Additionally, too many restrictions result in small changes in expressions, which is hard for users to distinguish. On the contrary, it leads to excessive displacement, resulting in exaggerated or distorted expressions.

In addition, in the case of constant boundary restrictions and load positions, several sets of different displacements are applied as shown in Table 1, among which all loads of groups a-e increase proportionally. Results of total five surprised expressions are displayed in Fig. 6. From group a to group e, expressions are gradually strengthened. Subjectively, the expression effect of judging the magnitude of displacement load in group c is better than other groups. Relatively, loads of groups a and b are not obvious enough to be noticed by the users, which even may cause misunderstanding that two expressions are in a neutral state. Although the expressions of groups d and e are obviously characterized by expressive surprise due to excessive loading. But at the same time, the expressions are too exaggerated, distorted and unnatural.

Table 1. Simulation effects of surprised expressions with different load settings.

group number	AU1 on both sides			AU2 on both sides			AU25/26		
	X	Y	Z	X	Y	Z	X	Y	Z
a	0	−1	0.2	0	−1	0.2	0	−2	0.2
b	0	−2	0.3	0	−2	0.3	0	−3	0.5
c	0	−4	0.5	0	−4	0.5	0	−5	1
d	(±) 1	−5	1	(±) 1	−5	1	1	−7	2
e	(±) 1.5	−8	2	−1.5	−8	2	0	−9	3

Note: ± indicates load directions on the left and right sides are opposite

Based on variations of boundary restrictions, load displacements and positions, optimal solutions of finite element simulation for six basic expressions including happy, sad, surprise, fear, anger and disgust are obtained as shown in Fig. 7. Four expressions (happiness, surprise, anger and disgust) are similar to the real expressions and have higher authenticity. However, the expressions of fear and sadness have high similarities that are difficult to distinguish. The main reason may be the movement differences between these two AUs are not obvious, owing to the contact positions and directions of AU15 and AU20 at corners of the mouth are relatively close. Simultaneously, the similarity of AU mechanisms may lead to difficult distinctions between these two expressions as well, the former direction is downward while the latter direction has a certain angle.

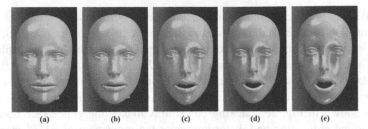

(a)   (b)   (c)   (d)   (e)

Fig. 6. Surprised expression simulations of five groups under different load conditions.

Therefore, future remedial measures will include, but are not limited to, the following methods: increasing the number of AUs reasonably and optimizing the distribution of AUs nearby the corner of the mouth.

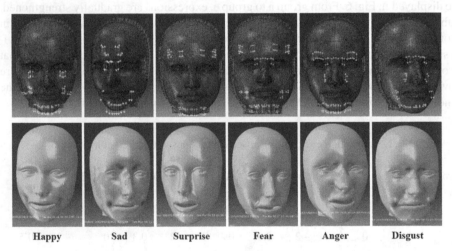

Happy   Sad   Surprise   Fear   Anger   Disgust

Fig. 7. Loads, restrictions and simulation results of six expressions.

4   Conclusion

In this research, the FECS theory-based multi-DoF mechanisms of the robotic head for humanoid facial expression imitation were designed, including neck, eyeball-eyelid, and facial expression mechanisms have been validated to working well. Topic proposes the design of a humanoid expression robotic head. While reasonable synthesis rules of AUs were proposed. Based on the finite element analysis, the effect of six humanoid facial expressions under various boundary restrictions and load displacements and positions were verified and qualitative expression results were obtained. However, the actual effect of 6 humanoid facial expressions still needs to be confirmed. In future work, a physical facial expression robotic head will be constructed and integrated onto a humanoid robot specifically designed for homecare purposes. Further related experiments and demonstration regarding human-robot interaction will be conducted, focusing on daily care tasks. These efforts aim to initially assess the feasibility and practicality of utilizing such technology for indoor elderly care.

Acknowledgment. This work was supported in part by the National Natural Science Foundation of China (No. 51975513), the Natural Science Foundation of Zhejiang Province, China (No. LR20E050003), the Major Research Plan of National Natural Science Foundation of China (No. 51890884), the Major Research Plan of Ningbo Innovation 2025 (No. 2020Z022), and the Bellwethers Research and Development Plan of Zhejiang Province (No. 2023C01045). Some image elements were downloaded from https://www.freepik.com.

References

1. Wu, L., Huang, Z., Pan, Z.: The spatiality and driving forces of population ageing in China. PLoS ONE **16**(1), e0243559 (2021)
2. Tu, W.J., Zeng, X., Liu, Q.: Aging tsunami coming: the main finding from China's seventh national population census. Aging Clin. Exp. Res. **34**(5), 1159–1163 (2022)
3. Eshkoor, S.A., Hamid, T.A., Mun, C.Y., et al.: Mild cognitive impairment and its management in older people. Clin. Interv. Aging **10**, 687–693 (2015)
4. Sakagami, Y., Watanabe, R., Aoyama, C., et al.: The intelligent ASIMO: system overview and integration. In: IEEE/RSJ International Conference on Intelligent Robots and Systems, **3**, pp. 2478–2483. IEEE, Lausanne (2002)
5. Shamsuddin, S., Ismail, L.I., Yussof, H., et al.: Humanoid robot NAO: review of control and motion exploration. In: 2011 IEEE International Conference on Control System, Computing and Engineering, pp. 511–516. IEEE, Penang (2011)
6. Tanaka, F., Isshiki, K., Takahashi, F., et al.: Pepper learns together with children: development of an educational application. In: IEEE-RAS 15th International Conference on Humanoid Robots (Humanoids), pp. 270–275. IEEE, Seoul (2015)
7. Hashimoto, T., Hiramatsu, S., Tsuji, T., et al.: Realization and evaluation of realistic nod with receptionist robot SAYA. In: RO-MAN 2007 - The 16th IEEE International Symposium on Robot and Human Interactive Communication, pp. 326–331. IEEE, Jeju (2007)
8. Hashimoto, T., Hitramatsu, S., Tsuji, T., et al.: Development of the face robot SAYA for rich facial expressions. In: SICE-ICASE International Joint Conference, pp. 5423–5428. IEEE, Busan (2006)
9. Zecca, M., Endo, N., Momoki, S., et al.: Design of the humanoid robot KOBIAN - preliminary analysis of facial and whole body emotion expression capabilities. In: Humanoids 2008 - 8th IEEE-RAS International Conference on Humanoid Robots, pp. 487–492. IEEE, Daejeon (2008)
10. Kishi, T., Otani, T., Endo, N., et al.: Development of expressive robotic head for bipedal humanoid robot. In: IEEE/RSJ International Conference on Intelligent Robots and Systems, pp. 4584–4589. Vilamoura-Algarve (2012)
11. Miwa, H., Okuchi, T., Takanobu, H., et al.: Development of a new human-like head robot WE-4. In: IEEE/RSJ International Conference on Intelligent Robots and Systems, **3**, pp. 2443–2448. IEEE, Lausanne (2002)
12. Takanishi, A., Takanobu, H., Kato, I., et al.: Development of the anthropomorphic head-eye robot WE-3RII with an autonomous facial expression mechanism. In: Proceedings 1999 IEEE International Conference on Robotics and Automation (Cat No99CH36288C), **4**, pp. 3255–3260. IEEE, Detroit (1999)

13. Zecca, M., Roccella, S., Carrozza, M.C., et al.: On the development of the emotion expression humanoid robot WE-4RII with RCH-1. In: IEEE/RAS International Conference on Humanoid Robots, 1, pp. 235–252. IEEE, Santa Monica (2004)
14. Shayganfar, M., Rich, C., Sidner, C.L.: A design methodology for expressing emotion on robot faces. In: IEEE/RSJ International Conference on Intelligent Robots and Systems, pp. 4577–4583. IEEE, Vilamoura-Algarve (2012)
15. Ekman, P., Friesen, W.V.: Measuring facial movement. Environ. Psychology Nonverbal Behav. 1(1), 56–75 (1976)
16. Ekman, P., Friesen, W.V.: Facial action coding system. Environmental Psychology & Nonverbal Behavior (1978)
17. Ekman, P.: Pictures of Facial Affect. Consulting Psychologists Press (1976)

Adversarial Attacks on Skeleton-Based Sign Language Recognition

Yufeng Li[1], Meng Han[2(✉)], Jiahui Yu[3], Changting Lin[4], and Zhaojie Ju[5]

[1] School of Automation and Electrical Engineering, Shenyang Ligong University,
Shenyang 110159, China
liyufeng2187@163.com

[2] College of Computer Science and Technology, Zhejiang University, Hangzhou, China
mhan@zju.edu.cn

[3] Department of Biomedical Engineering, Zhejiang University, Hangzhou 310058, China
jiahui.yu@zju.edu.cn

[4] College of Computer Science and Technology, Zhejiang University, Hangzhou 310058, China
linchangting@zju.edu.cn

[5] School of Computing, University of Portsmouth, Portsmouth PO13HE, UK
Zhaojie.Ju@port.ac.uk

Abstract. Despite the impressive performance achieved by sign language recognition systems based on skeleton information, our research has uncovered their vulnerability to malicious attacks. In response to this challenge, we present an adversarial attack specifically designed to sign language recognition models that rely on extracted human skeleton data as features. Our attack aims to assess the robustness and sensitivity of these models, and we propose adversarial training techniques to enhance their resilience. Moreover, we conduct transfer experiments using the generated adversarial samples to demonstrate the transferability of these adversarial examples across different models. Additionally, by conducting experiments on the sensitivity of sign language recognition models, we identify the optimal experimental parameter settings for achieving the most effective attacks. This research significantly contributes to future investigations into the security of sign language recognition.

Keywords: Sign language recognition · Adversarial attacks · Robustness

1 Introduction

In recent years, the field of sign language recognition (SLR) has gained increasing importance, thanks to the rapid advancements in deep learning [1, 3] and computer vision [2, 6]. Compared to traditional action recognition, sign language recognition presents unique challenges. Sign language involves full-body movements, precise arm and gesture motions, and the utilization of facial expressions to convey emotions. Additionally, similar gestures can hold different meanings based on the number of repetitions. These factors pose challenges to the accuracy and robustness of sign language recognition

The authors would like to acknowledge the support from the National Natural Science Foundation of China (52075530).

H. Yang et al. (Eds.): ICIRA 2023, LNAI 14267, pp. 33–43, 2023.
https://doi.org/10.1007/978-981-99-6483-3_4

models. The introduction of the Spatial-Temporal Graph Convolutional Network (ST-GCN), which models dynamic patterns in skeleton data using Graph Convolutional Networks (GCNs), has achieved remarkable results [7, 9].

Despite the successful application of deep learning [4, 5, 8] in various complex problems, it has been discovered that these models are vulnerable to adversarial attacks, where slight, imperceptible perturbations can arbitrarily alter their predictions [10]. As a result, numerous adversarial attacks targeting different visual tasks have emerged [11, 12]. Studying these attacks not only enhances our understanding of neural network principles but also provides insights into improving the robustness of deep learning in real-world adversarial environments [13].

Skeleton-based sign language recognition models are also susceptible to such risks. When deploying sign language recognition models in critical communication scenarios with economic significance, the robustness of these models becomes paramount. If an attacker successfully targets the sign language recognition model, they can disrupt machine translation results without raising suspicion from human observers (e.g., individuals with disabilities). This makes it difficult to trace the attacker during post-event investigations. However, adversarial attacks on these models are still being explored. One of the main challenges in this area is that skeleton data representation significantly differs from image representation, and existing attacks are primarily designed for image-based models. Human skeleton data is sparse, discrete, and evolves over time within a rigid spatial configuration [13]. So in this paper, we abandon the idea of changing the connection relationship of the skeleton structure. Instead, we focus on modifying the node feature information that each joint can form for the spatiotemporal graph composed of the same joint connecting naturally between frames and within a single frame of the skeleton. Our main contributions can be summarized as follows:

- We preliminarily explore the robustness of the privacy security model of sign language recognition model, which is very rare as we know.
- We propose a novel perturbation design for skeleton feature information. By changing the characteristics of joint nodes, bone flow and other characteristics of second-order vectors obtained by the calculation of first-order vectors are changed. We also tested the sensitivity of the sign language model to the antagonistic samples generated by different training batches and disturbance factors.
- We conducted an experiment on adversarial sample generation to study the privacy of feature extraction of skeleton flow in a multi-stream gesture recognition model. And the robustness of sign language recognition model is improved by using these adversarial samples for adversarial training in Fig. 1.

In this paper, we first review the principles of sign language recognition and spatiotemporal graph neural networks using skeleton. And then describes the attacker's attack. Finally, generate adversarial samples to test the robustness and sensitivity of the model, and improve the anti-jamming ability of the model through adversarial training.

2   Related Work

Skeleton-Based Sign Language Recognition. The use of skeleton data in action recognition has become popular, as reliable skeleton data can be obtained from modern RGB-D sensors (such as Microsoft Kinect) or extracted from images captured by a single RGB camera. [8, 14, 15, 29] Skeletal actions are represented as a series of human bones that encode rich spatiotemporal information about human motion. [9] First attempted to design a graph-based approach called ST-GCN, which models dynamic patterns in skeleton data using a Graph Convolutional Network (GCN). [9] This approach has attracted much attention and there have been some improvements. Specifically, [16] proposed an AS-GCN to mine potential co-connections for improved recognition performance. [17] extended this to two-stream, [18] further extended to four-stream. [7] developed a Decoupled GCN to increase model capacity without additional computational cost. ResGCN, proposed in [19], adopts the bottleneck structure of ResNet [20] to reduce parameters while increasing model capacity.

Adversarial Attacks on Sign Language Recognition. With the development of deep learning, there has been a significant research focus on adversarial attacks in recent years [10–12, 24, 30]. For networks that use convolutional layers to extract features, the principles of inherent adversarial attacks also apply. However, direct transfer of these attacks can lead to various problems. Adversarial attacks on graph-structured data have become increasingly prevalent, but new challenges have arisen compared to attacking traditional image data. Firstly, the structure of the graph and the features of its nodes exist in a discrete domain with certain predefined structures, which limits the degrees of freedom for creating adversarial perturbations. Secondly, the imperceptibility of adversarial perturbations in graph data is difficult to define and achieve, as discrete graph data inherently prevents infinitesimal changes [21]. In human body skeletons, graph edges represent rigid human bones, which connect a limited number of human joints to form a standard spatial configuration. Unlike graph data with variable graph structures (e.g. social network graphs [22]), human skeletons are fixed in terms of joint connections and bone lengths. The spatiotemporal skeleton graph not only inherits these characteristics of the human skeleton graph, but also has fixed edges between frames, which, if arbitrarily modified, can lead to a visually disorienting effect. Wang et al. [23] used a new perceptual loss to achieve better attack results, which minimized the dynamic differences between the original motion and the adversarial motion. Furthermore, extensive

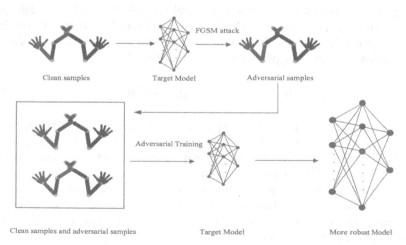

Fig. 1. Attacks on skeleton-based sign language recognition schematics

perceptual research has also demonstrated this performance. Zheng et al. [24] formulated adversarial attacks as an optimization problem with joint angle constraints in Euclidean space, and then solved it using the alternating direction method of multipliers (ADMM) [24].

3   Sign Language Recognition Model

We have selected SL-GCN [26], which achieved the highest performance in both RGB (98.42%) and RGBD (98.53%) tracks in the 2021 "Looking at People Large Scale Signer Independent Isolated SLR Challenge". Due to the particularity of sign language recognition task, the models with good performance adopt multimodal fusion methods, and skeleton information flow is one of the essential ways to express the intrinsic correlation features of human dynamics. Therefore, its security is of great importance. So, we will only select the modality network that utilizes the skeleton flow information as our attack target. To better understand the attacks we have designed, it is first necessary to understand our target model. Using this prerequisite knowledge, we subsequently formalize our problem of adversarial attacks on skeleton sign language recognition.

3.1   Spatial-temporal Convolution Network

An action in skeleton domain is represented as a sequence of T skeleton frames, where every skeleton consists of N body joints [9]. Given such N × T volumes of joints, an undirected spatio-temporal graph G = (V, E) can be constructed [10], where V denotes the node set of graph and E is the edge set. A representative description of the graph structure in matrix form; summarized in a N × D feature matrix X (N: number of nodes, D: number of input features). A representative description of the graph structure in matrix form; typically in the form of an adjacency matrix A (or some function thereof). And produces a node-level output Z (an N × F feature matrix, where F is the number of output features per node).

As a transfer attempt of convolutional neural networks to topological data, graph convolutional neural networks aim to learn a function G = (V,E) that operates on signals or features on graphs. For each layer of the network, the feature extraction is designed with the following formula applied to the feature matrix H,

$$f\left(H^{(l)}, A\right) = \sigma(\widehat{D}^{-\frac{1}{2}}\widehat{A}\widehat{D}^{-\frac{1}{2}}H^{(l)}W^{(l)}) \tag{1}$$

Here, $V = \{v_{ti} | t = 1,..., T, i = 1,..., N\}$ encodes the skeleton joints. An element 'v' of this set can also be considered to encode a joint's Cartesian coordinates. Two kinds of graph edges E are defined for joints, namely; intra-body edge ES and inter-frame edge EF. Specifically, ES is represented as an N × N adjacency matrix of graph nodes, where the matrix element ES ij = 1|i 6 = j identifies that a physical bone connection exists between the body joint vi and vj. The interframe edges EF denotes the connections of the same joints between consecutive frames, which can also be treated as temporal trajectories of the skeleton joints.

Given the spatio-temporal skeleton graph G, a graph convolution operation is defined by extending the conventional image-based convolution. Along the spatial dimension, graph convolution is conducted on a graph node vi around its neighboring nodes $v_j \in B(v_i)$,

$$f_{out}(v_i) = \sum_{v_j \in B(v_i)} \frac{1}{Z_i(v_j)} f_{in}(v_j) \cdot w(l_i(v_j))$$ (2)

3.2 Sign Language Graph Convolution Network

SL-GCN Block is constructed with decoupled spatial convolutional network, self-attention and graph dropping module inspired by [9, 16]. As illustrated in Fig. 2, a basic GCN block of our proposed SL-GCN network consists of a decoupled spatial convolutional layer (Decouple SCN), a STC (spatial, temporal and channelwise) attention module, a temporal convolutional layer (TCN) and a DropGraph module.

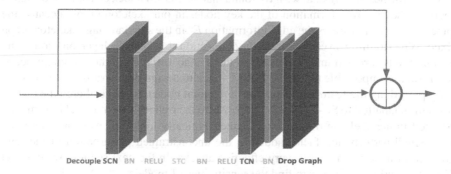

Decouple SCN BN RELU STC BN RELU TCN BN Drop Graph

Fig. 2. SL-GCN single block

Except for the joint feature information 1st-order representation (joints coordinate), 2nd-order representation (bone vector), and their motion vectors are trained four stream separately and save the output of the last fully-connected layers of each modality before softmax layer. Those outputs have the size nc where nc is the number of classes. We assign weights to the every modality according to their accuracy on validation set and sum them up with weights as our final predicted score.

As for how the feature information of the other three streams, apart from the joint feature information, is calculated, I will introduce it in detail in the next section.

4 Attacker Implementation

4.1 Attack for Skeleton Coordinate

The uniqueness of sign language recognition tasks typically assumes that different patterns contain unique motion information, which may complement each other and ultimately obtain a comprehensive and unique representation of motion. However, to explore the explorability of adversarial sample generation in representing skeleton information, we focus our research on the flow of skeleton information.

When designing attack samples on sign language recognition models that use skeletal information, we attempted to utilize the Fast Gradient Sign Method (FGSM) [10] as the primary attack, to create a skeletal perturbation V^0 in a single step. This approach, which is the most fundamental way of designing perturbations in image data, is feasible when extended to the field of topological data. For our FGSM-based attack setup, the perturbation calculation for joint features can be expressed as follows,

$$V' = V^0 + \epsilon sign\left(\nabla_{V^0}\mathcal{L}\left(\mathcal{F}_\theta\left(V^0, E^0\right), c_{gt}\right)\right) \tag{3}$$

where $\mathcal{F}_\theta$ denotes trained Sl-GCN [28] model, $\mathcal{L}$ is the crossentropy loss for action recognition, and ∇_{V^0} is the derivative operation that computes the gradient of ST-GCN loss w.r.t. V^0, given the current model parameters θ and the ground truth action label c_{gt}. The sign of gradient is scaled with a parameter ϵ, and added to the original graph V^0. The FGSM-based attack is computationally efficient as it takes only a single step in the direction of increasing the recognition loss of the target model.

It is worth mentioning that, we have found that the FGSM attack can only be designed to perturb the feature information of the key nodes in our skeleton graph, because the adjacency matrix that stores the edge information E^0 in the sign language skeleton graph is fixed. When training on each sample, the connections between each person's joints and the same joints across frames are fixed, so there is no variation in the training process. Therefore, it is impossible to use the FGSM attack to design perturbations that target E.

By perturbing the feature information at the joint nodes, we have altered the feature information inputted to SL-GCN. However, due to the richness of structural information contained in the skeleton diagram, its input is typically high-dimensional. Therefore, even a small perturbation factor added to the unconstrained perturbation of the joint feature information can lead to very effective attacks. In the next section, we have set different perturbation factors to find the sensitivities of models.

4.2 Attack for Sign Language Recognition

In order to find out the vulnerability of skeleton flow information input in sign language recognition system and seek the practical significance of adversarial samples. We also focused on bone data features, bone motion features, and joint motion features. Bone features are represented as vectors by connecting joints in the human body from the source joint to the target joint in Fig. 3. Motion features are generated by calculating the differences between adjacent frames in the joint and bone flow. For example [26], in a gesture recognition task, the nose node is used as the root joint, so its bone vector is assigned a value of zero. If the features of the source joint and the target joint are represented respectively as,

$$v_{i,t}^J = \left(x_{i,t}, y_{i,t}, s_{i,t}\right) v_{j,t}^J = \left(x_{j,t}, y_{j,t}, s_{j,t}\right) \tag{4}$$

(x; y; s) represents the x-y coordinates and confidence score, then the calculation method for bone features is as follows,

$$v_{j,t}^B = \left(x_{j,t} - x_{i,t}, y_{j,t} - y_{i,t}, s_{j,t}\right) \tag{5}$$

The calculation method for joint motion characteristics is as follows,

$$v_{i,t}^{JM} = \left(x_{i,t+1} - x_{i,t}, y_{i,t+1} - y_{i,t}, s_{i,t} \right) \tag{6}$$

The calculation method for bone motion features is as follows,

$$v_{i,t}^{BM} = v_{i,t+1}^{B} - v_{i,t}^{B} \tag{7}$$

If we follow the approach of FGSM to design perturbations, the spatial coordinate information of the node will be changed. The bone features with perturbations will increase the difference between the source joint and the target joint in the same frame, and the connection length between joints in the human body will be changed in the same frame. If we design perturbations for joint movement and bone movement, it will increase the differences in motion between the same joint and different joints.

5 Experiments

We first introduce our experimental settings. Then, we present the results of our proposed attack. Finally, we attempt to defend against our attack.

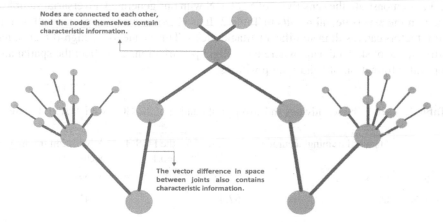

Fig. 3. Single frame skeleton graph. The nose is the root node, but the characteristic information provided by the nose itself as the node is composed of a high-dimensional array [N, C, V, T, M]. N is numbers of samples; C is numbers of channels; V is numbers of joints; T is numbers of frames; M is numbers of people.

5.1 Datasets and Evaluation Metric

AUTSL Dataset [27]. It is a Turkish SLR dataset collected using Kinect V2 sensor [28]. Statistically, 226 different sign glosses are performed by 43 signers with 20 backgrounds. The dataset contains 38,336 videos that split into training, validation, and testing subsets.

Evaluation Metric. As there has been limited exploration of attack methods for sign language recognition tasks, we chose to use the same evaluation metrics as those for generating adversarial samples for action recognition, as described in [12]. The lower the accuracy, the more effective our generated adversarial samples are.

Attack Results and Adversarial Training. Our attack employs FGSM to design perturbations targeted at the skeletal flow feature information in gesture recognition tasks. We use the accuracies on AUTSL dataset as the attack metrics across ST-GCN and multi-stream SL-GCN to demonstrate the transferability of our generated adversarial samples.

We designed perturbation for the characteristic of joint nodes, and the disturbance of joint characteristic was used to calculate the second-order vector characteristic. Finally, we combine their predicted results by adding them together with weights using the ensemble strategy.

We attempted to defend against our attacks by conducting adversarial training on the AUTSL dataset, using a setting of $\epsilon =0.1$. As shown in Table 1, the ST-GCN and SL-GCN models with adversarial training were more robust than the models trained on raw data. We can also see that sl-gcn has better robustness than ST-gcn after adversarial training. We think this case is that SL-GCN reduces the number of identification points compared with ST-GCN. This also may be related to the fact that the SL-GCN model incorporated attention mechanisms and GCN decoupling modules to better extract features compared to the ST-GCN model.

We also conducted experiments in Table 2. With different perturbation factors ϵ in Eq. 3 to demonstrate the sensitivity of SL-GCN with our generated adversarial samples. Based on the experimental results in Table 2. It can be observed that even small perturbation factors can result in significant attack effects. This is due to the high-dimensional feature space of skeletal data, where even slight perturbations can affect the spatial and temporal information of hand joint positions.

Table 1. $\epsilon =0.1$, the sensitivities and adversarial training of SL-GCN with AUTSL Dataset

	Standard training accuracy	Accuracy for the FGSM attack with $\epsilon =0.1$	Adversarial training accuracy
SL-GCN	94.68	71.94	98.23
ST-GCN	89.67	67.48	92.47

In Fig. 4, we can observe that even with the same perturbation factor ϵ, , the size of the batch affects the impact of each generated adversarial sample on the accuracy of the model. From the four different perturbation factors, smaller batch sizes result in better perturbation effects for the generated adversarial samples. However, when the batch size reaches or approaches one, the perturbation effects contradict the conclusions drawn. This may be related to the preprocessing of the dataset, where sign language gestures in a video are extracted as images with different frame rates to extract key points. Indeed, the loss of relevant features across different frames of a video is not significant. Therefore, for attack methods like one-step FGSM (Fast Gradient Sign Method), the generated perturbation effects are limited. However, when the batch size slightly increases, the perturbation effects become more effective due to the high-dimensional characteristics of skeleton data in different frames of various videos. Under the setting of perturbation

Table 2. Accuracy of using different ϵ generated against samples on the SL-GCN and ST-GCN model with the AUTSL dataset

ϵ	SL-GCN	ST-GCN
0	94.68	89.67
0.02	88.13	80.45
0.06	80.53	74.83
0.1	71.94	67.48
0.2	47.98	40.42
0.4	17.78	8.42

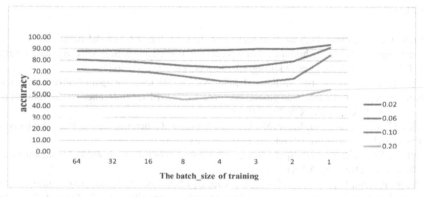

Fig. 4. With different ϵ, the sensitivities of SL-GCN for different batch sizes in training. The discounting of different colors corresponds to the sensitivity of the model to batch_size under different disturbance factors.

factor $\epsilon = 0.1$, the model is most sensitive to adversarial examples generated from training batch size 3, with a decrease in accuracy of 60%. Across different training batches, the differences in the impact of generated adversarial examples on the model's accuracy reach as much as 20%. Even without considering the potential influence of training batch 1 due to data preprocessing, overall trends suggest that the differences in the impact of adversarial examples on the model's accuracy reach up to 10%. We only investigated the impact of adversarial samples from different training batches under perturbation factors of 0.02, 0.06, 0.1, and 0.2. Because, with a perturbation factor of 0.2, the perturbed skeleton data already exhibited an accuracy below 50%, which is even lower than the probability of random prediction, as a result, it lacks practical significance for our research.

Through this experiment, we discovered that the effectiveness of perturbations is related to our preprocessing of the original dataset. We also identified the most effective perturbation parameter settings for different perturbation factors and training batch sizes on the AUTSL dataset. This is of great significance for our subsequent search for the most effective and imperceptible adversarial examples.

6 Conclusion

We show the vulnerability of state-of-the-art sign language recognizers to adversarial attacks. To this end, we designed a targeted attack on a sign language recognizer based on skeleton. Through experiments, we show that sign language recognizers are also at risk from adversarial attacks. In addition, robustness can be enhanced by training sign language recognizers with adversarial samples generated under our adversarial attacks. In the future we will continue to explore other secure directions for sign language recognizers and make our attacks relevant to real world dangers.

Acknowledgement. Changting's work was partially supported by NSFC under No. 62102363 and No. 62072404, the Zhejiang Provincial Natural Science Foundation under No. LQ21F020010, Hangzhou Innovation Team under No. TD2022011.

References

1. Yu, J., Gao, H., Zhou, D., Liu, J., Gao, Q., Ju, Z.: Deep temporal model-based identity-aware hand detection for space human-robot interaction. IEEE Transactions on Cybernetics **52**(12), 13738–13751 (2022). https://doi.org/10.1109/TCYB.2021.3114031
2. Liao, F., Liang, M., Dong, Y., Pang, T., Hu, X., Zhu, J.: Defense against adversarial attacks using high-level representation guided denoiser. In: The IEEE Conference on Computer Vision and Pattern Recognition (CVPR) (2018)
3. Xiao, C., Li, B., yan Zhu, J., He, W., Liu, M., Song, D.: Generating adversarial examples with adversarial networks. In: IJCAI, pp. 3905–3911 (2018)
4. Yan, S., Xiong, Y., Lin, D.: Spatial temporal graph convolutional networks for skeleton-based action recognition. In: AAAI (2018)
5. Zhang, P., Lan, C., Xing, J., Zeng, W., Xue, J., Zheng, N.: View adaptive neural networks for high performance skeleton-based human action recognition. IEEE Trans. Pattern Anal. Mach. Intell. **41**(8), 1963–1978 (2019)
6. Yu, J., Gao, H., Chen, Y., Zhou, D., Liu, J., Ju, Z.: Adaptive spatiotemporal representation learning for skeleton-based human action recognition. IEEE Trans. Cognitive and Developmental Syst. **14**(4), 1654–1665 (2022). https://doi.org/10.1109/TCDS.2021.3131253
7. Cheng, K., Zhang, Y., Cao, C., Shi, L., Cheng, J., Lu, H.: Decoupling GCN with DropGraph module for skeleton-based action recognition. In: Proceedings of European Conference on Computer Vision (2020)
8. Xiao, Q., Qin, M., Yin, Y.: Skeleton-based chinese sign language recognition and generation for bidirectional communication between deaf and hearing people. Neural Networks, **125**, 41–55 (2020)
9. Yan, S., Xiong, Y., Lin, D.: Spatial temporal graph convolutional networks for skeleton-based action recognition. In: Proceedings of AAAI conference on artificial intelligence **32** (2018)
10. Goodfellow, I.J., Shlens, J., Szegedy, C.: Explaining and Harnessing Adversarial Examples. arXiv preprint arXiv:1412.6572 (20140
11. Diao, Y., Shao, T., Yang, Y.L., et al.: BASAR: black-box attack on skeletal action recognition. In: Proceedings of the IEEE/CVF Conference on Computer Vision and Pattern Recognition, pp. 7597–7607 (2021)
12. Tanaka, N., Kera, H., Kawamoto, K.: Adversarial bone length attack on action recognition. Proceedings of the AAAI Conference on Artificial Intelligence. **36**(2), 2335–2343 (2022)
13. Wang, H., He, F., Peng, Z., et al.: Understanding the robustness of skeleton-based action recognition under adversarial attack. Proceedings of the IEEE/CVF Conference on Computer Vision and Pattern Recognition, pp. 14656–14665 (2021)

14. Koller, O., Zargaran, S., Ney, H., Bowden, R.: Deep sign: enabling robust statistical continuous sign language recognition via hybrid CNN-HMMs. Int. J. Comput. Vision **126**(12), 1311–1325 (2018)
15. Du, Y., Wang, W., Wang, L.: Hierarchical recurrent neural network for skeleton based action recognition. In: Proceedings of the IEEE Conference on Computer Vision and Pattern Recognition, pp. 1110–1118 (2015)
16. Li, M., Chen, S., Chen, X., Zhang, Y., Wang, Y., Tian, Q.: Actional-structural graph convolutional networks for skeleton-based action recognition. In: Proceedings of the IEEE/CVF Conference on Computer Vision and Pattern Recognition, pp. 3595–3603 (2019)
17. Shi, L., Zhang, Y., Cheng, J., Lu, H.: Twostream adaptive graph convolutional networks for skeletonbased action recognition. In: Proceedings of the IEEE/CVF Conference on Computer Vision and Pattern Recognition, pp. 12026–12035 (2019)
18. Shi, L., Zhang, Y., Cheng, J., Hanqing, L.: Skeleton-based action recognition with multi-stream adaptive graph convolutional networks. IEEE Trans. Image Process. **29**, 9532–9545 (2020)
19. Song, Y.-F., Zhang, Z., Shan, C., Wang, L.: Stronger, faster and more explainable: a graph convolutional baseline for skeleton-based action recognition. In: Proceedings of ACM International Conference on Multimedia, pp. 1625–1633 (2020)
20. He, K., Zhang, X., Ren, S., Sun, J.: Deep residual learning for image recognition. In: Proceedings of the IEEE Conference on Computer Vision and Pattern Recognition, pp. 770–778 (2016)
21. Liu, J., Akhtar, N., Mian, A.: Adversarial attack on skeleton-based human action recognition. IEEE Trans. Neural Networks and Learning Syst. **33**(4), 1609–1622 (2020)
22. Newman, M.E., Watts, D.J., Strogatz, S.H.: Random graph models of social networks. Proc. Natl. Acad. Sci. **99**(suppl 1), 2566–2572 (2002)
23. Cao, Z., Hidalgo, G., Simon, T., Wei, S.-E., Sheikh, Y.: Openposc: Realtime Multi-Person 2d Pose Estimation Using Part Affinity Fields. arXiv preprint arXiv:1812.08008 (2018)
24. Zhou, Y., Han, M., Liu, L., et al.: The adversarial attacks threats on computer vision: a survey. In: 2019 IEEE 16th International Conference on Mobile Ad Hoc and Sensor Systems Workshops (MASSW), IEEE, pp. 25–30 (2019)
25. Zheng, T., Liu, S., Chen, C., Yuan, J., Li, B., Ren, K.: Towards Understanding the Adversarial Vulnerability of Skeleton-based Action Recognition. arXiv:2005.07151 [cs] (2020)
26. Jiang, S., Sun, B., Wang, L., et al.: Skeleton aware multi-modal sign language recognition. Proceedings of the IEEE/CVF Conference on Computer Vision and Pattern Recognition, 3413–3423 (2021)
27. Sincan, O.M., Keles, H.Y.: AUTSL: a large scale multi-modal turkish sign language dataset and baseline methods. IEEE Access **8**, 181340–181355 (2020)
28. Amon, C., Fuhrmann, F., Graf, F.: Evaluation of the spatial resolution accuracy of the face tracking system for Kinect for windows V1 and V2. In: Proceedings of AAAI Conference on Artificial, pp. 16–17 (2014)
29. He, S., Han, M., Patel, N., et al.: Converting handwritten text to editable format via gesture recognition for education. Proceedings of the 51st ACM Technical Symposium on Computer Science Education, pp. 1369–1369 (2020)
30. Zhou, Y., Han, M., Liu, L., et al.: Deep learning approach for cyberattack detection. IEEE INFOCOM 2018-IEEE Conference on Computer Communications Workshops (INFOCOM WKSHPS). IEEE, pp. 262–267 (2018)

Adaptive Goal-Biased Bi-RRT for Online Path Planning of Robotic Manipulators

Letian Fu, Xiaoben Lin, and Yunjiang Lou[✉]

Harbin Institute of Technology Shenzhen, Shenzhen 518055, China
louyj@hit.edu.cn

Abstract. Autonomous obstacle avoidance path planning plays a crucial role in enabling intelligent and safe operation of robotic manipulators. While the RRT algorithm exhibits promising performance in high-dimensional spaces by avoiding explicit environment modeling and exploring a wide search space, its efficiency is obstructed by random and blind sampling and expansion, limiting online planning and efficient motion capabilities. To address this, we propose the Adaptive Goal-Biased Bi-RRT (AGBBi-RRT) algorithm, which incorporates a goal-biased strategy and an adaptive step size strategy to enhance path planning efficiency in high-dimensional spaces. By combining the concept of Artificial Potential Fields (APF) with a goal-bias factor, we guide the expansion of tree nodes, mitigating the limitations of the RRT algorithm. Additionally, to overcome falling into 'local minimum', an adaptive step size strategy is proposed to enhance obstacle avoidance capabilities. Further improvements are achieved through bidirectional pruning and cubic non-uniform B-spline fitting, resulting in shorter and smoother paths. Simulation experiments are conducted to evaluate the performance of AGBBi-RRT algorithm on a six-dof robotic manipulator in single-obstacle and multi-obstacles scenarios, comparing three algorithms: Bi-RRT, GBBi-RRT, and AGBBi-RRT. The experimental results show significant improvements in AGBBi-RRT compared to the previous two algorithms. In the single-obstacle scenario, the AGBBi-RRT algorithm achieves a 15.28% and 9.11% reduction in calculation time, while in the multi-obstacles scenario, the reduction is 27.00% and 15.92% respectively. In addition, AGBBi-RRT exhibits encouraging performance in terms of number of nodes, number of waypoints, and path length.

Keywords: Path planning · Robotic manipulator · Bi-RRT · Goal-biased strategy · Adaptive step size

1 Introduction

Robotic manipulators have found applications in various fields, including human-robot collaboration in industrial production, fruit and vegetable picking in agriculture, coffee preparation and so on. These application scenarios are usually complex, with a large number of obstacles and constraints, requiring robotic manipulators to achieve intelligent and safe operation. In such situations, the

© The Author(s), under exclusive license to Springer Nature Singapore Pte Ltd. 2023
H. Yang et al. (Eds.): ICIRA 2023, LNAI 14267, pp. 44–56, 2023.
https://doi.org/10.1007/978-981-99-6483-3_5

ability to autonomously generate obstacle avoidance paths rapidly becomes crucial, calling for highly efficient algorithms. By enhancing algorithmic efficiency and minimizing computation time, a more adaptable, scalable, and practical solution can be provided. This empowers robotic manipulators to plan paths swiftly, enabling them to respond promptly and effectively in online path planning tasks. In recent years, research on path planning algorithms for robotic manipulators has received increasing attention [1]. Classical methods for path planning are commonly categorized into four types: search-based algorithms, optimization-based algorithms, sampling-based algorithms, and artificial potential field methods [2].

Search-based algorithms like A* and D* are widely used for path planning [3], but they have limitations in high-dimensional spaces due to the need for explicit environment modeling and resolution issues. Optimization-based algorithms such as CHOMP and STOMP offer optimal paths but can be sensitive to the initial path and lack guaranteed success rates [4]. The artificial potential field algorithm easily falls into a 'local minimum' [5]. In the field of high-dimensional path planning, the RRT algorithm proposed by LaValle et al. [6] has shown promising performance with probabilistic completeness and a wide search range. However, the basic RRT algorithm suffers from issues like redundant nodes, slow convergence, and poor path quality, which severely limit the efficiency of the algorithm.

To address these shortcomings, researchers have proposed various improvements to the RRT algorithm. The Bi-RRT algorithm and the idea of goal bias are proposed by LaValle and Kuffner [7,8]. Afterwards, several researchers have applied this idea in their work, Jiang et al. [9], Yuan et al. [10] and Liu et al. [11] used the idea of goal bias to guide the search, Sepehri et al. combined APF and RRT to achieve two-stage planning [12], and Chen et al. used the Sigmoid function to adjust the probability of sampling [13]. Zhen et al. [14] and Chen et al. [13] conduct research on adaptive step size to improve algorithm efficiency. These algorithms mainly used the idea of goal bias to improve the efficiency, but they did not solve the problem of falling into 'local minimum' well.

This paper presents the AGBBi-RRT algorithm, which improves path planning efficiency through a goal-biased strategy and an adaptive step size strategy. The goal-biased strategy guides the expansion direction of the tree by combining the idea of APF, and the adaptive step size strategy accelerates the expansion and improves the obstacle avoidance ability of the algorithm. We also reduce path cost and smooth the path using bidirectional pruning and cubic non-uniform B-spline fitting. Finally, a series of simulation experiments are carried out to verify the performance of proposed algorithm, and the experimental results show the feasibility, effectiveness and superiority of the algorithm.

The remainder of this paper is structured as follows. In Sect. 2, we provide an introduction to the basic Bi-RRT algorithm, followed by a discussion of our goal-biased and adaptive step size strategies. The path is bidirectional prunend and is fitted by cubic non-uniform B-Spline curve in Sect. 3. In Sect. 4, simulation experiments are carried out to verify the effectiveness of our algrorithm. Finally, a conclusion is summarized in Sect. 5.

2   Improved Bi-RRT Algorithm

2.1   Basic Bi-RRT

The core idea of the Bi-RRT algorithm proposed by Kuffner and LaValle is to construct two random trees rooted in the initial and goal configurations and alternate their growth to achieve a fast connection.

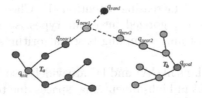

Fig. 1. Bi-RRT node expansion diagram

The specific node expansion diagram can be seen in Fig. 1. The algorithm first builds two random trees T_a and T_b rooted in the initial configuration q_{init} and the goal configuration q_{goal} respectively, and in each iteration of the algorithm, a sampling point q_{rand} is obtained by random sampling in the configuration space. Find the point q_{near1} closest to q_{rand} in T_a, then expand a fixed step from q_{near1} to q_{rand} to get a new node q_{new1}. Do a collision check between q_{new1} and q_{near1}, if passed, add q_{new1} to T_a, otherwise resample and expand. Then find the node q_{near2} closest to q_{new1} in T_b and greedily expand from q_{near2} to q_{near1} until a collision occurs or T_a and T_b complete the connection. If T_a and T_b have not finished connecting, swap the two trees for the next iteration. The specific process is shown in Algorithm 1.

Algorithm 1: Basic Bi-RRT

    Input: Initial and goal configuration q_{init}, q_{goal}, parameters
    Output: RRT trees T_a and T_b, waypoints set Q
1 $T_a.init(q_{init})$; $T_b.init(q_{goal})$
2   **while** *not connected and number of tree nodes* $< K$ **do**
3 q_{rand} = Random_sample();
4 q_{near1} = Find_nearest(T_a, q_{rand});
5 q_{new1} = Extend(T_a, q_{near1}, δ);
6   **if** *ObstacleFree(q_{near1}, q_{new1})* **then**
7 $T_a.add(q_{new1})$;
8 q_{near2} = Find_nearest(T_b, q_{new1});
9   GreedyExtend(T_b, q_{near2}, q_{new1});
10   **end**
11   Swap(T_a, T_b);
12 **end**
13 Q=find_path($T_a, T_b, q_{init}, q_{goal}$);
14 Return T_a, T_b, Q;

Bi-RRT still uses a random sampling method which leads to a large number of invalid nodes and poor path quality. This paper attempts to improve the Bi-RRT algorithm through the idea of goal bias and adaptive step size to improve the efficiency of the algorithm.

2.2   Goal-Biased Strategy

The current sampling method employed by the Bi-RRT algorithm is random and does not account for orientation. To enhance the algorithm's search efficiency, we adopt an improvement by drawing inspiration from heuristic search algorithms. Specifically, we introduce a goal-biased strategy into the Bi-RRT algorithm, which directs the expansion direction of random sampling towards the goal point.

The conventional approach for the goal-biased strategy involves setting a threshold value, denoted as p_{goal}. If a randomly generated probability value, p, is less than the threshold, the sampling point is considered as the goal point. Otherwise, random sampling is performed. The sampling and expansion procedure can be described using Eq. 1:

$$q_{rand} = \begin{cases} q_{goal} & p < p_{goal} \\ random\_sample() & else \end{cases}$$

$$q_{new} = q_{rand} + \delta \frac{q_{rand} - q_{near}}{\|q_{rand} - q_{near}\|} \tag{1}$$

In this paper, the concept of gravitational attraction in the artificial potential field method is used to guide the expansion direction of the random tree. To achieve rapid convergence, a goal-bias factor denoted as ϕ is introduced, which guides the direction of node expansion. The calculation for node expansion is expressed by the Eq. 2:

$$q_{new} = q_{rand} + \delta \left(\frac{q_{rand} - q_{near}}{\|q_{rand} - q_{near}\|} + \phi \frac{q_{goal} - q_{near}}{\|q_{goal} - q_{near}\|} \right) \tag{2}$$

In Eq. 2, δ represents the node expansion step size, ϕ is the goal-bias factor, and $\| \cdot \|$ is the Euclidean distance between nodes. The procedure outlined in Eq. 2 can be conceptualized as a process of vector superposition, as depicted in Fig. 2. This variant of the Bi-RRT algorithm, which incorporates goal-biased strategy, is denoted as the GBBi-RRT algorithm.

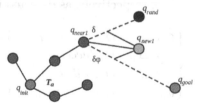

Fig. 2. Goal-biased node expansion diagram

2.3   Adaptive Step Size Strategy

When utilizing the random tree algorithm for search purposes within an obstacle-free space, the presence of a fixed step size can impose restrictions on the expansion speed. Furthermore, the setting of the goal-bias factor will make the expansion direction always biased towards the goal, and it is easy to fall into a "local minimum" case.

In order to speed up the convergence and to avoid falling into the "local minimum", an adaptive step size algorithm is designed for the expansion step size δ and the goal-bias factor ϕ, respectively. Specifically, the algorithm will adaptively adjust δ and ϕ according to the situation of expanding nodes. Considering that the random tree should be accelerated and expanded as much as possible in obstacle-free space, the goal orientation should be increased so that the manipulator can reach the goal configuration faster. But in the vicinity of obstacles, the randomness of sampling and expansion should be enhanced, the step size should be reduced, and the manipulator's ability to avoid obstacles should be enhanced. If there is no obstacle between the newly sampled node and the nearest node, i.e. if the manipulator configurations corresponding to the n interpolation points between the two configurations do not collide with obstacles, the extended function returns Succeed, otherwise it returns Failed, and the adaptive step size function adjusts the step size according to the two states.

We design to adjust δ through the function shown in Eq. 3. In this method, we exploit the properties of the sigmoid function to impose limitations on the value of δ. By doing so, we prevent δ from becoming excessively large, which could result in sampling beyond the desired limits. Simultaneously, we also avoid setting δ to be too small, as this could adversely affect the algorithm's efficiency. Furthermore, the sigmoid function can exhibit distinct sensitivities to changes in x during different stages of tree growth. The parameters in Eq. 3 need to be designed according to the actual situation.

$$\delta = a + \frac{b}{1 + e^{-kx}} \tag{3}$$

While adjusting ϕ, it is crucial to consider the possibility of encountering a 'local minimum' when increasing its value. Moreover, when faced with obstacles, it is vital to decrease ϕ at an accelerated rate to facilitate successful obstacle avoidance. To achieve this, we introduce distinct rates of change, Δ_+ and Δ_-, for increasing and decreasing ϕ, respectively, as depicted in Eq. 4:

$$\phi = \begin{cases} \phi_{max} & if \ \phi >= \phi_{max} - \Delta_+ \\ \phi + \Delta_+ & if \ Succeed \\ \phi - \Delta_- & if \ Failed \\ \phi_{min} & if \ \phi <= \phi_{min} + \Delta_- \end{cases} \tag{4}$$

According to the above analysis, the complete adaptive step-size adjustment algorithm is shown in Algorithm 2. When doing goal-biased expansion, the step size δ and the goal-bias factor ϕ are adjusted at the same time, but during the greedy expansion of the tree connection, only the step size δ is adjusted. This Bi-RRT algorithm with goal-biased strategy and adaptive step size strategy is denoted as AGBBi-RRT algorithm.

Algorithm 2: Adaptive Step Size Algorithm

    Input: $\Delta_+, \Delta_-, \Delta_x, \phi_{max}, \phi_{min}$
    Output: δ, ϕ

1 $\delta = \delta_{init}, \phi = \phi_{init}, x = 0;$
2 **if** $Extend(T){=}Succeed$ **then**
3 | $x \leftarrow x + \Delta_x, \delta = sigmoid(x);$
4 | $\phi = AdaptivePhi(\phi, \Delta_+);$
5 **end**
6 **if** $Extend(T){=}Failed$ **then**
7 | $x \leftarrow x - \Delta_x, \delta = sigmoid(x);$
8 | $\phi = AdaptivePhi(\phi, \Delta_-);$
9 **end**
10 Return $\delta, \phi;$

---

3 Path Smoothing

Based on the algorithm described in Sect. 2, we are able to obtain a collision-free initial path, but this path still contains some redundant nodes and exhibits jaggedness, resulting in poor path quality, which is not conducive to robotic manipulator motion. To mitigate these issues, we adopt a bidirectional pruning strategy to eliminate redundant nodes and reduce the path cost. Furthermore, we employ cubic non-uniform B-spline fitting to achieve path smoothing, so that the final path obtained is more suitable for robotic manipulator motion.

3.1 Bidirectional Pruning Strategy

Since the initial path obtained is jagged and there are some redundant nodes, we adopt a bidirectional pruning strategy to eliminate redundant nodes and lower the path cost.

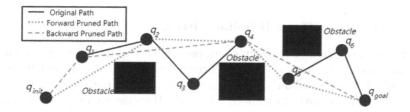

Fig. 3. An example of bidirectional pruning strategy

As shown in Fig. 3, the initial configuration is q_{init}, the goal configuration is q_{goal}, moving from q_{init} to q_{goal}, the initial path we get is $q_{init} - q_1 - q_2 - q_3 - q_4 - q_5 - q_6 - q_{goal}$. On the premise of no collision, starting from q_{init}, we can go directly from q_{init} to q_2 without going through q_1, similarly it is possible to go directly from q_2 to q_4. In this case we can do forward pruning to get a collision free path of $q_{init} - q_2 - q_4 - q_5 - q_{goal}$, as shown by the green line. To further reduce the path cost, we perform backward pruning from q_{goal} to obtain the path of $q_{goal} - q_4 - q_1 - q_{init}$, as shown by the orange line. We compute the path cost of the two paths separately, i.e. the sum of the Euclidean distances of the joint angles between the manipulator configurations corresponding to each node, and then select the path with the lower path cost as the pruned path.

Algorithm 3: Bidirectional Pruning Strategy

Input: Waypoints set $Q = \{q_0, q_1, \cdots, q_n\}$
Output: Pruned waypoints set Q_{new}
1 $i = 1, temp = 0, Q_1 = \{q_0\}$;
2 Q_1=forward_pruning($i, temp, Q_1$);
3 $i = n - 1, temp = n, Q_2 = \{q_n\}$;
4 Q_2=backward_pruning($i, temp, Q_2$);
5 Q_{new}=Compare_cost(Q_1, Q_2);
6 Return Q_{new};

Specifically, the process of bidirectional pruning is to traverse and search the initial path from q_{init} and q_{goal} respectively, as shown in Algorithm 3. Starting from the initial point, it is connected to the following waypoints in order, and the connection is interpolated n times to complete the collision detection of the robot arm. If no collision occurs, it is connected to the next waypoint until a collision occurs. After a collision, the previous point q_{i-1} of the current waypoint q_i is added to the new waypoint sequence and then searched backwards from q_{i-1} to the right. The entire path is searched to obtain a new sequence of waypoints. After completing the search from q_{init} and q_{goal} respectively, compare the costs of the two paths Q_1 and Q_2, select the path with the lower cost as the final result, and complete the bidirectional pruning.

3.2   Cubic Non-uniform B-Spline Fitting

The bidirectional pruning strategy produces a path with fewer waypoints and a lower path cost, but the path is still a broken line in space, and the path is still jagged, which is not conducive to the movement of the robot arm. Therefore, we need to smooth the path. Considering that the B-spline curve is widely used in the trajectory planning of the manipulator, and the waypoints we get are not evenly distributed, we use a cubic non-uniform B-spline curve to fit the path [10].

The mathematical expression of the non-uniform B-Spline curve is shown as Eq. 5:

$$c(u) = \sum_{i=0}^{n} d_i N_{i,k}(u) \tag{5}$$

where $d_i(i = 0, 1, 2, \cdots, n)$ are the control points sequentially connected to form the B-spline control polygon, and $N_{i,k}(u)$ is the k-order normal B-spline basis function defined on the non-uniform node vector U. The schematic diagram of the path smoothing using the cubic non-uniform b-spline interpolation method is shown in Fig. 4, where the black points are waypoints and the green points are control points $d_i, i = 0, 1, \cdots, n + 2$, the red curve is the smoothed path.

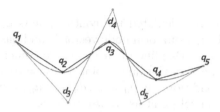

Fig. 4. An example of cubic non-uniform B-spline fitting

First, we obtain the pruned waypoint set $\mathcal{Q} = \{q_0, q_1, \cdots, q_n\}$ according to AGBBi-RRT, where $q_0 = q_{init}, q_n = q_{goal}$, each $q_i, i = 0, 1, \cdots, n$ is a vector composed of the joint angle of the robotic manipulator. Taking the six-dof robot arm as an example, each q_i is a six-dimensional vector, and each component corresponds to a joint angle of the robot manipulator. We use these $n + 1$ waypoints as the data points to be fitted by the cubic non-uniform B-spline, construct the non-uniform node vector U according to these $n + 1$ points, and then construct the basis function according to U, and then constructs the equation to solve control pointss. Finally, the waypoints is interpolated and fitted according to the solved control points. It should be noted that the cubic non-uniform B-spline curve fitting requires at least 4 data points, and there may be less than 4 way-points after pruning, so we need to limit it when pruning or interpolate to make the number of waypoints meet the fitting requirements.

Specifically, for $n + 1$ data points, these $n + 1$ points divide the curve into n segments, each segment being determined by 4 control points, so a total of n+3 control points are required Point $d_i, i = 0, 1, \cdots, n + 2$. The nonuniform node vector U is parameterized by chord length to implement the parameterization process for control points [15], where the first node and the last node both need $k + 1$ repetitions. Therefore, for the cubic non-uniform B-spline curve, $u_0 = u_1 = u_2 = u_3 = 0, u_{n+1} = u_{n+2} = u_{n+3} = u_{n+4} = 1$. According to the Riesenfeld method, assume the length of each side of the control polygon is $l_i = \|q_i - q_{i-1}\|, i = 1, 2, \cdots, n$, and the total side length is $L = \sum\limits_{i=1}^{n} l_i$. As shown in Eq. 6, we can obtain the non-uniform node vector U:

$$U = \left[0, 0, 0, 0, \frac{l_1 + l_2}{L}, \cdots, \frac{\sum\limits_{i=1}^{n-2} l_i}{L}, 1, 1, 1, 1\right] \tag{6}$$

Then the basis function of B-spline can be calculated by the Cox-deBoor recursion formula:

$$\begin{cases} N_{i,0}(u) = \begin{cases} 1, u_i \leq u \leq u_{i+1} \\ 0, others \end{cases} \\ N_{i,k}(u) = \frac{u-u_i}{u_{i+k}-u_i}N_{i,k-1}(u) + \frac{u_{i+k+1}-u}{u_{i+k+1}-u_{i+1}}N_{i+1,k-1}(u) \\ \frac{0}{0} = 0 \end{cases} \tag{7}$$

Next, we can reversely calculated the control points $d_i, i = 0, 1, \cdots, n+2$ using data points q_i, the non-uniform node vector U and basis functions $N_{i,k}(u)$. For the cubic non-uniform B-spline open curve, we coincide the control point with the beginning and end of the value point, i.e. $d_0 = q_0, d_{n+2} = q_n$, and then use the free endpoint condition, i.e. $d_0 = d_1, d_{n+1} = d_{n+2}$, we can construct the equation to solve the control point as shown in Eq. 8:

$$\begin{bmatrix} N_{1,3}(u_4) & N_{2,3}(u_4) & N_{3,3}(u_4) & & \\ & \ddots & \ddots & \ddots & \\ & & N_{n-1,3}(u_{n+2}) & N_{n,3}(u_{n+2}) & N_{n+1,3}(u_{n+2}) \end{bmatrix} \begin{bmatrix} d_2 \\ \vdots \\ d_n \end{bmatrix} = \begin{bmatrix} q_1 \\ \vdots \\ q_{n-1} \end{bmatrix} \tag{8}$$

Solving Eq. 8 to get all the control points d_i, then the waypoints are interpolated and fitted to obtain a smooth trajectory by using Eq. 5. The smoothed trajectory of the end of the robotic manipulator is shown in Fig. 5, where the orange robot is the initial configuration, the white robot is the goal configuration and the green ball is the obstacle. It can be seen from the figure that after smoothing, the entire trajectory has no jagged turning points, which is more suitable for the movement of the robotic manipulator.

Fig. 5. The smoothed trajectory of the robotic manipulator

However, after using non-uniform cubic B-spline curve fitting, the fitted path may collide with obstacles in narrow or multi-obstacles scenarios, so it may be necessary to modify the fitting curve in special scenarios to make adjustments.

4   Simulation and Verification

In this section, in order to verify the validity and reliability of our proposed algorithm, Dobot-CR5 manipulator is used for experiments. All experiments were performed on a computer configured with an InterCore i5-10400 and 2.9 Ghz processor, 15.4 GB of memory, and Ubuntu 20.04 operating system. The relevant parameters are set as follows: the initial step size $\delta = 0.02 * 2\pi$, the working space of the manipulator is $2m * 2m * 1m$, the maximum number of tree nodes is 2000, the initial goal-bias factor $\phi = 1.1$.

We conducted experiments in single-obstacle and multi-obstacles scenarios and compared three algorithms Bi-RRT, GBBi-RRT and AGBBi-RRT in each scenario. We select four performance indicators: planning time, number of tree nodes, number of waypoints, and path length (the sum of Euclidean distances between joint angles corresponding to each configuration).

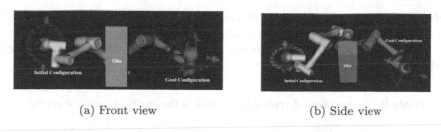

(a) Front view   (b) Side view

Fig. 6. Single-obstacle experimental scenario

The single-obstacle scenario is shown in Fig. 6, we choose configurations on both sides of the obstacle as the initial and goal configurations. Each joint angle of the initial configuration, represented by the yellow robot, is {-160,-47,-42,102,159,18}, while the goal configuration, represented by the orange robot, is {55,-71,101,-94,-72,-22}. This scenario was tested 500 times, and the experimental results are shown in Table 1.

Table 1. Comparison of typical indicators in the single-obstacle scenario.

Algorithm	Avg. Time of path planning(ms)	Avg. Number of tree nodes	Avg. Number of waypoints	Avg. Path length (rad)
Bi-RRT	3.1483	127.858	50.824	6.1991
GBBi-RRT	2.9346	95.084	27.708	4.0659
AGBBi-RRT	2.4672	100.162	31.65	4.5806

As shown in Table 1, in the single-obstacle scenario, the AGBBi-RRT has the shortest planning time, which is 15.28% shorter than Bi-RRT and 9.11% shorter than GBBi-RRT. In terms of the other three indicators, AGBBi-RRT performs slightly worse than GBBi-RRT due to the adaptive step size adjustment, but it still performs better than Bi-RRT with increases of 21.66%, 37.73% and 26.11% respectively.

The multi-obstacles scenario is shown in Fig. 7, we arbitrarily choose two collision-free configurations as the initial and goal configurations. Each joint

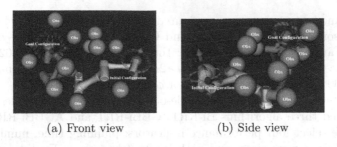

(a) Front view   (b) Side view

Fig. 7. Multi-obstacles experimental scenario

angle of the initial configuration, represented by the yellow robot, is {-36,-63,-48,118,36,0}, while the goal configuration, represented by the orange robot, is {58,-59,-56,10,-58,9}. This scenario was tested 100 times, and the experimental results are shown in Table 2.

Table 2. Comparison of typical indicators in the multi-obstacles scenario.

Algorithm	Avg. Time of path planning(ms)	Avg. Number of tree nodes	Avg. Number of waypoints	Avg. Path length (rad)
Bi-RRT	483.775	422.42	75.86	11.6054
GBBi-RRT	419.9946	371.26	60.2	8.9268
AGBBi-RRT	353.1386	310.84	68.05	9.7394

Table 3. Simulation results comparision before and after pruing.

Algorithm	Path length in single-obstacle scenario		Path length in multi-obstacles scenario	
	Before pruning	After pruning	Before pruning	After pruning
GBBi-RRT	4.0895rad	3.5298rad	8.7422rad	7.7329rad
AGBBi-RRT	5.1831rad	3.9629rad	10.091rad	8.0633rad

As shown in Table 2, in the multi-obstacles scenario, the effect of AGBBi-RRT on the reduction of planning time is more obvious, being 27.00% shorter than Bi-RRT and 15.92% shorter than GBBi-RRT. For the other three aspects, the last two are still slightly worse than GBBi-RRT, but compared to Bi-RRT they have increased by 26, 41%, 10.29% and 16.08% respectively.

Combining the bidirectional pruning strategy and cubic non-uniform B-spline fitting with AGBBi-RRT, the algorithm is tested in both single-obstacle and multi-obstacles scenarios for 200 times. The experimental results are shown in Table 3, demonstrating the significant improvements in path length after pruning. Specifically, in both single-obstacle and multi-obstacles scenarios, the algorithm achieved a reduction in path length of 23.54% and 20.09%, respectively. Notably, the gap in path length between the AGBBi-RRT and GBBi-RRT algorithms was considerably reduced after pruning.

5   Conclusion

This paper presents the AGBBi-RRT algorithm, aiming to enhance algorithm efficiency and enable its effective application in online path planning tasks. By incorporating the idea of artificial potential fields (APF), the algorithm enhances the expansion strategy of Bi-RRT, enabling improved obstacle avoidance in multi-obstacles environments and rapid convergence in open environments through an adaptive step size strategy. Moreover, the algorithm reduces redundant nodes and smooths the path by employing a bidirectional pruning strategy and cubic non-uniform B-spline fitting.

The effectiveness of the proposed algorithm is demonstrated through simulation experiments involving a six-dof robotic manipulator operating in both single-obstacle and multi-obstacles scenarios. The results validate the algorithm's outstanding performance in reducing planning time and its encouraging performance in terms of number of tree nodes, number of waypoints, and path length. Furthermore, the quality of the path is greatly enhanced, and its length is shortened through the process of pruning and curve fitting.

In future work, further research will be conducted on improving path quality and shortening planning time, and considering the idea of combining waypoints reuse to enhance the replanning ability of the algorithm.

Acknowledgements. This work was supported in part by the National Key Research and Development Program of China under Grant No. 2020YFB1313900 and in part by the Shenzhen Science and Technology Plan under Grant No. JSGG20210420091602008.

References

1. Wei, K., Ren, B.: A method on dynamic path planning for robotic manipulator autonomous obstacle avoidance based on an improved RRT algorithm. Sensors **18**(2) (2018). https://doi.org/10.3390/s18020571
2. Zhou, C., Huang, B., Fränti, P.: A review of motion planning algorithms for intelligent robots. J. Intell. Manuf. **33**, 387–424 (2021). https://doi.org/10.1007/s10845-021-01867-z
3. Le, A.T., Le, T.D.: Search-based planning and replanning in robotics and autonomous systems. Adv. Path Plann. Mobile Entities (2017). https://doi.org/10.5772/intechopen.71663
4. Zucker, M., et al.: CHOMP: covariant Hamiltonian optimization for motion planning. Int. J. Robot. Res. **32**, 1164–1193 (2013). https://doi.org/10.1177/0278364913488805
5. He, Z., He, Y., Zeng, B.: Obstacle avoidance path planning for robot arm based on mixed algorithm of artificial potential field method and RRT. Ind. Eng. J. **20**(2), 56 (2017). https://doi.org/10.3969/j.issn.1007-7375.e17-2002
6. LaValle, S.M.: Rapidly-exploring random trees : a new tool for path planning. Ann. Res. Rep. (1998)

7. Kuffner, J.J., LaValle, S.M.: RRT-connect: an efficient approach to single-query path planning. In: Proceedings 2000 ICRA. Millennium Conference. IEEE International Conference on Robotics and Automation. Symposia Proceedings (Cat. No.00CH37065). vol. 2, pp. 995–1001 (2000). https://doi.org/10.1109/ROBOT.2000.844730

8. LaValle, S.M., Kuffner, J.J.: Randomized kinodynamic planning. Int. J. Robot. Res. **20**(5), 378–400 (2001). https://doi.org/10.1177/02783640122067453

9. Jiang, R., Zhou, H., Wang, H., Ge, S.S.: Maximum entropy searching. CAAI Trans. Intell. Technol. **4**(1), 1–8 (2019). https://doi.org/10.1049/trit.2018.1058

10. Yuan, C., Zhang, W., Liu, G., Pan, X., Liu, X.: A heuristic rapidly-exploring random trees method for manipulator motion planning. IEEE Access **8**, 900–910 (2020). https://doi.org/10.1109/ACCESS.2019.2958876

11. Liu, H., Zhang, X., Wen, J., Wang, R., Chen, X.: Goal-biased bidirectional RRT based on curve-smoothing. IFAC-PapersOnLine **52**(24), 255–260 (2019). https://doi.org/10.1016/j.ifacol.2019.12.417

12. Sepehri, A., Moghaddam, A.M.: A motion planning algorithm for redundant manipulators using rapidly exploring randomized trees and artificial potential fields. IEEE Access **9**, 26059–26070 (2021). https://doi.org/10.1109/ACCESS.2021.3056397

13. Chen, Y., Wang, L.: Adaptively dynamic RRT*-connect: Path planning for UAVs against dynamic obstacles. In: 2022 7th International Conference on Automation, Control and Robotics Engineering (CACRE), pp. 1–7 (2022). https://doi.org/10.1109/CACRE54574.2022.9834188

14. Zhang, Z., Wu, D., Gu, J., Li, F.: A path-planning strategy for unmanned surface vehicles based on an adaptive hybrid dynamic stepsize and target attractive force-RRT algorithm. J. Marine Sci. Eng. **7**(5), 132 (2019). https://doi.org/10.3390/jmse7050132

15. Lü, W.: Curves with chord length parameterization. Comput. Aided Geom. Design **26**(3), 342–350 (2009). https://doi.org/10.1016/j.cagd.2008.08.001

A Novel 3-DOF Spherical Hybrid Mechanism for Wrist Movement: Design, Kinematics, and Simulation

Jingbo Yang[1,2] , Zhiwei Liao[1,2] , and Fei Zhao[1,2(✉)]

[1] School of Mechanical Engineering, Xi'an Jiaotong University, Xi'an 710049, China
ztzhao@mail.xjtu.edu.cn
[2] Shaanxi Key Laboratory of Intelligent Robots and School of Mechanical Engineering,
Xi'an Jiaotong University, Xi'an 710049, Shaanxi, China

Abstract. Wrist movement and rotational stiffness determine the flexibility of the human hand, which are also critical in skillful manipulation scenarios. But few rotational stiffness extraction mechanisms can adjust based on the hand lengths of subjects. To solve this problem, this paper first proposes a 3-degree-of-freedom (DOF) spherical hybrid mechanism driving wrists to rotate in three dimensions which can adapt to different individuals. And then, forward and inverse kinematics analyses are derived according to the hybrid structure. Besides, the kinematics simulation is also carried out to validate the derivation. And the workspace of the mechanism is calculated which satisfies the motion range of human wrist joints and is larger than most existing writs motion mechanisms.

Keywords: Wrist stiffness · Spherical hybrid mechanism · Kinematics

1 Introduction

Human-robot skill transfer (HRST) has become one of the most important ways for robot fast programming from human demonstration [1]. Existing research [2–4] on HRST endows robots with human skills mostly at the kinematic level. But the skill includes not only kinematics but also dynamics information. Dynamic characteristics of the human arm, referring to the compliance capability, are also significant and can be used to guide robot impedance parameters planning. For dynamic skills learning, existing work also focuses on the translational stiffness of the human arm [5, 6] and the lack of literature on rotational stiffness. With the development of robotic technology, next-generation robot is required to work in skillful manipulation scenarios wherein hand-like dexterous operation becomes a critical ability for them. Thus, rotational stiffness, related to human wrist movement, has recently achieved great attention in the HRST community.

It is the prerequisite work to design a mechanism that can drive wrist motion of obtaining wrist stiffness information through perturbation method. Human wrist has three DOFs, i. e., flexion and extension (FE), radial and ulnar deviation (RUD), pronation and supination (PS) (see Fig. 1) and the range of max and activities of daily living

H. Yang et al. (Eds.): ICIRA 2023, LNAI 14267, pp. 57–68, 2023.
https://doi.org/10.1007/978-981-99-6483-3_6

(ADLs) wrist motion is listed in Table 1 [8]. Wrist motion mechanism can help wrist realize movement in one or multiple DOFs and be generally divided into exoskeleton and non-exoskeleton mechanisms. For instance, for the exoskeleton mechanism. Raiano [9] proposes an exoskeleton robot that is portable and capable of real-time extraction for FE movement. Shi [10] develops a cable-driven 3-DOF wrist rehabilitation robot. Erwin et al. [11] propose 2-DOF wrist motion mechanism base on series elastic actuation capable of rotating in FE and RUD. Almusawi and Husi [12] present a finger and wrist grounded-exoskeleton rehabilitation system that can cover three DOFs of the wrist separately via different type of grasping handles and this approach to achieving multi-DOF wrist motion can also be found in [13]. For non-exoskeleton mechanism, Rijnveld and Krebs [14] propose a wrist motion robot being able to drive wrist rotation with 3-DOFs and succeed in extracting wrist stiffness. Wang [15] develops a wrist rehabilitation robot based on pneumatic artificial muscle (PAM) which can drive wrist motion in three DOFs. Allington et al. [16] present a pneumatically actuated robot to drive wrist rotate in FE and PS. Oblak [17] proposes a rehabilitation robot for the human arm and wrist. Furthermore, Molaei et al. [18] propose a 2-DOF, i. e. FE and RUD, wrist rehabilitation robot based on a remote center of motion mechanism.

Table 1. Range of wrist motion

	Max	ADLs
FE	[−73°–71°]	[−60°–54°]
RUD	[−33°–19°]	[−33°–19°]
PS	[−86°–71°]	[−85°–70°]

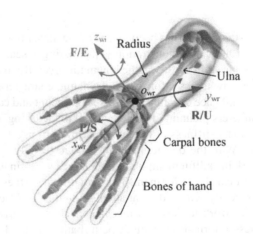

Fig. 1. Definition of the movement of human wrists [7]

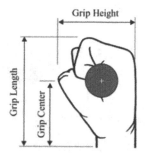

Fig. 2. Schematic diagram of hand gripping [18]

Both exoskeleton and non-exoskeleton mechanisms should cover the max range of wrist motion and adapt to the diversity (various arm/hand lengths) of different individuals to ensure the universality. Especially for the 3-DOF mechanism, the motion center of mechanisms should always coincide with the center of the wrist joint. According to [18], 90% of people's grip center, length and height (see Fig. 2) are less than 8.64, 14.22 and 10.41 cm respectively. However, existing mechanisms rarely meet both requirements simultaneously, even many researches only consider 2-DOF motion. On this basis, this paper proposes a 3-DOF spherical hybrid mechanism whose end position can be adjusted according to various subjects and workspace can cover the max wrist motion range. Kinematics analysis and simulation validation are carried out, successively.

2   Mechanical Design of the 3-DOF Spherical Hybrid Mechanism

The diagram of the 3-DOF spherical hybrid mechanism is shown in Fig. 3(1) which has 3 DOFs and mainly consists of two parts, i.e., a spherical parallel mechanism (SPM) and a round plate. As shown in Fig. 3(2), SPM mainly consists of two limbs that are connected through a rotation pair. In which limbs 1 and 2 are directly driven by motors 1 and 2, respectively. To be specific, limb 2 comprises three parts, i.e., limbs 2–1 and 2–2. Limb2–1 is directly driven by motor 2 through a rigid connector, and limb2–2 is connected to limb2–1 and end effector by rotation pair 1 and 2, respectively. It should be emphasized that according to the motion characteristics of the human wrist joint, the axes of motor 1, motor 2, and three rotation pairs in the mechanism should intersect at the same point which is also the center of the wrist joint. To this end, two positioning holes and the corresponding slots are designed on the platform (see Fig. 4) to move and fix the linkage to the suitable position for humans with various hand lengths. As shown in Fig. 4, d represents the adjustment range of the holes, that is 1.5cm, making the length of grip center, l_{GC}, can range from 7.1–8.6cm, which meets the variation of 90% of humans. Other requirements of linkage length are all based on the information mentioned in [18] which mainly are to provide enough space for the hand when the subject holds the handle. Furthermore, a 6 DOF Force/Torque sensor (ATI, mini45, 1 kHz) installed on the end-effector of the robot is used to record the interaction forces from human-robot interactions.

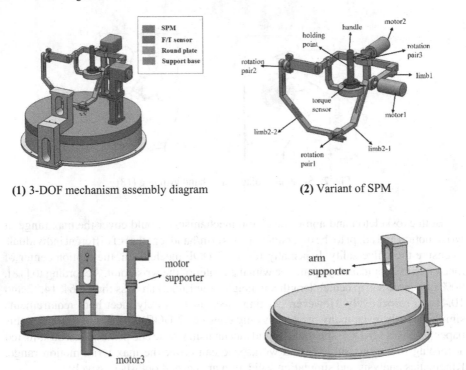

(1) 3-DOF mechanism assembly diagram

(2) Variant of SPM

(3) The round plate

(4) The support base

Fig. 3. 3-DOF spherical hybrid mechanism

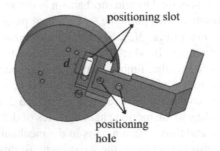

Fig. 4. Adjustment for various hand lengths

As shown in Fig. 3(3), the remaining part of the mechanism is a round plate equipped with two motor supporters, wherein the two motor supporters are designed to support motors 1 and 2, and motor 3 is placed in the center of the round plate to directly rotate the SPM. On this basis, the human hand can be rotated in all three DOF (FE, RUD and PS) with the help of the developed novel mechanism. The round plate is placed on the support base (see Fig. 3(4)) which is mainly for the stabilization of the mechanism.

Moreover, to support the human forearm, an arm supporter is designed on the support base to minimize the impact of the forearm on the wrist movement.

3 Kinematics Analysis

3.1 Forward Kinematics Solution

Since the SPM and the round plate constitute a hybrid mechanism, the rotation in RUD and PS is realized by SPM, and the rotation in FE is driven by the round plate, the kinematics of the whole mechanism can be divided into two parts. The first part is established for the SPM, as shown in Fig. 5. Establish the base coordinate system $O_0 - x_0y_0z_0$ which is fixed at the center of the support base and the distance between P and O_0 is denoted by l_{op}. Coordinate systems $O_i - x_iy_iz_i$ $(i = 1, \ldots, 5)$ are set with respect to each joint and coordinate system $P - x_Py_Pz_P$ represents the pose frame of the SPM. The purple point H is where human hands hold the handle (holding point in Fig. 3(2)) representing the end effector position of the SPM and the coordinate of H in $O_p - x_py_pz_p$ is $h^P = [-l_{GC}, 0, 0]^T$.

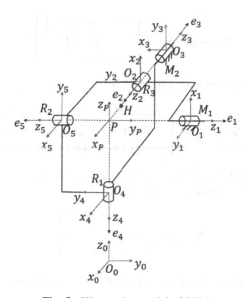

Fig. 5. Kinematics model of SPM

$e_i(i = 1, 2, \ldots., 5) \in R^3$ is used to denote z_i-axis. Since each axis of revolute pair always converges at P, when motor 1 rotates α, e_2 will rotate around axis y_p so

$$e_2' = R_y(\alpha) \cdot e_2 = \begin{bmatrix} cos\alpha & 0 & sin\alpha \\ 0 & 1 & 0 \\ -sin\alpha & 0 & cos\alpha \end{bmatrix} \begin{bmatrix} -1 \\ 0 \\ 0 \end{bmatrix} = \begin{bmatrix} -cos\alpha \\ 0 \\ sin\alpha \end{bmatrix} \tag{1}$$

When motor 2 rotates β, e_4 will rotate around axis x_p so

$$e_4' = R_x(\beta) \cdot e_4 = \begin{bmatrix} 1 & 0 & 0 \\ 0 & \cos\beta & -\sin\beta \\ 0 & \sin\beta & \cos\beta \end{bmatrix} \begin{bmatrix} 0 \\ 0 \\ -1 \end{bmatrix} = \begin{bmatrix} 0 \\ \sin\beta \\ -\cos\beta \end{bmatrix} \tag{2}$$

e_5 is perpendicular to both e_2 and e_4, that is:

$$e_5' = e_2' \times e_4' = \begin{bmatrix} -\sin\alpha\sin\beta \\ -\cos\alpha\cos\beta \\ -\cos\alpha\sin\beta \end{bmatrix} \tag{3}$$

y_p and e_5' are located on the same axis but in opposite direction:

$$y_p = -\frac{e_5'}{l} \tag{4}$$

where l denotes the modulus of e_5' and $l = \sqrt{1 - \sin^2\alpha\cos^2\beta}$. It's obvious that $x_p = -e_2'$ and we can easily infer

$$z_p = x_p \times y_p = \begin{bmatrix} \sin\alpha\cos\alpha\cos\beta/l \\ -\sin\beta/l \\ \cos^2\alpha\cos\beta/l \end{bmatrix} \tag{5}$$

On this basis, the rotation matrix of SPM is

$$R_{SPM} = \begin{bmatrix} x_p & y_p & z_p \end{bmatrix} = \begin{bmatrix} \cos\alpha & \sin\alpha\sin\beta/l & \sin\alpha\cos\alpha\cos\beta/l \\ 0 & \cos\alpha\cos\beta/l & -\sin\beta/l \\ -\sin\alpha & \cos\alpha\sin\beta/l & \cos^2\alpha\cos\beta/l \end{bmatrix} \tag{6}$$

Since the rotation in FE, along z_0-axis, is driven by motor 3 independently, the rotation caused by motor 3 when it rotates γ is

$$R_z(\gamma) = \begin{bmatrix} \cos\gamma & -\sin\gamma & 0 \\ \sin\gamma & \cos\gamma & 0 \\ 0 & 0 & 1 \end{bmatrix} \tag{7}$$

Then the rotation matrix of 3-DOF spherical hybrid mechanism is

$$R = R_z(\gamma)R_{SPM}$$

$$= \begin{bmatrix} \cos\alpha\cos\gamma & (\sin\alpha\sin\beta\cos\gamma - \cos\alpha\cos\beta\sin\gamma)/l & (\sin\alpha\cos\alpha\cos\beta\cos\gamma + \sin\beta\sin\gamma)/l \\ \cos\alpha\sin\gamma & (\sin\alpha\cos\beta\sin\gamma + \cos\alpha\cos\beta\cos\gamma)/l & (\sin\alpha\cos\alpha\cos\beta\sin\gamma - \sin\beta\cos\gamma)/l \\ -\sin\alpha & \cos\alpha\sin\beta/l & \cos^2\alpha\cos\beta/l \end{bmatrix} \# \tag{8}$$

Based on the result, the coordinate of H after rotation is

$$h = {}_P^0 T R h^P = \begin{bmatrix} -l_{GC}\cos\alpha\cos\gamma \\ -l_{GC}\cos\alpha\sin\gamma \\ l_{GC}\sin\alpha + l_{OP} \end{bmatrix} \tag{9}$$

where p^0T is the transformation matrix between $O_0 - x_0 y_0 z_0$ and $O_p - x_p y_p z_p$ and

$$p^0T = \begin{bmatrix} 1 & 0 & 0 & 0 \\ 0 & 1 & 0 & 0 \\ 0 & 0 & 1 & l_{OP} \\ 0 & 0 & 0 & 1 \end{bmatrix} \tag{10}$$

matics solution can be obtained:

$$T = \begin{bmatrix} R & h \\ 0 & 1 \end{bmatrix} \tag{11}$$

3.2 Inverse Kinematics Solution

Assuming $t_{mn}(m = 1, 2, 3; n = 1, 2, 3)$ is used to denote the elements of T:

$$T = \begin{bmatrix} t_{11} & t_{12} & t_{13} & t_{14} \\ t_{21} & t_{22} & t_{23} & t_{24} \\ t_{31} & t_{32} & t_{33} & t_{34} \\ t_{41} & t_{42} & t_{43} & t_{44} \end{bmatrix} \tag{12}$$

According to Eq. 11, the inverse kinematics solution of the 3-DOF spherical hybrid mechanism can be obtained from the elements of T:

$$\alpha = \left(-t_{31}, \sqrt{t_{11}^2 + t_{21}^2} \right) \tag{13}$$

$$\beta = (t_{32}\cos\alpha, t_{33}) \tag{14}$$

$$\gamma = (t_{21}, t_{11}) \tag{15}$$

4 Simulation Verification

4.1 Kinematics Simulation

To verify the kinematics derivation, corresponding simulation is carried. H is considered as the reference point of motion output. Based on the length mentioned before, set $l_{GC}=8.6$ cm and $l_{OP}=19$ cm. The motion input of each motor is shown in Fig. 6 and α, β, γ represent the rotation angle of motor1, 2, 3 respectively. And the corresponding motion trajectory of H is presented in Fig. 7(1), the trajectory comparisons in axis-x_0, y_0, z_0 are shown in Fig. 7(2)-(3), respectively. What's more, the comparison of end poses is presented in quaternion format (see Fig. 8).

It's obvious that theoretical results are consistent with simulation results which proves that the theoretical derivation is correct.

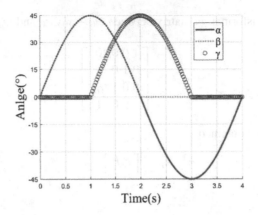

Fig. 6. Motor inputs

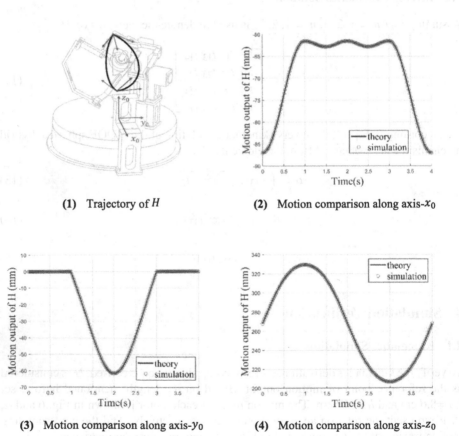

(1) Trajectory of H

(2) Motion comparison along axis-x_0

(3) Motion comparison along axis-y_0

(4) Motion comparison along axis-z_0

Fig. 7. Simulation result of displacement

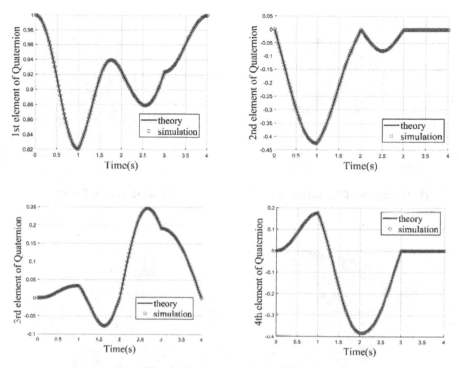

Fig. 8. Comparison of quaternion

4.2 Workspace Simulation

The workspace of 3-DOF spherical hybrid mechanism can also be obtained from forward kinematics solution. l_{GC} and l_{OP} are still the same as before and the range of α, β is $[-90°, 90°]$ and γ is $[-90°, 75°]$. The workspace obtained from h is shown in Fig. 9(1)-(4). To demonstrate the excellent workspace of the mechanism, the work comparison among our mechanism, some wrist motion mechanisms (SEU-WRE [10], CDWRR [19], NTU [20]) proposed before and human wrists is presented in Fig. 10. The proportion of workspace increase, compared with SEU-WRE, CDWRR, NTU, is listed in Table 2. It is clear that 3-DOF spherical hybrid mechanism's workspace is much larger than the others. What' more, it can cover the max range of wrist motion, which means the mechanism can satisfy the requirement of all kinds of application scenarios, i.e., wrist rehabilitation and wrist stiffness extraction.

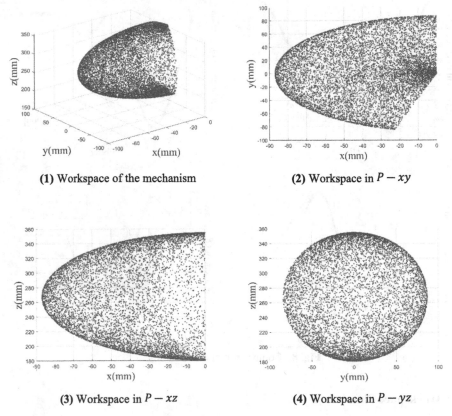

(1) Workspace of the mechanism

(2) Workspace in $P - xy$

(3) Workspace in $P - xz$

(4) Workspace in $P - yz$

Fig. 9. Workspace simulation

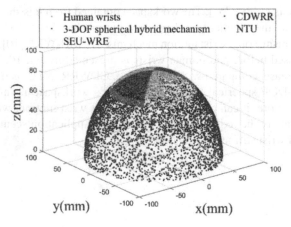

Fig. 10. Workspace comparison

Table 2. Workspace increase proportion

	SEU-WRE	CDWRR	NTU
FE	20%	137%	140%
RUD	125%	233%	125%
PS	−8%	112%	157%

5 Conclusion

In this work, a novel 3-DOF spherical hybrid mechanism that can drives wrist rotation in 3 DOFs is proposed. This mechanism can adapt to the various hand lengths ensuring it can be used by different subjects. The forward and inverse kinematics analyses are carried which are proven to be correct by the kinematics simulation. On this basis, the workspace is obtained which covers the wrist motion range and is much larger than the existing wrist motion mechanisms. The sufficient workspace indicates the mechanism can satisfy various scenarios, not only for wrist stiffness extraction, but also for wrist rehabilitation. In the future, the mechanism will be processed for the extraction of rotation stiffness firstly.

Acknowledgements. This work was supported in part by the National Natural Science Foundation of China (Grant No. 52175029).

References

1. Zeng, C., Yang, C.G., Li, Q., Dai, S.L.: Research progress on human-robot skill transfer. Acta Automatica Sinica **45**(10), 1813–1828 (2019)
2. Tang, T., Lin, H.C., Zhao, Y., Fan, Y.X., Chen, W.J., Tomizuka, M.: Teach industrial robots peg-hole-insertion by human demonstration. In: Proceedings of the 2016 IEEE International Conference on Advanced Intelligent Mechatronics, pp. 488−494. IEEE, Banff, Canada (2016)
3. Ajoudani, A., Fang, C., Tsagarakis, N.G., Bicchi, A.: A reduced-complexity description of arm endpoint stiffness with applications to teleimpedance control. In: Proceedings of the 2015 IEEE/RSJ International Conference on Intelligent Robots and Systems, pp. 1017−1023. IEEE, Hamburg, Germany (2015)
4. Yang, C., Wang, X., Cheng, L., Ma, H.: Neural-learning-based telerobot control with guaranteed performance. IEEE Trans. Cybernetics **47**(10), 3148–3159 (2016)
5. Gomi, H., Osu, R.: Task-dependent viscoelasticity of human multijoint arm and its spatial characteristics for interaction with environments. J. Neurosci. **18**(21), 8965–8978 (1998)
6. Perreault, E.J., Kirsch, R.F., Crago, P.E.: Effects of voluntary force generation on the elastic components of endpoint stiffness. Exp. Brain Res. **141**(3), 312–323 (2001)
7. Wyndaele, J.J.: Color atlas of human anatomy. Spinal Cord **47**(11), 838 (2009)
8. Tilley, A.R., Dreyfuss, H.: The Measure of Man and Woman: Human Factors in Design. 2nd edn. John Wiley & Sons, America (2001)

9. Raiano, L., Pino, G.D., Formica, D.: Flexion-extension wrist impedance estimation using a novel portable wrist exoskeleton: a pilot study. In: 8th IEEE RAS/EMBS International Conference for Biomedical Robotics and Biomechatronics (BioRob), pp. 440–445. IEEE, New York (2020)

10. Shi, K., et al.: A cable-driven three-DOF wrist rehabilitation exoskeleton with improved performance. Frontiers in Neurorobotics **15** (2021)

11. Erwin, A., McDonald, C.G., Moser, N., O'Malley, M.K.: The SE-assesswrist for robot-aided assessment of wrist stiffness and range of motion: development and experimental validation. J. Rehabilitation and Assistive Technologies Eng. **8**, 1–11 (2021)

12. Almusawi, H., Husi, G.: Design and development of continuous passive motion (CPM) for fingers and wrist grounded-exoskeleton rehabilitation system. Applied Sciences **11**(2), 815 (2021)

13. Khor, K., Chin, P., Hisyam, A., Yeong, C., Narayanan, A., Su, E.: Development of CR2-haptic: a compact and portable rehabilitation robot for wrist and forearm training. In: 2014 IEEE Conference On Biomedical Engineering And Sciences (IECBES), pp. 424–429. IEEE, Kuala Lumpur (2014)

14. Rijnveld, N., Krebs, H.I.: Passive wrist joint impedance in flexion - extension and abduction - adduction. In: IEEE 10th International Conference on Rehabilitation Robotics (ICORR), pp. 43–47. IEEE, Noordwijk (2007)

15. Wang, Y., Xu, Q.: Design and testing of a soft parallel robot based on pneumatic artificial muscles for wrist rehabilitation. Scientific Reports **11**(1), 1273 (2021)

16. Allington, J., Spencer, S.J., Klein, J., Buell, M., Reinkensmeyer, D.J., Bobrow, J.: Supinator extender (SUE): a pneumatically actuated robot for forearm/wrist rehabilitation after stroke. In: 2011 Annual International Conference of the IEEE Engineering in Medicine and Biology Society, pp. 1579–1582. IEEE, Boston, MA, USA (2011)

17. Oblak, J., Cikajlo, I.: Universal haptic drive: a robot for arm and wrist rehabilitation. IEEE Trans. Neural Syst. Rehabil. Eng. **18**(3), 293–302 (2010)

18. Molaei, A., Foomany, N.A., Parsapour, M., Dargahi, J.: A portable low-cost 3D-printed wrist rehabilitation robot: design and development. Mechanism and Machine Theory **171** (2022)

19. Chen, W., Cui, X., Zhang, J., Wang, J.: A cable-driven wrist robotic rehabilitator using a novel torque-field controller for human motion training. Rev. Sci. Instrum. **86**(6), 59–68 (2015)

20. Mustafa, S.K., Yang, G., Yeo, S.H., Lin, W.: Optimal design of a bio-inspired anthropocentric shoulder rehabilitator. Applied Bionics and Biomechanics, pp. 199–208 (2006)

Dimensional Synthesis of a Novel Redundantly Actuated Parallel Manipulator

Zhen He, Hangliang Fang, and Jun Zhang$^{(\boxtimes)}$

Fuzhou University, Fuzhou 350105, China
zhang_jun@fzu.edu.cn

Abstract. Redundantly actuated parallel manipulators (RAPMs) receive growing interest due to their enlarged dexterous workspace, higher stiffness and improved force distribution. The results of dimensional synthesis have an important influence on the comprehensive performance of RAPMs. Usually, dexterity index is one of the performance indices, which should be took into consideration. The dexterity index is based on the algebraic characteristics of the Jacobian matrix. However, for an RAPM with combined motilities of rotation and translation, its Jacobian matrix has inconsistent element units and un-clear physical meaning. This paper establishes a set of dexterity indices based on the dimensionally homogeneous Jacobian (DHJ) matrix of a 2UPR-2RPS RAPM for dimensional synthesis. Firstly, a local dexterity index is established to evaluate the dexterity of the 2UPR-2RPS RAPM at a certain posture. Meanwhile, a global dexterity index is determined in accordance with the local dexterity index. Secondly, a dimensional design method based on the parameter-finiteness normalization method (PFNM) is proposed to optimize the dimensional parameters of the 2UPR-2RPS RAPM. Finally, a set of dimensional parameters is optimized and a laboratory prototype of the 2UPR-2RPS RAPM is fabricated.

Keywords: Redundantly Actuated Parallel Manipulators · Dimensional Synthesis · Dexterity

1 Introduction

Parallel manipulators offer high rigidity, high accuracy, and large payload capability compared with serial manipulators. Therefore, parallel manipulators are regarded as an advantageous alternative solution for high-speed machining [1–3]. According to the relationship between degrees of freedom (DOFs) and number of actuators, parallel manipulators can be roughly classified into two categories, i.e., redundantly actuated parallel manipulators (RAPMs) and non-redundantly actuated parallel manipulators (NRAPMs). Many studies have focused on the former category because it offers the advantages of enlarged dexterous workspace, higher stiffness and improved force distribution [2, 4, 5].

Dimensional synthesis of the RAPM is indispensable in optimal kinematic design, which aims at obtaining better performances in the reachable workspace. One of the dimensional synthesis methods is optimal design with performance-chart, which include

H. Yang et al. (Eds.): ICIRA 2023, LNAI 14267, pp. 69–79, 2023.
https://doi.org/10.1007/978-981-99-6483-3_7

defining suitable performance indices, reducing the number of design variables, as well as employing proper search algorithms. Defining suitable performance indices is still challenging issues [6]. As indicated by the existing studies [7–9], there are mainly two types of performance index used for dimensional synthesis of RAPMs.

One type of index is called the motion / force transmission index. The motion / force transmission index indicates the capability of the linkages transmitting input motion / force to the output link. By tracking present literatures, one may find that the motion / force transmission index has been systematically formulated and applied to RAPMs. For example, Li et al. [10] proposed a new 2UPR-2PRU redundantly actuated parallel manipulator and a local transmission index (LTI) is defined as the minimum value of the index of output and input transmission performance. Zhang et al. [11] derived a set of motion / force transmission performance indices with an alternative screw theory based approach to evaluate the performance of a novel 2PRU-PRPS RAPM. The aforementioned studies indicate that the motion / force transmission index based dimensional design can improve the capability of transmission between the actuators and moving platform.

The other type of index that can be used for performance evaluation is the dexterity index. The dexterity index is proposed to evaluate the kinematic performance of parallel manipulators, which is based on the algebraic characteristics of the Jacobian matrix, such as manipulability [12], condition number [13], etc. For example, Zarkandi [14] used the condition number of the inverse and forward Jacobian matrix to construct the dexterity index for a 3-PRR spherical parallel manipulator and conducted an optimal design for this manipulator to achieve a workspace with good kinematic dexterity. Most literature focuses on the design of NRAPMs with symmetrical architectures associated with pure translation or pure rotational DOF. Since the Jacobian matrix is homogeneous, this type of RAPMs makes ease of analysis and dimensional design. However, for an NRAPM with combined motilities of rotation and translation, its Jacobian matrix has inconsistent element units and un-clear physical meaning. For this reason, the dimensionally homogeneous Jacobian (DHJ) matrix was formulated to deal with this inconsistency. Then, a local index of dexterity, which is adopted to evaluate an NRAPM with mixed motion capabilities, is established based on the DHJ matrix's condition number or its inverse. For example, Huang et al. [15] presented a general and systematic screw-based method to formulate the DHJ matrix for NRAPMs with mixed motion capabilities. Wang et al. [16] proposed a DHJ matrix by means of the concept of characteristic length using the Newton-Raphson method. Through the above literature review, one may find that the dexterity index, which is proposed based a DHJ matrix, has been systematically formulated and applied to the dimensional synthesis of NRAPMs. However, quite few investigations considered the dexterity formulations of RAPMs. Wang et al. [17] proposed the indices of manipulability and the condition number of the Jacobian matrix to evaluate the dexterity of a 3PRS-1UPS RAPM. It is worth pointing out that the dexterity index directly generated from a Jacobian matrix with inconsistent units is not appropriate for RAPMs with combined motilities of rotation and translation. To solve this problem, this paper will derive the DHJ matrix for an RAPM driven by prismatic actuators and propose a set of dexterity index to evaluate the dexterity of RAPMs with mixed motion capabilities. To be specific, a local dexterity index is defined as the reciprocal of the condition number of the DHJ matrix, while a global dexterity index is defined as the ratio of good dexterity workspace to the reachable workspace.

The rest of this paper is organized as follows: Sect. 2 briefly describes the 2UPR-2RPS RAPM. Section 3 formulates the DHJ matrix of the RAPM to establishes the local dexterity index and the global dexterity index. Section 4 give details of the dimensional synthesis of the 2UPR-2RPS RAPM. Finally, some conclusions are drawn to close the paper.

2 Description of the 2UPR-2RPS RAPM

A prototype of 2UPR-2RPS RAPM is shown in Fig. 1. The 2UPR-2RPS RAPM is composed of a fixed based, a moving platform and four limbs. Specially, limb 1 and limb 2 are two identical UPR limbs, while limb 3 and limb 4 are two identical RPS limbs. The moving platform is connected to the fixed based by the four limbs. Namely, limb 1 and limb 2 are fixed on the fixed based through universal joints and connected to the moving platform through revolute joints, while limb 3 and limb 4 are fixed on the fixed based through revolute joints and connected to the moving platform through spherical joints. Furthermore, the prismatic joint, which is to be an actuated joint, is actuated by a servo motor via a ball screw and two guide rails. To make the conformation compact, the passive actuated joints including the spherical joint, the universal joint, the revolute joint connected to moving platform and the revolute joint connected to fixed based are designed in a modular way.

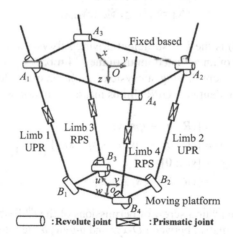

Fig. 1. Schematics of the 2UPR-2RPS RAPM

As shown in Fig. 1, A_i ($i = 1 \sim 4$) denote the central points of the joints connecting to the fixed based in i^{th} limbs; B_i ($i = 1 \sim 4$) denote the central points of the joints connecting to the moving platfrom in i^{th} limbs. For simplicity, the fixed base $A_1A_2A_3A_4$ and the moving platform $B_1B_2B_3B_4$ are set to be two quadrates. O and o are the central points of the quadrate of $\Box A_1A_2A_3A_4$ and $\Box B_1B_2B_3B_4$.

For ease of derivation, the coordinate frames are established as shown in Fig. 1. A reference coordinate system $O\text{-}xyz$ is established at O, with x axis pointing to A_3, y axis pointing to A_2 and z axis satisfying the right-hand rule. A moving coordinate system $o\text{-}uvw$ is established at o, with u axis pointing to B_3, v axis pointing to B_3 and w axis satisfying the right-hand rule. The architectural parameters of the 2UPR-2RPS RAPM are defined as follows: $oB_1 = oB_2 = R_1$, $OA_1 = OA_2 = R_2$, $oB_3 = oB_4 = R_3$, $OA_3 = OA_3 = R_4$ and $A_iB_i = q_i$ $(i = 1 \sim 4)$.

3 Dexterity Indices Formulation

3.1 A Local Dexterity Index Formulation

The non-redundantly actuated subsystem is named as 'sufficient driving subsystem' and the redundantly actuated subsystem is named as 'passive actuators with power inputs' [18]. The 2UPR-2RPS parallel manipulator is a three-DOF redundant actuated parallel manipulators with 4 actuated kinematic limbs and any three kinematic limbs can form a 'sufficient driving subsystem' by regarding any one actuator as a 'passive actuator with power input'. Therefore, this type of parallel manipulator can have four types of 'sufficient driving subsystems', namely:

$$
\begin{aligned}
\Lambda_1 &= \{\hat{\$}_{ta,1}, \hat{\$}_{ta,2}, \hat{\$}_{ta,3}\} \\
\Lambda_2 &= \{\hat{\$}_{ta,1}, \hat{\$}_{ta,2}, \hat{\$}_{ta,4}\} \\
\Lambda_3 &= \{\hat{\$}_{ta,1}, \hat{\$}_{ta,3}, \hat{\$}_{ta,4}\} \\
\Lambda_4 &= \{\hat{\$}_{ta,2}, \hat{\$}_{ta,3}, \hat{\$}_{ta,4}\}
\end{aligned}
\tag{1}
$$

where Λ_k $(k = 1,2,3,4)$ is the kth 'sufficient driving subsystem' and $\hat{\$}_{ta,i}$ $(i = 1,2,3,4)$ represents a unit screw of an actuated input of the ith limb.

Taking the 1st 'sufficient driving subsystem' Λ_1 as an example. The unit screws of permissions for the two identical 'UPR' limbs measured in $o\text{-}uvw$ can be given as

$$
\begin{aligned}
\hat{\$}_{ta,i,1} &= [(R \cdot b_i - q_i s_{i,3}) \times s_{i,1}; s_{i,1}] \\
\hat{\$}_{ta,i,2} &= [(R \cdot b_i - q_i s_{i,3}) \times s_{i,2}; s_{i,2}] \\
\hat{\$}_{ta,i,3} &= [s_{i,3}; \mathbf{0}] \\
\hat{\$}_{ta,i,4} &= [(R \cdot b_i) \times s_{i,4}; s_{i,4}]
\end{aligned}
\quad (i = 1, 2)
\tag{2}
$$

where $\hat{\$}_{ta,i,j}$ denotes the jth unit screw of permissions of the ith limb measured in $o\text{-}uvw$; R is the transformation matrix between $O\text{-}xyz$ and $o\text{-}uvw$; b_i denotes the position vector of point B_i measured in the reference coordinate frame $o\text{-}uvw$; $s_{i,j}$ denotes a unit vector along the jth single-DOF joint axis in the ith limb.

The proposed RAPM takes the prismatic joint as an actuated joint, thus the number of actuators l_a is three. According to the reciprocal screw theory, the unit wrench of constraints $\hat{\$}_{wc,i,lc}$ $(i = 1,2; lc = 1,2)$, the unit wrench of actuations $\hat{\$}_{wa,i,3}$ and the unit screw of restrictions $\hat{\$}_{tc,i,jc}$ ($jc = 1,2$) of limb 1 and limb 2 can be expressed as

$$
\begin{aligned}
\hat{\$}_{wc,i,1} &= [s_{i,4}; (R \cdot b_i - q_i s_{i,3}) \times s_{i,4}] \\
\hat{\$}_{wc,i,2} &= [0; s_{i,1} \times s_{i,2}] \\
\hat{\$}_{wa,i,3} &= [s_{i,3}; (R \cdot b_i - q_i s_{i,3}) \times s_{i,3}] \qquad (i = 1, 2) \\
\hat{\$}_{tc,i,1} &= [(R \cdot b_i - q_i s_{i,3}) \times (s_{i,1} \times s_{i,2}); s_{i,1} \times s_{i,2}] \\
\hat{\$}_{tc,i,2} &= [s_{i,4}; 0]
\end{aligned}
\tag{3}
$$

where $\hat{\$}_{wc,i,lc}$ denotes the lc^{th} unit wrench of constraints of the ith limb measured in o-uvw; $\hat{\$}_{wa,i,3}$ is the unit wrench of actuations of the ith limb measured in o-uvw; $\hat{\$}_{tc,i,jc}$ denotes the jc^{th} unit screw of restrictions of the ith limb measured in o-uvw.

By the same token, the unit screws of permissions for the two identical 'RPS' limbs measured in o-uvw can be obtained by

$$
\begin{aligned}
\hat{\$}_{ta,i,1} &= [(R \cdot b_i - q_i s_{i,2}) \times s_{i,1}; s_{i,1}] \\
\hat{\$}_{ta,i,2} &= [s_{i,2}; 0] \\
\hat{\$}_{ta,i,3} &= [(R \cdot b_i) \times s_{i,3}; s_{i,3}] \qquad (i = 3, 4) \\
\hat{\$}_{ta,i,4} &= [(R \cdot b_i) \times s_{i,4}; s_{i,4}] \\
\hat{\$}_{ta,i,5} &= [(R \cdot b_i) \times s_{i,5}; s_{i,5}]
\end{aligned}
\tag{4}
$$

Concurrently, the unit wrench of constraints $\hat{\$}_{wc,3,1}$, the unit wrench of actuations $\hat{\$}_{wa,3,2}$ and the unit screw of restrictions $\hat{\$}_{tc,3,1}$ of limb 3 can be expressed as follows.

$$
\begin{aligned}
\hat{\$}_{wc,3,1} &= [s_{3,1}; (R \cdot b_3) \times s_{3,1}] \\
\hat{\$}_{wa,3,2} &= [s_{3,2}; (R \cdot b_3) \times s_{3,2}] \\
\hat{\$}_{tc,3,1} &= [(R \cdot b_3 - q_3 s_{3,3}) \times (s_{3,1} \times s_{3,2}); s_{3,1} \times s_{3,2}]
\end{aligned}
\tag{5}
$$

The prismatic actuator of limb 4 is regarded as a 'passive actuator with power input', so there is no unit wrench of actuations. The unit wrench of constraints $\hat{\$}_{wc,4,1}$ and the unit screw of restrictions $\hat{\$}_{tc,4,1}$ of limb 4 can be given as

$$
\begin{aligned}
\hat{\$}_{wc,4,1} &= [s_{4,1}; (R \cdot b_4) \times s_{4,1}] \\
\hat{\$}_{tc,4,1} &= [(R \cdot b_4 - q_4 s_{4,3}) \times (s_{4,1} \times s_{4,2}); s_{4,1} \times s_{4,2}]
\end{aligned}
\tag{6}
$$

The Jacobian matrix of the parallel manipulator driven by the 1st 'sufficient driving subsystem' can be obtained as follows.

$$
J_1 \cdot \hat{\$}_t = \begin{bmatrix} q'_1 \\ 0 \end{bmatrix}, \; J_1 = \begin{bmatrix} J_{1a} \\ J_{1c} \end{bmatrix}, \; q'_1 = \begin{bmatrix} q'_{1,1} \\ q'_{1,2} \\ q'_{1,3} \end{bmatrix}
\tag{7}
$$

where

$$J_1 = \begin{bmatrix} J_{1a} \\ J_{1c} \end{bmatrix}, \; q_1' = \begin{bmatrix} q_{1,1}' \\ q_{1,2}' \\ q_{1,3}' \end{bmatrix}, \; \hat{\$}_t = \sum_{j=1}^{nj} q_{1,j}' \cdot \hat{\$}_{ta,i,j} + \sum_{jc=1}^{6-nj} 0 \cdot \hat{\$}_{tc,i,jc} = \begin{bmatrix} v^T & w^T \end{bmatrix}^T,$$

$$J_{1a} = \begin{bmatrix} s_{1,3}^T & ((R \cdot b_1 - q_1 s_{1,3}) \times s_{1,3}) \\ s_{2,3}^T & ((R \cdot b_2 - q_2 s_{2,3}) \times s_{2,3}) \\ s_{3,2}^T & ((R \cdot b_3) \times s_{3,2}) \end{bmatrix}, \; J_{1c} = \begin{bmatrix} s_{1,4}^T & ((R \cdot b_1 - q_1 s_{1,3}) \times s_{1,4})^T \\ 0 & (s_{1,1} \times s_{1,2})^T \\ s_{2,4}^T & ((R \cdot b_2 - q_2 s_{2,3}) \times s_{2,4})^T \\ 0 & (s_{2,1} \times s_{2,2})^T \\ s_{3,1}^T/q_3 & ((R \cdot b_3) \times s_{3,1})^T/q_3 \\ s_{4,1}^T/q_4 & ((R \cdot b_4) \times s_{4,1})^T/q_4 \end{bmatrix} \quad (8)$$

where J_1 is an $(f + \sum_{i=1}^{L}(6 - n_j)) \times 6$ matrix known as the generalized Jacobian of the 1st 'sufficient driving subsystem'; L is the number of kinematic limbs, where $L = 4$; n_j is the number of single-DOF joints of the ith limb; $\hat{\$}_t$ denotes the twist of the moving platform; $q_{1,j}'$ denotes the velocity of the jth single-DOF actuated joint of the 1st 'sufficient driving subsystem'; v and w represent the linear velocities of the reference point on the moving platform and angular velocities of the platform, respectively.

Taking B_i ($i = 1, 2, 3$) as three independent coordinates, the dimensionally homogeneous Jacobian matrix J_{pa}^1 can be obtained by substituting Eq. (8) in Eq. (9).

$$J_{pa}^1 = \left[J_{pa0}^1 \cdot A_g^T \cdot ((J_1)^T \cdot J_1)^{-1} \cdot (J_{1a})^T \right]^{-1} \quad (9)$$

where

$$J_{pa0}^1 = \begin{bmatrix} e_0 & e_0 & e_0 \\ b_1 \times e_0 & b_2 \times e_0 & b_3 \times e_0 \end{bmatrix}, \; e_0 = [0, 0, 1]^T, \; A_g = \begin{bmatrix} R & 0 \\ 0 & R \end{bmatrix} \quad (10)$$

The local dexterity index corresponding to the 1st 'sufficient driving subsystem' can be obtained from Eq. (11).

$$d_1 = 1/(\lVert J_{pa}^1 \rVert \cdot \lVert (J_{pa}^1)^{-1} \rVert) \quad (11)$$

In a similar manner, the dimensionally homogeneous Jacobian matrix J_{pa}^2, J_{pa}^3 and J_{pa}^4 of the proposed RAPM driven by the other three 'sufficiently driving subsystems' can be formulated. Then, the local dexterity indices d_2, d_3 and d_4 can be obtained.

Therefore, the local dexterity index d_L^R of the proposed RAPM can be obtained by Eq. (12) under any specified position and orientation.

$$d_L^R = \max\{d_1, d_2, d_3, d_4\} \quad (12)$$

where d_L^R is in the range of $(0, 1)$. The greater the value of d_L^R, the better the dexterity performance of the redundant actuated parallel manipulator.

3.2 Global Dexterity Index Formulation

It is necessary to define an index that can describe the manipulator's dexterity in a set of poses. When a RAPM works in the region in where the local dexterity index is lower than the allowable value, it suffers great loss in the dexterity. Considering the fact, we define the good dexterity workspace (GDW) as the region where $d_L^R > [d_L^R]$. In Ref. [7], if $d_L^R > 0.1$, the point will be excluded to calculate the GDW from the reachable workspace. In this study, to further improve the global dexterity of the 2UPR-2RPS RAPM, $[d_L^R] = 0.4$, i.e., the region where $d_L^R > [d_L^R]$ is the GDW.

Based on the above discussions, the index that measures the global dexterity of a RAPM is thus defined as

$$\sigma_G = \frac{\int_{S_G} dW_r}{\int_S dW_r} \tag{13}$$

where W_r is the reachable workspace; and S_G and S denote the areas of the GDW and overall possible workspace, respectively. σ_G is in the range of (0, 1); having a σ_G value that is closer to unity leads to better dexterity for a RAPM.

4 Dimensional Synthesis

The target workspace is introduced to replace the reachable workspace, that is, the target workspace is given by the designer as one of the design parameters. Exechon is a commercial parallel manipulator, whose rotation ranges of the precession angle and nutation angle are [-30,30] and [-30,30], respectively. Benchmarking Exechon and according to the characteristics of the workspace of the 2UPR-2RPS RAPM, a cuboid as the target workspace of 2UPR-2RPS RAPM is taken, which can be expressed as,

$$z \in [180\,\text{mm}, 260\,\text{mm}], \ \theta \in [-30°, 30°], \ \psi \in [-30°, 30°] \tag{14}$$

where z, θ and ψ represent three independent DOFs of the 2UPR-2RPS RAPM, where one translation along z-axis and two continuous rotations about the u and the y axes. In a given reachable workspace, the global dexterity index of a RAPM are determined by R_1, R_2, R_3 and R_4. For the 2UPR-2PRS RAPM, the moving platform and the fixed based are all rhombuses and the geometric parameters R_1, R_2, R_3 and R_4 satisfy $R_4 = R_2 R_3 / R_1$, which means R_1, R_2 and R_3 can be regarded as design parameters. Using the PFNM, this method reduces the boundary limitations of each normalized parameter and converts an infinite parameter space into a finite space. For the 2UPR-2PRS RAPM, the design parameters R_1, R_2 and R_3 are normalized as

$$D = (R1 + R2 + R3)/3, \ e_i = R_i/D \ (i = 1, 2, 3, 4) \tag{15}$$

where D is a normalized factor; e_i $(i = 1, 2, 3, 4)$ are the non-dimensional and normalized parameters, which is constrained by the following conditions:

$$\begin{cases} e_1 e_4 = e_2 e_3 \\ e_1 + e_2 + e_3 = 3 \end{cases}, \quad \begin{cases} e_2, e_4 > e_1, e_3 \\ 0 < e_1, e_2, e_3, e_4 < 3 \end{cases} \tag{16}$$

Figure 2(a) shows the generation of the parameter design space with constraints in Eq. (16). For convenience, the parameter design space can be transformed into a plan view to illustrate this region, which is shown in Fig. 2(b). The relationship between the parameters in three-dimensional space and those in planar space is derived as

$$\begin{cases} s = e_1 \\ t = \dfrac{3 + e_2 - e_3}{\sqrt{3}} \end{cases} \tag{17}$$

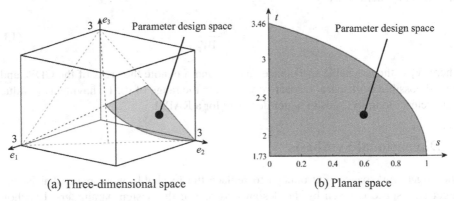

(a) Three-dimensional space   (b) Planar space

Fig. 2. Parameter design space

The steps required for dimensional synthesis are as follows:

Step 1: obtaining the distributions diagram of σ_G. Based on the above analysis, the distribution of σ_G in the parameter design space is searched in MATLAB environment. The distributions diagram of σ_G is obtained as shown in Fig. 3.

Step 2: selecting the data points. The parameters s and t are obtained from Fig. 3 and the non-dimensional parameters e_1, e_2 and e_3 can be obtained by using Eq. (17). For example, one group of the design parameters are selected as the optimal results, where $e_1 = 0.86$, $e_2 = 1.28$ and $e_3 = 0.86$. The σ_G value of this group of the design parameters is 1.0, which indicates that the 2UPR-2RPS RAPM has a good dexterity under any specified position and orientation of the reachable workspace.

Step 3: Determining the normalized factor D. By considering the occupied area and the non-dimensional parameters that were selected from the optimal design regions, the normalized factor D is determined to be 140 mm in this study. Then, the design parameters R_1, R_2, R_3 and R_4 can be obtained by using Eq. (15) and Eq. (16), giving R_1 = 120 mm, R_2 = 180 mm, R_3 = 120 mm and R_4 = 180 mm.

Step 4: Checking whether the dimensional parameters obtained in Step 3 are suitable for actual use. If the dimensional parameters are suitable for actual assembly conditions, then the design process is complete. Otherwise, the procedure is returned to Step 2 and another group of data is selected. Then, Step 3 and Step 4 are repeated.

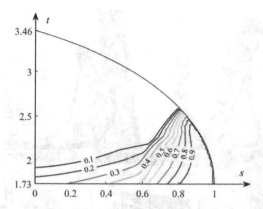

Fig. 3. Distribution diagram of σ_G for the 2UPR-2RPS RAPM

In addition to R_1, R_2, R_3 and R_4, there is also q_i ($i = 1 \sim 4$) that needs to be designed. Considering the dimension of the revolute joint and the universal joint connected with the fixed based and the size of the target workspace, a guide rail with a length of 340 mm is selected. When the revolute joint and the spherical joint connected with the moving platform are integrated on the kinematic branch chain, the minimum length value of q_i ($i = 1 \sim 4$) is 155 mm. By calculation, the maximum length value of q_i ($i = 1 \sim 4$) is 320 mm.

Based on the above analysis, the basic dimensional parameters of the prototype are listed in Table 1.

Table 1. The basic dimensional parameters of the prototype.

$R1$	R_2	R_3	R_4	q_{min}	q_{max}
120 mm	180 mm	120 mm	180 mm	155 mm	320 mm

As shown in Fig. 4, based on the dimensional parameters listed in Table 1, a laboratory prototype of the 2UPR-2RPS RAPM is fabricated.

Fig. 4. The laboratory prototype of the 2UPR-2RPS RAPM

5 Conclusion

In this paper, a dimensional synthesis of a RAPM with 2UPR-2RPS topology is proposed. Based on the studies, the following specific conclusions can be drawn.

(1) The DHJ matrix of the 2UPR-2RPS RAPM is established. Based on this, a set of local and global indices are proposed to evaluate the motion capabilities for the RAPM. The proposed dexterity indices provide general dexterity indices, which are with the consistent element units in the Jacobian matrix and clear physical meaning.

(2) Based on the PFNM, which make sure that the parameter design space is finite and the normalization factor does not change the similarity of manipulators' performances, a dimensional synthesis is proposed to design the dimensional parameters of the 2UPR-2RPS RAPM. Finally, a laboratory prototype of the 2UPR-2RPS RAPM is fabricated.

(3) Our future work will focus on the following issues. Firstly, it is important to consider dexterity and motion/force transmissibility simultaneously in the dimensional synthesis of a RAPM. Secondly, it is necessary to explore the influence of different spatial layouts on performance of RAPMs, for example, rigidity, dexterity, motion/force transmissibility and so on. They will be investigated in-depth in our future work.

References

1. López-Custodio, P.C., Fu, R., Dai, J.S., et al.: Compliance model of Exechon manipulators with an offset wrist. Mech. Mach. Theory **167**, 104558 (2022)
2. Liu, Z., Tao, R., Fan, J., et al.: Kinematics, dynamics, and load distribution analysis of a 4-PPPS redundantly actuated parallel manipulator. Mech. Mach. Theory **167**, 104494 (2022)

3. Yang, C., Ye, W., Li, Q.: Review of the performance optimization of parallel manipulators. Mech. Mach. Theory **170**, 104725 (2022)
4. Zhang, H., Fang, H., Zhang, D., et al.: Forward kinematics and workspace determination of a novel redundantly actuated parallel manipulator. International Journal of Aerospace Engineering, 2019 (2019)
5. Zhu, B., Wang, L., Wu, J.: Optimal design of loading device based on a redundantly actuated parallel manipulator. Mech. Mach. Theory **178**, 105084 (2022)
6. Cardou, P., Bouchard, S., Gosselin, C.: Kinematic-sensitivity indices for dimensionally nonhomogeneous jacobian matrices. IEEE Trans. Rob. **26**(1), 166–173 (2010)
7. Liu, X., Cai, Y., Liu, W., et al.: Performance evaluation of a special 6-PUS type parallel manipulator. Robotica **40**(3), 505–519 (2022)
8. Shen, X., Xu, L., Li, Q.: Motion/Force constraint indices of redundantly actuated parallel manipulators with over constraints. Mech. Mach. Theory **165**, 104427 (2021)
9. Boudreau, R., Nokleby, S., Gallant, M.: Wrench capabilities of a kinematically redundant planar parallel manipulator. Robotica **39**(9), 1601–1616 (2021)
10. Zhang, N., Li, Q., Wang, F.: New indices for optimal design of redundantly actuated parallel manipulators. J. Mechanisms and Robotics: Transactions of the ASME **9**(1) (2017)
11. Zhang, H., Fang, H., Jiang, B.: Motion-force transmissibility characteristic analysis of a redundantly actuated and overconstrained parallel machine. Int. J. Autom. Comput. **16**(2), 150–162 (2019)
12. Stoughton, R.S., Arai, T.: A modified stewart platform manipulator with improved dexterity. IEEE Trans. Robot. Autom. **9**(2), 166–173 (1993)
13. Angeles, J., López-Cajún, C.S.: Kinematic isotropy and the conditioning index of serial robotic manipulators. Int. J. Robotics Res. **11**(6), 560–571 (1992)
14. Zarkandi, S.: Kinematic analysis and optimal design of a novel 3-PRR spherical parallel manipulator. Proc. Inst. Mech. Eng. C J. Mech. Eng. Sci. **235**(4), 693–712 (2021)
15. Huang, T., Yang, S., Wang, M., et al.: An approach to determining the unknown twist/wrench subspaces of lower mobility serial kinematic chains. J. Mech. Robot. **7**(3), 031003 (2015)
16. Wang, Y., Belzile, B., Angeles, J., et al.: Kinematic analysis and optimum design of a novel 2PUR-2RPU parallel robot. Mech. Mach. Theory **139**, 407–423 (2019)
17. Wang, D., Fan, R., Chen, W.: Performance enhancement of a three-degree-of-freedom parallel tool head via actuation redundancy. Mech. Mach. Theory **71**, 142–162 (2014)
18. Fang, H., Tang, T., Zhang, J.: Kinematic analysis and comparison of a 2R1T redundantly actuated parallel manipulator and its non-redundantly actuated forms. Mech. Mach. Theory **142**, 103587 (2019)

A Novel Hyper-Redundant Manipulator Dynamic Identification Method Based on Whale Optimization and Nonlinear Friction Model

Yufei Zhou[1,2], Zhongcan Li[1,2], Angang Feng[1,2], Xianke Zhang[1,2], and Mingchao Zhu[1(✉)]

[1] ChangChun Institute of Optics, Fine Mechanics and Physics, Chinese Academy of Sciences, Changchun 130033, China
2313297208@qq.com
[2] University of Chinese Academy of Sciences, Beijing 100049, China

Abstract. To achieve accurate dynamic model identification of the hyper-redundant manipulator, a novel identification method based on whale optimization algorithm is proposed. Firstly, the dynamic model of the hyper-redundant manipulator and the base parameter set are introduced, and a joint nonlinear friction model is established. The excitation trajectory is generated using genetic algorithm to optimize the condition number of the regression matrix. Secondly, physical feasibility constraints of the manipulator dynamic model are established, and the whale optimization algorithm (WOA) is applied for dynamic parameter identification under nonlinear constraints. Finally, experiments are conducted to verify the effectiveness of the identification method. The experimental results demonstrate that, compared with the traditional least squares (LS) algorithm and weighted least squares (WLS) algorithm, the proposed identification algorithm can improve the sum of identify torque residual root mean square (RMS) of joints by 11.51 N·m and 6.29 N·m, respectively. The experimental results demonstrate the superiority of the algorithm proposed in this paper.

Keywords: Dynamic model identification · Hyper-redundant manipulator · Whale optimization algorithm · Nonlinear friction model

1 Introduction

Robotics is a rapidly growing field that has seen significant advancements in recent years. One of the key areas of research in robotics is the development of accurate and reliable dynamic model for robot. These dynamic models are essential for the control and manipulation of robots in various applications, such as advanced control algorithm design [1], collision detection [2], human-robot interaction [3], multi-arm collaboration [4]. However, industrial manipulators do not provide accurate dynamic parameters, and experimental identification is a reliable way to get the accurate dynamic parameters.

The dynamic parameter identification of the manipulator in the experiment involves four steps: dynamics modeling, excitation trajectory design, parameter estimation, and

H. Yang et al. (Eds.): ICIRA 2023, LNAI 14267, pp. 80–91, 2023.
https://doi.org/10.1007/978-981-99-6483-3_8

dynamic model validation. The Newton-Euler method is commonly used for dynamic modeling, and by linearizing dynamics, dynamic parameters can be separated from the regression matrix. Khalil's method eliminates redundant dynamic parameters and establishes a minimum parameter set, effectively reducing the number of dynamic parameters that require identification and improving the identification accuracy [5]. The friction model plays a crucial role in the dynamic modeling process. While the Coulomb + viscous friction model is commonly used [3, 6], it fails to accurately capture the nonlinear effects of joint friction. Thus, this article adopts a nonlinear friction model to better fit the friction force.

The design of an excitation trajectory is a critical aspect of identifying the dynamic parameters. Commonly used excitation trajectory measurement indicators include the condition number of the regression matrix [7, 8], the condition number of the sub-regression matrix [9], and the value of $log\{det(\cdot)\}$ [10, 11]. While a fifth-order polynomial excitation trajectory requires fewer parameters to be optimized [12], periodic Fourier series excitation trajectories offer advantages in data processing [13]. Combining the trajectories of fifth-order polynomials and periodic Fourier series can integrate the characteristics of both. This approach can reduce the constraints of optimization problems and minimize data errors by averaging the data. Therefore, the use of combined trajectories is a promising method for designing excitation trajectories that can accurately identify the dynamic model of a manipulator.

The LS [5] and WLS [14] methods are commonly employed for parameter estimation in dynamic model identification due to their fast data processing, simplicity, and efficiency. However, these algorithms are susceptible to abnormal data and exhibit poor generalization ability for the obtained dynamic parameters. To address these limitations, scholars have proposed iterative reweighted least squares and geometric optimization identification methods [15, 16], which improve identification accuracy. Nevertheless, these methods are characterized by complex algorithm structures and long processing times. Furthermore, the Coulomb linear friction models utilized by these algorithms fail to account for the nonlinear characteristics of friction, thereby resulting in inaccurate friction models that significantly impact the identification results. Therefore, there is a need for novel optimization estimation methods that can accurately identify dynamic parameters in the presence of nonlinear friction models.

This article introduces a novel optimization estimation method for identifying the dynamic parameters of a manipulator with nonlinear friction models. Specifically, the proposed approach involves establishing a nonlinear friction model of the joint and utilizing the whale optimization algorithm [17] to solve for the optimal dynamic parameters. Notably, the solved dynamic parameters include an additional nonlinear friction model parameter, which effectively enhances the identification accuracy. Experimental comparisons of different identification methods demonstrate that our method outperforms other approaches.

The article is arranged as follows. In Sect. 2, we introduce the joint friction model and manipulator dynamic model. Section 3 introduces the design of excitation trajectory. Section 4 introduces the dynamic identification schematic, detailing the proposed method. Section 5 conductes a series of experiments. We conclude the paper in Sect. 5 by summarizing the main contributions of our research.

2 Dynamic Modeling of Hyper-Redundant Manipulator

The hyper-redundant modular manipulator comprises 9 modular joints, each equipped with an encoder for measuring joint position. Figure 1 depicts the joint coordinate system diagram of the hyper-redundant modular manipulator, while Table 1 shows the modified DH modeling parameters and joint motor parameters. As joint torque sensors are not available, joint torque needs to be calculated by collecting joint current information.

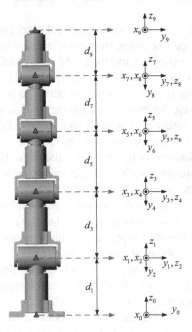

Fig. 1. Structure of the hyper-redundant modular manipulator

The dynamic model of the manipulator is shown in the following formula:

$$\tau = M_I(q)\ddot{q} + V(q,\dot{q})\dot{q} + G(q) + F_f(\dot{q}) \tag{1}$$

where $M_I(q)\ddot{q}$ represents the inertia term. $V(q,\dot{q})\dot{q}$ represents the centrifugal and Coriolis forces. $G(q)$ denotes the gravity term. $f(\dot{q})$ is joint friction force.

The conventional friction model for joint friction is the Coulomb + viscous friction model. This model is linear and can be expressed as follows:

$$F_{fi}(\dot{q}_i) = f_{ci}sign(\dot{q}_i) + f_{vi}\dot{q}_i + S_i \tag{2}$$

Among them, f_{ci} represents the Coulomb friction coefficient. f_{vi} Represents the viscous friction coefficient. S_i Represents the joint friction offset.

In the above-mentioned friction model, the viscous friction force is linearly proportional to the joint angular velocity. However, this linear relationship is considered

Table 1. Hyper-redundant modular manipulator joint motor parameters

Joints	α	a	d	offset	rated torque (N·m)	Torque coefficient
1	0	0	0.2878	0	2.3	0.21
2	$\pi/2$	0	0	π	2.3	0.21
3	$\pi/2$	0	0.3498	π	1.43	0.13
4	$\pi/2$	0	0	π	1.43	0.13
5	$\pi/2$	0	0.3187	π	0.74	0.106
6	$\pi/2$	0	0	π	0.74	0.106
7	$\pi/2$	0	0.2941	π	0.27	0.057
8	$\pi/2$	0	0	π	0.27	0.057
9	$\pi/2$	0	0.2351	π	0.27	0.057

inaccurate by many researchers as it fails to account for the nonlinear effects of joint friction. Therefore, a nonlinear friction model has been proposed in [3] to more accurately describe the friction force, as shown below:

$$F_{fi}(\dot{q}_i) = f_{ci}sign(\dot{q}_i) + f_{vi}|\dot{q}_i|^{\alpha_i}sign(\dot{q}_i) + S_i \tag{3}$$

The viscous friction force in the above friction model is proportional to the α_i power of the joint angular velocity.

Substituting (3) into Eq. (1) can construct dynamic equations of manipulators based on different friction models. In order to identify dynamic parameters, linearizing the dynamic model is a necessity. By using the symPybotics toolbox, the minimum parameter set can be quickly derived. The dynamic linearization takes the following form:

$$\tau = Y(q, \dot{q}, \ddot{q})\varphi_b$$

$$\varphi_b = \left[I_{ixx}, I_{ixy}, I_{ixz}, I_{iyy}, I_{iyz}, I_{izz}, m_i p_{ix}, m_i p_{iy}, m_i p_{iz}, m_i, I_{a_i}, f_{ci}, f_{vi}, S_i\right]^T \tag{4}$$

where $Y(q, \dot{q}, \ddot{q})$ represents the regression matrix, φ_b represents the full parameter set. Each joint in contains 14 parameters. By extracting the maximum linearly independent group from the regression matrix, a new regression matrix that matches the minimum parameter set can be obtained.

$$\tau = Y^*(q, \dot{q}, \ddot{q})\varphi_{min} \tag{5}$$

The 9-DOF hyper-redundant modular manipulator identified in this paper has 126 dynamic parameters, and the minimum parameter set contains 91 parameters. To achieve more precise identification of the friction model, using Eq. (3) for identification entails an inclusion of 9 additional friction parameters. Deriving the φ_{min} matrix based on collected torque and joint angle information is the primary objective of dynamic identification.

3   The Design of Excitation Trajectory

To enhance the effectiveness of data, this study employs a periodic excitation trajectory, which comprises a fifth-order Fourier series. By repeatedly executing the excitation trajectory and averaging the data, the data error can be minimized, and the selection of an appropriate filtering frequency during data processing can be facilitated. The excitation trajectory model is presented below:

$$
\begin{cases}
q_i = \sum_{l=1}^{5} \left[\frac{{}^i a_l}{\omega_f l} \sin(\omega_f l \cdot t) - \frac{{}^i b_l}{\omega_f l} \cos(\omega_f l \cdot t) \right] + q_{0i} \\
\dot{q}_i = \sum_{l=1}^{5} \left[{}^i a_l \cos(\omega_f l \cdot t) + {}^i b_l \sin(\omega_f l \cdot t) \right] \\
\ddot{q}_i = \sum_{l=1}^{5} \left[-{}^i a_l \omega_f l \sin(\omega_f l \cdot t) + {}^i b_l \omega_f l \cos(\omega_f l \cdot t) \right]
\end{cases}
\tag{6}
$$

where ω_f is the fundamental frequency of the excitation trajectory. q_{0i} is the initial joint angle of the excitation trajectory. a, b is the parameter need to be optimized in the excitation trajectory.

The aforementioned excitation trajectory comprises 99 optimized parameters. The optimization process aims to minimize the sum of the condition numbers of the regression matrix and the sub-regression matrix, thereby ensuring sufficient excitation of the inertia, gravity, and friction terms. The excitation trajectory must account for constraints regarding joint angle, velocity and acceleration. The excitation trajectory defined in this study has a period of 25s and a frequency of f=0.04Hz. The excitation trajectory is optimized using classical genetic algorithms. This optimization problem can be regarded as a nonlinear constrained minimization problem, which is described below:

$$
\arg(a, b, q_0) \min_{\forall q, \dot{q}, \ddot{q}} (5 \cdot cond(Y^*) + cond(Y_I^*) + cond(Y_g^*) + cond(Y_f^*))
$$

$$
subject\ to : \begin{cases}
q_{i,min} \leq q_i(t) \leq q_{i,max} \\
\dot{q}_{i,min} \leq \dot{q}_i(t) \leq \dot{q}_{i,max} \\
\ddot{q}_{i,min} \leq \ddot{q}_i(t) \leq \ddot{q}_{i,max} \\
\dot{q}_i(t_0) = \dot{q}_i(t_f) = \sum_{l=1}^{N} {}^i a_l = 0 \\
\ddot{q}_i(t_0) = \ddot{q}_i(t_f) = \sum_{l=1}^{N} {}^i b_l \omega_f l = 0
\end{cases} , \forall i, t
\tag{7}
$$

Two excitation trajectories are obtained through optimization: one trajectory is used for experiments, while another trajectory is employed to validate the identified dynamic model. Due to low-speed bandwidth of the self-developed 9-DOF hyper-redundant manipulator, the maximum joint speed is set to 30°/s, and the optimized regression matrix condition number is 341. The optimized excitation trajectory parameters are shown in Table 2. The trajectory of the manipulator's joints and end-effector is shown in Fig. 2.

Table 2. Identification trajectory parameters for hyper-redundant manipulator

Joints	a_1	a_2	a_3	a_4	a_5	
1	0.24529	0.44483	-0.00105	-0.03119	-0.0606	
2	0.04478	0.13335	-0.01824	-0.00873	-0.0109	
3	0.87644	-0.40796	-0.06577	0.0235	0.0389	
4	-0.16260	-0.0186	0.0821	0.16626	-0.1266	
5	-0.00431	0.00153	0.00576	-0.07611	0.04679	
6	-0.67595	-0.00746	-0.01372	0.120159	-0.0438	
7	-1.55605	0.0051	-0.00108	0.00455	0.05906	
8	-0.136723	-0.0077	-0.0401	-0.0650	0.06278	
9	0.048681	-0.0184	0.0965	-0.0622	0.00603	
Joints	b_1	b_2	b_3	b_4	b_5	q_0
1	-0.16546	0.0390	-0.0724	0.2287	-0.12186	0.18081
2	0.829112	-0.1354	0.3654	-0.171	-0.19371	0.01994
3	-0.14353	-0.3378	0.0429	0.0327	0.11200	-0.3410
4	0.65913	-0.00179	0.0261	-0.1735	-0.0084	0.03832
5	-0.01279	-0.3075	-0.0684	-0.0488	0.20564	-0.6336
6	0.02990	0.00617	0.00937	-0.0174	-0.00058	-0.0213
7	0.01848	0.01562	0.0073	-0.0237	0.00485	0.10479
8	0.21118	0.01983	0.02769	-0.1405	0.04488	0.03315
9	0.52366	-0.04477	-0.0041	-0.0283	-0.06239	-0.10719

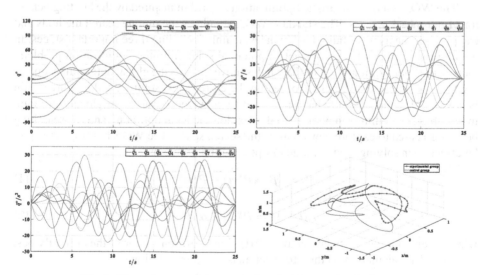

Fig. 2. The trajectory of the manipulator's joints and end-effector

4 Parameters Identification

Upon finalizing the excitation trajectory design, the manipulator is executed along the trajectory to collect joint angle and joint torque information, which is utilized to construct a hyper-positive equation:

$$\tau = \begin{bmatrix} \tau_{t_1}^* \\ \tau_{t_2}^* \\ \vdots \\ \tau_{t_M}^* \end{bmatrix} = \begin{bmatrix} Y_{t_1}^*(q_{t_1}, \dot{q}_{t_1}, \ddot{q}_{t_1}) \\ Y_{t_2}^*(q_{t_2}, \dot{q}_{t_2}, \ddot{q}_{t_2}) \\ \vdots \\ Y_{t_M}^*(q_{t_M}, \dot{q}_{t_M}, \ddot{q}_{t_M}) \end{bmatrix} \varphi_{\min} \tag{8}$$

The simplest method to identify the minimum parameter set is the LS and WLS. The relevant calculation formula is shown as follows:

$$\varphi_{LS} = (Y^{*T} Y^*)^{-1} Y^{*T} \tau^* \tag{9}$$

$$\begin{cases} \varphi_{WLS} = (Y^{*T} G^{-1} Y^*)^{-1} Y^{*T} G^{-1} \tau^* \\ G = diag(\Lambda_1, \Lambda_2, \ldots \Lambda_n) \end{cases} \tag{10}$$

In the above formula, Λ_i is calculated based on the identification residuals of each joint. The above identification methods are all based on a linear friction model as shown in Eq. (2). The drawback of this method is its incompatibility with nonlinear friction models. To address this limitation, this study introduces the use of the whale algorithm to identify the minimum parameter set and nonlinear friction model parameters, thereby producing identification outcomes that are most applicable to the actual robot model.

The WOA is a meta-heuristic optimization algorithm inspired by the hunting behavior of humpback whales. The standard WOA simulates the unique search methods and trapping mechanisms of humpback whales, mainly including three important stages. In the algorithm, each whale represents a potential solution to the optimization problem. During the optimization process, the whales move towards the global optimum by updating their positions and velocities based on the current best solution and the three main behaviors. The encircling behavior is used to converge towards the global optimum, the bubble-net feeding behavior is used to exploit the local optimum, and the searching behavior is used to explore new areas of the search space. The WOA has been shown to be effective in solving a wide range of optimization problems.

$$D = |\beta \cdot *P^*(t) - P(t)| \tag{11}$$

$$P(t+1) = P^*(t) - \alpha \cdot *D \tag{12}$$

where α and β are coefficient vectors. $P^*(t)$ is the position vector of the currently best solution. The calculation method for vectors α and β is as follows:

$$\alpha = 2a \times \eta_1 - a \tag{13}$$

$$\beta = 2 \times \eta_2 \tag{14}$$

where η_1 and η_2 are random vectors in $[0, 1]$.

There are two main prey method for humpback whales: surround predation and bubble net predation. When using a bubble-net for predation, the position update is represented by a logarithmic spiral equation, as shown in follows:

$$P(t + 1) = \begin{cases} P^*(t) - \alpha \cdot D & \gamma \leq 0.5 \\ D\prime \times e^{xl} \times \cos(2\pi l) + P^*(t) & \gamma \geq 0.5 \end{cases} \tag{15}$$

where γ is a random number with a range of $[0,1]$. As the number of iterations t increases, the parameter α and convergence factor a gradually decrease. If $|\alpha| < 1$, whale gradually surrounds the current optimal solution.

In order to ensure all whales to explore the solution space thoroughly, WOA updates the position based on the distance between whales, achieving the goal of random search. Therefore, when $|\alpha| > 1$, search for individuals swimming towards random whales.

$$D^{''} = |\beta \cdot P_{rand}(t) - P(t)| \tag{16}$$

$$P(t + 1) = P_{rand}(t) - \alpha \cdot D \tag{17}$$

If nonlinear model Eq. (3) is applied for dynamic identification, 100 parameters require to be optimized, including 91 minimum parameters and 9 friction model parameters. The dynamic parameters can be calculated by solving the following optimization problems with nonlinear physical feasibility constrains [18]. The overall procedure of the proposed approach is shown in Fig. 3.

$$\arg(\varphi_{\min}, \alpha_i \, or f_1, f_2) \min_{\forall q, \dot{q}, \ddot{q}} (\|Y^* \cdot \varphi_{\min} - \tau\|_2)$$

$$subject \, to : \begin{cases} f_{vi} > 0 \\ f_{ci} > 0 \\ I_{ai} > 0 \\ \begin{bmatrix} I_i & S(p_i)^T \\ S(p_i) & m_i \end{bmatrix} > 0 \end{cases}, i = 1, 2, \ldots 9 \tag{18}$$

5 Experiments

To validate the novel dynamic identification algorithm based on WOA, a 9-DOP hyper-redundant modular manipulator is used for dynamic model identification. The overall identification experimental platform and process are shown in Fig. 4. The hardware platform includes a computer, Beckhoff controller, communication module, motor driver, and manipulator. The software platform includes TwinCAT motion control system and EtherCAT communication protocol. The communication cycle is 5ms, and the data sampling frequency is 200Hz. The excitation trajectory cycle is 25s, so it can collect 5000 sets of data.

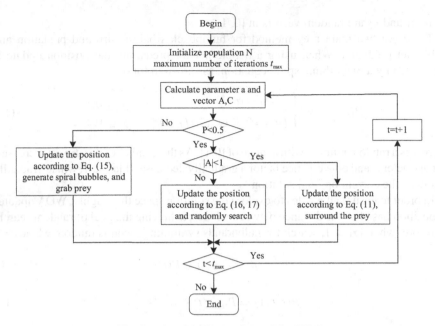

Fig. 3. The overall procedure of the WOA

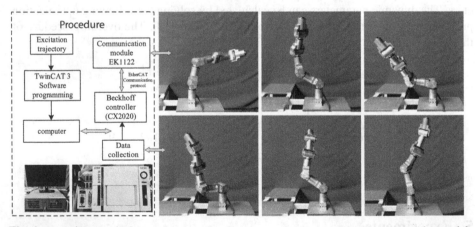

Fig. 4. Experiment platform and process of hyper-redundant manipulator dynamic model identification

During the experiment, the collected joint angle and joint torque are filtered using a zero-phase Butterworth filter. One set of experimental trajectories is utilized for parameter identification, while another set is reserved for verifying the identification efficacy. The experimental outcomes of various algorithms, such as LS, WLS, and the whale optimization algorithm based on different friction models, are compared. The identification accuracy of the experimental results is quantified using the residual RMS between the estimated and measured values, as shown in Eq. (19). The experimental identification results are shown in Table 3.

$$\varepsilon_{RMS} = \sqrt{\frac{1}{M} \sum_{M=1}^{M} (\tau_m(t_M) - \tau_{est}(t_M))^2} \qquad (19)$$

Table 3. Identify torque residual RMS values using various methods[1]

Methods		Joint 1	Joint 2	Joint 3	Joint 4	Joint 5	Joint 6	Joint 7	Joint 8	Joint 9	sum
1	①[2]	5.74	10.15	5.68	5.10	3.08	3.00	1.55	1.62	1.43	37.35
	②[3]	7.76	11.4	11.1	7.44	4.88	4.84	1.88	2.01	1.66	52.97
2	①	6.09	11.02	5.51	4.77	2.41	2.75	1.32	1.45	1.35	36.67
	②	7.80	10.6	10.0	6.46	3.24	4.12	1.38	1.68	1.40	46.68
3	①	4.78	10.8	5.78	4.41	2.45	3.14	1.70	2.35	1.43	36.8
	②	3.95	9.88	9.13	6.71	2.77	2.99	1.71	2.44	1.88	41.46

[1]Method 1 represents LS; Method 2 represents WLS; Method 3 represents WOA + nonlinear friction model Eq. (3); [2] ① represents experimental group; [3] ② represents validation group

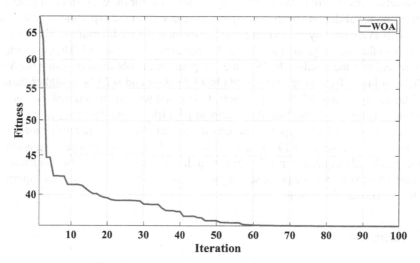

Fig. 5. Fitness convergence curves of the WOA

In this experiment, the maximum number of iterations is 100 and the initialization population to 30 for the WOA. The fitness convergence curves of the WOA are presented in Fig. 5. Initially, due to inaccurate identification of the dynamic parameters and non-linear friction model parameters, a high fitness value is obtained, leading to a significant identification error. As the iterative optimization process continues, the fitness function

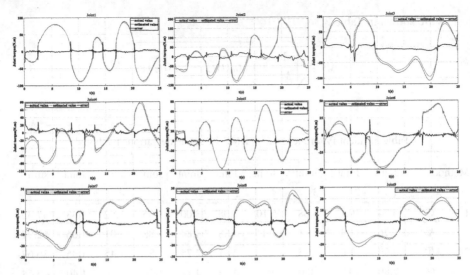

Fig. 6. Identification model verification results

gradually decreases, indicating an improvement in identification accuracy. Eventually, the WOA achieved a convergent fitness function value of 36.8, which is similar to the WLS algorithm.

Two sets of results are obtained from algorithms, one for the experimental group and the other for the validation group. All algorithms can well fit the experimental data. Nevertheless, as evidenced by the experimental outcomes, the traditional algorithm fails to accurately fit the control group data due to the inaccuracy of the model. The experimental results reveal that the residual RMS values of joint torque obtained by using the WOA and the non-linear friction model Eq. (3) is 11.51 N·m and 6.29 N·m higher than the sum obtained by LS and WLS, respectively. Compared with the traditional method, this algorithm can effectively combine the nonlinear joint friction model to improve the identification accuracy. 9-DOF hyper-redundant manipulator dynamic identification results are shown in Fig. 6. Based on Fig. 6, it is evident that the measured torque aligns closely with the predicted torque. The results show that the dynamic model of the manipulator is identified effectively and the proposed algorithm in this study demonstrates superiority over the traditional algorithms.

6   Conclusion

In this paper, a novel manipulator dynamic identification method based on whale optimization is proposed for a 9-DOF modular manipulator. This method can identify the nonlinear joint friction model effectively. The experimental results show that the sum of RMS of joint identification torque in this paper is decreased by 11.51 N·m and 6.29 N·m respectively compared with the traditional LS and WLS algorithms. The proposed novel identification algorithm can effectively and accurately identify the dynamic model parameters of the manipulator.

Acknowledgements. This research was supported by the National Natural Science Foundation of China (Grant No. 62173047).

References

1. Xiao, B., Yin, S.: Exponential tracking control of robotic manipulators with uncertain dynamics and kinematics. IEEE Trans. Industr. Inf. **15**(2), 689–698 (2019). https://doi.org/10.1109/TII.2018.2809514
2. Li, Y., Li, Y., Zhu, M., Zhenbang, X., Deqiang, M.: A nonlinear momentum observer for sensorless robot collision detection under model uncertainties. Mechatronics **78**, 102603 (2021). https://doi.org/10.1016/j.mechatronics.2021.102603
3. Han, Y., Wu, J., Liu, C., et al.: An iterative approach for accurate dynamic model identification of industrial robots. IEEE Trans. Rob. **99**, 1–18 (2020)
4. Dehio, N., Smith, J., Wigand, D.L., et al.: Enabling impedance-based physical human–multi–robot collaboration: experiments with four torque-controlled manipulators. Int. J. Robot. Res. **41**(1), 68–84 (2022)
5. Khalil, W., Bennis, F.: Direct calculation of minimum set of inertial parameters of serial robots. IEEE Trans. Robot. Autom. **6**(1), 368–373 (1994)
6. Dong, J., Jianming, Xu., Zhou, Q., Zhu, J., Li, Yu.: Dynamic Identification of Industrial robot based on nonlinear friction model and LS-SOS algorithm. IEEE Trans. Instrum. Meas. **70**, 1–12 (2021). https://doi.org/10.1109/TIM.2021.3124039
7. Presse, C., Gautier, M.: New criteria of exciting trajectories for robot identification. Int. Conf. Robot. Autom. **3**, 907–912 (1993)
8. Galafiore, G., Indri, M., Bona, B.: Robot dynamic calibration: Optimal excitation trajectories and experimental parameter estimation. J. Robot. Syst. **18**(2), 55–68 (2001)
9. Gautier, M., Bonnet, V.: Optimal Exciting Dance for Identifying Inertial Parameters of an Anthropomorphic Structure. IEEE Trans. Robot. (2016)
10. Jin, J., Gans, N.: Parameter identification for industrial robots with a fast and robust trajectory design approach. Robot. Comput. Integr. Manuf. **31**(1), 21–29 (2015)
11. Swevers, J., Ganseman, C., Tukel, D.B.: Optimal robot excitation and identification. IEEE Trans. Robot. Autom. **13**, 730–740 (1997)
12. Atkeson, C.G., An, C.H., Hollerbach, J.M.: Estimation of Inertial parameters of manipulator loads and links. Int. J. Robot. Res. **5**(3), 101–119 (1986)
13. Wu, W., Zhu, S., Wang, X., et al.: Closed-loop dynamic parameter identification of robot manipulators using modified fourier series. Int. J. Adv. Rob. Syst. **9**(1), 1 (2012)
14. Gautier, M.: Dynamic identification of robots with power model. Int. Conf. Robot. Autom. **3**, 1922–1927 (1997)
15. Lee, T., Park, F.C.: A geometric algorithm for robust multibody inertial parameter identification. IEEE Robot. Autom. Lett., 1 (2018)
16. Lee, T., Wensing, P.M., Park, F.C.: Geometric robot dynamic identification: a convex programming approach. IEEE Trans. Rob. **36**(2), 348–365 (2020)
17. Mirjalili, S., Lewis, A., et al.: The Whale Optimization Algorithm. Adv. Eng. Softw. **95**, 51–67 (2016)
18. Sousa, C.D., Cortesao, R.: Physical feasibility of robot base inertial parameter identification: a linear matrix inequality approach. Int. J. Robot. Res. **33**(6), 931–944 (2014)

Study on Shared Compliance Control of Teleoperated Abdominal Ultrasonic Robot

Ying-Long Chen[1,2](✉), Peng-Yu Zhao[1], Qing Sun[1], Fu-Jun Song[1], and Yong-Jun Gong[1]

[1] Dalian Maritime University, Dalian 116026, China
chenyinglong@dlmu.edu.cn

[2] Key Laboratory of Rescue and Salvage Engineering Liaoning Province, Dalian 116026, China

Abstract. As an important auxiliary tool in the diagnosis and treatment of many diseases, ultrasound examination has become one of the most routine examinations in clinical application due to its advantages of non-invasive and radiation-free. However, in practical application, sonographers are prone to fatigue damage and lack of talent resources, and there are also risks of cross infection between doctors and patients during the COVID-19. The full use of doctors' clinical experience and the appropriate intensity of examination in the actual ultrasound examination are the key issues concerned by both doctors and patients. Therefore, a set of shared compliance control system of teleoperation ultrasound robot was built in this paper. In order to make the robot have a certain degree of environmental adaptability, an adaptive impedance control method was introduced. In the process of ultrasound examination, the fusion of human-machine shared control methods was used to apply clinical examination experience or respond to clinical conditions. The proposed control strategy aims to focus on the study of ultrasonic doctors in giving full play to clinical examination experience while ensuring examination strength and human safety, giving full play to the advantages of human and machine respectively, so that ultrasonic doctors and robots "each play their own roles" and complement each other, improving ultrasound examination efficiency.

Keywords: Abdominal Ultrasound Robot · Shared Control · Adaptive Impedance Control

1 Introduction

1.1 A Subsection Sample

In the medical field, ultrasonic diagnosis has been applied more and more widely. Its advantages are also obvious. Compared to other technologies, ultrasound diagnosis has less radiation damage to the human body, low price, less non-invasive pain, and relatively simple operation by doctors, which can be observed in real-time. The real-time anatomical body structure information provided by ultrasound imaging technology has become an important source of information in the diagnosis and treatment of diseases. However, in reality, ultrasound diagnosis also faces the following problems:

© The Author(s), under exclusive license to Springer Nature Singapore Pte Ltd. 2023
H. Yang et al. (Eds.): ICIRA 2023, LNAI 14267, pp. 92–103, 2023.
https://doi.org/10.1007/978-981-99-6483-3_9

Firstly, there is a shortage of talent resources for ultrasound physicians. One of the reasons for this is that compared to other imaging technologies, such as magnetic resonance imaging, higher requirements for doctors' work experience and professional knowledge [1]. Secondly, the sonographer is easy to suffer from fatigue damage due to heavy operation during work. Moreover, the high coordination of eye, hand and brain, as well as the different operation tasks of both hands also aggravate the instability of ultrasonic detection [2]. At the same time, there is still an uneven distribution of medical resources in various countries. The number of experienced sonographers is limited, but they cannot perform remote operations, and patients cannot get timely inspection. Therefore, mechanized and intelligent equipment is urgently needed. Ultrasound robots can perform autonomous testing while also integrating the sonographer's instructions for operation. Fully leverage the advantages of robot remote assistance technology to extend the inspection distance and ability of sonographer.

So far, some researchers have been designing robot-assisted ultrasound diagnostic systems that use control algorithms (impedance control, fuzzy control, etc.) or modified end-force actuators to provide auxiliary support to sonographers [3–5]. Most of researchers are mainly focused on developing remote imaging systems, with path planning and force control of ultrasound probes being the main research topics. During the COVID-19 pandemic, researchers have used the MGIUS-R3 commercial remote robot ultrasound system for heart and lung imaging information [6, 7]. The system can reproduce doctor actions and scanning force through flexible contact control algorithms, Moreover, researchers have conducted practical verification of the accuracy of remote ultrasound robots in clinical application examinations of common abdominal, vascular, and superficial organ pathologies [8]. In practical medical ultrasound examinations, the application of ultrasound robots can reduce the operational pressure of doctors or reproduce the examination techniques of sonographer. However, how to not only reduce the operational pressure of doctors but also reproduce the examination techniques of sonographer, while also ensuring the safety of the machine and the test subjects, is the focus of this paper's research. Therefore, this paper aims to propose a control method that can meet the above requirements simultaneously, and realize remote ultrasound examination more humanized and intelligent.

This paper focuses on the application of doctors' clinical experience in ultrasonic examination, the self adjustment of human Contact force and the response to various clinical situations. Adaptive impedance control is applied to the adjustment of human abdominal examination force, and it is integrated into shared control to achieve master-slave man-machine coordinated control of the entire ultrasonic robot system to complete ultrasonic examination.

2 Master-Slave Shared Control System

2.1 Three State Human-Machine Negotiation Mechanism

In the human-machine shared control system, robots can plan long-distance rough tasks, and the fine short distance task execution can be completed by human operators. It makes up for the limitations of robot autonomy and human operator in task execution, human-robot shared control can fully leverage the advantages of robot and human operator's respective intelligence level and executive ability to achieve a balance between the robot and human operator's respective ability level. Therefore, the negotiation strategy is introduced into the model to exert the autonomous planning and control ability of the slave robot as much as possible.

During the examination phase in contact with the human body, in the human-robot collaboration process, the arbitration of authority weights between operators and robots in task execution has always been a research hotspot. In order to reasonably adjust the authority weights of robots and human operators in the process of ultrasound examination, better complete various real-life examination tasks and cope with emergencies during the process. Based on feedback information, three different system working modes are defined in this paper. The specific adjustment modes are shown in Eq. (1). When the operator observes that the robot operation does not meet the task safety requirements or the system issues an alert, the operator's execution state transitions from upper level supervision to decision execution, and the system switches modes based on negotiation strategies.

$$When\ C > C_{threshold}\ or\ V_B > V_{B\,threshold}, counting;\ when\ T > T_{threshold}, triggered;\ conf = 1.$$

$$When\ C < C_{threshold}\ \&\ V_B < V_{B\,threshold}, counting;\ when\ T > T_{threshold}, triggered;\ conf \in (0, 1).$$
(1)

$$When\ C < C_{threshold}\ \&\ V_B < V_{B\,threshold}, counting;\ when\ T < T_{threshold}, triggered;\ conf = 0.$$

where, C, T and V_B are operator intervention signal, operator continuous intervention time and change rate of impedance control strategy compensation value respectively. $C_{threshold}$, $T_{threshold}$ and $V_{B\,threshold}$ are respectively operator intervention signal threshold, operator continuous intervention time threshold and change rate threshold of impedance control strategy compensation value.

In the process of human-robot cooperation, the control includes three modes: S1 direct control, S2 human-robot shared control, and S3 autonomous control. Direct control means that the operator directly controls the robot movement, mainly occurring when encountering lesions or when the subject is moving their body posture (i.e. $C > C_{threshold}$ or $V_B > V_{B\,threshold}$). It requires sonographer to fully utilize professional experience or manually change the inspection trajectory, and execute satisfactory action instructions for long-term robot control. The autonomous control mode means that the robot runs independently after autonomous intelligent planning, with the operator in an upper level supervisory state and able to provide certain support (i.e., guidance within the command time threshold of $T_{threshold}$ that does not exceed the human threshold of $C_{threshold}$). The human-robot shared control mode requires the operator to provide continuous operational support for a period of time in case of sudden encounters with obstacles, or changes in bearing capacity caused by differences in human body structure during the inspection process (i.e. $T > T_{threshold}$ and $C < C_{threshold}$), and the human-robot can jointly complete the expected work task.

By introducing three threshold signals as the basis for judgment, a human-robot shared control model framework was established. The three modes correspond to three working states throughout the collaboration process, describing the state of human-robot collaboration. As shown in Eq. (1), the framework of three-state human-robot negotiation model is shown in Fig. 1 below.

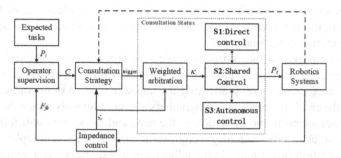

Fig. 1. Human-robot shared control mode framework.

As shown in Fig. 1, when performing task operations, the operator first specifies the expected task P_i. The robot acts autonomously based on task decomposition, and sends the returned remote environmental monitoring data to the image monitor. The operator determines whether interference is necessary and provides instruction C. The negotiation module receives instruction C, instruction interference time T, and impedance control compensation change rate V_B to trigger the weight arbitration module to arbitrate the weight κ, thus adjusting the shared control status of the current system. Subsequently, the system negotiates the status and outputs task execution information P_t, which is then executed by the robot and fed back to the impedance controller.

2.2 Master-Slave Sharing Control Framework

The focus of the negotiation is on adjusting the authority weight, reasonably allocating the weight of operators and robots participating in system control, releasing the advantages of their respective control and execution capabilities, and fully leveraging the role of shared control. The framework of human-robot shared control is shown in Fig. 2.

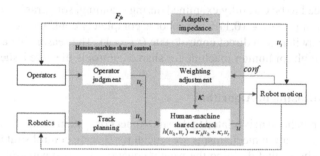

Fig. 2. Human-robot shared control framework

The motion command for autonomous trajectory planning of robots is u_r; When the operator interferes with the operation of the system, the motion command input by the operator is u_h; Whether a sonographer interferes with the autonomous movement of the robot is based on fully utilize clinical experience, which means whether robot can achieve the same inspection effect as sonographer's clinical inspection when the robot autonomously performs inspection tasks, that is the empirical confidence *conf* of sonographer in the completion of the task, and the system adjusts the control weight based on the current confidence *conf*.

Of course, throughout the entire task execution process, both the empirical operation of sonographer and the actual task execution reliability of robot have an impact on the confidence *conf*, thereby affecting the adjustment of system control weight κ. Throughout the entire process, the sonographers also continuously adjust the amount of intervention according to the execution of the task, and the system will follow suit by continuously adjusting the authority weight value until the task is completed. The key to the task execution process lies in the adjustment of experience confidence *conf* and weight. The state equation of the robot system can be expressed as follows:

$$\tilde{x}(t) = f(x(t), u(t)) \tag{2}$$

$$u(t) = h_\theta(u_h(t), u_r(t); \theta(t)) \tag{3}$$

where, x represents the robot state and u represents the control input. Arbitration function combination u_r and u_h, which are autonomous control and human control respectively, determine the level of autonomy of the robot system. Here, θ Simulated the robot's understanding of human and autonomous controller inputs through arbitration functions.

$$h(u_h, u_r) = \kappa_h u_h + \kappa_r u_r \tag{4}$$

where, κ represents the proportion of distribution rights between humans and robot. According to the definition of system control permissions, including: $\kappa_r + \kappa_h = 1$, $0 \leq \kappa_h, \kappa_r \leq 1$. κ_r, κ_h represented as the weight of the robot and the weight of the sonographer, different weight values represent different negotiation states: during normal system operation, the sonographer supervises the system in the background and does not directly interfere with the robot's motion ($\kappa_r = 1$); When unexpected situations occur or when lesions need to be carefully examined during scanning, sonographer participate in task manipulation ($\kappa_r, \kappa_h \in (0,1)$); The robot is completely controlled by sonographer, and the system switches to direct control state ($\kappa_h = 1$). The reasonable adjustment of the authority weight of human-machine for shared control is the core issue.

2.3 Weight Adjustment Algorithm

The arbitration mechanism is related to the smoothness of system control authority transfer. Therefore, arbitration mechanisms are crucial for sharing control strategies. Dragan et al., research shows that dividing the weight equation into two parts through the sigmoid function and linetype formula can improve the stability and high response of the operation [9]. Therefore, this paper adopts a segmented function to adjust the system control authority weights. Linear formula is used to make the robot run smoothly, an exponential formula was used to improve response speed. The adjustment of control weights mainly depends on the reliability of the current task execution and the system feedback information to adjust confidence *conf*. The sonographer's control weight value is positively correlated with the confidence *conf*, and the less reliable the robot task execution, the greater the control weight of sonographer, until the sonographer completely takes over the system.

$$\kappa_h = \begin{cases} 0 & conf < 0.2 \\ 1.825conf - 0.365 & 0.2 \leq conf < 0.6 \\ \frac{1}{1+\exp(-25conf+14)} & 0.6 \leq conf \leq 0.8 \\ 1 & 0.8 < conf \leq 1 \end{cases} \tag{5}$$

where, *conf* represents the empirical confidence level, which is the level of untrustworthiness of sonographer to perform current tasks of robot. The weight adjustment stage is divided into three stages: when the confidence *conf* is lower than 0.2, the corresponding weight value κ_h is adjusted to 0, corresponding to the system negotiation state S3; If the confidence *conf* is higher than 0.8, corresponding to the weight value $\kappa_h = 1$, system negotiation status S1; When the confidence value *conf* $\in$ (0.2,0.8), the corresponding weight $\kappa_h \in$ (0, 1), negotiation state S2.

According to the intuitive representation variable of sonographer's empirical confidence in actual task execution, the confidence formula can be expressed as follows:

$$conf = a \cdot \eta_T + b \cdot \eta_B + c \cdot \eta_x \tag{6}$$

where, η_T, η_B and η_x are the direct characterization variables of confidence: interference time, interference displacement, and the change rate of adaptive impedance compensation value. *a*, *b*, and *c* are the influence coefficients of the variables. The direct addition of various characteristic variables can directly reflect the trend of the influence of various variable factors. In general literature, η is expressed in the form of exponential function, the calculation formula of each variable is as follows:

$$\begin{cases} \eta_T = 1 - e^{-\Delta T} \\ \eta_\varsigma = 1 - e^{-v_B} \\ \eta_\varsigma = 1 - e^{-\Delta P} \end{cases} \tag{7}$$

$$\Delta P = \gamma(\Delta P_x + \Delta P_y + \Delta P_z) \tag{8}$$

where, γ is the coefficient of interference displacement, ΔT, ΔP and V_B represents the actual interference time, interference displacement, and the change rate of adaptive impedance compensation value respectively.

3 Master-Slave Shared Control Based on Adaptive Impedance

In the extensive research on robot remote operation, more and more researchers begin to realize the importance of impedance in robot operation. In addition, the ability to adjust the impedance of remote robots in the process of physical interaction can be helpful to avoid high impact when interacting with uncertain environments [6, 7]. However, impedance regulation is not autonomous, as the compliance of the slave robot must be physically presented by the operator, who must understand the requirements of the slave robot in terms of impedance regulation during the interaction. For operators, this may not be an intuitive task, especially considering the high visibility requirements of perception conditions in remote environments. Therefore, this paper focuses on reducing the control requirements for operators while enhancing the control robustness of slave robots in physical interaction processes under unexpected circumstances.

Under normal circumstances during the examination process, robot can inspect autonomously without human participation, but when the following situations occur, the sonographer will intervene in adjustment of the control authority of the robot system:

(1) Due to differences in the body structure of the test subject, the local skin tissue of the test subject may feel uncomfortable with the force applied during the inspection. (2) If the sonographer believes that the current motion path or position cannot meet the actual inspection requirements during the inspection process, the sonographer will not trust the current path, and sonographer will work with the robot to control the examination path. (3) Due to differences in hardness and subcutaneous position between potential lesion and normal human skin tissue, the impedance controller will generate a different change rate in impedance compensation values when the potential lesion is located than that through normal skin tissue, which can serve as an early warning signal for the potential lesion and provide decision-making assistance to sonographer, indicating that sonographer may need detailed examination here. (4) During the ultrasound examination process, if the patient's body posture changes, the examination site performed by the robot will be different from that expected by the sonographer.

In the actual process of ultrasound examination, sonographer evaluate and make corresponding adjustments to various actual conditions based on years of clinical experience, so the above situations are all included in the range of experience confidence of sonographer. Therefore, this strategy structure fully combines the mechanism of experience confidence to adjust the control authority weight of the human-machine, in order to better complete the ultrasound examination.

As shown in Fig. 3, the information fed back by the visual system is artificially input into the system to enable the robot to perform inspection instructions autonomously. When the sonographer determines that empirical operations need to be performed based on the visual information fed back, the sonographer's instructions and the robot's autonomous motion instructions are shared and fused through weight adjustment. During the inspection process, adaptive impedance control also maintains the contact force between the robot and human skin, so as to ensure the comfort of the test subject as much as possible during the inspection process, and ensuring the safety of human and robot system.

Moreover, adaptive impedance control can reduce the communication delay and the challenges of physical interaction stability caused by the decline of perception ability in remote operations. The control state equation of the system is:

$$u(t) = h_\theta(u_h(t), u_r(t), u_i(t); \theta(t)) \tag{9}$$

$$h(u_h, u_r) = \kappa_h u_h + \kappa_r u_r + u_i \tag{10}$$

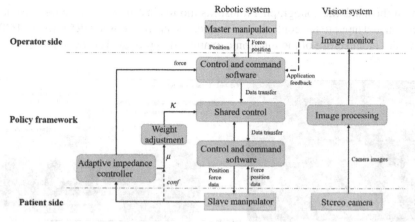

Fig. 3. Human-robot shared control process

where, u_i represents the system control input variable of adaptive impedance control. The input of adaptive impedance control is as follows [8]:

$$m\ddot{e}(t) + (b + \Delta b(t))\dot{e}(t) = f_e(t) - f_d(t) \tag{11}$$

$$\begin{cases} \Delta b(t) = \frac{b}{\dot{e}(t)} \rho(t) \\ \rho(t) = \rho(t - \lambda) + \Omega \frac{f_d(t-\lambda) - f_e(t-\lambda)}{b} \end{cases} \tag{12}$$

where, m and b are the expected inertia and expected damping, f_e and f_d are the actual contact force and expected contact force, λ is the sampling period of the controller, and Ω is the update rate.

After the sonographer fully utilizes clinical experiences and performs ultrasound examination, the system continues to operate autonomously to complete the remaining planned actions. During the ultrasound examination process, adaptive impedance always plays a role, especially during sonographer's experience examination, which can reduce the requirements for system control by physicians, especially for novice doctors more friendly. It will also be an effective method to address the challenges brought by the possible limitations in remote perception.

4 Experimental Results and Analysis

This section aims to verify the feasibility of the shared adaptive impedance control strategy through experiments. Firstly, a complete remote ultrasonic inspection robot system and test environment are built. The system equipment uses UR5 robotic and Geomagic Touch as master-slave manipulator and actuators. The experimental system uses MATLAB/Simulink and VS to build the control strategy and communication link of the system, which was verified through dynamic experiments.

The physical objects of the test system is shown in Fig. 4. The environmental information of the experiment was obtained by two binocular cameras. By operating Geomagic

Touch on the hand, the sonographer transmits motion instructions to the remote end for conversion and input to the controller, and sends the instructions to UR5 through TCP/IP. The system architecture of the ultrasonic examination process is shown in Fig. 4.

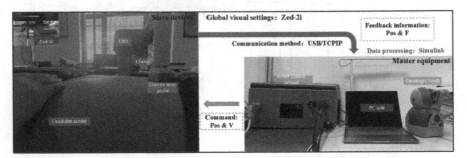

Fig. 4. Physical diagram of the experimental system

Ultrasound robots can autonomously complete ultrasound examinations under normal circumstances, but in clinical situations, ultrasound robots sometimes cannot rely on themselves to complete the ideal examination actions of sonographer or cope with some emergencies. At this point, the shared control mechanism will be triggered only when the sonographer interferes with the task execution of the robot according to the information returned. Then, the system calculates *conf* and triggers weight adjustment. After calculating the weights of human and robot, the control command information is integrated, and integrates the control quantity of adaptive impedance control. It is input into the robot executive controller until the target pose is reached. If the input quantity of the system control changes, the system negotiation state follows the adjustment. After the inspection is completed, the system ends its running.

Verification tests were conducted based on the above test program and the selected hardware of the master-slave devices, as shown in Fig. 5. The entire experimental process mentioned above is as follows: first, the robot located above the abdomen of the test subject and had just come into contact with the human skin, and ultrasound examination begins. The robot first moves autonomously, and the sonographer was in a supervised state; Then, due to differences in body structure, the patient's ability to withstand contact force decreases. At this time, the sonographer remotely lifts probe at the surface of the human skin. After crossing this section, the sonographer manipulates the probe to contact the human skin for a fixed point inspection for 5 s. Then, the sonographer manipulates the probe to move on the surface of human skin for about 5 s. Finally, the sonographer does not manipulate main device, and the robot continues to complete the examination task autonomously.

In order to simplify the experiments, sonographer only manipulate the slave device to move on the y-z plane during the entire experimental process. To ensure personal safety of the test subject, the maximum contact force and maximum movement displacement of the robot were also limited. After multiple adjustments in the experiment, $m_d = 1$ kg, $b_d = 220$ Ns/m, variable influence coefficient a is 8, and all other parameters are 1. Figures 6, 7 show the variation curves of confidence *conf* and weight κ_h when

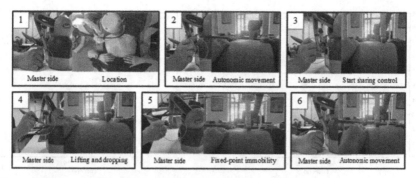

Fig. 5. Ultrasonic examination experiment

sonographer participates in system control. In the first 5 s, person pulls out the joystick of the master Geomagic Touch device. Due to the large displacement, the confidence *conf* suddenly changes, but it does not affect the change of weight, making it convenient for sonographer to adjust the manipulation posture. During this process, hand shaking was inevitable. At the beginning of the manipulation, due to the need to have an adjustment phase and familiarize oneself with the size of the control displacement, confidence and weight have significant changes, and the subsequent changes in confidence and weight curves are in line with actual situation.

From Fig. 8, it can be seen that the actual force change curve of the robot end probe in contact with human skin fluctuates in a small range due to the influence such as shaking of the sonographer's hand. As the probe is lifted by sonographer, the force decreases to zero. Later, as sonographer manipulates the probe to contact the skin, the contact force increases. During this process, due to the effect of impedance control, the force change is not smooth. Then, after pressing the probe onto the human skin, although the sonographer remains motionless, the impedance compensation makes the contact force between the probe and human skin gradually approximate to the expected force, and the force adjustment amount is about 20% of the expected force. If you want to maintain a constant force during the fixed-point inspection, you need to overcome the influence of adaptive impedance control compensation, which need to make real-time adjustments based on the tactile sensation generated by Geomagic Touch. After the contact force gradually stabilizes, the probe was manipulated to move in a straight line on the surface of human skin. Slight force fluctuations occurred due to hand shaking. Finally, the desired force was steadily tracked when the robot moved autonomously.

To ensure safety, an abdominal silicone model was made to carry out 10 tests on the above process, and the above operations were repeated in the way of complete human manipulation. The time of the two groups of experiments was compared, and the experiment could not exclude the influence of the operator's improved proficiency with the increase of the number of times after performing the same action. Figure 9 shows the comparison results. From Fig. 9, it can be seen that shared control improves work efficiency by about 30% compared to direct control mode, and can reduce the physical burden and pressure of sonographer during the examination process when completing the same examination task.

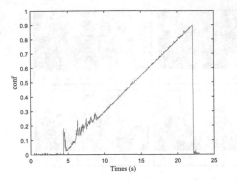

Fig. 6. The change of confidence –conf

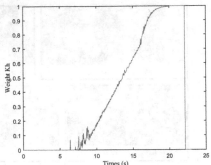

Fig. 7. The change of physician operating weight

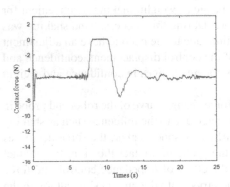

Fig. 8. Shared control of the actual contact force

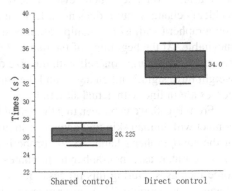

Fig. 9. Time consumed comparison

In this paper, a shared compliance control method for remote ultrasonic robot was proposed for abdominal ultrasound examination. This system provides a feasible control method for fully utilizing the clinical examination experience of sonographers and leveraging the autonomous planning ability of robots to alleviate operating pressure of sonographer. But the method has not been tested on multiple subjects; The adaptive impedance control method cannot automatically update the update rate and has limited environmental adaptability; And the sense of touch is not fully utilized. Our future work will attempt to automatically update the adaptive update rate to better adapt to changes in different abdominal environments. And apply the combination strategy of adaptive control and shared control to the direction and force adjustment of probe. The probe fixture will also be optimized. Finally, we will conduct a large-scale evaluation of the system's performance in remote control.

References

1. Peng, J.: Preliminary exploration on the effective mode of ultrasound diagnosis thinking – summary of 20 years of misdiagnosis cases experience. Kunming Medical College, Kunming (2008)
2. Swerdlow, D.R., Cleary, K., Wilson, E., et al.: Robotic arm–assisted sonography: review of technical developments and potential clinical applications. Am. J. Roentgenol. **208**(4), 733–738 (2017)
3. Liu, X., Ran, C., Wang, Q., Zhang, P.: Research on control of auxiliary robot for ultrasonic diagnosis. In: IEEE International Conference on Robotics and Biomimetics (ROBIO), Kuala Lumpur, Malaysia, pp. 2133–2140 (2018)
4. Bao, X., Wang, S., Housden, R., Hajnal, J., Rhode, K.: A constant-force end-effector with online force adjustment for robotic ultrasonography. IEEE Robot. Autom. Lett. **6**(2), 2547–2554 (2021)
5. Koizumi, N., Warisawa, S., Nagoshi, M., Hashizume, H., Mitsuishi, M.: Construction methodology for a remote ultrasound diagnostic system. IEEE Trans. Robot. **25**(3), 522–538 (2009)
6. Wang, J., Peng, C., Zhao, Y., Ye, R., Hong, J., Huang, H., Chen, L.: Application of a robotic tele-echography system for COVID-19 pneumonia. J. Ultrasound Med. **40**(2), 385–390 (2021)
7. Wu, S., Li, K., Ye, R., Lu, Y., Xu, J., Xiong, L., et al.: Robot-assisted teleultrasound assessment of cardiopulmonary function on a patient with confirmed COVID-19 in a cabin hospital. Adv. Ultrasound Diagn. Therapy **4**(2), 128–130 (2020)
8. Jiang, W., et al.: Application of a tele-ultrasound robot during COVID-19 pandemic: a feasibility study. J. Ultrasound Med. **42**(3), 595–601 (2023)
9. Dragan, A.D., Srinivasa, S.S.: A policy-blending formalism for shared control. Int. J. Robot. Res. **32**(7), 790–805 (2013)
10. Albu-Schäffer, A., Ott, C., Hirzinger, G.: A unified passivity-based control framework for position, torque and impedance control of flexible joint robots. Int. J. Robot. Res. **26**(1), 23–39 (2007)
11. Vanderborght, B., Albu-Schaeffer, A., Bicchi, A., et al.: Variable impedance actuators: a re-view. Robot. Auton. Syst. **61**(12), 1601–1614 (2013)
12. Seul, J., Hsia, T.C., Bonitz, R.G.: Force tracking impedance control of robot manipulators under unknown environment. IEEE Trans. Control Syst. Technol. **12**(3), 474–483 (2004)

Construction of Control System on Kinematic Redundant Hybrid Parallel Mechanism for Micro-assembly

Fen-hua Zhang[⊠], Xian-min Zhang, Rui-da Zheng, Tian-yu Xie,
Jian-qin Zhang, and Hai Li

Guangdong Province Key Laboratory of Precision Equipment and Manufacturing
Technology, South China University of Technology, Guangzhou, Guangdong 510641,
China
1041271418@qq.com

Abstract. The Kinematic Redundant Hybrid Parallel Mechanism has
advantages over traditional parallel mechanisms such as large motion
posture angles and large working space. It can play its advantages
in adaptive assembly of small parts. However, there is currently little
research on the control of motion redundant mechanisms. To make this
mechanism work effectively, a reliable and effective control system is
essential. This paper first introduces the architecture of KRHPM, then
starts with, lower industrial control computer PLC program writing,
upper computer C++ program writing logic, motor selection and controller design to describe in detail the construction process of the control
system, supplemented by experimental verification of its feasibility, lay-
ing the foundation for subsequent research on high-precision control.

Keywords: Control system · Kinematic Redundant Hybrid Parallel
Mechanism · Micro-assembly

1 Introduction

Precision intelligent equipment is a cutting-edge research field that includes
precision manufacturing, micro-assembly, intelligent manufacturing and so on.
Micro-assembly is widely used in fields such as micro-electromechanical systems
and precision sensor assembly. Micro-assembly related research has become a
hot topic in disciplines such as robotics and machine vision. It also presents new
demands for the macro-micro integration, cross-scale, and adaptive assembly of
precision components, gradually becoming a research trend.

Parallel mechanisms have advantages such as no cumulative error, good
dynamic response, strong load-bearing capacity, and good flexibility. They show
good application prospects in micro-assembly and have attracted widespread
attention in academia, they are also widely used in industry [1,2]. However,
compared with serial mechanisms, parallel mechanisms have the disadvantages

Supported by National Natural Science Foundation of China (Grant No. 52130508).

H. Yang et al. (Eds.): ICIRA 2023, LNAI 14267, pp. 104–115, 2023.
https://doi.org/10.1007/978-981-99-6483-3_10

of small workspace and limited rotation angle [3]. To overcome these shortcomings, this paper studies the kinematically redundant (6+3)-dof hybrid parallel mechanism (KRHPM), which adopts a hybrid form of serial and parallel connections and combines redundant symmetrical structures to give KRHPM larger motion posture angles and a wider dexterous workspace than general parallel mechanisms [4].

With the development of industrial robot technology and high-end manufacturing equipment technology, scholars have carried out extensive research on the control methods of parallel and hybrid mechanisms. Gao et al. proposed a fractional-order PID+ feedforward compensation control strategy to improve the control performance of the hybrid conveyor mechanism under high-speed motion conditions, by using a genetic algorithm to optimize the controller parameters, reducing trajectory tracking errors and improving trajectory tracking performance [?]. Jorge et al. proposed an algebraic constraint-based non-linear computational torque control method to improve the trajectory tracking control performance of ankle rehabilitation parallel robots [5]. Lin et al. studied the robust sliding mode control of uncertain hybrid mechanisms for parallel-serial hybrid mechanisms, and they, considering various disturbances, proposed a hybrid H_2/H_∞ control strategy to achieve optimal control at different configurations and processing speeds for curved surface machining machine tools with high precision and high efficiency requirements [6]. Koessle et al. used adaptive control methods to solve the problem of model degradation around singular points in parallel structures [7]. Chen et al. proposed a composite control strategy that combines time-varying sliding mode control with RBF neural networks for trajectory tracking control of two-degree-of-freedom parallel robots. They used a radial basis function (RBF) compensator to estimate actuator nonlinearity and its upper bound [8]. Qin et al. proposed an intelligent high-robust fast integer-power superhelix second-order sliding mode dynamic control method for uncertain hybrid mechanisms with optimal robust performance when there are matching uncertainties, non-matching uncertainties, and changes in expected motion requirements under different loads [?]. Chen et al. proposed an observer-based inversion control method to improve the trajectory tracking performance of a 6-dof hydraulic Stewart platform while considering the nonlinear characteristics of hydraulic actuators [9].

This paper mainly describes the process of building the KRHPM electromechanical coupling control system, including PLC program writing for lower industrial computers, communication and solution calculation program logic for upper computers, motor selection, controller design, semi-closed-loop control experiments for the system, and conclusions.

2 Mechanical Architecture of KRHPM

The control system to be built in this paper is based on the 3-[R(RR-RRR)SR] motion redundant hybrid parallel mechanism (see Fig. 1). From the figure, it can be seen that the mechanism is composed of a fixed base, a moving platform, three

R(RR-RRR)SR support chains, and three equivalent ball hinges. Among them, R represents an positive rotation joint, while R represents a negative rotation joint. The motor A in each support chain is fixed on the base through a frame. Motors B and C are fixed on the output end of motor A and respectively drive the long rod and short rod in the connecting rod mechanism to push the output end of the planar connecting rod mechanism to move. The output ends of the planar connecting rod mechanisms of the three support chains are connected to the moving platform through tiger hinges equivalent to ball hinges. They together with the fixed base constitute the overall mechanical structure.

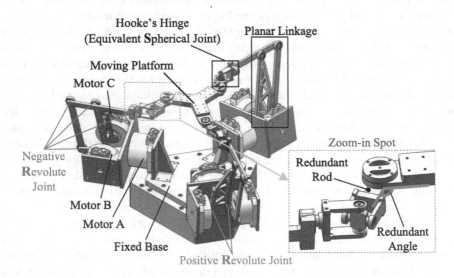

Fig. 1. Architecture of KRHPM.

The redundancy of KRHPM is reflected in the connecting rods between the center of tiger hinges and three vertices of the moving platform. The existence of redundant rods can keep the pose of the mechanism's end moving platform unchanged, but the input angle of the motor may not be a unique fixed value. This means that when KRHPM moves to a certain position or needs to cross a singularity point, it can ensure that the mechanism will not become singular or lose control by switching positions, thus expanding the flexible workspace of the mechanism.

3   Building Control System

3.1   Logical Framework of Entire Control System

In order to clarify the workflow of the control system more clearly, Fig. 2 arranges the core content according to the logical relationship into an entire structural framework.

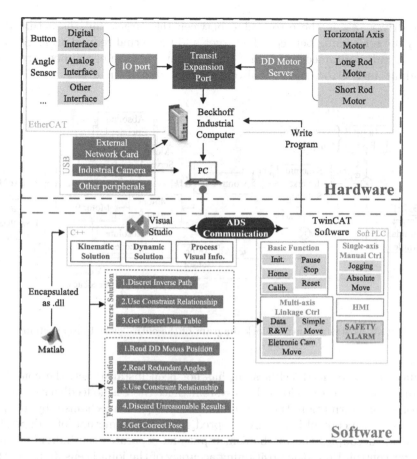

Fig. 2. Entire logical framework of control system.

3.2   Controller Design

KRHPM's complex motion redundant mechanical structure and the precision of micro-assembly working conditions, as well as the large number of components in the whole machine, will result in various nonlinear errors such as joint internal clearance and parts processing assembly. Therefore, it is reasonable to use a closed-loop system to build the control system. In actual motion control, since the movement of the mechanism, data sampling, analysis and processing all require a certain amount of time, continuous control algorithms cannot be used directly for control. Therefore, this paper designs a discrete closed-loop system for KRHPM, and its abstract control block diagram can be seen in Fig. 3.

In the figure, (x_t, y_t, z_t) and $\boldsymbol{Qp}_t$ is the target position and rotation matrix of the moving platform, (x_r, y_r, z_r) and $\boldsymbol{Qp}_r$ is the actual position of the moving platform solved by visual feedback. φ_t is the target redundant angle of the moving platform, φ_r is the redundant angle of the moving platform measured by the angle sensor. $\overrightarrow{\boldsymbol{u}}$ is the output function of the controller acting on the motor driver. $\vec{e}_p$ is the error value between the target and the actual pose, $\vec{e}_{rd}$ is the error value between the target and the actual redundant angle, $\vec{e}$ is the error value obtained by solving the kinematic inverse of the pose error and redundant angle error, and it is also the input value of the driver.

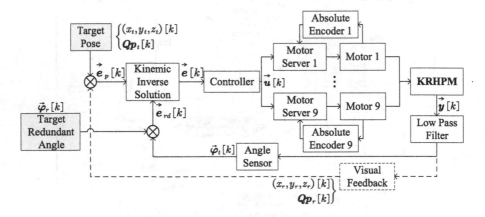

Fig. 3. Abstract control block diagram of the entire closed-loop system.

Since the visual feedback system has not been installed yet, the completed system belongs to a semi-closed-loop system. Since there is no feedback of the end effector state information, the method of controlling the mechanism by independent joint space control is usually adopted. The control method of independent joint space decouples the mechanism input and separates the individual drive joints for control. First, the positioning accuracy of the joint is ensured, and then the end positioning accuracy of the mechanism is improved by identifying kinematic parameters and system calibration methods. The motor driver selected in this paper has conducted a detailed analysis of the matching motor, so the semi-closed-loop control of this mechanism can achieve a good level.

3.3 Lower Computer Program Development

In order to ensure the stability of KRHPM in completing micro-assembly tasks, a control system in the form of upper and lower computers will be adopted. The lower computer is responsible for controlling the basic movement of the motor, while the upper computer is responsible for complex calculations, ensuring that the control system does not reduce its computing power and thus reduce overall control accuracy and response speed, or even cause computer crashes or other accidents, resulting in safety hazards caused by motor out-of-control when it needs a large amount of resources to solve nonlinear equations while driving the motor at the same time.

Programming Language Selection. Nowadays, among many controllers, compared with microcontrollers and embedded chips, Programmable Logic Controller (PLC) is used as the main controller for various modern industrial automation equipment due to its high reliability, easy programming, easy maintenance, and wide applicability. With the popularization of PCs and increasingly powerful computing performance, soft PLCs have emerged, which essentially use high-performance PC equipment to simulate traditional PLC hardware for control.

The architecture of the soft PLC is shown in Fig. 4. Its development environment is based on the IEC61131-3 compilation system. All PLC functions such as logic control, motion control, visualization, and safety are implemented in a development environment. The compiled code of the source program is parsed and executed by RunTime, which is also the highest priority task within RTOS. Unlike ordinary office operating systems, RTOS can ensure that PLC tasks have the highest priority and real-time performance comparable to hard PLCs.

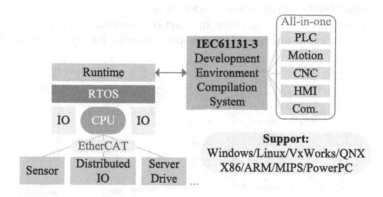

Fig. 4. The framework of Soft PLC.

This article will use Beckhoff's TwinCAT system as the control software and the company's C6030-0060 industrial computer based on Windows embedded operating system as the controller. They have several advantages: first, they can be compatible with multiple brands of motors; secondly, they have modular components for easy expansion; thirdly, they have mature and rich software packages that support development in multiple languages such as C++, PLC, Matlab (Simulink), etc.; fourthly, they can support up to 25 axes of common motion (depending on computational load and bus cycle); fifthly, they use EtherCAT bus protocol for easy expansion and good working stability.

PLC Program Internal Logic Architecture. The internal logic of the PLC program can be roughly divided into 5 major functions: basic system function, single-axis manual control, multi-axis linkage control, safety alarm, and HMI. The core work of the lower computer is centered around the stable operation of the motor.

(1) The basic system function is mainly the fundamental guarantee that the entire lower computer controller can complete the axis work tasks, including the following modules: "Initialization" module, "Reset" module, "Pause & Stop"module , "Return to zero position" module, "Motor and sensor calibration" module, "Peripheral device settings" module.

(2) The single-axis manual control function is mainly used for initial axis-by-axis debugging, testing drive commands such as jogging and absolute motion, monitoring various states of axes, etc., and is a foundation for multi-axis linkage control.

(3) Multi-axis linkage control simultaneously controls 9 motors for coordinated motion, including several modules: Reading module, "All axes reach corresponding discrete points before starting simultaneously" motion mode and "Electronic cam" motion mode.

(4) The safety alarm function mainly handles error/alarm information from various functional blocks and integrates them together for easy maintenance and debugging later. Emergency stop function is also included in this module to ensure operator safety during system operation.

(5) HMI provides human-machine interaction functions for convenient monitoring and operation of machines by operators. Specific interfaces can see Fig. 5.

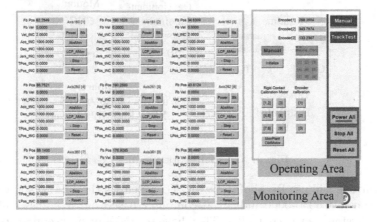

Fig. 5. HMI of lower computer in TwinCAT software.

3.4   Upper Computer Program Development

The focus of the upper computer is to use high-level languages to solve non-linear complex operations such as kinematic inverse solutions and forward solutions. At the same time, the upper computer also needs to read important information from the lower industrial control machine and send discrete data groups and custom command information to the lower industrial control machine.

Kinematic Solution Logic. The solution logic of kinematic inverse solution is: After discretizing the trajectory inverse solution into n+1($n \geq 1$, $n \in \mathbb{N}$) points, solve each point according to the support chain kinematic constraint relationship. After integrating the 9 absolute motor angle discrete values obtained by all discrete points in sequence, a motor operation discrete data table of $9 \times (n+1)$ can be obtained and handed over to the lower machine for execution.

The solution logic of kinematic forward solution is: Read the current position of 9 DD motors, and also need to read 3 redundant angles. Use geometric constraints and vector relationships of support chains, and calculate several possible results under different positions according to motor position parameters. Then judge and discard unreasonable positions through redundant angles, leaving only one result closest to Matlab theoretical calculation. Finally, output the end effector pose parameters and theoretical redundant angle at this time to complete the forward solution.

Packaging Matlab Calculation Code. In the process of theoretical calculation by Maltab software, solving nonlinear equation group instructions will be used for inverse solution, while forward solution will also involve solving nonlinear equation group using "symbol" variables. If both solving processes are reproduced in C++ in the upper computer program, although it can improve the operation efficiency to a certain extent, it is difficult to implement and cannot guarantee the accuracy and correctness of the solution.

Therefore, using the **mcc** command to translate a M file into C/C++ file for encapsulation into a corresponding package file is an ideal way for C++ calling. This package file contains interfaces required between codes generated by C/C++ compiler and executable file types supported by it, including .h header files, .ctf files, .dll dynamic link libraries, .lib static data link library files. If the entire extern folder under Matlab directory is retained, then the upper computer can run core operation code independently without relying on Matlab environment, which is conducive to code confidentiality and adaptation to different motion environments.

ADS Communication. ADS stands for Automation Device Specification, which is an application layer communication protocol based on TCP transport layer. It supports multiple protocols such as TCP/IP communication between applications, web-based HTTP communication, and other third-party protocols (such as serial ports). Its framework in TwinCAT system is shown in Fig. 6. Each module in TwinCAT system is an independent device. The information between them is not directly communicated but needs to be exchanged uniformly through ADS routers. Each task has a service module that exchanges data by sending requests from clients and returning requests from servers.

In the upper computer program, an ADS client needs to be applied for reading and writing variables inside TwinCAT of lower machine from server side. By writing AmsNetID and AdsPortNr to locate hardware devices and software services, and then completing read-write tasks through variable handles, the upper computer can read important information from the lower computer and send data and commands to the lower industrial control machine.

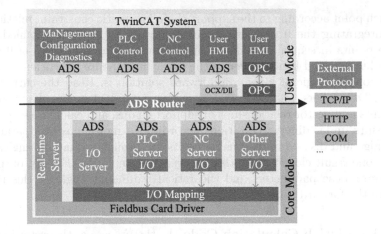

Fig. 6. The framework of ADS communication.

3.5 Motor Selection

Motor is an important driving component in the control system. A suitable motor can better play the advantages of the mechanism. The motor selection of KRHPM needs to consider the following points: The shape of the motor should be flat enough; The motor needs to integrate an absolute value encoder; The motor needs to provide sufficient torque; The motor needs sufficient accuracy; The driver matched with the motor can use EtherCAT protocol communication. Considering the requirements above, three direct-drive torque motors with different continuous torques in the same series for three branches are selected for each support chain. (see Fig. 7)

Company Name	FvMotor Corporation		
Type Name	D-1160SL2N	D-1161SL2N	D-1162SL2N
Continuous Torque	1.3Nm	3Nm	5Nm
Peek Torque	3.9Nm	9Nm	15Nm
Positioning Accuracy	Absolute: ±20 arc sec Repetitive: ±2 arc sec		
Absolute Encoder Resolution PPR	16,777,216		

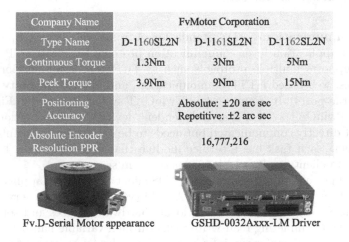

Fv.D-Serial Motor appearance   GSHD-0032Axxx-LM Driver

Fig. 7. Motor selection result.

3.6   Experiment

The first-generation experimental prototype of KRHPM has been completed as shown in Fig. 8.

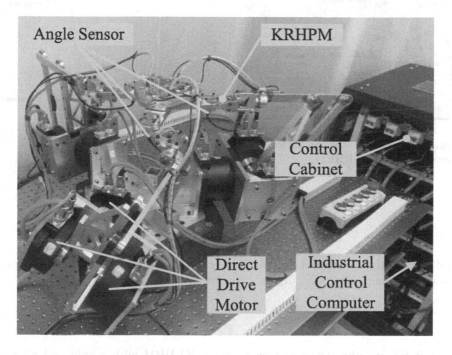

Fig. 8. First-generation experimental prototype of KRHPM.

This experiment will use a laser tracker to measure the position trajectory of the moving platform in circular motion parallel to the base plane at zero position to verify whether the functionality of the experimental platform meets the standard. The laser tracker used is the German Leica AT901-B, which has a super high resolution of $0.01\,\mu m$ and an accuracy of up to $10.00\,\mu m$, which can meet the measurement needs of this experiment. The data acquisition experiment site is arranged as shown in Fig. 9. The laser tracker software continuously measures at equal time intervals with a speed of $0.5\,s$ per measurement, which is relatively slow. Therefore, in order to obtain enough data, the physical moving platform is set to continuously perform 10 rounds of circular motion, with a radius of $50\,mm$ and KRHPM speed set at $\pi/10(rad/s)$.

The theoretical discrete points are fitted into a circular trajectory and the moving platform motion position trajectory is plotted into two groups in the same figure. The experimental results are shown in Fig. 10. The experimental results indicate that from this trajectory, KRHPM's moving platform position trajectory basically coincides with the ideal one. Under the condition of lack of

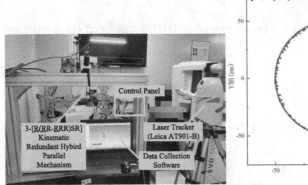 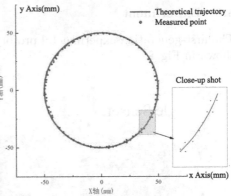

Fig. 9. Experimental scene of testing control system of KRHPM.

Fig. 10. Theoretical trajectory and actual position map of the dynamic platform walking a 50 mm radius circle in the plane where it is located at zero position.

feedback, KRHPM can not only achieve control goals but also achieve qualified semi-closed-loop control accuracy.

4 Conclusion

This article mainly discusses how to equip KRHPM with a safe and reliable control system that meets the requirements of assembly operations for small parts. It mainly elaborates on the overall control framework, the core logic of the upper and lower computer programs, motor selection, etc. Finally, a semi-closed-loop control experiment is conducted to verify the feasibility of the control system. The innovation point of this article is mainly in the theoretical system that regulates the overall construction framework of the KRHPM control system and constructs a control block diagram based on kinematics, which lays a foundation for improving complex mechanism control systems. In future work, this control system will be used in conjunction with visual feedback to complete closed-loop control and further improve the operating accuracy of KRHPM. At the same time, combined with dynamic models, model reference adaptive methods are used to complete control, so that the machine can better cooperate with micro-actuators to complete micro-assembly operations.

References

1. Wang, R., Zhang, X.: Parameters optimization and experiment of a planar parallel 3-DOF nanopositioning system. IEEE Trans. Ind. Electron. (2017)

2. Tang, T., Fang, H., Luo, H., Song, Y., Zhang, J.: Type synthesis, unified kinematic analysis and prototype validation of a family of Exechon inspired parallel mechanisms for 5-axis hybrid kinematic machine tools. Robot. Comput.-Integr. Manuf. **72** (2021)
3. Hunt, K.H.: Structural kinematics of in-parallel-actuated robot-arms. J. Mech. Transmiss. Automat. Des. **105** (1983)
4. Wen, K., Harton, D., Laliberte, T., Gosselin, C.: Kinematically redundant (6+3)-DOF hybrid parallel robot with large orientational workspace and remotely operated gripper. In: 2019 International Conference on Robotics and Automation (ICRA), Montreal, QC, Canada, May 2019, pp. 1672–1678. IEEE (2019)
5. Alvarez, J., Arceo, J.C., Armenta, C., Lauber, J., Bernal, M.: An extension of computed-torque control for parallel robots in ankle reeducation. In: IFAC Conference on Intelligent Control and Automation Sciences (2020)
6. Lin, W., Li, B., Yang, X., Zhang, D.: Modelling and control of inverse dynamics for a 5-DOF parallel kinematic polishing machine. Int. J. Adv. Robot. Syst. **10**(8), 1 (2013)
7. Koessler, A., Bouton, N., Briot, S., Bouzgarrou, B.C., Mezouar, Y.: Linear adaptive computed torque control for singularity crossing of parallel robots. In: Arakelian, V., Wenger, P. (eds.) ROMANSY 22 – Robot Design. Dynamics and Control, volume 584, pp. 222–229. Springer International Publishing, Cham (2019)
8. Chen, H., Wo, S.: RBF neural network of sliding mode control for time-varying 2-DOF parallel manipulator system. Math. Probl. Eng. **1**–**10**, 2013 (2013)
9. Chen, S.H., Fu, L.C.: Observer-based backstepping control of a 6-DOF parallel hydraulic manipulator. Control. Eng. Pract. **36**, 100–112 (2015)

Multimodal Collaborative Perception and Fusion

Influence of Contact Characteristics on Pressure Sensing of IPMC Sensors

Gangqiang Tang🄳, Xin Zhao, Yujun Ji, Chun Zhao, Dong Mei,
and Yanjie Wang(✉) 🄳

Jiangsu Provincial Key Laboratory of Special Robot Technology, Hohai University,
Changzhou Campus, Changzhou 213022, China
yj.wang1985@gmail.com

Abstract. Ionic flexible sensors have shown broad application prospects in wearable devices, special environmental monitoring and intelligent human-computer interaction. As a typical kind of ionic flexible sensor, ionic polymer (IPMC) metal composite can response to stimuli like bending, pressure, humidity and so on. However, the current researches about pressure sensing of IPMC mainly considers that IPMC is in full contact with the object, but how the characteristics of the contact object affect the pressure sensing performance of IPMC have not been revealed. In this paper, we studied the influence of different contact characteristics on the pressure sensing signal of IPMC by designing a series of contact objects with cone, prism and planar structures through 3D printing. Then the pressure sensing process were simulated in multi-physical fields based on Zhu's model to verify the experimental results. The conclusion may provide a potential for the identification of different contact characteristics using ionic flexible sensors.

Keywords: IPMC · Pressure sensing · Contact characteristics · Multi-physical fields · Simulation

1 Introduction

With the development of material science, robotics and bionics, the concept of bionic skin has been put forward and developed rapidly, which shows broad application prospects in wearable devices, special environmental monitoring, intelligent human-computer interaction and other fields [1]. Flexible sensors are an important part of bionic skin, which can be divided into capacitive, resistive, piezoelectric, triboelectric and ionic sensors according to the working principle [2]. Among them, ionic flexible sensors have attracted wide attention of researchers because of their close bioelectrical sensing mechanism, and have great research prospects in the field of bionics [3].

Ionic polymer metal composite (IPMC) is a typical kind of ionic flexible sensor, which is composed of two layers of conductive electrodes and an ionic polymer matrix to form a sandwich structure. [4] The backbone structure of the ionomer is composed of C-F long chains, and the negative sulfonic groups are fixed at the end of the side chains and agglomerated to form nanochannels. The nanochannel contains liquid electrolyte,

H. Yang et al. (Eds.): ICIRA 2023, LNAI 14267, pp. 119–127, 2023.
https://doi.org/10.1007/978-981-99-6483-3_11

which is mainly composed of water and free cations. Under the external stimulation, IPMC will deform, resulting in uneven stress distribution in the polymer. At this time, the free cations will redistribute under the stress gradient, thus generating voltage signals between the two electrodes. Based on the aforementioned mechanism, IPMC can sense bending, pressure, humidity and other stimuli. [5–7] As a part of tactile sensing, pressure sensing is one of the most important functions of bionic skin. However, the current researches about pressure sensing of IPMC mainly considers that the whole body is subjected to pressure load [8], as shown in Fig. 1 A. In fact, in practical applications, the IPMC is generally in local contact with the object, as shown in Fig. 1 B. Therefore, how the characteristics of the contact object affect the pressure sensing performance of the IPMC remains to be revealed.

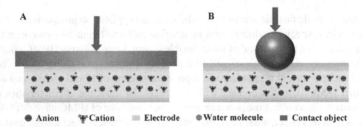

Fig. 1. Pressure sensing mechanism of IPMC. A. Pressure sensing of full contact. B. Pressure sensing of local contact.

In this paper, we studied the influence of different contact characteristics (point contact, line contact, surface contact) on the pressure sensing signal of IPMC. Then based on the sensing model of Zhu et al.'s, the pressure sensing signals of IPMC under different contact areas are simulated in multi-physical fields. The results show that the simulation and experimental results are in good agreement. This work will provide a potential for the identification of different contact characteristics using ionic flexible sensors.

2   Experiments

In this work, Nafion117 is served as the interlayer of the IPMC while palladium and gold were served as the composite electrode. The IPMC was prepared through a combination of immersion reduction plating and electroplating method as described in Reference [9], which has a size of 10 mm × 10 mm and a thickness of 0.2 mm.

In order to explore the influence of different contact characteristics on the pressure sensing signal of IPMC, we set up a test platform that integrates pressure application and signal acquisition. As shown in Fig. 2, the platform consists of a fixed base, a vibration exciter (SA-JZ002), a signal generator (SA-SG030A), a load cell (ZNLBM-3KG), an NI USB-6001 data acquisition card and a PC. The vibration exciter is controlled by the signal generator and is used to apply pressure to the surface of the IPMC. The pressure generated by the vibration exciter can be controlled by adjusting the amplitude of the exciter according to the value fed back by the load cell. The voltage generated by the IPMC and the real-time signal of the load cell are recorded in the Labview software in the PC through the NI USB-6001 data acquisition. During the test, the IPMC was fixed vertically on a rigid plate of the fixed base with the upper surface covered by layer of Polyimide (PI) tape, which can effectively prevent humidity from interfering with electrical signals. When the output voltage of IPMC was measured, the lower electrode was connected to the positive electrode while the upper electrode was connected to the negative one.

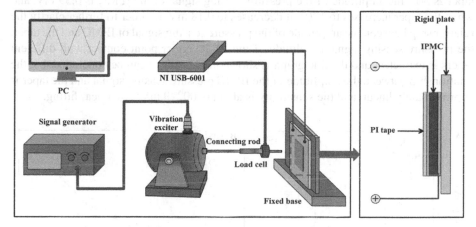

Fig. 2. Test platform of pressure sensing.

Different contact characteristics are realized through 3D printed method. As shown in Fig. 3, a series of contact objects were printed with cone, prism and planar structures to realize point, line and surface contact, respectively. These elements can be installed at the front end of the exciter to contact the surface of IPMC with convenient disassembly and replacement.

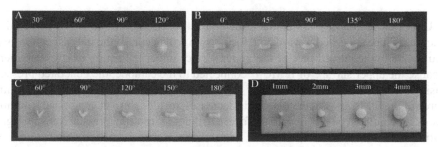

Fig. 3. Contact objects with different characteristics. A. Cone structures with different tapers for point contact. B. Prism structures with different radians for line contact. C. Prism structures with different angles for line contact. D. Planar structures with different radii for surface contact.

3   Results and Discussions

3.1   Point Contact

A periodic pressure with a frequency of 1 Hz was applied to the surface of IPMC, and the amplitude of the pressure was controlled to 5 N. The pressure sensing signals generated by point contact with different tapers are shown in Fig. 4 A. It can be seen that if the pressure remains unchanged, the amplitude of the pressure sensing signal of the IPMC decreases with the increase of the taper of the conical structure. When the taper is 30°, the amplitude of the pressure sensing signal of the IPMC is 0.39 mV, and when the taper increases to 120°, it decreases to 0.18 mV. In order to further clarify the relationship between the amplitude of the pressure sensing signal of IPMC and the taper, the pressure sensing signal amplitude of the IPMC under point contact with different tapers is extracted, and the line graph is shown in Fig. 4 B. It can be concluded that the relationship between the amplitude of the IPMC pressure sensing signal and the taper is approximately linear, and the sensitivity is about 0. 00229 mV/° by linear fitting.

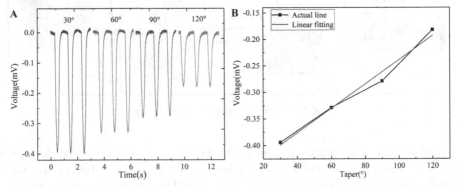

Fig. 4. Pressure sensing performance under point contact. A. Pressure sensing signals generated by point contact with different tapers. B. Evolution of the pressure sensing signal amplitude of the IPMC with taper.

Under the action of point contact, the contact position between IPMC and conical structure will be squeezed inward, and local strain will occur, so the internal cations will accumulate in the curved part of the upper surface under the action of stress gradient. Because the upper surface of IPMC is connected to the cathode, the generated pressure sensing signal is negative. As the taper of the conical structure increases, the deforming degree of the IPMC toward the inner side decreases, resulting in a decrease in the number of ions accumulated on the upward surface, and thus the resulting pressure sensing signal continues to decrease.

3.2   Line Contact

In this section, we mainly studied the influence of radians in arc contact and the angles in broken line contact on pressure sensing of IPMC. When the pressure amplitude is 5 N, the pressure sensing signals generated by line contact with different radians are shown in Fig. 5 A. It can be seen that as the radian increases, the amplitude of the pressure sensing signal of the IPMC is essentially unchanged, remaining about 0.28 mV. Therefore, it can be concluded that the amplitude of the pressure sensor signal basically does not change with the radian. The reason may lie on that when the radian changes, the length of the contact line does not change, so the area of the strain region generated on the IPMC surface and the depth of the upper surface depression will not change, resulting in pressure sensing signal unchanged.

The pressure sensing signals generated by broken line contacts with different angles under the pressure of 5 N are shown in Fig. 5 B. When the contact angle increases from 60° to 180°, the pressure sensing signal amplitude of IPMC increases from 0.14 mV to 0.28 mV, and the relationship between them is approximately linear. Different from arc contact, in the broken line contact, the contact line is composed of two straight lines, and the strain areas generated by the two lines exerting pressure on the IPMC are overlapped, resulting in interference. The smaller the angle of the broken line is, the larger the interference area is. Therefore, as the angle increases, the pressure sensing signal of the IPMC increases.

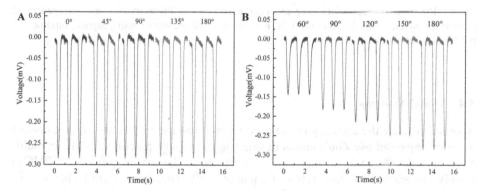

Fig. 5. Pressure sensing performance under line contact. A. Pressure sensing signals generated by arc contact with different radians. B. Pressure sensing signals generated by broken line contact with different angles.

3.3 Surface Contact

Circular planes with different radii were used to investigate the influence of surface contact characteristics on pressure sensing of IPMC. When the pressure amplitude is 5 N, the pressure sensing signals generated by the surface contact with different radii are shown in Fig. 6 A. It can be seen that the amplitude of the pressure sensing signal of the IPMC decreases with the increase of the contact radius. When the contact radius increases from 1 mm to 4 mm, the pressure sensing signal amplitude of IPMC declines from 0.136 mV to 0.016 mV.

To further reveal the evolution of the pressure signal of the IPMC with the contact radius, the response signal values at different contact radii were extracted and shown in

Fig. 6 B. It indicates that the voltage decrease rate is getting slower during the changing progress. In fact, in planar contact, the pressure sensing signal of IPMC is mainly affected by the pressure intensity. When the applied force is constant, the pressure intensity decreases with the increase of contact area, so the deformation of IPMC decreases, which leads to the decrease of output voltage.

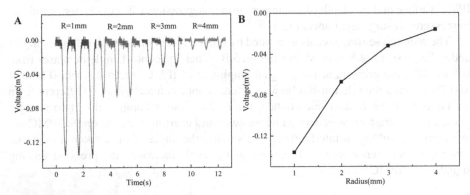

Fig. 6. Pressure sensing performance under surface contact. A. Pressure sensing signals generated by surface contact with different radii. B. Evolution of the pressure sensing signal amplitude of the IPMC with radius.

3.4 Model Analysis

In order to verify the accuracy of the experimental results, we take the surface contact as an example and use Zhu's model to simulate the sensing process of IPMC in multi-physical fields. According to the theory of Zhu et al., the sensing process of IPMC is mainly constrained by three types of equations [10]. One is the Nernst-Planck (NP) equation describing the mass transfer process and the mass continuity equation, which can be expressed as follows.

$$\begin{cases} J_I = -d_{II}\left(\nabla c_I + \frac{z_I c_I F}{RT}\nabla\phi\right) - n_{dI}d_{WW}\nabla c_W - c_I K\nabla P \\ J_W = -d_{WW}\nabla c_W - n_{dW}d_{II}\left(\nabla c_I + \frac{z_I c_I F}{RT}\nabla\phi\right) - c_W K\nabla P \end{cases} \tag{1}$$

where J_I is the flux of cations, J_W is the flux of water molecules, d_{II} is he diffusion coefficient of the cations, d_{WW} is he diffusion coefficient of the water molecules, c_I is the concentration of cations, c_W is the concentration of water molecules, n_{dI} is the drag coefficient of cations, n_{dW} is the drag coefficient of water molecules, z_I is the sodium ion valence, F is the Faraday constant, R is the gas constant, T is the temperature, ϕ is the potential, K is the hydraulic permeability coefficient and P represents the pressure.

Then combining the electrostatic field equation,

$$\nabla^2\phi = -\frac{z_I F\left(c_I - c^-\right)}{\varepsilon} \tag{2}$$

and mechanical equation,

$$\begin{cases} \varepsilon_i = \frac{\partial u_i}{\partial i} \\ \sigma_i = \varepsilon_i E \end{cases} (i = x, y, z) \tag{1}$$

the sensing process of the IPMC can be described. Where ε is the dielectric constant, c^- is the concentration of anion, E is the elastic modulus of the IPMC, ε_i, u_i, and σ_i represent the strain, displacement, and normal stress, respectively.

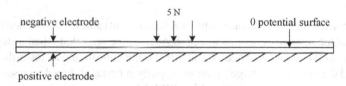

Fig. 7. Schematic diagram of the two-dimensional model of IPMC.

Based on the above theoretical analysis, the sensing process of IPMC is analyzed by the multi-physical field simulation in Comsol software, regarding the substrate membrane of IPMC as a homogeneous linear elastic material. In order to simplify the simulation process, it is carried out in two-dimensional state. As shown in Fig. 7, the two-dimensional model was established with a length of 10 mm and a thickness of 0.2 mm. The lower surface of the two-dimensional model was completely fixed, and the upper surface was subjected to pressure loads of different line lengths (static force with magnitude of 5 N and duration of 20 s). In the electric field, the middle symmetry axis is set as a 0 potential surface, the upper surface is a negative electrode, and the lower surface is a positive electrode. The numerical values of each physical parameter in the simulation process are shown in Table 1.

Table 1.

Variables	Value	Unit	Implication
d_{II}	2.5×10^{-11}	m²/s	Self-diffusion coefficient of Sodium ions
d_{WW}	1.2×10^{-10}	m²/s	Self-diffusion coefficient of water molecules
c_I	1353	mol/m³	Initial concentration of cations
c_W	17965	mol/m³	Initial concentration of water molecules
c^-	1353	mol/m³	Concentration of fixed anions
n_{dW}	7	—	Drag coefficient of water molecules
E	1×109	Pa	Elastic modulus of IPMC
ε	4.4×10^{-4}	—	Dielectric constant

(*continued*)

(*continued*)

Variables	Value	Unit	Implication
T	300	K	Temperature
z	1	—	Sodium ion valence
K	2×10^{-17}	$m^2(s \cdot Pa)$	Hydraulic permeability
F	96485	C/mol	Faraday constant

The response process of surface contact with different radii was simulated by Comsol software, and the results are shown in Fig. 8 A. It can be seen that when a step pressure load applied to the upper surface of the IPMC, the cations move towards the upper surface. And the response voltage increases rapidly at first and then decreases slowly. In addition, the response voltage amplitude of IPMC decreases with the increase of contact radius. The peak value of voltage response under different contact radii is extracted, and its variation with the contact radius is shown in Fig. 8 B. The growth rate of the response voltage gradually decreases with the increase of the contact radius, which is consistent with the experimental results in the change trend.

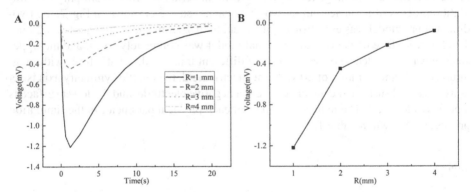

Fig. 8. Simulation results. A. Simulated response process of surface contact with different radii. B. Evolution of the simulated pressure sensing signal amplitude of the IPMC with radius.

4 Conclusion

In this paper, we investigated the influence of different contact characteristics on the pressure sensing performance of IPMC. First, a series of contact objects with cone, prism and planar structures were fabricated through 3D printing. Then, by applying a periodic pressure with a frequency of 1 Hz an amplitude of 5 N, the pressure sensing signals under point contact, line contact and surface contact were test. In the condition of point contact, there is nearly a linear relationship between the amplitude of the IPMC pressure sensing signal and the taper. In the condition point contact, the amplitude of the pressure sensor signal basically does not change with the radian of the arc while it decreases with the decrease of the angle of broken line. And under surface contact, the amplitude of the pressure sensing signal of the IPMC decreases with the increase of the contact radius. Finally, the experimental results were verified by simulating the pressure sensing process in in multi-physical fields based on Zhu's model. This work may shed light on the identification of different contact characteristics using a single piece of ionic flexible sensor.

Acknowledgement. This research was supported by the National Natural Science Foundation of China (51975184), the National Key Research and Development Program of China (2020YFB1312900). The authors gratefully acknowledge the supports.

References

1. Hu, H., Huang, H., Gao, X., et al.: A wearable cardiac ultrasound imager. Nature **613**, 667–675 (2023)
2. Zhu, J., Zhou, C., Zhang, M.: Recent progress in flexible tactile sensor systems: from design to application. Soft Sci. **1**, 3 (2021)
3. Zhao, C., Wang, Y., Tang, G., et al.: Ionic flexible sensors: mechanisms, materials, structures, and applications. Adv. Funct. Mater. **17**, 2110417 (2022)
4. Tang, G., Mei, D., Zhao, X., et al.: A comprehensive survey of ionic polymer metal composite transducers: preparation, performance optimization and applications. Soft Sci. **3**, 9 (2023)
5. Zhao, C., Wang, Y., Tang, G., et al.: Biological hair-inspired AgNWs@Au-embedded nafion electrodes with high stability for self-powered ionic flexible sensors. ACS Appl. Mater. Interfaces **14**, 46023–46031 (2022)
6. Wang, Y., Tang, G., Zhao, C., et al.: The effects of contact area on pressure sensing of ionic polymer metal composite sensor with a soft substrate. Smart Mater. Struct. **31**(6), 065013 (2022)
7. Wang, Y., Tang, G., Zhao, C., et al.: Experimental investigation on the physical parameters of ionic polymer metal composites sensors for humidity perception. Sens. Actuators B Chem. **345**, 130421 (2021)
8. Gudarzi, M., Smolinski, P., Wang, Q.: Compression and shear mode ionic polymer-metal composite (IPMC) pressure sensors. Sens. Actuators A **260**, 99–111 (2017)
9. Wang, Y., Liu, J., Zhu, Y., et al.: Formation and characterization of dendritic interfacial electrodes inside an ionomer. ACS Appl. Mater. Interfaces **9**, 30258–30262 (2017)
10. Zhu, Z., Chang, L., Horiuchi, T., et al.: Multi-physical model of cation and water transport in ionic polymer-metal composite sensors. J. Appl. Phys. **119**(12), 124901 (2016)

Optimization-Based Motion Planning Method for a Robot Manipulator Under the Conditions of Confined Space and Heavy Load

Tianyu Zhang[1,2,3], Hongguang Wang[1,2(✉)], Peng Lv[1,2], Fanxu Kong[1,2], Daqian Wang[1,2], and Xin'an Pan[1,2]

[1] State Key Laboratory of Robotics, Shenyang Institute of Automation, Chinese Academy of Sciences, Shenyang 110016, China
hgwang@sia.cn
[2] Institutes for Robotics and Intelligent Manufacturing, Chinese Academy of Sciences, Shenyang 110169, China
[3] University of Chinese Academy of Sciences, Beijing 100049, China

Abstract. The current aircraft refueling method relies heavily on manual labor, resulting in high labor intensity, a cumbersome refueling process, and low efficiency. Therefore, extensive research is crucial to explore the use of robot manipulators for autonomous refueling. However, implementing robot arms encounters challenges such as confined workspace and the heavy weight of fueling tools. This paper proposes a motion planning method for a robot manipulator operating within confined areas to address these issues. The method considers obstacle avoidance constraints, dynamic joint torque allocation, and physical limitations. To characterize the dynamic transmission performance between joint torque output and end force while considering joint torque limitations, we introduce the Inertia Matching Index (IMI). The IMI and minimum joint angles serve as cost functions in our approach. Given the confined environments and various types of refueling equipment, we incorporate collision distance as a constraint to avoid collisions between the robot arm and other objects. To ensure effective resolution, we reformulate these non-convex objectives and constraints to solve them using the ADMM algorithm. The experimental results demonstrate the effectiveness of our proposed motion planning method in improving IMI while ensuring safe trajectories and optimal joint torque allocation. This study has significant theoretical and practical value for autonomous robot operations and autonomous aerial refueling applications in confined spaces.

Keywords: Confined space · Heavy load · Inertial Matching Index (IMI) · Motion planning · Manipulator

1 Introduction

In the aviation industry, aircraft refueling is a critical process that requires maximum attention to safety and efficiency. Manual operations are mainly used,

H. Yang et al. (Eds.): ICIRA 2023, LNAI 14267, pp. 128–138, 2023.
https://doi.org/10.1007/978-981-99-6483-3_12

which can be labor-intensive, time-consuming, and inefficient. Therefore, conducting research and implementing autonomous refueling using robot manipulators is essential. However, refueling activities usually occur in confined areas where various fixed equipment such as fuel trucks, tanks, and auxiliary fueling devices are present [1]. It means that the robot arm must have higher requirements for obstacle avoidance accuracy and efficiency to ensure complete safety for both the robotic arm and the equipment involved.

In addition, when performing autonomous refueling tasks, the robot arm's end-effector is required to support a heavy weight in the form of a refueling hose that is attached to the fuel port of an aircraft. However, the joint torque of a robot manipulator has inherent limitations that make it challenging to ensure high-performance stability when applying force in any configuration of the robot. To effectively address this issue, it is essential to allocate joint torques reasonably, based on dynamic load changes, to enhance the transmission performance of joint torques within the constraints imposed by joint torque limitations. Given these limitations, it is essential to investigate how motion planning techniques for robotic arms can effectively balance obstacle avoidance constraints, dynamic joint torque allocation, and physical restrictions within a restricted workspace.

This paper propose a motion planning method for a robot manipulator under the conditions of confined space and heavy load to address the issues above. The Inertia Matching Index (IMI) [2], a dynamic transfer performance index, is introduced as an optimization objective to represent the joint torque output to the end force. This objective ensures minimal joint position changes and adherence to physical constraints, enabling redundant robot manipulators to function optimally. The main contributions of this paper can be summarized as follows:

- We propose a motion planning approach incorporating obstacle avoidance constraints, dynamic joint torque allocation, and physical constraints.
- We address the challenge of effectively distributing joint torque during motion planning under dynamic loads, while also maximizing joint performance utilization.
- We confirm the algorithm's effectiveness by conducting experiments. Our work offer valuable references and insights for future research on robots' autonomous refueling capabilities.

The subsequent sections of this paper are structured as follows: Sect. 2 presents an overview of relevant research and theoretical methods. Section 3 discusses inertia-matching ellipsoids and redefines the Inertia Matching Index (IMI). Section 4 formulates objective functions and constraint conditions using optimization theory, solving them effectively using the ADMM algorithm. Section 5 establishes an experimental platform to verify the algorithm's efficacy. Finally, Sect. 6 summarizes this paper.

2 Related Work

This section will discuss research on motion planning, performance evaluation indicators, collision distance calculation methods for robot arms.

For robot arms motion planning, sampling-based [3,4] and optimization-based planning methods [4–6] enjoy widespread utilization. These methods integrate collision avoidance technologies throughout the movement process to prevent collisions between robots and physical environments. However, sampling-based planners predominantly rely on "yes" or "no" collision detection to determine the feasibility of sampling points or edge paths. This approach needs to provide insights into collision trends and enable their decoupling, thus making it challenging to meet the requirements for safe obstacle avoidance within constrained workspace. Conversely, optimization-based planning methods allow the calculation of collision distances by utilizing algorithms such as approximate geometry, bounding volume hierarchy, and convex polyhedron. Although these algorithms perform well in specific spatial environments, they encounter difficulties in accurately and efficiently calculating distances in constrained workspace with various obstacles and varying shapes. When dealing with issues like the limited torque output of a robot manipulator carrying a heavy load, sampling-based algorithms do not consider the dynamic characteristics of the arm's movement. On the other hand, optimization-based methods rarely address how to allocate joint torque based on changes in dynamic loads. Convex optimization has been widely applied in robotic motion planning fields. Recently many convex optimization algorithms, like the Alternating Direction Method of Multipliers (ADMM) or Augmented Lagrangian Method (ALM), have achieved significant results when solving non-convex optimization problems.

In robotics, researchers commonly use manipulability ellipsoid [7], the manipulability force ellipsoid [8], dynamic manipulability ellipsoid [9], and inertia matching ellipsoid [2] to evaluate a robot's operational capabilities and performance. These tools improve manipulation accuracy and stability. The manipulability ellipsoid describes all movements a robot can perform in its current posture. It determines a robot's best position and posture given a specific task. The force manipulability ellipsoid evaluates a robot's maximum manipulation force under given tasks by describing all forces and torques it can apply in its current posture. The dynamic manipulability ellipsoid evaluates a robot's manipulation ability under different motion states. In contrast, inertia-matching ellipsoids describe dynamic transfer performance between joint torque and load-applied forces at end-effector when evaluating their performances with loads.

Avoiding collisions is crucially essential in robot arm motion planning. Researchers have proposed various collision distance calculation methods, which mainly fall into three categories: approximate geometric algorithm, bounding volume hierarchy algorithm [10], and convex polytope algorithm [11,12] - these methods have different impacts on the precision and efficiency of collision detection algorithms. In confined spaces where obstacles with diverse shapes interfere seriously with robot manipulator autonomous movement, safety must be ensured by fast yet accurate collision distance calculations involving key technologies such as the modeling method or model state representation.

Based on previous research, this paper proposes a self-refueling method for robot manipulators in environments where refueling is restricted. The proposed method achieves efficient motion planning of the robot manipulator by maximizing the Inertial Matching Index (IMI) along its trajectory. Additionally, collision distance is a constraint to ensure the robot arm does not collide with objects in its environment. Experimental results demonstrate that this algorithm can reduce human errors, lower labor intensity, and improve refueling speed and efficiency. This study has significant research implications and practical applications for robotics and autonomous refueling.

3   Preliminary

This section reviewed the Inertial Matching Ellipsoid and Inertial Matching Index (IMI) [2], which are used to evaluate the performance of a 7-DoF collaborative robot when subjected to loads at its end effector.

3.1   Inertia Matching Ellipsoid

Considering the end effector load, the dynamic equation of an n-DoF collaborative robot is defined as:

$$\tau = \mathbf{M}(\mathbf{q})\ddot{\mathbf{q}} + \mathbf{C}(\mathbf{q}, \dot{\mathbf{q}}) + \mathbf{G}(\mathbf{q}) + \mathbf{J}(\mathbf{q})^{\mathbf{T}}\mathbf{F_e} \tag{1}$$

Here, n and m represent the number of joints and the dimensions of the end effector load, respectively. $\tau \in \mathbf{R^n}$ denotes the joint torques, $\mathbf{M}(\mathbf{q}) \in \mathbf{R^{n \times n}}$ represents the inertia tensor of the robot arm in joint space, $\mathbf{C}(\mathbf{q}, \dot{\mathbf{q}}) \in \mathbf{R^n}$ includes Coriolis and centrifugal forces, $\mathbf{G}(\mathbf{q}) \in \mathbf{R^n}$ denotes the gravitational forces, and $\mathbf{J}(\mathbf{q}) \in \mathbf{R^{m \times n}}$ is the Jacobian matrix of the robot arm at configuration $\mathbf{q}$.

Taking into account the inertia of the end effector load, the joint torques can be expressed as:

$$\tau = \mathbf{Q}(\mathbf{q})\left(\mathbf{F_e} - \mathbf{F_{bias}}\left(\mathbf{q}, \dot{\mathbf{q}}\right)\right) \tag{2}$$

where $\mathbf{F_{bias}}\left(\mathbf{q}, \dot{\mathbf{q}}\right)$ represents the bias term related to the joint angles $\mathbf{q}$ and angular velocities $\dot{\mathbf{q}}$, and $\mathbf{Q}(\mathbf{q})$ is defined as:

$$\mathbf{Q}(\mathbf{q}) = \mathbf{J}(\mathbf{q})^{\mathbf{T}} + \mathbf{M}(\mathbf{q})\mathbf{J}(\mathbf{q})^{\dagger}\mathbf{M_p^{-1}} \tag{3}$$

Here, $\mathbf{J}(\mathbf{q})^{\dagger}$ denotes the pseudo-inverse of the Jacobian matrix $\mathbf{J}(\mathbf{q})$, and $\mathbf{M_p} \in \mathbf{R^{m \times m}}$ represents the inertia matrix of the end-effector load. This equation describes the relationship between the torques generated at the joints and the forces and torques applied to the end effector.

The Inertial Matching Ellipsoid corresponds to the forces and torques exerted at the end effector when the joint torques satisfy $\|\tau\|^2 = 1$, forming a unit sphere in the n-dimensional joint torque space. The condition for unit joint torques can be written as follows:

$$\|\tau\|^2 = (\mathbf{F_e} - \mathbf{F_{bias}})^T \mathbf{Q}^T \mathbf{Q} \, (\mathbf{F_e} - \mathbf{F_{bias}}) \tag{4}$$

This equation describes the ellipsoid of forces and torques from the joints to the end effector, defined as the Inertial Matching Index (IME).

3.2 Inertia Matching Index

Based on the knowledge of linear algebra, it is known that the scaling of joint torques to task space depends on the condition number of the symmetric positive semi-definite matrix $\mathbf{Q}^T\mathbf{Q}$. Letting $\mathbf{A} = \mathbf{Q}^T\mathbf{Q}$ and λ_i be the eigenvalues of A, the Inertial Matching Index (im) can be expressed as:

$$im = \sqrt{\det(\mathbf{A})} = \sqrt{\det(\mathbf{Q}^T\mathbf{Q})} \tag{5}$$

The magnitude of this index, im, represents the efficiency of torque transmission from each joint to the forces and torques exerted on the load by the end effector. It can evaluate the performance when applying loads at the end effector.

Considering the constraints on joint torques and assuming symmetric limits for torques, $|\tau_i| \leq \tau_i^{\text{limit}}$, we have:

$$\mathbf{A} = \mathbf{Q}^T\mathbf{L}^{-2}\mathbf{Q} \tag{6}$$

where $\mathbf{L}$ is defined as $\mathbf{L} = diag\left(\tau_1^{\text{limit}}, \tau_2^{\text{limit}}, \cdots, \tau_n^{\text{limit}}\right)$.

4   Problem Formulation

Considering the attachment of a load to a collaborative robot in a constrained workspace, maximizing the Inertial Matching Index can enhance the transfer performance between joint torques and forces exerted on the load. Additionally, efficient collision detection is of utmost importance to ensure the safety of the robot arm and refueling equipment. This paper adopts an optimization-based [13] motion planning method to generate a collision-free trajectory that maximizes the Inertial Matching Index, given a desired target position. The motion planning problem can be expressed as a general nonlinear optimization, with equality and inequality constraints, taking advantage of a number of software packages to solve such problems. The general formulation of this method is as follows:

$$\begin{aligned} \min_{\mathbf{q}(t)} \quad & \mathcal{F}[\mathbf{q}\,(t)] \\ \text{s.t.} \quad & \mathcal{G}_i[\mathbf{q}\,(t)] \leq 0, \quad i = 1, \ldots, p \\ & \mathcal{H}_i[\mathbf{q}\,(t)] = 0, \quad i = 1, \ldots, q \end{aligned} \tag{7}$$

Here, $\mathbf{q}(t) \in R^n$ represents the decision variables, indicating the variation of joint angles of the robot arm over time $t \in [t_0, t_f]$. $\mathcal{F}[\mathbf{q}(t)]$ is the objective function that measures the performance of the robot arm, including minimizing the Inertial Matching Index, joint angles, and more. $\mathcal{G}_i[\mathbf{q}(t)]$ represents the inequality constraints that impose physical limitations on the robot arm, such as joint angles, torque range, and obstacle avoidance. $\mathcal{H}_i[\mathbf{q}(t)]$ denotes the equality constraints that ensure the robot arm's end effector reaches a specified position or orientation.

4.1 Object Function

This paper aims to maximize the Inertial Matching Index and minimize the joint angles to meet the task's requirements. The objective function is defined as follows:

$$\min_{\mathbf{q}(t)} -\sqrt{\det\left(A\left(\mathbf{q}\left(t\right)\right)\right)} + \frac{1}{2}\|\mathbf{q}\left(t\right)\|_2^2 \tag{8}$$

The objective function is non-convex, categorizing the problem as a non-convex optimization problem. To transform this problem into a convex optimization problem, techniques such as logarithmic transformation and Schur complement [13] are employed to reformulate Eq. (8) as follows:

$$\min_{\mathbf{q}(t)} -\ln\det\left(\mathbf{A}\left(\mathbf{q}\left(t\right)\right)\right) + \frac{1}{2}\|\mathbf{q}\left(t\right)\|_2^2$$

$$s.t. \qquad \begin{bmatrix} \mathbf{A}\left(\mathbf{q}\left(t\right)\right) & \mathbf{0} \\ \mathbf{0} & 1 \end{bmatrix} \succeq \mathbf{0} \tag{9}$$

Here, $\mathbf{0}$ is the zero vector of the same dimension as $\mathbf{q}(t)$, $\mathbf{0}^T$ denotes the transpose of $\mathbf{0}$, and $A(\mathbf{q}(t))$ is a matrix function with respect to $\mathbf{q}(t)$.

4.2 Inequality Constraints

Obstacle Avoidance. Collision avoidance is achieved by calculating the distances between the robot arm's joints and obstacles. The accuracy and efficiency of distance calculation are crucial for ensuring task safety. Firstly, a convex superquadric is used to model the robot arm and the environment, as shown in Fig. 1-b. This surface modeling technique provides high accuracy and converts the distance calculation between the robot arm and obstacles into the problem of finding the distance between convex superquadrics. Next, based on parameterized Minkowski sum and the computation of distances between superquadric surfaces [14], the distance is determined by the spatial positions of the geometric center of the bodies, denoted as $d_{L_iO_j}\left(\mathbf{X}\left(\mathbf{q}\right)\right)$, where the superquadric center is connected to the adjacent links. The following PoE-based [15] extended form of forward kinematics is utilized to represent the pose of any superquadric surface relative to the base coordinates, given the initial position X_{SQ}^0 of the superquadric center as shown in Fig. 1-c:

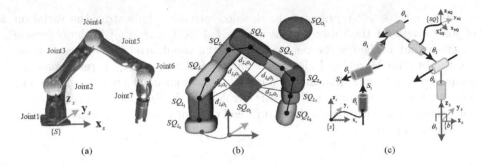

Fig. 1. Robot arm modeling, obstacle avoidance constraints, and forward kinematics model.

$$\mathbf{T}^0_{\mathbf{SQ}}\left(\mathbf{q}\left(t\right)\right) = \left(\prod_{i=1}^{n} e^{[S_1]q_1} \cdots e^{[S_{i-1}]q_{i-1}} e^{[S_i]q_i}\right) \mathbf{X}^0_{\mathbf{SQ}} \tag{10}$$

Here, the homogeneous transformation matrix T^0_{SQ} represents the coordinates of the center of the superquadric surface. This matrix can determine the pose $\mathbf{X}\left(\mathbf{q}\left(t\right)\right)$ of a convex superquadric surface at any given moment. The motion twist of unit screw axis i relative to the base coordinates is denoted by $S_i = (w_i, v_i) \in \mathbf{R}^6$, where $[S_i]$ is its corresponding matrix representation as follows:

$$[S_i] = \begin{bmatrix} [\omega_i] & v_i \\ 0 & 1 \end{bmatrix} \tag{11}$$

To ensure a certain safety margin between the robot arm links and obstacles, assuming the same safety distance between the robot arm and objects in the environment, the obstacle avoidance constraint is expressed as follows:

$$d_{L_i O_j}\left(\mathbf{X}\left(\mathbf{q}\left(t\right)\right)\right) \geq d_{safe}, i = 1, 2, \cdots, n+1; j = 1, 2, \cdots \tag{12}$$

Joint Angle and Torque Limits. The matrix A in Eq. (6) includes torque limits and does not require additional expression in the constraints.

The joint angle range is determined by the collaborative robot and defined as:

$$\mathbf{q}^- \leq \mathbf{q}(t) \leq \mathbf{q}^+ \tag{13}$$

4.3   Equation Constraints

The equation constraint is formulated through the kinematic equation of a manipulator arm, which is conceptualized as an arbitrary superquadric surface in a given position. This equation establishes the kinematic relationship between the redundant joint space of the robotic system and the superquadric surface in Cartesian space.

$$\dot{X} = \mathbf{J}\left(\mathbf{q}\right)\dot{\mathbf{q}} \tag{14}$$

Here, $\dot{\mathbf{X}}$ represents the velocity vector of an arbitrary convex superquadric surface in Cartesian space, while $\dot{\mathbf{q}}$ denotes the joint angles associated with the forward kinematic chain of the present superquadric surface. The function $\mathbf{J}(\mathbf{q})$ corresponds to the Jacobian matrix.

4.4   Reformulation and Nonlinear Optimization

In this section, by integrating the constraint conditions and the redefined objective function, we formulate a optimization problem that maximizes the IMI while avoiding obstacles as key constraints. The problem is defined as follows:

$$
\begin{aligned}
\min_{\mathbf{q}(t)} \quad & -\ln \det\left(\mathbf{A}\left(\mathbf{q}\left(t\right)\right)\right) + \tfrac{1}{2}\left\|\mathbf{q}\left(t\right)\right\|_2^2 \\
\text{s.t.} \quad & \begin{bmatrix} \mathbf{A}\left(\mathbf{q}\left(t\right)\right) & 0 \\ 0 & 1 \end{bmatrix} \succeq 0 \\
& \dot{\mathbf{X}} = \mathbf{J}\left(\mathbf{q}\right)\dot{\mathbf{q}} \\
& d_{L_i O_j}\left(\mathbf{X}\left(\mathbf{q}\left(t\right)\right)\right) \geq d_{safe}, i = 1,2,\cdots, n+1; j = 1,2,\cdots \\
& \mathbf{q}^- \leq \mathbf{q}(t) \leq \mathbf{q}^+
\end{aligned}
\tag{15}
$$

The objective function presented above is convex, while the matrix inequality constraint can be categorized as semi-definite. The optimization problem can be classified as a nonlinear optimization problem. To address this, we employ an efficient Alternating Direction Method of Multipliers (ADMM) algorithm, which decomposes the original problem into multiple sub-problems, allowing for an effective optimization solution.

Firstly, the objective function is decomposed as follows:

$$
\min_{\mathbf{q}(t)} f\left(\mathbf{q}\left(t\right)\right) + g\left(\mathbf{q}\left(t\right)\right)
\tag{16}
$$

where $f\left(\mathbf{q}(t)\right) = -\ln \det\left(\mathbf{A}\left(\mathbf{q}(t)\right)\right)$ and $g\left(\mathbf{q}(t)\right) = \tfrac{1}{2}\left|\mathbf{q}(t)\right|_2^2$.

Next, an auxiliary variable $z(t)$ is introduced to transform the objective function into the following form:

$$
\begin{aligned}
\min_{\mathbf{q}(t)} \quad & f\left(\mathbf{q}\left(t\right)\right) + g\left(\mathbf{z}\left(t\right)\right) \\
\text{s.t.} \quad & \mathbf{q}\left(t\right) - \mathbf{z}\left(t\right) = 0
\end{aligned}
\tag{17}
$$

The ADMM algorithm is then employed to iteratively solve this problem while satisfying the constraints of the original convex optimization problem. Nishihara et al.'s study provided a new proof of the linear convergence of the alternating direction method of multipliers (ADMM) when one of the objective terms is strongly convex [16].

5   Experiments and Results

This section will demonstrate how to use our method to obtain a trajectory that maximizes the IMI while satisfying constraints. We will also show that the planned trajectory is collision-free. To conduct our experiment, we utilized a 7-DOF collaborative robot developed by our laboratory, as shown in Fig. 2-a. In order to simulate restricted working space for refueling aircraft and obstacle situations, we set up a test environment in the lab. Figure 2-b displays an environment model established by the method introduced in this paper for the arm's understanding of environmental information. All planning calculations were performed on a computer with an Intel® Core™ i7-1165G7 CPU (12M Cache, up to 4.70 GHz), 16 GB of RAM, and a Linux 64-bit operating system. Given the robot arm's starting and ending positions, its end effector's inertia parameters, and physical constraints, a path that maximizes the IMI is planned while recording joint angle data, as shown in Fig. 3. Time was not used as a constraint or optimization criterion in this experiment. The algorithm's effectiveness has yet to be verified by using IMI as an optimization criterion to execute planning algorithms and comparing changes in the IMI over time for different trajectories. Meanwhile, this algorithm is compared with typical sampling algorithms such as

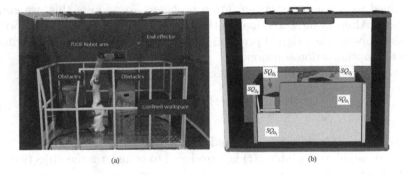

Fig. 2. Experiment on motion planning of a robot manipulator in confined space. The end-effector replacing heavy load modeling.

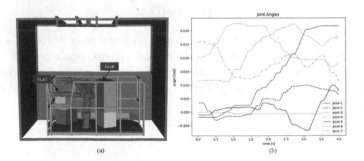

Fig. 3. Motion performance testing and results.

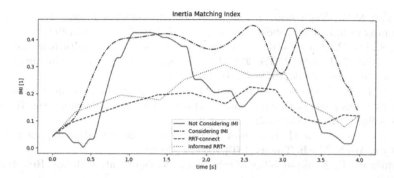

Fig. 4. Comparison results and data with other algorithms.

RRT-connect algorithm and Informed-RRT* algorithm. The comparison results and data are shown in Fig. 4. This algorithm can significantly improve the IMI through comparative data analysis while avoiding collisions.

6   Conclusion and Future Work

This paper presents a solution to traditional refueling methods' safety and efficiency issues by using robot manipulators. A motion planning method based on optimization is proposed to achieve autonomous refueling of robot arms in confined space. This approach can adapt to complex and narrow refueling environments. The Inertia Matching Index (IMI) is utilized as the cost function, and collision distance constraints are implemented to avoid any collisions between the robot arm and other objects. The experimental results demonstrate that this method of motion planning significantly enhances IMI, thereby ensuring safe and dependable refueling operations. In the Future, We will further study more advanced sensor technology and perception algorithms to improve obstacle avoidance performance so robot arms can accurately perceive their surroundings. The proposed method can provide valuable references for research on autonomous robot refueling. This technology has potential uses in comparable situations, such as industrial assembly and material handling. We intend to investigate these applications further to confirm its versatility and usefulness across various fields.

Acknowledgment. This work was supported by the Basic Research Program of Shenyang Institute of Automation, Chinese Academy of Sciences (No. 2022JC3K06).

References

1. Civil Aviation Administration of China. Aircraft hydrant dispenser. MH/T 6100-2013 (2013)
2. Kurazume, R., Hasegawa, T.: A new index of serial-link manipulator performance combining dynamic manipulability and manipulating force ellipsoids. IEEE Trans. Rob. **22**(5), 1022–1028 (2006)

3. Tamizi, M.G., Yaghoubi, M., Najjaran, H.: A review of recent trend in motion planning of industrial robots. Int. J. Intell. Robot. Appl. 1–22 (2023)

4. Liu, S., Liu, P.: A review of motion planning algorithms for robotic arm systems. In: Chew, E., et al. (eds.) RiTA 2020. LNME, pp. 56–66. Springer, Singapore (2021). https://doi.org/10.1007/978-981-16-4803-8_7

5. Li, Z., Li, S.: A sparse optimization-based control method for manipulator with simultaneous potential energy minimization. IEEE Trans. Circuits Syst. II Express Briefs **68**(6), 2062–2066 (2020)

6. Yang, C., Ye, W., Li, Q.: Review of the performance optimization of parallel manipulators. Mech. Mach. Theory **170**, 104725 (2022)

7. Yoshikawa, T.: Manipulability of robotic mechanisms. Int. J. Robot. Res. **4**(2), 3–9 (1985)

8. Yoshikawa, T.: Dynamic manipulability of robot manipulators. Trans. Soc. Instrum. Control Eng. **21**(9), 970–975 (1985)

9. Rosenstein, M.T., Grupen, R.A.: Velocity-dependent dynamic manipulability. In: Proceedings 2002 IEEE International Conference on Robotics and Automation (Cat. No. 02CH37292), vol. 3, pp. 2424–2429. IEEE (2002)

10. Dinas, S., Bañón, J.M.: A literature review of bounding volumes hierarchy focused on collision detection. Ingeniería y competitividad **17**(1), 49–62 (2015)

11. Jingjing, X., Liu, Z., Yang, C., Li, L., Pei, Y.: A pseudo-distance algorithm for collision detection of manipulators using convex-plane-polygons-based representation. Robot. Comput.-Integr. Manuf. **66**, 101993 (2020)

12. Ruan, S., Wang, X., Chirikjian, G.S.: Collision detection for unions of convex bodies with smooth boundaries using closed-form contact space parameterization. IEEE Robot. Autom. Lett. **7**(4), 9485–9492 (2022)

13. Boyd, S.P., Vandenberghe, L.: Convex Optimization. Cambridge University Press, Cambridge (2004)

14. Ruan, S., Chirikjian, G.S.: Closed-form Minkowski sums of convex bodies with smooth positively curved boundaries. Comput.-Aided Des. **143**, 103133 (2022)

15. Lynch, K.M., Park, F.C.: Modern Robotics. Cambridge University Press, Cambridge (2017)

16. Nishihara, R., Lessard, L., Recht, B., Packard, A., Jordan, M.: A general analysis of the convergence of Admm. In: International Conference on Machine Learning, pp. 343–352. PMLR (2015)

Vision-Based Categorical Object Pose Estimation and Manipulation

Qiwei Meng[1,2], Jianfeng Liao[1,2], Shao Jun[1,2,3], Nuo Xu[1,2], Zeming Xu[1,2],
Yinan Sun[1,2], Yao Sun[1,2], Shiqiang Zhu[1,2], Jason Gu[4], and Wei Song[1,2(✉)]

[1] Center for Intelligent Robotics, Zhejiang Lab, Hangzhou, China
weisong@zhejianglab.com
[2] Zhejiang Engineering Research Center for Intelligent Robotics, Hangzhou, China
[3] School of Mechanical Engineering, Zhejiang University, Hangzhou, China
[4] Department of Electrical and Computer Engineering, Dalhousie University,
Halifax, Canada

Abstract. Object manipulation and environment interaction are of great
significance for intelligent robots, especially service robots working under
unstructured household and office scenarios. This paper proposes a novel
approach for categorical unseen object grasping and manipulation. Different from recently popular end-to-end reinforcement learning methods,
we develop models for geometric primitive abstraction of target objects,
and accordingly estimate their pose as well as generate task-orientated
grasp points. Such design emphasizes visual perception in guiding robotic
manipulation, thereby enhancing model interpretability and reliability
during implementation. In addition, we also conduct object grasping
experiments both under simulation and real-world settings, which further
verify the effectiveness and superiority of our method.

Keywords: Robotic Manipulation · Object Representation · Pose
Estimation

1 Introduction

As technology advances, intelligent robots become able to interact with their
environment rather than just perceive it [8], which gradually evolves into extensive applications ranging from autonomous driving [35], tour guiding [7], space
exploration [12] and household services [26]. These robotic applications have the
potential to revolutionize many aspects of human lives [11,22]. However, within
these applications, the object 3D perception and manipulation are acknowledged
to be the common difficulty, especially under unstructured household and office
scenarios, limiting the widespread implementation of robotics technology [28].

Generally, object perception and manipulation consist of four major steps [8]:
1) object localization; 2) pose estimation; 3) grasp detection; 4) motion planning.
Although reinforcement learning once leads the trend of end-to-end networks to
generate robotic motion from raw scene images [16,19], these methods are widely
concerned for their robustness and reliability in real-world applications [8,14].
Therefore, we follow the traditional technical route and design a vision-based

H. Yang et al. (Eds.): ICIRA 2023, LNAI 14267, pp. 139–150, 2023.
https://doi.org/10.1007/978-981-99-6483-3_13

categorical object manipulation scheme. In the main framework, we apply the off-shelf Mask-RCNN [13] and RRT-connect [15] algorithms for object localization and robot arm motion planning respectively, while major attention is focused on the object pose estimation and grasp points generation, which are also regarded as core algorithms influencing the overall performance of object manipulation [8, 14].

Different from 2D perception like object detection and segmentation, pose estimation involves information processing in high-dimensional 3D space, thereby being more sensitive to background variations and scene cluttering [21,24]. Additionally, in household and office environments, the exact CAD models of most target objects are unavailable beforehand [29], so instance-level approaches applying rigid model transformation for pose estimation become less effective [28], which further increases its difficulty. Besides, another challenge is that the grasp points cannot be preset without object CAD models, and they are supposed to be dynamically generated for various manipulation tasks [20].

To resolve the aforementioned difficulties and promote robotic development, we propose a novel approach for 3D object perception and grasp points generation. Its semantic illustration is shown in Fig. 1. Through predefining geometric primitives as categorical object representations, the common objects in office and household scenarios can be abstracted as variable-size geometric primitives and their affine deformation [10]. This module bridges target unseen objects with their geometric characteristics, so accordingly we can construct the approximate CAD model for target object in a real-time manner. Afterwards, the constructed model could be applied for scene object feature extraction, pose estimation, and grasp points generation. The proposal and representation of object geometric primitives significantly contribute to the generalization ability and robustness of our method, particularly under unstructured environments.

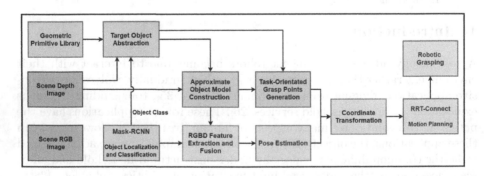

Fig. 1. Semantic Illustration of Our Approach.

Overall, the primary contributions of this paper are summarized as follows:

1. We develop a novel approach for object 3D perception and grasp generation, which has great potential in robotic manipulation under unstructured household and office scenarios;

2. To improve model robustness and generalization ability on categorical unseen objects, we propose the concept of geometric primitive abstraction, which can construct approximate CAD models for unseen objects in a real-time manner;
3. For different manipulation tasks, we design the dynamic grasp points generation scheme based on the functionality and approximate model of target objects.
4. We conducted a series of robotic grasping and object manipulation experiments in both simulation and real-world environments, and the results can prove the effectiveness of our vision-based manipulation method.

2   Related Work

2.1   Object Grasping and Manipulation

Object grasping and manipulation is a significant capability for robots [1], as it allows them to interact with their surroundings similar to humans, and it has important implications for a variety of fields, from intelligent manufacturing to household service [7,26,35].

This technology mainly involves robotic perception, planning and control [8]. Some reinforcement-learning methods attempt to resolve them in an end-to-end manner and have achieved satisfying results in simulation environments [18,25,34], but their robustness and generalization ability in practical applications are widely concerned [8,14,28]. Hence, to improve the reliability of manipulation under real-world scenarios, the preferable technical route divides this task into several substeps [8,14]: object detection and pose estimation for target localization in image and camera coordinate systems respectively; grasp detection to generate grasp points based on robotic gripper and object properties; motion planning and arm control for grasp execution. The distributed approach not only enhances the overall interpretability and robustness, but also makes it much easier to debug and fine-tune the sub-module using prior expert knowledge [15], especially in grasp points generation and motion planning. Following this technical route, our approach provides targeted optimizations in the perception section to enable robots to perform more complex and diverse manipulation tasks.

2.2   Category-Level Object Pose Estimation

According to the availability of preknown CAD models for target objects, pose estimation algorithms are generally divided into instance-level and category-level [9,28,29]. It is acknowledged that under unstructured household and office scenarios, creating exact CAD models for each potential target could be time-consuming and even impossible. Therefore, category-level approaches are considered to be more effective and promising in robotic applications [9,29].

As a developing frontier research field, there has not formed a widely recognized and adopted method [9,24]. Some researchers [31,32] attempt to establish large datasets and resolve categorical object pose estimation through an end-to-end neural network. Wang [29] proposes the concept of Normalized Object Coordinate Space (NOCS) and combines Umeyama algorithms to recover object pose, which imposes geometric constraints in network training. SPD [27] and SGPA [5] establish standard categorical models as templates for pose estimation. However, none of the aforementioned methods combine categorical object pose estimation with robotic grasping, so their performance in real-world applications is questioned [8]. Additionally, on the basis of categorical prior models, we propose geometric primitive for scene objects abstraction, which not only enhances the generalization ability of our approach, but also facilitates object grasp points generation and manipulation.

2.3   Grasp Detection

Grasp detection is defined as recognizing the gripper pose or grasp points for object manipulation [17]. It is a complex process that involves analyzing the geometry and properties of target objects, as well as the shape and size of the robotic gripper [23]. Typically, there are three commonly-used approaches for this task: empirical methods presetting grasp points for known and familiar objects in advance [2]; analytical methods combining kinematics and dynamics formulation for object point cloud analyzing [23]; learning-based methods applying deep learning and reinforcement learning for end-to-end grasp detection [6]. In this paper, the robotic end effector is parallel jaws, and we will incorporate empirical knowledge and force-closure for task-specific grasp points generation of previously unseen objects.

3   Method

3.1   Method Overview

This paper presents a novel vision-based approach for categorical object pose estimation and manipulation. As illustrated in Fig. 2, given the scene RGBD image, the off-the-shelf Mask-RCNN is firstly applied for target object detection, segmentation and classification. Subsequently, the point cloud of target object is abstracted into predefined geometric primitives, which will then be leveraged for object representation after size variation and affine deformation. On the one hand, the refined object model can be used for task-specific grasp points generation, and on the other hand, it is combined with the cropped object image for RGBD feature extraction and pose estimation. Lastly, the generated grasp points are transformed into robot coordinate system, and RRT-connect algorithms are applied for motion planning and grasp execution. Details about primary model components and innovations are discussed in following sections.

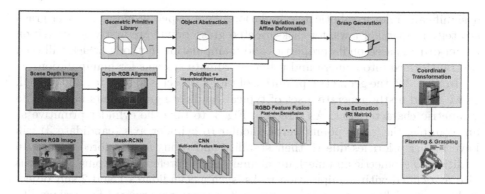

Fig. 2. Detailed Model Design and Structure.

3.2 Geometric Primitive Abstraction

It is widely acknowledged that creating prior CAD models of individual or categorical objects for pose estimation and grasping could be fairly time-consuming, while end-to-end methods are not robust and reliable, thereby limiting widespread applications of robotic manipulation. Therefore, to enhance the robustness and generalization ability of robotic grasping under unstructured environments, we propose the geometric primitive representation for target object abstraction in our paper.

To be specific, we predefine a geometric primitive library including 4 types of primitives: sphere, cuboid, cylinder and cone. For common office and household items, they can be abstracted into a certain primitive aforementioned, like cylinder for water bottle, cuboid for boxed milk and notebook, sphere for orange and sport ball, etc. Accordingly, by combining 2D shapes and classification of target unseen objects, we could identify their most similar primitives from the geometric primitive library. The selected primitives can generally represent geometric characteristics of target objects, but their sizes and surface details need to be fine-tuned. Therefore, we propose to apply the segmented object point cloud for size estimation through RANSAC clustering algorithms, while for surface refinement, a multi-layer perceptron is designed to calculate pointwise deformation offsets. With size variation and affine deformation, the fine-tuned geometric primitive can be applied for object pose estimation and manipulation in the following steps.

As a broadly applicable module, the geometric primitives abstraction enables unseen object representation in a real-time manner, which helps robots form a general impression of target objects while avoiding time-intensive prior model construction.

3.3 Grasp Points Generation

Grasp points generation is supposed to ensure the stability, task compatibility and adaptability of object grasping under various scenes, thereby performing a significant role in robotic manipulation. This paper proposes a novel grasp strategy for parallel jaws, for task-oriented grasp points are firstly generated on target object based on its properties and manipulation methods, which will then be transformed into camera and robot coordinate systems for manipulation.

In Sect. 3.2, the geometric primitive of target object is abstracted and refined, so we could firstly generate a set of typical candidate grasp points based on its geometric characteristics. As shown in Fig. 3, to take the cylinder primitive as an example, the grasp points perpendicular to cylinder axis (candidate 3) will have higher priorities due to their stability and robustness in force-closure. In addition to geometric and mechanical analysis, the preferred grasping strategy is also associated with manipulation tasks, such as candidates 1 and 2 suit object picking and delivering, while candidate 3 is more appropriate for actions like water pouring. These correlations and grasp selection are fairly complicated, so we apply a large language model (LLM) with prompt learning [3] for this process. Our approach combines the advantages of empirical knowledge and physical analysis for grasp generation, which ensures the final grasping strategy is reliable and appropriate for specific tasks.

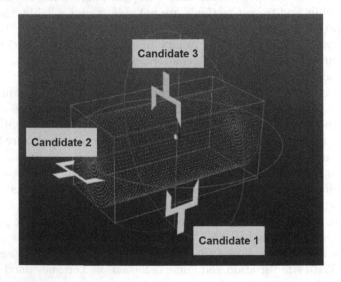

Fig. 3. Illustration of Grasp Points Generation on Cylinder Primitive.

3.4   Pose Estimation

After determining robotic grasp points under object coordinate system, one last step before manipulation is to transform grasp pose into robotic coordinate system, so end-effector can execute grasping accordingly.

To achieve this, we propose key-point matching and point cloud registration approach for object pose estimation. Specifically, a pointnet-like model [20] is trained to extract geometric features of target object through its abstracted primitive, while meantime convolutional neural networks (CNN) will be applied for object appearance feature extraction from cropped RGB image, which are then fused together for target object representation. Afterwards, we design a multi-layer perceptron with object fused features as inputs, and it will output a correspondence matrix of object key points between scene point cloud and abstracted primitive, which can be applied to identify the matching points between camera and object coordinate systems. The final object pose can be calculated by regressing optimal solution for Eq. (1)

$$Error(R, t) = \sum_{i=0}^{N} \|p_i - (R \times p'_i + t)\|^2 \tag{1}$$

where N is the total number of preset matching points; p_i and p'_i are i^{th} matching points on scene point cloud and abstracted primitive, respectively; R and t are rotation matrix and translation vector of target object. Through applying the least-squared fitting algorithms, the R and t are refined to minimize the total error, and the optimal R, t values are used as object pose.

4   Experiment

4.1   Experimental Setting

In this paper, the hardware environments for model training are 24 Intel(R) Xeon(R) Gold 6248R CPU @ 3.00 GHz and 1 T V100S-PCIE-32GB GPU.

Additionally, to verify the effectiveness of our proposed approach, we design elaborate experiments both under simulation and real-world scenarios. For simulation experiments, the OMG-Planner [30] is utilized to construct virtual environments, where various synthetic objects from ShapeNet [4] and YCB-Video [33] datasets are added into it, together with the KINOVA® Gen3 as robot arm to evaluate model performance. As for the real-world experiments, we apply RealSense D455 as "eye-to-hand" camera for sensing data acquisition, and KINOVA® Gen3 as robotic platform for object grasping and manipulation.

It is noteworthy that the main purpose of these experiments are investigating our innovations in pose estimation and grasp generation, so off-the-shelf Mask-RCNN and RRT-connect are deployed for object localization and motion planning, respectively.

4.2   Simulation Experiments

Under OMG-Planner simulation environments, we conduct robotic manipulation experiments 1000 times for 20 categorical unseen objects in four basic geometries. During grasping, we apply ground truth values for target objects detection and segmentation, then accordingly our approach can estimate pose and grasp points for these objects.

The experiments results are summarized in Table 1, and it is manifest that our vision-based manipulation approach achieves satisfying performance for most daily objects, especially the cuboid-shaped and sphere-shape ones, while for cone-shaped objects, the primitive abstraction and grasp points generation processes are fairly difficult, causing the degradation of overall model performance. Partial visualization results of simulation experiments are demonstrated in Fig. 4.

Table 1. Quantitative Results for Simulation Experiments.

Geometry Basis	Object	Test Times	Success Times	Success Rate(%)
Cylinder	master_chef_can	50	42	84
	tomato_soup_can	50	38	76
	tuna_fish_can	50	41	82
	mug_YCB	50	27	54
	mug_ShapeNet	50	32	64
	bottle_Shapenet	50	47	94
	coke_can	50	41	82
	skinny_can	50	47	94
	pitcher_base	50	44	88
Cuboid	cracker_box	50	44	88
	sugar_box	50	40	80
	wood_block	50	37	74
	pudding_box	50	40	80
	bleach_cleanser	50	38	76
	mustard_bottle	50	39	78
Cone	large_clamp	50	17	34
	extra_large_clamp	50	22	44
Sphere	sport_ball	50	48	96
	tennis_ball	50	47	94
	ocean_ball	50	44	88
Total		1000	775	77.5

4.3 Real-World Experiments

In simulation experiments, we generally verify the effectiveness of our method for unseen objects manipulation. However, the sim-to-real has long been considered as one of the significant problems in robotics and engineering applications. Therefore, we further deploy our algorithms and evaluate them in real-world environments. Since cone-shaped objects are unusual in daily life, and they have been proven difficult for grasping in simulation tests, we only conduct experiments for cylinder-shaped, sphere-shaped and cuboid-shaped objects. The results

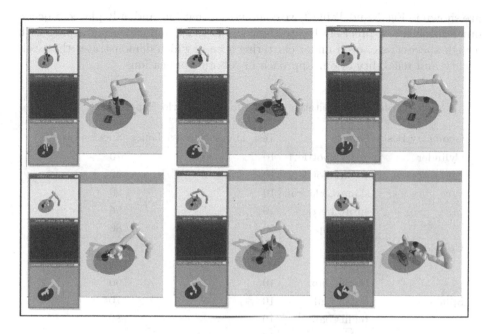

Fig. 4. Visualization of Simulation Experiments.

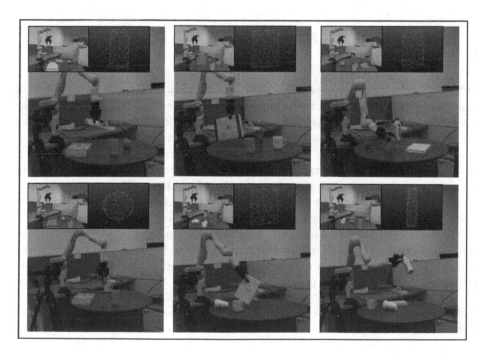

Fig. 5. Visualization of Real-World Experiments.

are shown in Fig. 5 and Table 2, we could notice that for randomly placed objects, our approach can precisely locate them in 3D space and execute grasping with a high success rate, even under cluttering scenes, which demonstrates the availability and reliability of our approach in robotic applications.

Table 2. Quantitative Results for Real-World Experiments.

Geometry Basis	Object	Test Times	Success Times	Success Rate(%)
Cylinder	yogurt_bottle_1	10	7	70
	yogurt_bottle_2	10	6	60
	skinny_coke_can	10	8	80
	sprite_bottle	10	5	50
	water_cup	10	8	80
Cuboid	book_1	10	4	40
	book_2	10	6	60
	biscuit_box	10	6	60
Sphere	ocean_ball	10	7	70
	tennis_ball	10	8	80
Total		100	65	65

5 Conclusion

To conclude, we propose a novel vision-based approach for categorical objects manipulation under unstructured environments. Different from end-to-end reinforcement learning methods, we introduce geometric primitive abstraction of target objects in model design, which significantly facilitates grasp points generation and pose estimation through forming a general impression of the target in a real-time manner. To evaluate its effectiveness, we conduct robotic grasping experiments both under simulation and real-world settings. Their results demonstrate that our approach can precisely estimate pose and generate task-orientated grasp points for target unseen objects, even with heavy scene cluttering.

This research performs a critical role in promoting the widespread applications and implementations of robotic manipulation. Following it, future works can further explore how to represent complex compound objects and combine object affordance for grasp points generation.

Acknowledgment. Supported by Key Research Project of Zhejiang Lab (No. G2021NB0AL03).

References

1. Babin, V., Gosselin, C.: Mechanisms for robotic grasping and manipulation. Annual Review of Control, Robotics, and Autonomous Systems **4**, 573–593 (2021)
2. Bohg, J., Morales, A., Asfour, T., Kragic, D.: Data-driven grasp synthesis-a survey. IEEE Trans. Rob. **30**(2), 289–309 (2013)
3. Brown, T., et al.: Language models are few-shot learners. Adv. Neural. Inf. Process. Syst. **33**, 1877–1901 (2020)
4. Chang, A.X., et al.: Shapenet: an information-rich 3d model repository. arXiv preprint arXiv:1512.03012 (2015)
5. Chen, K., Dou, Q.: Sgpa: structure-guided prior adaptation for category-level 6d object pose estimation. In: Proceedings of the IEEE/CVF International Conference on Computer Vision, pp. 2773–2782 (2021)
6. Chu, F.J., Vela, P.A.: Deep grasp: detection and localization of grasps with deep neural networks. arXiv preprint arXiv:1802.00520 1 (2018)
7. Diallo, A.D., Gobee, S., Durairajah, V.: Autonomous tour guide robot using embedded system control. Procedia Comput. Sci. **76**, 126–133 (2015)
8. Du, G., Wang, K., Lian, S., Zhao, K.: Vision-based robotic grasping from object localization, object pose estimation to grasp estimation for parallel grippers: a review. Artif. Intell. Rev. **54**(3), 1677–1734 (2021)
9. Fan, Z., Zhu, Y., He, Y., Sun, Q., Liu, H., He, J.: Deep learning on monocular object pose detection and tracking: a comprehensive overview. ACM Comput. Surv. **55**(4), 1–40 (2022)
10. Filonik, D., Bednarz, T., Rittenbruch, M., Foth, M.: Glance: generalized geometric primitives and transformations for information visualization in ar/vr environments. In: Proceedings of the 15th ACM SIGGRAPH Conference on Virtual-Reality Continuum and Its Applications in Industry-Volume 1, pp. 461–468 (2016)
11. Gonzalez-Aguirre, J.A., et al.: Service robots: trends and technology. Appl. Sci. **11**(22), 10702 (2021)
12. Gul, F., Mir, I., Abualigah, L., Sumari, P.: Multi-robot space exploration: an augmented arithmetic approach. IEEE Access **9**, 107738–107750 (2021)
13. He, K., Gkioxari, G., Dollár, P., Girshick, R.: Mask R-CNN. In: Proceedings of the IEEE International Conference on Computer Vision, pp. 2961–2969 (2017)
14. Kleeberger, K., Bormann, R., Kraus, W., Huber, M.F.: A survey on learning-based robotic grasping. Current Robot. Rep. **1**, 239–249 (2020)
15. Kuffner, J.J., LaValle, S.M.: Rrt-connect: an efficient approach to single-query path planning. In: Proceedings 2000 ICRA. Millennium Conference. IEEE International Conference on Robotics and Automation. Symposia Proceedings (Cat. No. 00CH37065), vol. 2, pp. 995–1001. IEEE (2000)
16. Lobbezoo, A., Qian, Y., Kwon, H.J.: Reinforcement learning for pick and place operations in robotics: a survey. Robotics **10**(3), 105 (2021)
17. Mahler, J., et al.: Dex-net 2.0: deep learning to plan robust grasps with synthetic point clouds and analytic grasp metrics. arXiv preprint arXiv:1703.09312 (2017)
18. Matas, J., James, S., Davison, A.J.: Sim-to-real reinforcement learning for deformable object manipulation. In: Conference on Robot Learning, pp. 734–743. PMLR (2018)
19. Mohammed, M.Q., Chung, K.L., Chyi, C.S.: Review of deep reinforcement learning-based object grasping: techniques, open challenges, and recommendations. IEEE Access **8**, 178450–178481 (2020)

20. Ni, P., Zhang, W., Zhu, X., Cao, Q.: Pointnet++ grasping: learning an end-to-end spatial grasp generation algorithm from sparse point clouds. In: 2020 IEEE International Conference on Robotics and Automation (ICRA), pp. 3619–3625. IEEE (2020)
21. O'Mahony, N., Campbell, S., Krpalkova, L., Riordan, D., Walsh, J., Murphy, A., Ryan, C.: Computer vision for 3d perception: a review. In: Intelligent Systems and Applications: Proceedings of the 2018 Intelligent Systems Conference (IntelliSys) Volume 2, pp. 788–804. Springer (2019)
22. Rosete, A., Soares, B., Salvadorinho, J., Reis, J., Amorim, M.: Service robots in the hospitality industry: an exploratory literature review. In: Exploring Service Science: 10th International Conference, IESS 2020, Porto, Portugal, February 5–7, 2020, Proceedings 10, pp. 174–186. Springer (2020)
23. Sahbani, A., El-Khoury, S., Bidaud, P.: An overview of 3d object grasp synthesis algorithms. Robot. Auton. Syst. **60**(3), 326–336 (2012)
24. Sahin, C., Garcia-Hernando, G., Sock, J., Kim, T.K.: A review on object pose recovery: from 3d bounding box detectors to full 6d pose estimators. Image Vis. Comput. **96**, 103898 (2020)
25. Sharif, M., Erdogmus, D., Amato, C., Padir, T.: End-to-end grasping policies for human-in-the-loop robots via deep reinforcement learning. In: 2021 IEEE International Conference on Robotics and Automation (ICRA), pp. 2768–2774. IEEE (2021)
26. Thosar, M., Zug, S., Skaria, A.M., Jain, A.: A review of knowledge bases for service robots in household environments. In: AIC, pp. 98–110 (2018)
27. Tian, M., Ang, M.H., Lee, G.H.: Shape prior deformation for categorical 6d object pose and size estimation. In: Computer Vision-ECCV 2020: 16th European Conference, Glasgow, UK, August 23–28, 2020, Proceedings, Part XXI 16, pp. 530–546. Springer (2020)
28. Wang, C., et al.: Densefusion: 6d object pose estimation by iterative dense fusion. In: Proceedings of the IEEE/CVF Conference on Computer Vision and Pattern Recognition, pp. 3343–3352 (2019)
29. Wang, H., Sridhar, S., Huang, J., Valentin, J., Song, S., Guibas, L.J.: Normalized object coordinate space for category-level 6d object pose and size estimation. In: Proceedings of the IEEE/CVF Conference on Computer Vision and Pattern Recognition, pp. 2642–2651 (2019)
30. Wang, L., Xiang, Y., Fox, D.: Manipulation trajectory optimization with online grasp synthesis and selection. arXiv preprint arXiv:1911.10280 (2019)
31. Wang, Y., Tan, X., Yang, Y., Liu, X., Ding, E., Zhou, F., Davis, L.S.: 3d pose estimation for fine-grained object categories. In: Proceedings of the European Conference on Computer Vision (ECCV) Workshops (2018)
32. Wang, Z., Li, W., Kao, Y., Zou, D., Wang, Q., Ahn, M., Hong, S.: Hcr-net: a hybrid of classification and regression network for object pose estimation. In: IJCAI, pp. 1014–1020 (2018)
33. Xiang, Y., Schmidt, T., Narayanan, V., Fox, D.: Posecnn: a convolutional neural network for 6d object pose estimation in cluttered scenes. arXiv preprint arXiv:1711.00199 (2017)
34. Yuan, W., Hang, K., Kragic, D., Wang, M.Y., Stork, J.A.: End-to-end nonprehensile rearrangement with deep reinforcement learning and simulation-to-reality transfer. Robot. Auton. Syst. **119**, 119–134 (2019)
35. Yurtsever, E., Lambert, J., Carballo, A., Takeda, K.: A survey of autonomous driving: common practices and emerging technologies. IEEE access **8**, 58443–58469 (2020)

Animal-Like Eye Vision Assisted Locomotion of a Quadruped Based on Reinforcement Learning

Xiaojian Wei, Qing Wei[✉], Honglei An, Zhitong Zhang, Junwei Yu, and Hongxu Ma

National University of Defense Technology, Changsha, China
wien1993@163.com

Abstract. The legged robot is only satisfied with walking on flat ground, it obviously does not take advantage of its locomotion performance, especially in the real environment where the robot may encounter various complex terrains. It is a highly nonlinear system for the quadruped robot, so it is very hard to model the dynamics accurately and achieve high performance locomotion control. In recent years, with the emerging of reinforcement learning, there are more possibilities to improve the locomotion ability of legged robots. To address the problem of how to improve the ability of a quadruped robot to negotiate complex terrains, this paper proposes a method to provide an animal-like eye for a quadruped robot to obtain a control strategy based on reinforcement learning. The method uses only the terrain information in front of the quadruped robot as the input state of the robot, and uses a curriculum training method to make the quadruped robot negotiate complex terrains such as the stairway terrain and the gap terrain constructed in the simulation environment smoothly. Compared with the motion strategy based on proprioception only, the vision-assisted motion strategy is safer and smoother, and we utilize less and simpler visual information than other methods based on visual information.

Keywords: Quadruped Robot · Reinforcement Learning · Complex terrains

1 Introduction

Legged robots make their capability of terrain crossing superior to that of wheeled and tracked robots, with their selectable discrete landing points. However, this unique advantage of legged robots has not been explored in many previous studies fully. We suggest that studying the locomotion control of legged robots only on relatively flat terrain deviates from the original purpose of developing legged robots and does not exploit the potential of their powerful capability of traversing. In our real-world environment, there are many kinds of complex terrain in urban environments, such as stairs and gullies, besides relatively flat and continuous terrain. Many universities and research institutions are working to improve the locomotion of the robots, so the ability of robots to negotiate such terrains is a major focus of our work, improving the capability should be paid more attention.

© The Author(s), under exclusive license to Springer Nature Singapore Pte Ltd. 2023
H. Yang et al. (Eds.): ICIRA 2023, LNAI 14267, pp. 151–161, 2023.
https://doi.org/10.1007/978-981-99-6483-3_14

In the study of quadruped robots, MIT has already shown us the powerful locomotion of quadruped robots by using a model predictive control approach [1]. Many research institutions have implemented some human and animal-like behaviors based on this approach, but the approach relies on building complex models. In the last few years, with the rise of reinforcement learning, especially deep reinforcement learning, which benefits from the absence of the need for accurate modeling, there has been a rapid development in the field of quadruped robot locomotion control. The ETH Robotics Lab has made amazing achievements with reinforcement learning control methods for quadruped robots [2–4]. From the research of ETH, it is easy to find that providing visual information to the robot can greatly improve the robot's movement ability. During the training of the control strategy, they collected information about the terrain around the four legs for the quadruped robot, so that the robot learned to walk on complex terrain. Nowadays, it is common for robots to perform stable walking on flat terrains, but there are more complex terrains in the human living environment, such as the common stairs and gap terrains. Although various advanced control networks based on reinforcement learning have been proposed by many scholars [5–9], we believe that adding visual information to quadruped robots is essential to achieve more efficient locomotion in real-world environments while ensuring their locomotion safety (e.g., reduce injury phenomena such as falls and bumps). Currently, the use of external sensors to provide terrain information for robots and to obtain control strategies has gradually become a new direction of research by scholars [4, 10–13]. However, the method they used was to sample the elevation near the robot's four legs or to directly use the camera frame as the robot's state input, which we believe aggravates the instability of the input state and computational burden.

Fig. 1. In the simulation environment, the quadruped robot uses visual information to pass through the terrain with a step size of 0.3 m * 0.15 m.

Compared to sampling elevation information around the four legs of a quadruped robot, our proposed method requires less information and is simpler in that we only sample topographic information at the location of the robot's front legs, similar to the visual information acquired by animals, which greatly reduces the need for vision equipment and computing power. The yellow points appearing in Fig. 1 are the scanned points of the terrain in front of the robot. Based on reinforcement learning, without changing the overall structure of the network, we obtained the control strategies without and with visual information, respectively. We compared the control performance of the two strategies in a simulation environment with different terrains, as shown in Fig. 1 and Fig. 2, and verified that the vision-assisted control strategy performs better in terms of safety and reliability.

Fig. 2. In the simulation environment, the quadruped robot uses visual information to pass through the gap with a width of 0.2 m.

The main contributions of this paper are that we trained the available control network to enable the quadruped robot to travel smoothly through complex terrain using only the terrain information in front of the quadruped robot and that we consider success rate and number of bumps as the specific metrics to evaluate the ability of a quadruped robot to negotiate the complex terrain in this work [14].

2 Related Work

Whether a quadruped robot can successfully pass through complex terrains has been a hot issue for scholars to study. Both classical approaches based on models and reinforcement learning methods have made a lot of achievements, driving the research on the control of quadruped robots forward.

Model-based Predictive Control (MPC). Promising results have been achieved using model predictive control through complex terrain. MIT used MPC to enable Cheetah 3 to jump over obstacles by simplifying the dynamics to construct a model [1]. Ruben Grandia et al. proposed a multilayer control framework that combines control barrier functions (CBF) with model predictive control (MPC) to achieve a quadruped robot walking on stepping stones [15]. The ANYmal robot [16] achieved this by using a model based on an inverted pendulum model [17] to optimize parametric controllers and planning to move. Qi et al. used a model predictive control-based approach to accomplish the task of a quadruped robot climbing stairs by visually acquiring the structural information of the stairs, calculating kinematically feasible velocity commands, and then selecting the footprint location based on the stair conditions and velocity commands [18]. However, these methods not only require accurate modeling of the real environment, but also involve a large amount of computation and parameter tuning, which is obviously not friendly enough.

Based on reinforcement learning without visualization. Model-free reinforcement learning allows a robot to learn control strategies over complex terrain. Most current approaches rely only on robot proprioceptive states and do not incorporate visual information. Lee et al. proposed to incorporate proprioceptive feedback into motion control to build a reinforcement learning control network that enables a quadrupedal robot to continuously learn new skills and generalize to new environments through domain randomization using sequential models [3], cheat learning, and automated course training. They deployed the trained control network on ANYmal robot to complete the DARPA Underground Challenge [19–21]. Tan et al. introduced a hierarchical learning framework to design a trajectory generator guided by the robot's pose, trained a control strategy by using reinforcement learning methods, and then the trajectory generator performed inverse kinematics to calculate the foot trajectory based on the output of the control strategy to better adapt to the terrain [22] A. Kumar et al. proposed a fast motor adaptive (RMA) algorithm to pass complex terrain in a realistic environment [23]. Although their proposed method also possesses some robustness, the reality given by them shows that there is some damage to the robot, which we expect to avoid.

Based on reinforcement learning with visualization. Recent research has added visual information to the state input of the robot with good results. Antonio Loquercio et al. proposed the cross-modal monitoring (CMS) algorithm, which trains a vision module that predicts upcoming terrain in the real world through a reinforcement learning approach, and then uses the predicted terrain information as input to train a control strategy [12]. However, this method is prone to fall and cause damage to the robot when it is first deployed due to the poor training of the vision module. This is a situation we would like to avoid. Takahiro Miki et al. proposed a control method for quadruped robots that combines external sensing and proprioception [4]. They used an attention-based cyclic encoder that integrates proprioceptive and external sensing inputs. The encoder was trained end-to-end to obtain a motion controller with high robustness and high speed. However, they provide the quadruped robot with information around the four legs, which increases the amount of information and is more difficult. In this work, we obtained a strategy that successfully avoids collisions when passing through step terrain by using the elevation information in front of the robot as a state input, and trained a strategy that can pass through gap terrain in the same way.

3   Method

3.1   Reinforcement Learning Framework

We formulate the interaction of a quadruped robot with its environment as a partially observable Markov decision process (POMDP) defined by a tuple (S, A, P, R, γ), where $s \in S$ is the set of states, $a \in A$ is the set of actions, $P(s'|s, a)$ is the transfer function of states for a given action, R is the reward function, and γ is the discount factor. The objective of reinforcement learning is to find an optimal strategy π^* that maximizes the expected reward (the sum of discounted rewards):

$$\pi^* = \arg\max_{\pi} \mathbb{E}[\sum_{t=0}^{\infty} \gamma^t r(s_t, a_t)] \tag{1}$$

Observation Space. In this work, we take the robot's proprioceptive state and a privileged elevation map containing height samples from the 0.5 m × 1.0 m grid in front of the robot as input. For instance, at time t, the state space consists of the following components, joint position $q_t \in \mathbb{R}^{12}$, joint velocity $\dot{q}_t \in \mathbb{R}^{12}$, previous joint position $q_{t-1} \in \mathbb{R}^{12}$, base body linear velocity $v \in \mathbb{R}^3$, base body angular velocity $\omega \in \mathbb{R}^3$, projected gravity vector $g \in \mathbb{R}^3$, command velocity $(v_x, v_y, \omega_z) \in \mathbb{R}^3$ and terrain elevation information $H \in \mathbb{R}^{100}$.

Action Space. The output of the control strategy consists of the joint target position $q \in \mathbb{R}^{12}$ which is used as the target position for the PD motor controller, which is converted to torque $\tau = K_p(\hat{q} - q) + K_d(\hat{\dot{q}} - \dot{q})$ by the PD controller, where K_p and K_d are manually set gains respectively and the target joint speed $\hat{\dot{q}}$ is set to 0.

Figure 3 shows the structure of the training network we used.

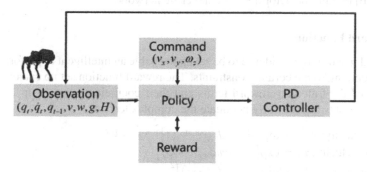

Fig. 3. The training network architecture used in this work

3.2 Training Curriculum

In the Isaac Gym simulation environment [24, 25], we constructed complex terrains commonly found in daily life, namely a staircase terrain with a width of 0.3 m and a height of 0.15 m as shown in Fig. 1 and a gap terrain with a width range of 0.05–0.2 m as shown in Fig. 2. The object in the simulation training is the Unitree A1 quadruped robot. In order to effectively train usable control strategies that allow the robot to negotiate staircase terrain and gap terrain, we designed a course training. Similar to the growth of human, our job was first to get the robot to learn to walk on flat terrain. Then we set the difficulty (stair terrain refers to the height of the steps and gap terrain refers to the width of the gap) to gradually increase so that the robots learn to smoothly negotiate the set terrains. The highest difficulty level we set in the simulation environment was 15 cm for the height of the steps and 20 cm for the width of the gap to train the robot to adapt to the complex terrain. Although the difficulty level can be increased, we are not aiming for the limit, but we need the quadruped robot to pass through the complex terrain safely and smoothly. Figure 4 shows a snapshot of the quadruped robot crossing a 20-cm wide gap.

Fig. 4. Snapshot of the robot crosses a gap with a width of 20 cm

3.3 Network Architecture

Our neural network structure is an A2C network, which consists of two parts, an actor network and a critic network. They are designed as a multilayer perceptron (MLP) networks with a structure of (512 × 256 × 64). Our system takes the sensor data as input, trains the network to obtain the optimal control strategy, and then outputs the desired joint positions for each actor. We use the Proximal Policy Optimization (PPO) method [26] to train the actor network and critic network.

3.4 Reward Function

The reward function is considered to be set up to enable an intelligent to perform motion control according to the certain constraints. The reward function set up can express our purpose, and the following reward terms and their coefficients are set up in order to enable the robot to successfully negotiate the complex terrain,

- Linear velocity: $r_1 = \exp\left[-4\left(cmd_{v_{xy}} - V_{xy}\right)\right]^2$, $r_2 = V_z^2$
- Angular velocity: $r_3 = \exp\left[-4\left(cmd_{w_z} - w_z^2\right)\right]$
- Orientation: $r_4 = \left[angle\left(\phi_{body,z}, \phi_{world,z}\right)\right]^2$
- Joint torque: $r_5 = \tau^2$
- Joint acceleration: $r_6 = \left(\dot{q}_t - \dot{q}_{t-1}\right)^2$
- Air time: $r_7 = T$
- Action smoothness: $r_8 = \left(\delta_{q_t} - \delta_{q_{t-1}}\right)^2 + 2\left(\dot{q}_t - \dot{q}_{t-1}\right)^2$

The coefficients of each of these reward items are shown in Table 1. Ultimately, the reward obtained is the sum of the above reward items,

$$R = \sum_{i=1}^{8} k_i r_i \qquad (2)$$

Table 1. The coefficients of the reward items

Reward coefficients			
k_1	1	k_5	−0.00002
k_2	−4	k_6	−0.0005
k_3	0.5	k_7	2
k_4	−1	k_8	−0.005

4 Simulation

To illustrate our work better, we set up two scenarios in the simulation environment, one with visual information added to the robot, as shown in Fig. 1, and the other with the robot in a proprioceptive state only, as shown in Fig. 5. With our proposed method, two available control strategies are obtained for π_{blind} and π_{bright} respectively. We constructed the same size staircase terrain in the simulation environment to examine the performance of the two control strategies. Figure 1 shows the quadruped robot passing the stairs under the control of the strategy π_{bright}. Figure 5 shows a quadruped robot is passing the stairs under the control of the strategy π_{blind}.

Fig. 5. Without visual information, the robot is climbing the steps under the control of the strategy π_{blind}

4.1 Simulation Result

In order to show that the obtained strategy enables the quadruped robot to pass through complex terrain smoothly, the trajectory of the robot's center of mass change when passing through complex terrain is obtained. Figure 6 shows the change of leg lift and the undulation of the body center of mass of the robot through the complex terrain under the control strategy. Figure 7 shows the variation of leg lift and the undulation of the center of mass of the robot through the complex terrain under the control strategy. From the figure, we can see that the robot is able to traverse complex terrain with a trained strategy.

In the left of Fig. 6, the robot's center-of-mass curve appears to fall sharply in the final stage because the robot does not perceive that it has reached the end of the stair terrain after walking up the stairs, but continues to walk forward, resulting in a fall from the stairs. In the right of Fig. 6, the irregularity of the foot-end trajectory at the beginning of the phase is caused by the bump that occurs when the robot has not yet perceived the change of the terrain when it first goes up the stairs based on the ontological perception case. In Fig. 7, the center of mass remains constant in the final stage because the robot has traveled to the end of the stairs at this time, and the control strategy gets the terrain information and controls the robot not to continue moving forward, avoiding the danger of falling down.

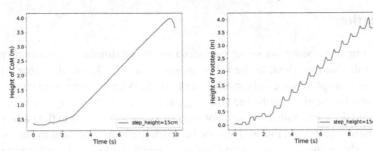

Fig. 6. Quadruped robot climbs stairs under the control of strategy π_{blind}. Left, the change in the height of the center of mass of the robot. Right, the change in height of the robot's footstep. The end of the curve indicates that the robot has fallen off the edge.

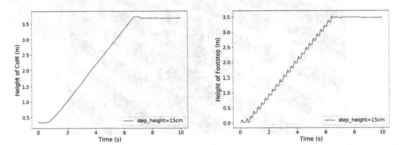

Fig. 7. Quadruped robot climbs stairs under the control of strategy π_{bright}. Left, the change in the height of the center of mass of the robot. Right, the change in height of the robot's footstep. The end of the curve indicates that the robot is risk-aware and remains stationary at the edges.

It is important to note here that in training both strategies, we did not change any other parameters or network details other than increasing the input visual information (i.e., the elevation information in front of the robot).

4.2 Comparison and Analysis

Comparing the results presented in Fig. 6 and Fig. 7, we can see that in the same staircase terrain condition, the robot has obvious advantages with the control strategy π_{bright}.

1. better safety in walking without falling down the stairs and bumping.
2. better performance in speed tracking with the control strategy π_{bright}, although the robot can pass two steps at a time with a higher height per leg lift with the control strategy π_{blind}.
3. when training to cross the gap terrain, robots based on proprioception never learn to cross the gap; robots aided by visual information can do so.

In order to better explain the importance of terrain information to the robot, we use the ability of the robot to pass the set terrain smoothly as a measure, although there is no unified standard yet, in this work, we use the pass rate and the number of collisions as indicators to evaluate the two strategies. We tested the two control strategies 100 times under two simulated terrains with the same structure, take the average of it as the final result and the result is shown in Table 2.

Table 2. Average success rate and number of collisions of robots negotiating different terrains

	Success rate		number of collisions
Type of terrain	Staircase	Gap	Staircase
π_{bright}	100%	44%	0.08
π_{blind}	91%	0	3.87

We observed that the control strategy with visual information did not achieve a high throughput rate when passing through gap terrain, which we believe is related to the terrain information acquired by the robot, since we only provided the robot with information around the front legs, and in the next step, we will try to provide the terrain information in front of the quadruped robot to the back two legs using neural networks.

Another point worth noting is the improvement in training speed, as we can demonstrate in the simulation that the strategy π_{bright} with visual information obtained better results in only 5300 generations of training, from learning to walk standing up to steadily passing a 15 cm high step in a stair terrain environment. We used a desktop computer with a 12 GB Nvidia RTX3060 GPU in 0.4 h, which is about 2 times faster than the blind strategy π_{blind}.

5 Conclusion and Future Work

In this paper, by using reinforcement learning to provide a quadruped robot with information on the terrain sampled ahead, the quadruped robot has been able to pass stairs and gap-like terrain smoothly in a simulated environment and compared with a blind controller, confirming that a control strategy based on visual information enables the robot to pass complex terrain faster and safer. Although the proposed method in this paper obtained a feasible control strategy, it did not make the robot appear to behave in an animal-like manner with linked front and hind leg muscles and coordination, which is the goal of our continued research in the future. Additionally, the work of this paper was completed in a simulation environment, it has been our pursuit to accomplish the research goal in a realistic environment. In the next step, we will migrate the trained vision information-based control strategy to the real environment through methods such as domain randomization [7] to achieve a powerful passage of the quadruped robot in the real environment.

References

1. Kim, D., Di Carlo, J., Katz, B.: Highly dynamic quadruped locomotion via whole-body impulse control and model predictive control. arXiv preprint arXiv:1909.06586 (2019)
2. Hwangbo, J., et al.: Learning agile and dynamic motor skills for legged robots. Sci. Robot. **4**(26), eaau5872 (2019). 2470-9476
3. Lee, J., Hwangbo, J., Wellhausen, L., Koltun, V., Hutter, M.: Learning quadrupedal locomotion over challenging terrain. Sci. Robot. **5**(47), eabc5986 (2020). 2470-9476
4. Miki, T., Lee, J., Hwangbo, J., Wellhausen, L., Koltun, V., Hutter, M.: Learning robust perceptive locomotion for quadrupedal robots in the wild. Sci. Robot. **7**(62), eabk2822 (2022). 2470-9476
5. Zhang, H., Starke, S., Komura, T., Saito, J.: Mode-adaptive neural networks for quadruped motion control. ACM Trans. Graph. **37**(4), 145 (2018). 0730-0301
6. Jain, D., Iscen, A., Caluwaerts, K.: 2019 IEEE/RSJ International Conference on Intelligent Robots and Systems, IROS 2019, Macau, SAR, China, November 3–8, 2019, pp. 7551–7557. IEEE (2019a). https://doi.org/10.1109/IROS40897.2019.8967913
7. Xie, Z., Da, X., van de Panne, M., Babich, B., Garg, A.: Dynamics randomization revisited: a case study for quadrupedal locomotion. In: 2021 IEEE International Conference on Robotics and Automation (ICRA), Xi'an, China (2021)
8. Peng, X., Coumans, E., Zhang, T., Lee, T.-W.E., Tan, J., Levine, S.: Learning agile robotic locomotion skills by imitating animals. Robot. Sci. Syst. **07** (2020). https://doi.org/10.15607/RSS.2020.XVI.064
9. Ji, G., Mun, J., Kim, H., Hwangbo, J.: Concurrent training of a control policy and a state estimator for dynamic and robust legged locomotion. IEEE Robot. Autom. Lett. **7**(2) (2022). 4630-4637
10. Agarwal, A., Kumar, A., Malik, J., Pathak, D.: Legged locomotion in challenging terrains using egocentric vision. arXiv e-prints (2022)
11. Kareer, S., Yokoyama, N., Batra, D., Ha, S., Truong, J.: ViNL: visual navigation and locomotion over obstacles. arXiv:2210.14791 (2022)
12. Loquercio, A., Kumar, A., Malik, J.: Learning visual locomotion with cross-modal supervision. arXiv:2211.03785v1 (2022)
13. Yang, R., Zhang, M., Hansen, N., Xu, H., Wang, X.: Learning vision-guided quadrupedal locomotion end-to-end with cross-modal transformers. arXiv:2107.03996 (2021)
14. Torres-Pardo, A., et al.: Legged locomotion over irregular terrains: state of the art of human and robot performance. Bioinspir. Biomim. **17**(6) (2022). 1748-3190
15. Grandia, R., Taylor, A.J., Ames, A.D., Hutter, M.: Multi-layered safety for legged robots via control barrier functions and model predictive control. In: International Conference on Robotics and Automation (ICRA 2021), Xi'an, China (2021)
16. Hutter, M., et al.: ANYmal-a highly mobile and dynamic quadrupedal robot. In: 2016 IEEE/RSJ International Conference on Intelligent Robots and Systems (IROS). IEEE (2016)
17. Gehring, C., et al.: Practice makes perfect: an optimization-based approach to controlling agile motions for a quadruped robot. IEEE Robot. Autom. Mag. **23**(1), 34–43 (2016). 1070-9932
18. Qi, S., Lin, W., Hong, Z., Chen, H., Zhang, W.: Perceptive autonomous stair climbing for quadrupedal robots. In: 2021 IEEE/RSJ International Conference on Intelligent Robots and Systems (IROS), Prague, Czech Republic (2021)
19. Zico Kolter, J., Ng, A.Y.: The Stanford LittleDog: a learning and rapid replanning approach to quadruped locomotion. Int. J. Robot. Res. **30**(2), 150–174 (2011). 0278-3649
20. Zucker, M., Andrew Bagnell, J., Atkeson, C.G., Kuffner, J.: An optimization approach to rough terrain locomotion. In: 2010 IEEE International Conference on Robotics and Automation. IEEE (2010)

21. Zucker, M., et al.: Optimization and learning for rough terrain legged locomotion. Int. J. Robot. Res. **30**(2), 175–191 (2011). 0278-3649
22. Tan, W., et al.: A hierarchical framework for quadruped locomotion based on reinforcement learning. In: 2021 IEEE/RSJ International Conference on Intelligent Robots and Systems (IROS), Prague, Czech Republic (2021)
23. Kumar, A., Fu, Z., Pathak, D., Malik, J.: RMA: rapid motor adaptation for legged robots. In: Robotics: Science and Systems XVII (2021). https://doi.org/10.15607/RSS.2021.XVII.011
24. Makoviychuk, V., et al.:: Isaac Gym: high performance GPU-based physics simulation for robot learning. arXiv preprint arXiv:2108.10470 (2021)
25. Nikita, R., David, H., Philipp, R., Marco, H.: Learning to walk in minutes using massively parallel deep reinforcement learning. In: Proceedings of Machine Learning Research, vol. 164, pp. 91–100 (2022). 2640-3498
26. Schulman, J., Wolski, F., Dhariwal, P., Radford, A., Klimov, O.: Proximal policy optimization algorithms. arXiv preprint (2017). https://doi.org/10.48550/arXiv.1707.06347

Abnormal Emotion Recognition Based on Audio-Visual Modality Fusion

Yutong Jiang, Kaoru Hirota, Yaping Dai, Ye Ji, and Shuai Shao[✉]

Beijing Institute of Technology, Beijing 100081, People's Republic of China
{jiangyutong1,hirota,daiyaping,jiye521,shaoshuai}@bit.edu.cn

Abstract. In indoor places, such as homes or offices, when abnormal events occur, the behavior and voice of individuals or groups will display abnormal signals. These signals can be both visual and auditory, and they interact and complement each other to jointly create a sense of emotional atmosphere within the scene. In order to achieve effective and accurate perception and response of abnormal emotion during the interaction in smart home, a model of abnormal emotion recognition based on audio-visual modality fusion is proposed. Human skeleton motion data and audio data are utilized to construct separate deep learning networks for action recognition and speech emotion recognition. The accuracy rate achieved on the G3D dataset is 100% and the accuracy rate achieved on the CASIA corpus is 90.83%. For decision-level multimodal fusion, the predicted results of actions and speech emotions are mapped to the "abnormal" axis through fuzzification and weighted average methods. In this process, considerations are taken into account for the varying contributions of different speech emotions and behaviors to the abnormal emotion, as well as the recognition recall rates of the unimodal emotion models. Then the two modalities are allowed to mutually modify each other and achieve quantitative analysis of abnormal emotion through weighted additive fusion.

Keywords: Speech emotion recognition · Abnormal emotion · Fuzzification · Action recognition · Multimodal fusion

1 Introduction

The rapid development and widespread application of smart homes provide new opportunities for improving human living environments [1]. As people's demands for quality of family life and safety continue to grow, abnormal emotion recognition has become an important research direction in smart home systems. Abnormal emotion recognition aims to effectively identify and respond to abnormal emotions related to safety, health, and other aspects by analyzing external cues

---

Supported by the National Natural Science Foundation of China under Grant No. 82201753.

from the human body in residential environments such as facial expressions [2], speech [3], body movements [4], and biological signals [5].

Speech and action are two essential modalities for emotion recognition as they are not only used to convey information but also contain rich emotional elements that can provide insights into a human's affective state [6]. Speech-based emotion recognition is studied extensively in the literature. For example, Abdelhamid A A et al. [7] combine a CNN and LSTM to propose an optimized model, achieving accuracies 98.13%, 99.76%, 99.47%, and 99.50% on IEMOCAP, Emo-DB, RAVDESS, and SAVEE, respectively. Apeksha Aggarwal et al. [8] explore two feature extraction methods: utilizing super convergence with principal component analysis (PCA) and using mel-spectrogram images with a pre-trained VGG-16 model. Action recognition is the task of identifying human actions from video sequences. Various deep learning models have been developed for action recognition. For example, et al. [9] design a compound scaling strategy to expand the model's width and depth synchronously, and obtain a family of efficient GCN baselines, achieving 92.1% accuracy on the cross-subject benchmark of NTU 60 dataset. Muhammad K al. [10] propose a BiLSTM-based attention mechanism with a DCNN that achieves recognition rates of 98.3%, 99.1%, and 80.2% on UCF11, UCF sports, and J-HMDB datasets, respectively.

However, Unimodal emotion identification lacks diversity and comprehensiveness due to the complex and variable nature of human emotions. Using single action or speech signal for emotion recognition may be affected by various factors such as environmental noise, accent, speech rate, etc., leading to a decrease in accuracy [11]. While cross-modal emotion recognition, which combines information from multiple modalities, can achieve even higher accuracy and robustness [12]. In recent years, with the development of multimodal data processing and artificial intelligence technologies, the fusion of audio-visual modalities has become one of the hot research areas in abnormal emotion recognition [13,14].

In light of the limitations of unimodal identification, an abnormal emotion recognition model based on audio-visual modality fusion is proposed in this paper. By integrating speech and action data, we aim to develop a more robust and reliable approach to measure the abnormal emotion indoor living environments.

2   Model Structure of Speech Emotion Recognition and Action Recognition

2.1   Speech Feature Set Extraction

In order to effectively analyze speech signals, it is essential to extract characteristic parameters that can accurately represent the essence of the speech. Several spectrum-based features are selected in this study, including Mel Frequency Cepstrum Coefficient (MFCC), Filter Bank (Fbank), Perceptual Linear Prediction (PLP), and Linear Predictive Cepstrum Coefficient (LPCC).

MFCC is based on the critical bandwidth of the human ear and uses a frequency filter to extract the key features of speech signals. Its extraction method

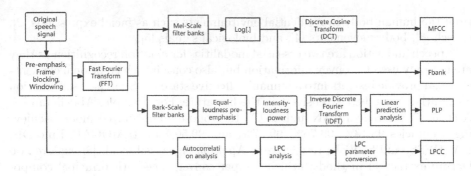

Fig. 1. Speech feature set extraction

mimics the human auditory system and uses a low-frequency linear interval and a high-frequency logarithmic interval [15]. In contrast, Fbank's extraction method removes the Discrete Cosine Transform (DCT) as it may cause the loss of critical features. PLP combines multiple processes such as key frequency band, intensity-loudness compression, and equal loudness pre-emphasis to extract speech-related information. It simulates various important features of the human auditory system and combines spectral analysis and linear prediction analysis [16]. The Linear Prediction Coefficient (LPC) simulates the human vocal tract and has strong robustness. It evaluates speech signals by approximating resonance peaks, removes the influence of resonance peaks from speech signals, and estimates the concentration and frequency of residual speech signals [17]. LPCC is the Fourier transform coefficient of the logarithmic amplitude spectrum of LPC.

To enrich speech features and improve network performance, a combination of different feature extraction methods is used to form feature sets in Fig. 1.

2.2   Architecture of the Speech Emotion Recognition Model

To accurately identify speech emotion, the CNN-Attention-BiLstm model is proposed as depicted in Fig. 2. The model is divided into two parts: convolutional neural network (CNN) and bidirectional Long Short-Term Memory (BiLSTM) neural network. It finally outputs six emotion classification results through the fully connection layer.

The BiLSTM network can process the time series positively and inversely, and effectively utilize the forward and backward features of the input to better analyze the bidirectional semantic dependence of the signal. The convolutional neural network can extract local features and focus on the most critical local information for the current task. The attention mechanism is adopted in the CNN feature extraction channel that prioritizes the emotion-related features in the speech sequence, while filtering out irrelevant information.

The CNN module consists of six convolutional layers and three pooling layers with four of the convolutional layers forming a residual block. Residual block structure mitigates issues such as gradient vanishing and network degradation,

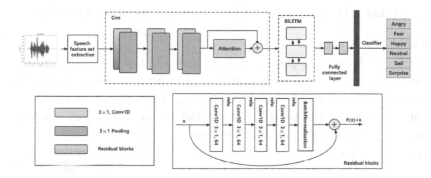

Fig. 2. Model structure of CNN-Attention-BiLstm

resulting in smoother forward and backward propagation of information. After inputting x, the model performs convolution and relu. Then it is followed by Batch Normalization to obtain f(x), which is added to the original x. The output of the residual block is f(x) + x.

The proposed CNN-Attention-BiLstm structure can compensate for the limitations of CNN's lack of global attention and BiLSTM's lack of local prominence. It can learn deeper emotional features in speech, and improve the efficiency and accuracy of speech recognition.

2.3 Action Data Acquisition and Processing

Action data is acquired by the Kinect sensor. Kinect is a vision sensor that integrates many advanced vision technologies, and can directly record skeleton data for action recognition [18]. Kinect identifies 20 joint points, including: Head, Shoulder-center, Shoulder-left, Elbow-left, Wrist-left, Hand-left, Shoulder-right, Elbow-right, Wrist-right, Hand-right, Spine, Hip-center, Hip-left, Knee-left, Ankle-left, Foot-left, Hip-right, Knee-right, Ankle-right and Foot-right.

Action recognition need to recognize different actions performed by humans based on the motion patterns of their skeletal poses. The collected data during an action comprises a sequence of three-dimensional skeletal poses captured over time. Each action can be further broken down into several sub-actions, for instance, boxing comprises a stand, punch-half, punch-full, punch-half, and stand sequence, which can be identified from the overall action sequence. Recognizing actions differs from recognizing emotions in speech, as speech emotions are complex and require the listener to hear the entire sentence to infer the mood and intent of the speaker. Action recognition requires identifying sub-actions as they happen, as opposed to waiting for the whole action to finish. This is because when people engage in action interaction, both parties can often comprehend and react to the other party's actions before the entire action is completed. To accurately sense the abnormal emotion of action, it is essential to identify the sequence of sub-actions accurately. The action and its corresponding sequence of sub-actions are shown in Table 1.

Table 1. Complete action and the sub-action sequences it contains

Action	Sub-actions
Left-Punch	Stand, Left-punch-half, Left-punch-full, Left-punch-half, Stand
Right-Punch	Stand, Right-punch-half, Right-punch-full, Right-punch-half, Stand
Left-Kick	Stand, Left-kick-half, Left-kick-full, Left-kick-half, Stand
Right-Kick	Stand, Right-kick-half, Right-kick-full, Right-kick-half, Stand
Run	Stand, Left-run, Stand, Right-run, Stand
Wave	Wave

2.4   Architecture of the Sub-action Sequence Recognition Model

Figure 3 illustrates the architecture of the model, which consists of three parts: Encoder, CNN-Attention-c and Decoder. The three-dimensional position of the skeleton in each frame of the complete action is taken as input by the model, which then generates a sequence of sub-actions as output. Sub-action recognition is a sequence-to-sequence problem, so the Encoder-Decoder framework is utilized. The BiLstm and Lstm structures are employed to implement the encoder and decoder, respectively. There are two ways to connect the encoder and the decoder.

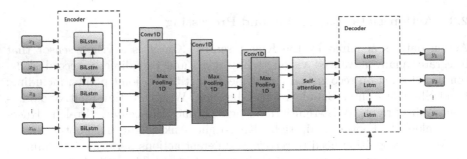

Fig. 3. Model structure of Encoder-CNN-Attention-C-Decoder

One approach is to stitch the cell state of the last time step of the forward and backward Lstm network together to obtain a fixed-length semantic vector C. It serves as the initial value of the decoder's cell state. Another approach is to pass the encoder's hidden state values of the entire time step into the CNN-Attention structure. Then, the CNN-Attention structure shortens the sequence length while retaining critical sequence features, resulting in sequence information of length n, which serves as input for the decoder.

3   Abnormal Emotion Recognition Based on Multimodal Fusion

The overall structure of the abnormal emotion recognition model based on multimodal fusion is shown in Fig. 4. Multimodal integration combines expressions or perceptions of things from multiple modes. Due to the varying expressions of different modalities, perspectives on things can also differ, resulting in overlapping and complementary phenomena. If multimodal information can be processed appropriately, rich emotion information can be obtained. The recognition results of speech emotion and action are subjected to decision-level fusion, which involves two parts: fuzzification and weighted average, as well as audio-visual emotion fusion.

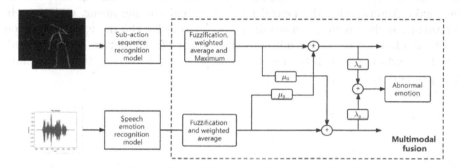

Fig. 4. Recognition model of abnormal emotion based on multimodal fusion

3.1   Fuzzification and Weighted Average

In the speech emotion recognition space, emotion are expressed by 6 binary vectors as

$$SE = \{Angry, Happy, Fear, Sad, Surprise, Neutral\} \in \{0,1\}^6 \qquad (1)$$

While in the action recognition space, emotion are expressed by 12 binary vectors as

$$
\begin{aligned}
AE = \{&Stand, Left - punch - half, Left - punch - full,\\
&Right - punch - half, Right - punch - full, Left - kick - half,\\
&Left - kick - full, Right - kick - half, Right - kick - full,\\
&Left - Run, Right - Run, Wave\} \in \{0,1\}^{12}
\end{aligned}
\qquad (2)
$$

To quantitatively analyze the level of abnormal emotion in indoor places, all emotional expressions are mapped to the "abnormal" axis.

$$EA = f(E) = e_{abnormal} \in [-1, 1] \qquad (3)$$

Taking the various contributions of emotions to the abnormal emotion into consideration, fuzzification and the weighted average method are adopted to construct function f:

$$f: \frac{\sum_{i=1}^{n} w_i Fuzzication(E_i)}{\sum_{i=1}^{n} w_i} \tag{4}$$

There are 6 and 12 emotional labels on speech and action, respectively. Based on the prediction probability of the classifier, each emotional label is fuzzified to a value between 0 and 1, which is then mapped to a corresponding position on the 'abnormal' axis. The membership functions as shown in Fig. 5–6. Each mode's classification result is represented by the probability of identifying each class of results output by the network softmax layer $P = [p_1, p_2, p_3, ..., p_n]$. n is the number of categories. The greater the predicted probability of the output, the more significant the corresponding emotion's contribution on the "abnormal" axis. Additionally, the neural network model has significant variations in recognizing each classification result, so accounting for the model's recognition recall calculation weight can mitigate the impact of different recognition recall rates to a certain extent. If the recall rate $K = [k_1, k_2, k_3, ..., k_n]$, then the weight $w_i = p_i k_i, i = 1, 2, 3, ..., n.$

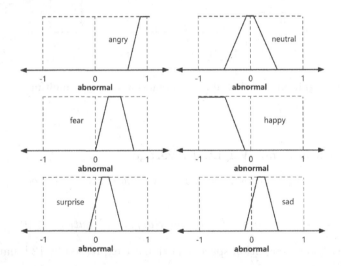

Fig. 5. Membership function of the speech emotion labels on the abnormal axis

The level of abnormal emotion of an action is measured by the intensity of its most violent movement. Therefore, the abnormal emotion of an action should take the maximum value of the fuzzy emotional abnormality of its sub-actions.

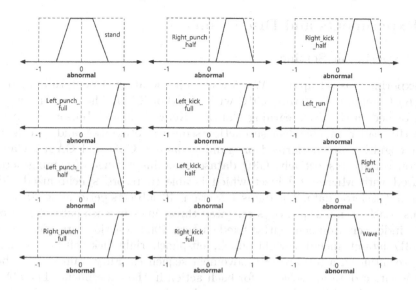

Fig. 6. Membership function of the sub-action labels on the abnormal axis

$$EA_{action} = max(EA_{sub-action1}, EA_{sub-action2}, ..., EA_{sub-actionl}) \qquad (5)$$

where, l is the sequence length.

3.2 Audio-Visual Emotion Fusion

Multiple modes work together, and the emotional information of the visual and auditory senses can be enhanced or corrected for each other. On the one hand, Human emotions are complex. In many situations, the emotion displayed in the voice or body action may not always indicate the real or absolute emotion of the individual. Compared with single modal, multimodal data has higher robustness and accuracy in interaction. On the other hand, it is not independent between the different modal data. The process of human sensing emotion using vision and hearing is coupled and complementary. For example, a fight that accompanies an argument tends to look more dangerous than a single fight. By simulating this characteristic of human emotional expression, the action emotion EA_{action} on the "abnormal" axis are multiplied by an adjustment coefficient μ_a, then added to the emotional abnormality of speech. The speech emotion EA_{speech} on the "abnormal" axis are multiplied by an adjustment coefficient μ_s, then added to the emotional abnormality of action.

$$EA'_{speech} = \mu_a EA_{action} + EA_{speech} \qquad (6)$$

$$EA'_{action} = \mu_s EA_{speech} + EA_{action} \qquad (7)$$

So the fuzzy emotional abnormality in indoor places:

$$EA'_{multimodal} = \lambda_s EA_{speech} + \lambda_a AE_{action} \qquad (8)$$

$$\lambda_s + \lambda_a = 1 \qquad (9)$$

4   Experiments and Discussion

4.1   Experiment Setting

Our experiment is set up on a Windows 64-bit operating system, running on an Intel(R) Core(TM) i7-10510U CPU with 16 GB of RAM. The entire framework is performed on the deep learning platform Keras 2.8.0 and Tensorflow 2.8.0.

In this paper, independent sub-action sequence recognition and speech emotion recognition are performed on gaming dataset–G3D and CASIA Chinese emotion corpus, respectively. G3D dataset contains a range of gaming actions captured with Microsoft Kinect which is able to record synchronized video, depth and skeleton data. The dataset contains 10 subjects performing 20 gaming actions. Each action sequence is repeated three times by each subject in a controlled indoor environment with a fixed camera [19]. Six actions are selected from the G3D dataset, including right punch, left punch, right kick, left kick, run, and wave, resulting in a total of 180 movement sequences. Fifty frames of 3D bone point position data are selected for each action in the experiment. The CASIA Chinese Emotional Speech Corpus is obtained through multiple emotional performances by four test subjects (2 males and 2 females) in a clean recording environment at the Institute of Automation, Chinese Academy of Sciences. The emotions are discretely represented as six categories: angry, happy, fear, sad, surprise, and neutral. This study selected 1200 recordings from the CASIA corpus to conduct speech emotion recognition experiments. The two datasets each took 80% as the training set and 20% as the test set.

4.2   Experimental Results and Discussion

Speech Emotion Recognition Experiment. The CNN-Attention-BiLstm network is compared with other structures, and the results are illustrated Table 2. It has shown that in experiments with the same feature set, the structure of CNN-Attention-BiLstm has a higher accuracy.

Table 2. Comparison of different models on CASIA

Models	ACC (%)	UAR (%)	WAR (%)
BiLstm	58.33	58.62	58.33
BiLstm+attn	79.58	79.59	79.58
6*CNN+attn+BiLstm	84.58	84.22	84.58
Resblock+2*CNN+attn+BiLstm	90.83	90.98	90.83

Then the recognition for several different feature sets are compared, as shown in Table 3. The combination of Fbank and LPCC gives the best recognition effect.

Table 3. Comparison of different feature sets

Feature Sets	ACC (%)	UAR (%)	WAR (%)
MFCC	83.75	83.42	83.42
MFCC+delta1+delta2	81.55	81.67	81.55
Fbank	88.33	88.02	88.33
Fbank+delta1+delta2	82.08	81.83	82.08
Fbank+LPCC	90.83	90.98	90.83
Fbank+PLP	87.50	88.01	87.50
Fbank+PLP+LPCC	88.75	89.20	88.75

To further analyze the classification performance of each emotion, the recognition recall rate for each category is calculated in Table 4.

Table 4. Recognition recall rate for each emotion

Emotions	Angry	Happy	Fear	sad	Surprise	Neutral
Recall (%)	91.43	87.76	91.18	94.74	91.30	89.47

Sub-action Sequence Recognition Experiment. The recognition result of the different model structures are compared as shown in Table 5. It can be seen that the Encoder-CNN-Attention-C-Decoder structure improves the accuracy up to 100%.

Multimodal Fusion Experiment. According to the above experimental results, p is the predicted probability from the output layer, $k_{speech} = [\ 91.43,\ 87.76,\ 91.18,\ 94.74,\ 91.30,\ 89.47\ ]$, the value of each element of k_{action} is 1. Assuming that vision and hearing play the same role in specific settings, $\mu_a = \mu_s = 0.5$, adjustment coefficient $\lambda_a = \lambda_s = 0.2$.

To compare multimodal fusion result across diverse contexts, a method is devised to combine speech and action data, which ensuring emotional consistency and expressive richness, thus creating a range of distinct multimodal emotion occasions. In Table 6, occasion 1 is interaction in abnormal atmosphere, occasion 2 is interaction in restless atmosphere, occasion 3 is interaction in peace atmosphere, and on occasion 4, angry speech emotion is misidentified as sad.

It is shown that the multimodal fusion can effectively quantify the abnormal emotion in scenes. On occasion 4, angry speech emotion is misidentified, but the degree of its emotional abnormality can be identified as a higher value after adjustment by right-punch-full action. Therefore, Multimodal emotion recognition model can make effective enhancement or complementarity of single modalities.

Table 5. Comparison of different models on G3D

Models	ACC (%)	UAR (%)	WAR (%)
3*CNN	91.67	95.26	91.67
Encoder-c-Decoder	97.22	98.96	97.22
Encoder-CNN-Decoder	99.78	99.17	99.78
Encoder-CNN-attention-c-Decoder	100	100	100

Table 6. The fusion results in several occasions

Occasion	Modal	Category	Abnormal emotion	Fusion results
1	Speech	Angry	1.08	1.08
	Action	Left-punch-full	1.08	
2	Speech	Fear	0.375	0.483
	Action	Left-punch-half	0.609	
3	Speech	Happy	−0.441	−0.19
	Action	Wave	0.032	
4	Speech	Sad	0.515	0.724
	Action	Right-punch-full	0.933	

5   Conclusion

Overall, the abnormal emotion recognition model based on audio-visual modality fusion is composed by speech emotion recognition, action recognition and multimodal fusion. The speech emotion recognition network achieved an accuracy rate of 90.83% on the CASIA corpus, while the action recognition achieved a 100% accuracy rate on the G3D dataset. After mapping recognition results to the "abnormal" axis and count abnormal emotion by weighted additive fusion. This model offers the quantitative analysis of abnormal emotion and reduces the risk of unimodal recognition errors. It contributes to the development of smart homes capable of effectively recognizing and responding to abnormal emotions in some indoor settings. In future studies, we plan to integrate more emotion recognition channels to develop more reliable multimodal recognition models that can accommodate more complex scenarios.

References

1. Liu, J., Wang, M., Wang, X.: Research on general model of intelligence level for smart home. In: 2022 7th International Conference on Computer and Communication Systems, pp. 123–129 (2022)
2. Canal, F.Z., Müller, T.R., Matias, J.C., et al.: A survey on facial emotion recognition techniques: a state-of-the-art literature review. Inf. Sci. 582 (2022)

3. Morais, E., Hoory, R., Zhu, W., et al.: Speech emotion recognition using self-supervised features. In: ICASSP 2022–2022 IEEE International Conference on Acoustics, Speech and Signal Processing (ICASSP). IEEE, 6922–6926 (2022)

4. Wang, S., Li, J., Cao, T., Wang, H., Tu, P., Li, Y.: Dance emotion recognition based on laban motion analysis using convolutional neural network and long short-term memory. IEEE Access **8**, 124928–124938 (2020)

5. Zhang, J., Yin, Z., Chen, P., et al.: Emotion recognition using multi-modal data and machine learning techniques: a tutorial and review. Inf. Fusion **59**, 103–126 (2020)

6. Middya, A.I., Nag, B., Roy, S.: Deep learning based multimodal emotion recognition using model-level fusion of audio-visual modalities. Knowl.-Based Syst. **244**, 108580 (2022)

7. Abdelhamid, A.A., El-Kenawy, E.S.M., Alotaibi, B., et al.: Robust speech emotion recognition using CNN+ LSTM based on stochastic fractal search optimization algorithm. IEEE Access **10**, 49265–49284 (2022)

8. Aggarwal, A., Srivastava, A., Agarwal, A., et al.: Two-way feature extraction for speech emotion recognition using deep learning. Sensors **22**(6), 2378 (2022)

9. Song, Y.F., Zhang, Z., Shan, C., et al.: Constructing stronger and faster baselines for skeleton-based action recognition. IEEE Trans. Pattern Anal. Mach. Intell. **45**(2), 1474–1488 (2022)

10. Muhammad, K., Ullah, A., Imran, A.S., et al.: Human action recognition using attention based LSTM network with dilated CNN features. Futur. Gener. Comput. Syst. **125**, 820–830 (2021)

11. Cai, L., Dong, J., Wei, M.: Multi-Modal Emotion Recognition From Speech and Facial Expression Based on Deep Learning. Chinese Autom. Congress (CAC) **2020**, 5726–5729 (2020)

12. Koromilas, P., Giannakopoulos, T.: Deep multimodal emotion recognition on human speech: a review. Appl. Sci. **11**(17), 7962 (2021)

13. Aggarwal, S., Sehgal, S.: Text independent data-level fusion network for multi-modal sentiment analysis. Int. J. Performability Eng. **18**(9) (2022)

14. Tan, Y., Sun, Z., Duan, F., et al.: A multimodal emotion recognition method based on facial expressions and electroencephalography. Biomed. Signal Process. Control **70**, 103029 (2021)

15. Jin, S., Wang, X., Du, L., et al.: Evaluation and modeling of automotive transmission whine noise quality based on MFCC and CNN. Appl. Acoust. **172**, 107562 (2021)

16. Bhatt, S., Dev, A., Jain, A.: Effects of the dynamic and energy based feature extraction on Hindi speech recognition. In: Recent Advances in Computer Science and Communications (Formerly: Recent Patents on Computer Science) **14**(5), 1422–1430 (2021)

17. Paseddula, C., Gangashetty, S.V.: Late fusion framework for Acoustic Scene Classification using LPCC, SCMC, and log-Mel band energies with Deep Neural Networks[J]. Appl. Acoust. **172**, 107568 (2021)

18. Zhang, Z.: Microsoft kinect sensor and its effect. IEEE Computer Society Press (2012)

19. Bloom, V., Argyriou, V., Makris, D.: Hierarchical transfer learning for online recognition of compound actions. Comput. Vision Image Understanding **144**, 62–72 (2016)

Powerful Encoding and Decoding Computation of Reservoir Computing

Weian Li[1], Huiwen Wu[2], and Dongping Yang[1(✉)]

[1] Research Center for Augmented Intelligence, Research Institute of Artificial Intelligence, Zhejiang Lab, Hangzhou 311101, Zhejiang, China
dpyang@zhejianglab.com
[2] Research Center for Basic Theories of Intelligent Computing, Research Institute of Basic Theories, Zhejiang Laboratory, Hangzhou 311100, China

Abstract. Reservoir computing (RC) has been widely applied in the fields of time series data processing and time series prediction due to its powerful data representation capability. The reservoir exhibits non-linear dynamics, and its internal dynamics have infinitely long correlations when the system settles at the edge of chaos, rendering the system to achieve excellent computational performance. However, the encoding and decoding performance of RC is still unclear. This paper investigates the encoding and decoding abilities of the classic RC model, Echo State Network (ESN), on an image reconstruction task. The results show that ESN could greatly reconstruct grey images as well as color images, and demonstrate excellent generalization. Furthermore, a deep neural network based on ESN is proposed to resist the attacks on the trained model in experiments, showing that ESN enables the model to have excellent privacy protection ability. Our results demonstrate that the ESN's powerful encoding and decoding computational performance makes it highly promising in facilitating tasks, such as few-shot learning and privacy computing.

Keywords: Reservoir computing · Encoding and decoding · Private protection

1 Introduction

Artificial Neural Networks (ANNs) have experienced rapid development and have played a significant role in various fields, including object detection [1], natural language processing [2], autonomous driving, and more [3]. However, popular large-scale models like Vision Transform (VIT) [4], suffer from some disadvantages, such as complex structures, a large number of parameters, overfitting, and high computational costs, which makes it difficult to deploy on edge devices [5]. On the other hand, classical Recurrent Neural Networks (RNNs) [6]

Supported by the National Natural Science Foundation of China under Grant 12175242
Supported by Youth Foundation Project of Zhejiang Lab (No. 111012-AA2306).

face some challenges including gradients vanishing and exploding, which hinder the training of the model. These issues can be naturally avoided in the paradigm called Reservoir Computing (RC) [7], which has attracted wide attention, with more and more researchers focusing on its study and engineering applications, such as speech signal recognition [8], temporal pattern classification [9], and action sequence prediction [10].

In RC, the internal parameters of the reservoir remain fixed and only the weights of the readout layer need to be trained. This characteristic significantly reduces the computational cost during the training phase. Besides, this nonlinear dynamical system can map low-dimensional inputs to the high-dimensional state of the network, exhibiting strong representation capacity. Although the RC framework is frequently applied in engineering and mostly used for tasks, such as prediction and classification, the research on the encoding and decoding computation of RC is still few, and its inherent computational capacity remains unclear. Therefore, it is essential to investigate the encoding and decoding performance of RC to gain deeper insights into this model.

In this paper, we study the encoding and decoding performance of the Echo State Network (ESN) [11], a classic RC model, specifically based on an image reconstruction task. Firstly, we compared the model's reconstruction accuracy using different network parameters on the MNIST dataset. The results demonstrated that the ESN effectively reconstructed the grey images, highlighting its strong encoding and decoding abilities. Furthermore, our findings indicated that ESN exhibited remarkable generalization capabilities in image reconstruction tasks, even when trained on a small number of samples. We extended the scope of the task to the color images [12], where the ESN continued to demonstrate excellent generalization and achieves favorable results. Finally, we found that the deep network incorporating ESN modules was more resistant to attacks and better at preserving data privacy, compared to traditional Convolutional Neural Networks (CNNs). These results indicate the significant potential of RC in encoding and decoding, warranting further research and development, which provides new insights and directions for some applications such as privacy protection and edge computing [13].

2   Preliminaries

2.1   Model Structure of ESN

ESN is a classical RC model, which consists of an input layer, a reservoir, and a readout layer, as shown in Fig. 1, where x_{in} represents the input data and $\boldsymbol{W_{in}}$ represents the input weights. The input layer is fully connected to the reservoir, with connection weights first randomly and uniformly sampled from the range [0,1], and then scaled by a scaling factor inScaling. The reservoir is a sparse recurrent neural network with connection weights $\boldsymbol{W_{res}}$, as described in detail in the next paragraph; x_i represents the voltage state of neuron i in the reservoir; $\boldsymbol{W_{out}}$ represents the readout weights, which connect the reservoir to the readout layer and map the network state to a desired output.

The construction of $\boldsymbol{W}_{res}$ follows a special design approach by creating a reservoir with hybrid oscillators [14]. Firstly, the number of oscillators N_{osc}, and the range of period parameter for each oscillator, Period $= [P_{min}, P_{max}]$, are determined as follows: All periods are uniformly sampled within this range, forming a set of oscillator periods $(P_1, ..., P_{N_{osc}})$, and sorted in ascending order; Then, some linear oscillator matrices $\boldsymbol{W}_i$ are constructed using each period, which can be described as:

$$\boldsymbol{W}_i = \begin{pmatrix} \cos(\phi_i) & -\sin(\phi_i) \\ \sin(\phi_i) & \cos(\phi_i) \end{pmatrix} \tag{1}$$

with the rotation angle $\phi_i = P_i/2\pi$. Then these N_{osc} rotation matrices are sequentially placed on the main diagonal of the top-left of a blank $\boldsymbol{W}$. The remaining lower-right elements of $\boldsymbol{W}$ are set as values sparsely and randomly sampled from -1 to 1. Finally, the spectral radius SR of this matrix is scaled to 1 to obtain the final $\boldsymbol{W}_{res}$.

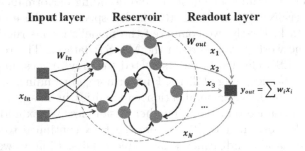

Fig. 1. Model structure of ESN.

The update of the neuron's voltage in the reservoir can be described as:

$$\mathbf{x}(n+1) = (1-\alpha)\mathbf{x}(n) + \alpha\tanh(\boldsymbol{W}_{res}\mathbf{x}(n) + \boldsymbol{W}_{in}\mathbf{x}_{in}(n+1)) \tag{2}$$

where $\mathbf{x}(n)$ is the column vector consisting of the neuron's voltages at time step n, and the size of the reservoir is represented by the symbol N; α represents the leakage rate, which takes values in the range [0,1]; tanh represents the nonlinear activation function, which transforms the input from other neurons and external inputs, and then updates the neuron's membrane voltage.

The linear readout of ESN is given as follows:

$$\mathbf{y}(n) = \boldsymbol{W}_{out}\mathbf{x}(n) \tag{3}$$

where $\mathbf{y}$ represents the output of the RC. The readout weights $\boldsymbol{W}_{out}$ of ESN are calculated by performing linear regression on the network state and target output, described as:

$$\boldsymbol{W}_{out} = ((\boldsymbol{S}^T)^\dagger \boldsymbol{T}^T)^T \tag{4}$$

where S is the state collection matrix of ESN, and T is the target output matrix. The symbol † in the upper right corner represents the pseudoinverse operation of a matrix, and the symbol T in the upper left corner represents the transpose operation of a matrix.

2.2   Data Preprocessing

The encoding and decoding performance of ESN is performed on image reconstruction tasks. Firstly, the image data are dimensionally reduced using Singular Value Decomposition (SVD) [15] at first. SVD is widely used in data dimensionality reduction, and the main formula for is given:

$$M = U\Sigma V^{T} \tag{5}$$

where M represents a $m \times n$ image with a single channel; Σ is a $m \times n$ semi-positive definite diagonal matrix, whose diagonal elements are the singular values of M; U is a $m \times m$ matrix, whose columns are the left eigenvectors corresponding to eigenvalues of M, while V is a $n \times n$ matrix, whose columns are the corresponding right eigenvectors. The square root of each diagonal element in Σ is multiplied with the corresponding eigenvectors in U and V. Then, the eigenvectors are sorted by the real part of eigenvalues and stacked together as the input data. The eigenvectors of different images are concatenated in order and fed into ESN, as shown in Fig. 2A, where U(1) and V(1) represents the eigenvector corresponding to the first largest eigenvalue. In the image reconstruction task, the above image data sequence is used as the network's input as well as the target of the output during training. The model framework based on ESN for the image reconstruction task is shown in Fig. 2B.

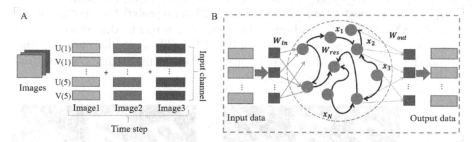

Fig. 2. Description of the data preparation and the framework of the network in an image reconstruction task. A: The input sequence of ESN corresponds to images after SVD; B: The model framework of ESN for the image reconstruction task.

2.3   Evaluation

The evaluation of the image reconstruction task was obtained by comparing the corresponding pixels between the input image and the reconstructed image, and the absolute error of all pixels was calculated [14]. If the absolute error of a pixel is less than 0.1, it is considered a successful reconstruction of this pixel. The number of successfully reconstructed pixels was counted, and the ratio to the total number of pixels of the image was used to obtain the final image reconstruction accuracy. The accuracy was calculated according to:

$$\text{Accuracy} = \frac{\text{correct}}{\text{correct} + \text{incorrect}} \tag{6}$$

where correct or incorrect represents the number of pixels predicted correctly or incorrectly, respectively.

3   Codec Performance of ESN

3.1   Image Reconstruction of a Gray Image on MNIST Dataset

We first tested the performance of image reconstruction of ESN with different parameters on the MNIST dataset. Several important parameters which affect the network are the size of reservoir N, the spectral radius of reservoir connectivity weights SR, the input weight scaling factor inScaling, the leaky rate of neurons in the reservoir α, and the rank numbers of eigenvectors selected after SVD processing. We first used the classical parameter settings which come from the previous paper [14] to perform the image reconstruction task: N = 300, SR = 1, inScaling = 0.2, Rank = 10, and set the reservoir connectivity probability p = 0.05. In the nominal experiments, 60000 images were used as the training set, and the remaining 10000 images were used as the test set.

The experiment result showed that the test accuracy of image reconstruction of ESN was 99.44%. Figure 3A showed the examples of input images and the corresponding reconstructed images. Figure 3B represented the reconstruction result of ESN which only read out a part set of neurons in the reservoir when SR = 1, and the accuracy could achieve 95.4439%. These results indicated that ESN on the edge of chaos has a great capacity for reconstructing grey images.

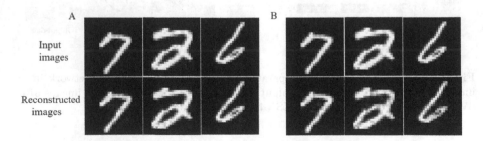

Fig. 3. Examples of input and reconstructed images in image reconstruction task. A: The result reconstructed from the signals of all neurons of the reservoir; B: The reconstruction result of ESN which only reads out 200 neurons of the reservoir.

Additionally, we tested the codec performance of ESN under different values of Rank, with the reconstruction accuracy as listed in Table 1. As more eigenvectors were concatenated as input data, the input channels of the network are also increased, thus making the task more complicated. Table 1 revealed that even when all 28 eigenvectors of the image were used, the reconstruction performance of ESN was still great.

Table 1. Images reconstruction accuracy under different Rank

Rank	N	SR	inScaling	α	Acc.[%]
5	300	1	0.2	1	99.9773
10	300	1	0.2	1	99.44
15	300	1	0.2	1	98.7207
20	300	1	0.2	1	98.4757
28	300	1	0.2	1	98.4757

We further tested the generalization of image reconstruction of ESN on the MNIST dataset by reducing the number of training samples. The model parameters used were set as N = 300, SR = 1, inScaling = 0.2, Rank = 10. Table 2 showed the accuracy of ESN in reconstructing 10000 test images under different numbers of training samples. As shown in the Table 2, ESN only required about 50 images for training to achieve 99.0385% reconstruction accuracy among all test images, greatly reducing the computational cost during the training period, which indicated excellent generalization of encoding and decoding of ESN.

Table 2. Images reconstruction accuracy under different sample numbers

number of training samples	number of testing samples	number of readout neurons	N	Acc.[%]
10	10000	300	300	81.2967
20	10000	300	300	92.5139
30	10000	300	300	96.8201
40	10000	300	300	97.7987
50	10000	300	300	98.1457
100	10000	300	300	98.7322
500	10000	300	300	99.0385

Additionally, our research further tested the readability of ESN, which means training the readout weights by only reading the voltage of a subset of neurons in the reservoir. The model parameters were set the same as those in Table 3: N = 300, SR = 1, inScaling = 0.2, Rank = 10.

Table 3 showed the reconstruction accuracy of ESN on the MNIST dataset under different numbers of readout neurons, using 60,000 images for training and 10,000 images for testing. As shown in Table 3, ESN had a certain degree of redundancy on representation, and it is possible to greatly reconstruct the image without reading the voltages of all neurons, which implicated excellent readability. When using only 150 readout neurons (half of the size of the reservoir), the reconstruction accuracy of ESN could also reach 87.4254%. When the number of readout neurons increased to 200, the reconstruction accuracy can be further raised to 95.4439%.

Table 3. Images reconstruction accuracy under different readout numbers

number of readout neurons	number of training samples	number of testing samples	N	Acc.[%]
50	60000	10000	300	62.2744
100	60000	10000	300	73.3253
150	60000	10000	300	87.4254
200	60000	10000	300	95.4439
250	60000	10000	300	98.5047
300	60000	10000	300	99.44

To demonstrate that the readability of ESN was not due to a large number of training samples, ESN was further trained to reconstruct images with a small number of training samples with a reduced number of readout neurons. Table 4 showed the reconstruction accuracy of ESN with different numbers of training samples and readout neurons. According to the Table 4, the reconstruction accuracy of the model using only 50 training samples and 250 readout neurons was 96.3696%, revealing that great performance could be achieved with a small number of training samples when reducing the number of readout neurons. However, insufficient training samples and incomplete readout neurons would jointly lead to a decrease in accuracy. For example, In the experiments of Table 4, with 200 readout neurons but only 20 training samples, the reconstruction accuracy dropped to 86.7225%. Therefore, effective trade-offs need to be made between reducing the number of readout neurons and increasing the number of training samples appropriately.

Table 4. Images reconstruction accuracy under different training samples numbers and readout numbers

number of training samples	number of readout neurons	number of testing samples	N	Acc.[%]
20	150	10000	300	78.7473
20	200	10000	300	86.7225
20	250	10000	300	91.1346
50	150	10000	300	83.8141
50	200	10000	300	92.3721
50	250	10000	300	96.3696

3.2   Reconstruction of Color Images on FFHQ Dataset

The image reconstruction ability of ESN is also further demonstrated on the color image dataset Flickr-Faces-HQ (FFHQ), which is a high-quality dataset [12] of human face images created as a benchmark for generative adversarial networks. Each image has a size of 128×128, with 60,000 training samples and 10,000 test samples. Here, a specific type of tensor low-rank decomposition, Canonical Polyadic decomposition (CP decomposition) [16], was applied to the color images for dimensionality reduction. CP decomposition of a tensor refers to decomposing the tensor into a collection of vectors, which can be given as:

$$\chi = \sum_{i=1}^{R} a_r \circ b_r \circ c_r \tag{7}$$

where χ is a 3-dimensional tensor; $\circ$ denotes the outer product; R is a positive integer representing the rank; $a_r \in R^I, b_r \in R^J, c_r \in R^K$ are 3 vectors or rank-1 tensors. As shown in Fig. 4, we arranged the selected eigenvectors corresponding to three-dimensionality into a row as the input sequence of ESN. Figure 4A illustrated the concatenation of the first 100 ranking eigenvectors of the three-dimensionality of a color image.

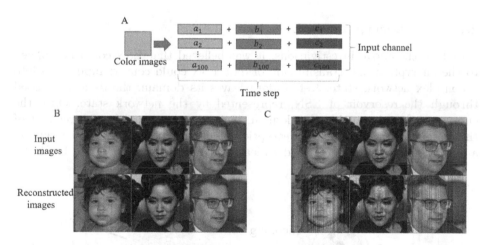

Fig. 4. CP decomposition and reconstruction of color images. A: The arrangement of color images as the input after CP decomposition. B: Examples of image reconstruction results reconstructed from the signals of all neurons of the reservoir. C: Examples of image reconstruction results when only 800 neurons of the reservoir were read out. (Color figure online)

The model parameters for the reconstruction of FFHQ images were set as follows: N =1000, inScaling = 0.002, SR = 1, α = 1, and 100 eigenvectors were selected as the input sequence in the CP decomposition. Our experiments used 500 training images and tested on the 10,00 images, finally achieving a testing accuracy of 99.9629%. Figure 4B showed the part result of input and reconstructed images by ESN. When reducing the number of readout neurons in the reservoir, such as using 800 readout neurons, the reconstruction accuracy was reduced to 81.7867%. The result was illustrated in Fig. 4C.

4   Important Privacy Protection

With the advent of the big data era, the protection of data privacy has become increasingly important. How to ensure the security of data is a crucial question. Privacy-preserving computation refers to the techniques that enable data analysis and computation while protecting the data itself from being leaked. It allows for the discovery of data value without the data leaving its domain. Privacy-preserving computation encompasses various approaches, including federated learning [17] in the context of distributed machine learning, secure multi-party computation based on complex cryptography [18], homomorphic encryption [19], differential privacy [20], and so on. Currently, privacy-preserving computation is primarily used in data-driven sectors, such as finance, the internet industry, and the healthcare sector, which require the exchange of large amounts of data while maintaining privacy.

4.1   Data Encryption by ESN

Based on the above investigations, it was believed that ESN could be applied to the encryption and transmission of data ESN could convert input data into a complex network state. Before data leaves its domain, the data are passed through the reservoir of ESN, represented by the network state. Once the encrypted data is outside the domain, it can be decrypted by the readout of the trained ESN, enabling the decryption of all encrypted data. The encryption and decryption process of ESN data leaving the domain is illustrated in Fig. 5.

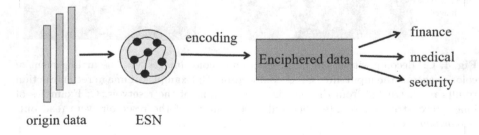

Fig. 5. The process of encrypting based on ESN when data is out of the domain.

4.2   The Anti-attack Performance of ESN Deep Network

When using general neural networks for some tasks, such as image classification, the trained networks are vulnerable to attacks, which means that the data from a certain layer downstream of the network can be used by a pre-trained network to reconstruct the original input image. Regarding the attacker, the input is embedded in a broad deep CNN or a reservoir, respectively. The output is the potential reconstructed data. The attacker is a trained network with style-GAN [21]. The goal is to find the nearest location of the target embedding in the latent space; Thus, the reconstructed is nearest to the target figure in the original space. The attacked results of a deep CNN trained on the FFHQ dataset are shown in Fig. 6B, where the reconstructed images after the attack bear a high resemblance to the input images. It indicated that the security of ordinary deep networks was not sufficient, as the data can be easily attacked, leading to information leakage. Although currently popular networks demonstrate excellent performance on various tasks, there is a need for further improvement in the security of these models.

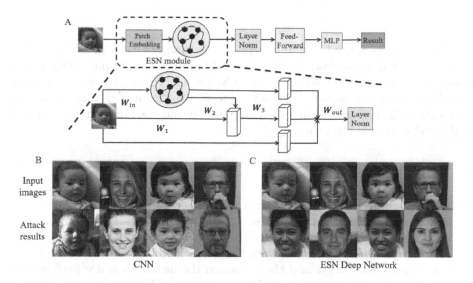

Fig. 6. ESN Deep network structure and attack results of CNN and ESN deep network. A: The structure of a deep network with an ESN module. B: Examples of attack results on CNN. C: Examples of attack results on ESN deep network.

Here, we tested the security of the proposed deep network model based on ESN in the same way. Our model consists of an ESN module, normalization, a feed-forward layer, and the MLP layer. By adding several neural network layers after the reservoir, the information from the reservoir could be read out by nonlinear methods, which replaced the traditional linear readout structure. The structure of our model was illustrated in Fig. 6A, the upper depicts the overall framework of the network, and the bottom part provided a detailed description of the ESN module of our network, where the W_{in}, W_1, W_2, W_3, W_{out} represent the weights of state layers. The ESN module operated at Edge of Chaos with SR = 1 in experiments. The same attack network was used to perform attacks on our network, and the results of the attacked network were shown in Fig. 6C, where the recovered results exhibit significant differences from the original inputs.

Some metrics were adopted to quantitatively validate how well the proposed method could recover the identity of the subject, such as Frechet Inception Distance (FID). Table 5 showed the compared results of FID of CNN and ESN deep network.

Table 5. FID between input and attacked results of CNN and ESN Deep Network

Model	FID
CNN	343.71
ESN deep network	407.41

The results indicated that the original data had not been leaked, revealing that the ESN deep network could effectively protect private data. Due to the complex dynamics in the reservoir of ESN, the encrypted data were not easily attacked. The great capacity of data protection makes it highly promising for applications in the field of privacy computation and warrants further research and development in the future.

5   Conclusion

In this paper, our study focused on exploring the coding and decoding capacity of ESN to discover new application scenarios. We utilized an image reconstruction task as a benchmark to evaluate the network's performance. To adapt the recurrent structure of the network, we first performed the dimensionality reduction on images using SVD and then assessed the network's codec performance by reconstructing these input eigenvector sequences. The result of reconstructing grey images revealed the strong capacity of the codec of ESN, and there was an excellent generalization on the network, which implies potential advantages. Besides, ESN could be easily extended to encode and decode color images.

Building upon these advantages, we proposed a novel idea for the protection of sensitive information based on ESN. We constructed a deep network incorporating an ESN module and subjected it to attacks from a specific adversarial network after training. The anti-attack performance of this network surpasses that of using CNN, highlighting the exceptional ability of ESN in safeguarding information and suggesting potential applications in the finance and security domains. In future work, further exploration of the mechanisms of information encoding, as well as the application of ESN in information encryption, would be conducted in greater detail.

Acknowledgment. Weian and Dongping's work is supported in part by the National Natural Science Foundation of China (Grant No. 12175242). Huiwen's work is supported in part by the Youth Foundation Project of Zhejiang Lab (Grant No. 111012-AA2306).

References

1. Redmon J., Divvala S., Girshick R., et al.: You only look once: unified, real-time object detection. In: Proceedings of the IEEE Conference on Computer Vision and Pattern Recognition (CVPR), pp. 779–788. IEEE, Las Vegas, NV, USA (2016)
2. Deng, L., Li, J., Huang, J.T., et al.: Recent advances in deep learning for speech research at Microsoft. In: IEEE International Conference on Acoustics, Speech and Signal Processing (ICASSP), pp. 8604–8608. IEEE, Vancouver, BC, Canada (2013)
3. Chen, C., Seff, A., Kornhauser, A., et al.: Deepdriving: learning affordance for direct perception in autonomous driving. In: Proceedings of the IEEE International Conference on Computer Vision (ICCV), pp. 2722–2730. IEEE, Santiago, Chile (2015)
4. Dosovitskiy, A., Beyer, L., Kolesnikov, A., et al.: An image is worth 16×16 words: transformers for image recognition at scale. eprint arXiv: 2010.11929 (2020)
5. Chen Z., Xie L., Niu J., et al.: Visformer: the vision-friendly transformer. In: Proceedings of the IEEE/CVF International Conference on Computer Vision (ICCV), pp. 589–598. IEEE, virtually (2021)
6. Hochreiter, S., Schmidhuber, J.: Long short-term memory. Neural Comput. **9**(8), 1735–1780 (1997)
7. Schrauwen B., Verstraeten D., Van Campenhout J.: An overview of reservoir computing: theory, applications, and implementations. In: Proceedings of the 15th European Symposium on Artificial Neural Networks (ESANN), pp. 471–482. DBLP, Bruges, Belgium (2007)
8. Skowronski, M.D., Harris, J.G.: Automatic speech recognition using a predictive echo state network classifier. Neural Netw. **20**(3), 414–423 (2007)
9. Lukoševičius, M., Jaeger, H., Schrauwen, B.: Reservoir computing trends. Künstl Intell. **26**(4), 365–371 (2012)
10. Lukoševičius, M., Jaeger, H.: Reservoir computing approaches to recurrent neural network training. Comput. Sci. Rev. **3**(3), 127–149 (2009)
11. Jaeger, H.: Echo state network. Scholarpedia **2**(9), 2330 (2007)
12. Karras T., Laine S., Aila T.: A style-based generator architecture for generative adversarial networks. In: Proceedings of the IEEE/CVF Conference on Computer Vision and Pattern Recognition (CVPR), pp. 4401–4410. IEEE, Long Beach (2019)
13. Hadaeghi, F.: Neuromorphic electronic systems for reservoir computing. In: Nakajima, K., Fischer, I. (eds.) Reservoir Computing. Natural Computing Series, pp. 221–237. Springer, Singapore (2021)
14. Jaeger, H.: Long short-term memory in echo state networks: details of a simulation study. Jacobs University Bremen (2012)
15. Abdi, H.: Singular value decomposition (SVD) and generalized singular value decomposition. In: Encyclopedia of Measurement and Statistics, pp. 907–912 (2007)

16. Kolda, T.G., Bader, B.W.: Tensor decompositions and applications. SIAM Rev. Soc. Ind. Appl. Math. **51**(3), 455–500 (2009)
17. Yang, H., Lam, K.Y., Xiao, L., et al.: Lead federated neuromorphic learning for wireless edge artificial intelligence. Nat. Commun. **13**(1), 4269 (2022)
18. Lindell, Y.: Secure multiparty computation for privacy preserving data mining. In: Wang, J. (eds.) Encyclopedia of Data Warehousing and Mining, pp. 1005–1009. IGI Global (2005)
19. Gentry, C.: Fully homomorphic encryption using ideal lattices. In: Proceedings of the forty-first annual ACM Symposium on Theory of Computing (STOC), pp. 169–178. Association for Computing Machinery, NY (2009)
20. Dwork, C.: Differential privacy: a survey of results. In: Theory and Applications of Models of Computation: 5th International Conference (TAMC), pp. 25–29. DBLP, Xi'an, China (2008)
21. Karras, T., Laine, S., Aila, T.: A style-based generator architecture for generative adversarial networks. In: Proceedings of the IEEE/CVF Conference on Computer Vision and Pattern Recognition (CVPR), pp. 4401–4410. IEEE, Long Beach (2019)

Bidirectional Delay Estimation of Motor Control Systems at Different Muscle Contraction Levels

Jinbiao Liu[1], Xinhang Li[1], Lijie Wang[1], Manli Luo[1], Tao Tang[1,2], Linqing Feng[1,2], and Yina Wei[1,2(✉)]

[1] Research Center for Augmented Intelligence, Zhejiang Lab, Hangzhou 311100, Zhejiang, China
weiyina039@zhejianglab.com

[2] Zhejiang Provincial Key Laboratory of Cardio-Cerebral Vascular Detection Technology and Medicinal Effectiveness Appraisal, Zhejiang University, Hangzhou 310027, China

Abstract. Reliable estimation of bidirectional delays in motor control systems is crucial for uncovering underlying physiological mechanisms. However, previous studies have largely overlooked the delay in information transmission from the perspective of movement levels, limiting the understanding of physiological delays. This study aims to investigate the conduction delay between the brain and muscles, and uncover the underlying physiological mechanisms of hand motor function through delay estimation. Based on the analogous cumulant density method, the delay between the brain cortex and hand muscles was evaluated at different levels of force contraction. We found that there was no significant difference in delay observed at different levels of force, regardless of whether the analysis was based on the raw electromyography (EMG) or EMG signals synthesized from motor unit (MU). In the descending pathway from the brain to the muscles, it was observed that the positive delay was significantly shorter at low force levels compared to moderate force levels. Moreover, by utilizing the features of the minimum spanning tree (MST) graph to characterize changes in the brain functional network at different levels of movement, it was found that in the beta frequency band, both the diameter and radius descriptors of the MST graph were significantly larger during low and high force movements compared to moderate force movement. This study suggests a potential correlation between physiological delays and muscle performance. Sustaining balance during low-force movements requires the integration of more resources, resulting in lower information transmission efficiency. Conversely, in the motor control loop, information is transmitted more quickly from the central nervous system to peripheral muscle tissues during low-force contraction.

Keywords: Electromyography · electroencephalography · delay estimation

1 Introduction

The motor cortex sends oscillatory outputs downward and also receives oscillatory inputs through afferent pathways [1]. This bidirectional coupling effect between the cortex and muscles results in different information transmission delays in both the descending and

H. Yang et al. (Eds.): ICIRA 2023, LNAI 14267, pp. 187–199, 2023.
https://doi.org/10.1007/978-981-99-6483-3_17

ascending pathways. Reliable estimation of these time delays could be beneficial in uncovering the underlying physiological mechanisms of motor control.

Based on the inverse Fourier transform and the Hilbert transform methods, the estimation accuracy of time delays for cortico-peripheral relations was improved in simulation experiments [2]. However, it has been demonstrated to produce conflicting results in human reflex experiments, which do not satisfy human physiological characteristics [3]. Although linear Granger causality measures such as directed transfer function and directed coherence can estimate bidirectional delays, recent study has shown that delays based on directed coherence are overestimated in limited-bandwidth bidirectional communication [4]. In contrast, the nonparametric directionality measures [5] can achieve accurate delay estimation in situations with a wide range of spectral frequencies. The study also found that decomposing EMG into single motor unit (MU) and extracting the spiking activity of pools of MUs improved the delay estimates and was more consistent with the cortical-spinal transmission delay determined by non-invasive brain stimulation. However, Ibáñez et al. only focused on low-force contraction levels and did not explore the potential delay variations caused by differences in muscle performance at different force levels [4]. The oscillatory activity of the motor cortex is closely related to the movement state of the response muscles. It remains unclear whether the varying degrees of oscillatory activity generated by the motor cortical circuits affects information transmission delay, which is crucial for understanding the mechanisms of motor control.

In this study, we evaluated the delay time between cerebral cortex and hand muscles under different force contraction levels based on the analogous cumulant density function, compared the difference of delay estimation under EMG and collective MUs, and further explored the potential relationship between delay time and changes in brain network using functional connectivity features. Our study represents a pioneering attempt to explore the delay in brain-muscle conduction as an effective indicator for uncovering the physiological mechanisms of motor control relevant to hand function.

2 Materials and Methods

2.1 Subjects

Ten participants (aged 25–33, two females) were recruited for the hand motor function experiment. All participants reported being right-handed, with no history of severe limb injuries, and no symptoms or signs of neuromuscular disorders. The experimental procedures of this study were approved by the ethics committee of Zhejiang Lab. For all participants, we provided a detailed description of the experiment both oral and written form, and obtained informed consent in accordance with the Helsinki declaration.

2.2 Experiment Procedures

The participants sat naturally beside a table and performed a sustained isometric contraction task with their index finger in abduction using dominant hand (right hand). Throughout the test, the participants were required to keep their head as stable as possible. Prior to the experiment, the maximum voluntary contraction (MVC) of the index finger abduction was measured for each participant. During the task, the participants performed the contraction at 20%, 40%, 60%, and 80% of their MVC. Each sustained contraction trial lasted for 20 s, including a 2-s preparation phase. Three sets of data (each set consisting of three trials) were collected for different levels of contraction force from each participant, with at least 2-min of rest between each set to avoid the possibility of fatigue.

2.3 Recordings and Preprocessing

During the experiment, we synchronously collected 64-channel high-density surface electromyography (HD-sEMG) signals and 64-channel electroencephalography (EEG) signals, while force information was displayed and fed back in real-time through a digital grip force sensor. The electrode position of the HD-sEMG device (GR04MM1305, Quattrocento, OT Bioelettronica) was located on the first dorsal interosseous muscle (FDI), with a sampling frequency of 2000 Hz (down-sampled to 1000 Hz in subsequent analysis). The EEG device (Neuracle-NSW364, China) were sampled at 1000 Hz, and the impedance of the electrodes was maintained below 50 KΩ. The synchronization between EEG and HD-sEMG signals was achieved by sending triggers through a marking box. To minimize noise and artifacts in the EEG signal, we applied a band-pass filter from 0.5 Hz to 45 Hz using the EEGLAB plugin, followed by the Runica algorithm and the multiple artifact rejection algorithm (MARA) to eliminate artifacts and obtained clean EEG signals.

Given that all participants were right-handed, C3 was selected as the channel for subsequent EEG analysis. Based on the distribution of average signal amplitudes of HD-sEMG channels during isometric contraction tasks performed by the participants, the channel with the highest muscle activation was chosen for subsequent EMG analysis. Each trial contained 18 s of valid data, and a continuous 10-s segment with dense firings was extracted for analysis.

2.4 Delay Estimation Based on Analogous Cumulant Density

In order to estimate the delay with the strongest correlation between EEG and hand muscle activity in this study, it is necessary to first define the coherence between EEG and EMG signals. Let x and y represent the time series of EEG and EMG respectively. Traditionally, coherence between x and y can be represented by the formula $|R_{yx}(\omega)|^2 = |f_{yx}(\omega)|^2 / f_{xx}(\omega) f_{yy}(\omega)$, where $f_{xx}(\omega)$, $f_{yy}(\omega)$ and $f_{yx}(\omega)$ represent the auto-power spectrum and cross-power spectrum at frequency ω, respectively.

To reduce interference within the signal, Eldar et al. [6] proposed the use of optimal whitening filter to multiply the self-spectrum by the whitening coefficient $f(\omega)^{-1/2}$, resulting in the whitened self-spectrum $f_{xx}^w(\omega) = 1$ and $f_{yy}^w(\omega) = 1$. Therefore, the coherence between whitened sequences has no denominator term and can be decomposed into directional measures. We further defined the coherence measure R_{yx}^2 as follows:

$$R_{yx}^2 = \frac{1}{2\pi} \int_{-\pi}^{\pi} \left| f_{yx}^w(\omega) \right|^2 d\omega \tag{1}$$

Further, we defined a correlation measure in the time domain with time delay τ, denoted as $\delta_{yx}(\tau)$, which forms a Fourier transform pair with the whitened cross-spectrum. This allows for the directional decomposition of R^2_{yx} and is expressed as follows:

$$\delta_{yx}(\tau) = \frac{1}{2\pi} \int_{-\pi}^{\pi} \left| f^w_{yx}(\omega) e^{i\omega\tau} \right|^2 d\omega \tag{2}$$

The function $\delta_{yx}(\tau)$ captures the temporal correlation structure between two whitened processes in the time domain, in a way that resembles the time structure captured by cumulant density of the original process as represented in the cross spectrum, $f^w_{yx}(\omega)$. Therefore, we defined $\delta_{yx}(\tau)$ as analogous cumulant density function. It should be noted that $\delta_{yx}(\tau)$ is not affected by any internal variables, and the whitening process has the same coherence and phase estimation as the original process [5]. Thus, all significant features in the estimation of $\delta_{yx}(\tau)$ will reflect the interaction between the cortex and muscles.

Based on the analogous cumulant density function (2), R^2_{yx} can be decomposed with respect to the time delay τ, as expressed below:

$$R^2_{yx} = \int_{-\infty}^{\infty} \left| \delta_{yx}(\tau) \right|^2 d\tau \tag{3}$$

Next, by selecting the desired lag range in Eq. (3), R^2_{yx} can be decomposed based on different lags to obtain directional measure, expressed as follows:

$$R^2_{yx} = \int_{\tau<0} \left| \delta_{yx}(\tau) \right|^2 d\tau + \left| \delta_{yx}(0) \right|^2 + \int_{\tau>0} \left| \delta_{yx}(\tau) \right|^2 d\tau \tag{4}$$

To characterize the interaction between the cortex and muscles in the time domain, a confidence interval of 95% was set for the significant peaks to determine the significant values. The confidence limit was defined as $\pm\frac{1.96}{\sqrt{R}}$, where R is the number of data points considered.

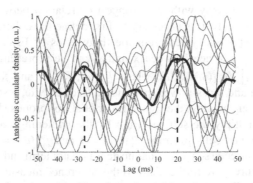

Fig. 1. An example of average (black) and single-trial (gray) normalized analogous cumulant densities obtained between the EEG and EMG data. The blue and red circles represent the delay PL and NL corresponding to the highest peak in the positive and negative directions, respectively.

Finally, in order to estimate the transmission delays in the motor cortical circuits for both the descending and ascending paths (brain→muscle/muscle→brain), we identified the time points where the maximum peaks were found at positive lags (PL) and negative lags (NL), respectively, as the bidirectional delay estimates (Fig. 1). The reason for using peak time is that the EEG recording is done with the reversed polarity (negative upward), which is related to the period when the dendritic trees of pyramidal cells in the motor cortex receive the main excitatory inputs [4].

2.5 Synthetic EMG based on collective MUs

Under low-force condition, Ibáñez et al. found that using MU discharge activity instead of EMG signals resulted in improved estimation of EEG → MU delay [4]. To evaluate the effectiveness of estimating delay time between cortex and muscles using MUs at different force levels, we further constructed synthetic EMG signals from the collective MU (CMU) activities. Specifically, we utilized the convolutional kernel compensation (CKC) algorithm to decompose the HD-sEMG signals into motor unit spike trains (MUSTs) [7]. Subsequently, spike-triggered averaging was performed to obtain the waveform of MU spatial distribution on each channel, representing the shape of MU on the i-th channel:

$$y_t = \frac{1}{N_i} \sum_{n=1}^{N_i} y_{s_{i,n}+t}, t = -\frac{L}{2} + 1, \cdots, L/2 \tag{5}$$

where y represents the original EMG signal, $s_{i,n}$ denotes the firing time of the n-th discharge of the i-th MU, and L = 50 ms.

Finally, the waveforms of CMU on the i-th channel were convolved with the MUSTs and then summed together to obtain the synthesized EMG signal on that channel.

2.6 Brain Functional Connectivity Analysis Based on Minimum Spanning Tree Graph

Previous studies have demonstrated that functional connectivity can be used to characterize the interactions between neurons and capture the multivariate characteristics of brain activity [8, 9]. Further investigation is required to elucidate the physiological significance of delay between brain and muscle tissues. In this study, we employed a global functional connectivity network, which reflects the underlying structure of oscillatory EEG activity, to elucidate the potential mechanisms behind the observed variations in delay at different force levels.

Specifically, graph theory analysis was utilized to examine the functional connectivity and activation patterns in the brain [10, 11]. Additionally, the potential relationship between delays and differences in brain activities within network configurations was further evaluated through Minimum Spanning Tree (MST) analysis. MST offers the advantage of providing an unbiased representation of the network by integrating features of small-worldness (clustering/path length) and scale-free properties (hubs). The weighted connectivity matrices were firstly computed using the imaginary part of coherence (iCOH) in multiple frequency bands [12]. Then, we extracted the MST graph that represents the subnetwork with the highest connectivity based on the functional connectivity matrices. Finally, in this study, local and global MST descriptors including degree, betweenness centrality (BC), leaf fraction (LF), eccentricity (EC), tree hierarchy (TH), diameter (Di), radius (Rad) and degree correlation (DC) were averaged across epochs and computed within each frequency band.

2.7 Statistical Analysis

To validate the statistical significance of bidirectional delay estimation between the cortex and muscles, this study proposed delay time as a statistical metric to quantify potential differences across various levels of contraction and different signal combination patterns. The beta frequency band (13 Hz–30 Hz) was chosen for the analysis of delay estimation. Statistical analysis was performed using SPSS 22.0 (IBM SPSS Statistics, Chicago, USA) through independent sample two-tailed t-tests, with a significance level set at 0.05.

3 Results

3.1 Comparison of Bidirectional Delay Between Two Signal Source Combinations

We compared the statistical distributions of delay time estimated using the analogous cumulative density function for two source signal combinations: EEG-EMG and EEG-CMU. Each pair of signal sources was treated as a matched time series pair, and the signal length for delay estimation analysis was set to T = 5 s. Delay values for the descending (brain→muscle) and ascending (muscle→brain) paths were separately calculated for different force levels. In this experiment, for each contraction condition, the total number of valid segments across all participant groups was no less than 20. Taking the 40% MVC condition as an example, the delay estimation results for the two signal source combinations are shown in Fig. 2, where the black dashed line represents the average positive delay (lag) and the green dashed line represents the average negative delay. From the overall distribution, it can be observed that the delays calculated using the EEG-EMG combination (Fig. 2a) exhibited greater fluctuations compared to the EEG-CMU combination (Fig. 2b), but there was basically the same in the overall mean values. Furthermore, irrespective of whether it involved the EEG-EMG combination or the EEG-CMU combination, no notable difference in the delays between the two directions was observed.

Further statistical comparisons of delay estimation for the two signal source combinations were conducted at four different force levels, as shown in Fig. 3. Although no significant differences were observed between the two combinations at different force levels, there was a trend of decreased delay for both low-force (20% MVC) and high-force (80% MVC) conditions compared to the moderate-force (40% MVC and 60% MVC) condition, particularly noticeable in the positive and negative directions for 20% MVC. Additional comparing the delay estimation at different force levels within the EEG-EMG or EEG-CMU combination separately, as shown in Fig. 4, it can be observed that in the positive direction of the EEG-EMG combination, the estimated delay at 20%

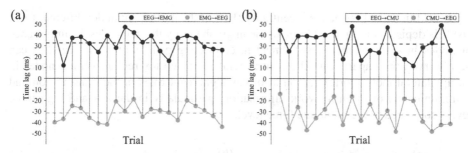

Fig. 2. The delay estimation of the two signal source combinations. (a) EEG-EMG combination. (b) EEG-CMU combination. The solid black circles and solid green circles represent positive and negative delays, respectively. The dashed black line and dashed green line represent the average delays, respectively.

MVC was significantly lower than at 40% MVC (p = 0.049). Similarly, in the positive direction of the EEG-CMU combination, the estimated delay at 20% MVC was significantly lower than at both 40% MVC (p = 0.022) and 60% MVC (p = 0.033).

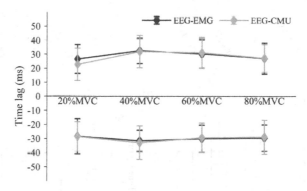

Fig. 3. Delay estimation of two signal source combination patterns at different force contraction.

3.2 Comparison of Brain Functional Connectivity Characteristics Under Different Force Levels

In order to gain insight into the physiological significance of brain-muscle delay and explore the underlying mechanisms of individual differences, we calculated the MST structure of functional connectivity and quantified the multivariate properties of brain activity across different force conditions using MST descriptor features. Node degree is one of the significant characteristics of MST graph that can reveal the importance, stability, and information transmission capability of nodes in the network. Based on MST graph computation, brain topographic mapping of node degrees for a typical participant was shown in Fig. 5. It can be found that nodes with higher degrees are primarily located in the contralateral motor cortex area. Moreover, the node degrees are higher in the moderate force level compared to the low and high force levels.

In addition, the betweenness centrality (BC) of the participant under different force levels is depicted in Fig. 6. BC is a metric in graph theory that measures the importance of nodes in terms of their involvement in connecting paths within the graph. It can be observed that, apart from the contralateral motor cortex region, certain nodes in the ipsilateral motor cortex region also play significant roles in the transmission and communication of brain network information, particularly in the low and high force levels compared to the moderate force level.

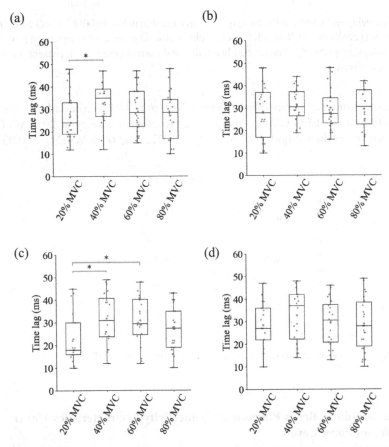

Fig. 4. The delay estimation at different force levels within the EEG-EMG or EEG-CMU combination at the positive and negative directions. (a) EEG→EMG. (b) EMG→EEG. (c) EEG→CMU. (d) CMU→EEG. * p < 0.05.

Table 1 further presented the overall statistical results of each MST descriptor in the beta frequency band under different force levels. The analysis revealed significant differences in the diameter (Di) and radius (Rad) metrics across the force levels. Specifically, the Di was significantly longer at 20% MVC compared to 60% MVC, while at 80% MVC, the Di was significantly longer than at both 40% MVC and 60% MVC. Similarly, the Rad was significantly greater at 20% MVC compared to 60% MVC, while at 80% MVC, the Rad was significantly higher than at both 40% MVC and 60% MVC.

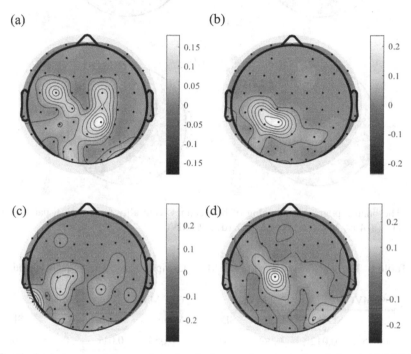

Fig. 5. The brain topographic mapping of node degrees for a typical participant. (a) 20% MVC. (b) 40% MVC. (c) 60% MVC. (d) 80% MVC.

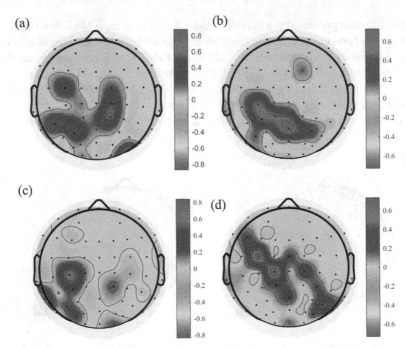

Fig. 6. The brain topographic mapping of betweenness centrality for a typical participant. (a) 20% MVC. (b) 40% MVC. (c) 60% MVC. (d) 80% MVC.

Table 1. The statistical results of each MST descriptor in the beta frequency band.

	20% MVC		40% MVC		60% MVC		80% MVC	
	Mean	SD	Mean	SD	Mean	SD	Mean	SD
BC	0.075	0.012	0.069	0.014	0.068	0.011	0.075	0.013
EC	0.773	0.025	0.769	0.031	0.761	0.024	0.777	0.027
LF	0.653	0.059	0.664	0.051	0.670	0.048	0.659	0.064
TH	0.455	0.060	0.450	0.058	0.454	0.041	0.476	0.050
DC	−0.407	0.092	−0.392	0.183	−0.424	0.083	−0.431	0.084
Di	**95.864**	**20.332**	**86.740**	**20.852**	**83.870**	**23.943**	**95.699**	**18.945**
Rad	**49.690**	**10.469**	**45.146**	**10.763**	**43.495**	**12.468**	**49.873**	**9.423**

SD: standard deviation.

4 Discussion

Cortical activity is propagated to muscle groups through motor neurons, while peripheral feedback inputs, including sensory information, are transmitted from muscle proprioceptors to the motor cortex. In the process of sensorimotor control, information transmission is not instantaneous but involves a time delay, which reflects at least the time of neural conduction [3]. Reliably characterizing the time delays between cortex and muscles can quantify the process by which oscillatory activity generated in the motor cortical circuits is transmitted through the corticospinal tract. In this study, we employed the analogous cumulant density function to estimate the transmission delay between the brain and hand muscles, and the estimated delay was consistent with previous findings [4, 13]. Furthermore, we found that the delay in both directions was not significantly affected by different levels of force, regardless of whether the analysis based on raw EMG or EMG signals synthesized from MUs. However, our study revealed a potential correlation between the delay time in the descending pathway (EEG→EMG) and motor performance of hand muscles. Specifically, we observed that the positive delays were significantly greater at the moderate force level compared to the low force level. While there is currently no definitive physiological explanation for this observation, it is speculated that maintaining continuous muscle contraction at a low force level may require higher motor performance, resulting in faster information transmission within the motor loop. Previous studies have demonstrated that damage to the corticospinal tract following a stroke can alter the time delay from the cortex to the periphery in the motor control process, involving indirect pathways that are less dominant in healthy individuals, potentially leading to increased delays [14]. Thus, conduction delay may serve as an important physiological indicator for uncovering the intrinsic mechanisms of brain injury and diagnosing the location of lesions in neurological disorders.

Studying the dynamic changes of brain functional networks under different tasks or states contributes to our understanding of their plasticity and adaptability, as well as how brain function is organized and integrated under various conditions. By constructing a MST graph, the brain functional network can be simplified into an acyclic subnetwork from a global perspective. This helps identify key nodes that play important functional and regulatory roles, thereby revealing functional connectivity and information transmission pathways between brain regions [15]. In this study, we observed that in the beta frequency band, during low and high force movements, both the Di and Rad descriptors of the MST graph were significantly greater compared to moderate force movement. Larger values of Di and Rad indicate higher overall integrity and expansiveness of the graph, implying the involvement of more steps in information propagation. Conversely, smaller values suggest closer proximity between nodes, indicating more efficient information transfer. Interestingly, we found that the descending pathway delay between the brain and hand muscles during low force movement was lower compared to moderate force movement. Further speculation suggests that maintaining a balanced low force movement requires the integration of more resources, with more nodes participating in the brain network, resulting in relatively less efficient information transmission compared to moderate force movement. However, in the sensorimotor circuit, the time required for information to be transmitted from the central nervous system to the peripheral system is shortened.

5 Conclusion

There are bidirectional coupling effects between the cerebral cortex and muscle, with delayed information transfer in both directions of the descending and ascending pathways. This study aims to explore the conduction delay between the brain and muscles and utilize delay estimation to reveal the physiological mechanisms underlying hand motor control. By employing the analogous cumulant density method, the delay between the motor cortex and the hand muscles was assessed at different levels of force contraction. The results indicated that there was no significant difference in the delay between EMG and collective MUs calculations. However, in the descending pathway (EEG→EMG), the positive delay during low-force movement was significantly shorter than during moderate-force movement, suggesting a potential correlation between delay and muscle movement performance. Furthermore, utilizing MST graph features to characterize brain network changes at different movement levels, it was observed that in the beta frequency band, during low and high-force movements, both the diameter and radius descriptors of the MST graph were significantly larger than during moderate-force movement. The execution of balanced low-level movement requires the integration of more resources, resulting in lower efficiency of information transmission. On the contrary, information travels more rapidly from the central nervous system to the peripheral muscle tissues within the motor control loop during this process.

Acknowledgment. This work was supported by the National Natural Science Foundation of China under Grant 62201515 and Grant 12101570, the China Postdoctoral Science Foundation under Grant 2021M702974, and Key Research Project of Zhejiang Lab (2022KI0AC01).

References

1. Yang, Y., Dewald, J.P., van der Helm, F.C., Schouten, A.C.: Unveiling neural coupling within the sensorimotor system: directionality and nonlinearity. Eur. J. Neurosci. **48**(7), 2407–2415 (2018)
2. Lindemann, M., Raethjen, J., Timmer, J., Deuschl, G., Pfister, G.: Delay estimation for cortico-peripheral relations. J. Neurosci. Methods **111**(2), 127–139 (2001)
3. Xu, Y., McClelland, V.M., Cvetković, Z., Mills, K.R.: Corticomuscular coherence with time lag with application to delay estimation. IEEE Trans. Biomed. Eng. **64**(3), 588–600 (2016)
4. Ibáñez, J., Del Vecchio, A., Rothwell, J.C., Baker, S.N., Farina, D.: Only the fastest corticospinal fibers contribute to β corticomuscular coherence. J. Neurosci. **41**(22), 4867–4879 (2021)
5. Halliday, D.M.: Nonparametric directionality measures for time series and point process data. J. Integr. Neurosci. **14**(02), 253–277 (2015)
6. Eldar, Y.C., Oppenheim, A.V.: MMSE whitening and subspace whitening. IEEE Trans. Inf. Theory **49**(7), 1846–1851 (2003)
7. Holobar, A., Zazula, D.: Multichannel blind source separation using convolution kernel compensation. IEEE Trans. Signal Process. **55**(9), 4487–4496 (2007)
8. Horwitz, B.: The elusive concept of brain connectivity. Neuroimage **19**(2), 466–470 (2003)
9. Ahmadlou, M., Adeli, H.: Functional community analysis of brain: a new approach for EEG-based investigation of the brain pathology. Neuroimage **58**(2), 401–408 (2011)

10. Reijneveld, J.C., Ponten, S.C., Berendse, H.W., Stam, C.J.: The application of graph theoretical analysis to complex networks in the brain. Clin. Neurophysiol. **118**(11), 2317–2331 (2007)
11. Ponten, S.C., Douw, L., Bartolomei, F., Reijneveld, J.C., Stam, C.J.: Indications for network regularization during absence seizures: weighted and unweighted graph theoretical analyses. Exp. Neurol. **217**(1), 197–204 (2009)
12. Dal Maso, F., Desormeau, B., Boudrias, M.H., Roig, M.: Acute cardiovascular exercise promotes functional changes in cortico-motor networks during the early stages of motor memory consolidation. Neuroimage **174**, 380–392 (2018)
13. Ushiyama, J., Takahashi, Y., Ushiba, J.: Muscle dependency of corticomuscular coherence in upper and lower limb muscles and training-related alterations in ballet dancers and weightlifters. J. Appl. Physiol. **109**(4), 1086–1095 (2010)
14. Liu, J., Tan, G., Sheng, Y., Wei, Y., Liu, H.: A novel delay estimation method for improving corticomuscular coherence in continuous synchronization events. IEEE Trans. Biomed. Eng. **69**(4), 1328–1339 (2021)
15. Tewarie, P., van Dellen, E., Hillebrand, A., Stam, C.J.: The minimum spanning tree: an unbiased method for brain network analysis. Neuroimage **104**, 177–188 (2015)

Growing Memory Network with Random Weight 3DCNN for Continuous Human Action Recognition

Wenbang Dou$^{(\boxtimes)}$, Wei Hong Chin, and Naoyuki Kubota

Graduate School of Systems Design, Tokyo Metropolitan University, Tokyo, Japan
dou-wenbang@ed.tmu.ac.jp

Abstract. Recent research has shown that continuous learning models, which emulate the learning mechanisms of the human brain, can effectively learn new data over time. However, many of these models require significant amounts of task-specific data to extract visual and temporal features using convolutional neural networks (CNNs) and recurrent neural networks (RNNs). Additionally, pre-training these data feature extractors is often computationally expensive and time-consuming. Furthermore, traditional continuous learning models require data labeling before learning new data, which is difficult to achieve in real-world applications such as human action recognition. To address these limitations, we present a novel Random Weight Convolutional-Growing Memory Network (RWC-GMN) model that enables real-time continuous learning of new human actions in the real world. Our model uses a fixed random weight 3DCNN as a feature extractor, thereby eliminating the need for pre-training and enabling our model to start learning new actions immediately. The random weight features will be fed into the Growing Memory Network (GMN) for learning. GMN is a self-organizing incremental network that emulates human episodic memory. The network size can grow and shrink to adapt to input data continuously. Moreover, our model does not require pre-labeling of new human actions, allowing for label-free learning in real-time. Finally, our model can learn new actions continuously while retaining previously acquired knowledge, avoiding the problem of catastrophic forgetting.

Keywords: Random Weight 3DCNN · Continuous Learning · Human Action Recognition

1 Introduction

Humans have remarkable learning abilities, gradually acquiring knowledge as a fundamental characteristic of learning [1]. Traditional deep learning algorithms have demonstrated excellent performance in various fields. However, continuously learning multiple tasks remains an important challenge in deep learning. In conventional scenarios, deep learning models may gradually forget the knowledge acquired in previous tasks when learning new tasks. This is referred to as the "catastrophic forgetting" [2] problem. To

H. Yang et al. (Eds.): ICIRA 2023, LNAI 14267, pp. 200–211, 2023.
https://doi.org/10.1007/978-981-99-6483-3_18

overcome this problem and achieve a more human-like continuous acquisition of knowledge, Ring [3] proposed continual learning. Continual learning is a task that requires machine learning to continuously learn data, adapt to new knowledge without forgetting previous knowledge. In recent years, research on continual learning has been frequently conducted. Shin et al. [4] proposed Deep Generative Replay (DGR), which uses a generative model to replay past data and maintains a generative model for each task. During learning, the generative model generates samples for each task, and this is used to train the feature extractor for the current task. However, DGR requires enormous computational resources because it learns multiple generative models for each task. Rebuffi et al. [5] proposed iCaRL, which uses correct samples from previous tasks to maintain a knowledge buffer for each task. The correct samples are selected based on the distance from the current decision boundary and are used to train the classifier for the current task. However, iCaRL requires a large amount of memory to store correct samples from previous tasks. Li et al. [6] proposed a method to learn without forgetting using meta-learning. The proposed method maximizes transfer learning between tasks and minimizes interference between tasks by optimizing model parameters using gradient descent algorithms. However, because the model parameters are optimized for each new task, the computational cost increases with the number of tasks. Lopez-Paz et al. [7] proposed Gradient Episodic Memory (GEM), which uses episodic memory to store past gradients and minimizes interference between tasks. GEM updates the feature extractor based on gradients from past tasks and uses an episode memory buffer to store gradients. The disadvantage of GEM is that a large memory is required to store the episode memory buffer. Chaudhry et al. [8] proposed Experience Replay (ER), which uses a replay buffer to store past data and alleviate catastrophic forgetting. The replay buffer generates samples for each task during training, which are then used to train the feature extractor for the current task.

Since continuous learning always involves learning from unknown data, feature extraction from data is particularly important. Current research on continuous learning involves extracting relevant features from input data and using feature extractors to represent them in a low-dimensional space to stabilize the model's performance. Conventional continuous learning models require feature extractors to be constantly updated, which increases computational costs every time new data is learned. To overcome this problem, recent studies have proposed using feature extractors with random weights that do not require learning. Shmelkov et al. [9] proposed an online EWC method that uses a feature extractor with random weights to learn from continuous data and adapt to new tasks. The feature extractor is trained using the Elastic Weight Consolidation (EWC) regularization method to prevent catastrophic forgetting. Zenke et al. [10] proposed a method for learning from the flow of continuous data and adapting to new tasks using a feature extractor with random weights and a replay buffer. The feature extractor is trained using a regularization method that encourages it to be orthogonal to the previous feature extractor. Rusu et al. [11] proposed a method for learning from continuous data and adapting to new tasks using a feature extractor with random weights and Knowledge Transfer (KT). KT allows the feature extractor to reuse the weights of previous tasks and learn new weights for the current task.

In addition, the techniques for continuous learning can be divided into three categories: dynamic architecture, regularization, and memory replay, in order to mitigate the "catastrophic forgetting" problem of traditional deep learning models. i) Dynamic architecture: This technique uses a flexible network architecture that can be dynamically changed in response to new inputs. B. Fritzke et al. [12] proposed the Grow Neural Gas (GNG) that gradually increases the network complexity in response to continuous inputs. Parisi et al. [13] proposed a Dual Memory Network that inserts nodes into the network over time for continuous object recognition. Dou et al. [14] proposed an episodic memory network that can generate a topological map over time for gesture recognition. Kato et al. [15] proposed a three-layered Multi-channel Episodic Memory Adaptive Resonance Theory (McEM-ART) for human behavior recognition. ii) Regularization: Regularization is a method that adds regularization terms to the objective function during learning to constrain the weight updates of the network structure in order to prevent catastrophic forgetting [16]. iii) Memory replay: Memory replay is a technique that typically uses generative models such as Variational Autoencoders (VAE) [17] or Generative Adversarial Networks (GAN) [18].

In this study, we propose a Random Weight Convolutional-Growing Memory Network (RWC-GMN) that continuously extracts and learns temporal features from sequential data, using human behavior as an example. To address the catastrophic forgetting problem in traditional methods, we incorporate a topology map that mimics human episodic memory, enabling the network size to change according to the input data. To extract the spatial-temporal features of the sequential data for continuous learning, we use a 3D convolutional neural network with random weights as the feature extractor. Additionally, the system automatically generates and reinforces episodic memory from the network structure using previously learned knowledge. Furthermore, to apply the proposed method to real-world scenarios, we automatically label new data by referencing stored knowledge within the network, allowing for continuous learning of new data.

2   Proposed Model

The proposed Random Weight Convolutional-Growing Memory Network (RWC-GMN) consists of two parts: a random weight 3D convolutional neural network (CNN) feature extractor and a growing memory network (GMN). The feature extractor can transform high-dimensional data into a low-dimensional representation using related features. As real-world data often contains time-series information, the proposed system uses a 3D CNN that can extract features from spatiotemporal correlations. The GMN is composed of a self-organizing topological network that mimics human episodic memory. To learn the input data, the GMN continuously generates new nodes by using encoded data information and the relationships between them as topological connections. To encode spatiotemporal information, the GMN learns the activation patterns of episode memory nodes. To maintain network stability and flexibility, the GMN continuously generates new nodes and updates the weights of existing nodes when input data is similar to previously learned knowledge. Figure 1 provides an overview of the proposed approach. Data is input from the sensor and transformed into a low-dimensional representation containing spatiotemporal features using the 3D CNN feature extractor. The GMN is used for learning the data and storing knowledge. If sensory data is not input, the GMN retrieves episodic memories. Table 1 shows the notation used for the GMN.

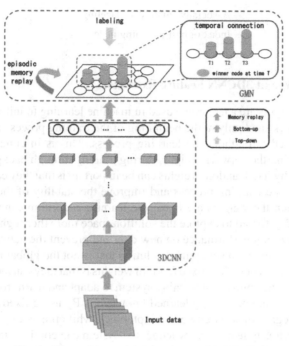

Fig. 1. The architecture of the proposed RWC-GMN

Table 1. Notation of GMN

Notation	Definition
$\mathbb{G}_{max}$	Maximum value of long-term memory weight
$\mathbb{G}_{min}$	Minimum value of long-term memory weight
$T_j(t)$	Activation value of node j at t
$w_b(t)$	Best matching node weights at t − 1
r_j	Regularity counter of node j
γ_j	Contributing factor of node j
τ_j, λ	Decay factors for regularity counter
ρ	Learning threshold

(*continued*)

Table 1. (*continued*)

Notation	Definition
$P_{(m,n)}$	Temporal connection between node m and n
V	Associative matrix for labeling
b	Index of best matching node

2.1 Random Weight 3DCNN Feature Extractor

Fixed random weights are a technique used in machine learning to initialize the weights of a neural network randomly at the beginning of the training process and then to keep these weights fixed throughout the learning process. This is in contrast to the usual practice of updating the network weights during training through backpropagation.

The reason why fixed random weights can be important is that they can help to reduce the variability in the learning process and improve the stability of the learned policy. In particular, when the weights are fixed, the learning algorithm cannot overfit to the training data, and is forced to explore the solution space more thoroughly. This can lead to better generalization performance on new data and prevent the network from getting stuck in a local minimum, a suboptimal solution that is not the global minimum.

Another important benefit of fixed random weights is that they can facilitate continual learning, which is the ability of a learning system to adapt and learn from new data over time without forgetting previously learned knowledge. By using fixed random weights to retain some degree of plasticity and adaptability, while preventing the catastrophic forgetting of previously learned knowledge, the system can continue to learn from new data, while preserving the knowledge learned from previous tasks.

2.2 Learning Process of GMN

Based on sensory input, the network first generates two episode nodes and updates the long-term memory weight. For time $t = 1$, each element of the long-term memory weight becomes as follows.

$$\mathbb{G}_{max} = \mathbb{G}_{min} = x(1) \tag{1}$$

Afterwards, the long-term memory weight is updated as follows.

$$\mathbb{G}_{max} \leftarrow \mathbb{G}_{max} + \beta \cdot (\max_{i \in (0,N)} (\mathbb{G}_{max,i}, x_i(t)) - \mathbb{G}_{max,i}) \tag{2}$$

$$\mathbb{G}_{min} \leftarrow \mathbb{G}_{min} + \beta \cdot (\min_{i \in (0,N)} (\mathbb{G}_{min,i}, x_i(t)) - \mathbb{G}_{min,i}) \tag{3}$$

Here, i represents the index of each element in long-term memory weight. $\max(a, b)$ calculates the maximum value for each element, and $\min(a, b)$ calculates the minimum value for each element.

Due to the characteristics of the long-term memory weight, the system is less affected by the setting of vigilance parameters and can continue learning without normalizing input data.

Next, each episode node in the network is composed of a weight vector w_j. Using Eqs. (4) and (5), the network selects the winner node for the current input data $x(t)$ for the next learning process.

$$b = \text{arg}, min\big(T_j(t)\big), \tag{4}$$

$$T_j(t) = \frac{\|x(t)-w_j\|^2}{\|\mathbb{G}_{max}-\mathbb{G}_{min}\|^2}. \tag{5}$$

Then, the activation value of the winning node J is calculated as follows.

$$a_b(t) = exp(-T_b). \tag{6}$$

If the activation value $a_b(t)$ is less than the threshold a_T that was initially set, a new node N is added to the network with new weights as follows.

$$w_N = 0.5 \cdot (x(t) + w_b). \tag{7}$$

To connect the selected best winner node b and the second winner node, it is necessary to generate a new edge. If $a_b(t)$ is greater than a_T, best winner node b can represent the input $x(t)$. As a result, best winner node b and its neighbor node n are updated using the input $x(t)$ as follows.

$$w_j \leftarrow w_j + \gamma_j \cdot r_j \cdot (x(t) - w_j) \tag{8}$$

If there is no edge between the best winner node b and the second winner node, a new edge is generated to connect them. For each learning iteration, the age counter of each edge is increased by one. The age counter of the edge between the best winner node and the second winner node is initialized to zero. Nodes without edges, nodes with habituation counter greater than the threshold, and edges with age counter greater than the threshold are removed from the network. Additionally, each episode node has a regularity counter r_j indicating the firing strength over time, ranging from $[0, 1]$. The regularity counter of the newly formed episode node is initialized to $r_j = 1$. The regularity counter of the best winner node and its neighbor nodes are decayed for each learning iteration using the following formula.

$$r_j \leftarrow r_j + \tau_j \cdot \lambda \cdot (1 - r_j) - \tau_j. \tag{9}$$

As a result, the regularity counter of a node can express the relevance and importance of the information stored in that node. The regularity counter indicates the regularity value of a node that is triggered over time depending on the learning input. If the age counter of edge greater than the threshold, these independent nodes and edges are removed from the network. To prevent the removal of useful edges generated at the beginning of learning, we remove nodes according to the criteria introduced in a previous study [19], as follows.

$$v = \mu(H) + \sigma(H). \tag{10}$$

Here, H is a vector representation of the regularity counter of all nodes in the network, μ is the mean function, and σ is the standard deviation. Nodes with regularity counter greater than threshold are removed.

The new episode node is connected to the network only if $b_J(t) < \rho_b$ and $r_J < \rho_r$. If both the activation threshold and regularity threshold are met, the node is updated using Eq. (8). In the GMN network, a succession of events creates an episode that recalls distinctive prior experiences and episodes related to one another to simulate episodic memory properties. The activation patterns of episode nodes in the network are learned using temporal connections. Temporal connections represent the order in which the activated nodes occurred during the learning stage. If the best winner node b is activated at time t and other nodes were activated at time $t - 1$, the temporal connection between them is reinforced.

$$P_{(b(t),b(t-1))} \leftarrow P_{(b(t),b(t-1))} + 1. \tag{11}$$

Therefore, for each episode node m of the encoded time series, the next node g can be obtained by selecting the maximum value of P as follows.

$$g = \arg maxP_{(m,n)}. \tag{12}$$

Here, n is the neighbor node of m. The activation time sequence of episode nodes can be restored without requiring input data.

2.3 Memory Replay of GMN

Inspired by previous research, the episode memory network utilizes the spatiotemporal connectivity of existing nodes to replay meaningful temporal data. The episode memory network is capable of replaying temporal data when sensory input is not provided. For example, best winner node b which the first node of the episode memory network is activated by input. The next temporal connection can be generated by selecting the node with the highest activation value P. For each node j, the replay memory of length $K + 1$ is calculated as follows.

$$U_j = \langle w_{u(0)}, w_{u(1)}, \cdots, w_{u(K)} \rangle, \tag{13}$$

$$u(i) = \arg max P_{(j,u(i-1))}. \tag{14}$$

Here, $P(i, j)$ is a matrix of temporal connections for episode, with $u(0) = j$. It is possible to automatically generate a sequence of memories and replay them in the network without storing previously learned data, by establishing temporal connections for existing episode nodes in the network.

2.4 Labeling of GMN

During the learning phase, class label l can be assigned to each node based on the input data. L classes generate l class labels. In this labeling method, the frequency of each label in the network is stored in $V(j, l)$. Using this, each node j holds a distribution counter that maintains the frequency of the specific label assigned to it. A new node N is created, and the label ζ associated with input data $x(t)$ is determined. The matrix V is extended by one row, and $V(N, \zeta) = 1$ and $V(N, l) = 0$ are initialized. When an existing winning node b is selected for weight updating, the V matrix is also updated as follows.

$$V(b, \zeta) \leftarrow V(b, \zeta) + \varphi^+, \tag{15}$$

$$V(b, l) \leftarrow V(b, l) + \varphi^-. \tag{16}$$

Note that φ^+ must always be smaller than φ^-, and the label ζ belongs to the class L. If the data label ζ does not exist in class L, a new column is added to V, and $V(b, \zeta) = 1$, $V(b, l) = 0$. If it does not match the label of the given input data, the matrix V is not updated. The selected label ζ_j for node j is calculated as follows.

$$\zeta_j = label(j) \equiv \arg max \, V(j, l). \tag{17}$$

Here, the label l is a label within class L. The advantage of this labeling method [20] is that it is not necessary to determine the class labels in advance. This method enables learning when the number of data classes is unknown.

3   Experimental Results

To demonstrate the effectiveness of the proposed system, we conducted a continuous learning experiment of RWC-GMN using six human daily behaviors, as shown in Fig. 2 Each collected behavioral pattern was composed of a 3-s video. To extract the 3D human skeleton model from the environment, a motion capture system called Kinect [21] was used, as shown in Fig. 3. The collected human action dataset used the 3D skeleton coordinates from Kinect as the input data. In addition, for all human behavior data, we split the dataset into 80% for training and 20% for validation data.

Fig. 2. Example of behaviors data

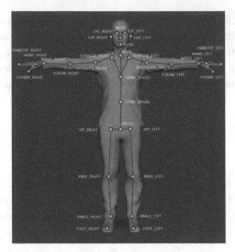

Fig. 3. Example of behaviors data

In training phase of RWC-GMN, the first four behaviors are learned. During training, all data is sequentially input to the model. To achieve continual learning, the training epoch is set to 1, and all data is trained only once. The results of verification using the trained model are shown in Fig. 4 and Table 2.

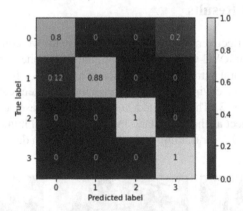

Fig. 4. Class 0–3 validation results by using trained RWC-GMN

In addition, the following process is used for continuous learning of new behaviors for the two unlearned behavioral patterns:

i) Validation experiments are conducted on the data of new and previous behavioral patterns using the previously trained model.
ii) For each input behavioral pattern, similarity is calculated by referencing the knowledge base of the trained model, and automatic labeling of new data is performed to continue learning the data.
iii) The validation experiments on the data of new and previous behavioral patterns are conducted again using the newly trained model.

Table 2. Training Results of Class 0–3

Accuracy	0.93
Precision	0.92
Recall	0.92
F1	0.92
Number of nodes	18

By following this process, the continuous learning results for the three unlearned behavioral patterns are shown in Fig. 5 and 6. The validation results before and after learning the new behavioral patterns and the number of nodes in RWC-GMN are shown in Table 3.

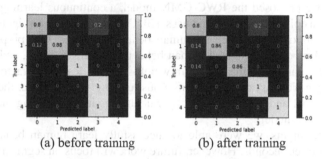

(a) before training   (b) after training

Fig. 5. Validation results of Class 4 before and after continuous learning

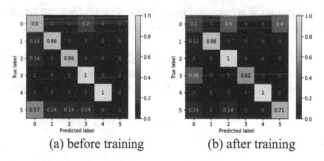

(a) before training   (b) after training

Fig. 6. Validation results of Class 5 before and after continuous learning

As the results, RWC-GMN was able to learn and recognize the first four patterns of behavior. Furthermore, in the continuous learning of new behavior patterns using the learned model, the recognition rate for new behavior patterns after learning improved compared to before learning. As the number of data classes learned simultaneously increased, the structure of RWC-GMN changed, resulting in an increase in the number of nodes in the network. Based on these results, it is considered that the proposed system, RWC-GMN, is effective for continuous learning of real-world data.

Table 3. Results of Class 4–5 Before and After Training

	Class 4		Class 5	
	before	after	before	after
Accuracy	0.66	0.90	0.73	0.75
Precision	0.64	0.76	0.56	0.65
Recall	0.74	0.73	0.63	0.61
F1	0.66	0.74	0.58	0.62
Number of nodes	18	22	22	23

4 Conclusion

In this study, we proposed the RWC-GMN model, a continuous learning system that emulates human episodic memory and uses a 3DCNN with random weights as a feature extractor for temporal data, such as human behavior patterns. Our proposed system takes a skeletal model of collected human behavior patterns as input, and extracts the features of these patterns using a random weight 3DCNN feature extractor that can be used without pre-training, enabling continuous learning. Furthermore, the system can automatically label and learn new data by calculating similarity using the knowledge base of the trained model.

In our experiments, we were able to successfully learn human behaviors with a fixed length of three seconds. However, future work will focus on segmenting temporal and spatial data to enable the continuous learning of variable-length temporal data. Additionally, we believe that applying this approach to real-world scenarios requires a multi-channel continuous learning and recognition system that can handle various data from different sensors in complex environments.

Acknowledgment. This work was (partially) supported by JST, [Moonshot R&D] [Grant Number JPMJMS2034] and [the establishment of university fellowships towards the creation of science technology innovation] [Grant Number JPMJFS2139], and TMU local 5G research support.

References

1. Flesch, T., Balaguer, J., Dekker, R., Nili, H., Summerfield, C.: Comparing continual task learning in minds and machines. Nat. Commun. **10**(1), 1 (2019). https://doi.org/10.1038/s41 467-019-11861-2
2. McCloskey, M., Cohen, N.J.: Catastrophic interference in connectionist networks: the sequential learning problem. In: Psychology of Learning and Motivation, vol. 24, pp. 109–165 (1989)
3. Ring, M.B.: Continual learning in reinforcement environments. University of Texas at Austin, Austin, Texas 78712, August 1994 (1994)
4. Shin, H., Lee, J.K., Kim, J., Kim, J.: Continual learning with deep generative replay. In: Advances in Neural Information Processing Systems, pp. 2990–2999 (2017)

5. Rebuffi, S.A., Kolesnikov, A., Sperl, G., Lampert, C.H.: iCaRL: incremental classifier and representation learning. In: Proceedings of the IEEE Conference on Computer Vision and Pattern Recognition, pp. 2001–2010 (2017)
6. Li, Z., Hoiem, D.: Learning to learn without forgetting by maximizing transfer and minimizing interference. In: Proceedings of the IEEE Conference on Computer Vision and Pattern Recognition (CVPR), pp. 4427–4435 (2017)
7. Lopez-Paz, D., Ranzato, M.: Gradient episodic memory for continual learning. In: Advances in Neural Information Processing Systems, pp. 6467–6476 (2017)
8. Chaudhry, A., Dokania, P.K., Ajanthan, T., Torr, P.H.S.: Experience Replay for Continual Learning. In: Proceedings of the 32nd AAAI Conference on Artificial Intelligence, pp. 1120–1127 (2018)
9. Shmelkov, K., Schoenholz, S.S., Bahdanau, D., Metz, L., Bengio, Y.: Online continual learning with random task ordering. In: Proceedings of the 34th International Conference on Machine Learning, vol. 70, pp. 3079–3088 (2017)
10. Zenke, F., Poole, B., Ganguli, S.: Random feature replay: a compact representation for incremental learning. In: Proceedings of the 34th International Conference on Machine Learning (ICML-2017), pp. 4055–4064 (2017)
11. Rusu, A.A., et al.: Progressive neural networks. arXiv:1606.04671 (2016)
12. Fritzke, B.: A growing neural gas network learns topologies. In: Advances in Neural Information Processing Systems, vol. 7, pp. 625–632 (1995)
13. Parisi, G.I., Jun, T., Cornelius, W., Stefan, W.: lifelong learning of spatiotemporal representations with dual-memory recurrent self- organization. Front. Neurorobot. 12 (2018)
14. Dou, W., Chin, W., Kubota, N.: Multi-scopic cognitive memory system for continuous gesture learning. Biomimetics 8, 88 (2023). https://doi.org/10.3390/biomimetics8010088
15. Kato, K., Chin, W.H., Toda, Y., Kubota, N.: A multi-channel episodic memory model for human action learning and recognition. In: 2018 IEEE International Conference on Systems, Man, and Cybernetics (SMC), Miyazaki, Japan, pp. 843–849 (2018). https://doi.org/10.1109/SMC.2018.00151
16. Hinton, G., Vinyals, O., Dean, J.: Distilling the knowledge in a neural network. In: NIPS Deep Learning and Representation Learning Workshop (2014)
17. Shin, H., Lee, J.K., Kim, J., Kim, J.: Continual learning with deep generative replay. In: Advances in Neural Information Processing Systems (NIPS), pp. 2990–2999 (2017)
18. Rezende, D.J., Mohamed, S., Wierstra, D.: Stochastic backpropagation and approximate inference in deep generative models. In: Proceedings International Conference on Machine Learning (ICML), vol. 32, no. 2, pp. 1278–1286. PMLR (2014)
19. Liew, W.S., Kiong Loo, C., Gryshchuk, V., Weber, C., Wermter, S.: Effect of pruning on catastrophic forgetting in growing dual memory networks. In: 2019 International Joint Conference on Neural Networks (IJCNN), Budapest, Hungary, pp. 1–8 (2019)
20. Parisi, I.G., Tani, J., Weber, C., Wermter, S.: Lifelong learning of spatiotemporal representations with dual-memory recurrent self- organization. Front. Neurorobot. 12 (2018)
21. Kinect. https://learn.microsoft.com/ja-jp/azure/kinect-dk/body-joints. Accessed 24 May 2023

Sleep-Dependent Memory Replay Enables Brain-Like Robustness in Neural Networks

Siwei Xie[1], Tao Tang[1,2], Linqing Feng[1,2], Feng Lin[1], and Yina Wei[1,2(✉)]

[1] Research Institute of Artificial Intelligence, Zhejiang Lab, Hangzhou 311100, China
weiyina039@zhejianglab.com
[2] Zhejiang Provincial Key Laboratory of Cardio-Cerebral Vascular Detection Technology and Medicinal Effectiveness Appraisal, Zhejiang University, Hangzhou 310027, China

Abstract. Sleep is known to play a crucial role in memory and learning processes. During sleep, the replay of neural activity patterns associated with recent memories is believed to contribute to memory consolidation. Inspired by the sleep replay process in the biological system, we proposed a brain-like memory replay algorithm consisting of three phases. First, an artificial neural network (ANN) underwent learning, mimicking the cognitive processes of the awake stage. Next, we conducted a simulation where slow oscillation sleep or awake stages were simulated in a spiking neural network (SNN). The network connections and initial synaptic weights are identical to those of the trained ANN. Lastly, the performance of the ANN is evaluated and validated during the awake phase using the synaptic weights converted from the SNN. We applied this brain-inspired memory replay algorithm to a two-digit MNIST classification task. We found that as the level of noise increases, the model exhibits a significant improvement in performance after a period of sleep compared to the awake state. These findings provide compelling evidence that sleep-dependent memory consolidation can significantly enhance the network performance and improve its the robustness. Overall, this study sheds light on the potential advantages of incorporating sleep-like processes into neural networks, offering valuable insights into the field.

Keywords: Artificial intelligence · Sleep-inspired algorithm · Memory replay · Robustness

1 Introduction

Artificial neural networks (ANNs), have been widely used in areas such as computer vision and language processing [1–3]. Despite the success, they often face challenges such as overfitting and limited robustness to noisy or sparse data [3]. In contrast, humans exhibit remarkable performance even under conditions of limited or noisy stimuli [4]. This discrepancy has motivated researchers to explore the potential benefits from biological brains [5].

From an information processing perspective, memory formation depends on three general processes: encoding, consolidation and retrieval. In biological brains, sleep has been reported to play an important role in memory consolidation [6]. During sleep,

© The Author(s), under exclusive license to Springer Nature Singapore Pte Ltd. 2023
H. Yang et al. (Eds.): ICIRA 2023, LNAI 14267, pp. 212–221, 2023.
https://doi.org/10.1007/978-981-99-6483-3_19

although the brain is primarily decoupled from external sensory input, the brain activity remains high across sleep stages [7]. Specifically, slow-wave sleep (SWS), characterized by repetitive Up and Down states (~1 Hz) [8], has been hypothesized to support the reactivation and redistribution of memory representations [9]. Previous computational modelling studies have shown that SWS facilitates the consolidation of memory through the replay of temporally ordered spike sequences associated with recent memories [10–12].

An increasing number of studies have been devoted to implementing brain-like activities with spiking neural networks (SNNs) to improve network performance [13–22]. SNNs facilitate the temporal encoding process by addressing information through time intervals with biologically plausible neurons [19, 20]. This also benefits the implementation of multiple biological mechanisms from neuroscience to artificial networks, including biological spatial-temporal constraints [21], and timing dependent learning rules [13, 15, 16, 18]. Furthermore, researchers have successfully implemented SNN algorithms on neuromorphic computing hardware [23–28]. Recently, the sleep-inspired replay algorithm was developed to reduce catastrophic forgetting in the ANN [14, 17]. Another study also demonstrated that the information stored initially in the hippocampus can help to build neocortical representations during sleep, and the alternation between non–rapid eye movement (NREM) and REM sleep across the night facilitated the integration of new information with existing knowledge [22]. However, none of them has incorporated slow wave sleep dynamics into neural network models and taken advantages of memory consolidation during slow wave sleep.

In this work, we proposed a brain-like algorithm with a process of memory consolidation by simulating the sleep slow oscillations embedded with synaptic plasticity. The algorithm includes three phases: 1) An ANN with rectified linear unit (ReLU) activation was trained with backpropagation. 2) An SNN, converted equivalently from the trained ANN, went into sleep stages characterized by slow oscillations. During this phase, the synaptic weights were modified based on the spike-timing dependent plasticity (STDP) rule. For comparison, the control group of the SNN went into an awake stage with random neural activities. 3) Finally, the model performance was evaluated using the ANN, whose weights was converted from the SNN. We demonstrated a significant improvement in model performance when dealing with images containing noise. Specifically, the sleep phase enhanced the robustness of the neural network, surpassing the performance of both the awake state and the original ANN. This study suggests that spontaneous replay of neural activity during slow wave sleep can improve the overall robustness of neural networks.

2   Methods

2.1   Main Procedure

The proposed brain-inspired algorithm consists of three phases (Fig. 1). First, an artificial neural network (ANN) with ReLU activation was trained with backpropagation a two-digit MNIST classification task. The architecture of the ANN was fully connected with 4-layer feedforward architecture of [784, 1200, 1200, 2]. In the second phase, the trained ANN was converted into an equivalent spiking neural network (SNN), as adapted from

Tadros [17]. The SNN went into either an awake or sleep stage. The network connectivity was adjusted based on the spike-timing dependent plasticity (STDP) rule. In the final phase, the modified weights of the SNN were transferred back to an ANN. The model performance of this ANN was evaluated in the classification task using noisy images, to explore the robustness of the network.

2.2 The SNN Model

Leaky integrate-and-fire (LIF) neurons were most widely used in the SNN. The network connections and initial weights of the SNN were directly inherited from the trained ANN. This allowed for a seamless transition from the ANN to the SNN. The dynamics of the LIF neurons in the SNN were given as follows:

$$\tau_m \frac{du}{dt} = -[u(t) - u_{rest}] + R_m I(t) \tag{1}$$

where u represents the membrane potential, I represents synaptic inputs ($\tau_m = 10$ ms, $u_{rest} = -75$ mV, $R_m = 10$ MΩ). Spikes were triggered when u was accumulated to the threshold $u_{thresh} = -55$ mV, and membrane potential was reset to u_{rest} simultaneously.

The input layer of the SNN is activated with Poisson-distributed spike trains. The mean firing rates of these spike trains were determined by the corresponding ANN node activation, which were calculated based on the average image of all task inputs during initial training phase. This process ensures that the SNN receives input patterns that are consistent with the training data used by the ANN, facilitating a smooth transition between the two models.

The nodes of subsequent layers integrate the input from the previous layer:

$$I(t) = aW\dot{x} \tag{2}$$

where $\dot{x}$ is the binary spiking activity of the previous layer, W is the connectivity weight matrix, and a represents the layer-specific scaling factor, which was used to adjust the firing rate of the network to a specific target value.

2.3 Simulation of Awake and Sleep Stages

As a control group, Eq. (2) was used to simulate the awake stage of the SNN. Additionally, to model cortical rhythmic activity during slow oscillation sleep, we introduced the external synchronized rectification operation to induce the slow oscillation in the network:

$$I(t) = aW\dot{x} \cdot \left[sign(sin(2\pi t/T)) \right]_+ \tag{3}$$

where $\left[sign(z) \right]_+$ is a function that returns 1 when z is greater than zero and 0 otherwise. To generate 1 Hz sleep slow oscillations, we set $1/T$ to be 1 Hz.

By adjusting the layer-specific scaling factor a, the network achieved an averaged population firing rate of approximately 2.5 Hz during the awake stage and 4 Hz during the Up state of slow oscillations. These rates were chosen to simulate neural activities similar to those observed in humans [29, 30]. The network underwent sleep or awake stages for a duration of 2000 ms.

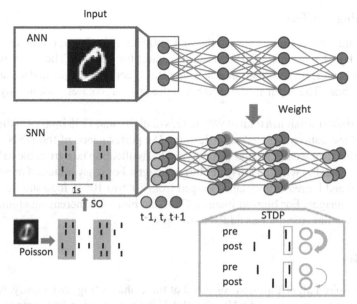

Fig. 1. Schematic of learning paradigm. The model was trained and tested by an artificial neural network (ANN), and went into sleep (blue block) stages by a spiking neural network with synaptic plasticity. The input layer of the SNN is activated with Poisson-distributed spike trains. To simulate slow oscillation, an external synchronized rectification operation was applied on the Poisson-distributed spike trains. (Color figure online)

2.4 Spike-Timing Dependent Plasticity (STDP)

The synaptic connections between neurons was adjusted according to the STDP rule [31], which was based on the relative timing of pre- and post-synaptic spikes. The change in synaptic connections is determined by the relative timing ($\Delta t = t_{post} - t_{pre}$) of pre- and post-synaptic spikes as follows:

$$\Delta w_{ij} = \begin{cases} \varepsilon(w_{ij}) \cdot (A_+ e^{-\frac{\Delta t}{\tau_+}}), & if\ \Delta t > 0 \\ \varepsilon(w_{ij}) \cdot (-A_- e^{\frac{\Delta t}{\tau_-}}), & if\ \Delta t < 0 \end{cases} \tag{4}$$

$$\varepsilon(w) = 2 \cdot \min(sigmoid(w), 1 - sigmoid(w)) \tag{5}$$

$$sigmoid(w) = 1/\left(1 + e^{-w/0.0002}\right) \tag{6}$$

where w_{ij} represents the synaptic weight between pre- and post-synaptic neuron, A and τ are parameters that determine the maximal amplitude and time constant of synaptic modification, and $\varepsilon(w)$ denotes a symmetric weight-dependent changing rate [32]. We set $A_+ = 0.0103$, $A_- = 0.0051$, $\tau_+ = 14$ ms and $\tau_- = 34$ ms, as biologically constrained parameters according to experimental observations of cortical neurons [33].

2.5 Training and Test

During the training session, we used the first 5000 images of digit 0 and the first 5000 images of digit 1 from the MNIST training dataset for training. The ANN was firstly trained on a two-digit classification task, using ReLU activation units and a learning rate 0.1 without bias. The input to the ANN was the original dataset without any noise or blur.

During the test session, a total of 980 images of digit 0 and 1135 images of digit 1 from the MNIST test dataset were used for testing. The performance of the ANN converted back from the SNN was evaluated in a two-digit classification task from the MNIST test dataset (digit 0 and 1) with the noisy or blurred images. For noisy images, Gaussian noise with mean 0 and increasing variance ranged from 10^{-1} to 10^2 in logarithmic steps was added to the images. For blurred images, Gaussian blur with increasing sigma ranging from 1 to 10 in linear steps was added to images.

3 Results

The brain-inspired algorithm was consisted of three phases (Fig. 2a). Firstly, we trained an artificial neural network (ANN) with ReLU activation using backpropagation in a two-digit classification task from the MNIST dataset. Secondly, the network went into either awake (Fig. 2a, pink block) or sleep (Fig. 2a, blue block) stages by a spiking neural network (SNN) with synaptic plasticity. The network connections and initial synaptic weights of the SNN were set to mirror those of the previously trained ANN. To investigate the role of sleep, we conducted a simulation in the SNN by introducing sleep slow oscillations at a frequency of 1 Hz across all layers of the network. During the Up state, the population firing rate approximated 4 Hz, while no neurons fired during the Down state (Fig. 2f–i). As a control, random neural activities around 2.5 Hz were simulated to represent the awake stage (Fig. 2b–e). During both awake and sleep stages, synaptic weights in the SNNs were adjusted according to a symmetric weight-dependent STDP rule.

During biological sleep, cortical rhythms coordinate to reactivate memory traces and consolidate task-related connections, resulting in the strengthening of these connections within the network. To assess the robustness of the neural network, we conducted experiments comparing its performance under increasing levels of noise (Fig. 3) or blur (Fig. 4) in the input images. The ANN was trained on the original dataset without any noise or blur, and tested using noisy or blurred images.

In the different levels of noise input, the classification accuracy of the network after sleep was notably improved, as shown in Fig. 3. Specifically, when the noise variance was set to 10^0, the performance after sleep was significantly enhanced compared to the awake state (one-way ANOVA with Bonferroni's post hoc test, p = 1.5×10^{-14}), and the original ANN (one-way ANOVA with Bonferroni's post hoc test, p = 1.3×10^{-11}). The performance improvement resulted in an approximate 22% increase in accuracy, with the accuracy after the awake stage at 58.9% and the accuracy after the sleep stage reaching 81.3%.

In the different levels of blur, sleep also demonstrated an improvement in the classification performance. Specifically, when blur sigma was set to 5, there was a significant

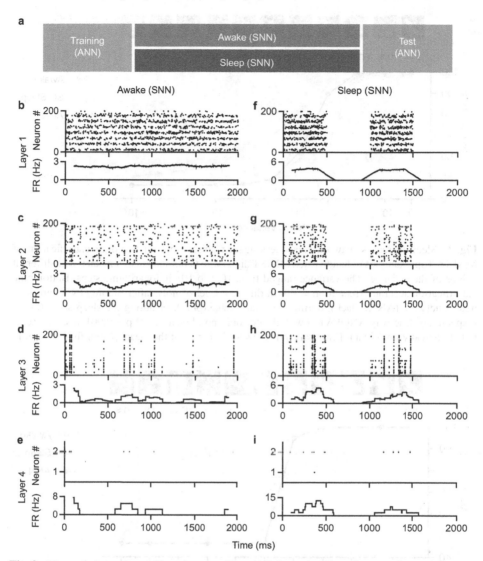

Fig. 2. Network dynamics and learning paradigm. **a)** Schematic of learning paradigm. The model was trained and tested by an artificial neural network (ANN), and went into either awake (pink block) or sleep (blue block) stages by a spiking neural network with synaptic plasticity. The neural network activity during awake stage (**b–e**) and sleep stage (**f–i**). Raster plot (*top*) shows the spike activities of 200 neurons from layer 1 (**b, f**, n = 784 neurons), layer 2 (**c, g**, n = 1200 neurons), layer 3 (**d, h**, n = 1200 neurons), respectively, and all two neurons from layer 4 (**e, i**, n = 2 neurons). Population firing rate (*bottom*) was averaged within a sliding window (window size = 200 ms, window step = 1 ms).

increase in accuracy after sleep compared to the awake state (one-way ANOVA with Bonferroni's post hoc test, $p = 7.8 \times 10^{-4}$) and the original ANN (one-way ANOVA with Bonferroni's post hoc test, $p = 2.7 \times 10^{-7}$). The sleep stage resulted in a net

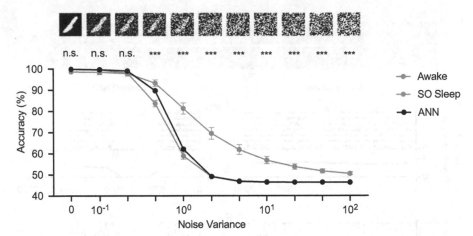

Fig. 3. Sleep increases network robustness against noise input on two-digit classification of MNIST. Top: examples of handwritten MNIST digits with Gaussian noise at mean 0 with different values of the variance. The variance ranged from 10^{-1} to 10^2 in logarithmic steps. Bottom: the classification accuracy (repetition $= 40$) at different level of noise after training by an artificial neural network (ANN, black), during the awake stage (pink), or during the sleep stage (blue), respectively. One-way ANOVA test with Bonferroni's post hoc test, *** $p < 0.001$, n.s. represents not statistically significant. Error bars indicate standard error of the mean. (Color figure online)

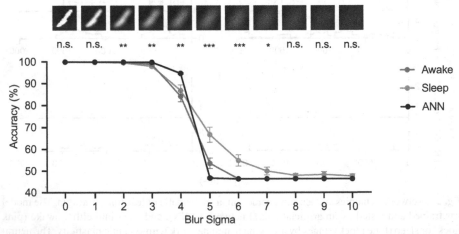

Fig. 4. Sleep increases network robustness against blur input on two-digit classification of MNIST. Top: examples of handwritten MNIST digits with different levels of blur. Blur sigma ranged from 1 to 10 in linear steps. Bottom: the classification accuracy (repetition $= 40$) at different levels of blur after training by an artificial neural network (ANN, black), during the awake stage (pink), or during the sleep stage (blue), respectively. One-way ANOVA test with Bonferroni's post hoc test, *** $p < 0.001$, ** $p < 0.01$, * $p < 0.05$, n.s. represents not statistically significant. Error bars indicate standard error of the mean. (Color figure online)

increase in accuracy of up to 13%, with the accuracy after the awake stage at 53.5% and the accuracy after the sleep stage reaching 66.6%. It is worth noting that at certain levels of blur, the ANN without SNN exhibited the best performance, suggesting that the ANN may have already been well-trained and reached its optimal performance, leaving little room for further improvement through memory consolidation.

Overall, our results suggest that sleep can enhance the robustness of network classification in the noisy or blurred images.

4 Discussion

This study demonstrated that a sleep-inspired algorithm implemented with slow wave sleep and synaptic plasticity can improve network robustness to the noisy or blurred input. When evaluated on a two-digit MNIST classification task, the network's performance exhibited significant improvement through sleep, compared to the awake or the original network. Specifically, the classification accuracy was improved through sleep by up to 22% for noisy images and 13% for blurred images.

One of the major advantages of our algorithm was embedding the network into the sleep phase. The SNN, which shared identical network connections and initial synaptic weights with the trained ANN, underwent sleep slow oscillations, which facilitated memory consolidation [6, 10, 34]. Remarkably, we simulated the model with bio-constraints, such as the frequency of the oscillations and firing rates during sleep or awake, as well as the parameters in the STDP rule. The networks integrated with sleep stage exhibited superior performance compared to the awake stage, suggesting the important role of sleep in memory consolidation.

However, there are some shortcomings of this study. First of all, the slow oscillation in the model was generated by an external rectification operation function, which is not quite biologically. In the future, we will improve the model to make it generate slow oscillations automatically as during our deep sleep. In addition, the memory consolidation during sleep might decrease the performance if the ANN has already been well trained, indicating that no further memory consolidation is needed in such case.

In conclusion, our study introduced a novel and robust brain-like algorithm implemented with slow wave sleep. The spontaneous replay during slow wave sleep can enhance the overall robustness of neural networks. Importantly, this sleep-inspired algorithm can be applied independently to other state-of-the-art artificial intelligent algorithms. Further, the potential application of the algorithm in multiple tasks may alleviate catastrophic forgetting and improve the performance of the ANN in the context of continual learning.

Acknowledgement. This work was supported by the National Natural Science Foundation of China (12101570), Zhejiang Lab & Pujiang Lab (K2023KA1BB01), and Scientific Projects of Zhejiang Lab (K2023KI0AA02, 2021KE0PI03).

References

1. Abiodun, O.I., et al.: Comprehensive review of artificial neural network applications to pattern recognition. IEEE Access **7**, 158820–158846 (2019)
2. Wu, Y., Feng, J.: Development and application of artificial neural network. Wirel. Pers. Commun. **102**, 1645–1656 (2018)
3. Abiodun, O.I., Jantan, A., Omolara, A.E., Dada, K.V., Mohamed, N.A., Arshad, H.: State-of-the-art in artificial neural network applications: a survey. Heliyon **4**, e00938 (2018)
4. Geirhos, R., Temme, C.R.M., Rauber, J., Schütt, H.H., Bethge, M., Wichmann, F.A.: Generalisation in humans and deep neural networks. http://arxiv.org/abs/1808.08750 (2020)
5. Hassabis, D., Kumaran, D., Summerfield, C., Botvinick, M.: Neuroscience-inspired artificial intelligence. Neuron **95**, 245–258 (2017)
6. Rasch, B., Born, J.: About sleep's role in memory. Physiol. Rev. **93**, 681–766 (2013)
7. Frank, M.G.: Erasing synapses in sleep: is it time to be SHY? Neural Plast. **2012**, 264378 (2012)
8. Achermann, P., BorbÉly, A.: Temporal evolution of coherence and power in the human sleep electroencephalogram. J. Sleep Res. **7**, 36–41 (1998)
9. Girardeau, G., Lopes-dos-Santos, V.: Brain neural patterns and the memory function of sleep. Science **374**, 560–564 (2021)
10. Wei, Y., Krishnan, G.P., Komarov, M., Bazhenov, M.: Differential roles of sleep spindles and sleep slow oscillations in memory consolidation. PLoS Comput. Biol. **14**, e1006322 (2018)
11. Wei, Y., Krishnan, G.P., Marshall, L., Martinetz, T., Bazhenov, M.: Stimulation augments spike sequence replay and memory consolidation during slow-wave sleep. J. Neurosci. **40**, 811–824 (2020)
12. Wei, Y., Krishnan, G.P., Bazhenov, M.: Synaptic mechanisms of memory consolidation during sleep slow oscillations. J. Neurosci. **36**, 4231–4247 (2016)
13. Bellec, G., Salaj, D., Subramoney, A., Legenstein, R., Maass, W.: Long short-term memory and learning-to-learn in networks of spiking neurons. Presented at the 32nd Conference on Neural Information Processing Systems (NIPS 2018) (2018)
14. Krishnan, G.P., Tadros, T., Ramyaa, R., Bazhenov, M.: Biologically inspired sleep algorithm for artificial neural networks (2019). http://arxiv.org/abs/1908.02240
15. Lee, C., Panda, P., Srinivasan, G., Roy, K.: Training deep spiking convolutional neural networks with STDP-based unsupervised pre-training followed by supervised fine-tuning. Front. Neurosci. **12**, 435 (2018)
16. Liu, F., Zhao, W., Chen, Y., Wang, Z., Yang, T., Jiang, L.: SSTDP: supervised spike timing dependent plasticity for efficient spiking neural network training. Front. Neurosci. **15** (2021)
17. Tadros, T., Krishnan, G.P., Ramyaa, R., Bazhenov, M.: Sleep-like unsupervised replay reduces catastrophic forgetting in artificial neural networks. Nat. Commun. **13**, 7742 (2022)
18. Yi, Z., Lian, J., Liu, Q., Zhu, H., Liang, D., Liu, J.: Learning rules in spiking neural networks: a survey. Neurocomputing **531**, 163–179 (2023)
19. Yu, Q., Tang, H., Tan, K.C., Yu, H.: A brain-inspired spiking neural network model with temporal encoding and learning. Neurocomputing **138**, 3–13 (2014)
20. Zhang, T., Zeng, Y., Zhao, D., Xu, B.: Brain-inspired balanced tuning for spiking neural networks. In: Proceedings of the Twenty-Seventh International Joint Conference on Artificial Intelligence, Stockholm, Sweden, pp. 1653–1659. International Joint Conferences on Artificial Intelligence Organization (2018)
21. Chen, G., Scherr, F., Maass, W.: A data-based large-scale model for primary visual cortex enables brain-like robust and versatile visual processing. Sci. Adv. **8**, eabq7592 (2022)
22. Singh, D., Norman, K.A., Schapiro, A.C.: A model of autonomous interactions between hippocampus and neocortex driving sleep-dependent memory consolidation. Proc. Natl. Acad. Sci. U.S.A. **119**, e2123432119 (2022)

23. Marković, D., Mizrahi, A., Querlioz, D., Grollier, J.: Physics for neuromorphic computing. Nat. Rev. Phys. **2**, 499–510 (2020)
24. Pei, J., et al.: Towards artificial general intelligence with hybrid Tianjic chip architecture. Nature **572**, 106–111 (2019)
25. Wu, Y., et al.: Brain-inspired global-local learning incorporated with neuromorphic computing. Nat. Commun. **13**, 65 (2022)
26. Zenke, F., Neftci, E.O.: Brain-inspired learning on neuromorphic substrates. Proc. IEEE **109**, 935–950 (2021)
27. Zhang, Y., et al.: A system hierarchy for brain-inspired computing. Nature **586**, 378–384 (2020)
28. Zhao, R., et al.: A framework for the general design and computation of hybrid neural networks. Nat. Commun. **13**, 3427 (2022)
29. Nir, Y., et al.: Regional slow waves and spindles in human sleep. Neuron **70**, 153–169 (2011)
30. Miyawaki, H., Watson, B.O., Diba, K.: Neuronal firing rates diverge during REM and homogenize during non-REM. Sci. Rep. **9**, 689 (2019)
31. Bi, G., Poo, M.: Synaptic modifications in cultured hippocampal neurons: dependence on spike timing, synaptic strength, and postsynaptic cell type. J. Neurosci. **18**, 10464–10472 (1998)
32. Park, Y., Choi, W., Paik, S.-B.: Symmetry of learning rate in synaptic plasticity modulates formation of flexible and stable memories. Sci. Rep. **7**, 5671 (2017)
33. Froemke, R.C., Dan, Y.: Spike-timing-dependent synaptic modification induced by natural spike trains. Nature **416**, 433–438 (2002)
34. Klinzing, J.G., Niethard, N., Born, J.: Mechanisms of systems memory consolidation during sleep. Nat. Neurosci. **22**, 1598–1610 (2019)

Improving Motor Imagery Brain-Computer Interface Performance Through Data Screening

Shiwei Zheng[1], Lizi Jiang[1], Xun Mai[1], Tao Tang[1,2], Linqing Feng[1,2], Feng Lin[1], and Yina Wei[1,2(✉)]

[1] Research Institute of Artificial Intelligence, Zhejiang Lab, Hangzhou 311100, Zhejiang, China
weiyina039@zhejianglab.com

[2] Zhejiang Provincial Key Laboratory of Cardio-Cerebral Vascular Detection Technology and Medicinal Effectiveness Appraisal, Zhejiang University, Hangzhou 310027, China

Abstract. Brain-computer interface (BCI) technology enables the direct transmission of human control intentions to external devices, allowing direct control of external devices through the human brain. However, the current implementation of BCIs is limited by the low accuracy of electroencephalogram (EEG) classification. In this study, we applied Gaussian distribution model as a preprocessing tool to screen and filter EEG training data samples, aiming to improve the classification accuracy of motor imagery tasks. Firstly, the Gaussian distribution model was established through small sample pre-training. Subsequently, a probability threshold was determined based on the two types of Gaussian model distributions corresponding to the imagery of the left and right hands. This threshold was used to screen and filter subsequent training samples. Our results demonstrated that this proposed method effectively enhanced the accuracy of motor imagery task classification, and significant improvements were observed in public datasets. This study emphasizes the importance of data screening in ensuring the quality and reliability of training data, thereby presenting promising opportunities for the practical implementation of BCI technology.

Keywords: Brain Computer Interface · Gaussian Distribution Model · EEG Data Screening · Motor Imagery

1 Introduction

Brain-computer interface (BCI) is a communication system that establishes direct communication between the human brain and external devices, bypassing the peripheral nervous system [1]. The concept of BCI was first proposed by Vidal in the 1970s, aiming to explore the feasibility and practicality of direct communication between the brain and controlled machines [2]. Since then, various prototype BCI systems utilizing different types of electroencephalogram (EEG) signals have been developed, including slow

---

S. Zheng and L. Jiang—These authors contributed equally.

cortical potentials (SCPs) based BCI [3, 4], event-related brain potentials (ERP) based BCI [5], mu rhythm or motor imagery (MI) based BCI [6, 7] and steady-state visual evoked potential (SSVEP) based BCI [8]. Among these paradigms, motor imagery (MI) is particularly noteworthy as it does not require external stimuli and directly reflects the subject's motor intentions [9]. In the field of medical rehabilitation, such as exoskeleton control, nerve repair, and assisted rehabilitation, MI-BCI holds significant potential for widespread application.

The fundamental principle underlying MI-BCI involves event-related desynchronization (ERD) and event-related synchronization (ERS). Typically, ERD indicates cortical activity, while ERS is observed as a rebound after ERD or during cortical idling [10, 11]. In recent years, significant progress has been made in the field of MI-BCI. Ramoser et al. introduced an optimized common spatial pattern (CSP) algorithm that incorporates channel selection for both left and right-hand motor imagery tasks [12]. Dornhege et al. proposed feature integration and fusion of various experimental paradigms to enhance classification accuracy [13]. Moreover, machine learning [14, 15], deep learning [16–19], and other methods have been widely employed for decoding motor imagery signals. However, most of these studies have remained in the laboratory stage, and further improvement of classification accuracy remains a key factor in the development of BCI.

In online MI-BCI experiments, the classifier is built using calibrated training EEG data, and the quality of this data directly impacts the performance of the classifier. However, during long and monotonous training sessions, subjects often struggle to maintain concentration, leading to poor signal robustness and even shifts in data distribution, resulting in a subpar learning effect for the classifier. To address this issue, several adaptive methods have been proposed to align data from an algorithmic perspective, aiming to improve classification accuracy. However, the problem of poor training effect on the subjects' side has not been effectively resolved.

In this study, we propose an innovative approach to EEG data screening and filtering, which can significantly enhance classification accuracy based on traditional EEG processing and classification methods. Firstly, the EEG data undergo noise reduction and filtering as part of the preprocessing stage. Then, the traditional common spatial pattern (CSP) algorithm is utilized to extract features. Following feature extraction, a small sample selection and Gaussian mixture model modeling are performed on the two-dimensional EEG data. This step is crucial for screening subsequent training samples. Finally, the support vector machine (SVM) algorithm is employed for classification, and the accuracy of classification is cross-verified. Experimental results demonstrate that this method greatly improves classification accuracy. Additionally, real-time feedback can be provided to the subjects during the data screening process, facilitating the implementation of the brain-computer interface.

2 Methods

2.1 Data Description

2.1.1 Public Datasets

The effect of the Gaussian distribution model for data screening was verified using two public motor imagery datasets: BNCI2014 [20] and Cho2017 [21]. BNCI2014 is an open-access dataset from the BNCI Horizon 2020 (http://bnci-horizon-2020.eu/dat abase/data-sets), specifically Dataset IIa in BCI Competition IV. It consists of 9 subjects performing 4 types of motor imagery tasks: imagining the movement of the left hand (class 1), right hand (class 2), foot (class 3), and tongue (class 4). Each subject completed 144 trials, and the EEG data was sampled at 250 Hz from 22 channels. For this study, we selected data from the first 6 subjects (A01, A03, A04, A07, A08, A09) with a duration of 4 s following the imaginary cue. Specifically, we focused on the binary classification task of left-hand and right-hand imagination. Cho2017 is another commonly used motor imagery dataset for left-right hand binary classification. It includes data from 52 subjects, with each subject performing 200 trials. The EEG data was sampled at 512 Hz from 64 channels. For this study, we selected data from 6 subjects (s01, s03, s14, s35, s41, s43) with a duration of 3 s following the imagery cue.

2.1.2 NSW364 Experiment Dataset

In addition, we also conducted MI experiments using the wireless digital EEG acquisition system NSW364. This portable BCI device, developed by Neuracle, is widely used for EEG recordings. The system consists of five components (Fig. 1a): ① EEG amplifier, ② EEG cap, ③ synchronizer, ④ intelligent synchronization center, and ⑤ computer. In this experiment, we focused on a binary classification task involving the imagination of grasping actions using the left and right hands. The dataset was collected from 5 subjects. Each subject performed a total of 5 runs, with each run comprising 20 trials. Within each run, 10 trials were dedicated to the left-hand imagery task, and the remaining 10 were for the right-hand imagery task. The order of the trials was randomized to minimize potential bias. This dataset provides valuable data for evaluating the proposed EEG data screening and filtering methods and assessing their impact on the classification accuracy of the motor imagery task.

Each trial consists of different stages (Fig. 2b):

(1) Blank stage (0–2 s): this is the initial period where the subject is at rest.
(2) Preparation stage (2–4 s): a cross appears in the middle of the screen, signaling the subject to prepare for the upcoming task.
(3) Grasp animation cue stage (4–5.5 s): after four seconds, a grasp animation of either the left or right hand randomly appears on one side of the screen. The subject is prompted to imagine performing the corresponding grasping action.
(4) Motor imagery stage (5.5–9 s): after the cue ended, a white dot appeared in the middle of the screen, prompting the subject to continue imagining until the end of the trial.

For our analyses, we focused on the data captured from 0.5 s to 3.5 s after the imagery cue appeared, which corresponds to the period when the subject is actively engaged in motor imagery.

Table 1 provides the relevant parameters for the three datasets, including the number of subjects, the number of trials per subject, duration of the data used for analysis, EEG sampling rate, and the number of channels.

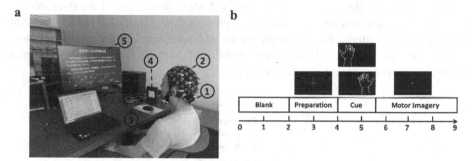

Fig. 1. EEG acquisition system and experiment paradigm. **a** NSW364 EEG acquisition system. The system consists of five components: ①EEG amplifier, ② EEG cap, ③ synchronizer, ④ intelligent synchronization center, and ⑤ computer. **b** Experimental paradigm, included 2 s blank stage, 2 s preparation stage, 1.5 s cue stage and 3.5 s motor imagery stage. The motor imagery stage included left and right-hand motor imagery, and 3 s data appeared after cue was adopted in data analysis.

Table 1. Public datasets and NSW364 experiment datasets.

Dataset	No. of subjects	No. of trials	Data length (s)	Sample rate (Hz)	No. of channels
BNCI2014 [20]	6	144	4	250	22
Cho2017 [21]	6	200	3	512	64
NSW364	3	100	3	1000	64

2.2 The Proposed Data Screening and Filtering Module

The conventional MI-BCI classification algorithm typically involves three main steps: signal preprocessing, feature extraction, and classification. In the signal preprocessing process, a Butterworth filter with a frequency range of 8–30 Hz was applied to the raw EEG data. Then, feature extraction was performed using a common spatial pattern (CSP) algorithm, which yields a 2D feature dimension. To classify left and right hand motor imagery, a support vector machine (SVM) is utilized. The dataset is divided into training and test sets with a 7:3 ratio enable cross-verification of the classification results.

In order to improve the quality and reliability of the training set, we incorporated the data screening and filtering modules before classification, as illustrated in Fig. 2. The newly introduced module consists of two main processing steps: (i) Pre-training data, consisting of the first 20 samples, was selected to fit the Gaussian distribution model for both left and right-hand motor imagery. The goal is to achieve a good separation between the two distributions. Subsequently, an appropriate confidence level was chosen as the threshold for data screening. (ii) Each subsequent sample is screened individually, and samples within the threshold range are retained while those beyond the threshold are discarded. This process ensures that the training set consists of data points that align with the desired criteria. By implementing the data screening and filtering procedures, we aim to enhance the overall quality and reliability of the training set, leading to improve performance in subsequent classification tasks.

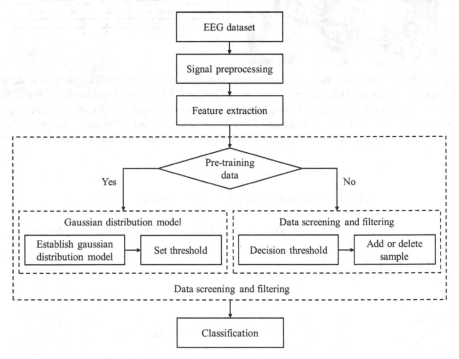

Fig. 2. Schematic illustration of the proposed method

2.2.1   The Use of Gaussian Distribution Model and Malhalanobis Distance for Data Screening

Gaussian mixture model (GMM) is a probabilistic model that assumes data points are generated from a mixture of several Gaussian distributions. The probability density function of GMM can be expressed as follows:

$$P(x; u; \sum) = \frac{1}{2\pi^{n/2}\left|\sum\right|^{1/2}}\exp(-\frac{1}{2}(x - u)^T \Sigma^{-1}(x - u) \tag{1}$$

where x represents the observed data, n represents data dimension, u and $\sum$ represent mean and covariance of Gaussian distribution. In our study, we utilized the GMM to estimate the probability distribution of the pre-training data by incorporating two-dimensional Gaussian models with different parameters. The contour lines of its probability density form ellipses, each representing a different confidence level. These ellipses provide valuable information about the probability of a sample point belonging to the Gaussian distribution.

To assess the probability of a new sample point belonging to a Gaussian distribution, we utilize the Mahalanobis distance (MD) between the sample point and the center of the distribution. The MD takes into account the covariance structure of the distribution and provides a more accurate representation of the sample's relationship to the distribution compared to the Euclidean distance, which was introduced by an Indian statistician P.C. Mahalanobis in 1936 [22]. It can be defined as follows:

$$d(\vec{x}, \vec{y}) = \sqrt{(\vec{x} - \vec{y})^T \Sigma^{-1}(\vec{x} - \vec{y})} \tag{2}$$

where $\vec{x}$ represents the new sample point and $\vec{y}$ represents the center of a Gaussian distribution, $\sum$ is the covariance matrix of the Gaussian distribution. By calculating the Mahalanobis distance, we obtain a quantitative measure of how closely the sample aligns with the Gaussian distribution.

Different distances correspond to different confidence levels, which can be used as thresholds for data screening. For instance, when considering confidence levels of 99%, 95%, and 90%, the corresponding MD threshold values are 9.21, 5.99, and 4.61, respectively. Samples within the threshold range are considered to have a higher probability of belonging to the distribution and are retained, while those beyond the threshold are deemed less likely to belong and are discarded.

By employing the Mahalanobis distance and setting appropriate thresholds, we can effectively screen and filter the data, improving the quality and reliability of the training dataset for subsequent analysis and classification tasks.

3 Results

3.1 The Gaussian Mixture Models of MI Pre-training Data

To construct the Gaussian mixture model, we utilized the first 20 training samples from the training set as pre-training data. An example of the Gaussian mixture models is illustrated in Fig. 3a, in which green and orange colors represent sample points from left and right-hand MI, respectively. The curve represents the probability density contours corresponding to a confidence level of 99% (Fig. 3a), indicating that two distributions are separable. In Fig. 3b, the probability density distribution terrain map also showed two distinct distributions of the pre-training samples. This map provides a visual representation of the probability density across the feature space. It helps us understand the distribution of the pre-training samples and provides valuable insights into the underlying patterns and structure of the data. By leveraging the Gaussian mixture model and analyzing the probability density contours and terrain map, we gain a better understanding of the classification potential and discriminative power of the pre-training data. These visualizations aid in comprehension of the data distribution and lay the foundation for subsequent classification tasks.

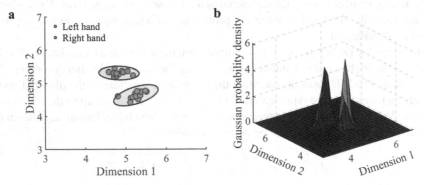

Fig. 3. Gaussian mixture models and their probability density. **a** Two distinct Gaussian mixture models are obtained from the data of left (green) and right (orange) hand motor imagination, respectively. **b** Topographic map of probability density distributions. Data comes from the public dataset BNCI2014S01. (Color figure online)

3.2 Enhancing Training Set Quality and Reliability Through Data Screening and Filtering

Firstly, we selected the first 20 sample points as the pre-training sample set. We then constructed the Gaussian mixture models using these samples. Subsequently, we proceeded to screen and filter the remaining samples in the dataset one by one. The Gaussian mixture models were fitted at different confidence levels: 99% (Fig. 4a), 95% (Fig. 4c), and 90% (Fig. 4e). These curves depict the probability density contours, where the smaller the confidence level, the tighter and smaller the corresponding confidence ellipse. The example of screening sample points was shown at different confidence levels: 99% (Fig. 4b), 95% (Fig. 4d), and 90% (Fig. 4f). As the confidence level decreases, the filtered training set becomes more distinguishable, with clearer boundaries between the sample points. These findings demonstrate the effectiveness of the Gaussian distribution model and the screening process in identifying and eliminating outlier samples. By varying the confidence level, we can fine-tune the screening process and improve the quality and reliability of the training set for subsequent classification tasks.

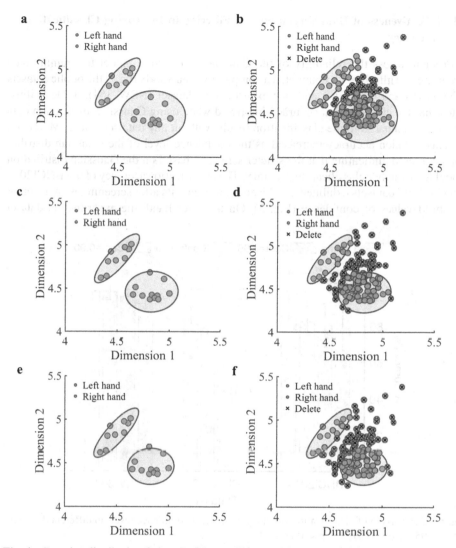

Fig. 4. Gaussian distribution fitting confidence ellipse and the process of data screening. **a, c** and **e** represent Gaussian distribution fitting at confidence levels of 99%, 95% and 90%, respectively. **b, d** and **f** are the examples of data screening at confidence levels of 99%, 95% and 90%, respectively. Green and orange dots represent sample points from left and right hand motor imagery respectively, and 'x' indicates that the sample point outside the ellipse and needs to be filerted. Data comes from the public dataset BNCI2014S01.

3.3 Effectiveness of Data Screening and Filtering in Improving Classification Accuracy

In order to assess the reliability of the Gaussian distribution model for training data screening and filtering, we conducted a comparative analysis between the public datasets (BNCI2014 and Cho2017) and our experimental dataset (NSW 364). Table 2 illustrates that the classification accuracy improved when using Gaussian distribution data screening compared to the classification results without any data screening. Moreover, the classification accuracy increased as the confidence level of the Gaussian distribution decreased, indicating that the stricter screening based on the Gaussian distribution model led to higher classification accuracy. The classification accuracy of the BNCI2014 and Cho2017 datasets exhibited significant improvements after screening with different threshold values of confidence (Fig. 5). On the other hand, the experimental dataset

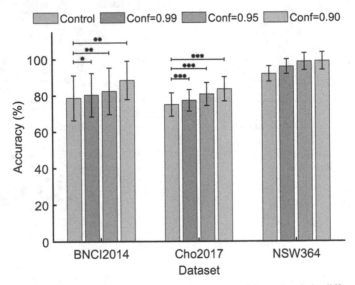

Fig. 5. Comparison of classification accuracy at different confidence levels in different data sets. * p < 0.05, ** p < 0.01, *** p < 0.001.

Table 2. Classification accuracy (%) at different confidence levels in different data sets

Methods	Datasets		
	BNCI2014	Cho2017	NSW364
Conf = 1 (Control)	78.72 ± 12.38	75.04 ± 6.46	92.00 ± 4.25
Conf = 0.99	80.40 ± 11.93	77.33 ± 5.97	95.98 ± 4.05
Conf = 0.95	82.49 ± 12.83	80.77 ± 6.34	98.70 ± 4.69
Conf = 0.90	88.44 ± 10.59	83.64 ± 6.71	98.94 ± 4.84

Data are presented as mean ± SD (standard deviation).

(NSW 364) exhibited a higher classification accuracy across different confidence levels (Fig. 5), indicating that this dataset has a smaller variance compared to the other datasets. These findings highlight the effectiveness of the Gaussian distribution model for data screening and filtering in improving classification accuracy. By applying the Gaussian mixture model with appropriate confidence levels to screen the data, we showed that this approach enhances the reliability and performance of BCI.

4 Discussion

In this study, we introduced a data screening and filtering method as an enhancement to the traditional EEG processing and classification. The first step involved collecting a small sample of data for pre-training the Gaussian distribution model. This model served as the basis for defining a probability threshold for data screening. Subsequently, we conducted experiments using data collected from the Neuracle device and public datasets to verify the effectiveness of data screening. The results demonstrated that the classification accuracy was improved using the Gaussian model data screening method compared to the traditional method without data screening. Moreover, a smaller probability threshold yielded a higher improvement in classification accuracy.

In addition, during the experiment, we discovered that providing real-time feedback on the quality of subsequent training based on the pre-training model enhanced the subjects' understanding and memory of the specific training. This approach has the potential to improve the effectiveness of online experiments.

Overall, the process of data screening and filtering by the Gaussian distribution model showed promise in enhancing the classification accuracy of EEG-based motor imagery tasks. The findings from public datasets support the effectiveness of this approach.

5 Conclusion

In summary, the utilization of the Gaussian mixture model for modeling small sample data, followed by the screening of training samples, proves to be an effective approach for enhancing the reliability of the training set and improving classification accuracy. Additionally, providing participants with real-time feedback during online training can further enhance their understanding and memory of different motor imagery tasks. These advancements contribute to the practical implementation and application of BCI in real-world scenarios.

Acknowledgment. This work was supported by the National Natural Science Foundation of China (12101570), Zhejiang Lab & Pujiang Lab (K2023KA1BB01), and Key Research Project of Zhejiang Lab (2022KI0AC01).

References

1. Wolpaw, J.R., Birbaumer, N., McFarland, D.J., Pfurtscheller, G., Vaughan, T.M.: Brain-computer interfaces for communication and control. Clin. Neurophysiol. Off. J. Int. Fed. Clin. Neurophysiol. **113**(6), 767–791 (2002)

2. Vidal, J.J.: Toward direct brain-computer communication. Annu. Rev. Biophys. Bioeng. **2**(1), 157–180 (1973)
3. Elbert, T., Rockstroh, B., Lutzenberger, W., Birbaumer, N.: Biofeedback of slow cortical potentials. I Electroencephalogr. Clin. Neurophysiol. **48**(3), 293–301 (1980)
4. Birbaumer, N., Elbert, T., Canavan, A.G., Rockstroh, B.: Slow potentials of the cerebral cortex and behavior. Physiol. Rev. **70**(1), 1–41 (1990)
5. Farwell, L.A., Donchin, E.: Talking off the top of your head: toward a mental prosthesis utilizing event-related brain potentials. Electroencephalogr. Clin. Neurophysiol. **70**(6), 510–523 (1988)
6. Wolpaw, J.R., McFarland, D.J., Neat, G.W., Forneris, C.A.: An EEG-based brain-computer interface for cursor control. Electroencephalogr. Clin. Neurophysiol. **78**(3), 252–259 (1991)
7. Wang, Y., Gao, S., Gao, X.: Common spatial pattern method for channel selelction in motor imagery based brain-computer interface. In: 2005 IEEE Engineering in Medicine and Biology 27th Annual Conference, pp. 5392–5395. IEEE, January 2006
8. Cheng, M., Gao, X., Gao, S., Xu, D.: Design and implementation of a brain-computer interface with high transfer rates. IEEE Trans. Biomed. Eng. **49**(10), 1181–1186 (2002)
9. Shih, J.J., Krusienski, D.J., Wolpaw, J.R.: Brain-computer interfaces in medicine. In: Mayo Clinic Proceedings, vol. 87, no. 3, pp. 268–279. Elsevier, March 2012
10. Pfurtscheller, G., Da Silva, F.L.: Event-related EEG/MEG synchronization and desynchronization: basic principles. Clin. Neurophysiol. **110**(11), 1842–1857 (1999)
11. Pfurtscheller, G., Brunner, C., Schlögl, A., Da Silva, F.L.: Mu rhythm (de)synchronization and EEG single-trial classification of different motor imagery tasks. Neuroimage **31**(1), 153–159 (2006)
12. Ramoser, H., Muller-Gerking, J., Pfurtscheller, G.: Optimal spatial filtering of single trial EEG during imagined hand movement. IEEE Trans. Rehabil. Eng. **8**(4), 441–446 (2000)
13. Dornhege, G., Blankertz, B., Curio, G., Muller, K.R.: Boosting bit rates in noninvasive EEG single-trial classifications by feature combination and multiclass paradigms. IEEE Trans. Biomed. Eng. **51**(6), 993–1002 (2004)
14. Nisar, H., Boon, K.W., Ho, Y.K., Khang, T.S.: Brain-computer interface: feature extraction and classification of motor imagery-based cognitive tasks. In: 2022 IEEE International Conference on Automatic Control and Intelligent Systems (I2CACIS), pp. 42–47. IEEE (2022)
15. Guerrero, M.C., Parada, J.S., Espitia, H.E.: EEG signal analysis using classification techniques: logistic regression, artificial neural networks, support vector machines, and convolutional neural networks. Heliyon **7**(6), e07258 (2021)
16. Liu, X., Shen, Y., Liu, J., Yang, J., Xiong, P., Lin, F.: Parallel spatial–temporal self-attention CNN-based motor imagery classification for BCI. Front. Neurosci. **14**, 587520 (2020)
17. Lawhern, V.J., Solon, A.J., Waytowich, N.R., Gordon, S.M., Hung, C.P., Lance, B.J.: EEGNet: a compact convolutional neural network for EEG-based brain–computer interfaces. J. Neural Eng. **15**(5), 056013 (2018)
18. Sakhavi, S., Guan, C., Yan, S.: Learning temporal information for brain-computer interface using convolutional neural networks. IEEE Trans. Neural Netw. Learn. Syst. **29**(11), 5619–5629 (2018)
19. Jing, L., Yaojie, W., Guangming, L., Xiaofan, W., Xiaofeng, L., Xinhong, H.: Mirror convolutional neural network for motor imagery electroencephalogram recognition. J. Image Graph. **26**(9), 2257–2269 (2021)
20. Tangermann, M., et al.: Review of the BCI competition IV. Front. Neurosci. **6**, 55 (2012)
21. Cho, H., Ahn, M., Ahn, S., Kwon, M., Jun, S.C.: EEG datasets for motor imagery brain–computer interface. GigaScience **6**(7), gix034 (2017)
22. Mahalanobis, P.C.: On the generalised distance in statistics. Proc. Natl. Inst. Sci. India. **2**(1), 49–55 (1936)

The Impact of Three-Week Passive Robotic Hand Therapy on Stroke Patients

Xinhang Li[1], Minjun Zheng[2], Jinbiao Liu[1], Li Zhang[3], Lizi Jiang[1], Shiwei Zheng[1], Linqing Feng[1,4], Tao Tang[1,4], Lei Ling[3(✉)], Xiangming Ye[3(✉)], and Yina Wei[1,4(✉)]

[1] Research Center for Augmented Intelligence, Zhejiang Lab, Hangzhou 311100, Zhejiang, China
weiyina039@zhejianglab.com
[2] The Second School of Clinical Medicine, Zhejiang Chinese Medical University, Hangzhou 310053, China
[3] Zhejiang Provincial People's Hospital, Hangzhou 310027, China
linglei@hmc.edu.cn, yexmdr@126.com
[4] Zhejiang Provincial Key Laboratory of Cardio-Cerebral Vascular Detection Technology and Medicinal Effectiveness Appraisal, Zhejiang University, Hangzhou 310027, China

Abstract. Robotic hand therapy is widely used in rehabilitation for patients with hand dysfunction caused by stoke. However, the effectiveness of passive robotic hand training for rehabilitation is still unknown. In this study, we assessed the impact of three-week passive robotic hand therapy on stroke patients based on electroencephalography (EEG) and electromyography (EMG). We employed localization techniques to identify the source of electrical activity and compared the brain activity between the left and right regions of sensorimotor. Despite the limited improvements in hand function, the results showed that there was an overall improvement in brain activity. Although no significant difference was observed in the change of brain activity at the sensorimotor regions after the training in three movement modes, the EEG-EMG coherence in the beta and gamma frequency bands were increased after training in the active mode, suggesting an increase in the efficiency of nerve signals driving muscle activity. This study contributes to a better understanding of the effectiveness of various neurological rehabilitation training methods for stroke patients undergoing robotic hand therapy.

Keywords: Electroencephalography · electromyography · robotic hand therapy

1 Introduction

The stoke is a severe medical event which could cause severe disability or fatality, resulting in a serious impact on patients' quality of life. There are various rehabilitation treatments for stroke [1]. Rehabilitation training aims to enable individuals with impairments to achieve their optimal physical, cognitive, and emotional well-being [2]. In recent years, there are many novel therapeutic interventions proposed for the recovery of upper-limb function after a stroke. However, the outcomes of patients after rehabilitation often remain disappointing despite these new treatments [3].

X. Li and M. Zheng—These authors contributed equally.

H. Yang et al. (Eds.): ICIRA 2023, LNAI 14267, pp. 233–243, 2023.
https://doi.org/10.1007/978-981-99-6483-3_21

Due to the repeated practice of skilled movements in rehabilitation treatment, the robotic assisted therapy for rehabilitation seems more prevalent [4]. Robot-assisted therapy will improve activities of daily living, arm function, and arm muscle strength [5]. Generally, the robot provides passive, active-assisted or active-resisted movement of the hand and visual feedback via a screen to motivate the patient [6]. Grace et al. found that robotic hand training was feasible, safe, and well tolerated. Their results showed that patients had improved hand motor function after six-week training [7]. Similarly, Calabrò et al. observed that robotic hand therapy led to significant improvements in hand motor function recovery. Their findings demonstrated that the patients who underwent robotic hand therapy exhibited clinical improvements compared to those received intense occupational therapy [8]. While there are many rehabilitation strategies in routine clinical examination, there remains a lack of comprehensive approaches that can effectively assess the direct impact of neuromotor disorders.

Clinical assessment of upper limb function in stroke patients mainly includes several assessment tests. The Fugl-Meyer assessment (FMA) is commonly used to assess the global motor impairment by examining movement speed, force, and range of motion through the upper limb. However, interpretations of FMA results may differ across different regions [9]. On the other hand, Wolf motor function test (WMFT) evaluation is often considered tedious, which may easily reduce patient compliance. However, these methods exhibit a certain degree of subjectivity, and no single test is universally applicable for assessing hands dysfunction. To address this limitation, it's crucial to select assessment tools that are tailored to the residual motor function level of individual patients [10].

The coherence between electroencephalography (EEG) and electromyography (EMG) is a recognized neurophysiological measure and has been widely used in the coherence analysis of EEG and EMG [11]. Matthias et al. found that an increase of force within the low-level range is associated with enhanced coupling between sensorimotor cortex and muscle in health people. This suggests a role for beta-range corticomuscular coherence in effective sensorimotor integration, which in turn can stabilize corticospinal communication [12]. In this study, the participants underwent three distinct types of robotic hand therapy training sessions: passive, active, and mirror training. During these sessions, the EEG and EMG signals were recorded to analyze the neural and muscular activities. We compared localized brain signal before and after three-week passive robotic hand therapy on stroke patients. Despite the potential of EEG-EMG coherence as a valuable tool to analyze outcomes of the robotic hand therapy, few studies have been conducted specifically on this measure. In this study our goal was to assess the impact of passive robotic hand therapy on motor function by EEG-EMG coherence. This study enhances our understanding of the effectiveness of passive robotic hand training as a rehabilitation approach for stroke patients. The findings shed light on the benefits and outcomes associated with passive robotic hand therapy, contributing valuable insights to the field of stroke rehabilitation.

2 Materials and Methods

2.1 Subjects

Nine participants with stroke were recruited for the hand motor function experiment from Zhejiang Provincial People's Hospital. The experimental procedure of this study has been approved by the Ethics Committee of the Zhejiang Provincial People's Hospital (No. ChiCTR2200063682). All participants were given a detailed verbal and written description of the experiment and signed an informed consent form in accordance with the Helsinki Declaration.

Patients were rated as eligible according to the following criteria: (i) age between 18–70 years; (ii) a chronic-stage stroke caused by initial intracerebral hemorrhage and cerebral infarction, or prior lacunar infarction without sequelae at least six months after the event; (iii) Brunnstrom stage $\geq$III; (iii) no metal implants, such as stents; (iv) no previous history of mental disorders or drug use causing symptoms of mental disorders; (v) a Mini–Mental State Examination score (MMSE) >20 points, indicating that patients can follow instructions; (vi) no history of tumor, epilepsy or secondary epilepsy. Table 1 summarizes the clinical-demographics characteristics of patients.

2.2 Experiment Procedures

The subjects participated in 20-min passive robotic-assisted training each day for three weeks. To evaluate the effect of three-week training, we recorded EEG and EMG signals before and after the training at three movement modes, including passive, mirror and active training. Throughout three movement modes, the subjects naturally sat in a chair and their affected hand was wearing an assistive glove of robotic rehabilitation equipment (SY-HR08P, Shanghai Siyi Intelligence Technology Co., Ltd.). During the passive training, the gloves drove the affected hand flexion and extension. During the mirror training, the healthy hand flexed voluntarily while the affected side hand was driven by the robotic rehabilitation equipment simultaneously. During the active training, the affected hand flexed and extended voluntarily.

2.3 Data Description and Preprocessing

During the experiment, high density surface EMG (HD-sEMG) signals were recorded using an electrode grid containing 64 channels (GR04MM1305, Quattrocento, OT Bioelettronica). EEG signals were recorded synchronously using a Neuracle-NSW364 system (Neuracle, China). HD-sEMG signals were recorded on the flexor digitorum superficialis muscle at a sampling frequency of 2000 Hz, and downsampled to 1000 Hz for subsequent analysis. To remove noise components and power frequency interference from the EMG signals, a bandpass filter from 0.5 Hz to 45 Hz and a notch filter of 50 Hz were applied.

Similarly, EEG signals were recorded at a sampling rate of 1000 Hz using 64 channels, and the impedance of the electrodes was kept below 50 KΩ. EEG signals were synchronized in real-time by sending tags through a trigger box. To remove noise components from the EEG signals, a bandpass filter from 0.5 Hz to 45 Hz was applied using the EEGLAB plugin. Additionally, the Runica algorithm combined with multiple arti-fact suppression algorithms was employed to remove various EEG artifacts [13]. We simultaneously recorded EEG and EMG signals for a duration of 300 s. From these recording, we extracted a 240-s segment during different training sessions for further analysis.

Table 1. The clinical-demographics characteristics of patients

Patient	Age	Gender	Affected	BS	FMUL (Prior)	FMUL (Post)	Lesion side
S01	59	M	R	III	4	13	L basal ganglia
S02	57	M	L	V	14	14	R Cerebellum and brain stem
S03	55	M	R	III	4	5	R Parietal and basal ganglia
S04	42	M	R	IV	6	10	L frontotemporal parietal lobe
S05	41	M	R	III	6	8	L basal ganglia
S06	64	M	R	III	7	9	L basal ganglia Lateral ventricle
S07	65	M	R	IV	7	13	L basal ganglia
S08	68	F	L	IV	8	9	R Periventricular-basal ganglia
S09	66	M	R	IV	8	11	L thalamus

F: female; M: male; R: right; L: left; BS: Brunnstrom; FMUL: Fugl-Meyer Upper Limb Subscale.

2.4 Dynamic Statistical Analysis

2.4.1 Signal Reconstruction in the Cerebral Cortex

In order to accurately investigate the brain activity, we used the standardized low-resolution brain electromagnetic tomography (sLORETA) to localize the source of elec-trical activity using EEG signals. The localized brain source signals can be used for a better diagnosis and treatment of neurological disorders including depression [14]. The current density J at the cortex was calculated as follows:

$$J = L^T(LL^T + \alpha H)^{-1}M \tag{1}$$

where L represents the lead field which related to the geometry and conductivity profile of the head, α represents Tikhonov regularization parameter, H means the center matrix and M represents the scalp potential. Then the statistically standardized current density is defined as z_i:

$$z_i = \frac{[j]_i}{S_{J_{ii}}^{1/2}} \tag{2}$$

where $[j]_i$ is the estimated current density at the i-th voxel, S_J represents the covariance matrix for the current density J.

We first computed the cross-spectra of each channel at various frequency bands, including alpha (8–13 Hz), beta (15–28 Hz) and gamma (30–70 Hz), for each subject. Subsequently, utilizing LORETA-KEY (KEY Institute for Brain-Mind Research, Switzerland) software, we mapped these cross-spectra back to the cerebral cortex. To visualize the changes in brain activity before and after the three-week therapy, we performed an averaging process of the brain source activity across all subjects. This averaged brain source activity allowed us to obtain a comprehensive representation of the overall patterns before and after the therapy.

2.4.2 Difference Between Left and Right Sensorimotor Cortex

To assess the activity of sensorimotor cortex, we focused on the specific regions as known as the Brodmann areas 1, 2, 3, 4 and 6 (Fig. 1). These areas are associated with somatic sensory sensations and motor execution [15, 16]. Then we compared the difference between the left and right sides of the brain. Despite all the participants being right-handed, the stroke led to variations in the level of their hand dysfunction, which poses a challenge to quantify the effects of stroke on the left and right brain regions. Thus, we defined the sum of brain activity at the Brodmann areas 1, 2, 3, 4 and 6 as the sensorimotor relative brain activity. Then we examined the variations in brain activity before and after three weeks of training across different frequency bands.

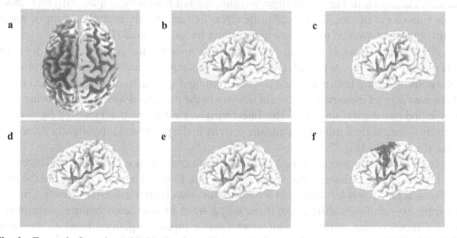

Fig. 1. Example for selected ROI (Region of Interest) of sensorimotor cortex. (a) ROI of the left and right sensorimotor cortex. (b) Brodmann area 1. (c) Brodmann area 2. (d) Brodmann area 3. (e) Brodmann area 4. (f) Brodmann area 6.

2.4.3   The EEG-EMG Coherence

The EEG-EMG coherence has been widely used in recognized neurophysiological measure. It can be applied to characterize the functional status between neurons and muscle activity. To estimate the coherence of EEG and EMG, we selected the EEG channel C3 if the right hand was affected or C4 if the left hand affected. EMG channel 32 was selected to represent the activity of muscles. The coherence was estimate as follows [17]:

$$C_{xy}(\omega) = \frac{\left|f_{yx}(\omega)\right|^2}{f_{xx}(\omega)f_{yy}(\omega)} \tag{3}$$

where $f_{yx}(\omega)$ represents the cross power spectral density between signal x and y, $f_{xx}(\omega)$ and $f_{yy}(\omega)$ represents the power spectral densities of signal x and y at frequency ω respectively. Independent sample two-tailed t-tests were used to assess significant differences between groups by MATLAB Inc. USA, with a significance level set at 0.05.

Among the three movement modes, only the active mode showed a stronger control of brain over muscles. We segmented the EEG and EMG signals recorded during active mode and calculated their coherence at each hand flexion. To investigate the impact of three-week passive therapy, we compared the average coherence of patients across three frequency bands before and after training.

3   Results

3.1   The Change of Brain Activity Before and After Three-Week Passive Therapy

By localizing the source of EEG signals and averaging them across nine subjects, we obtained the cortical activity of different frequency bands under three distinct movement modes. As shown in Fig. 2, we observed that the brain activity is quite different under three movement modes. Specifically, the alpha frequent band generally exhibited lower brain activity compared to the beta and gamma frequency band (Fig. 2a).

After three weeks of training, we observed a notable change in brain activity even within the same frequency band. In the alpha band, there was an increase in the prefrontal lobe activity during both active and passive training (Fig. 2a). Similarly, in the beta band, there was also an increase in the brain activity in the prefrontal lobe activity during both active and passive training (Fig. 2b). Interestingly, the gamma band showed the highest activity during mirror training, while the activity in the prefrontal lobe slightly decreased after three weeks (Fig. 2c).

Generally, the sensorimotor cortex of the brain controls body movement. Therefore, we focused on the sensorimotor areas, as shown in Fig. 1. Then, we compared the sum of brain activity over left and right sensorimotor areas before and after therapy (Fig. 3). Despite no significant difference, there was a trend of decreased brain activity in the sensorimotor cortex during the mirror and active modes at gamma band as shown in Fig. 3.

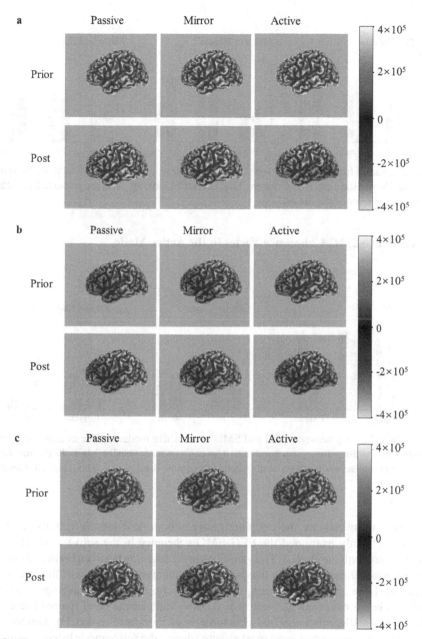

Fig. 2. The examples of brain source activity at different frequent bands during three movement modes. (a) Alpha band. (a) Beta band. (c) Gamma band.

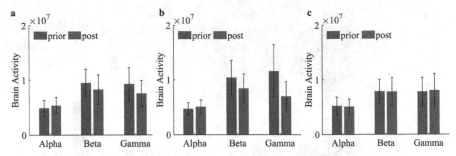

Fig. 3. The sum of brain activity between left and right sensorimotor areas under three movement modes. (a) Passive training. (b) Mirror training. (c) Active training. Data are presented as mean ± SEM (standard error of the mean).

3.2 The EEG-EMG Coherence Varies in the Active Mode

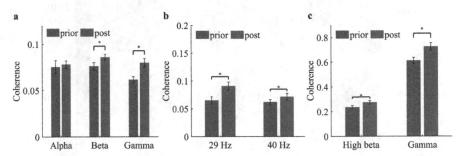

Fig. 4. The coherence between EEG and EMG in the active mode. (a) The averaged coherence of patients across three frequency bands. (b) The coherence across all trials at 29 Hz and 40 Hz. (c) The coherence across all trials at high beta and gamma band. * p < 0.05. Data are presented as mean ± SEM.

In order to investigate the coupling between brain and muscle activity in stroke patients, we mainly examined the EEG-EMG coherence in the active mode (Fig. 4a) across various frequency bands. The variations in the coupling between brain and muscles observed across these frequency bands, indicated the dynamic nature of the interaction between the brain and muscles during active modes. Importantly, the average coherence of patients in the beta (paired t-test, p = 0.0409) and gamma band (paired t-test, p < 0.001) were significantly enhanced after three-week therapy (Fig. 4a). Furthermore, we explored which frequencies were most affected during the active mode by comparing the coherence at different frequencies across all trials. We found that the coherence at 29 Hz (two-sample t-test, two-sided, p = 0.0116) and 40 Hz (two-sample t-test, two-sided, p = 0.0128) was significantly increased after three-week therapy (Fig. 4b). Additionally, the summation of coherence at 25–30 Hz (two-sample t-test, two-sided, p = 0.0495) and 30–50 Hz (two-sample t-test, two-sided, p = 0.0055) representing high beta band and gamma band respectively, also showed a significant enhancement (Fig. 4c).

4 Discussion

Rehabilitation training is essential for stroke patients to improve their quality of life. The rehabilitation training for patients can span several weeks to months, and there are numerous rehabilitation strategies available. Among these, the robotic-assisted therapy is more prevalent due to its multiple training modes. However, there remains a lack of accurate and reliable methods for effectively detecting subtle changes after the passive robotic hand therapy. In this study, we localized the source of electrical activity to estimate the brain activity at three distinct movement modes. Our findings indicate that there were minimal changes in brain activity within the alpha band following three weeks of training, suggesting a lower correlation between the alpha band and movement. Previous study showed that neuro-oscillatory desynchronization in the alpha band is thought to direct resource allocation away from the internal state and towards the processing of salient environmental events, such as reward feedback [18]. Next, we compared the sum of activity over the left and right brain regions in the sensorimotor cortex. Several people tended to have lower activity at beta band at mirror training. This suggests that it is possible that this passive training did not significantly improve the brain function during three-week training. This is to be expected because about 60% failing to achieve some dexterity at 6 months after stroke [1].

Different training modalities have varying effects on rehabilitation outcomes. In this study, we employed the EEG-EMG coherence as a measure of the function status in stroke patients, providing insights into the changes observed during a short three-week training period. Notably, we found that the coherence at beta and gamma bands increased significantly in the active movement mode after three-week training. These changes were consistent with the previous research which demonstrated that corticomuscular synchronization occurs in beta and gamma range during isometric compensation of static and dynamic low-level forces [12]. The increased coherence with lower brain activity suggesting increased recruitment efficiency of muscles and the involvement of a smaller group of neurons in muscle control. Although there was limited improvement in hand function over the three-week passive robotic hand therapy (Table 1), changes in brain activity were evident.

5 Conclusion

In conclusion, this study provides valuable insights into the use of robotic hand therapy for stroke patients with hand dysfunction. By exploring the impact of three-week passive robotic hand therapy on stroke patients during three distinct movement modes, this study demonstrates that despite observing limited improvement in hand function, there was an overall enhancement in brain activity. These findings suggest that passive robotic hand therapy may not lead to distinct improvement in the hand function for stoke patients in a short time. However, it is worth noting that mirror or active training modes may have positive effects on brain activity, as indicated by changes observed in brain activity during various training modes. Additionally, the increase in EEG-EMG coherence at active mode after training indicates an increase in the efficiency of nerve signals driving muscle activity. These findings contribute to a better understanding of the potential benefits of robotic hand therapy and different neurological rehabilitation training methods for stroke patients. Further research is needed to identify the most effective training methods and protocols for different types of stroke and severity of hand dysfunction.

Acknowledgement. This work was supported by the National Natural Science Foundation of China under Grant 62201515 and Grant 12101570, the China Postdoctoral Science Foundation under Grant 2021M702974, and Key Research Project of Zhejiang Lab (2022KI0AC01).

References

1. Hatem, S.M., et al.: Rehabilitation of motor function after stroke: a multiple systematic review focused on techniques to stimulate upper extremity recovery. Front. Hum. Neurosci. **10**, 442 (2016)
2. Hebert, D., et al.: Canadian stroke best practice recommendations: stroke rehabilitation practice guidelines, update 2015. Int. J. Stroke **11**(4), 459–484 (2016)
3. Roby-Brami, A., Jarrassé, N., Parry, R.: Impairment and compensation in dexterous upper-limb function after stroke. From the direct consequences of pyramidal tract lesions to behavioral involvement of both upper-limbs in daily activities. Front. Hum. Neurosc. **15**, 662006 (2021)
4. Stein, J.: Robotics in rehabilitation: technology as destiny. Am. J. Phys. Med. Rehabil. **91**(11), S199–S203 (2012)
5. Mehrholz, J., Pohl, M., Platz, T., Kugler, J., Elsner, B.: Electromechanical and robot-assisted arm training for improving activities of daily living, arm function, and arm muscle strength after stroke. Cochrane Database Syst. Rev. **9**, CD006876 (2018)
6. Hidler, J., Nichols, D., Pelliccio, M., Brady, K.: Advances in the understanding and treatment of stroke impairment using robotic devices. Top. Stroke Rehabil. **12**(2), 22–35 (2005)
7. Kim, G.J., Taub, M., Creelman, C., Cahalan, C., O'Dell, M.W., Stein, J.: Feasibility of an electromyography-triggered hand robot for people after chronic stroke. Am. J. Occup. Ther. **73**(4), 1–9 (2019)
8. Calabrò, R.S., et al.: Does hand robotic rehabilitation improve motor function by rebalancing interhemispheric connectivity after chronic stroke? Encouraging data from a randomised-clinical-trial. Clin. Neurophysiol. **130**(5), 767–780 (2019)
9. Kim, T., et al.: The Korean version of the Fugl-Meyer assessment: reliability and validity evaluation. Ann. Rehabil. Med. **45**(2), 83–98 (2021)
10. Thompson-Butel, A.G., Lin, G., Shiner, C.T., McNulty, P.A.: Comparison of three tools to measure improvements in upper-limb function with poststroke therapy. Neurorehabil. Neural **29**(4), 341–348 (2015)
11. Poortvliet, P.C., Tucker, K.J., Finnigan, S., Scott, D., Sowman, P., Hodges, P.W.: Cortical activity differs between position- and force-control knee extension tasks. Exp. Brain Res. **233**(12), 3447–3457 (2015)
12. Witte, M., Patino, L., Andrykiewicz, A., Hepp-Reymond, M.-C., Kristeva, R.: Modulation of human corticomuscular beta-range coherence with low-level static forces: beta coherence varies with low-level force. Eur. J. Neurosci. **26**(12), 3564–3570 (2007)
13. Delorme, A., Makeig, S.: EEGLAB: an open source toolbox for analysis of single-trial EEG dynamics including independent component analysis. J. Neurosci. Methods **134**(1), 9–21 (2004)
14. Zhang, Y., Gong, T., Sun, S., Li, J., Zhu, J., Li, X.: A functional network study of patients with mild depression based on source location. In: 2020 IEEE International Conference on Bioinformatics and Biomedicine (BIBM), pp. 1827–1834 (2020)

15. Sánchez-Panchuelo, R.-M., et al.: Regional structural differences across functionally parcellated Brodmann areas of human primary somatosensory cortex. Neuroimage **93**, 221–230 (2014)
16. Shah, K.B., et al.: Glial tumors in Brodmann area 6: spread pattern and relationships to motor areas. Radiographics **35**(3), 793–803 (2015)
17. Liu, J., Sheng, Y., Liu, H.: Corticomuscular coherence and its applications: a review. Front. Hum. Neurosci. **13**, 100 (2019)
18. Fryer, S.L., et al.: Alpha event-related desynchronization during reward processing in schizophrenia. Biol. Psychiatry Cognit. Neurosci. Neuroimaging **8**(5), 551–559 (2023)

A Six-Dof Parallel Robot-Assisted Dispensing Platform with Visual Servoing and Force Sensing for Accurate Needle Positioning and Mass Control

Jingyuan Xia[1,2], Zecai Lin[1,2], Huanghua Liu[1,2], and Anzhu Gao[1,2(✉)]

[1] Department of Automation, School of Electronic Information and Electrical Engineering, Shanghai Jiao Tong University, Shanghai 200240, China
anzhu_gao@sjtu.edu.cn
[2] Institute of Medical Robotics, Shanghai Jiao Tong University, Shanghai 200240, China

Abstract. Traditional manual dispensing of intravenous drugs needs the pharmacist to work in a pharmacy intravenous admixture services (PIVAS), leading to low efficiency, heavy physical labor, and the potential toxic drug exposure risk. There exist some automatic systems for drug dispensing. However, they may lead to inaccurate positioning and mass control due to various vial sizes and assembly errors. To solve this, this paper develops a compact dispensing platform with a six-DOF parallel robot, force sensing module, and visual servoing module for routine work in the biosafety cabinet. First, a customized robot to work inside the biosafety cabinet is developed using the configuration of 6-PSS parallel robot with three single-axis force sensors, enabling accurate needle positioning and mass control. Then, the forward and inverse kinematics are built to analyze and optimize its operational workspace and performance. Second, a visual servoing algorithm using a binocular camera is used to align the injection needle and the vial hole and a force-sensing module is incorporated onto the parallel robot to achieve real-time onsite measurement and evaluation of mass changes in the aspirated liquid. Finally, experiments are carried out to validate the effectiveness of the proposed robotic dispensing platform, and results indicate that the average positioning error is 0.41 mm, and the average mass error is 0.3 g. The developed robotic dispensing platform shows the merits of unmanned working inside the biosafety cabinet without occupying additional space, also makes accurate robotic positioning be adapted to the various sizes of commercial vials.

Keywords: 6-PSS Parallel Robot · Visual Servoing · Kinematic Analysis · Mass Control

1 Introduction

Currently, people face numerous diseases and the primary methods of medication for their treatment involve utilizing intravenous infusions, oral and intramuscular injections. Unfortunately, these delivery methods frequently rely on manual dispensing, which can be time-consuming and dangerous [1]. Often, such dispensing scenarios fail to ensure adequate air cleanliness standards, leaving them prone to the intrusion of fine particles and microorganisms which can have negative effects on the body [2]. Furthermore, the extended exposure of dispensers to antiviral drugs, chemotherapeutic drugs and immunosuppressive drugs carries considerable risks to their safety. Negative health consequences, such as hair loss, cancer, infertility, and miscarriage, can arise even with the use of protective clothing due to their prolonged exposure to such toxic materials [3–6]. As a result, the introduction of dispensing robots as a replacement for manual dispensing is deemed necessary to mitigate these risks and ensure safe and efficient drug delivery within clinical settings [7, 8].

Some companies and institutes have developed dispensing robots for medical applications. Intelligent Hospital Systems, a leading Canadian medical device company, has successfully designed and manufactured the RIVA (Robotic IV Automation) medication dispensing robot, which utilizes a six-degree-of-freedom robotic arm and can be integrated with hospital management systems to enhance operational efficiency [9–11]. However, due to their large overall size, significant footprint, and high production cost, dispensing robots equipped with a six-degree-of-freedom robot arm for docking are currently not a widely adopted solution. The Italian healthcare robot company, Health Robotics, has successfully launched the i.v.STATION robot, which is an automated device designed specifically for the preparation of non-toxic medical liquids. This small and cost-effective system includes an air treatment unit [12]. However, because of the lack of weight feedback, the robot system is unable to achieve precise mass control during the drug delivery process. Kiro Grifols Medical Devices, a Spanish company, has introduced the Kiro Oncology intravenous medication dispensing robot, which features two six-degree-of-freedom robotic arms that collaborate to dispense drugs. The robot utilizes a multi-sensor control approach, including vision and mass measurements, to ensure accurate identification and aspiration of drugs [13]. However, the collaborative dispensing speed of the robot is currently slow, with each pair of drugs taking approximately fifteen minutes to dispense. Y.C. He, et al. have developed an Intravenous Medication Dispensing Robot. They designed and implemented an expert system-based robot control system, and finally built a platform for a dispensing robot system [14], but these robotic systems lack mass acquisition and are designed to handle ampoules. H.Y. Jin, et al. have developed dispensing robots for toxic drugs in pharmacy intravenous admixture services [15]. It has a clean environment control system to clean the blended drugs. Despite the ongoing challenges and limitations, advancements in dispensing robot technology undoubtedly hold significant potential for streamlining medical processes and improving patient outcomes.

To solve the above limitations, this paper develops a six-DOF parallel robot-assisted dispensing platform with visual servoing and force sensing, featuring high-precision robotic positioning and mass control for drug dispensing medication. We develop a compact dispensing platform with a 6-PSS parallel robot, force sensing module. The visual servoing method is to achieve accurate alignment of the syringe and the vial. The paper also introduces a mass control method during the aspirating process. The robot prototype is developed and experiments are conducted to test the precise positioning and mass control modules, which demonstrates an average positioning error of 0.41 mm and a mass error of 0.3 g. The developed robotic dispensing platform shows the merits of unmanned working inside the biosafety cabinet without occupying additional space, and also enables accurate robotic positioning to adapt to the various sizes of commercial vials.

2   Design of the 6-PSS Parallel Robot-Assisted Dispensing Platform

2.1   Mechanical Design

The overall design requires a compact and small size that can be embedded inside the biosafety cabinet, as shown in Fig. 1. Dispensing in a fume hood can prevent the dispersal of toxic substances and can be adapted to any confined environment. Since the direction of the injection needle needs to be tilted upward and downward during actual operation, we designed a mechanism that allows the robot system to be tilted. There is a 6-PSS parallel robot on the button and six screw modules are laid on the button surface. During movement, the servo drives the gears to rotate and the gears drive the screw shaft to rotate, thus driving the motion of the bottom slider. The movement of the slider changes the position of the spherical on the motion platform. Therefore, the pose of the motion platform are adjusted to make the needle aligned to the vial. Since the entire motion chain is at the button, the 6-PSS parallel robot has good motion stability and high load capacity. Three force sensors were put symmetrically on the 6-PSS parallel robot. They are used to achieve the mass of the top platform. Two screw modules are put on the top platform, which is used to control the motion of the syringe and piston pusher to complete the injection and aspiration of liquid. Besides, a binocular camera was fixed on the platform, which is used to get the pose of the vial.

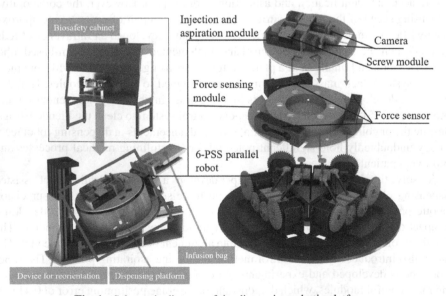

Fig. 1. Schematic diagram of the dispensing robotic platform.

The complete workflow of the dispensing platform in biosafety cabinet is shown in Fig. 2. In Step.1, the directional device is first moved so that the entire dispensing platform tilts upward. The syringe and piston pusher are then inserted into the infusion bags. Piston push rod is pushed back to aspirate the liquid from the infusion bags. In Step.2, the 6-PSS parallel robot was controlled by visual servoing to align the syringe end with the vial center. In Step.3, the directional device is first moved so that the entire dispensing platform tilts down, and then the syringe and piston push rod are inserted into the vial. Piston push rod is pushed forward to inject the liquid from the syringe into the vial. In step.4, the screw module is moved back and forth to shake the vial and accelerate the dissolution of the solute inside the vial. In Step.5, the directional device is first moved so that the entire dispensing platform tilts upward, and then the syringe and piston push rod are inserted into the vial. Piston push rod is pushed backward to aspirate the liquid from the vial into the syringe, force sensors here are used as feedback to control the mass of liquid in syringe. In Step.6, the directional device is first moved so that the entire dispensing platform tilts down, and the syringe and piston pushrod are inserted into the infusion bag. Piston rod is pushed forward to inject the liquid into the infusion bags.

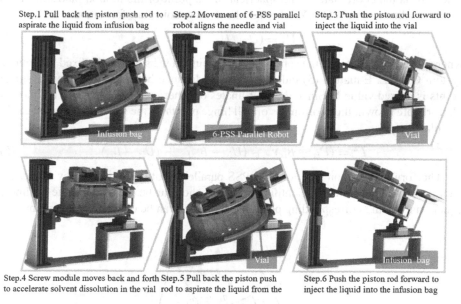

Step.1 Pull back the piston push rod to aspirate the liquid from infusion bag

Step.2 Movement of 6 PSS parallel robot aligns the needle and vial

Step.3 Push the piston rod forward to inject the liquid into the vial

Step.4 Screw module moves back and forth to accelerate solvent dissolution in the vial

Step.5 Pull back the piston push rod to aspirate the liquid from the

Step.6 Push the piston rod forward to inject the liquid into the infusion bag

Fig. 2. Workflow of the dispensing platform.

2.2 Inverse and Forward Kinematics Analysis of 6-PSS Parallel Robot

The parallel robot in the robotic system employs a 6-PSS parallel robot , as illustrated in the schematic diagram in Fig. 3. The desired trajectory in space of the motion platform is achieved by changing the position of the slider. The position of the moving stage is represented by six quantities, namely translation along the X, Y and Z axes and rotation around the X, Y and Z axes. The homogeneous transformation matrix with translation and rotation is denoted in Eq. (1).

$$FH(\alpha, \beta, \gamma, x, y, z) = \begin{pmatrix} c\alpha c\beta & c\alpha s\beta s\gamma - s\alpha c\gamma & s\alpha s\gamma + c\alpha s\beta c\gamma & x \\ s\alpha s\beta & c\alpha c\gamma + s\alpha s\beta s\gamma & s\alpha s\beta cr - s\gamma c\alpha & y \\ -s\beta & c\beta s\gamma & c\beta c\gamma & z \\ 0 & 0 & 0 & 1 \end{pmatrix} \tag{1}$$

where α, β and γ represent the angles of rotation of the motion platform around the x, y and z axes respectively in the O-XYZ fixed coordinate system. $c\alpha$ represents $\cos\alpha$, $s\alpha$ represents $\sin\alpha$ and so on. x, y and z represent the distance of translation of the motion platform along the X, Y and X axes in the O-XYZ fixed coordinate system.

$$B_i^* = (B_{ix}{}^*, B_{iy}{}^*, B_{iz}{}^*, 1)^T \tag{2}$$

where $B_i{}^*$ is the coordinate of the spherical hinge in the moving coordinate system.

$$B_i = (B_{ix}, B_{iy}, B_{iz}, 1)^T = FH(\alpha, \beta, \gamma, x, y, z) * B_i^* \tag{3}$$

where B_i is the coordinate of the spherical hinge point of the motion platform in the fixed coordinate system O-XYZ through the homogenous transformation.

$$U_i = (U_{ix}, U_{iy}, U_{iz},)^T \tag{4}$$

where U_i is coordinates of the spherical hinge point on the slider in the fixed coordinate system O-XYZ. Equation (5) indicates that the distance between two spherical hinge points is a fixed value L. Since the coordinates of spherical hinge points in the motion platform are known, the coordinates of ball hinge points on the slide block can be easily calculated.

$$L^2 = (U_{ix} - B_{ix})^2 + (U_{iy} - B_{iy})^2 + (U_{iz} - B_{iz})^2 \tag{5}$$

The forward position solution of 6-PSS parallel robot can be solved by numerical method. [16, 17]. The SciPy scientific library in python can be used to solve the nonlinear equations, and the corresponding positions and poses can be obtained at this point.

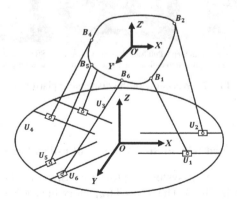

Fig. 3. The structure sketch of 6-PSS parallel robot.

3 Vision-Based Needle Positioning and Force Sensor-Based Mass Control

3.1 Visual Servoing for Needle Positioning

Because of the complexity of the actual work, it is difficult to obtain the contours of the vial directly by using the traditional image processing algorithm. An object detection algorithm based on machine learning is used here. The Yolo_v3 algorithm [18–20] is used to complete the target detection, and the region of interest was extracted. We collect 90 photos as a data set. Image enhancement was carried out on these 90 photos to change their exposure and brightness and simulate the complex conditions of the actual situation. The whole data set has 630 photos. Let batch = 64, learning rate = 0.001, max batches = 1500, momentum = 0.9, decay = 0.005 and the model is trained. Test set and the validator surface of the model can recognize the vial well, which is shown in Fig. 4.

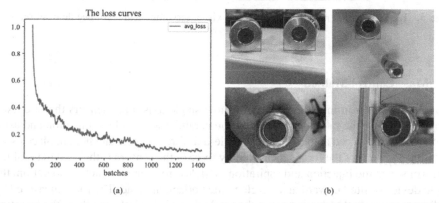

(a)   (b)

Fig. 4. The loss function of yolo training process and the training effect of the model. (a) The loss function of the training process. (b) The training model is tested on the validation set, and the results show that it can identify different types of vials well.

When the region of interest is extracted, there will be some error if the center of the detection frame is directly used as the coordinates of the returned pixel points. Therefore, we do image processing on the extracted region of interest. First, it is converted into grayscale map to reduce its noise and increase the processing speed. The brightness of the image changes because the lighting conditions in the actual working situation, so the image mechanical energy adaptive thresholding is processed. After that, the image is through closed-operator corrosion to make the contour of the vial smoother. Finally, the image is subjected to Hough circle detection, and the coordinates of the circle's center are returned as the pixel coordinates of the center point of the vial. The depth is found as

$$D = (b * f)/d \tag{6}$$

where D is the depth information, f is the focal length of the camera, b is the baseline distance of the binocular camera, and d is the pixel parallax of the center point in the two images. The ICP algorithm is used to align the extracted 3D point cloud with the pre-defined 3D plane of the vial, thus determining the pose of the vial. As a result, the relative position and posture difference of the vial concerning for the end of the injector can be ascertained. The dispensing robotic platform uses a position-based visual servoing method. The error of the end of the vial relative to the end of the camera can be obtained. The error is used as feedback to conduct inverse kinematics calculation of the robot and perform trajectory planning. Then we control the movement of the 6-PSS parallel robot to align the end of the syringe with the center of the vial. The control flow is shown in Fig. 5.

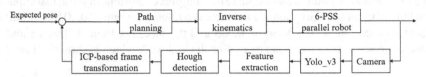

Fig. 5. The control diagram of position-based visual servoing control for needle positioning.

3.2 Mass Control Method

The mass acquisition module consists of three single-axis force sensors that are fixed symmetrically on the moving platform of the parallel robot, and the injection and aspiration module is placed above the three single-axis force sensors and held in place using six bolts. The sum of the forces measured by three of the sensors is the total mass of the platform where the injection and aspiration modules are located. In actual operation, the whole device is tilted upward at an angle to the horizontal plane. The force measured by the force sensors is the component of the total mass of the platform where the injection and aspiration module are located along the direction perpendicular to the plane of the force sensors. We fixed the position of the platform. Weights were placed on it and the data variation of the sensor was recorded, and finally this scale factor was obtained as 0.95. During the process of aspirating liquid from a vial, it is necessary to control the mass of the liquid. The desired mass is inputted and the system starts working. After each process, the syringe is taken out of the vial and checked to see if the desired mass has been obtained. If not, the process is repeated until the desired quality is achieved.

4 Experiment

To demonstrate the feasibility of this robotic system, we built a prototype of the dispensing platform and carried out two experiments. The prototype of the dispensing platform is shown in Fig. 6. The resolution of binocular camera (Shenzhen Rongyang Electronic Technology Co., Ltd) is 1280*720. The accuracy of screw modules (Haijie Technology Co., Ltd) is 0.1 mm. The resoultion of single-axis force sensors (Qishensensor Technology Co., Ltd) is 0.1 g.

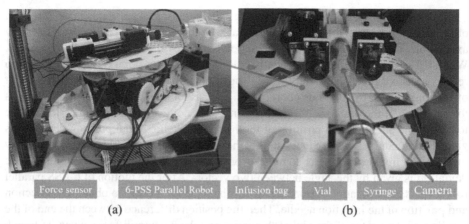

| Force sensor | 6-PSS Parallel Robot | Infusion bag | Vial | Syringe | Camera |

(a)   (b)

Fig. 6. Prototype of dispensing platform. (a) Prototype of dispensing robotic platform and experimental platform. (b) Physical view of the upper platform.

4.1 Vial Positioning Experiment

In this experiment, electromagnetic tracking system (Aurora, Northern Digital Inc., Canada) is used to obtain the real position and direction of the target as an accuracy evaluation. The experimental setup and software platform is shown in Fig. 7. When the vial is fixed, the meter pen is placed at the center point of the vial mouth to record its coordinates, and then the NDI positioning pen is placed at the center point of the vial bottom to obtain its coordinates. The vector between the two coordinates is the direction of the vial axis. The same operation is done again for the injection needle to obtain the direction and position of the injection needle.

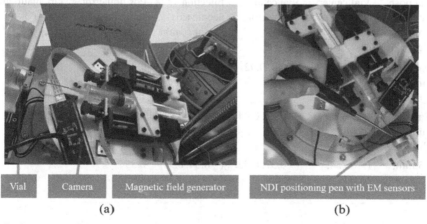

| Vial | Camera | Magnetic field generator | NDI positioning pen with EM sensors |

(a)   (b)

Fig. 7. Prototype of the visual servoing experiment. (a) Schematic diagram of the experimental setup. (b) The coordinates of the vial and the puncture needle are obtained by tapping them with NDI positioning pen with embedded EM sensors.

Initial position deviation is given by the camera sensor. Since z axis is the direction of the injection needle, the screw module has free degrees here, so only error of x and y axis is considered. Initial orientation deviation is given by the angle between two vectors. When the vial is fixed, the meter pen is placed at the center point of the vial mouth to record its coordinates, and then the NDI positioning pen is placed at the center point of the vial bottom to obtain its coordinates. The vector between the two coordinates is the direction of the vial axis. the same operation is done again for the injection needle to obtain the direction and position of the injection needle. Initial position deviation is given by the camera sensor. Since z axis is the direction of the injection needle, the screw module has free degrees here, so only error of x and y axis is considered. Initial pose deviation is given by the angle between two vectors. After the motion of 6-PSS parallel robot, the same operation is done again for the injection needle to obtain the direction and position of the injection needle. Then the position difference between the end of the needle and the center of the vial at this point and the posture difference can be found. Since only the relative position and attitude errors are measured during the experiment, the coordinates of the magnetic field generator and the world coordinate system do not need to be calibrated with the change matrix. As a result of the experiment, we can obtain the vector of the axis of the vial and the coordinates of the midpoint of the vial, and the vector of the injection needle and the coordinates of the end of the needle. The difference between the coordinates of the end of the needle and the coordinates of the midpoint of the mouth of the vial is used as the final position error, and the angle between the vector of the needle and the vector of the axis of the vial is evaluated as the orientation error. The deviations were obtained by placing the vial in different initial positions and three experiments were conducted. Experimental results are shown in Table 1.

Table 1. Three sets of experimental data of visual servoing.

Initial pose error (x, y, deviation angle)	Vial center coordinate (mm)	Vial central axis vector (mm)	Injection needle axis vector (mm)	Position error (mm)	Orientationm error (°)
(−0.4 mm, 3.2 mm, 5.4°)	(−68.01, 69.35, − 155.36)	(−0.4, 0.92, -0.02)	(−0.41, 0.91, −0.03)	0.33	0.59
(1.8 mm, − 2.6 mm, 7.1°)	(−67.54, 65.94, -151.47)	(−0.32, 0.94, −0.07)	(−0.39, 0.92, −0.02)	0.54	5.2
(0.25 mm, 0.1 mm, 6.3°)	(−68.54, 67.21, − 153.32)	(−0.37, 0.93, −0.03)	(−0.34, 0.94, −0.02)	0.35	2.1

Through three experiments, it is shown that when there is angular deviation and positional deviation in the initial position of the vial, the position error can be less than 1 mm by adjusting the 6-pss parallel robot, and the deviation in the angle direction is also reduced to a certain extent. In the actual working situation, the error of the position of the vial is more influential, and the angle within 5° can make the needle enter the vial. Therefore, the impact of the position error was mainly considered, and it is obvious that the position error of the three experiments finally reached the ideal situation.

4.2 Mass Control Experiments

During the experiment, the whole device is placed tilting so that the direction of the injection needle faces upward diagonally, as shown in Fig. 2(5). 5 g, 10 g, 15 g of liquid is aspirated from the vial, with each group being repeated five times. The experimental results are shown in Table 2. The average error is the average of the errors of the five experiments in each group). Fig. 8 displays the real-time data obtained by the sensor during the aspiration of 5 g of liquid. The results indicate that the system can effectively control the mass of the extracted liquid, with an average error within acceptable limits.

Table 2. Experimental data of liquid aspiration experiment.

Expected mass (g)	1	2	3	4	5	Average error (g)
5	4.7	4.6	5.2	5.0	5.3	0.24
10	9.7	9.9	9.1	9.8	10.4	0.38
15	15.2	15.4	14.5	15.0	14.7	0.28

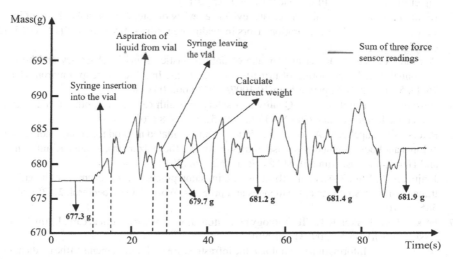

Fig. 8. The graph of the change of the real-time value of the mass during the aspirating process. (the first group of experiments with 5 g aspirated.)

In the working process, each action is divided into four cycles, which is shown in Fig. 8. After the completion of a cycle, repeat the action of the next cycle according to the current error, knowing that the quality error detected meets the requirements. Based on the experimental data in Table 2, it can be concluded that the aspiration process is stable and reliable, achieving high accuracy mass and the average error is 0.3 g.

5 Conclusions

This paper develops a six-DOF parallel robot-assisted dispensing platform with visual servoing module and force sensing module, which can achieve high precision robotic positioning and mass control for liquid drug dispensing medication. The precise positioning and mass control modules are shown to achieve an average error of 0.41 mm and 0.3 g respectively. The entire dispensing platform is compact and can be embedded inside a small biosafety cabinet. The dispensing platform will be further improved and enhanced to ensure full machine functionality about the sterilization and dissolution.

Acknowledgement. This work was supported in part by the Science and Technology Commission of Shanghai Municipality (22511101602); the National Natural Science Foundation of China (62003209); the Natural Science Foundation of Shanghai (21ZR1429500); the Shanghai Rising-Star Program (22QC1401400).

References

1. Pépin, J.C.N., et al.: Evolution of the global burden of viral infections from unsafe medical injections 2000–2010. PLoS One **9**(6), e99677 (2014)
2. Hedlund, N., Beer, I., et al.: Systematic evidence review of rates and burden of harm of intravenous admixture drug preparation errors in healthcare settings. BMJ Open. **7**(12), e015912 (2017)
3. Pethran, A., Schierl, R., et al.: Uptake of antineoplastic agents in pharmacy and hospital personnel. Part I: monitoring of urinary concentrations. Int. Arch. Occup. Environ. Health **76**(1), 5–10 (2003). https://doi.org/10.1007/s00420-002-0383-8
4. Harolds, J.A., Harolds, L.B.: Quality and safety in health care, part x: other technology to reduce medication errors. Clin Nucl Med. **41**(5), 376–378 (2016)
5. Peters, B.J., Capelle, M.A., et al.: Validation of an automated method for compounding monoclonal antibody patient doses: case studies of Avastin (bevacizumab), Remicade (infliximab) and Herceptin (trastuzumab). MAbs. **5**(1), 162–170 (2012)
6. Janjua, N.Z., Butt, Z.A., et al.: Towards safe injection practices for prevention of hepatitis C transmission in South Asia: Challenges and progress. World J. Gastroenterol. **22**(25), 5837–5852 (2016)
7. Felkey, B.G., Barker, K.N.: Technology and automation in pharmaceutical care. J. Am. Pharm. Assoc. (Wash). **36**(5), 309–314 (1996)
8. Murray, M.D.: Information technology: the infrastructure for improvements to the medication-use process. Am. J. Health Syst. Pharm. **57**(6), 565–571 (2000)
9. Jodi, F.: Robotic products to assist the aging population. Interactions. **12**(2), 16–18 (2005)
10. Urbine, T.F., Schneider, P.J.: Estimated cost savings from reducing errors in the preparation of sterile doses of medications. Hosp. Pharm. **49**(8), 731–739 (2014)
11. Sivlee, L., Morgan, L.: Implementation of wireless "intelligent" pump iv Infusion technology in a not-for-profit academic hospital setting. Hosp. Pharm. **12**, 832–840 (2001)

12. Yagüe, C., Maqueda, G, et al.: Characteristics of turbulence in the lower atmosphere at Halley IV station, Antarctica. In: Dynamics of Atmospheres and Oceans, pp.205–223(2001)
13. Schoening, T., Artes, A., et al.: Semiautomated aseptic preparation of patient-individual antineoplastic intravenous solutions: first experiences in a German hospital pharmacy. Eur. J. Hosp. Pharm. **23**(1), 44–49 (2016)
14. He, Y.C., et al.: Design and implementation of an intravenous medication dispensing robot. In: 2019 IEEE International Conference on Cyborg and Bionic Systems (CBS), pp. 191–196 (2019)
15. Jin, H.Y., et al.: Dispensing robot for toxic drugs in pharmacy intravenous admixture services. In: 2021 IEEE International Conference on Real-time Computing and Robotics (RCAR), pp. 905-909 (2021)
16. Arshad, M., et al.: Solution of forward kinematics model of six degrees of freedom parallel robot manipulator. In: Proceedings of the IEEE Symposium on Emerging Technologies, pp. 393-398 (2005)
17. Merlet, J.P., et al.: Solving the forward kinematics of a gough-type parallel manipulator with interval analysis. Int. J. Robot. Res. **23**(3), 221–235 (2004)
18. Jiang, P.Y., et al.: A review of yolo algorithm developments. Procedia Comput. Sci. **199**, 1066–1073 (2022)
19. Zhao, Z.Q., et al.: Object detection with deep learning: a review. In: IEEE Transactions on Neural Networks and Learning Systems, vol.30, pp. 3212–3232 (2019)
20. Maity, M., et al.: Faster r-cnn and yolo based vehicle detection: a survey. In: 5th International Conference on Computing Methodologies and Communication (ICCMC), pp. 1442–1447 (2021)

Post-Stroke Motor Function Assessment Based on Brain-Muscle Coupling Analysis

Hui Chang[1], Ruikai Cao[1], YiXuan Sheng[1], Zhiyong Wang[1], Pu Wang[2], Rong Xin[2], XianXian Yu[2], and Honghai Liu[1(✉)]

[1] Harbin Institute of Technology (Shenzhen), Shenzhen 518055, China
honghai.liu@icloud.com
[2] The Seventh Affiliated Hospital, Sun Yat-sen University, Shenzhen 518107, China

Abstract. The interaction of information between the brain and muscles is widely present in human activities. Brain-muscle coupling has been proven to quantify the amount of information transmission between the cortex and muscles. Motor dysfunction is a typical sequela of stroke. Accurate quantitative assessment of motor function is the basis for formulating rehabilitation strategies. The application of brain-muscle coupling analysis to stroke patients' motor evaluation has received extensive attention from researchers. In this study, brain and muscle data were collected synchronously from 6 healthy subjects and 2 stroke patients during an upper limb iso-velocity motion paradigm. Linear brain-muscle coupling results were obtained based on the method of wavelet coherence. The results revealed that CMC during the dynamic force output process predominantly manifested in the gamma band. The CMC strength of stroke patients was significantly lower than that of healthy individuals. Furthermore, stroke patients exhibited a shift of CMC towards the lower frequency band (beta band). This study proves the effectiveness of brain-muscle coupling in quantifying stroke patients' motor function and has certain value in promoting motor rehabilitation.

Keywords: Stroke · Motor Rehabilitation · Cortico-muscular coupling

1 Introduction

The assessment of motor function is an important component in the process of motor rehabilitation [1]. Neurological disorders such as stroke are often accompanied by motor impairments in 80% of survivors [2]. Accurate evaluation of motor function not only helps physicians understand the patient's condition but also enables the measurement of the effectiveness of rehabilitation interventions.

Currently, clinical assessments are performed using scales such as the Fugl-Meyer Assessment and the Motor Assessment Scale [3]. These qualitative assessment methods are susceptible to the subjective perception of the physician. Furthermore, these evaluations are based on the patient's completion of specific motor tasks, lacking information about the underlying mechanisms of motor

H. Yang et al. (Eds.): ICIRA 2023, LNAI 14267, pp. 256–267, 2023.
https://doi.org/10.1007/978-981-99-6483-3_23

control. Therefore, there is a clinical need for quantitative assessment methods that incorporate physiological information.

During limb movement, there is a degree of information transmission and interaction between the cerebral cortex and the responding muscles [4]. The neural coupling phenomenon between the central nervous system and the periphery is essential for motor control. This coupling between the brain and muscles originates from the descending motor commands and the ascending somatosensory feedback [5], commonly referred to as corticomuscular coupling (CMC) or corticomuscular coherence. CMC was initially discovered between MEG and EMG signals [6] and has since been widely utilized for analyzing coherence between EEG and EMG signals [7]. It has been proven to be an effective indicator for evaluating synchronized activities or interactions between the cerebral cortex and muscles in the sensorimotor system [8]. Based on the complex interaction between the brain and muscles at different levels, the analysis methods of corticomuscular coupling (CMC) can be broadly classified into linear coupling and nonlinear coupling. Coherence analysis, as a linear analysis method, is the most commonly used approach in the analysis of corticomuscular coupling. It involves normalizing the cross-spectral density of two signals by their respective spectral densities to obtain coherence [9].

Studies have found a significant relationship between the state of corticomuscular coupling (CMC) and the patterns of movement. Omlor et al. utilized squared coherence analysis to evaluate CMC during the generation of constant force and force with periodic modulation in a force feedback task. They explored the neural mechanisms associated with muscle output force in the hand and reported significant differences in CMC between constant force and dynamic force, accompanied by characteristic coherence frequency shifts [10]. Fu et al. estimated CMC in dynamic finger movement tasks using wavelet coherence and found that the strength of CMC increases with the increment of force [11].

Current clinical research on corticomuscular coupling (CMC) has yielded certain conclusions. In general, muscle atrophy in stroke patients typically leads to a decrease in coupling strength [12]. Stroke patients often exhibit lower coupling strength compared to healthy individuals and may experience intermittent loss phenomena. Studies have also indicated that stroke patients demonstrate a broader distribution of coupling peak cortical locations than healthy subjects, which is consistent with the plastic reorganization of sensorimotor functions and suggests the involvement of the contralesional hemisphere in the affected muscles' activity [13,14]. Furthermore, as motor function recovers, the CMC strength in stroke patients gradually increases. Carlowitz-Ghori et al. found that in patients with post-acute stroke-induced motor impairments, the coupling strength increased in the unaffected hemisphere while decreasing in the affected hemisphere. Subsequently, the coupling strength normalized as the functional recovery improved. However, chronic stroke patients did not exhibit significant hemispheric differences in coupling strength [15]. Increased coupling strength has also been reported in patients who showed good recovery after receiving transcranial magnetic stimulation treatment [16]. Similar studies have shown that coupling strength increases with the recovery of impaired limb motor function. Graziadio et al. proposed that the overall degree of recovery in chronic unilateral stroke is associated with the symmetry of the interdependent damaged and non-damaged cortical spinal systems at the level of CMC [17].

In order to investigate the mechanisms of CMC during dynamic force generation and the differences in CMC between stroke patients and healthy individuals, we recruited two stroke patients as the experimental group and six healthy individuals as the control group. The experimental results revealed significant differences in CMC outcomes between the experimental and control groups. The following section of this paper, Sect. 2, will introduce the materials and methods, including the participants, experimental paradigm, data collection, and analysis procedures. Section 3 will present the results of the data analysis, while Sect. 4 will provide a discussion and summary.

2   Materials and Methods

2.1   Subject

The information of the participants is presented in Table 1. The healthy participants involved in the experiment were all right-handed and had no underlying medical conditions. Both stroke patients experienced their first-ever stroke within the past year. The upper limb Brunnstrom stage for P-subj1 was classified as stage 4, while the upper limb Brunnstrom stage for P-subj2 was classified as stage 2. All subjects gave signed informed consent according to the Helsinki Declaration, and all measurements were approved by the local ethics committee.

Table 1. Information of stroke patients and healthy controls.

Subject	Gender	Age	Hemiplegia side
P-subj1	Male	62	Left
P-subj2	Female	68	Right
H-subj1	Female	65	-
H-subj2	Female	56	-
H-subj3	Female	52	-
H-subj4	Female	25	-
H-subj5	Male	22	-
H-subj6	Male	26	-

P: Patients; H: Healthy controls; subj: subject

2.2   Experiment Paradigm

The participants were instructed to sit at an appropriate distance directly in front of the upper limb rehabilitation robot, as shown in Fig. 1(a). The height-adjustable operating plane of the robot was tailored to the height of each participant. During the experiment, the position and trajectory of the handle were displayed on a screen. The robot was set to operate in passive mode with a constant resistance. During the experiment, participants were required to exert a certain amount of force to initiate the movement of the handle according to the information displayed on the screen. When the applied force exceeded the resistance, the handle moved linearly at a constant velocity.

The movement trajectory of the handle is illustrated in Fig. 1(b). The starting point is the center, and the handle sequentially moves towards eight directions, labeled as a to h. Each direction consists of both pushing and pulling processes, as indicated by the red straight arrows in the figure. After completing the movement in each direction, the handle returns to the center point. The distance for each one-way push or pull is 20 cm, and the total duration for each push and pull is 3 s. Starting from direction a, the first rotation is clockwise, and the second rotation is counterclockwise, continuing in this alternating pattern. Each test lasted for 3 min and consisted of 60 trials. After each test, there was a 3-minute rest period to prevent muscle fatigue in the participants. During the experiment, participants were instructed to keep their trunk and head as still as possible and rely solely on their upper limbs to exert force for pushing the handle. They were required to maintain their gaze on the screen and refrain from speaking throughout the duration of the experiment. Healthy participants used their right hand to push the handle, while stroke patients used their affected hand for the experiment.

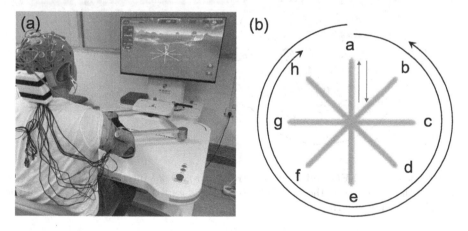

Fig. 1. Upper extremity iso-velocity motion paradigm: (a) Upper limb rehabilitation training robot; (b) Trajectory of motion.

2.3   Data Recording

In this study, a custom-designed integrated acquisition system with 16 channels for electroencephalography (EEG) and 16 channels for electromyography (EMG) was utilized for simultaneous data collection of the two signals. The system had a 24-bit analog-to-digital conversion precision and a common mode rejection ratio of up to 110 decibels. The quality of the acquired EEG and EMG signals has been confirmed to be comparable to commercial devices. Furthermore, the synchronization accuracy between the two signals could reach the nanosecond level, eliminating the need for offline synchronization. The sampling rate for both the EEG and EMG signals was set to 1000 Hz, meeting the requirements of the Nyquist-Shannon sampling theorem. In this experiment, we employed a 16-channel setup that primarily covered the brain regions associated with motor function, as illustrated in Fig. 2(a). Following the international 10–20 system for EEG electrode placement, these electrode positions were labeled as C1, C2, C3, C4, F3, F4, FC1, FC2, FC5, FC6, CP1, CP2, CP5, CP6, P3, and P4. We employed 10 channels for EMG, covering the major muscles of the upper arm and forearm. These channels were specifically placed over the flexor digitorum superficialis (FDS), flexor carpi urinaris (FCU), flexor carpi radialis (FCR), extensor carpi ulnaris (ECU), extensor carpi radialis longus (ECRL), biceps brachii (BB), triceps brachii (TB), deltoid medius (DM), deltoid anterior (DA), and deltoid posterior (DP). As illustrated in Fig. 2(a) and (b), the electrode positions for EMG are displayed from both the front and back views.

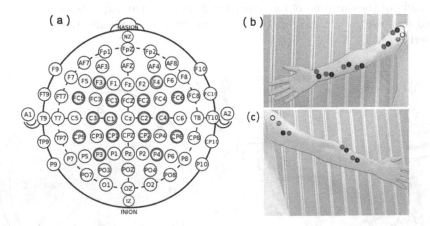

Fig. 2. Location of EEG and EMG electrodes: (a) 10–20 International EEG system topology, the red circle is the area collected in this experiment; (b) front view of the arm; (c) back view of arm.

2.4 Data Analysis

Data Preprocessing. The typical frequency range of EEG signals is 1–100 Hz, with the main energy concentrated below 50 Hz [18]. Therefore, for EEG preprocessing, the first step is to apply band-pass filtering, which can be performed in MATLAB or using EEGLAB, a specialized MATLAB toolbox for EEG signal processing. EEG signals are susceptible to contamination from environmental factors, muscle activity, cardiac signals, eye movements, and other sources. Therefore, after filtering, artifact removal is necessary. Initially, the EEG signals are visualized using EEGLAB, and based on experience, manual removal of artifacts is performed. This step focuses on removing parts of the signal with noticeable variations in amplitude and frequency. Subsequently, the EEG signals are subjected to Independent Component Analysis (ICA), and using frequency spectra and scalp topography, certain artifacts are identified and removed.

The typical frequency range of electromyographic (EMG) signals spans from 20 to 500 Hz, with the majority of energy concentrated between 50 and 150 Hz [19]. Hence, it is imperative to apply bandpass filtering and power-line notch filtering techniques to the EMG signals. Subsequently, rectification becomes a vital step in CMC analysis, often necessitating the preprocessing of EMG signals.

As depicted in Fig. 3, the final step involves segmenting the EEG and EMG signals. To facilitate the identification of the starting point of the motor paradigms, we employed a camera to capture the experimental footage. The clock of the camera and the acquisition device were synchronized through a shared computer. Once the starting point was accurately determined, segmentation was performed using a 3-second window, corresponding to the eight directions labeled as a to h.

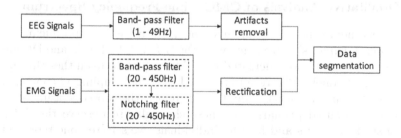

Fig. 3. Framework of data preprocessing.

Wavelet Coherence. Due to its inherent capabilities in conducting time-frequency analysis, as well as multi-resolution analysis, wavelet transform has gained wide acceptance in the analysis of physiological signals such as EEG and EMG [20]. In this study, wavelet transform was employed to perform spectral analysis on EEG and EMG signals, followed by segmentation into distinct frequency bands, including theta band (4–7 Hz), alpha band (8–13 Hz), beta band (14–30 Hz), and gamma band (30–49 Hz).

The commonly used algorithms for CMC (Corticomuscular Coherence) are developed based on measures of coherence, Granger causality, mutual information, and transfer entropy. Among these, coherence is the most widely applied linear analysis method. The calculation formula for coherence is as follows:

$$Coh_{XY}(f) = \frac{|P_{XY}(f)|^2}{|P_{XX}(f)| \times |P_{YY}(f)|} \tag{1}$$

where, $P_{XY}(f)$ is cross-spectrum density of EMG and EEG, $P_{XX}(f)$ and $P_{YY}(f)$ are the auto-power spectral density of EMG and EEG, respectively. The value range of CMC is 0 to 1, approaching 1 indicates high interdependence.

In this study, we performed CMC calculations for each trial of the same movement direction. Subsequently, based on the mean and standard deviation of all trials, certain trials were excluded. The specific criterion was as follows: if the CMC value of a particular trial exceeded the mean plus or minus 1.5 times the standard deviation, it was considered as an abnormal trial and excluded from further analysis.

Statistical Analysis. To analyze the differences between stroke patients and healthy individuals, as well as the effects of frequency band and pushing/pulling states on CMC results, we performed one-way and two-way ANOVA analyses using SPSS (SPSS Inc., Chicago, IL, USA).

3   Results

3.1   Qualitative Analysis of CMC Time-Frequency Spectrum

In the experimental paradigm of this study, the main force-producing muscles during the participants' movements were the BB, TB, DM, DA, and DP muscles. In the pre-experiment, we calculated the CMC values between these five muscles and all EEG channels. The results revealed that the coupling phenomenon was most prominent in channels C3 and C4. Therefore, the subsequent investigations in this study focused primarily on these channels. To observe the differences between stroke patients and healthy individuals, we selected one representative healthy participant and one stroke patient for comparison. The CMC results were then visualized using a time-frequency two-dimensional plot.

As shown in Fig. 4(a), the CMC results during the push and pull cycles in direction "a" for healthy participant 5 are displayed. The leftmost column of five plots represents the coupling results between channel C3 and the five EMG channels. The middle column represents the coupling results between channel C4 and the five EMG channels. The rightmost column displays the activation patterns of the five EMG channels during the push-pull process. Figure 4(b) shows the results for the stroke patient. From the figures, it can be observed that both in healthy participants and stroke patients, under this motor paradigm, the coupling strength between the motor muscles and the contralateral brain region is significantly higher than the coupling strength with the ipsilateral brain region. However, based on the scale, it can be observed that the CMC values of stroke patients are significantly lower than those of healthy participants. Furthermore, in healthy participants, strong coupling is mainly observed in the gamma band, whereas in stroke patients, coupling has shifted towards lower frequency bands (beta band). Additionally, the muscle activation patterns of stroke patients differ slightly from those of healthy participants.

3.2   Quantitative Analysis Based on CMC Mean Value

For each participant, the average CMC values in the three frequency bands were calculated after excluding bad trials during the push and pull phases in the a-direction. Subsequently, statistical analysis was conducted on the CMC values across different frequency bands for both healthy participants and stroke patients. As shown in Fig. 5(a), which represents the results during the push phase, and Fig. 5(b), which represents the results during the pull phase, it can be observed that, regardless of the phase, healthy participants exhibited significantly higher CMC values in the gamma band compared to the alpha and beta bands. On the other hand, stroke patients showed higher CMC values in the beta and gamma bands compared to the alpha band. These findings align with the qualitative analysis, indicating a shift of CMC towards the beta band in stroke patients. However, it is worth noting that the gamma band CMC values of stroke patients were significantly lower than those of healthy participants. During the pull phase, the CMC values of healthy participants exhibited a decrease and were not higher than those of stroke patients.

4   Discussion and Conclusion

4.1   Discussion

Effectiveness of CMC as a Motor Function Evaluation Index. The findings of this study confirm significant differences in CMC between stroke patients and healthy individuals, indicating that CMC can serve as an effective measure to evaluate post-stroke motor impairments. These results align with previous studies conducted by peers in the field. However, the robustness of CMC still needs further improvement, particularly when investigating the performance of specific muscles at certain moments or time intervals. Therefore, future research endeavors are warranted to provide additional evidence in this regard.

The Influence of Individual Differences on CMC Stability. During the course of our study, we observed significant individual variations among participants. It is understandable that stroke patients exhibited substantial variability due to differences in their medical conditions. However, it was surprising to note

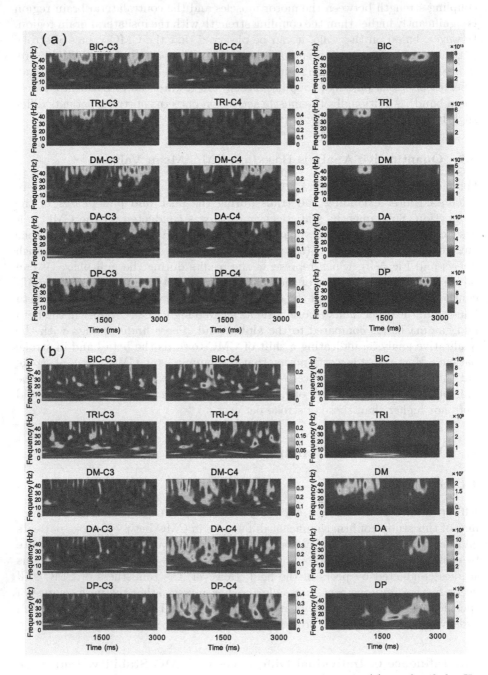

Fig. 4. Time-frequency two-dimensional visualization of CMC: (a) result of the H-subj5; (b) result of the P-subj1.

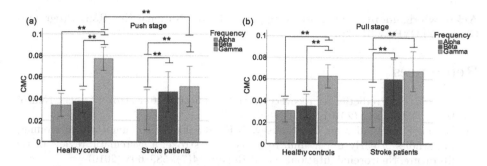

Fig. 5. CMC in three frequency bands of healthy controls and stroke patients in different stage: (a) push stage; (b) pull stage.

considerable variations even among healthy individuals. In some cases, individuals demonstrated stronger CMC during the muscle rest phase compared to the muscle exertion phase, which contradicts our conventional understanding. This highlights the need for extensive physiological experiments to validate the substantial inter-individual differences observed.

Benefits of Dynamic Force Output Experimental Paradigm. In CMC research, the commonly adopted experimental paradigms involve static force outputs, such as clenched fists or finger gripping. We believe that these highly standardized paradigms may be too detached from everyday motor tasks, limiting their clinical applicability. The contribution of this study lies in aiding the identification of stable characteristics of the CMC during dynamic movements, thereby facilitating the application of CMC-based measures in clinical assessments.

4.2   Conclusion

The aim of this study was to investigate the characteristic changes in CMC after stroke and to validate its utility for motor function assessment. We designed a constant velocity motion experiment using an upper limb rehabilitation robot. A total of six healthy participants and two stroke patients were recruited for the study. Wavelet coherence analysis was employed to calculate CMC in the alpha, beta, and gamma frequency bands during different movement directions and stages. The results demonstrated that gamma band coupling exhibited the most significant patterns during dynamic force output. The CMC strength in stroke patients was significantly lower than that of healthy individuals. Furthermore, stroke patients exhibited a shift towards lower frequency bands in CMC, with stronger beta band CMC compared to healthy participants. This work confirms the effectiveness of CMC as an evaluation metric and demonstrates the potential of CMC for clinical motor function assessment.

Acknowledgement. This work is supported by the National Key R&D Program of China (2022YFC3601702).

References

1. Stinear, C.: Prediction of recovery of motor function after stroke. Lancet Neurol. **9**(12), 1228–1232 (2010)
2. Buma, F.E., Lindeman, E., Ramsey, N.F., Kwakkel, G.: Functional neuroimaging studies of early upper limb recovery after stroke: a systematic review of the literature. Neurorehabilitation Neural Repair **24**(7), 589–608 (2010)
3. Gor-García-Fogeda, M.D., et al.: Scales to assess gross motor function in stroke patients: a systematic review. Arch. Phys. Med. Rehabil. **95**(6), 1174–1183 (2014)
4. Liu, J., Sheng, Y., Honghai Liu, H.: Corticomuscular coherence and its applications: a review. Front. Human Neurosci. **13**, 100 (2019)
5. Yang, Y., Dewald, J.P.A., van der Helm, F.C., Schouten, A.C.: Unveiling neural coupling within the sensorimotor system: directionality and nonlinearity. Eur. J. Neurosci. **48**(7), 2407–2415 (2018)
6. Kilner, J.M., Baker, S.N., Salenius, S., Hari, R., Lemon, R.N.: Human cortical muscle coherence is directly related to specific motor parameters. J. Neurosci. **20**(23), 8838–8845 (2000)
7. Lattari, E., et al.: Corticomuscular coherence behavior in fine motor control of force: a critical review. Rev. Neurol. **51**(10), 610–623 (2010)
8. Mima, T., Toma, K., Koshy, B., Hallett, M.: Coherence between cortical and muscular activities after subcortical stroke. Stroke **32**(11), 2597–2601 (2001)
9. Liu, J., Sheng, Y., Zeng, J., Liu, H.: Corticomuscular coherence for upper arm flexor and extensor muscles during isometric exercise and cyclically isokinetic movement. Front. Neurosci. **13**, 522 (2019)
10. Omlor, W., Patino, L., Hepp-Reymond, M.-C., Kristeva, R.: Gamma-range corticomuscular coherence during dynamic force output. Neuroimage **34**(3), 1191–1198 (2007)
11. Anshuang Fu, A., et al.: Corticomuscular coherence analysis on the static and dynamic tasks of hand movement. In: 2014 19th International Conference on Digital Signal Processing, pp. 715–718. IEEE (2014)
12. Fang, Y., et al.: Functional corticomuscular connection during reaching is weakened following stroke. Clin. Neurophys. **120**(5), 994–1002 (2009)
13. Farmer, S.F., Swash, M., Ingram, D.A., Stephens, J.A.: Changes in motor unit synchronization following central nervous lesions in man. J. Physiol. **463**(1), 83–105 (1993)
14. Rossiter, H.E., et al.: Changes in the location of cortico-muscular coherence following stroke. NeuroImage Clin. **2**, 50–55 (2013)
15. von Carlowitz-Ghori, K, et al.: Corticomuscular coherence in acute and chronic stroke. Clin. Neurophys. **125**(6), 1182–1191 (2014)
16. Gerloff, C., Braun, C., Staudt, M., Hegner, Y.L., Dichgans, J., Krägeloh-Mann, I.: Coherent corticomuscular oscillations originate from primary motor cortex: evidence from patients with early brain lesions. Human Brain Mapp. **27**(10), 789–798 (2006)
17. Graziadio, S., Tomasevic, L., Assenza, G., Tecchio, F., Eyre, J.A.: The myth of the 'unaffected' side after unilateral stroke: is reorganisation of the non-infarcted corticospinal system to re-establish balance the price for recovery? Exp. Neurol. **238**(2), 168–175 (2012)

18. Subha, D.P., Joseph, P.K., Acharya U.R., Lim, C.M.: EEG signal analysis: a survey. J. med. Syst. **34**, 195–212 (2010)
19. Wang, J., Tang, L., Bronlund, J.E.: Surface EMG signal amplification and filtering. Int. J. Comput. Appl. **82**(1), 2013
20. Akin, M.: Comparison of wavelet transform and FFT methods in the analysis of EEG signals. J. Med. Syst. **26**, 241–247 (2002)

Factors Affecting the Perception Performance of Biomimetic Tactile Sensing System

Yicheng Yang[1], Xiaoxin Wang[2], Ziliang Zhou[1], and Honghai Liu[2]([✉])

[1] Shanghai Jiao Tong University, Shanghai 200240, China
[2] Harbin Institute of Technology (Shenzhen), Shenzhen 518055, China
honghai.liu@hit.edu.cn

Abstract. To address the issue of the unclear factors affecting the perception performance of biomimetic tactile sensing system, FEM and cantilever beam model are firstly employed to analyze the effects of the physical properties of biomimetic multi-layer elastomer on the deformation and vibration tactile signals. Next, the impacts of physical properties and data processing methods on the perception performance are evaluated through fabrics recognition experiments sensitive to vibration signals. The results indicate that simultaneous change in the hardness and thickness of the multi-layer elastomer leads to stable tactile perceptual capability. Detrending data improves the consistency in temporal sequence , but weakens the continuity, and exhibits various impacts on different perception tasks. Taking absolute value helps to focus on the vibration characteristic. Additionally, based on the physical properties changes during human skin growth, sorting the corresponding elastomers shows nearly consistent tactile perception performance, suggesting a similar regularity of maintaining tactile perceptual capability throughout human skin growth. This study provides new ideas for optimizing the biomimetic tactile sensors design and exploring the factors that affect human tactile perceptual capability.

Keywords: Tactile sensing · Tactile perception · Biomimetic sensing

1 Introduction

Biomimetic tactile sensors have become a highly researched area in robot tactile perception in recent years [1]. Through flexible materials and structural design, biomimetic tactile sensors simulate the physical structure of human skin and tissue and are used for various tactile information like contact force and object

This work is supported by the Shenzhen Science and Technology Program (Grant No. JCYJ20210324120214040) and Guangdong Basic and Applied Basic Research Foundation (Grant No. 2020B1515120064).

shape by tactile sensing signals [2]. Some biomimetic tactile sensors also simulate the human's mechanoreceptors for sensitive and accurate tactile perception [3]. However, the diverse biomimetic design schemes result in considerable differences in the characteristics, that could affect the tactile perceptual capability [4]. Current biomimetic tactile sensing researches focus on simulating human skin physiological structure and mechanoreceptors characteristics [5]. However, the research on how biomimetic designs affect perceptual capability is scarce [6]. Hence, understanding the influencing factors of biomimetic tactile sensing systems can optimize the design of the biomimetic system and provide new insights into the exploration of the mechanism of human tactile perception, which is of great practical and theoretical significance.

Meanwhile, texture perception with tactile sensors has a wide range of applications [7]. Related researches usually use tactile sensor arrays to obtain deformation and vibration signals, analyzed with machine learning algorithms to achieve texture perception [8]. There is also research indicating that biomimetic tactile sensors can achieve more fine-grained texture perception capability [9]. Researchers have designed a biomimetic reflective tactile sensor array, which can recognize textures across materials like wood, fabric, and metal [10]. Other researchers have developed multi-layered biomimetic tactile sensors that have improved the sensitivity and resolution for accurate texture perception [11]. Finally, some studies adopt deep learning methods, using a large amount of sensing data from biomimetic tactile sensors to train neural networks, also achieving high-precision texture perception [12,13]. Among them, the long short-term memory (LSTM) network has significant advantages in processing temporal sensing signals [14]. In summary, these studies indicate that biomimetic tactile sensors have shown great advantages in texture perception.

The rest of this paper is organized as follows. Section 2 analyzes the effects of the physical proportion of multi-layer elastomer on the deformation and vibration tactile signals through FEM and cantilever beam model. Section 3 evaluates the influence of physical properties and data processing methods on the tactile perception performance in fabrics recognition tasks. Section 4 discusses the experimental results and Sect. 5 draws the conclusion.

2   Analysis of the Physical Properties Influence

This study is based our previous work [15], which proposed the customized biomimetic visual-tactile sensor based on FingerVision [16]. Its working principle is to visualize the deformation of the elastomer surface when contacting objects through tracking the marker array with computer vision (CV) algorithm. As shown in Fig. 1(a), the sensor can conduct pressing and sliding on the two-axis platform. As shown in Fig. 1(b), the multi-layer silicone elastomer simulates the physiological structure of human skin and tissue.

To study the effects of physical properties on the tactile perception performance, four types of silicone with different hardness (0HA, 5HA, 8HA, 15HA) are employed to customize eight elastomers with different hardness and thickness

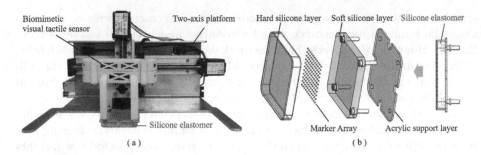

Fig. 1. The customized biomimetic visual tactile sensor. (a) The sensor on experimental platform. (b) The multi-layer silicone elastomer structure.

combinations, as shown in Fig. 2. The silicone layers with the hardness of 8HA or 15HA and thickness of 1 mm simulate the skin, while those with the hardness of 0HA or 5HA and thickness of 5 mm or 7 mm simulate the subcutaneous tissue. Hence, a total of eight silicone elastomers with different hardness and thickness combinations are obtained and denoted as follows: (1) outer 8HA/1 mm - inner 0HA/5 mm (8/1-0/5), (2) 15/1-0/5, (3) 8/1-5/5, (4) 15/1-5/5, (5) 8/1-0/7, (6) 15/1-0/7, (7) 8/1-5/7, (8) 15/1-5/7.

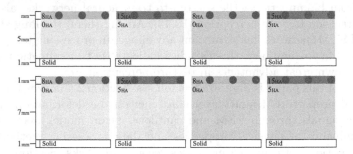

Fig. 2. Eight silicone elastomers with different hardness and thickness combinations.

The hardness and thickness combination design also refers to the physical properties changes during human growth. For the skin and subcutaneous tissue, their hardness and thickness both increase with age. However, the skin thickness remains relatively stable during the middle age. Thus, the hard layer only changes hardness (8HA and 15HA). Meanwhile, both the hardness (0HA and 5HA) and thickness (5 mm and 7 mm) of the soft layer change. According to the physical properties change during growth, the silicone elastomers can be sorted in the order of 1-2-4-8 or 1-3-4-8 (the skin's hardness change is pronounced), 1-5-6-8 or 1-5-7-8 (the tissue's thickness change is pronounced), 1-2-6-8 or 1-3-7-8 (their physical properties change synchronously).

In addition, human tactile perception is sensitive to deformation and vibration signals. They are reflected by the marker displacement and vibration in the customized sensor. With the friction force applied on the entire surface during sliding, the camera records the marker displacement, and the force distribution is even. Thus, according to the finite element method (FEM), the elastomer can be regarded as a series of composite cantilever beams, with one end fixed to the support layer and the other end subjected to friction force. The physical properties effects on the deformation and vibration signals are further analyzed based on the cantilever beam model.

2.1 Physical Properties Influence on Tangential Deformation

Considering the composite cantilever beam model, one end is fixed and the other end is subjected to friction force F, as shown in Fig. 3. Segment AB corresponds to the soft layer with the thickness d_1 and stiffness $E_1 I$ (E_1 is the elastic modulus and I is the inertia moment of the cross-section). Segment BD corresponds to the hard layer with the thickness d_2 and stiffness $E_2 I$ (E_2 is greater than E_1). The displacement of the marker recorded is at point C, that is, the deflection ω_C. The distance BC is denoted as d_3.

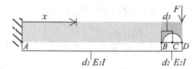

Fig. 3. Tangential deformation model of the free-end two-segment composite cantilever beam with frictional tangential force.

The deflection ω_C can be obtained by the Incremental Rigid Method and Superposition Principle, calculating the deflection curves of each uniform stiffness cantilever beam respectively. Thus, segment AB is analyzed first for the deflection and rotation at point B, marked as ω_B and θ_B. Then, the deflection curve ω_{BD} and the rotation θ_{BD} of segment BD are calculated. Finally, the deflection ω_C and rotation θ_C are calculated. Particularly, when analyzing segment AB, the force on the cross-section at point B is F, and the bending moment of segment BD to point B is Fd_2. According to the Superposition Principle, the deformation caused by multiple loads is equal to the sum of the deformation caused by each individual load.

(1) Segment BD is regarded as a rigid body to calculate the deflection curve of segment AB. Firstly, the deformation caused by force F at point B is calculated. The bending moment equations of segment AB are:

$$M_{1,AB}(x) = -F(d_1 - x), \quad E_1 I \omega''_{1,AB}(x) = -M_{1,AB}(x) = F(d_1 - x)$$

$$s.t. \ E_1 I \omega_{1,AB}(0) = 0, \quad E_1 I \omega'_{1,AB}(0) = 0$$

Thus, the deflection $w_{1,AB}(x)$ and rotation $\theta_{1,AB}(x)$ of segment AB caused by force F can be calculated as:

$$w_{1,AB}(x) = \frac{Fx^2}{6E_1I}(3d_1 - x), \ \theta_{1,AB}(x) = \frac{Fd_1x}{E_1I} - \frac{Fx^2}{E_1I}$$

Thus, the deflection $w_{1,B}$ and rotation $\theta_{1,B}$ are:

$$w_{1,B} = w_{1,AB}(d_1) = \frac{Fd_1^3}{3E_1I}, \ \theta_{1,B} = \theta_{1,AB}(d_1) = \frac{Fd_1^2}{2E_1I}$$

Secondly, the deformation caused by bending moment Fd_2 of segment BD to point B is calculated. The bending moment equations of segment AB are:

$$M_{2,AB}(x) = -Fd_2, \ E_1Iw_{2,AB}''(x) = -M_{2,AB}(x) = Fd_2$$

$$s.t. \ E_1Iw_{2,AB}(0) = 0, \ E_1Iw_{2,AB}'(0) = 0$$

Thus, the deflection $w_{2,AB}(x)$ and rotation $\theta_{2,AB}(x)$ of segment AB caused by bending moment Fd_2 can be calculated to be:

$$w_{2,AB}(x) = \frac{Fd_2}{2E_1I}x^2, \ \theta_{2,AB}(x) = \frac{Fd_2x}{E_1I}$$

Thus, the deflection $w_{2,B}$ and rotation $\theta_{2,B}$ are:

$$w_{2,B} = w_{2,AB}(d_1) = \frac{Fd_1^2d_2}{2E_1I}, \ \theta_{2,B} = \theta_{2,AB}(d_1) = \frac{Fd_1d_2}{E_1I}$$

Finally, the deflections and rotation are superimposed as:

$$w_B = w_{1,B} + w_{2,B} = \frac{Fd_1^3}{3E_1I} + \frac{Fd_1^2d_2}{2E_1I}, \ \theta_B = \theta_{1,B} + \theta_{2,B} = \frac{Fd_1^2}{2E_1I} + \frac{Fd_1d_2}{E_1I}$$

(2) Calculate the deflection at point C caused by the deflection of segment AB.

$$w_{1,C} = w_B + \theta_B d_3 = \frac{Fd_1^3}{3E_1I} + \frac{Fd_1^2d_2}{2E_1I} + \frac{Fd_1^2d_3}{2E_1I} + \frac{Fd_1d_2d_3}{E_1I},$$

(3) Calculate the deformation of segment BD under force F. The deformed segment AB is rigidified, and segment BD is regarded as a cantilever beam only with force F. The calculation process is similar to that before. The deflection $w_{2,C}$ and the rotation $\theta_{2,C}$ of point C at a distance of d_3 can be calculated as:

$$w_{2,C} = w_{BC}(d_3) = \frac{Fd_2d_3^2}{2E_2I} - \frac{Fd_3^3}{6E_2I}, \ \theta_{2,C} = \theta_{BC}(d_3) = \frac{Fd_2d_3}{E_2I} - \frac{Fd_3^2}{2E_2I}$$

(4) Apply the superposition principle. The deflection and rotation at point C equal to the superposition of the deformation of segment BC caused by segment AB and the bending deformation of segment BC, expressed as:

$$w_C = w_{1,C} + w_{2,C} = \frac{F}{E_1I}\left(\frac{d_1^3}{3} + \frac{d_1^2d_2}{2} + \frac{d_1^2d_3}{2} + d_1d_2d_3\right) + \frac{F}{E_2I}\left(\frac{d_2d_3^2}{2} - \frac{d_3^3}{6}\right)$$

As the elastomer designed to be $d_1 > d_2 > d_3$, w_C is mainly affected by E_1 and d_1, determined by the hardness and thickness of the soft layer.

2.2   Physical Properties Influence on Tangential Vibration

According to multi-layer elastomer properties, d_1 is significantly larger than d_3, and the deformation of segment AB is much larger than that of BC, as shown in Fig. 4. Thus, the vibration model can be simplified by regarding section BD as a rigid body. The problem is to analyze the vibration of point B.

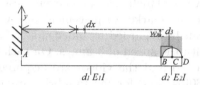

Fig. 4. Tangential vibration model of the free-end two-segment composite cantilever beam with an initial displacement at the free end.

Generally, the differential equations of equal-section beam free bending vibration and the deflection of the cantilever beam AB are:

$$E_1 I \frac{\partial^2 y}{\partial x^2} = M(x), \; E_1 I \frac{\partial^4 y}{\partial x^4} = -\rho \frac{\partial^2 y}{\partial t^2}$$

where E is the elastic modulus, I is the inertia moment of the section, ρ is the density, and $M(x)$ is the bending moment at the section. The characteristic equation and natural resonant frequency are:

$$1 + ch\lambda cos\lambda = 0, \; \omega_i = \frac{\lambda_i^2}{d_1^2} \sqrt{\frac{E_1 I}{\rho}}$$

Actually, this model can be regarded as giving a tangential displacement ω_B to the free end of the cantilever beam firstly and then releasing it, as shown in Fig. 4. It indicates that unless the initial displacement ω_B exactly equals to any vibration mode, the free vibration of the system is generally a superposition of infinite vibration mode components. And the natural resonant frequency is expressed as ω_i, which is also mainly affected by E_1 and d_1, determined by the hardness and thickness of the soft layer.

3   Influence on Fabrics Texture Perception Performance

Referring to the analysis above, obtaining the larger deformation signal requires the elastomer to have lower hardness and large thickness. While the higher natural resonant frequency requires the elastomer to have higher hardness and smaller thickness. It means that in tasks sensitive to vibration signals, the physical properties have contradictory requirements. Thus, this section studies how the physical properties affect the tactile perception performance related to vibration signals by fabrics texture recognition experiments.

3.1   Experimental Setup

The experimental platform is shown in Fig. 1(a). The experimental objects are 15 fabrics of different linear mass densities in the unit of denier (D), as shown in Fig. 5. The perception paradigm is lateral pressing sliding in contact with the fabrics. The maximum pressing depth is set as 1mm by the limit switch on the vertical screw, to keep the same pressure distribution. Specially, the sliding is horizontal with a slight vertical incline for an uneven pressure distribution among the marker array. Thus, the marker displacement and vibration states in each row are different and can be regarded as independent features. Moreover, one sliding trial lasts 40 s with the speed of 3 mm/s. On each fabric, 6 reciprocating sliding trials are conducted and the videos are acquired. Thus, a total of 90 videos (1080 × 1080P, 60fps, 40 s) for the 15 fabrics are acquired.

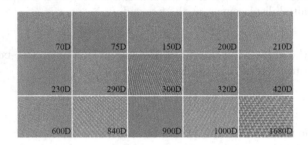

Fig. 5. 15 fabrics of different linear mass densities as the experiment objects.

3.2   Feature Extraction

In each frame, the 11 × 11 marker coordinates are extracted by CV algorithm, as discussed in our previous work [15]. Coordinate of the marker at row-i, column-j in frame-f is denoted as (x_f^{ij}, y_f^{ij}). In uncontacted state, it is denoted as (x_0^{ij}, y_0^{ij}). As the sliding is along the row, only the component $(x_f^{ij} - x_0^{ij})$ is considered. Moreover, the markers in the same row are under the same pressure. Their displacements should be similar, and are averaged to reduce feature dimension, defined as Ave_f^i for row-i. Besides, the markers displacement states are different between rows, and the Ave_f^is are independent. Thus, the features of each frame, defined as Ft_f^{11}, consisted of 11 Ave_f^is, is expressed as Equ. 1.

$$Ave_f^i = \sum_{j=1}^{11}(x_f^{i,j} - x_0^{i,j})/11, \ Ft_f^{11} = (Ave_f^1, Ave_f^2, \ldots, Ave_f^{10}, Ave_f^{11}) \quad (1)$$

Feature Extraction According to Tasks. For the recognition task, the 15 objects are first divided into 15 classes. Moreover, 30 classes are considered by distinguishing sliding direction, with suffix '_DD (distinguish direction)'. Considering the vibration signal has strong temporal correlation between features, the recognition tasks are based on the LSTM network. Moreover, two types of LSTM networks are employed, the sequence-to-label classification (S2LC) and sequence-to-sequence classification (S2SC) LSTM network. The former uses a sliding window with the length of 40 and step of 40 frames to extract 60 segments of temporal sequence data from each video containing 2400 frames, with each feature denoted as Ft_s^{11}, expressed as Equ. 2. While the S2SC LSTM network considers the feature Ft_f^{11} of each frame.

$$Ft_s^{11} = (Ft_f^{11}, Ft_{f+1}^{11}, \ldots, Ft_{f+39}^{11}) \tag{2}$$

Feature Extraction According to Data Processing. Different features are further constructed with data processing. First, as the elastomer lateral displacement during the sliding may change and the markers do not always vibrate near stable locations, the sequence date is detrended to weaken the overall lateral displacement impact. It is implemented with the 'detrend' function in MATLAB. The data detrended is denoted as '**Modified Value**', and the original data is denoted as '**Original Value**'. Meanwhile, the marker displacement values have positive and negative signs. Taking absolute value is considered to only retaining the magnitude of the displacement, which could help to focus on the vibration information. The data that takes absolute value is denoted as '**Absolute Value**', and the original data is denoted as '**True Value**'. Thus, four data processing methods are obtained, namely, 'Original True Value (**OTV**)', 'Original Absolute Value (**OAV**)', 'Modified True Value (**MTV**)', and 'Modified Absolute Value (**MAV**)', with the processing degree increasing.

3.3   Influence of Physical Properties and Data Processing on Tasks

The influence of the physical properties and data processing methods on tactile perception performance is tested by fabrics texture recognition tasks. Specifically, eight silicone elastomer with different hardness and thickness combinations, and four data processing methods are considered.

Sequence-to-Label Texture Recognition Task. The S2LC LSTM network is constructed in MATLAB. The input size is 11, a Bi-LSTM layer with 100 hidden network units is specified, and the last element of the sequence is output. For the recognition of 15 classes, the subsequent fully connected layer, softmax layer, and classification layer of size 15 are specified. For the recognition of 30 classes distinguishing the sliding direction, the subsequent classification layer's size is 30, with suffix '_DD'. Thus, two recognition targets and four data processing methods make up eight tasks, **OTV**, **OTV_DD**, **OAV**, **OAV_DD**, **MTV**, **MTV_DD**, **MAV**, and **MAV_DD**. Considering the eight elastomers, there are 64 task scenarios. The recognition rates are calculated using three-fold cross-validation in each scenario, and are grouped and analyzed according to the specific elastomer or data processing method, as shown in Fig. 6(a) and (b), respectively. The box plots show the comprehensive results of each group. The overall recognition rates of the sequence-to-label recognition task is between 80% to 99%. In most scenarios, the recognition rates reach 95%. Generally, with the increase of the overall elastomer hardness, the recognition rates also increase. The overall hardest elastomer (15/1-5/5) shows the best recognition result. In addition, the performance of the detrended data is better than that of original data, while taking absolute value does not improve the recognition rates.

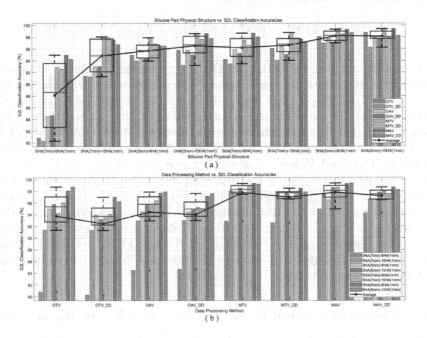

Fig. 6. Experiment results of the sequence-to-label recognition task.(a) The silicone elastomer's physical structure *vs.* the recognition rates. (b) The data processing method *vs.* the recognition rates.

Sequence-to-Sequence Texture Recognition Task. The S2SC LSTM network is also constructed in MATLAB. The input size is 11, and the LSTM layer contains 200 hidden units, outputting the complete sequence. For the recognition of 15 classes, a fully connected layer of size 15, a softmax layer, and a classification layer are followed. For the recognition of 30 classes , the fully connected layer's size is 30, with suffix '_DD'. Similar to the previous task, there are still 64 task scenarios, and the recognition rate is also calculated with the three-fold cross-validation method, as shown in Fig. 7(a) and (b). It can be seen that the overall recognition rate is between 55% and 96%, much lower than that of the former task. Moreover, the difference between the maximum and minimum recognition rates exceeds 40%. Only a few scenarios achieve recognition rates of over 90%, and most scenarios have recognition rates of 70% to 90%. In addition, there is no overall correspondence between the physical properties and recognition rates. When the thickness of each layer is the same, the harder elastomer does not always perform better. For example, the recognition rate corresponding to the elastomer of 15/1-0/5 is lower than that of 8/1-0/5. For the data processing methods, in contrast to the former task, the overall performance of the original data is better than that of the detrended data. Moreover, taking absolute value improves the recognition rate in this task.

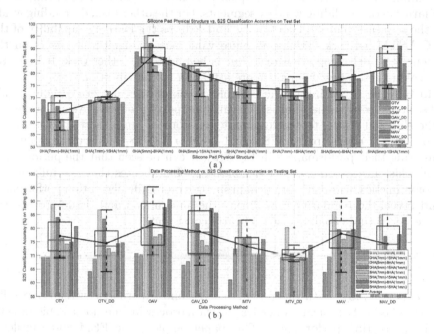

Fig. 7. Experiment results of the sequence-to-sequence recognition task. (a) The silicone elastomer's physical structure *vs.* the recognition rates. (b) The data processing method *vs.* the recognition rates.

4   Discussion

This paper firstly analyze the influence of the elastomer's physical properties on tangential deformation and vibration signals. The results show the deformation is mainly influenced by the hardness and thickness of the soft layer. The greater hardness or the larger thickness of the soft layer, the greater deformation. Moreover, considering the free vibration with initial tangential deformation, the smaller elastic modulus (the greater hardness) or the larger thickness of the soft layer, the smaller natural resonant frequency. And it is more likely for resonance phenomenon, corresponding to the smaller frequency response range.

Next, this paper discusses the influence factors on tactile perception performance related to vibration signals by fabrics recognition tasks, with the S2LC and S2SC LSTM network considered. As for the physical properties, the results show that the harder elastomer, the better performance of the sequence-to-label recognition. However, there is no such correspondence for the other task. Results of the other task indicates that stable performance could be achieved when the hardness and thickness change synchronously. For data processing methods, detrending only helps the sequence-to-label recognition. It can be explained that detrending improves the feature sequence consistency, thereby achieving better similarity between sliding window segments. For the other task, detrending weakens the sequence temporal continuity, and reduces the learning capability of the S2SC LSTM network. Taking absolute value has no significant effects on the sequence-to-label recognition task, but is helpful to the other task. It indicates that taking absolute value pays more attention to the vibration.

In the end, according to the possible developmental pattern of human skin and subcutaneous tissue, that is, the variation pattern of the physical properties of the skin and tissue, the corresponding elastomers can be sorted, such as 1-2-4-8 or 1-3-4-8, 1-5-6-8 or 1-5-7-8, and 1-2-6-8 or 1-3-7-8, as discussed above. By comparing their performances in Fig. 7(a), it can be seen that the performance of the elastomers sorted is nearly consistent. It indicates that the influence of the biomimetic elastomer's physical properties on tactile perception performance could reveal the regularity that during the human skin and tissue growth, the tactile perceptual capability keeps nearly consistent.

5   Conclusion

This paper employs both theoretical analysis and experiment evaluation to discuss the effects of physical properties and data processing methods on biomimetic tactile perception performance. This paper employs the FEM and cantilever beam model to analyze the effects of the physical properties on deformation and vibration tactile signals. The results show that the smaller hardness or the larger thickness of the soft layer, the greater deformation. While the smaller hardness or the larger thickness corresponds to the smaller natural resonant frequency and the smaller frequency response range. It further evaluates the tactile perception performance through fabrics texture recognition tasks sensitive to vibration signals. Considering the sequence-to-sequence recognition, the results show that the simultaneous change in hardness and thickness of the multi-layers elastomer leads to stable tactile perception performance. Regarding data processing methods, detrending improves the consistency in temporal sequence but weakens the continuity, and exhibits various impacts on different tasks. Meanwhile, taking absolute value helps to focus on the vibration of the signals. In addition, based on the physical properties change during human growth, sorting the corresponding elastomers shows that the tactile perception performance is nearly consistent, providing new ideas for optimizing the design of biomimetic tactile sensors and exploring the factors that affect human tactile perceptual capability.

References

1. Lee, Y., Ahn, J.H.: Biomimetic tactile sensors based on nanomaterials. ACS Nano **14**(2), 1220–1226 (2020)
2. Wang, C., et al.: Tactile sensing technology in bionic skin: a review. Biosens. Bioelectron. **220**, 114882 (2022)
3. Duan, S., et al.: A skin-beyond tactile sensor as interfaces between the prosthetics and biological systems. Nano Energ. **102**, 107665 (2022)
4. Sayegh, M.A., Daraghma, H., Mekid, S., Bashmal, S.: Review of recent bio-inspired design and manufacturing of whisker tactile sensors. Sensors **22**(7), 2705 (2022)
5. Lu, X., et al.: 3D tactile based object recognition for robot hands using force-sensitive and bend sensor arrays. IEEE Trans. Cogn. Dev. Syst. (2022)
6. Pestell, N.J.: Human inspired multi-modal robot touch. Ph.D. thesis, University of Bristol (2021)
7. Kappassov, Z., Corrales, J.A., Perdereau, V.: Tactile sensing in dexterous robot hands. Robot. Auton. Syst. **74**, 195–220 (2015)
8. Rongala, U.B., Mazzoni, A., Oddo, C.M.: Neuromorphic artificial touch for categorization of naturalistic textures. IEEE Trans. Neural Netw. Learn. Syst. **28**(4), 819–829 (2015)
9. Lima, B.M.R., da Fonseca, V.P., de Oliveira, T.E.A., Zhu, Q., Petriu, E.M.: Dynamic tactile exploration for texture classification using a miniaturized multimodal tactile sensor and machine learning. In: 2020 IEEE International Systems Conference (SysCon), pp. 1–7. IEEE (2020)
10. Sankar, S., et al.: Texture discrimination with a soft biomimetic finger using a flexible neuromorphic tactile sensor array that provides sensory feedback. Soft Rob. **8**(5), 577–587 (2021)
11. Dai, K., et al.: Design of a biomimetic tactile sensor for material classification. In: 2022 International Conference on Robotics and Automation (ICRA), pp. 10774–10780. IEEE (2022)
12. Yuan, X., Li, L., Shardt, Y.A., Wang, Y., Yang, C.: Deep learning with spatiotemporal attention-based LSTM for industrial soft sensor model development. IEEE Trans. Industr. Electron. **68**(5), 4404–4414 (2020)
13. Taunyazov, T., Chua, Y., Gao, R., Soh, H., Wu, Y.: Fast texture classification using tactile neural coding and spiking neural network. In: 2020 IEEE/RSJ International Conference on Intelligent Robots and Systems (IROS), pp. 9890–9895. IEEE (2020)
14. Tan, Y., Zhao, G.: Transfer learning with long short-term memory network for state-of-health prediction of lithium-ion batteries. IEEE Trans. Industr. Electron. **67**(10), 8723–8731 (2019)
15. Yang, Y., Wang, X., Zhou, Z., Zeng, J., Liu, H.: An enhanced fingervision for contact spatial surface sensing. IEEE Sens. J. **21**(15), 16492–16502 (2021)
16. Yamaguchi, A.: Fingervision for tactile behaviors, manipulation, and haptic feedback teleoperation. In: the 4th IEEJ International Workshop on Sensing, Actuation, Motion Control, and Optimization (SAMCON2018) (2018)

Intelligent Robot Perception
in Unknown Environments

Air-Ground Robots' Cooperation-Based Mountain Glaciers Thickness Continuous Detection: Systems And Applications

Jikang Zhong[1,2,3,4], Peng Li[1,2,3]($\boxtimes$), Xu Liu[1,2,3,4], Pinhui Zhao[1,2,3,4], Han Jiang[1,2,3,4], Liying Yang[1,2,3], Decai Li[1,2,3], Chunguang Bu[1,2,3], and Yuqing He[1,2,3]

[1] State Key Laboratory of Robotics, Shenyang Institute of Automation, Chinese Academy of Sciences, Shenyang 110016, China
{zhongjikang,lipeng,liuxu,zhaopinhui,jianghan,lidecai,cgbu,
heyuqing}@sia.cn

[2] Key Laboratory of Networked Control Systems, Chinese Academy of Sciences, Shenyang 110016, China

[3] Institutes for Robotics and Intelligent Manufacturing, Chinese Academy of Sciences, Shenyang 110169, China

[4] University of Chinese Academy of Sciences, Beijing 100049, China

Abstract. In this article, we present a multi-robot continuous ice thickness measurement system that can operate in plateau glacial environments with natural slopes up to 30°, large crevasses of glacier, slippery snow/ice ground surface, and inevitable terrain undulations. The ground station operator can operate the unmanned ground vehicle (UGV) with improved safety driving ability by following the optimal driving advice provided by the driving skill learning model. The air-ground robot collaboration algorithm coordinated the operation of the UGV with the unmanned aerial vehicle (UAV) to improve the mobility of the UGV in complex glacier environments. We obtain multi-scale and multi-aspect environmental information through air-ground collaboration and use a lightweight environmental modeling method to obtain a three-dimensional model of the glacier surface and subglacial terrain. The system was applied in the Korchung Gangri Glacier in the Tibet Plateau in June 2022. The experimental results show that the system can operate in the extreme environment of plateau glaciers and collect high-precision continuous ice thickness distribution data.

Keywords: Human machine collaboration · Multi-machine collaboration · Air-ground collaboration · Ice penetrating radar · Lightweight modeling · Driving Skills Model · Korchung Gangri glacier · Tibet Plateau

1 Introduction

With the continuous development of robotics technology, multirobot collaboration systems have become a hot topic in the field of robotics research and application due to their many advantages [1]. Unlike traditional robots that perform repetitive tasks, collaborative robots tend to work as partners who cooperate with each other in their work. Or

© The Author(s), under exclusive license to Springer Nature Singapore Pte Ltd. 2023
H. Yang et al. (Eds.): ICIRA 2023, LNAI 14267, pp. 283–295, 2023.
https://doi.org/10.1007/978-981-99-6483-3_25

when humans are in a safe environment, operating multiple robots to adapt to dynamic environments and complete multifunctional tasks in complex and dangerous environments. In the 2011 Great East Japan Earthquake, the Robotic Assisted Search and Rescue Center (USA) and the International Rescue System Research Institute (Japan) used multiple robots to collaborate in victim rescue and post-disaster environmental mapping [2]. Danilo et al. [3] introduced a rescue robot team for intervention tasks in restricted and structured environments such as mining accidents or tunnel collapses.

The Tibet Plateau and its surrounding areas are known as the "Water Tower of Asia" and the "Third Pole" of the world [4]. Affected by the Indian monsoon, the southeast of the Tibet Plateau (TP) is the most important and concentrated area for the development of marine (temperate) glaciers [5], and the second largest glacier gathering place in the world except for the polar ice sheet. In recent decades, glaciers around the world have experienced significant retreat and mass loss. The disaster caused by glacier loss will have a negative impact on the population living in its downstream basin [9, 10]. As the cradle of more than ten major rivers in Asia, TP also affects the social and economic activities of more than two billion people on the earth. Relevant research on the TP glacier has attracted wide attention [6, 7]. Using robots to explore glaciers is one possible solution, and there have been many research results in recent years. Drones have been used in a large number of studies to detect glaciers [8–13], but in most cases, drones can only be used to obtain the surface parameters of glaciers. Glacier exploration based on unmanned ground vehicles has also been studied, but rarely [13–15]. The assistance of robots accelerates the collection of scientific data and increases the density of data in time and space. However, the current ground robot operation scene is usually relatively simple, flat terrain, gentle slope, small area, cannot be competent for the exploration task in extremely complex environment.

In this article, we aim to complete the collection of high range and high-density surface environment and ice thickness data of Korchung Gangri glacier of TP by using an air-ground cooperative and human-machine cooperative robotic system equipped with instruments including Ice-penetrating radar (IPR) and monocular camera. The final results verified that multi-robot cooperation can complete the high-altitude glacier exploration tasks well. Our original system, as a new scheme of plateau mountain glacier investigation, can provide more methods for glacier research and become a new tool to obtain continuous large-scale transition data.

2 System Architecture

Figure 1 shows the surface characteristics of Korchung Grangri glacier on the TP. It is very difficult for ground robots to traverse, mainly due to the following challenges:

1. First, the glacial terrain is typically a steep slope covered with snow and ice. According to the measured data, the average slope is about 15°, and the maximum slope is above 35°, which may cause the ground robot to slip, roll over, and lack of power.
2. Second, the surface of the glacier is covered with streams ranging from a few centimeters to a few meters wide, which could create potential traps for the robot.
3. Finally, different glacier regions, temperature changes and abrupt weather changes lead to drastic changes in the physical characteristics of the terrain surface.

In fact, navigation and exploration in unknown and extreme conditions is one of the top 10 challenges of scientific robotics. In addition, driving on rough terrain is a big problem for unmanned ground vehicles (UGVs). Our goal is to efficiently capture intensive ice thickness measurements using a complex multi-robotic system. For this purpose, a human and air-ground robot collaborative system shown in Fig. 2 is designed to traverse the surface of the glacier. The drone flies up to 6,500 m in low pressure and strong winds, while the UGV is equipped with four tracked wheels to adapt to glacial terrain covered with snow, ice and crevices.

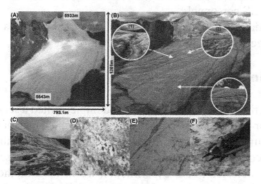

Fig. 1. The surface features of the Korchung Gangri glacier on Tibetan Plateau

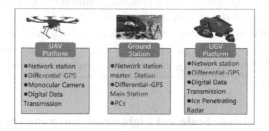

Fig. 2. System architecture overview

Our system architecture consists of a UAV, an UGV, and two ground stations (GSs). The UAV platform is designed to perform three functions:

1. Equipped with a monocular camera to collect multi-perspective images and obtain glacier surface information.
2. Equipped with an airborne network radio and plays the role of aerial communication relay between UGV and ground station.
3. Using a digital data transmission (DDT) and a monocular camera to track and capture UGV and transmit video back to the GS.

The UGV platform is design to perform three functions:

1. Roaming on the glacier surface under manual remote operation.
2. Learning driving skills and providing optimal driving suggestions to operators.

3. Carrying IPR to detect ice thickness information.

For UAV and UGV, the differential global positioning system (DGPS) receivers are used to receive high-precision location information. The GS is mainly responsible for:

1. Based on the vehicle status information and environment information returned by the UGV, as well as the driving suggestions given by the incremental driving skill model, determine the next task for the UGV.
2. Three-dimensional reconstruction and lightweight of the images collected by the monocular camera are carried out to generate the glacier surface model and display the model to the GS personnel.
3. Processing IPR data to obtain ice thickness, and com-posing a three-dimensional glacier model together with the glacier surface model.

3   Field Experiment

As mentioned in section II, we have designed and implemented a set of human-machine collaboration and air-ground collaboration system, which can adapt to extremely complex plateau mountain and glacier environments. In order to verify the capability of this system, we conducted field experiments on Korchung Gangri in Lasa in June 2022. The length of the glacier detected in our experiment is about 1192 m, the width is about 81 m, and the height difference is about 230 m. Figure 3 shows the schematic diagram of field experiment scheme.

We completed the application of the ground-ground robot collaborative system and obtained the 3D model of the glacier on Korchung Gangri Glacier by four steps, which are: large-scale lightweight environment modeling of the glacier surface, learning and training of UGV traffic capacity and driving skills, human-machine collaboration and ground-ground collaborative exploration, IPR data processing and three-dimensional modeling of the glacier.

3.1   Glacier Surface Large Scale and Lightweight Environment Modeling

In Fig. 3 Step 1, the UAV single-sided camera was used to collect glacier surface image data, and UGV carried IPR to collect ice thickness data. Then, we use motion structure (SFM) and splicing techniques to generate a three-dimensional point cloud model of the surface. We then used a lightweight terrain modeling and pre-diction approach to transform the point cloud model into a smaller model without significant loss of accuracy. Finally, we obtain a full range, accurate and light-weight 3D model of the large-scale glacier surface.

However, in practical applications, the field un-structured environment modeling faces four problems:

1. Terrain data collected by rangefinder or camera will generate centimeter-unit errors due to the sensor noise and robot positioning errors.
2. Due to the viewing angle and other reasons, some terrain gaps are blocked or not observed, resulting in in-complete data.

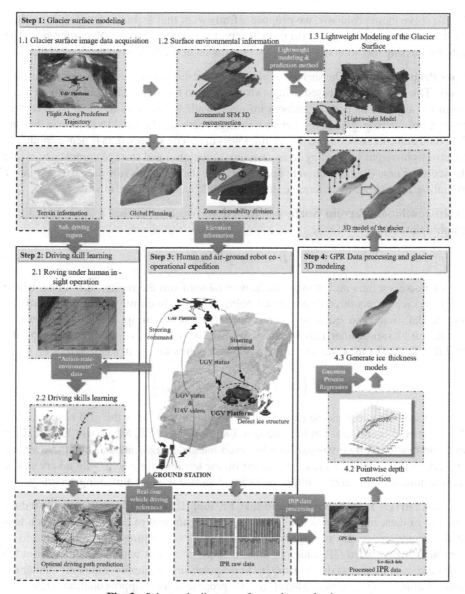

Fig. 3. Schematic diagram of experimental scheme

3. In large-scale terrain, due to the complex terrain structure and large amount of data captured, the computation and memory consumption are large.
4. The unstructured environments are more complex and possess more attributes, such as the terrain gradients, posing challenges for adaptable terrain characterization.

To solve these problems, we propose a framework that includes data preprocessing, multi-resolution elevation filtering, surface partitioning and topographic inference. The data processing methods will be briefly introduced in the following sections [16].

Data Preprocessing: The surface of glacier and ice thickness data are processed respectively. The former is processed using a structure from motion (SFM) and stitching algorithm for airborne monocular camera im-ages, while the latter is acquired by IPR after correction, filtering, gain and other processing. There are 21,638,316 points on the surface data and 18,776 points on the ice thickness data. The surface data is dense enough to require lightweight processing to re-duce computational and storage complexity, while the ice thickness data is relatively sparse. We use these data as raw data for the glacier modeling framework to generate compact, complete and accurate models.

Multi-resolution Terrain Surface Extraction: We assume that a large-scale topographic data set:

$$D = \{(x_i, y_i, z_i)\}_{i=1}^{N} \tag{1}$$

full of noise, outliers and missing data, is obtained from the region of interest, where (x_i, y_i, z_i) represents three-dimensional points. In order to eliminate noise and outliers, reduce data size, and establish correct regression relationship, we propose a multi-resolution elevation filter (MEF) based on EF. EF is a kind of method based on the grid that keeps the maximal elevation among all points falling in a cell, which is:

$$S = \left\{ (x_i, y_i, z_i) \middle| z_i = max\{z_i\}_{i=1}^{N_i} \right\}_{i=1}^{n} \tag{2}$$

where S could be seen as the extraction of terrain data set, n as the grid number, N_i is the number of points that fall into the cell. On the basis of EF, MEFs will further allow variable resolution by distinguishing between flat and rugged areas. Therefore, we can preserve surface detail in areas of interest on the terrain, while achieving a very sparse representation on flat areas, further reducing data size while maintaining accuracy.

Terrain Surface Partition with Boundary Fusion: Even if MEF can effectively reduce the size of data, in many practical applications, the amount of data will still reach tens of thousands, especially in large terrain and complex structures. It is unfeasible to be computed by standard GP, which is limited to the problems with fewer than about ten thousand training points due to its $O(n^3)$ computation complexity, especially under the limited computing resource. Therefore, we propose a local approximation strategy to divide the large-scale mapping region into several sub-regions. We take Gaussian mixture model (GMM) as a clustering method and adopted GMM to its favorable probabilistic interpretation of the cluster results. Besides, these posteriori probabilities can be further used to identify the boundaries between adjacent subregions and extend them to overlap each other to fully consider the intrinsic relationship between actual terrain structures, thereby improving the accuracy of the inference of points near the boundaries.

Terrain Elevation Inference: We treat terrain modeling as a regression problem and use accurate interpolation to fill in the terrain gaps. Considering the uncertainty and correlation of terrain data can be incorporated into the kernel matrix, Gaussian process

(GP) is adopted to deduce terrain. By training the aggregation of local terrain points obtained from surface partitioning, the customized model will be more suitable for local terrain. For a subsurface S_i with M points, we construct a Gaussian process regression (GPR) to obtain a posteriori Gaussian distribution with new input X_{M+1}, who's mean $m(\mathbf{x}_{M+1})$ and variance $v(\mathbf{x}_{M+1})$ are given by

$$m(\mathbf{x}_{M+1}) = \mathbf{k}^T \mathbf{C}_M^{-1} z_M \tag{3}$$

$$v(\mathbf{x}_{M+1}) = c - \mathbf{k}^T \mathbf{C}_M^{-1} \mathbf{k} \tag{4}$$

where $\mathbf{C}_M$ is the covariance matrix, $\mathbf{k}$ is a kernel with element $k(\mathbf{x}_j, \mathbf{x}_{M+1}), j = 1, \ldots, M$. $k(\mathbf{x}_j, \mathbf{x}_{M+1})$ is a kernel fuction to capture terrain correlation according to the actual terrain. Notice that all Gaussion distributions at the query point constitute GP. In particular, considering the uncertain of the terrain, the estimated variance can be applied to the path planning of robots.

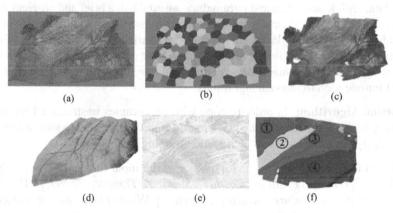

Fig. 4. (a) Elevation filtering, (b) Terrain segmentation, (c) Glacier surface model; (d) Global planning; (e) Terrain information; (f) Zone accessibility division (The smaller the number, the higher the risk factor of the area)

After the elevation filtering, the surface data is filtered from 21,638,316 points to 514,735 points, accounting for only 2.1% of the original data (shown in Fig. 4(a)). We set the data of terrain segmentation to 100 (shown in Fig. 4(b)), and the average number of point clouds in each subregion to 5140, which greatly reduces the total calculation amount of Gaussian process regression. We used 2,000,000 for topographic reasoning, and the mean square error of the final reasoning is approximately 0.10 m^3 compared to the original data.

By using this method, we can obtain a full range, accurate and lightweight 3D model of the glacier surface (shown in Fig. 4(c)). The model can:

1. Generate feasible path through a prior map of global path planner and provide route reference for operators (shown in Fig. 4(d)).
2. The UAV can refer to the elevation information in the terrain model to adjust the flight height in the air-ground cooperative mission (shown in Fig. 4(e)).
3. As one of the input features, namely terrain information, the optimal driving behavior will be determined by the driving skill learning module.
4. Combined with the ice thickness model to get the 3D model of the glacier.

3.2 UGV Trafficability and Driving Skill Learning and Training

In Fig. 3 Step 2, we first analyze the glacier surface model obtained in Step 1 to get the safe driving area of UGV (shown in Fig. 4(f)). The UGV is then controlled by an operator as it patrols a safe area on the glacier, picking up a stream of data. This data is then used to form input data to the model, through the correlation analysis between driving data, vehicle state data and terrain data, we establish a brief and efficient driving skill model. Then an incremental learning method is constructed to make the driving skill model adapt quickly from glacial environment and variable surface structure. Finally, an iterative prediction algorithm is established, so as to provide drivers with reasonable driving suggestions and visual future vehicle condition prediction [17]. The following is a brief introduction to relevant algorithms:

Incremental Algorithm: In order to cope with the complex unstructured terrain and changeable surface properties of the glacier surface and enable the model to adapt to the model quickly, we constructed an incremental learning method.

The data form is: $\{(X_{t-n}, \ldots, X_{t-1}), Y_t\}$, and the input data is $(X_{t-n}, \ldots, X_{t-1})$, where $X_t = \{Terrain_t, Position_t, Posture_t, Steering_t, Throttle_t, Target_t\}$. The output data $Y_t = \{Position_t, Posture_t, Steering_t, Throttle_t\}$. Where $k(x)$ is the eigenspace projection function at time t, D_t is the dictionary at time t and $\Phi_t = [k_t(X_1), \ldots, k_t(X_t)]^T$ is the characteristic matrix at time t.

The driving skill model can provide recommended operation and predict the future conditions of UGV:

$$Y_t = \sum_{i=1}^{n} k(X_{t-n}, \ldots, X_{t-1})\omega_{i,j}, j = 1, 2, \ldots, m \qquad (5)$$

where n is the number of nodes, m is the output dimension, and $\omega_{i,j}$ is the continuous weight obtained from the ith node to the jth output. When new data comes in, the approximate linear independence criterion is used to deter-mine whether the data belongs to a new mode. If it is a new mode, the model structure is extended by increasing the length of the mode dictionary S_t:

$$S_t^{-1} = \begin{bmatrix} A & b \\ b^t & d \end{bmatrix} \qquad (6)$$

where:

$$S_t^{-1} = \Phi_t^{-1}\Phi_t + \lambda I$$
$$a_t = [0^T, 1]^T$$
$$A = S_t^{-1} + k_{t-1}(x_1)k_{t-1}^T(x_t)$$
$$b = S_t^{-1}a_t + k_{t-1}(x_t)k_{tt} - \lambda a_t$$
$$d = \lambda + a_t^T\left(S_t^{-1} - \lambda I\right)a_t + k_{tt}^2$$

If it is an old mode, fine-tune the relevant structure to make the model more general, and the new parameters can be calculated by the formula:

$$S_t^{-1} = S_t^{-1} + k_{t-1}(x_t)k_{t-1}^T(x_t) \tag{7}$$

Iterative Algorithm: In order to provide the operators with reasonable operating range and visualized vehicle future condition prediction, we use the one-step predictive driving skill model obtained before to make multi-step iterative prediction. The model uses the historical data series $(X_{t-n}, \ldots, X_{t-1})$ from the time of $t - n$ to $t - 1$ to predict the vehicle's recommended throttle and steering values, as well as the future state and position information Y_t at time t, as shown in Eq. (5).

Next, using the sliding window to delete the data X_{t-n} and add the data X_t at time t to the front of the queue. Input the new data sequence $(X_{t-n+1}, \ldots, X_t)$ into the model and predict the value X_{t+1} at time $t + 1$:

$$Y_{t+1} = \sum_{i=1}^n k(X_{t-n+1}, \ldots, X_t)\omega_{i,j}, j = 1, 2, \ldots, m \tag{8}$$

The future time is predicted iteratively by repeating the above steps, and the predicted positions are finally connected to form a forecast trajectory. In addition, multiple alternative target points are generated near the target points, the target points in the model input are replaced by the input of alternative target points, and the prediction is made in the same way to obtain multiple alternative predicted trajectories. Multiple recommended operations guided by multiple alter-native target points are weighted into one operating range by comprehensive evaluation of alternative predictive trajectories to help operators operate safely in foreseeable future vehicle conditions.

3.3 Human and Air-ground Robot Cooperative Exploration

In Step 3, we demonstrated the system's ability to work continuously in complex environments. Based on the global path obtained in Step 1 and the real-time vehicle driving reference given by the driving model in Step 2, the UGV is remotely controlled to roam the glacier surface. During the glacier exploration, we used the UAV as a relay platform to ensure communication between the UGV and the GS beyond the visual range. The UAV tracks and locates the UGV based on the location information sent by it and uses the camera to capture and return images in real time. During the second process, the UAV will constantly adjust its position and attitude to ensure the best communication quality and ensure the safety of the UGV. To this end, we abstract the cooperation problem of air-ground robots into a trajectory planning problem considering UAV mobility, UAV energy consumption, horizontal distance constraints and line of sight (LOS) constraints [18].

Optimization Function: In general, the energy consumption of UAV in vertical flight is far greater than that in horizontal flight, that is, low altitude usually means low energy consumption. Therefore, the flight height of UAV is taken as the optimization function, and the vertical flight distance of UAV is minimized to reduce energy consumption. The optimization function is defined as follows:

$$J = \sum_{k=1}^{p} |z_{UAV}(t+k) - z_{UAV}(t+k-1)| \tag{9}$$

where p is the prediction step, $z_{UAV}(t+k)$ and is the height of UAV at time $t+k$.

Constraints: LOS constraints restrict the construction of LOS links between UAV and GS to maintain smooth communication. Constraints are given as follows:

$$min\{\Delta Z_1(P_{UAV}, P_{GS}), \ldots, \Delta Z_i(P_{UAV}, P_{GS})\} \geq 0 \tag{10}$$

$$min\{\Delta Z_1(P_{UAV}, P_{UGV}), \ldots, \Delta Z_i(P_{UAV}, P_{UGV})\} \geq 0 \tag{11}$$

where $P_{UAV} = (x_{UAV}, y_{UAV}, z_{UAV})$ is the location of UAV, $P_{GS} = (x_{GS}, y_{GS}, z_{GS})$ is the location of GS, $P_{UGV} = (x_{UGV}, y_{UGV}, z_{UGV})$ is the location of UGV. $\Delta Z_i(P_{UAV}, P_{GS}) = z_i - f(x_i, y_i)$ is the height difference derived from the P_{GS} finally P_{UAV} of the ith point on the spatial line of the UAV. Take a point within the specified interval d_s, and then there are $i(i = INT((x_{UAV} - x_{GS})/d)$ total points with the function $INT(\cdot)$ indicating that decimal is deleted and rounded to the nearest integer. The height value on the space line is $z_i = z_{GS} + ((x_i - x_{GS})/(x_{UAV} - x_{GS})) \times (z_{UAV} - z_{GS})$, and the surface elevation value corresponding to the coordinates in the actual elevation diagram.

Horizontal range constraints:

$$\|P_{UAV,h}(t+k) - P_{UGV,h}(t+k)\|_2 \leq d \tag{12}$$

are used to ensure that UAVs always track UGVs to capture and transmit video to operators, simplifying remote connections. Where $P_{UAV,h} = (x_{UAV}, y_{UAV})$, d is the maxi-mum horizontal distance between the UAV and UGV, $P_{UGV,h} = (x_{UGV}, y_{UGV})$.

The height difference constraint:

$$\Delta z_{UAV}(t+k) \leq h$$

limits the minimum and maximum flight height of UAV in order to ensure the flight safety and proper visual field of UAV during video transmission. Where $\Delta z_{UAV}(t+k) = z_{UAV}(t+k) - z_{UGV}(t+k)$ is the maximum vertical height difference.

3.4 IPR Data Processing and Glacier 3D Modeling Results

We processed the original IPR data as shown in Fig. 5(a) obtained in the experiment, which mainly included data preprocessing, routine correction and image interpretation. Firstly, we improve data quality by eliminating noise caused by vehicle interference and system error through data preprocessing, including data sorting, elimination of waste channels, alignment of measurement lines and signal extraction. Secondly, we then perform routine processing such as correction, gain, filtering and migration on the pre-processed data to obtain a better interpreted signal. Finally, we can obtain a clear ice-rock structure image, and extract ice thickness data with GPS data of each measuring point according to the image and obtain ice thickness distribution data with GPS information (shown in Fig. 5(b)). Finally, we used the existing ice thickness data to train the Gaussian process regression model to interpolate the new thickness data, thus generating the ice thickness distribution model (shown in Fig. 5(c)). Finally, KD tree was applied to match the lightweight surface model with the ice thickness model to obtain a complete three-dimensional glacier model (shown in Fig. 5(d)).

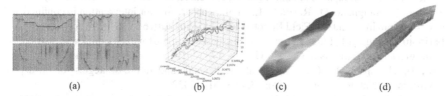

(a)   (b)   (c)   (d)

Fig. 5. (a) IPR raw data, (b) ice thickness with GPS, (c) ice thickness distribution and (d) 3D ice thickness model

4 Conclusion

In order to achieve continuous, efficient and accurate ice thickness distribution and volume estimation, we designed and implemented a cooperative detection system for ground robots to safely and intelligently traverse the extremely complex plateau and mountain glacier environment. The air-ground coordination strategy assists the UGV platform in large-scale exploration on the glacier. The Driving skills model provides safer and more reliable driving recommendations for UGV, making glacier exploration safer and smarter. Lightweight modeling frameworks help us model complex, inaccurate surface environments with lightweight, accurate models. We conducted validation experiments on the Korchung Gangri Glacier in the Tibetan Plateau and obtained glacier surface and ice thickness data, using these data, we established a continuous ice thickness distribution model. The whole system formed a new glacier survey scheme.

While the system is useful and has yielded some new scientific data, there are some limitations to our approach. Better travers ability than ground-based robots is difficult to determine in some special areas, and due to the complex terrain and high risk, our systems are still semi-autonomous and require constant human intervention. Future work will focus on ways to train robots to improve their resilience to weather conditions, environments and tasks. These are difficult because these conditions are time-varying and regionally different.

Acknowledgement. This work was supported by National Natural Science Foundation of China (No. 91948303), National Natural Science Foundation of China (No. 61991413), National Natural Science Foundation of China Innovative Research Group Project (No. 61821005), Shenyang science and technology plan (No. 21–108-9–18) Science and Technology Department of Shenyang (No. RC210477), Youth Innovation Promotion Association (No. Y2022065).

References

1. Yan, Z., Guan, W., Wen, S., Huang, L., Song, H.: Multirobot cooperative localization based on visible light positioning and odometer. IEEE Trans. Instrum. Measur. **70**, 1–8 (2021). 7004808
2. Murphy, R.R., Dreger, K.L., Newsome, S., et al.: Marine heterogeneous multirobot systems at the great Eastern Japan Tsunami recovery. J. Field Robot. **29**(5), 819–831 (2012)
3. Tardioli, D., Sicignano, D., Riazuelo, L., et al.: Robot teams for intervention in confined and structured environments. J. Field Robot. **33**(6), 765–801 (2016)
4. Farinotti, D., Huss, M., Fürst, J.J., et al.: A consensus estimate for the ice thickness distribution of all glaciers on Earth. Nat. Geosci. **12**, 168–173 (2019)
5. Yao, T., Thompson, L., Chen, D., et al.: Reflections and future strategies for third pole environment. Nat. Rev. Earth Environ. **3**, 608–610 (2022)
6. Liu, J., Milne, R.I., Cadotte, M.W., et al.: Protect third pole' fragile ecosystem. Science **362**(6421), 1368 (2018)
7. Jouvet, G., Weidmann, Y., Kneib, M., et al.: Short-lived ice speed-up and plume water flow captured by a VTOL UAV give insights into subglacial hydrological system of Bowdoin Glacier. Remote Sens. Environ. **217**, 389–399 (2018)
8. Woodward, J., Burke, M.J.: Applications of ground-penetrating radar to glacial and frozen materials. J. Environ. Eng. Geophys. **12**(1), 69–85 (2007)
9. Bash, E.A., Moorman, B.J., Gunther, A.: Detecting short-term surface melt on an Arctic glacier using UAV surveys. Remote Sens. **10**(10), 1547 (2018)
10. Rohner, C., Small, D., Beutel, J., et al.: Multisensor validation of tidewater glacier flow fields derived from synthetic aperture radar (SAR) intensity tracking. Cryosphere **13**(11), 2953–2975 (2019)
11. Bash, E.A., Moorman, B.J.: Surface melt and the importance of water flow–an analysis based on high-resolution unmanned aerial vehicle (UAV) data for an Arctic glacier. Cryosphere **14**(2), 549–563 (2020)
12. Dąbski, M., Zmarz, A., Rodzewicz, M., et al.: Mapping glacier forelands based on UAV BVLOS operation in Antarctica. Remote Sens. **12**(4), 630 (2020)
13. Williams, S., Parker, L.T., Howard, A.M.: Terrain reconstruction of glacial surfaces: robotic surveying techniques. IEEE Robot. Autom. Mag. **19**(4), 59–71 (2012)
14. Das, R.K., Upadhyay, A., Garg, R.K.: An unmanned tracked vehicle for snow research applications. Defence Sci. J. **67**(1) (2017)
15. Williams, R.M., Ray, L.E., Lever, J.:An autonomous robotic platform for ground penetrating radar surveys. In: 2012 IEEE International Geoscience and Remote Sensing Symposium, Munich, Germany, pp. 3174–3177 (2012)

16. Liu, X., Li, D., He, Y., Gu, F.: Efficient and multifidelity terrain modeling for 3D large-scale and unstructured environments. J. Field Robot. **39**, 1286–1322 (2022)
17. Hu, Y., Li, D., He, Y., Han, J.: Incremental learning framework for autonomous robots based on Q-learning and the adaptive kernel linear model. IEEE Trans. Cogn. Dev. Syst. **14**(1), 64–74 (2022)
18. Jiang, H., Chang, Y., Sun, X., Liu, X., Yang, L., He, Y.: Autonomous communication relay position planning based on predictive model. In: 2022 IEEE International Conference on Unmanned Systems (ICUS), Guangzhou, China, pp. 102–108 (2022)

A Modified Artificial Potential Field Method Based on Subgoal Points for Mobile Robot

Jixue Mo[1], Changqing Gao[2], Fei Liu[3], Qingkai Yang[4], and Hao Fang[4(✉)]

[1] Department of Mathematics and Theories, Pengcheng Laboratory, Shenzhen 518055, China
[2] School of Mechanical Engineering and Automation, Harbin Institute of Technology, Shenzhen 518055, China
[3] Industrial Training Center, Shenzhen Polytechnic, Shenzhen 518055, China
[4] Key Laboratory of Intelligent Control and Decision of Complex Systems, Beijing Institute of Technology, Beijing 100081, China
fangh@bit.edu.cn

Abstract. In this paper, a modified artificial potential field (MAPF) method was proposed for general mobile robot navigation system. This MAPF method can effectively solve the unreachable goal problem and the local minima problem of traditional APF method. The first key idea of MAPF method is to modify the repulsive force function and thus optimize the direction of total repulsive force; the second key idea is to generate a serials of subgoal points around obstacles with specific method, so as to help the robot escape from or keep away from local minima area. By comparing with other similar algorithms in simulation environment, the MAPF algorithm can generate shorter paths efficiently. More importantly, it also can generate effective paths in multi-obstacle environment where other algorithms cannot. Finally the simulation results verified the reasonability and practicability of the proposed MAPF method.

Keywords: Path planning · Artificial potential field · Subgoal points · Mobile robot

1 Introduction

The path planning and navigation function is usually quite important for autonomous mobile robot. Path planning refers to how the robot can generate an optimal path from initial position to destination based on certain indicators in a specific environment [1], and it mainly includes global path planning and local path planning. Global path planning, such as A* method [2], is an offline path planning method which can generate a complete collision-free path in known environment. However, the A* method is often computationally complex, time-consuming and vulnerable to unexpected obstacles. Therefore, the D* Lite method [3] was introduced as a modified algorithm for A*. Although D* Lite can effectively change the cost function while unexpected obstacles occurs, it still cannot deal with the essential problems of global path planning desirably. On the other hand, the local path planning is especially suitable for handling accidental situations in

H. Yang et al. (Eds.): ICIRA 2023, LNAI 14267, pp. 296–307, 2023.
https://doi.org/10.1007/978-981-99-6483-3_26

known or unknown environment. It often applies sensors to detect surrounding obstacles by consuming few processing time in real task. The artificial potential field (APF) is the most commonly used local path planning method due to its advantages such as quick response time and low computational complexity. However, the APF method usually has two disadvantages: the local minima problem and the unreachable goal problem. The first one means the mobile robot could be trapped in a local area when its attraction force equals to its repulsive force; the second one means the mobile robot can just wander around the goal due to its repulsive force outweigh its attraction force obviously.

After the APF method being firstly put forward by Knatib [4] in 1986, its different improved methods were proposed successively in the last few decades [5–9]. The "Going along obstacle's edge" method was proposed in [5] to solve the local minima problem in complex environment, but its generated path was undesirably long and had limited application value. Reference [6] analyzed the connectivity of different obstacles and set up temporary goals to help robot escape from local minima area. Although this method can reduce searching space and improve searching efficiency, it still didn't consider the situation of U-shape trap. An APF path planning algorithm based on electric potential field was brought forward in [7]. It can solve the trap problem but the modelling and computation processes were also complex. Reference [8] set up temporary obstacles in sector area to break force equilibrium in the local minima area, but the method of setting up temporary obstacles was not specific enough. Reference [9] introduced the idea of direction vector and virtual goal points to solve the local minima and escape from trap. However, the selection of virtual goal was not quite reasonable, and the generated path was also too long and contained excessive corners.

This paper proposed a modified artificial potential field (MAPF) method to solve both the unreachable goal problem and the local minima problem. Firstly, the repulsive force function of traditional APF was modified to optimize the direction of total repulsive force and thus make the goal reachable. Then a serials of new points around the obstacles were created, if necessary, to be the subgoals and thus help the robot escape from local minima area. The effectiveness and advantage of MAPF compared with other similar algorithms were finally verified by a serials of simulations. The MAPF method is especially suitable for mobile robot equipped with a 2D LiDAR. Because the LiDAR can cover a 360° horizontal field and detect the borders of different obstacles rapidly, thus contributing to creating subgoal points more efficiently.

2 Methodology

2.1 Traditional Artificial Potential Field

The traditional artificial potential field is mainly composed of the attractive potential field of the goal U_{att} and the repulsive potential field U_{rep} of the obstacles, that is:

$$U(X) = U_{att}(X) + U_{rep}(X) \tag{1}$$

where $X = (x, y)^T$ is current position of the mobile robot.

Then the mobile robot's total force vector $F(X)$ is the sum of the attractive force vector $F_{att}(X)$ and the repulsive force vector $F_{rep}(X)$:

$$F(X) = -\nabla U(X) = F_{att}(X) + F_{rep}(X) \tag{2}$$

The general equation of attractive potential field of the goal U_{att} is:

$$U_{att}(X) = \frac{1}{2}k_{att}\rho^2(X, X_g) \tag{3}$$

where k_{att} is the proportional gain factor of the attractive potential field, X_g is the goal's position and $\rho(X, X_g)$ is the Euclidean distance between robot and goal.

Then the direction of the attractive force vector $F_{att}(X)$ is from robot to the goal, and it magnitude can be obtained as:

$$F_{att}(X) = -\nabla U_{att}(X) = -k_{att}\rho(X, X_g) \tag{4}$$

In addition, the general equation of repulsive potential field of the obstacle U_{rep} is:

$$U_{rep}(X) = \begin{cases} \frac{1}{2}k_{rep}\left(\frac{1}{\rho(X,X_0)} - \frac{1}{\rho_0}\right)^2 & \rho(X, X_0) \leq \rho_0 \\ 0 & \rho(X, X_0) > \rho_0 \end{cases} \tag{5}$$

where k_{rep} is the proportional gain factor of the repulsive potential field, $\rho(X, X_0)$ is the Euclidean distance between robot and obstacle, and ρ_0 is the maximum operating distance of the obstacle.

Thus the direction of the repulsive force vector $F_{rep}(X)$ is from obstacle to robot, and its magnitude can be obtained as:

$$F_{rep}(X) = \begin{cases} k_{rep}\left(\frac{1}{\rho(X,X_0)} - \frac{1}{\rho_0}\right)\frac{\partial\rho(X,X_0)}{\rho^2(X,X_0)\partial X} & \rho(X, X_0) \leq \rho_0 \\ 0 & \rho(X, X_0) > \rho_0 \end{cases} \tag{6}$$

Therefore, the schematic diagram of mobile robot's force analysis under artificial potential field is shown in Fig. 1.

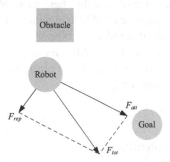

Fig. 1. Mobile robot's force analysis under artificial potential field.

2.2 Shortcomings in Traditional Potential Field

Although the traditional artificial potential field method can generate smooth and feasible paths in simple environment, it is not applicable in complex environment due to its two shortcomings: the unreachable goal problem and the local minima problem.

Figure 2 shows the force analysis of unreachable goal problem. If there is an obstacle around the goal, the mobile robot would suffer larger repulsive force F_{rep} and smaller attraction force F_{att} as it progresses towards the goal. Then the total potential field force F_{tot} would make the robot keep away from the goal, which causes the repulsive force F_{rep} become smaller and attraction force F_{att} become larger again. Therefore the robot would wander around the goal while cannot reach the goal forever.

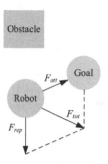

Fig. 2. Force analysis of unreachable goal problem.

The local minima problem means the robot is trapped in a local area where its attraction force equals to its repulsive forces, and thus the robot cannot progress towards goal any further. Due to the different distribution conditions of goal and obstacles in real environment, there might be different conditions for local minima problem. Figure 3 illustrates four typical conditions as well as force analysis of local minima problem. Figure 3(a)–(d) shows the distal end single-obstacle condition, proximal end single-obstacle condition, interval double-obstacle condition and U-shape obstacle condition respectively. As the APF method lacks global information while performing local path planning, it usually cannot prevent from local minima area. In addition, the local minima area would appear more easily if the mutual distances of obstacles become smaller and the sphere of influence of each obstacle becomes larger.

2.3 Modified Artificial Potential Field

For the unreachable goal problem of traditional APF method, the common solution is introducing the parameter of distance between robot and goal to the original repulsive force Eq. (6) [10]. Then the repulsive potential field of the goal point would be zero, and therefore the goal is also the global minimum point of the total potential field. So the modified repulsive force function is:

$$
U_{rep}^*(X) = \begin{cases} \frac{k_{rep}}{2}\left(\frac{1}{\rho(X,X_0)} - \frac{1}{\rho_0}\right)^2 \rho^n(X,X_g) & \rho(X,X_0) \le \rho_0 \\ 0 & \rho(X,X_0) > \rho_0 \end{cases} \tag{7}
$$

where k_{rep} is the proportional gain factor of the repulsive potential field, $\rho(X, X_g)$ is the Euclidean distance between robot and goal, ρ_0 is the maximum operating distance of the obstacle, and n is the modified repulsive force factor (the setting value of n is 1).

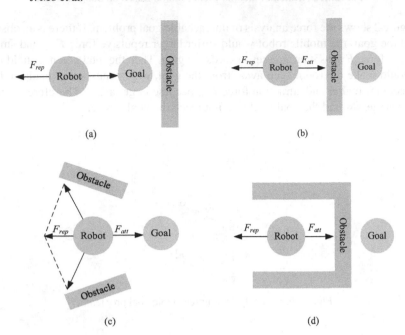

Fig. 3. Force analysis of local minima problem.

Similarly, the modified repulsive force is the negative gradient of the repulsive potential field, that is:

$$F_{rep}^*(X) = -\nabla U_{rep}^*(X) = \begin{cases} F_{rep1}^* + F_{rep2}^* & \rho(X, X_0) \le \rho_0 \\ 0 & \rho(X, X_0) > \rho_0 \end{cases} \tag{8}$$

When the robot is within the influence scope of obstacle, it would suffer two different repulsive forces, that is:

$$\begin{cases} F_{rep1}^*(X) = k_{rep}\left(\dfrac{1}{\rho(X, X_0)} - \dfrac{1}{\rho_0}\right)\dfrac{\partial \rho(X, X_0)}{\rho^2(X, X_0)\partial X}\rho^n(X, X_g) \\ F_{rep2}^*(X) = -\dfrac{1}{2}k_{rep}\left(\dfrac{1}{\rho(X, X_0)} - \dfrac{1}{\rho_0}\right)^2 \dfrac{\partial \rho^n(X, X_g)}{\partial X} \end{cases} \tag{9}$$

If $n = 1$, then (9) can be simplified as follows:

$$\begin{cases} F_{rep1}^*(X) = k_{rep}\left(\dfrac{1}{\rho(X, X_0)} - \dfrac{1}{\rho_0}\right)\dfrac{\rho(X, X_g)}{\rho^2(X, X_0)} \\ F_{rep2}^*(X) = -\dfrac{1}{2}k_{rep}\left(\dfrac{1}{\rho(X, X_0)} - \dfrac{1}{\rho_0}\right)^2 \end{cases} \tag{10}$$

Thus the schematic diagram of modified repulsive force analysis are shown in Fig. 4. The direction of F^*_{rep1} is from obstacle to the robot while the direction of F^*_{rep2} is from the robot to the goal. It can be seen that the direction of modified total repulsive force F^*_{tot} is obviously closer to the goal compared with original total repulsive force F_{tot}. According to (10), the modified repulsive force can ensure the goal as the global minimum point of the total potential field, and hence the robot can keep progressing towards the goal.

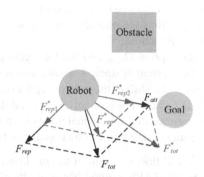

Fig. 4. Schematic diagram of the modified repulsive force analysis.

On the other side, for the local minima problem, it is applicable to set several temporary subgoal points when the robot realizes it is being trapped in a local minima area. Then the attractive potential field would be temporarily generated by the subgoal point until the robot escapes from the local minima area.

It is noteworthy that the amount and specific positions of the subgoal points are quite important for robot's success escape from local minima area and the escaping efficiency. Then a subgoal points establishment method with sweeping process was proposed here. Its main idea is to generate a serials of temporary subgoal points by sweeping process given the global position information of robot, final goal and all obstacles, so as to escape from local minima area successfully.

Firstly, each obstacle of the map is composed of a group of points which mutual distances are small enough, and the single obstacle can be seen as a common geometry or limited combination of common geometries. Taking the U-shape obstacle as example, the basic steps of subgoal points establishment method with sweeping process are described as follows, and the related schematic diagram is shown in Fig. 5:

1. Connect the starting point and the goal point with a line segment, determine which obstacle was passed through in sequence (each obstacle is recorded as k_i, $i = 1, 2, 3,$ ...);
2. For the current obstacle k_i, connect the starting point S or last subgoal point O_{last} and the goal E with line segment l_{i0}, and record the current angle of l_{i0} as θ_{i0}. Calculate the maximum left and right vertical distance of l_{i0} with k_i, then mark the corresponding point as A and B respectively, their distances to l_{i0} are d_{max1} and d_{max2} respectively. If $d_{max1} > d_{max2}$, then l_{i0} should take O_{last} as the origin and sweep towards point B, otherwise it should sweep toward point A. The sweeping angle of each step $\Delta\theta_i$ is previously given, and the length of rotated line segment l_{ij} ($j = 1, 2, 3,$ ...) is the distance between O_{last} and k_i along the direction of l_{ij};

3. Repeat step 2 until it is the last time which line segment l_{ij} can contact the obstacle k_i. Record the current angle of l_{ij} as θ_{ij}, then make l_{ij} rotate once again to $\theta_{ij} + \tau$ and extend the length of l_{ij} to αl_{ij}. It is worth noting that both τ and α are hyper-parameters whose values are also given previously, and the different values of τ and α would affect the amount of generated subgoal points and whether the robot can escape from local minima area obviously. The end of the rotated line segment l'_{ij} is the new subgoal point O_{new}, thus the planning path between O_{last} and O_{new} can be generated by traditional APF method;

4. Connect the current subgoal point O_{new} and the final goal point with line segment l_{i0}. If l_{i0} passes through the current obstacle k_i again, then repeat step 2 and step 3 to generate new subgoal point, else shift to the next sweeping obstacle k_{i+1} and then also repeat step 2 and step 3. If l_{i0} does not pass through k_i and there is not next obstacle anymore, then it can be assumed that all subgoal points have been generated and thus the total planning path from starting point to final goal can be obtained.

Figure 6 presents the overall flow diagram of the modified artificial potential field (MAPF) method. Therefore the MAPF method based on the aforementioned modified repulsive force function and subgoal points establishment method with sweeping process can be proposed to perform path planning for mobile robot. It usually can generate applicable mobile path in complex environment and escape from local minima area successfully.

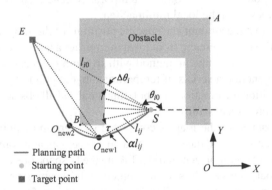

Fig. 5. Subgoal points establishment method with sweeping process.

3 Result and Discussion

In order to verify the effectiveness of the proposed MAPF method, it can be tested in the MATLAB simulation environment. Firstly, in consideration of safety, each obstacle should be appropriately expanded. Then the edge of single obstacle should be extracted and discretized with a group of peripheral points.

Mark the artificial potential field method with only the modified repulsive force function as algorithm A, then mark the VP-90 artificial potential field method in reference

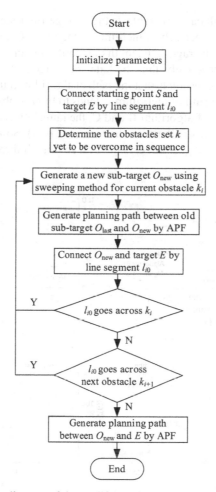

Fig. 6. Flow diagram of the modified artificial potential field method.

[11] as algorithm B and mark the proposed modified artificial potential field method as algorithm C. Then treat the mobile robot as a mass point, and the values of initial parameters were set as follows: $k_{rep} = 15$, $k_{att} = 10$, $\rho_0 = 10$ m, the robot's moving distance of each step $\Delta l = 1$ m, the hyper parameters of algorithm C$\tau = 8°$ and $\alpha = 1.3$. Thus the path planning effects of three algorithms in different environments can be analyzed by the simulation of MATLAB, so that the characteristics of different algorithms can also be obtained.

Figure 7 shows the planning effects of three APF methods in four different environments, and Table 1 presents the effect details of different APF methods. It can be seen from Fig. 7 that the planning path of algorithm A was trapped in local minima area for all cases and did not reach the goal point finally. Algorithm B used the strategy that generated a series of subgoal points along the obstacle's edge to escape from local minima area, while algorithm C generated limited subgoal points near the obstacle to keep away from it. For all cases in Table 1, the average run time of algorithm B and C were 0.28s and 1.38 s respectively, which means the latter's run time was 1.1s slower than the former. Then the average path length of algorithm B and C in Table 1 were 244.5 steps and 204.2 steps respectively, thus the latter's average path length was only 83.5% of the former's. This main reason is that the path of algorithm B usually goes along with obstacle's edge while the path of algorithm C tends to bypass obstacle. In addition, due to the strategy difference of algorithm B and C, the latter's average amount of subgoal points (2.5) was also much smaller than the former (116.5). So it can be observed that the path planning effect of algorithm C is the best among all three APF algorithms.

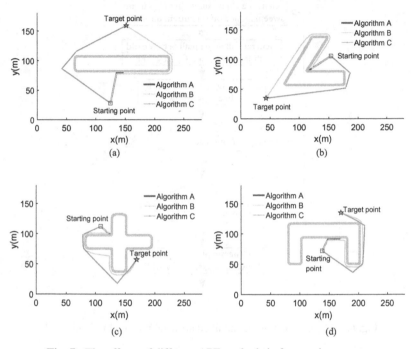

Fig. 7. The effects of different APF methods in four environments.

On the other side, neither algorithm A and B can deal with overcoming different types of obstacles in succession because algorithm A cannot generate subgoal points and algorithm B did not consider the case of overcoming multiple obstacles [11]. On the contrary, algorithm C still has obvious advantage in overcoming successive obstacles. Figure 8 presents the planning effects of algorithm C in four different environments. It can be seen that algorithm C can successfully generate planning paths in all multi-obstacle environments where traditional APF method is not qualified. Table 2 lists the path planning effects of algorithm C for all four cases (from case V to case VIII). According to Table 2, the average run time and average path length for four cases are 1.75s and 279.2 steps respectively. Therefore it can be concluded that the proposed MAPF algorithm has better local path planning performance than other similar APF algorithms, hence it has wider range of application and better practicability.

Table 1. Effect details of different APF methods.

	Starting point	Goal point	Operation effect	Algorithm A	Algorithm B	Algorithm C
Case I	(125, 28)	(152, 159)	Algorithm run time (s)	0.10	0.27	1.25
			Reachability of the goal point	No	Yes	Yes
			Total path length (step)	107	264	234
			Amount of subgoal points	0	126	2
Case II	(154, 106)	(43, 35)	Algorithm run time (s)	0.08	0.29	1.37
			Reachability of the goal point	No	Yes	Yes
			Total path length (step)	87	267	205
			Amount of subgoal points	0	98	2
Case III	(109, 112)	(169, 57)	Algorithm run time (s)	0.05	0.24	1.25
			Reachability of the goal point	No	Yes	Yes
			Total path length (step)	62	215	185
			Amount of subgoal points	0	124	3
Case IV	(138, 72)	(170, 135)	Algorithm run time (s)	0.09	0.30	1.64
			Reachability of the goal point	No	Yes	Yes
			Total path length (step)	91	232	193
			Amount of subgoal points	0	118	3

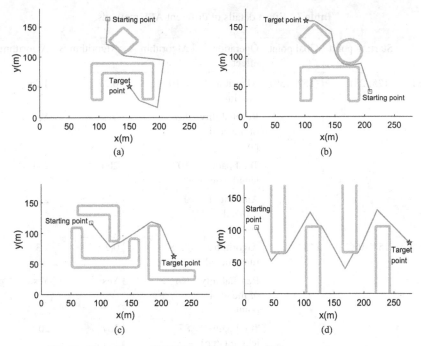

Fig. 8. The effects of MAPF method in four different environments.

Table 2. Effect details of robot's overcoming success obstacles.

	Starting point	Goal point	τ	α	Algorithm run time (s)	Reachability of the goal point	Total path length (step)	Amount of subgoal points
Case V	(115, 163)	(150, 51)	7°	1.2	1.58	Yes	283	4
Case VI	(209, 41)	(102, 160)	7°	1.2	0.92	Yes	184	5
Case VII	(84, 117)	(221, 62)	7°	1.2	1.65	Yes	199	4
Case VIII	(21, 104)	(276, 80)	8°	1.3	2.87	Yes	451	4

4   Conclusion

In order to solve the typical shortcomings of traditional artificial potential field (APF) method, this paper came up with a modified artificial potential field (MAPF) method. In the first place, the repulsive force function of traditional APF was modified to optimize the direction of total repulsive force and thus make the goal reachable. On the other side, a serials of subgoal points were generated around obstacles with specific method to escape from or keep away from local minima area. Then the improvement effect of MAPF algorithm was verified by comparing with other similar algorithms in MATLAB simulation environment. The simulation results showed that MAPF algorithm can generate shorter paths and also still worked well in multi-obstacle environment, thus verified effectiveness of modification methods.

Acknowledgment. This work is mainly supported by National Key Research and Development Program of China (No. 2022YFB4702000) and Shenzhen Polytechnic Research Fund (6023310005K).

References

1. Sombolestan, S.M., Rasooli, A., Khodaygan, S.: Optimal path-planning for mobile robots to find a hidden target in an unknown environment based on machine learning. J. Ambient. Intell. Humaniz. Comput. **10**, 1841–1850 (2019). https://doi.org/10.1007/s12652-018-0777-4
2. Hart, P.E., Nilsson, N.J., Raphael, B.: A formal basis for the heuristic determination of minimum cost paths. IEEE Trans. Syst. Sci. Cybern. **4**(2), 28–29 (1972)
3. Koenig, S., Likhachev, M.: Fast replanning for navigation in unknown terrain. IEEE Trans. Rob. **21**(3), 354–363 (2005)
4. Khatib, O.: Real-time obstacle avoidance for manipulators and mobile robots. Int. J. Robot. Res. **5**(1), 90–98 (1986)
5. Huang, Y., Hu, H., Liu, X.: Obstacles avoidance of artificial potential field method with memory function in complex environment. In: Proceedings of the 8th World Congress on Intelligent Control and Automation, pp. 6414–6418 (2010)
6. Qian, C., Qisong, Z., Li, H.: Improved artificial potential field method for dynamic target path planning in LBS. In: Proceedings of Chinese Control and Decision Conference (CCDC), pp. 2710–2714 (2018)
7. Fang, W., Fengyu, Z., Lei, Y.: Global path planning algorithm of mobile robot based on electric potential field. Robot. **41**(6), 742–750 (2019)
8. Liang, X., Liu, C., Song, X., et al.: Research on improved artificial potential field approach in local path planning for mobile robot. Comput. Simul. **35**(4), 291–361 (2018)
9. Wang, S., Zhao, T., Li, W.: Mobile robot path planning based on improved artificial potential field method. In: Proceedings of IEEE International Conference of Intelligent Robotic and Control Engineering (IRCE), pp. 29–33. IEEE (2018)
10. Chen, W., Wu, X., Lu, Y.: An improved path planning method based on artificial potential field for a mobile robot. Cybern. Inf. Technol. **15**(2), 181–191 (2015)
11. Wang, D., Li, C., Guo, N., et al.: Local path planning of mobile robot based on artificial potential field. In: Proceedings of 39th Chinese Control Conference (CCC), pp. 25–30 (2021)

A Modular Tensegrity Mobile Robot with Multi-locomotion Modes

Qi Yang, Ze Yu, Binbin Lian, and Tao Sun[✉]

Key Laboratory of Mechanism Theory and Equipment Design of Ministry of Education,
Tianjin University, Tianjin 300350, China
stao@tju.edu.cn

Abstract. Tensegrity mobile robots have merits of high stiff-to-mass ratio and superior structural compliance, making them a hot research topic recently. In this work, a novel modular tensegrity mobile robot with multi-locomotion modes is proposed. Unlike the existing conventional tensegrity robots, the robot in this work has abundant deformation ability, and can achieve four locomotion modes in terms of earthworm-like, inchworm-like, tumbling and hybrid locomotion. Afterwards, motion planning of the four locomotion modes based on the kinematic model is implemented, and the driving law of the motors under each locomotion mode can be obtained. A prototype of the robot is developed, and experimental results show that the robot can effectively adjust to five types of terrains by the four locomotion modes (maximum velocity on flat ground 33.90 BL/min, minimum height of confined space 1.18 BH, maximum angle of slope 9°, maximum height of obstacle 0.55 BH and maximum width of gap 0.21 BL. BL and BH represent the body length and body height of the robot, respectively). This work provides a useful reference for the application of tensegrity structures in the field of multi-locomotion mobile robot.

Keywords: Tensegrity robot · multi-locomotion · motion planning

1 Introduction

Tensegrity structures have become a hot research topic recently owing to their superior structural compliance [1, 2] and high stiff-to-mass ratio [3, 4]. Based on the tensegrity structures, a variety of mobile robots have been developed, which can be used for planetary exploration and disaster rescue [5, 6].

Currently, the tensegrity mobile robots can be divided into two categories, namely spherical tensegrity robot and spine-like tensegrity robot [7, 8]. The locomotion mode of the spherical tensegrity robot is mainly rolling, and a typical representative is SUPERball developed by NASA [9, 10]. The length of cables of SUPERball can be changed by motors to achieve the rolling locomotion, and thus it can be used to carry out the space exploration mission to Titan. Researchers from the UC Berkely have proposed many spherical tensegrity mobile robots called TT-1, TT-2, TT-3, and TT4-mini [11–13]. These robots can be applied in the ruins of a disaster to search and transmit on-site data, and this is the first practical application of a tensegrity robot in a disaster occasion. In addition, Hao et al. [14] and Littlefield et al. [15] have also conducted research on the spherical tensegrity mobile robots. Spine-like tensegrity mobile robots' locomotion mode is mainly crawling, and the common configurations of the robot mainly include three-rod structure [16, 17] and four-rod structure [18]. In particular, due to the fact that the spine-like tensegrity robots can only achieve crawling locomotion, their adaptability to multiple terrains is weak.

It can be seen from the above research status that the existing tensegrity mobile robots have very limited locomotion modes, further leading to the weak adaptability under the multiple terrains. To the best of our knowledge, a multi-locomotion tensegrity mobile robot with the adaptability to various terrains has not been reported so far. In this study, we propose a modular tensegrity mobile robot with multi-locomotion modes. The robot can achieve four locomotion modes in terms of earthworm-like, inchworm-like, tumbling and hybrid locomotion, and can adapt to five typical terrains, namely flat ground, confined space, ascending slope, gap and obstacle. The experiments show the effectiveness of the robot in passing through different terrains. This study fully utilizes the deformability of the tensegrity structures and demonstrates their potential applications in the fields of multi-locomotion mobile robots.

The rest of this study is organized as follows. In Sect. 2, the overall structure of the modular tensegrity mobile robot is described. In Sect. 3, a generalized kinematic model is established, and on this basis, the motion planning on the four locomotion modes is conducted. In Sect. 4, experiments on the prototype are conducted to show the environmental adaptability of the proposed tensegrity mobile robot. Section 5 concludes this study.

2 Overall Design of the Robot

The tensegrity mobile robot proposed in this study consists of two identical modules, as is shown in Fig. 1(a), and the two modules are connected by electromagnets. The size and weight of each module are 11 cm × 9 cm × 5.5 cm and 160 g, respectively. In particular, each module of the robot is composed of two frames, four crossed struts, two elastic cables, and four sliding cables (Fig. 1(b)), and the parameters of each module can be seen in Table 1. The four sliding cables are divided into two groups (i.e., the upper two being a group, and the lower two being a group), and each group of cables is driven by one motor mounted on the frame. The different steering of the two motors can make the four sliding cables lengthen or shorten, ensuring that the robot can achieve different forms of deformation. In addition, each joint of the robot is provided with a ratchet-based "foot" (Fig. 1(c)), which can rotate clockwise but not counterclockwise, and the ratchet-based "foot" can provide friction for the robot to move forward. The locomotion mechanism is presented as follows.

The diagram of the module of the robot is shown in Fig. 1(e). Δs_1 (Δs_2) means the length variation of the sliding cable 1 (sliding cable 2), and $\Delta s_i > 0$ (or $\Delta s_i < 0$, $i = 1$–2) represents the sliding cable i is extended (or shortened). When $\Delta s_1 = \Delta s_2$, the module of the robot undergoes the contraction/ extension deformation, as is shown in Fig. 1(e). When $\Delta s_1 > 0$ and $\Delta s_2 < 0$, the module of the robot undergoes the bending deformation. The different deformation forms of the two modules endows the robot with rich deformable ability, such as the contraction and bending deformation shown in the right section of Fig. 1(e). On the basis of different deformation forms of the robot, the ratchet-based "foot" can make the robot move forward. The ratchet-based "foot" is composed of a pawl, an inner ratchet and an external ratchet (Fig. 1(c)), and the external ratchet can rotate clockwise but not counterclockwise. When the robot tends to contract, the external ratchet in the front section of the robot tends to turn counterclockwise but stuck, while the ratchet in the rear section tends to turn clockwise and move forward. The locomotion tendency is the opposite when the robot stretches. Therefore, the robot can achieve the locomotion sequence as shown in Fig. 1(d). In order to acquire the multiple locomotion modes accurately, the kinematic-based motion planning of the robot is conducted.

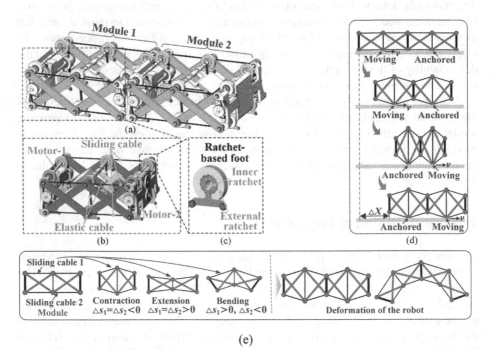

Fig. 1. Overall structure and locomotion mechanism of the tensegrity mobile robot. (a) Structure of the robot; (b) Structure of the module; (c) Ratchet-based feet; (d) Locomotion sequence of the robot; (e) Deformation mechanism of the module and overall structure

Table 1. Parameters of each module

Category	Size/ m	Weight/ g	Number of sliding cables	Number of elastic cables
Value	$11 \times 9 \times 5.5$	160	4	2
Category	Number of crossed struts	Length of crossed struts/ m	Stiffness of elastic cable/ N/m	Original length of elastic cable/ m
Value	6	0.06	100	0.02

3 Motion Planning of Different Locomotion Modes

3.1 Generalized Kinematic Modelling

The generalized kinematic modelling of the robot is mainly to obtain the relationship between the input angles of motors of the two modules and the posture of the robot. The diagram of the robot is shown in Fig. 2, and the coordinate system O-XY is established. In the i-th ($i = 1,2$) module, the following vector equation holds,

$$\begin{cases} A_{1,k}A_{2,k} + A_{2,k}A_{1,k+1} + A_{1,k+1}A_{2,k+1} + A_{2,k+1}A_{1,k} = 0 \\ A_{1,k}A_{2,k} + A_{2,k}A_{2,k+1} + A_{2,k+1}A_{1,k+1} + A_{1,k+1}A_{1,k} = 0 \\ A_{1,k}A_{2,k} + A_{2,k}A_{2,k+1} + A_{2,k+1}A_{1,k} = 0 \\ A_{1,k}A_{2,k} + A_{2,k}A_{1,k+1} + A_{1,k+1}A_{1,k} = 0 \end{cases}, \ i-1-2, \ k=(2i-1), 2i \quad (1)$$

where, $A_{i,k}$ (i-1-2, $k = (2i$-1), $2i$) is the node of the robot, as is shown in Fig. 2.

According to Eq. (1), the joint angles of the robot and the lengths of the two elastic cables can be obtained as follow

$$\begin{cases} \theta_{q,k} = f_{q,k}\left(s_{j,1}^{(i)}, s_{j,2}^{(i)}\right) & q = 1 - 3, k = (2i - 1), 2i \\ \theta_{4,k+1} = f_{4,k+1}\left(s_{j,1}^{(i)}, s_{j,2}^{(i)}\right) & s = 1, 3, i = 1-2 \\ \gamma_{s,k} = g_{s,k}\left(s_{j,1}^{(i)}, s_{j,2}^{(i)}\right) & j = 1-2 \end{cases} \quad (2)$$

$$L_{spi} = \begin{cases} \sqrt{L_{st}^2 + \left(s_{2,1}^{(i)}\right)^2 - 2L_{st}s_{2,1}^{(i)} \cdot \cos\left(\theta_{1,k} - \gamma_{1,k}\right)}, \ k = 2i - 1 \\ \sqrt{L_{st}^2 + \left(s_{2,2}^{(i)}\right)^2 + 2L_{st}s_{2,2}^{(i)} \cdot \cos\left(\gamma_{3,k} - \theta_{1,k}\right)}, \ k = 2i \end{cases}, \ i = 1-2 \quad (3)$$

where, L_{st} is the length of the crossed link, and L_{spi} is the length of the i-th elastic cables shown in Fig. 2. $\theta_{1,k}$ ($\theta_{2,k}, \theta_{3,k}, \theta_{4,k}, \theta_{4,k+1}$) is the angle between $A_{1,k}A_{1,k+1}, (A_{1,k+1}A_{2,k+1}, A_{2,k+1}A_{2,k}, A_{2,k}A_{1,k}, A_{2,k+1}A_{1,k+1})$ and $A_{1,1}A_{2,1}$. $\gamma_{1,k}$ ($\gamma_{3,k}$) is the angle between the link $A_{1,k}A_{2,k+1}$ ($A_{1,k+1}A_{2,k}$) and $A_{1,1}A_{2,1}$. In particular, $\theta_{4,1} = \pi$. $vsgn(x) = \begin{cases} 0, & x = 1 \\ 1, & x \geq 2 \end{cases}$.

It is worth noting that, in Eqs. (2)–(3), $s_{j,1}^{(i)}$ and $s_{j,2}^{(i)}$ ($i = 1-2, j = 1-2$) represent the lengths of cable segments in the i-th module, and they satisfy the following equation,

$$s_{j,1}^{(i)} = s_{j,2}^{(i)} = \frac{1}{2} \cdot s_{j\_Total}^{(i)} = \frac{1}{2}\varphi_j^{(i)} \cdot R_j^{(i)}, \ i = 1 - 2, j = 1 - 2 \quad (4)$$

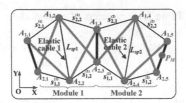

Fig. 2. Diagram of the robot

where, $s^{(i)}_{j\_\text{Total}}$ is the total length of each sliding cable in the module. $\varphi^{(i)}_j$ is the input angle of each motor. $R^{(i)}_j$ is the radius of the spool.

Therefore, on condition that the input angles of all the motors are given, the position and posture of the robot can be known on compliance with Eqs. (1)–(4). The position of the end point P_M (Fig. 2) of the robot can be expressed as

$$
\begin{cases}
X_{PM} = \dfrac{1}{2}L_{fr}\left(1-\cos\theta_{2,8}\right) - \displaystyle\sum_{i=1}^{4}\left(s^{(i)}_{1,1}\cos\theta_{3,2i-1} + s^{(i)}_{1,2}\cos\theta_{3,2i}\right) \\[4mm]
Y_{PM} = -\displaystyle\sum_{i=1}^{4}\left(s^{(i)}_{1,1}\sin\theta_{3,2i-1} + s^{(i)}_{1,2}\sin\theta_{3,2i}\right) - \dfrac{1}{2}L_{fr}\sin\theta_{2,8}
\end{cases}
\tag{5}
$$

where, L_{fr} is the length of links of the robot except the crossed links

3.2 Motion Planning Based on the Kinematic Model

According to the generalized kinematic model and the locomotion mechanism, the robot has four basic locomotion modes in terms of earthworm-like locomotion, inchworm-like locomotion, tumbling locomotion and hybrid locomotion. The motion planning of the robot aims at acquiring the driving law of each motor under the four locomotion modes.

For the earthworm-like locomotion, in one cycle, the sliding cables in the two modules are contracted uniformly first and then extended consistently. The locomotion sequence of the earthworm-like locomotion can be seen in Fig. 3(a). Therefore, the driving law of each motor in the two modules can be formulated as

$$
\varphi^{(i)}_1 = \varphi^{(i)}_2 \in [0, \varphi_E], \; i = 1-2
\tag{6}
$$

where, φ_E is the rotation angle of the motors when the robot is in its middle state of the earthworm-like locomotion (Fig. 3(a)), and can be given according to experience.

For the inchworm-like locomotion, in one cycle, the sliding cable 1 is first extended and then shortened, while the sliding cable 2 is first shortened and then extended. It is worth noting that when the frames of the robot are parallel to the ground, the robot is in its middle state of the inchworm-like locomotion. The locomotion sequence of the inchworm-like locomotion can be seen in Fig. 3(b).

During the inchworm-like locomotion of the robot, the lengths of the two elastic cables (i.e., L_{spi}, $i = 1-2$) are unchanged and equal to the length of link $A_{1,1}A_{2,1}$ (i.e.,

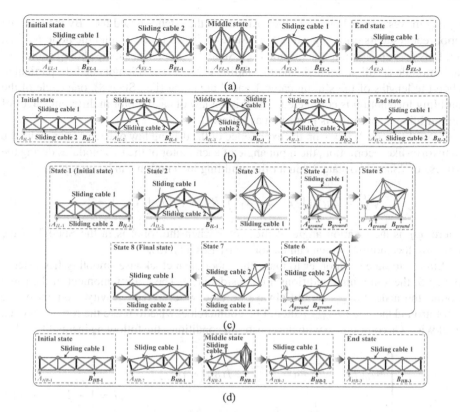

Fig. 3. Four locomotion modes of the robot. (a) Earthworm-like locomotion. (b) Inchworm-like locomotion. (c) Tumbling locomotion. (d) Hybrid locomotion

L_{fr}). Based on this, the relationship between $S_{j,1}^{(i)}$ and $S_{j,2}^{(i)}$ ($j = 1$–2) can be obtained by substituting $L_{spi} = L_{fr}$ into Eq. (3),

$$s_{2,1}^{(i)} = f_{IL}\left(s_{1,1}^{(i)}\right), \ s_{2,2}^{(i)} = f_{IL}\left(s_{1,2}^{(i)}\right), \ i = 1 - 2 \tag{7}$$

Equation (7) can be inserted into Eq. (4), and the driving law of each motor in the two modules can be written as

$$\varphi_2^{(i)} = 2f_{IL}\left((1/2) \cdot \varphi_1^{(i)} R_1^{(i)}\right) / R_2^{(i)} \in [0, \varphi_I], \ i = 1 - 2 \tag{8}$$

where, φ_I is the rotation angle of the motor when the robot is in the middle state of the inchworm-like locomotion (Fig. 3(b)), and can be solved according to Eqs. (1)–(5).

For the tumbling locomotion, in one cycle, the sliding cable 1 of each module is lengthened, and the sliding cable 2 is shortened until the two frames of the robot are parallel to each other (i.e., State 3). Then, the robot falls forward to the ground under the effect of inertial force (i.e., State 4). After that, the sliding cable 1 is shortened, and the sliding cable 2 is lengthened so that the robot can open clockwise. It is worth noting that in this process, the node B_{ground} of the robot is anchored to the ground, and the node

A_{ground} moves forward owing to the structure of the ratchet-based feet. By the time the robot reaches to its critical posture (i.e., State 6), it will rotate around the node B_{ground}, and falls forward again to the ground (i.e., State 7). On this basis, the sliding cable 1 of each module is still shortened, and the sliding cable 2 is still lengthened. In particular, when the lengths of the sliding cable 1 and 2 are equal (i.e., State 8), one cycle of the tumbling locomotion is completed. The driving law of each motor in different stages of the tumbling locomotion is presented as follow.

State 1 to state 3. Draw on the experience of the driving law of each motor under the inchworm-like locomotion, the input angle of each motor of the two modules during the process of "State 1 to state 3" under the tumbling locomotion can be written as

$$\varphi_2^{(i)} = 2f_{IL}\left((1/2) \cdot \varphi_1^{(i)} R_1^{(i)}\right)/R_2^{(i)} \in [0, \varphi_T], \ i = 1 - 2 \tag{9}$$

where, φ_T is the rotation angle of the motor when the robot is in the State 3 of the tumbling locomotion, which can be solved by Eqs. (1)–(5).

State 4 to state 6. In order to make the robot open clockwise smoothly from step 4 to step 5, the following conditions are considered: ① The gravity moment of the robot around the node A_{ground} should always be clockwise. ② The gravity moment of the robot around the node B_{ground} should be counterclockwise to make the robot can open clockwise. On compliance with the constraint conditions, the following inequality holds,

$$\begin{cases} M_{Gravity}^{A_{ground}} = \sum_{t=1}^{11} m_t g r_t^{A_{ground}} = f_{TB,1}\left(s_{j,1}^{(i)}, s_{j,2}^{(i)}\right) \leq 0 \\ M_{Gravity}^{B_{ground}} = \sum_{t=1}^{11} m_t g r_t^{B_{ground}} = f_{TB,2}\left(s_{j,1}^{(i)}, s_{j,2}^{(i)}\right) \geq 0 \end{cases}, i = 1 - 2 \tag{10}$$

where, $M_{Gravity}^{A_{ground}}$ and $M_{Gravity}^{B_{ground}}$ are the gravity moments of the robot around the node A_{ground} and B_{ground}. In particular, in this study, it is assumed that the torque is negative value when it is clockwise and positive value when it is counterclockwise. m_t is the mass of the t-th link, and $r_t^{A_{ground}}$ and $r_t^{B_{ground}}$ are the horizontal distances from the center of mass of each link to the node A_{ground} and B_{ground}.

Insert inequality (10) with Eq. (1), the driving law of each motor can be expressed as

$$\varphi_2^{(i)} = g_{TB}\left(\varphi_1^{(i)}\right), \ \varphi_2^{(i)} \in \left[\varphi_T, \varphi_{Tf}^{(i)}\right], \ \varphi_1^{(i)} \in \left[\varphi_E, \varphi_{Ef}^{(i)}\right] \tag{11}$$

where, φ_E is the rotation angle of the motor when the robot is in the State 3. When $\varphi_1^{(i)} = \varphi_{Ef}^{(i)}$ and $\varphi_2^{(i)} = \varphi_{Tf}^{(i)} (i = 1 - 2)$, the robot is in the critical posture (i.e., State 6), and $\varphi_{Ef}^{(i)}(\varphi_{Tf}^{(i)})$ can be solved by letting $M_{Gravity}^{B_{ground}}$ be equal to zero.

State 7 to state 8. Based on the formulated locomotion process and Eq. (9), the input angle of motors in this stage can be expressed as

$$\varphi_2^{(i)} = 2f_{IL}\left((1/2) \cdot \varphi_1^{(i)} R_1^{(i)}\right)/R_2^{(i)}, \ \varphi_2^{(i)} \in \left[\varphi_{Tf}^{(i)}, 0\right], \ \varphi_1^{(i)} \in \left[\varphi_{Ef}^{(i)}, 0\right] \tag{12}$$

For the hybrid locomotion, it is the combination of the earthworm-like and inchworm-like locomotion, which can be seen in Fig. 3(d). One module exerts the bending deformation, and the other achieves the contraction/extension deformation. Hence, the driving law of each motor is similar to Eq. (6) and Eq. (8).

Table 2. Locomotion modes and terrains the robot can adapt to.

Modes	Earthworm-like locomotion			Inchworm-like mode		
Ter-rains	Flat ground	Confined space	Slope	Flat ground	Slope	
Modes	Tumbling locomotion			Hybrid locomotion		
Ter-rains	Flat ground	Gap	Obsta-cle	Flat ground	Confined space	Slope

Based on the four locomotion modes, the robot can adapt to five typical terrains, namely flat ground, confined space, ascending slope, gap and obstacle, as is shown in Table 2. In particular, on the flat ground, the robot can move by all the four locomotion modes. When it encounters the ascending slope, the robot can climb up by earthworm-like, inchworm-like and hybrid locomotion. The robot will transform to earthworm-like and hybrid locomotion when the confined space is in the front. When the robot meets the gap and obstacle, it can pass through by tumbling locomotion. Next, experiments on the robot are conducted to obtain the kinematic characteristic of the robot under different terrains.

4 Experiments

4.1 Prototype of the Robot

A prototype of the robot is manufactured, as is shown in Fig. 4. The size and weight of the prototype are consistent with the theoretical design. The crossed links in the robot are made of carbon fiber, and the two frames and "ratchet-based feet" are fabricated using 3D printing, in photosensitive resin material. For the control system, the controller is powered by 5V power supply, and has serial communication interface/ SPI interface/ I2C interface and number of timers and counters. In particular, in the experiment, the motors of the robot under each locomotion mode are controlled by the corresponding driving law shown in Eqs. (6)–(12), and we use a high-definition camera to capture and record the kinematic status of the robot during its locomotion process, thereby obtaining information such as displacement and velocity.

4.2 Locomotion Test on Different Terrains

4.2.1 Earthworm-Like Locomotion

The displacement and velocity of the robot moving on the flat ground, confined space and ascending slope under the earthworm-like locomotion can be seen in Fig. 5. For

Fig. 4. Prototype of the robot

the confined space, the smaller its height, the lower the average velocity of the robot passing through it, as is shown in Fig. 5(a). The average velocities of the robot when passing through the confined spaces with heights of 6.5 cm and 11.5 cm are 1.84 cm/s (5.0 BL/min) and 5.32 cm/s (14.5 BL/min), respectively. Hence, in order to enable the robot to pass through the narrow spaces quickly and effectively, the minimum height of the confined space that the robot can pass through in the earthworm-like locomotion can be determined as 6.5 cm (1.18 BH). The locomotion sequence of the robot passing through the confined space can be seen in Fig. 5(c). For the ascending slope, the change of displacements of the robot when moving on slopes with inclined angles of 5°, 6°, 7° and 8° is shown in Fig. 5(b). It can be seen that when the inclined angle of the slope is relatively large (i.e., 8°), the velocity of the robot is negative. This indicates that the robot slides downwards along the ascending slope, resulting in failure of the locomotion. Therefore, it can be concluded that the maximum inclined angle of the slope that the robot can climb up is 7°. The locomotion sequence of the robot moving on the slope can be seen in Fig. 5(d).

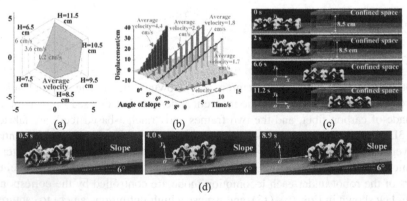

Fig. 5. Earthworm-like locomotion of the robot under different terrains. (a) The relationship between the average velocity of the robot and the height of the confined space that the robot can pass through. (b) Change of displacement of the robot on the slopes with different angles. (c) Locomotion sequence of the robot passing through the confined space. (d) Locomotion sequence of the robot on the slope.

4.2.2 Inchworm-Like Locomotion

Figure 6 shows the displacement and locomotion sequence of the robot moving on the flat ground and ascending slope under the inchworm-like locomotion. Apparently, the displacement of the robot decreases as the angle of the slope increases. This is because the larger the angle of the slope, the easier it is for the robot to slide down the slope under the action of gravity. When the robot moves on the slope with an angle of 10°, it slides down the slope obviously within 8–16 s, as is shown in Fig. 6(a). To this end, the maximum angle of the slope that the robot can pass under the inchworm-like locomotion can be regarded as 9°. The locomotion sequence of the robot when it moves on the 8°-slope can be seen in Fig. 6(b).

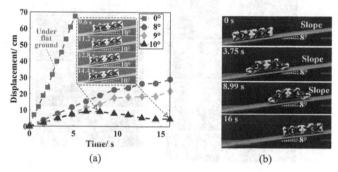

(a)   (b)

Fig. 6. Inchworm-like locomotion of the robot under different terrains. (a) Change of displacement of the robot when it moves on the flat ground and ascending slopes. (b) Locomotion sequence of the robot when moving on the 8° slope.

4.2.3 Tumbling Locomotion

The locomotion of the robot under the tumbling mode can be seen in Fig. 7. When the robot moves on the flat ground in the tumbling locomotion, its displacement is shown in Fig. 7(a). It can be obtained that the average velocity of the robot is 12.43 cm/s (33.90 BL/min) on the flat ground. For the gap, the process of the robot crossing the gap with width of 4.5 cm and 5.5 cm is shown in Fig. 7(b). At first, the tumbling locomotion is carried out, and the node H crosses the gap when $t = 1.12$ s. Then the robot continues the tumbling locomotion, and the whole robot crosses the gap when $t = 2.16$ s. In particular, the node H may fall into the gap during the tumbling locomotion ($t = 0.77$ s, Fig. 7(b)) when the width of the gap is 5.5 cm. Therefore, the maximum width of the gap that the robot can cross is 4.5 cm (0.21 BL). For the obstacle, the process of the robot climbing obstacle with the height of 3 cm is shown in Fig. 7(c). When a cycle of tumbling locomotion completes ($t = 2.61$ s), the node H climbs onto the obstacle. After that, the earthworm-like locomotion is conducted to make the robot continue moving forward. If the height of the obstacle increases to 4 cm, the node H cannot be up the obstacle at the end of the tumbling locomotion ($t = 2.61$ s, Fig. 7(d)). The subsequent earthworm-like locomotion cannot be realized, and the robot cannot climb up the obstacle. Therefore, the maximum height of the obstacle that the robot can climb over is 3 cm (0.55 BH).

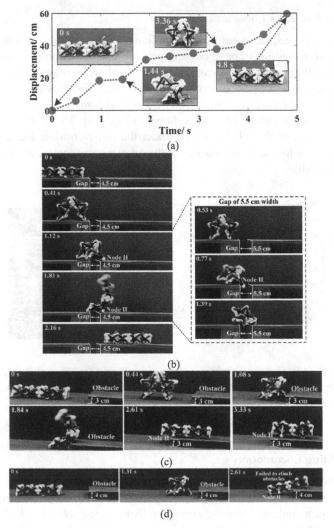

Fig. 7. Tumbling locomotion of the robot under different terrains. (a) Change of displacement of the robot under flat ground; (b) Locomotion sequence of the robot passing through gaps with different widths; (c) Locomotion sequence of the robot climbing up 3 cm-height obstacle; (d) Locomotion sequence of the robot climbing up 4 cm-height obstacle.

4.2.4 Hybrid Locomotion

When the robot passes through the confined space in the hybrid locomotion, the relationship between the average velocity of the robot and the height of the confined space can be seen in Fig. 8(a). Similar to the earthworm-like locomotion, the smaller the height of the confined space, the lower the average velocity of the robot. Therefore, the minimum height of the confined space that the robot can pass through in the hybrid locomotion can be regarded as 6.5 cm (1.18 BH). The locomotion sequence of the robot passing through

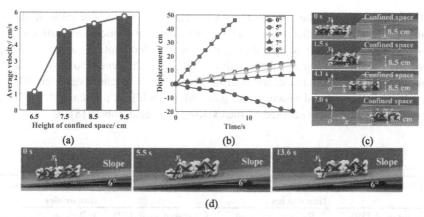

Fig. 8. Hybrid locomotion of the robot under different terrains. (a) The relationship between the average velocity of the robot under the hybrid locomotion and the height of the confined space that the robot can pass through. (b) Change of displacement of the robot on the slopes with different angles. (c) Locomotion sequence of the robot passing through the confined space. (d) Locomotion sequence of the robot on the slope.

the confined space can be seen in Fig. 8(c). When the robot moves on the ascending slope in the hybrid locomotion, its displacement is shown in Fig. 8(b). It can be seen that when the inclined angle of the slope is 8°, it slides down the slope and cannot move forward normally. Hence, it can be concluded that the maximum angle of the slope that the robot can climb up in the hybrid locomotion is 7°. The hybrid locomotion sequence of the robot moving on the slope can be seen in Fig. 8(d).

To sum up, the locomotion ability of the robot under the five typical terrains is shown in Table 3. The maximum velocity of the robot under the flat ground is 33.90 BL/min. The minimum height, maximum angle, maximum height and maximum width of the confined space, slope, obstacle and gap that the robot can pass through are 1.18 BH, 9°, 0.55 BH and 0.21 BL.

Table 3. Locomotion ability of the robot under different terrains

Terrains	Flat ground	Confined space	Ascending slope
Locomotion performance	Max.v = 33.90 BL/min	Min.H_C = 1.18 BH	Max.α = 9°
Terrains	Gap	Obstacle	
Locomotion performance	Max.D_g = 0.21 BL	Max.H_O = 0.55 BH	

4.2.5 Comparison of Our Proposed Robot and Other Related Tensegrity Robot

In Table 4, we summarize several relevant tensegrity robots and compare their number of locomotion modes with ours. In particular, the current tensegrity robots are mostly spherical structure, and they can only achieve one or at most two locomotion modes due to the limitation of their structures. As we can see from the comparison, the main advantage of our robot is that it can achieve four locomotion modes (i.e., earthworm-like, inchworm-like, tumbling and hybrid), and its number of locomotion modes is the largest among the existing tensegrity robots. This advantage brings benefit to the robot that the terrain adaptability is enhanced, and the robot can adapt to at least five different terrains (i.e., flat ground, confined space, slope, gap and obstacle). In particular, these terrains cannot be simultaneously adapted by the existing tensegrity robots [8].

Table 4. Comparison of our robot with other tensegrity robots.

Related robots	Number of locomotion modes	Related robots	Number of locomotion modes
Chung et al. [19]	2, Rolling, jumping	Khazanov et al. [22]	1, Rolling
Chen et al. [13]	2, Waking, rolling	Wang et al. [23]	1, Rolling
Kim et al. [20]	2, Hopping, rolling	Paul et al. [24]	1, Crawling
Koizumi et al. [21]	1, Rolling	Sabelhaus et al. [9]	1, Rolling
Our robot	4, Earthworm-like, inchworm-like, tumbling, hybrid locomotion (adapt to five terrains (flat ground, confined space, slope, gap and obstacle)		

5 Conclusion

This work presents a novel modular tensegrity mobile robot with multi-locomotion modes. The robot can achieve four locomotion modes, namely earthworm-like, inchworm-like, tumbling and hybrid locomotion. Naturally, motion planning of the four locomotion modes based on the kinematic model is conducted to obtain the driving law of the motors under each locomotion. Experiments are conducted to demonstrate the robot's locomotion abilities. The obtained results show that the robot can pass through different terrains effectively. The maximum velocity of the robot is 33.90 BL/min, and the minimum height (maximum angle, maximum height, maximum width) of the confined space (slope, obstacle, gap) that the robot can cross over is 1.18 BH (9°, 0.55 BH, 0.21 BL). By comparison, the tensegrity robot proposed in this work has the largest number of locomotion modes among the existing tensegrity robots, and its terrain adaptability is strong. Future work will focus on the self-adaptive mode switch and feedback control of the robot to motivate the autonomous exploration.

Acknowledgments. This work is funded by National Natural Science Foundation of China (grants 52275028).

References

1. Sychterz, A.C., Smith, I.F.C.: Using dynamic measurements to detect and locate ruptured cables on a tensegrity structure. Eng. Struct. **173**, 631–642 (2018)

2. Yang, S., Sultan, C.: Deployment of foldable tensegrity–membrane systems via transition between tensegrity configurations and tensegrity–membrane configurations. Int. J. Solids Struct. **160**, 103119 (2019)
3. Feng, X.D., Miah, M.S., Ou, Y.W.: Dynamic behavior and vibration mitigation of a spatial tensegrity beam. Eng. Struct. **171**, 1007–1016 (2018)
4. Wang, Y.F., Xu, X., Luo, Y.Z.: Minimal mass design of active tensegrity structures. Eng. Struct. **234**, 111965 (2021)
5. Luo, J.L., Rdmunds, R., Rice, F., Agogino, A.M.: Tensegrity robot locomotion under limited sensory inputs via deep reinforcement learning. In: 2018 IEEE International Conference on Robotics and Automation, pp. 6260–5267. IEEE Press, Brisbane (2018)
6. Savin, S., Badr, A.A., Devitt, D., Fedorenko, R., Klimchik, A.: Mixed–integer–based path and morphing planning for a tensegrity drone. Appl. Sci. **12**(11), 5588 (2022)
7. Liu, Y.X., Bi, Q., Yue, X.M., Wu, J., Yang, B., Li, Y.B.: A review on tensegrity structures–based robots. Mech. Mach. Theory **168**, 104571 (2022)
8. Shah, D.S., et al.: Tensegrity robotics. Soft Robotics **9**(4), 639–656 (2021)
9. Sabelhaus, A.P., et al.: System design and locomotion of SUPERball, an untethered tensegrity robot. In: 2015 IEEE International Conference on Robotics and Automation, pp. 1050–4729. IEEE Press, Seattle (2015)
10. Vespignani, M., Friesen, J.M., SunSpiral, V., Bruce, J.: Design of SUPERball v2, a compliant tensegrity robot for absorbing large impacts. In: Maciejewski, A.A., Okamura, A. (eds.) 2018 IEEE/RSJ International Conference on Intelligent Robots and Systems (IROS), pp. 2865–2871. IEEE Press, Madrid (2018)
11. Kim, K., Agogino, A.K., Agogion, A.M.: Emergent form–finding for center of mass control of ball–shaped tensegrity robots (2015)
12. Kim, K., Agogino, A.K., Toghyan, A., Moon, D., Taneja, L., Agogino, A.M: Robust learning of tensegrity robot control for locomotion through form–finding. In: 2015 IEEE/RSJ International Conference on Intelligent Robots and Systems (IROS), pp. 5824–5831. IEEE Press, Hamburg (2016)
13. Chen, L.H., et al.: Soft spherical tensegrity robot design using rod–centered actuation and control. In: 2016 ASME International Design Engineering Technical Conference/Computer and Information in Engineering Conference (IDETC/CIE), vol. 9, p. 025001. ASME, Charlotte (2016)
14. Hao, S.Q., et al.: Configuration design and gait planning of a six-bar tensegrity robot. Appl. Sci. **12**(22), 11845 (2022)
15. Littlefield, Z., Surovik, D., Vespignani, M., Bruce, J., Wang, W.F., Bekris, K.E.: Kinodynamic planning for spherical tensegrity locomotion with effective gait primitives. Int. J. Robot. Res. **38**(12), 1442–1462 (2019)
16. Paul, C., Roberts, J.W., Lipson, H., Cuevas, F.J.V: Gait production in a tensegrity based robot. In: 12th International Conference on Advanced Robotics, pp.216–222. IEEE Press, Seattle (2005)
17. Rovira, A.G., Tur, J.M.M.: Control and simulation of a tensegrity–based mobile robot. Robot. Auton. Syst. **57**(5), 526–535 (2009)
18. Luo, A., Wang, J.D., Liu, H.P.: Four–bar tensegrity robot based on ADAMS simulation. In: 2017 IEEE International Conference on Mechatronics and Automation (ICMA), pp.1463–1468. IEEE Press, Takamatsu (2017)
19. Chung, Y.S., Lee, J.H., Jang, J.H., Choi, H.R., Rodrigue, H.: Jumping tensegrity robot based on torsionally prestrained SMA Springs. ACS Appl. Mater. Interfaces. **11**(43), 40793–40799 (2019)
20. Kim, K., et al.: Hopping and rolling locomotion with spherical tensegrity robots. In: 2016 IEEE/RSJ International Conference on Intelligent Robots and Systems (IROS), pp. 4369–4376. IEEE Press, Daejeon (2016)

21. Koizumi, Y., Shibata, M., Hirai, S.: Rolling tensegrity driven by pneumatic soft actuators. In: 2012 IEEE International Conference on Robotics and Automation, pp. 1988–1993. IEEE Press, Paul (2012)

22. Khazanov, M., Humphreys, B., Keat, W., Rieffel, J.: Exploiting dynamical complexity in a physical tensegrity robot to achieve locomotion. In: The Twelfth European Conference on Artificial Life, pp. 965–972. ASME, Sicily (2013)

23. Wang, Z.J., Li, K., He, Q.G., Cai, S.Q.: A light–powered ultralight tensegrity robot with high deformability and load capacity. Adv. Mater. **31**(7), 1806849 (2019)

24. Paul, C., Valero–Cuevas, F.J., Lipson, H: Design and control of tensegrity robots for locomotion. In: 2006 IEEE/RSJ International Conference on Intelligent Robots and Systems, vol. 22, pp. 944–957. IEEE Press, Edmonton (2005)

Quantum Genetic Algorithm with Fuzzy Control Based on Clustering Analysis

Weipeng Tang[1] (ID), Yan Pan[2] (ID), Haojie Xu[2] (ID), and Yisu Ge[1(✉)] (ID)

[1] College of Computer Science and Artificial Intelligence, Wenzhou University, Wenzhou, China
ysg@wzu.edu.com
[2] State Grid WenZhou Electric Power Supply Company, Wenzhou, China

Abstract. Finding the solution of NP hard problem is an interesting puzzle, and numerous evolutionary algorithms are proposed to accelerate the speed of searching. In recent decades, the quantum computer technology has gradually improved, which is a new tool to reduce the searching time. In order to extend the genetic algorithm in quantum computer for faster convergence, the quantum genetic algorithm with fuzzy control based on clustering analysis is proposed. The operations of genetic algorithm are replaced by the quantum gate circuit First, quantum genetic algorithm is put forward, and the quantum superposition is applied to replace the mutation operation in genetic algorithm. Second, clustering analysis is employed to depict the distribution of solutions. Third, fuzzy control is used to adjust the reproduction parameter adaptively based on the results of clustering analysis. The experiments are designed for proving the performance of the proposed method with different algorithms.

Keywords: Genetic Algorithm · Quantum Computer · Clustering analysis · Fuzzy Control

1 Introduction

With the rapid development of computer technology, more and more evolutionary algorithms emerged endlessly, but finding the solution of NP hard problems with fast speed is still a pursed goal. The NP hard problems contains various interesting puzzles with practical applications, such as traveling salesman problem [1], multimodal optimization problems [2, 3], electric vehicle charging scheduling [4], supply chain management [5], transport route optimization [6], and machine scheduling to drill holes in a circuit board [7], path planning in the field of robotics [8, 9] etc. The above problem is focusing on the optimal solution, and there are some dynamic problems with time limitation. Therefore, performance and efficiency of evolutionary algorithms are both important.

For further decreasing the solution search time in NP hard problem, quantum genetic algorithm(QGA) is proposed, and plenty of researches emerged endlessly in recent decades. On the basis of QGA, the quantum genetic algorithm with fuzzy control based on clustering analysis is proposed. The clustering analysis is utilized to evaluate the

H. Yang et al. (Eds.): ICIRA 2023, LNAI 14267, pp. 323–334, 2023.
https://doi.org/10.1007/978-981-99-6483-3_28

distribution of current solutions, and fuzzy control is employed to adaptively influent the probability amplitude of quantum bits.

There are 13 different test functions with single-peak and multi-peak in the experiments, and 3 different algorithms in competition to prove the performance of the proposed method.

The remaining part of the paper is organized as follows. Section 2 reviews the related works. Then, in Sect. 3, the basic knowledge of quantum computation and operation of quantum genetic algorithm are introduced. Next, the details of quantum genetic algorithm with fuzzy control based on clustering analysis is elaborated in Sect. 4, following which is the verification of the effectiveness and efficiency of the devised method by extensive experiments in Sect. 5. Finally, conclusions are given in Sect. 6.

2 Related Works

In 1996, the quantum theory was combined with the genetic algorithm, and the Quantum Inspired Genetic Algorithm (QIGA) is proposed by Narayanan et al. [10], which is put forward to solve the TSP traveling salesman problem. But the method cannot operated in quantum computer, and Han et al. advanced the Genetic Quantum Algorithm (GQA) [11] in 2000, and Quantum-inspired Evolutionary Algorithm (QEA) [12] in 2002. GQA and QEA used the quantum bit to code chromosomes and operate the quantum chromosomes by quantum gate circuit, which is the fundamental work in quantum genetic algorithm. For improving the QEA performance, the terminal criterion was further considered [13]. After that, numerous works were raised to improve the QEA.

In chromosomes coding, Cruz et al. [14] modified QEA by real-values coding to instead binary-coding. Li et al. [15] coded the chromosomes by bloch coordinate of qubits. Zhao et al. [16] mixed QEA with diploid coding, and inversely mapped the real chromosomes Q-bits in the solution space.

There were many work integrate the QEA with other evolutionary algorithm. Wang et al. [17] used the improved particle swarm optimization algorithm to update quantum angle, and quantum swarm evolutionary algorithm (QSwE) was studied. P-system is connected to QEA for knapsack problem by Zhang et al. [18]. Zhao et al. [19] equipped the QGA by multi-agent strategy for addressing multi-objective combinatorial optimization.

Hossain et al. [20] used the a qubit to represent a particle with position, and inserted the particle theory in QEA. The QEA was extend to multi-objective problem, and Quantum-inspired Multi-objective Evolutionary Algorithm (QMEA) was propose by Kim et al. [21]. After that, more and more works were focus on QEA with multi-objective optimization [22–25].

This article designing a real quantum genetic algorithm which both contains the quantum superposition and quantum gate circuit, and balances the convergence speed and immature convergence is valuable.

3 Basic Knowledge

3.1 Quantum Chromosomes

This article proposes a partitioning of each chromosome into two components namely; classical and quantum chromosomes.

The classical bit can only be either of two type: 0 or 1. In contrast, the superposition state of quantum bit can be 0 and 1 at the same time:

$$|\psi\rangle = \alpha|0\rangle + \beta|1\rangle = \alpha\begin{bmatrix} 1 \\ 0 \end{bmatrix} + \beta\begin{bmatrix} 0 \\ 1 \end{bmatrix} = \begin{bmatrix} \alpha \\ \beta \end{bmatrix} \tag{1}$$

$|\psi\rangle$ is a quantum bit, represented by ket vector, of which the superposition are consist of $|0\rangle$ and $|1\rangle$. Where $|0\rangle$ is the ket vector of 0, which means the part of 0 in superposition, and $|1\rangle$ is the ket vector of 1, which means the part of 1 in superposition. α and β is the probability amplitude of the quantum bit, $\alpha, \beta \in [0, 1]$. The constrain (2) must be satisfied:

$$\alpha^2 + b^2 = 1 \tag{2}$$

where α^2 is the probability when $|\psi\rangle$ collapses to 0, and β^2 is the probability when $|\psi\rangle$ collapses to 1.

3.2 Quantum Gate Circuit

Quantum gate circuit is the way of quantum algorithm to manipulate the quantum bits in quantum computer. The various quantum gates are the basic operation unit.

Hadamard gate is a basic operation to generate quantum superposition, and generally shortened to H gate.

$$H = \frac{1}{\sqrt{2}}\begin{bmatrix} 1 & 1 \\ 1 & -1 \end{bmatrix} \tag{3}$$

$$|+\rangle = H|0\rangle = \frac{1}{\sqrt{2}}\begin{bmatrix} 1 & 1 \\ 1 & -1 \end{bmatrix}\begin{bmatrix} 1 \\ 0 \end{bmatrix} = \frac{\sqrt{2}}{2}|0\rangle + \frac{\sqrt{2}}{2}|1\rangle \tag{4}$$

The quantum bit $|0\rangle$ inputs to the H gate, and the superposition $|+\rangle$ is outputted. It can be applied for initializing the quantum chromosomes.

$RY(\theta)$ gate is the gate used to special quantum bit preparation, which is the useful tool for convert classical chromosomes to quantum chromosomes.

$$RY(\theta) = \begin{bmatrix} cos\left(\frac{\theta}{2}\right) & -sin\left(\frac{\theta}{2}\right) \\ sin\left(\frac{\theta}{2}\right) & cos\left(\frac{\theta}{2}\right) \end{bmatrix} \tag{5}$$

where θ is the parameter which controls the probability amplitude of the quantum bit.

4 Quantum Genetic Algorithm with Fuzzy Control Based on Clustering Analysis

4.1 Quantum Genetic Algorithm

The quantum genetic algorithm (QGA) is modified from genetic algorithm, but there are some different within two algorithms. The QGA splits the GA processes, puts part of work in quantum computer, as presented in Fig. 1.

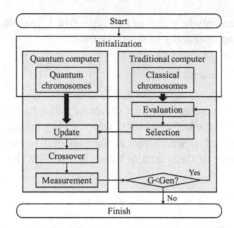

Fig. 1. The process of quantum genetic algorithm

The process is as follows:

Initialization: At the beginning of the algorithm, the chromosomes need to be initialized. There are N individuals in the population. All the quantum bits in quantum chromosomes are initialized from $|0\rangle$ with the H gate, and quantum bits obtain the superposition which collapses to 0 or 1 with the same probability. Then, the quantum measurement is applied, and the quantum chromosomes are collapsed to classical chromosomes.

Evaluation: The fitness evaluation process is only run in digital computer, and the fitness function is applied to calculate the classical chromosome fitness value.

Selection: The selection is process in digital computer based on the fitness value, and the roulette wheel selection operation is used. Before the roulette wheel selection, the tournament selection is worked between individual in previous and current generation, and only the better one can be reserved. The select probability is calculated by Eq. (6).

$$prob_i = \begin{cases} \dfrac{\sum_{j=0}^{N} fit_j - fit_i}{(N-1) \times \sum_{j=0}^{N} fit_j}, & minimum\ problem \\ \dfrac{fit_i}{\sum_{j=0}^{N} fit_j}, & maximum\ problem \end{cases} \tag{6}$$

where fit_i and $prob_i$ are the fitness and select probability of ith individual. The roulette wheel selection is operated N times to get a new population.

Update: After the new population selection, we need to update the quantum chromosomes based on the classical chromosomes, and the quantum computer can continue the subsequent steps. The classical chromosomes should transform to binary form, and one to one update each quantum bit. The R_y gate is utilized to prepare the specific quantum state, and the fuzzy control based on clustering analysis is applied.

Crossover: Crossover operation is worked in quantum computer, and the single point crossover is used in this paper, the process is present as follow:

Step1: Select two quantum chromosomes C^q_i and C^q_{i+1}, where $i = 2 \cdot j, j \in R, i < N$.

Step2: Obtain a random number r within $[0, 1]$, and contrast with the crossover probability parameter P_c. If $c > P_c$, repeat Step1; Else, pick a random number p within $[1, n_r \cdot n_b]$, where $p \in N$.

Step3: keep the state of quantum bits before the crossover position p in two picked chromosomes. The quantum state in the quantum bits after the position p is exchanged one by one by the swap gate.

Step4: repeat the Step1, until all the chromosomes are selected.

Due to the roulette wheel selection, the individuals are selected randomly. Therefore, the crossover operation selecting two adjacent individuals is equivalent to selecting the two individuals randomly.

Elite Strategy: The current best and worst individuals are picked out at first. We compare the current best individual with the global best one. If the current best fitness is better than the global best fitness, the global best individual will be updated. If the global best is better than the current best, the worst individual is replaced by the global best.

4.2 Fuzzy Control Based on Clustering Analysis for Quantum Bit State Update

The distribution of a population is indicative of the optimization stages, and the adaptability of parameter in reproductive processes enhances training efficiency.

Firstly, the clustering analysis should be operated to depict the distribution of population, and the K-means algorithm is employed. The details are as follow:

Step1: Randomly select n_s individuals in current classical chromosomes as the clustering center. This article chooses the first n_s individuals as the center points $CP = \{cp_i | i = 1,2,3,\ldots, n_s\}$, and set the iteration time t as 1.

Step2: Assign the individual p in population to the cluster C_j, $j \in \{1,2,3,\ldots,n_s\}$, where $dis(p, cp_j) < dis(p, cp_i)$, and $dis(a, b)$ is the distance between point a and b. The population is divided into n_s clusters, and clustering result in t^{th} iteration $CR^t = \{C_i | i = 1,2,3,\ldots, n_s\}$ is obtained.

Step3: If the $CR^t = CR^{(t-1)}$ and $t > 1$, the process will be terminated. Otherwise, set $t = t + 1$, and operate Step4.

Step4: update the center point of each cluster by Eq. (7):

$$cp_i^{new} = \frac{1}{M_i} \sum_{p_k \in C_i} p_k \qquad (7)$$

where M_i is the element number in cluster C_i.

Step5: The cp_i^{new} in CP^{new} are chosen as the new center point of each cluster, and Step2 will be started again.

After the clustering, the current population is divided into n_s clusters, and similar points are gathered in the same cluster.

The size of cluster is used to depict the population distribution. The best cluster represents the cluster contains the best individual, and the size of best cluster is S_b. On the contrary, the worst cluster denotes the cluster includes the worst individual, and the size of worst cluster is S_w. The S_b and S_w will the normalized by Eqs. (8) and (9):

$$\hat{S}_b = \frac{S_b - S_{min}}{S_{max} - S_{min}} \qquad (8)$$

$$\hat{S}_w = \frac{S_w - S_{min}}{S_{max} - S_{min}} \tag{9}$$

where S_{max} and S_{min} means the size of biggest cluster and smallest cluster, respectively.

Fuzzification: The inputs of the fuzzy system are variables $\hat{S}_b$ and $\hat{S}_w$, and the fuzzy system should map the input variables $\hat{S}_b$ and $\hat{S}_w$ into suitable linguistic values. Two fuzzy subsets positive small (PS) and positive big (PB) are defined. The degree of memberships are calculated by Eqs. (10) and (11).

$$\mu_0\left(\hat{S}\right) = \mu_{PS}\left(\hat{S}\right) = 1 - \hat{S} \tag{10}$$

$$\mu_1\left(\hat{S}\right) = \mu_{PB}\left(\hat{S}\right) = \hat{S} \tag{11}$$

where $\hat{S}$ equals to $\hat{S}_b$ or $\hat{S}_w$, respectively.

A value $m_{0,1}$ is settled by the algebraic multiplication fuzzy implication of μ_{PS} and μ_{PB}:

$$m_{0,1} = \mu_{PS}\left(\hat{S}_b\right)\mu_{PB}\left(\hat{S}_w\right) \tag{12}$$

The same operation is suitable for others.

Defuzzification: In this process, the fuzzy rules should convert to a crisp value. The output of the inference system is the change value of P_x and P_m, and the P_x and P_m are changed in each generation:

$$P_x(G) = P_x(G - 1) + K_x \delta p_x(G) \tag{13}$$

$$P_m(G) = P_m(G - 1) + K_m \delta p_m(G) \tag{14}$$

where K_x and K_m are the constraint of P_x and P_m, which limit the reproduce parameters to the value range. G is the generation number. The "center of sum method" is applied to compute the crisp value of δp_x and δp_m:

$$\delta p_x = d \frac{\sum_{i=0}^{1} \sum_{j=0}^{1} \mu_i\left(\hat{S}_b\right)\mu_j\left(\hat{S}_w\right)y_{ij}}{\sum_{i=0}^{1} \sum_{j=0}^{1} \mu_i\left(\hat{S}_b\right)\mu_j\left(\hat{S}_w\right)} \tag{15}$$

$$\delta p_m = \frac{\sum_{i=0}^{1} \sum_{j=0}^{1} \mu_i\left(\hat{S}_b\right)\mu_j\left(\hat{S}_w\right)z_{ij}}{\sum_{i=0}^{1} \sum_{j=0}^{1} \mu_i\left(\hat{S}_b\right)\mu_j\left(\hat{S}_w\right)} \tag{16}$$

where y_{ij} and z_{ij} are the center of the output fuzzy set δp_x and δp_m. d is the coefficient used to reduce the amplitude of P_x. Respectively, variation y_{ij} and z_{ij} are either $+1$ or -1, d equals to 0.01. The value setting of y and z are listed in Table 1.

Table 1. Value setting of y and z

(i, j)	$y_{i,j}$	$z_{i,j}$
$(0, 0)$	-1	-1
$(0, 1)$	1	-1
$(1, 0)$	1	1
$(1, 1)$	-1	1

5 Experiment Studies

For proving the performance and efficiency of the proposed method, the two experiments are designed. The first experiment is used to find the best super parameters for the proposed method, and evaluate the influence of parameter selection. Next, the effect of the reproduction parameter adjustment strategy is certificated in the second experiment. By comparing with the other methods in several test function, the problem solving ability of the proposed method is evaluated.

5.1 Experimental Configuration

The parameter setting of *Popsize, Gen, Bound$_q$, Px_init, Pm_init, n_r, n_b, n_s, Runtimes* are listed in Table 2.

Table 2. Parameter setting in experiments

Variable	Value
Popsize	40
Gen	1000
Bound$_q$	0.89
Px_init	0.3
Pm_init	0.05
n_r	5
n_b	20
n_s	9
RunTime	30

Where *Popsize* is the size of population, *Gen* I s the maximum generation size, p_r is the probability of selection operation, *Bound$_q$* means the bound of quantum probability, n_r represents the number of real number in chromosome, n_b is the bit number of each real, n_s denote the center number of cluster, *Runtimes* decides the repeat times of each experiments.

In the experiment, 13 test function is applied, the details are listed in Table 3.

Table 3. Test function

No	function	Value range	Optimal result
1	$f_1(x) = \sum_{i=1}^{D} x_i^2$	[−100, 100]	0
2	$f_2(x) = \sum_{i=1}^{D}|x_i| + \prod_{i=1}^{D}|x_i|$	[−10, 10]	0
3	$f_3(x) = \sum_{i=1}^{D}(\sum_{j=1}^{i} x_j)^2$	[−100, 100]	0
4	$f_4(x) = \max_i(|x_i|, 1 \le i \le D)$	[−100, 100]	0
5	$f_5(x) = \sum_{i=1}^{D}(\lfloor x_i + 0.5 \rfloor)^2$	[−100, 100]	0
6	$f_6(x) = \sum_{i=1}^{D} i x_i^4 + random[0, 1)$	[−1.28, 1.28]	0
7	$f_7(x) = \sum_{i=1}^{D-1}[100(x_{i+1} - x_i^2)^2 + (x_i - 1)^2]$	[−10, 10]	0
8	$f_8(x) = \sum_{i=1}^{D} - x_i \sin(\sqrt{|x_i|}) + 418.9829 \times D$	[−500, 500]	0
9	$f_9(x) = \sum_{i=1}^{D}[x_i^2 - 10\cos(2\pi x_i) + 10]$	[−5.12, 5.12]	0
10	$f_{10}(x) = -20\exp(-0.2\sqrt{\dfrac{1}{D}\sum_{i=1}^{D} x_i^2})$ $- \exp(\dfrac{1}{D}\sum_{i=1}^{D}\cos 2\pi x_i) + 20 + e$	[−32, 32]	0
11	$f_{11}(x) = \frac{1}{4000}\sum_{i=1}^{D} x_i^2 - \prod_{i=1}^{D}\cos(\frac{x_i}{\sqrt{i}}) + 1$	[−600,600]	0
12	$f_{12}(x) = \dfrac{\pi}{D}\{10\sin^2(\pi y_1) + \sum_{i=1}^{D-1}(y_i - 1)^2[1 + 10\sin^2(\pi y_{i+1})]$ $+ (y_D - 1)^2\} + \sum_{i=1}^{D} u(x_i, 10, 100, 4)$ $where\ y_i = 1 + \dfrac{1}{4}(x_i + 1),\ u(x_i, a, k, m) = \begin{cases} k(x_i - a)^m, & x_i > a \\ 0, & -a \le x_i \le a \\ k(-x_i - a)^m, & x_i < -a \end{cases}$	[−50,50]	0
13	$f_{13}(x) = 0.1\{\sin^2(3\pi x_1) + \sum_{i=1}^{D-1}(x_i - 1)^2[1 + \sin^2(3\pi x_{i+1})]$ $+ (x_D - 1)^2[1 + \sin^2(2\pi x_D)]\} + \sum_{i=1}^{D} u(x_i, 5, 100, 4)$	[−50,50]	0

5.2 Evaluate the Influence of Parameter Selection

The bound of quantum probability $Bound_q$ is similar with the mutation probability P_m in GA, which play vital roles in QGA. Therefore, a preliminary experiment is settled to evaluate the influence of $Bound_q$ parameter selection. The average fitness of best individuals is compared in 13 different test functions, and the results are similar. The results in test function 1 is chosen as the representation, of which h the convergence curves are presented in Fig. 2.

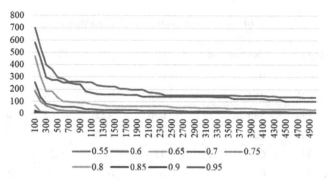

Fig. 2. Convergence curves of parameter selection in [0.5, 1]

As presented in Fig. 2, the changes of $Bound_q$ make great influence of model convergence, and models with $Bound_q$ in {0.85, 0.90, 0.95} can get the effective results. The bigger the $Bound_q$ is, the faster the model convergence. For further determining the crisp value of $Bound_q$, the experiment with range of $Bound_q$ in [0.85, 1.0] is settled. The average fitness in each test function is normalized to [0, 1] and presented in Fig. 3.

The average number of each parameter setting is calculated for evaluating the performance, which are drawn in Fig. 3 with red line. Because the all the test functions are minimum value problem, the smaller average value means the better result, and the model with 0.89 shows the best performance. This value was selected for remaining experiments.

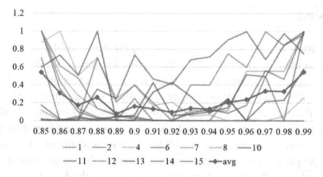

Fig. 3. Test function result with parameter setting in [0.85, 0.99]

5.3 Comparisons with Other Methods

For further proving the performance of the proposed method, the QGA with adaptive parameter adjustment is competed with other methods: GA, QGA-nonad(QGA with fixed Px and Pm) and QEA.

The stability and performance of solutions is listed in Table 4, which evaluates the algorithm by the average and standard deviation of the solution in replication.

Table 4. Comparisons with other methods

	Proposed QGA		QGA-nonad		QEA		GA		Scale
	μ	σ	μ	σ	μ	σ	μ	σ	
1	216	176	219	244	225	315	7354	6353	10–5
2	526	294	585	251	696	422	4362	2041	10–5
3	126	105	106	86	141	138	5517	4864	10–4
4	63	34	66	29	75	30	322	163	10–3
5	0	0	0	0	0	0	0	0	1
6	140	148	146	135	158	142	248	196	10–5
7	3.87	1.59	6.81	18.23	8.29	24.50	8.49	24.48	1
8	234	122	248	147	237	135	1762	6272	10–3
9	499	689	492	805	662	908	815	1057	10–3
10	10.1889	0.0099	10.1870	0.0069	10.1894	0.0098	10.3110	0.0963	1
11	103	71	109	64	91	50	237	87	10–3
12	56	80	58	58	65	60	51	49	10–2
13	24	9	30	13	26	11	31	18	10–2

6 Conclusion

Quantum algorithm is a good way to speed up the NP hard problem solving. The geneticalgorithm is an efficient way to search the optimal solution of NP hard problem. For further improving the solution finding efficiency, a new quantum genetic algorithm is proposed. The mutation operation is instead by the measurement process in quantum algorithm, and the probability of quantum bits is controlled by the adaptive reproduction parameter adjustment strategy which uses the fuzzy control based on the clustering analysis. 13 different test function is utilized in the experiment to prove the performance of the proposed method. And the experiments show the great potential of the proposed method, which get the more stable result with the less generation. However, the advantage of the method in the current experiment is not significant enough, so the improvement of the method will continue. How to use it well to solving the practical problem is our further work.

Acknowledgment. The authors would like to thank the associate editor and reviewers for their valuable comments and suggestions that improved the paper's quality.

References

1. Alhanjouri, M.A., Alfarra, B.: Ant colony versus genetic algorithm based on travelling salesman problem. Int. J. Comput. Tech. Appl **2**(3), 570–578 (2013)
2. Huang, T., Gong, Y.-J., Chen, W.-N., Wang, H., Zhang, J.: A probabilistic niching evolutionary computation framework based on binary space partitioning. IEEE Trans. Cybern. **52**(1), 51–64 (2020)
3. Chen, Z.-G., Zhan, Z.-H., Wang, H., Zhang, J.: Distributed individuals for multiple peaks: A novel differential evolution for multimodal optimization problems. IEEE Trans. Evol. Comput. **24**(4), 708–719 (2019)
4. Liu, W.-L., Gong, Y.-J., Chen, W.-N., Liu, Z., Wang, H., Zhang, J.: Coordinated charging scheduling of electric vehicles: A mixed-variable differential evolution approach. IEEE Trans. Intell. Transp. Syst. **21**(12), 5094–5109 (2019)
5. Rao, T.S.: An evaluation of ACO and GA TSP in a supply chain network. Mater. Today Proc. **5**(11), 25350–25357 (2018)
6. Hacizade, U., Kaya, I.: Ga based traveling salesman problem solution and its application to transport routes optimization. IFAC-PapersOnLine **51**(30), 620–625 (2018)
7. Zhou, Z.-W., Ding, T.-M.: Research on holes machining path planning optimization with tsp and ga. Modular Mach. Tool Autom. Manuf. Tech. **66**(7), 30–32 (2007)
8. Chen, Y., Wu, J.-F., He, C.-S., Zhang, S.: Intelligent warehouse robot path planning based on improved ant colony algorithm. IEEE Access **11**, 12360–12367 (2023)
9. Hu, X., Wu, H., Sun, Q.-L., Liu, J.: Robot time optimal trajectory planning based on improved simplified particle swarm optimization algorithm. IEEE Access **11**, 44496–44508 (2023)
10. Narayanan, A., Moore, M.: Quantum-inspired genetic algorithms. In: Proceedings of IEEE International Conference on Evolutionary Computation. IEEE, pp. 61–66 (1996)
11. Han, K.-H., Kim, J.-H.: Genetic quantum algorithm and its application to combinatorial optimization problem. In: Proceedings of the 2000 Congress on Evolutionary Computation. CEC00 (Cat. No. 00TH8512). IEEE, vol. 2, pp. 1354–1360 (2000)
12. Han, K.-H., Kim, J.-H.: Quantum-inspired evolutionary algorithm for a class of combinatorial optimization. IEEE Trans. Evol. Comput. **6**(6), 580–593 (2002)
13. Han, K.-H., Kim, J.-H.: Quantum-inspired evolutionary algorithms with a new termination criterion, H/sub/spl epsi//gate, and two-phase scheme. IEEE Trans. Evol. Comput. **8**(2), 156–169 (2004)
14. Cruz, A., Vellasco, M., Pacheco, M.:Quantum-inspired evolutionary algorithm for numerical optimization. In: 2006 IEEE International Conference on Evolutionary Computation, pp. 2630–2637 (2006)
15. Li, P., Li, S.: Quantum-inspired evolutionary algorithm for continuous space optimization based on Bloch coordinates of qubits. Neurocomputing **72**(1–3), 581–591 (2008)
16. Zhao, S., Xu, G., Tao, T., Liang, L.: Real-coded chaotic quantum-inspired genetic algorithm for training of fuzzy neural networks. Comput. Math. Appl. **57**(11–12), 2009–2015 (2009)
17. Wang, Y., et al.: A novel quantum swarm evolutionary algorithm and its applications. Neurocomputing **70**(4–6), 633–640 (2007)
18. Zhang, G.-X., Gheorghe, M., Wu, C.-Z.: A quantum-inspired evolutionary algorithm based on P systems for knapsack problem. Fund. Inform. **87**(1), 93–116 (2008)
19. Zhao, D., Tao, F.: A new idea for addressing multi-objective combinatorial optimization: Quantum multi-agent evolutionary algorithms. In: 2009 43rd Annual Conference on Information Sciences and Systems. IEEE, pp. 28–31 (2009)
20. Hossain, M.A., Hossain, M.K., Hashem, M.: Hybrid real-coded quantum evolutionary algorithm based on particle swarm theory. In: 2009 12th International Conference on Computers and Information Technology. IEEE, pp. 13–18 (2009)

21. Kim, Y., Kim, J.-H., Han, K.-H.: Quantum-inspired multiobjective evolutionary algorithm for multiobjective 0/1 knapsack problems. In: 2006 IEEE International Conference on Evolutionary Computation. IEEE, pp. 2601–2606 (2006)
22. Wang, Y., Li, Y., Jiao, L.: Quantum-inspired multi-objective optimization evolutionary algorithm based on decomposition. Soft. Comput. **20**(8), 3257–3272 (2016). https://doi.org/10.1007/s00500-015-1702-9
23. Dey, S., Bhattacharyya, S., Maulik, U.: Quantum inspired nondominated sorting based multi-objective GA for multi-level image thresholding. Hybrid Metaheuristics: Research and Applications, pp. 141–170 (2018)
24. Konar, D., Sharma, K., Sarogi, V., Bhattacharyya, S.: A multi-objective quantum-inspired genetic algorithm (Mo-QIGA) for real-time tasks scheduling in multiprocessor environment. Procedia Comput. Sci. **131**, 591–599 (2018)
25. Liu, T., Sun, J., Wang, G., Lu, Y.: A multi-objective quantum genetic algorithm for MIMO radar waveform design. Remote Sens. **14**(10), 2387 (2022)

Design and Research of a Snake-Like Robot Based on Orthogonal Joint and Wheel Modules

Ran Shi[1]($\boxtimes$), Hailong Zhang[1], Kaiwen Cheng[1], Yunjiang Lou[2], Zezheng Qi[2], Shibing Hao[2], Qianqian Zhang[2], and Danyang Bao[1]

[1] ShenZhen Polytechnic, Shenzhen, China
shiran@szpt.edu.cn
[2] Harbin Institute of Technology, Shenzhen, China

Abstract. Based on the research and analysis of the snake robot at home and abroad, combined with its structural design and theoretical status, a snake robot based on orthogonal joint and wheel modules connection is designed and studied, which can solve a variety of practical ground environment, overcome the limitation that the work space is two-dimensional plane, combined with the complex terrain environment of practical application scenes. Through the control terminal provided by the WEB service of Raspberry Pi deployed, the serpentine robot can realize 3D movement in the working space, high-speed movement on flat terrain, plane turning detour, and has the ability to cross obstacles, grooving terrain and other complex terrain environment. Meanwhile, users can record, take photos, move and other commands through the WEB interface. The motion control system of the snake robot mainly consists of four parts: main controller, visual imaging module, power module and signal source. Remote control can be realized by wireless remote control or WEB control. The WEB control end can provide real-time infrared thermal imaging, RGB images and audio feedback.

Keywords: Snake-like robot · Orthogonal-joint modules · Wheel modules · Disaster rescue

1 Introduction

Serpentine robot is a type of biomimetic robot that resembles a biological snake in appearance and can mimic its movements. Compared with other kinds of robots, snake robot has the advantages of flexible gait, lightness and strong adaptability. It can work in earthquake, fire, military investigation and other complex environments. Snake robot in the field of bionic robots has been a constant research, the results are not only reflected in the theory, the prototype

Supported by the National Key Research and Development Program of China (No. SQ2020YFB130197) and ShenZhen Polytechnic Program(6022310021K) and 2022 Shenzhen Outstanding Scientific and Technological Innovation Talents Training (Doctoral basic research start), Project number :RCBS20210706092213010.

H. Yang et al. (Eds.): ICIRA 2023, LNAI 14267, pp. 335–346, 2023.
https://doi.org/10.1007/978-981-99-6483-3_29

is also a variety of development. In 1970 s, Shigeo Hirose of Tokyo Institute of Technology in Japan proposed the Active Cord Mechanism snake-like robot. The research team led by him developed the world's first snake-like robot named ACM in 1972 [1], followed by continuous in-depth research. Developed representative ACM-III [2], ACM-R2 [3], ACM-R3 [4], ACM-R4 [5] and other land snake robots [6], these robots from simple two-dimensional movement, updated development to adapt to uneven ground. Although various snake-like robots in various research units have achieved fruitful research results, most of them have defects. The swing amplitude of the sinuous motion form will affect its narrow application environment. No matter the structure makes it difficult for the snake robot to travel on slopes or rugged terrain. In order to solve the existing practical problems, this paper designs a remote control snake robot, which is suitable for complex terrain, with high speed, strong obstacle crossing ability, multifunctional characteristics of the snake robot design and research. The purpose is to enter the narrow environment after the disaster to explore, understand the trapped information, in order to facilitate the search and rescue personnel to designate feasible programs, improve the rescue efficiency.

2   Structural Design of the Snake Robot

2.1   Mechanical Structure Design

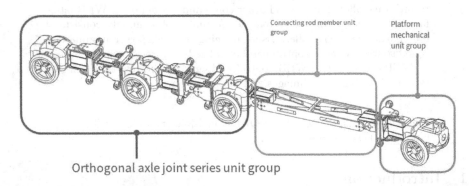

Fig. 1. Schematic diagram of the overall structure of the snake robot.

Aiming at the problems in the existing technology, this paper provides a series structure design of orthogonal shaft joint, which is arranged with the skeleton member for orthogonal connection arrangement. The beneficial effect is to realize the limitation that the working space is a two-dimensional plane, expand the range of activity and improve the flexibility of control. At the same time, combined with the complex terrain environment of the actual application scene, the modular snake robot based on the orthogonal joint connection, To realize 3D movement of the workspace, high-speed movement on flat terrain, plane turning detoured, and the ability to cross obstacles and groove terrain and other complex terrain environment. In terms of the overall mechanical structure, as shown in Fig. 1, it can be divided into three unit groups: orthogonal axis joint series unit group, connecting rod member unit group and platform mechanical unit group.

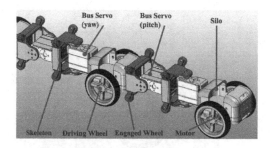

Fig. 2. Structure diagram of series unit group of orthogonal shaft joint.

As shown in Fig. 2, the series unit group of orthogonal shaft joint is composed of two bus steering gear through the skeleton structure orthogonal layout and through a single side open curved box appearance module connected in turn, which is mainly composed of bus steering gear, bin body, skeleton, driving wheel, driven wheel and reduction motor.

The snake robot is equipped with a driving wheel structure., the driving wheel is used to support the snake robot, relieve the impact from the road surface, generate driving force and braking force through the adhesion of the tire to the road surface, and keep the snake body running in a straight line. At the same time, ensure normal steering when doing left and right yaw Angle movement with the bus steering gear in the direction of yaw Angle movement at the skeleton connection. These are the necessary conditions for the robot to move smoothly. The connecting rod bracket of the connecting rod member unit group is H-shaped, and there is a rib plate to strengthen the design. The end is provided with a matching position with the bus steering machine, and the connecting rod matching end of the corresponding connecting rod bracket is arranged in the connecting rod bracket, which is convenient for the arrangement of the electrical control line of the robot. The platform mechanical unit group is composed of a platform silo body with a half-enveloped appearance as its main component. The holes of the platform silo body coincide with the central axis of the mounting hole of the camera case respectively. Two reduction motors are assembled at the bottom holes of the platform silo body, and the output shafts of the two reduction motors coincide with the driving wheels on the left and right sides of the linkage with the central axis.

As shown in Fig. 3 and Fig. 4, the mechanical unit of the platform of the snake robot is assembled with a set of camera modules, among which there is an infrared image transmission device and a conventional image transmission device. When the snake robot enters the working mode of the camera, it will set up the snake head through the snake body support between the snake head and the snake body to shoot and transmit the wounded and the scene situation. As shown in Fig. 3, in the normal state, the snake robot is stretched out. When it moves, it is driven by the bus steering gear and acts with the driving wheel.

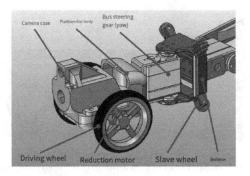

Fig. 3. Structure diagram of the platform mechanical unit group.

Fig. 4. Camera working mode of the snake robot.

2.2   Material Selection and Performance

In this paper, high performance nylon and resin materials are used for 3D printing of main parts, including silo body, skeleton, camera case, etc. The warehouse body parts are mainly made of resin material, which is a kind of ABS stereoscopic light modeling resin. The advantages of this material are that it can print parts with high precision and toughness requirements, good dimensional stability of the model, low shrinkage rate and excellent yellowing resistance, and machinability. The disadvantage is that the thermal deformation temperature is slightly low. The fracture elongation rate of resin material is $8 \sim 14\%$, suitable for tapping, buckle and other toughness requirements, the material is suitable for $1 \sim 3$ tapping; Notched impact strength (ASTM Method D256A) is $36 \sim 60 \, \mathrm{J/m}$, 4 mm thickness of the material product 30 cm height under the natural fall will not break; Material cost compared with the nylon material used in this paper has the advantage of lower cost, performance and cost comprehensive down, in line with the needs of the structure of the warehouse parts. The skeleton, camera box and other parts are mainly made of nylon material, which is a gray black polyamide 12. The advantages of this material are high temperature resistance, good toughness, high strength, and can be used as functional parts. There is no need for support when printing, which is suitable for proofing products with extremely complex structure. The disadvantage is that the surface has a sense of particle, the cost is relatively expensive with resin.

Nylon material fracture elongation of 36%, very suitable for tapping, buckle and other toughness requirements, the material is suitable for 5 ~ 10 tapping; Notched impact strength and non-notched impact strength are $4.9\,KJ/m^2$ and $13.2\,KJ/m^2$ respectively, respectively equivalent to ASTM Method D256A standard $49\,J/m$ and $130\,J/m$, 4mm thickness of the material product 70 cm height under the natural fall will not break, In line with the requirements of the strength of the snake robot parts materials.

2.3   Processing, Fabrication and Assembly

Fig. 5. Simplified prototype of snake robot.

By means of 3D printing additive manufacturing technology, the prototype is manufactured and assembled by itself. The simplified prototype of the assembled snake robot is shown in Fig. 5. It consists of a wheel set combined with two middle connection boxes and bus steering gear, and three middle parts of bus steering gear and skeleton, which are combined with the snake body support between the snake head and the snake body, together with the snake head part and the whole snake body. It is a structure with high redundancy, about 94 cm long, 12 cm wide and 7 cm high. In the attitude of camera working mode, as shown in Fig. 6, it is about 54 cm long, 12 cm wide and 23 cm high.

Fig. 6. Camera working mode attitude and ready to take pictures attitude of the snake robot.

3   Design of the Control System of the Snake Robot

3.1   Working Principle of the Control System

As shwon in Fig. 7, the snake-like robot currently developed has a WEB control terminal through the WEB service deployed in Raspberry PI. Users can record, take photos, move and other commands through the WEB interface. The Raspberry PI only needs to judge the command return symbol pressed by the user on the WEB end and then issue commands to different controllers. And then further calculate the requirements, and then speed up the response time of the main program, in order to deal with the problems caused by network delay.

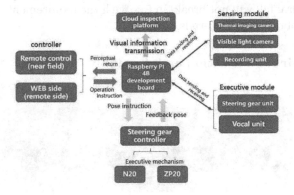

Fig. 7. Control principle of the current model.

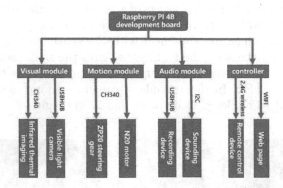

Fig. 8. Shows the communication structure topology.

The communication structure topology is shown in Fig. 8. This system mainly uses the four USB ports of the Raspberry PI as the connection mode. If other USB peripherals (such as remote control) are needed, the infrared thermal imaging device can be moved to the serial port pin of the Raspberry PI for communication. Since it uses USB as the connection mode, it can be directly powered by USB. Therefore, when the serial port connection is used, the external power supply needs to be carried out separately or the power supply cable should be introduced into the 5 V interface of the Raspberry PI.

3.2 Control Theory

According to the preliminary plan assignment and demand analysis, there are two theories for the application of snake robot, one is the theory of bionic meandering movement, and the other is the theory of planar 2R robot movement over obstacles. Although meandering motion is one of the most bionic motion modes, it will waste too much kinetic energy in the process of movement. Therefore, most practical snake robots do not rely too much on meandering motion. At the same time, since the theory itself is not calculated by itself, we will not elaborate too much. The meandering motion control function of the snake robot is

$$\begin{cases} \theta_t(t) = (\frac{e^{nt}-1}{e^{nt}+1})\alpha\sin(\omega t + (i-1)\beta) \\ \psi_i(t) = 0 \end{cases} \tag{1}$$

where, $\theta_t(t)$ is control function of the ith yaw joint of the snake robot; $\psi_i(t)$ is the control function of the ith pitching joint of the snake robot; α, β, ω are control parameters and η is the optimize parameters.

The turning motion control function of the snake robot is

$$\begin{cases} \theta_t(t) = (\frac{e^{nt}-1}{e^{nt}+1})\alpha\sin(\omega t + (i-1)\beta) + \gamma \\ \psi_i(t) = 0 \end{cases} \tag{2}$$

where, γ is the additional control parameters.

The realization of the lifting of the head joint of the snake robot can greatly expand the field of vision and improve the practical performance of the robot. The lifting of the front joint has practical research significance for the snake robot to enter the working mode of photographing. The rotation curve of each pitching joint in the lifting motion is planned as Follows,

$$\begin{cases} \varphi_{Yt}(t) = A_i\sin(\omega t) + B_i \\ \varphi_{pi}(t) = 0 \end{cases} \tag{3}$$

where, $\varphi_{Yt}(t)$ is the rotation value of the ith pitching joint, i = 1,2,3,4; $\varphi_{pi}(t)$ is the rotation value of the ith yaw joint, i=1,2,3... , 9; ω is the rotational angular frequency; A_i is the amplitude parameter; B_i is the center adjustment parameter.

And the current model of the final use of the theory for the plane 2R robot motion control theory, the theory is through a relatively simple geometric method of inverse kinematics calculated. According to the head motion control analysis, the head pitching motion of the snake robot can be regarded as a two-link mechanism, as shown in the right pose in Fig. 9.

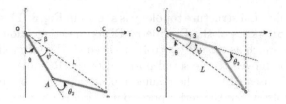

Fig. 9. Right side pose.

4   Prototype Experiment of Snake Robot

The grassland terrain marching experiment is shown in Fig. 10. Grass leaves are soft when rooted in the soil, which is a test of the driving wheel of the snake robot.

Fig. 10. Experimental walking of the snake robot on the grassland terrain.

Then sand and stone terrain walking experiment is shown in Fig. 11. There are many places in the outdoor environment with complex sand and stone terrain. Whether the snake robot can adapt to and march through the terrain is of great concern. In this kind of environment, the snake robot has relatively smooth moving ability.

Fig. 11. Experiment of the snake robot walking on sandy and gravel terrain.

Obstacle crossing experiment is shown in Fig. 12. By lifting the snake body, the snake robot can cross the steps with a height of 30 cm. The steps with a high drop are the key to test whether the snake robot can travel on the rugged terrain. The snake robot can successfully cross the steps with this height through attitude adjustment.

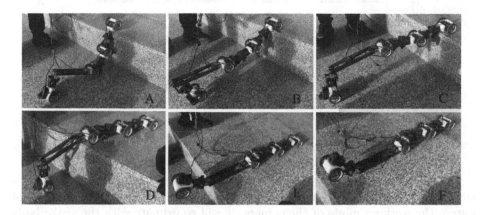

Fig. 12. Obstacle jumping experiment of snake robot.

The experiment of crossing gaps is shown in Fig. 13. The outdoor field inevitably has a wide void terrain, and whether it can cross the void alone without external help is a test of the capabilities of the snake robot in this paper. In the test of crossing the void, a void of 35 cm is set, so that the snake robot can coordinate and realize the crossing through the control system.

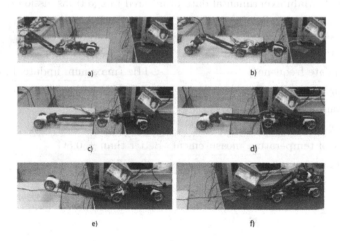

Fig. 13. Experiment of the snake robot crossing the gap.

The continuous obstacle crossing experiment is shown in Fig. 14. The snake-like robot can also realize the obstacle crossing of two steps by continuously passing obstacles at a height of 30 cm.

Fig. 14. Continuous obstacle crossing of a snake robot.

The camera module of the snake robot includes an infrared image transmission device and a conventional image transmission device. When the snake robot enters the working mode of the camera, it will coordinate with the snake body support between the snake head and the snake body, set up the snake head, take pictures of the wounded and the situation on the scene, and transmit pictures. Infrared image transmission device is composed of IRM-80X62-USB serial infrared thermal imager and its FPC line, circuit board, etc., which can directly output temperature data and heat source information, convenient and easy to use. The main experimental data of the device are shown in Table 1.

Table 1. Main experimental data of infrared image transmission device.

Project	Experimental data
Image array size	80 (H) x 62 (V)
Image update frequency	< 1 Hz (maximum update data 4 Hz)
Field Angle	44 x 35°C
Power consumption	0.5 W or less
Serial baud rate	921600
Accuracy of temperature measurement	Better than ± 0.5C
Operating temperature	−20 + 65

Table 2. Main experimental data of the conventional graph transmission device.

Project	Experimental data
Resolution	640 * 480
Camera size	25 * 30 * 22 (mm)
EFL	2.8
F/No	2.8
BFL(Optical)	3.6 mm
Pixel size	3.4 μm * 3.4 μm
Sensor type	(1/6 ")

The conventional image transmission device is composed of a USB drive-free HD camera suitable for Raspberry Pi. The main experimental data of the device are shown in Table 2.

There are 7 indexes in motion realization, which are walking speed, minimum passable hole, climbing Angle, obstacle height, passable step size, ditch width and turning radius. The results of the movement experiment data are shown in Table 3.

Table 3. Exercise realization index and experimental data results.

Project	Indicators	Experimental conditions
Walking speed	≮ 0.2 m/s	0.28 m/s
Available through minimum hole	0.25* 0.25 m	0.15 * 0.15 m
Angle of climb	≮ 30°	40°
Obstacle crossing height	≮ 0.25 m	0.35 m
Climbable step-over size	Height 0.175 m Width 0.26 m	Height 0.3 m Width 0.26 m
Width of the ditch	≮ 0.2 m	Up to 0.5 m
Turning radius	≯ 0.3 m	0.25 m

It can be seen from the data in Table 3 that the experimental conditions of the robot can pass the designed project and its indicators. Although there are slight errors in the experimental process, it meets the design requirements within the acceptable range.

5   Conclusion

In order to make up for the disadvantages of the current common snake robot such as low speed, poor obstacle crossing ability and poor flexibility, and at the same time meet the higher requirements of traveling in complex environment, passing in narrow space and cooperating with sensing instruments. In this paper, combined with the domestic and foreign snake robot research field analysis, combined with its actual needs, complete the structure of the snake robot design and describe the design and assembly of the way, and the key structure of the parts by 3D printing production. At the same time in the material selection and performance parameters of the study, and the design of its control system is described and the theoretical analysis of motion control. In order to verify the practical application of the snake robot designed in this paper and judge the rationality and reliability of its design, an engineering prototype of the snake robot was produced and tested in the complex environment such as outdoor field and sundry pile, to evaluate the situation in the process of moving. The experimental results show that the snake robot designed in this paper based on the orthogonal joint module connecting platform components can realize three-dimensional movement in the working space, high-speed movement on flat terrain, plane turning detour, can pass narrow space environment, has the ability to cross obstacles and grooving terrain and other complex terrain environment. It can be used with sensing instruments for different needs such as disaster relief, search and rescue exploration, environmental detection, anti-terrorism and anti-riot. It has the advantages of flexible control, reliable performance, multi-function and expansion.

References

1. Hirose, S.: Biologically Inspired Robots: Snake-like Locomotors and Manipulators. Oxford University Press, Oxford (1993)
2. Endo, G., Togawa, K., Hirose, S.: Study on self-contained and terrain adaptive active cord mechanism. In: IEEE International Conference on Intelligent Robots and Systems, pp. 1399–1405 (1999)
3. Mori, M., Hirose, S.: Three-dimensional serpentine motion an ad lateral rolling by active cord mechanism ACM-R3. In: Intelligent Robots and Systems. IEEE/RSJ International Conference on IEEE, vol. 1, pp. 829–834 (2002)
4. Takaoka, S., Yamada, H., Hirose, S.: Snake-like active wheel robot ACM-R4. 1 with joint torque sensor and limiter. In: Intelligent Robots and Systems (IROS), 2011 IEEE/RSJ International Conference on IEEE, pp. 1081–1086 (2011)
5. Yamada, H., Takaoka, S., Hirose, S.: A snake-like robot for real-world inspection applications (the design and control of a practical active cord mechanism). Adv. Robot. **27**(1), 47–60 (2013)
6. Ohashi, T., Yamada, H., Hirose, S.: Loop forming snake-like robot ACM-R7 and its Serpenoid oval control. In: Intelligent Robots and Systems (IROS), 2010 IEEE/RSJ International Conference on IEEE, pp. 413–418 (2010)

Multi-sensor Tightly Coupled SLAM Algorithm Based on Feature Planes in Indoor Scenes

Wenxue Hu[1], Zehua Wang[2], Kui Yang[1], Jiahui Zhu[1], and Dongtai Liang[1](✉)

[1] Ningbo University, Ningbo, China
liangdongtai@nbu.edu.cn
[2] Quanhang Technology Co., Ltd., Ningbo, China

Abstract. A tightly coupled multi-sensor SLAM algorithm based on feature planes in indoor scenes is proposed for laser SLAM algorithms in indoor environments affected by glass and mirrors and with few feature points. Firstly, the odometry motion estimation is performed by fusing inertial guidance, and the key frames are judged by the positional transformation. Secondly, the key frames are extracted based on RANSAC, matched with the data in the feature plane manager, and then the data are merged and expanded. Finally, the LIDAR data information, inertial guidance information and feature plane information are put into the sliding window optimizer and solved by nonlinear optimization to obtain the optimal poses and maps. To verify the effectiveness of the algorithm, experiments are conducted in real indoor scenes and detailed comparisons are made on the optimization time and localization accuracy. The experimental results show that this method achieves better positional estimation accuracy and shows good robustness and real-time performance compared with current advanced laser SLAM methods.

Keywords: SLAM · Indoor Environment · Feature Plane · Sliding Window

1 Introduction

To solve the indoor localization problem, in recent years, many researchers have focused on using airborne sensors to achieve simultaneous localization and mapping (SLAM). Although vision-based approaches have advantages in loop closure detection, the influence of the external environment makes visual SLAM limited. In contrast, LiDAR-based approaches can work even at night, and LiDAR has light invariance and accurate perception of the surrounding environment, which improves algorithmic robustness.

SLAM systems are coupled in two ways: loosely coupled and tightly coupled. Loosely coupled SLAM systems can fuse data from different sensors through recursive filters; this approach is usually more flexible and easy to deploy, but may lead to information loss and inaccurate estimation [1, 2]. Compared to loosely coupled systems, tightly coupled SLAM systems [3–5] use point cloud observation information directly

Supported by Zhejiang Province Public Welfare Technology Application Research Program Project (LGG21E050008) and Ningbo Public Welfare Science and Technology Program Project (2022S004).

in the back-end algorithm to optimize the localization and map building results, and also compensate and initialize the high-frequency motion information output from the combined system in the front-end point cloud matching to obtain higher accuracy [6].

Although existing laser-inertial odometry (LIO) systems have achieved very high accuracy and robustness, there are still many problems in practical applications. LIO has cumulative drift and requires optimization of many point cloud positions, key frame poses, and IMU states, making the algorithm difficult to solve in real time on mobile devices. There are many planar structures in indoor environments, and planar constraints have two main advantages. 1): planes are larger structural features compared to feature points, thus effectively suppressing the cumulative drift of SLAM; 2): planes can model larger environments using fewer parameters compared to feature points. Therefore, how to use planar features to improve the localization accuracy and stability of SLAM and reduce the system complexity is an important issue to be addressed. There are many algorithms [7–12] that use line and plane features to improve the accuracy and robustness of SLAM in complex environments. Taguchi Y et al. [7] used any combination of three point/plane primitives to register 3D data in two different coordinate systems. The Structure-SLAM algorithm [9] uses a convolutional neural network from each input RGB image to real-time predicting surface normals and calculating the bit-pose transformation based on point and line features. Li et al. [10] proposed visual SLAM based on fusion of point, line, and surface features. Paper [11] proposed π factors to significantly reduce the computational complexity of planar adjustment. The VIP-SLAM algorithm [12] proposed a tightly coupled visual/inertial/planar SLAM system. Most of the above algorithms are visual or pure laser SLAM, and no complete tightly coupled laser/inertial/planar SLAM system is proposed.

To further improve the trajectory accuracy and robustness of laser SLAM algorithm in indoor scenes, this paper proposes a tightly coupled SLAM algorithm that fuses LiDAR data information, IMU data information and structured plane information to address the above-mentioned problems of laser SLAM. The system framework is shown in Fig. 1, which is mainly divided into four modules: input, front-end odometry, feature plane manager, and back-end optimization.

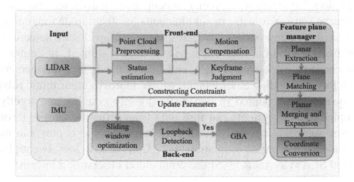

Fig. 1. Algorithm flow chart

The main contributions of this paper are as follows:

(1) Introducing the feature plane into the laser SLAM system and building a feature plane manager to manage its index, parameters and the contained point clouds.

(2) The residuals composed of point clouds contained in the planes are compressed into one to reduce the computational cost of planar constraints.

(3) Integrate all the information into a unified nonlinear optimization framework and update the parameters of the objects in the plane manager in real time.

2   Feature Planes Manager

Glass in indoor environment has a large interference to LiDAR, and plane is a common structure in buildings, especially in indoor environment, so a small number of planes can be used to represent large scenes. In this paper, $\varphi = [n; d]$ is used to represent the plane, where n is the normal vector of the plane, which satisfies $|n| = 1$, d is the signed distance from the coordinate origin to the plane φ. Since most of the planes in the indoor environment are horizontal or vertical, only the detection of horizontal and vertical planes are considered in this paper.

2.1   Key Frame Judgment

The key frame can effectively improve the real-time performance of the algorithm and the extraction of the plane is performed only when the current frame is the key frame due to the existence of the sliding window. The pre-integration of the IMU in the front-end odometer provides the initial value for the state of the platform, and the key frames are selected according to the results of the state estimation, which is judged by the following criteria:

1) whether the time interval between the current frame and the latest data frame is greater than 0.2 s;

2) whether the distance between the current frame and the latest key frame is greater than 0.15 m;

3) whether the rotation angle between the current frame and the latest key frame is greater than 10°;

2.2   RANSAC-Based Planar Extraction

The RANSAC algorithm [13] uses random sampling to fit the 3D point cloud data to estimate the planar mathematical model parameters, which is fast and effective. The number of point clouds, the number of iterations and the distance error threshold of the RANSAC algorithm are determined, and for the planar model fitted by RANSAC is set as:

$$Ax + By + Cz + D = 0 \tag{1}$$

For the current point cloud data P in the random 3 point clouds $P_1(x_1, y_1, z_1)$, $P_2(x_2, y_2, z_2)$, $P_3(x_3, y_3, z_3)$ for plane fitting, from which you can determine the four parameters A, B, C, D, calculate the point cloud data in any point $P_i(x_i, y_i, z_i)$ to the fitted out plane distance D_i.

$$D_i = \frac{|Ax_i + By_i + Cz_i + D|}{\sqrt{A^2 + B^2 + C^2}} \tag{2}$$

For the distance D_i less than the preset error threshold, the points are considered as local points (point clouds satisfying the fitted plane function), and the number of valid local points is counted. Iterate sequentially until the maximum number of iterations is satisfied, select the plane model with the most intra-local points, and repeat the procedure until

$$\frac{\text{Remaining}}{\text{Total}} < \eta \tag{3}$$

The plane filtering conditions are as follows:

1) the points matched by the plane are greater than N;
2) the plane $\varphi = [n; d]$ satisfies perpendicular or parallel to the direction of gravity, i.e. the angle of the normal vector is less than θ_1;
3) the plane is to be tracked by more than 3 key frames;

η, N and θ_1 are obtained according to the actual scene tuning, and will be assigned in Sect. 4.2. The extraction effect is shown in Fig. 2.

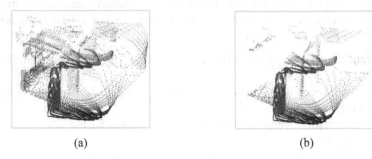

(a)   (b)

Fig. 2. Planar extraction. (a): before extraction; (b): after extraction

2.3 Plane Merging and Expansion

The feature plane manager is based on the world coordinate system, so the extracted planes are to be matched with the planes under the world coordinate system with the following conversion relations:

$$D_{ki} = t_{b_k}^W \cdot n_{W_i} + d_{W_i} \tag{4}$$

$$\theta_{W_{ikj}} = arccos\left(\left|n_{k_j} \cdot (R_W^{b_k} n_{W_i})\right|\right) \times 180 \div \pi \tag{5}$$

$$D_{W_{ik_j}} = \left| D_{ki} - d_{k_j} \right| \tag{6}$$

where $(\cdot)_{b_k}^{W}$ represents the data at the kth frame in world coordinates, R, t denotes rotation and translation, respectively, n_{W_i} and d_{W_i} denote the data of the ith plane under the world coordinate system, respectively, D_{ki} is the distance from the coordinate origin of the kth frame to the ith plane, n_{k_j} and d_{k_j} denote the data of the jth plane under the current frame, and $\theta_{W_{ik_j}}$, $D_{W_{ik_j}}$ denotes the distance and angle between the ith and j^{th} planes, respectively, and matching is completed when a certain angle θ_2 and distance threshold D_{dis} are satisfied, at which time the plane is merged. If it is not satisfied, the newly detected plane is converted to the world coordinate system, stored in the manager, and given a new index.

3   Sliding Window Nonlinear Optimization

The initial poses are obtained from the front-end odometer by fusing the IMU, and the initial values will be further optimized and updated by the back-end. The keyframe-based scheme was originally proposed and widely used for visual odometry, and the tightly coupled LIO in [14] achieves direct LiDAR-IMU fusion through sliding window optimization. However, since this scheme fuses each frame of LiDAR scans, real time is usually not achievable. Therefore, a sliding window is established using key frames to unify LiDAR data information, inertial guidance information, and planar information through nonlinear optimization, as shown in Fig. 3. Since IMU pre-integration constraints and line-plane feature constraints are common constraints in laser SLAM, this paper focuses on planar residual construction.

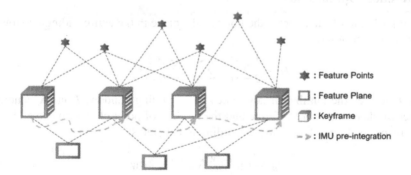

Fig. 3. Block diagram of tightly coupled nonlinear optimization

3.1   Planar Residual Construction

Above, operations such as plane extraction are performed on keyframes, where they are matched with the data in the plane manager according to their indexes, and then the plane

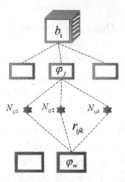

Fig. 4. Point face constraints on feature planes

parameters and keyframe poses are jointly optimized by constructing point-to-plane distance residuals, which are formed as shown in Fig. 4.

In the figure, b_i denotes the ith keyframe in the sliding window, φ_j denotes the jth plane extracted from the current keyframe, φ_w denotes the plane matched with φ_j in the plane manager, N_{ijk} denotes the kth point seen in the jth plane in the ith keyframe, and r_{ijk} denotes the plane distance from point N_{ijk} to φ_w. Then the point-to-plane residuals can be defined as:

$$r_{ijk} = [\varphi_W]_n^T (R_{b_i}^W N_{ijk} + t_{b_i}^W) + [\varphi_W]_d \tag{7}$$

where $[\varphi_W]_n$, $[\varphi_W]_d$ denotes the normal vector of the plane and the distance from the origin of the coordinates to the face, respectively.

3.2 Residual Optimization

From Eq. (7), the residuals from the point to the plane in the entire sliding window can be obtained as follows:

$$E = \frac{1}{2} \sum_{i=1}^{I} \sum_{j=1}^{J} \sum_{k=1}^{K} r_{ijk}^2 \tag{8}$$

where I denotes the number of keyframes in the sliding window, J and K denote the number of planes in each keyframe and the number of point clouds contained in each plane, respectively. r_{ijk}^2 Expanding according to (7) yields:

$$r_{ijk}^2 = \varphi_W^T T_{b_i}^W N_{ijk} N_{ijk}^T T_W^{b_i} \varphi_W \tag{9}$$

where $T_{b_i}^W$ represents the chi-square matrix in Eq. Then the residuals in each plane are:

$$E_{bj} = \sum_{k=1}^{K} r_{ijk}^2 = \varphi_W^T T_{b_i}^W \underbrace{\left(\sum_{k=1}^{K} N_{ijk} N_{ijk}^T \right)}_{G_{ij}} T_W^{b_i} \varphi_W \tag{10}$$

Thus, for each plane φ_j, only G_{ij} needs to be computed once. This consolidates numerous point cloud constraints into a single constraint, greatly reducing the computational cost of the optimizer.

4   Experiment

4.1   Experimental Hardware and Platform Construction

The hardware platform of the mobile robot used in this experiment is shown in Fig. 5, which consists of Scout four-wheel differential mobile robot, Livox-Avia LIDAR and built-in IMU and PC, where the CPU of the PC is Intel i5 processor with 16 GB memory and no GPU acceleration is used. The data processing side is the operating system of Ubuntu 18.04, and the individual sensor data is based on the ROS platform to achieve communication with the PC side.

Fig. 5. Experimental hardware platform

4.2   Experimental Analysis of Odometer Accuracy

Most of the open source datasets are mechanical radar and recorded under large outdoor scenes, while this paper aims to solve the indoor positioning and map building problem. Therefore, the dataset was recorded in a real indoor scene and divided into two sequences, Easy_Dataset and Medium_Dataset. Some of the algorithms [15] have requirements on the number of lines for online surface feature extraction, so the laser SLAM algorithms adapted to the Livox series were chosen: FAST-LIO [5], livox_horizon_loam, loam_livox [16], and LIO-Livox, and the comparison algorithms were taken from GitHub and performed as suggested by the authors The tuning was referenced and run five times on the same platform to take the best results. The performance of this algorithm is judged by running the Cartographer algorithm using the robot equipped with LIDAR and comparing the acquired trajectories as true values with those obtained by other algorithms. Since some of the algorithms do not have loopback function, for fairness, only the odometer accuracy is compared and the root mean square error (RMSE) of the absolute trajectory and the mean value are used for comparison.

Easy_Dataset. Easy_Dataset refers to the indoor closed corridor environment recorded using the experimental platform. Three constraints are involved in the back-end optimization of this algorithm, which are the IMU pre-integration constraint, the point-to-plane distance constraint of feature points, and the feature plane constraint. Among them, the most time-consuming for CPU computation is the feature point-to-plane distance constraint, and the plane is especially obvious in the indoor corridor environment, where the line surface features are contained in the extracted plane. Therefore, it is sufficient to consider only the remaining two constraints under this sequence. The proposed method requires setting some threshold parameters, which are obtained according to different scenario tuning, and the values of the parameters used in the Easy_Dataset sequence are shown in Table 1.

Table 1. Easy_Dataset sequence parameter settings

Parameter	Value	Parameter	Value
η	0.4	$D_{dis}/(m)$	0.15
N	1000	P_{e_filter}	0.1
$\theta_1/(°)$	7	P_{s_filter}	0.2
$\theta_2/(°)$	7	P_{f_filter}	0.2

P_{e_filter}, P_{s_filter}, and P_{f_filter} are the down-sampling parameters of corner points, surface points, and all points, respectively, and the performance of the system can be judged intuitively by the platform positional accuracy estimated by the system. In order to show the comparison effect more clearly, the optimal and suboptimal algorithms for this dataset are selected for comparison with the algorithms in this paper. The effect is shown as follows:

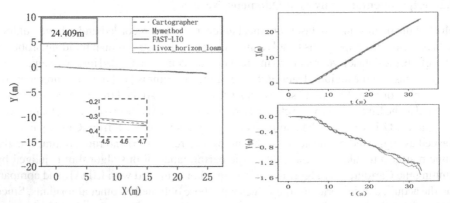

Fig. 6. Comparison between the estimated trajectory of the Easy_Dataset sequence algorithm and the actual trajectory

Figure 6 visualizes the comparison of the platform motion trajectory estimated by FAST-LIO, livox_horizon_loam algorithm and the method in this paper with the real trajectory of the platform under this sequence. The total mileage of the route is shown in the upper left corner, and the red box is a local zoomed-in view. Obviously, the trajectories obtained by the three algorithms are comparable to the real trajectories, and all of them show a high level of localization. For this sequence, this algorithm compares the back-end optimization time with other algorithms, and to avoid chance, the average value of ten optimization times is taken, and the results are shown in Table 2. The "/" in the table indicates that the algorithm has no corresponding time analysis results for this data set. According to the comparison results, it can be seen that the present algorithm saves a lot of time cost at the back-end optimization and also shows a great advantage over pure laser SLAM. The main reason is that the point cloud extracted from each radar frame is correlated with the feature planes and thus the residuals are optimized, effectively replacing the constraints of the line-plane features. The method streamlines thousands of point cloud residuals to single digits and improves the real-time performance of the system.

Table 2. Comparison of backend optimization time between this algorithm and the comparison algorithm (Unit: s)

Algorithm	FAST-LIO	Livox_horizon_loam	Livox_horizon_loam_imu	LIO-Livox	loam_livox	My method
Time	0.006142	0.005544	0.008453	/	0.012427	**0.001562**

Medium_Dataset. Medium_Dataset sequences, on the other hand, are recorded using the platform for indoor office and school building environments, and the consistent location of the start and end of the recording can be used for cumulative drift assessment for long time trajectory estimation. And due to the presence of glass and mirrors, the laser odometry method will inevitably experience cumulative drift, which in turn better validates the effectiveness of the algorithm in this paper.

Table 3. Medium_Dataset sequence parameter settings

Parameter	Value	Parameter	Value
η	0.2	$D_{dis}/(m)$	0.1
N	300	P_{e_filter}	0.2
$\theta_1/(°)$	5	P_{s_filter}	0.4
$\theta_2/(°)$	5	P_{f_filter}	0.3

Similar to Easy_Dataset, the optimal and suboptimal results of the comparison algorithm are selected for comparison with this algorithm, and the corresponding threshold parameters are also set for complex environments, as shown in Table 3. Figures 7 and 8 show the comparison of the platform motion trajectory estimated by FAST-LIO and livox_horizon_loam_imu algorithms with the present algorithm with the real trajectory under Medium_Dataset_01 and Medium_Dataset_02 sequences, respectively. The blue box in the upper left corner indicates the mileage of the route, and the scene plan is shown in the lower right corner.

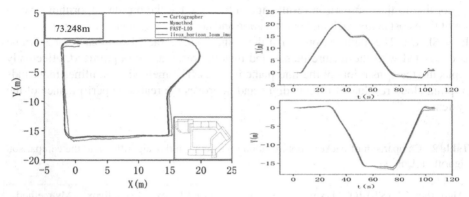

Fig. 7. Comparison between the estimated trajectory of the Medium_Dataset_01 sequence algorithm and the actual trajectory

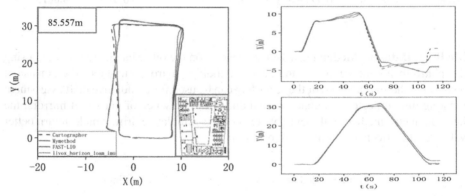

Fig. 8. Comparison between the estimated trajectory of the Medium_Dataset_02 sequence algorithm and the actual trajectory

From the data recorded in Table 4, it can be seen that in the wall-based Easy_Dataset sequence, both the present algorithm and the comparison algorithm exhibit higher localization accuracy, but for the time cost consumption of the optimizer, the present algorithm shows a greater advantage by using the feature plane optimization constraint, which provides an effective way for the real-time performance of the mobile platform. Medium_Dataset sequence, on the other hand, better Loam's livox series livox_horizon_loam algorithm, after incorporating IMU, the algorithm shows better localization performance, which is due to the fact that the initial value obtained by pre-integration of IMU in a short time is better than the constant velocity model estimation. Lio-livox and loam_livox algorithms, due to over-reliance on feature points, resulting in failure of tracking in the Medium_Dataset sequence, and even in the case that the algorithms do not work. Compared with the stability and high accuracy shown by each algorithm in the 01 sequence, the 02 sequence is quite different. Livox_horizon_loam algorithm has larger errors and even reverse direction odometer estimates due to the presence of a large number of mirrors and glass and narrow corners in the 02 sequence. The back-end optimization of laser SLAM depends on the point-plane residuals to optimize the relative poses between platforms, so the noise points as well as the fewer feature points are not enough to support robust platform poses estimation. The present algorithm is able to ensure good stability and accuracy regardless of the sequence, thanks to the constraint of planar features, which makes the system robust by constraining the odometer drift with fewer line surface features.

Table 4. Comparison of absolute trajectory error and mean between this algorithm and the comparison algorithm (Unit: m)

Sequence	FAST-LIO		Livox_horizon _loam		livox_horizon _loam_imu		loam_livox		Mymethod	
	RMSE	MEAN	RMSE	MEAN	RMSE	MEAN	RMSE	MEAN	RMSE	MEAN
Easy_Dataset	0.137	0.091	**0.083**	**0.052**	0.152	0.108	0.167	0.118	0.103	0.077
Medium _Dataset_01	0.437	0.401	0.784	0.696	0.530	0.491	6.492	5.416	**0.216**	**0.055**
Medium _Dataset_ 02	1.769	1.265	3.048	2.166	1.826	1.279	8.374	7.722	**0.549**	**0.285**

5   Conclusion

For the indoor scene, the shortage of specular interference and few line surface feature points, this paper proposes a multi-sensor tightly coupled SLAM algorithm based on feature planes. In the back-end optimization, the plane residuals are constructed and optimized, and put into the optimizer together with IMU pre-integration constraints and line-plane feature constraints to optimize the state information of key frames such as pose, which effectively The motion drift is suppressed. In order to verify the effectiveness of this algorithm, a comparison test is conducted in a real environment. Whether it is a simple or complex indoor environment, this algorithm shows higher localization accuracy and robustness compared with other laser SLAM algorithms.

In the experimental process, compared with the Medium_Dataset sequence, the Easy_Dataset sequence saves the computational cost by removing the constraint of line surface features, but it has certain limitations because of the high environmental requirements. Therefore, the algorithm has further room for improvement. The next step can integrate the camera to detect the complexity of the scene, set the threshold value, and determine whether to execute the constraint of the line surface features, so as to significantly save the computation time and improve the real-time performance of the system.

References

1. Tang, J., et al.: LiDAR scan matching aided inertial navigation system in GNSS-denied environments. Sensors **15**(7), 16710–16728 (2015)
2. Wang, Z.H., et al.: SLAM approach based on fusion of inertial/magnetic sensors and monocular vision. Robotics **40**(6), 933–941 (2018)
3. Qin, C., Ye, H., Pranata, C.E., et al.: LINS: a lidar-inertial state estimator for robust and efficient navigation. In: Proceedings of 2020 IEEE International Conference on Robotics and Automation (ICRA), Paris, France, pp. 8899–8906. IEEE (2020)
4. Shan, T., Englot, B., Meyers, D., et al.: LIO-SAM: tightly-coupled lidar inertial odometry via smoothing and mapping (2020)
5. Xu, W., Zhang, F.: FAST-LIO: a fast, robust lidar-inertial odometry package by tightly-coupled iterated Kalman filter. IEEE Robot. Autom. Lett., 1 (2021)
6. Shi, J.Y., et al.: Advances in visual inertial SLAM for mobile robots. Robotics **42**(6), 734–748 (2020)
7. Taguchi, Y., Jian, Y.D., Ramalingam, S., et al.: Point-plane SLAM for hand-held 3D sensors. In: 2013 IEEE International Conference on Robotics and Automation (ICRA). IEEE (2013)
8. Rosinol, A., Abate, M., Chang, Y., et al.: Kimera: an open-source library for real-time metric-semantic localization and mapping (2019). https://doi.org/10.1109/ICRA40945.2020.9196885
9. Li, Y., Brasch, N., Wang, Y., et al.: Structure-SLAM: low-drift monocular SLAM in indoor environments. IEEE (2020). https://doi.org/10.1109/LRA.2020.3015456
10. Li, H.F., et al.: PLP-SLAM: a visual SLAM method based on fusion of point, line and surface features. Robotics **39**(2), 214–220+229 (2017)
11. Zhou, L., Wang, S., Kaess, M.: π-LSAM: LiDAR smoothing and mapping with planes. In: 2021 IEEE International Conference on Robotics and Automation (ICRA). IEEE (2021)
12. Chen, D., Wang, S., et al.: VIP-SLAM: an efficient tightly-coupled RGB-D visual inertial planar SLAM (2022). https://arxiv.org/abs/2207.01158
13. Liu, Y.K., Li, Y.Q., Liu, H.Y., et al.: An improved RANSAC algorithm for point cloud segmentation of complex building roofs. J. Geo Inf. Sci. **23**(8), 1497–1507 (2021)
14. Ye, H., Chen, Y., Liu, M.: Tightly coupled 3D lidar inertial odometry and mapping. In: Proceedings of the 2019 International Conference on Robotics and Automation (ICRA 2019), Montreal, Canada, May 2019, pp. 3144–3150 (2019)
15. Zhang, J., Singh, S.: LOAM: lidar odometry and mapping in realtime. In: Robotics: Science and Systems, vol. 2, no. 9 (2014)
16. Lin, J., Zhang, F.: Loam_livox: a fast, robust, high-precision LiDAR odometry and mapping package for LiDARs of small FoV (2019)

Intelligent Perception Solution for Construction Machinery Based on Binocular Stereo Vision

Fangfang Lin[1,2], Tianliang Lin[1,2(✉)], Zhongshen Li[1,2], Qihuai Chen[1,2], Jiangdong Wu[1,2], and Yu Yao[3]

[1] College of Mechanical Engineering and Automation, Huaqiao University, Xiamen 361021, China
ltl@hqu.edu.cn
[2] Fujian Key Laboratory of Green Intelligent Drive and Transmission for Mobile Machinery, Xiamen 361021, China
[3] School of Mechanical Engineering and Automation, Beihang University, Beijing 102206, China

Abstract. In the field of construction machinery, the application of driverless technology can effectively improve operation efficiency, reduce labor costs, and lower the risks associated with driver. So it holds great potential for development. As a crucial component of driverless technology, perception technology plays a vital role in the intelligence of construction machinery. It not only enhances the efficiency, but also continuously monitors the surrounding environmental to ensure the safety. Aiming at the unstructured environmental conditions of construction machinery and the characteristics of special working objects, the advantages and disadvantages of sensors for realizing environmental perception are expounded. And a improved YOLOv7 network is proposed to realize real-time detection and segmentation of unstructured scenes. This achieves an intelligent perception solution for construction machinery based on binocular vision. In this paper, a novel attention module is proposed and combined with the YOLOv7 algorithm to enhance the accuracy of detection and segmentation. To better serve the real-world settings of construction machinery, a specialized image segmentation dataset is made. The improved network is evaluated and verified in the test set and the actual scenarios. The results indicate that the proposed intelligent perception solution is proficient in object detection and segmentation accuracy.

Keywords: Construction machinery · Driverless technology · Intelligent perception · Object detection · Semantic segmentation · Binocular vision

This work was supported by National Natural Science Foundation of China (Grant No.52175051&52275055), Fujian University industry university research joint innovation project plan (2022H6007), Key projects of natural science foundation of Fujian Province (2021J02013), Industry Cooperation of Major Science and Technology Project of Fujian Province (2022H6028).

1   Introduction

The construction machinery has a wide range of applications. Typically, it is utilized in harsh terrains such as unstructured roads, mountainous regions, mines, plateaus, as well as in challenging work conditions such as earthquakes, mudslides, explosions, and radiation [1]. When working in these complex environments, the drivers' physical and psychological standards need to meet extremely high demands. While for construction machinery with the intelligent technology, it not only significantly reduces labor intensity, decreases the possibility of human error, but also reduces the risk of accidents for driver operators while enhancing job safety. Additionally, it helps to lower the incidence rate of occupational diseases. Traditional construction machinery operations rely heavily on manual operations. With the implementation of intelligent construction machinery, it can continuously efficiently work for 24 h without manual interference. This not only increases productivity and quality of delivered projects, but also solves the problem of labor shortage.

As construction machinery moves towards driverless, intelligent perception technology is becoming increasingly important. This technology enables construction machinery to perceive and identify surrounding objects, such as pedestrians, other working vehicles, mounds, and drivable roads. So that they can provide accurate perception information for the decision-making and planning modules. This information enables construction machinery to make intelligent control and safe driving in complex environments and safe operation in harsh conditions. Environmental perception technology is a critical prerequisite for construction machinery to achieve unmanned driving and autonomous operation in unstructured environments.

The implementation of environmental perception technology primarily relies on various sensors to collect environmental data around vehicles and analyzes the data through algorithms. Due to the complex and harsh working environment of construction machinery, targets in the unstructured environment are variable and irregular in shape and cannot be recognized by low semantic features, which makes target detection and segmentation more difficult. In addition, the working conditions lead to large vibration during the movement of construction machinery, which affects the data obtained by sensors and reduces the effect of environmental perception. These objective reasons lead to the intelligent perception technology of construction machinery to put forward higher requirements for the accuracy of target detection and segmentation of neural network. Moreover, compared with the supervised training methods, the unsupervised or weakly supervised methods for intelligent perception technology are not mature enough and the implementation effect is poor. At present, the mainstream methods are based on supervised learning to realize intelligent perception technology. But there are almost no public datasets for construction machinery task scenes, which further hinders the research of intelligent perception technology of construction machinery.

Aiming at the above problems, an intelligent perception scheme based on binocular vision is proposed. This scheme is able to realize real-time object detection and segmentation tasks in the surrounding environment of construction machinery. YOLOv7 [2] algorithm can ensures high detection accuracy while achieving efficient target detection and segmentation in real-time scenarios. So the YOLOv7 algorithm is chosen as the neural network to implement these tasks. In addition, a new attention mechanism module is proposed to improve the YOLOv7 network structure. It further improves the accuracy of the network for object detection and segmentation. In this paper, an image segmentation dataset for construction machinery scenes is also made. The improved network performance is evaluated and verified in the dataset and the actual scene. By constructing an intelligent perception system of construction machinery, it can efficiently accomplish environment perception tasks while walking and working. It also makes the machinery output superior decision-making control under complex conditions.

2 Related Work

2.1 Construction Machinery Intelligence Research

At present, the research of unmanned driving technology mainly focuses on the field of passenger cars. Driverless technology in cars has been widely recognized and has been able to achieve automatic driving on city roads and highways. However, the complexity and variability of the working environment for engineering machinery present significant differences in application scenarios compared to autonomous cars. This poses higher technological challenges to the advancement of construction machinery intelligent technology. Currently, autonomous driving vehicles have already entered commercial operation stage and have been widely used in various countries. However, the research on autonomous construction machinery at home and abroad is relatively slow. Its development lags behind the driverless car and commercial-scale applications have not yet achieved.

Fortunately, there are various universities and companies that have been actively studying the technology of intelligent construction machinery. Caterpillar, Komatsu and other foreign enterprises, as well as SANY, XCMG, LiuGong and other domestic enterprises, have developed intelligent construction machinery products. In addition, foreign universities such as Carnegie Mellon University and Stanford University, and domestic universities such as Tsinghua University and Zhejiang University have conducted researchs on driverless technology and achieved certain results for specific construction scenarios at different times.

In 1999, Caterpillar Inc. made a breakthrough in the field of construction machinery by independently developing automatic bulldozers and underground loaders [3]. These machines were put into use in mining areas and improved work efficiency to a certain extent. In 2016, Komatsu Company developed a mine dump truck. The dump truck is equipped with wireless network, radar, camera and other sensors, which can realize environmental perception in the mining scene. Furthermore, this truck cancelled the cabin, which further moves closer to the unmanned operation. In 2021, the Baidu Autonomous Driving Lab proposed an Autonomous Excavator System (referred to as AES) [4]. As shown in Fig. 1, the system is equipped with a variety of sensors such as LIDAR and camera, which can realize 3D scene perception and target recognition tasks.

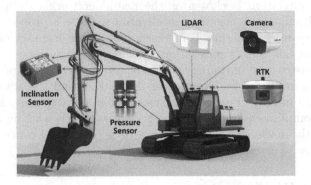

Fig. 1. Autonomous Excavator System of Baidu.

2.2   Intelligent Perception Technology Research

In the driverless system, the intelligent perception technology is mainly used to realize the perception and understanding of the surrounding environment, which is the basis of intelligent driving. Intelligent perception technologies ultimately equips the machinery with the human-like ability to sense and comprehend its surroundings. Thus, it helps to enhance the cognitive awareness and understanding of its environment.

The commonly used sensors of driverless perception system include camera, LIDAR, millimeter wave radar, etc. Each sensor has its own strengths and limitations, as shown in Table 1. Intelligent construction machinery requires high-quality image, as well as high frame rate in image output speed. Cameras are capable of continuously outputting real-time images, meeting the requirements of driverless construction machinery. Cameras rely on visual images to detect and measure distances to targets, and they offer high-resolution images at an affordable price. However, they are affected by adverse weather. Compared to monocular cameras, binocular cameras can achieve 3D imaging of the surrounding environment, and then realize the conversion from 2D image to 3D image. The LIDAR uses laser light to detect obstacles and measure distance. This makes them resistant to interference and measure distances with remarkable accuracy. They are also suitable for nighttime work. However, they cannot work properly in bad weather such as rain and heavy fog. Moreover, they are expensive and require frequent calibration. In harsh operating conditions, millimeter-wave radar has significant advantages over other sensors. It can penetrate obstacles such as dust, smoke, and fog to accurately provide information on the distance, speed, angle, and other characteristics of objects in the environment. However,

Table 1. Various environmental perception sensors.

Sensor	Advantage	Disadvantage
Monocular Camera	1. Fast dynamic response, perception of the scene within a certain angle range, rich information collection; 2. Low cost; 3. Mature technology.	1. It is greatly affected by light and weather; 2. Only scene 2D information can be obtained, and its depth information cannot be obtained. It is difficult to realize 3D modeling and precise positioning
Binocular Camera	1. The depth information of the scene can be perceived by using the principle of parallax. Then the 3D information of the object can be obtained; 2. Low cost.	1. It is greatly affected by light and weather; 2. Large amount of calculation; 3. The camera baseline limits the ranging range
LIDAR	1. 3D imaging has high resolution and high precision; 2. Strong anti-interference, high stability; 3. Wide detection range and long distance.	1. It is sensitive to suspended matter in the air and bad weather; 2. High cost; 3. The large amount of point clouds have certain requirements for the computing power platform. And the real-time performance of data processing is low
Millimeter-Wave Radar	1. Strong penetration, all-weather work, stable performance; 2. High resolution, small size; 3. The detection distance is far. And the measurement distance and speed information can be directly obtained.	1. Weak pedestrian perception ability and small detection angle; 2. The detection range is restricted by the frequency band loss; 3. High cost

its disadvantage is that it is high cost and can be affected by environmental factors such as rain and snow.

The performance of perception schemes that rely on vehicle-mounted sensors to detect surrounding environmental information is highly dependent on the performance of network algorithms and the scale of data. Currently, deep learning methods for image object detection tasks can be broadly classified into two categories: two-stage and one-stage. Typical examples of one-stage methods such as YOLO series algorithms [2,5–9], SSD series [10,11], and RetinaNet [12] exhibit fast detection speeds. On the other hand, typical examples of two-stage methods such as RCNN series algorithms [13–15] and FPN [16] exhibit high detection accuracy.

Using LIDAR for target detection tasks, based on different representations of point cloud data, point cloud object detection methods based on deep learning can be divided into four categories: view-based methods [17,18], voxel-based methods [19], point-based methods [20,21], and point-voxel-based methods [22].

2.3   Attention Mechanism

The attention mechanism mimics human visual attention by focusing on interest regions in an image. To enhance the performance of deep convolutional networks, an increasing number of attention blocks have been proposed and used in various tasks such as machine translation, object detection, semantic segmentation. And improved results have been obtained.

The self-attention mechanism [23] is first proposed to capture long-range dependencies from input sequences and applied to the field of machine translation. SENet [24] proposes an channel attention mechanism that recalibrates feature maps by using the squeeze-and-excitation module. scSE [25] fuses important information learned along both channel and spatial dimensions to enhance the representation of important features. CBAM [26] proposes an attention module that includes both channel and spatial attention to obtain important context information. CA [27] proposes a mobile network attention mechanism that embeds location information into channel attention. Inspired by these methods, an attention module is proposed to obtain important information about channel and spatial positions. It helps the network to distinguish the relationships between different objects and improves the network performance.

3   Proposed Work

An construction machinery perception solution based on binocular vision is proposed. The real-time images captured by the binocular camera are inputted into an improved YOLOv7 network for feature extraction. Then, the network realizes real-time object detection and segmentation. This paper introduces a novel attention module that is integrated with the YOLOv7 network to enhance its accuracy. An overview of the proposed attention module and the improved network structure will be introduced.

3.1   Proposed Attention Mechanism

In machine translation, the attention mechanism [23] has been proposed to focus on the key context of the sequence. Due to its powerful performance, the attention mechanism has also attracted widespread attention in the visual domain. The motivation of designing the attention module is to learn the interdependence between information and obtain important information positions of feature maps through learning. This allows more attention to be allocated to important information, while suppressing unimportant features by assigning low weight. Finally, the network is enable to learn more helpful information for the task.

Inspired by the CA attention module [27], a novel attention module is devised as shown in Fig. 2. CA encodes the channel attention through two 1D features, and performs the average pooling to aggregate features for the two spatial directions respectively. The proposed attention module is based on CA. It aggregates channel attention twice along each spatial direction by means of the average and max pooling. This enables features to capture more crucial and comprehensive positional information in the spatial domain. Finally, the generated pair of orientation and location sensitive attention maps are applied to the input feature map, thereby capturing the long-range dependencies with precise location information to enhance the feature representation of salient objects in an image.

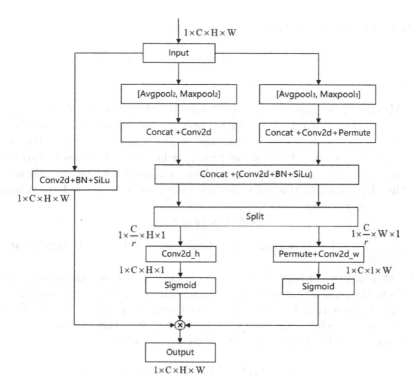

Fig. 2. The structure of our proposed attention module.

The proposed attention module is shown in Fig. 2. Specifically, given an input feature map $X \in R^{1 \times C \times H \times W}$ (where C represents the number of channels), it is passed through three branches. In the first branch, the average and max poolings along the 2nd dimension of the input feature map are performed, and then the pooled features are concatenated along the channel dimension. Subsequently, a convolution operation with 1×1 kernel size is applied. The formula described above is expressed as follows.

$$X_{\text{pool}_1} = [\text{MaxPool}_2(X), \text{AvgPool}_2(X)]_C \tag{1}$$

$$X_H = \text{Conv}(X_{\text{pool}_1}) \tag{2}$$

where $\text{MaxPool}_X(\cdot)$ is the maximum pooling operation and $\text{AvgPool}_X(\cdot)$ is the average pooling operation along the X-th dimension. $[\cdot, \cdot]_C$ denotes the concatenation operation along the channel dimension. $X_{\text{pool}_1} \in R^{1 \times 2C \times H \times 1}$ is the output after the concatenation. $X_H \in R^{1 \times C \times H \times 1}$ is the output after the convolution operation.

Similarly, the operations in the second branch are similar to those in the first branch. The main difference is that the second branch first performs two pooling operations on the 3rd dimension of the input feature map. The equation for the operation in the second branch is expressed as:

$$X_{\text{pool}_2} = [\text{MaxPool}_3(X), \text{AvgPool}_3(X)]_C \tag{3}$$

$$X_W = \text{Conv}(X_{\text{pool}_2}) \tag{4}$$

where $\text{MaxPool}_X(\cdot)$ and $\text{AvgPool}_X(\cdot)$ denotes the same as above. $X_{\text{pool}_2} \in R^{1 \times 2C \times H \times 1}$ is the output after the pooling connection of the second branch. $X_W \in R^{1 \times C \times H \times 1}$ is the output after the convolution operation of the second branch. The operations of the above two branches make features in two spatial directions be able to obtain more comprehensive contextual position information.

In the third branch, the input feature map is sent to a 1×1 convolutional function $F_1(\cdot)$, yielding:

$$y = \delta(BN(F_1(X))) \tag{5}$$

where $BN(\cdot)$ is a batch normalization layer and $\delta(\cdot)$ is a SiLU non-linear activation function.

The two outputs of Eqs. 2 and 4 are concatenated along the spatial dimension. Then, the concatenated feature are passed through a 1×1 convolutional transformation function $F_2(\cdot)$ to obtain the feature tensor $Z \in R^{1 \times \frac{C}{r} \times (H+W) \times 1}$. Here, r is the reduction ratio used to reduce the model, and in this paper a fixed value is taken $r = 16$. The formula is expressed as follows.

$$Z = \delta(BN(F_1([X_H, X_W]_S))) \tag{6}$$

where $[\cdot, \cdot]_S$ denotes the concatenation operation along the spatial dimension. The acquired feature tensor Z is the intermediate feature map, which encodes the spatial information in horizontal and vertical directions.

Then, Z is split along the spatial dimension into two feature tensors $Z_H \in R^{1 \times \frac{C}{r} \times H \times 1}$ and $Z_W \in R^{1 \times \frac{C}{r} \times 1 \times W}$ respectively. Another two 1×1 convolutional transformation functions $F_H(\cdot)$ and $F_W(\cdot)$ respectively convert Z_H and Z_W into tensors with the same number of the input channel, yielding:

$$G_H = \sigma(F_H(Z_H)) \tag{7}$$

$$G_W = \sigma(F_W(Z_W)) \tag{8}$$

where $\sigma(\cdot)$ is the sigmoid function. The generated $G_H \in R^{1 \times C \times H \times 1}$ and $G_W \in R^{1 \times C \times 1 \times W}$ are respectively used as attention weights.

Finally, the output G_H in Eq. 7 and the output G_W in Eq. 8 are used to calibrate the weight of the obtained y in Eq. 5. The generated $Y \in R^{1 \times C \times H \times W}$ can be formulated as:

$$Y = y \otimes G_H \otimes G_W \tag{9}$$

where $\otimes$ is the element-wise multiplication.

3.2 Proposed the Structure of Improved YOLOv7 Network

The network architecture of YOLOv7 can be defined as two parts: the backbone and the head. All modules before the SPPCSPC [2] module are combined to form the backbone module, while those after are combined to form the head module. In this article, the proposed attention module is referred to as EFA (Embedding Fusion Attention). The transition block [2] in the original YOLOv7 algorithm is combined with EMA to form a new module called EMATB (Embedding Fusion Attention Transition Block).

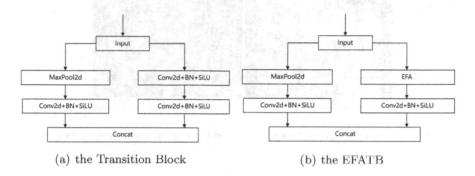

(a) the Transition Block   (b) the EFATB

Fig. 3. (a) The structure of the Transition Block in the original YOLOv7 algorithm. (b) The structure of Embedding Fusion Attention Transition Block.

In the improved overall structure of YOLOv7, all transition blocks in the original YOLOv7 network are replaced with EFATB modules. According to the experimental results, these operations can improve the improved model's ability to locate objects of interest, thereby helping to better detect and segment objects. The network structures of the transition block and the EFATB module are shown in Fig. 3.

4 Experiments

This article focuses on the practical working scenarios of construction machinery in unstructured environments and creates a specialized image segmentation dataset for construction machinery scenes. The dataset is used to train the improved YOLOv7 network. Then the target detection and segmentation network model is generated and it can operate effectively under actual working conditions for construction machinery. Finally, the model's performance is evaluated and verified on the test set and actual scenarios.

4.1 Datasets

Currently, the majority of vision datasets are composed of routine daily life scenarios. However, construction machinery is often applied in unstructured environments, and there is a lack of datasets specifically tailored to these conditions.

To further promote the development of intelligent construction machinery, it is crucial to construct the dataset that accurately reflects real working scenarios. To achieve this goal, we utilizes a ZED 2i stereo camera as the hardware device for data collection.

Fig. 4. Visualization of images acquired by binocular cameras on rviz.

In order to ensure real-time visualization of image data during the collection process, Rviz, a visualization tool within the Robot Operating System (ROS), is employed. As shown in Fig. 4, the acquired stereo camera images are displayed on Rviz. Ultimately, the total number of images in the constructed dataset are 667. Subsequently, the dataset is divided into the train and validation sets at a 10:1 ratio, thus the train set allocates 600 images and the validation set has 67 images.

After the data collection process described above, the required image dataset for the experiment is obtained. As YOLOv7 is a supervised method, it is necessary to annotate the images in the dataset to obtain image labels. The network can be trained by using the original images and their corresponding labels to achieve real-time detection and segmentation of objects in the surrounding environment.

LabelMe is a typical open source image annotation tool that can be used for object detection, segmentation, and classification tasks. Additionally, LabelMe is easy to install and operate. It outputs annotation data in various formats such as JSON, Pascal VOC, etc., which facilitates subsequent data processing and network model training. Therefore, LabelMe is chosen as the tool to perform segmentation annotation on the dataset. The experiment focused on 10 different classes for segmentation annotation including mound, clitter, bourock, gully, barrier, structual_road, off_road, person, gravel and engineering. The annotated results of image segmentation using LabelMe are shown in Fig. 5.

Fig. 5. The annotated results of image segmentation by LabelMe.

4.2 Comparision with Other Methods

Results of Objection Detection. To validate the effectiveness of the proposed EFA module, experimental comparison are conducted on different modified YOLOv7 networks and the baseline network YOLOv7. The modified YOLOv7 network refers to the structure that combines YOLOv7 with different attention modules. As shown in Table 2, YOLOv7_SE is the combination of SE [24] and the YOLOv7 network. YOLOv7_scSE is a combination of scSE [25] and YOLOv7. YOLOv7_CBAM combines CBAM [26] with the YOLOv7 network. YOLOv7_CA combines CA [27] with the YOLOv7 network. To ensure fairness in our experiments, all attention modules are combined with YOLOv7 at consistent positions. Furthermore, all network models in this paper are trained on our dataset with epoch=200 and batchsize=16.

Table 2. Comparative results of our improved YOLOv7 network (YOLOv7+EFA) and YOLOv7 networks combined with other attention modules on object detection task. P (%) is the precision. R (%) is the recall.

Model	P	R	mAP@.5	mAP@.5:0.95
YOLOv7	89.8	93.6	93.5	77.8
YOLOv7_SE	90.4	94.0	93.8	78.1
YOLOv7_scSE	90.5	94.8	93.7	78.4
YOLOv7_CBAM	91.1	94.2	93.8	77.6
YOLOv7_CA	90.8	94.5	94.1	78.2
Our	**91.3**	**95.0**	**94.9**	**78.5**

From the results in Table 2, it can be observed that the proposed EFA attention module improves the precision (P) by 1.5% and the recall (R) by 1.4% compared to YOLOv7 without any attention modules. Additionally, our proposed YOLOv7 network, which combines YOLOv7 with the introduced EFA module, outperforms other structures that combine different attention modules with YOLOv7 in terms of precision, recall, mAP@.5, and mAP@.5:0.95 performance metrics.

Table 3. Comparative AP (%) results of different YOLOv7 structures for various object classes in the detection task.

Model	YOLOv7	YOLOv7_SE	YOLOv7_scSE	YOLOv7_CBAM	YOLOv7_CA	Our
mound	94.3	93.7	94.1	94	95.3	95.2
clitter	98.7	97.2	96.2	96.4	98.1	98.4
bourock	97.3	97.4	98.0	97.4	97	97.6
gully	96.0	96.3	97.1	96.1	97.6	97.0
barrier	96.7	97.2	97.3	97.5	97.0	96.8
structual_roal	99.5	99.5	99.5	99.5	99.5	99.5
off_road	99.5	99.5	99.5	99.5	99.5	99.5
person	75.9	74.7	71.4	76.3	75.6	81.9
gravel	87.7	90.4	91.0	88.8	89.8	92.2
engineering	89.9	92.0	92.7	92.7	91.2	90.8

Table 3 presents the evaluation results of model performance on the test set for different YOLOv7 architectures. These architectures are trained on the created dataset with epochs=200 and batchsize=16, and the AP values of each object class in Table 3 are respectively measured by them. As our dataset contains relatively few labels for the class of person, the network's recognition accuracy for this class is relatively lower. However, compared to other YOLOv7 models, our proposed YOLOv7 network still achieves good detection results for the class of person. This indicates that the proposed EFA module can better recognize and locate the interested objects in images than other attention modules. Figure 6 shows a visualization of Table 3, which intuitively demonstrates that our improved YOLOv7 network achieves good detection accuracy for all target classes in our dataset.

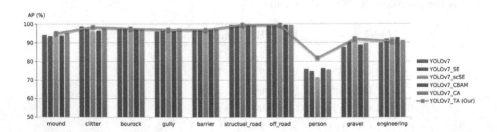

Fig. 6. Visualization of the AP results of different YOLOv7 models for each class in the object detection task.

Results of Semantic Segmentation. To validate that the proposed attention module is helpful for the downstream task of image segmentation, the performance of our improved YOLOv7 network is compared with the YOLOv7 benchmark network in the semantic segmentation task. To ensure the fairness of the experiment, both networks are trained for 200 epochs and 16 batchsize. As shown in Table 4, the improved YOLOv7 achieved better results in the semantic segmentation task compared to the original YOLOv7. The results of object detection and semantic segmentation achieved by the network in real time are shown in Fig. 7.

Table 4. Performance comparison of two different YOLOv7 structures in implementing the semantic segmentation task.

Model	P(M)	R(M)	mAP@.5(M)	mAP@.5:0.95(M)
YOLOv7	89.9	92.9	93.3	71.7
Our	91.0	94.1	93.6	72.3

Fig. 7. Visualization of the results of real-time object detection and semantic segmentation tasks based on our improved YOLOv7 network.

4.3 Ablation Studies

In this section, ablation studies about our proposed EFA module is conducted on the dataset made in actual construction machinery working scenarios. Furthermore, YOLOv7 [2] is adopted as our baseline network. The results of ablation experiments are shown in Table 5, and the mAP@.5 (%) and mAP@.5:0.95 (%) in the table are the mean average precision obtained when using the network for the object detection task. These two metrics are used as evaluation metrics of the network performance.

Table 5. Ablation study on the proposed dataset. EFA is our proposed embedded fusion attention module.

YOLOv7	EFA	mAP@.5	mAP@.5:0.95
√		93.5	77.8
√	√	**94.4**	**78.5**

To demonstrate the effectiveness of our proposed EFA module, the proposed attention module is only added to the baseline network at the transition block. As shown in Table 5, the improved YOLOv7 network (YOLOv7+EFA) achieves higher detection accuracy in terms of object detection performance compared to the baseline network YOLOv7. When the IOU threshold in the NMS is set to 0.5, our improved YOLOv7 network improves the mAP by 1.4% compared with the baseline network. By selecting 10 different values with a 0.05 interval within the range of IOU thresholds from 0.5 to 0.95, the mAP values under each threshold are calculated. Then, the obtained mAPs are averaged to acquire the mAP@.5:0.95. Our improved YOLOv7 network achieves a 0.7% increase in mAP@.5:0.95 compared to the baseline network.

From all the experimental results, it can be seen that the proposed intelligent perception solution can well satisfy the environmental perception tasks of construction machinery during operation and movement in terms of detection and segmentation accuracy. This provides necessary environmental knowledge for subsequent decision-making control and planning.

5   Conclusion

In this paper, the characteristics of several important sensors for automatic driving to achieve environmental perception are detailedly analyzed. In addition, an image segmentation dataset is created for the complex environment of construction machinery. A novel attention mechanism is proposed to improve the performance of the YOLOv7 algorithm, and the improved YOLOv7 network is trained and evaluated on the created dataset. The experimental results show that the improved algorithm is more accurate in object detection and segmentation tasks. Furthermore, the pricision and stability of our proposed scheme can better meet the requirements. This provides construction machineries with the ability to accurately perceive and interpret their surroundings.

References

1. Editorial Department of China Journal of Highway and Transport. Review on China's automotive engineering research progress: 2017. China J. Highw. Transp., **30**, 1–197 (2017)

2. Wang, C.Y., Bochkovskiy, A., Liao, H.Y.M.: YOLOv7: trainable bag-of-freebies sets new state-of-the-art for real-time object detectors. In: Proceedings of the IEEE/CVF Conference on Computer Vision and Pattern Recognition, pp. 7464–7475 (2023)
3. Cannon, H.N.: Extended earthmoving with an autonomous excavator[D]. Carnegie Mellon University (1999)
4. Zhang, L., et al.: An autonomous excavator system for material loading tasks. Sci. Robot. 6(55), (2021). https://doi.org/10.1126/scirobotics.abc3164
5. Redmon, J., Divvala, S., Girshick, R., et al.: You only look once: unified, real-time object detection. In: Proceedings of the IEEE Conference on Computer Vision and Pattern Recognition, pp. 779–788 (2016)
6. Redmon, J., Farhadi, A.: YOLO9000: better, faster, stronger. In: Proceedings of the IEEE Conference on Computer Vision and Pattern Recognition, pp. 7263–7271 (2017)
7. Redmon, J., Farhadi, A.: YOLOv3: an incremental improvement. arXiv preprint arXiv:1804.02767 (2018)
8. Bochkovskiy, A., Wang, C.Y., Liao, H.Y.M.: YOLOv4: optimal speed and accuracy of object detection. arXiv preprint arXiv:2004.10934 (2020)
9. Li, C., Li, L., Jiang, H., et al.: YOLOv6: a single-stage object detection framework for industrial applications. arXiv preprint arXiv:2209.02976 (2022)
10. Liu, W., et al.: SSD: single shot multibox detector. In: Leibe, B., Matas, J., Sebe, N., Welling, M. (eds.) ECCV 2016. LNCS, vol. 9905, pp. 21–37. Springer, Cham (2016). https://doi.org/10.1007/978-3-319-46448-0_2
11. Li, Z., Zhou, F.: FSSD: feature fusion single shot multibox detector. arXiv preprint arXiv:1712.00960 (2017)
12. Lin, T.Y., Goyal, P., Girshick, R., et al.: Focal loss for dense object detection. In: Proceedings of the IEEE International Conference on Computer Vision, pp. 2980–2988 (2017)
13. Girshick, R., Donahue, J., Darrell, T., et al.: Rich feature hierarchies for accurate object detection and semantic segmentation. In: Proceedings of the IEEE Conference on Computer Vision and Pattern Recognition, pp. 580–587 (2014)
14. Girshick, R.: Fast R-CNN. In: Proceedings of the IEEE International Conference on Computer Vision, pp. 1440–1448 (2015)
15. Ren, S., He, K., Girshick, R., et al.: Faster R-CNN: towards real-time object detection with region proposal networks. In: Advances in Neural Information Processing Systems 28 (2015)
16. Lin, T.Y., Dollár, P., Girshick, R., et al.: Feature pyramid networks for object detection. In: Proceedings of the IEEE Conference on Computer Vision and Pattern Recognition, pp. 2117–2125 (2017)
17. Ali, W., Abdelkarim, S., Zidan, M., et al.: YOLO3D: end-to-end real-time 3D oriented object bounding box detection from lidar point cloud. In: Proceedings of the European Conference on Computer Vision (ECCV) workshops (2018)
18. Simon, M., Milz, S., Amende, K., Gross, H.-M.: Complex-YOLO: an Euler-region-proposal for real-time 3d object detection on point clouds. In: Leal-Taixé, L., Roth, S. (eds.) Computer Vision – ECCV 2018 Workshops: Munich, Germany, September 8-14, 2018, Proceedings, Part I, pp. 197–209. Springer International Publishing, Cham (2019). https://doi.org/10.1007/978-3-030-11009-3_11
19. Zhou, Y., Tuzel, O.: VoxelNet: end-to-end learning for point cloud based 3D object detection. In: Proceedings of the IEEE Conference on Computer Vision and Pattern Recognition, pp. 4490–4499 (2018)

20. Qi, C.R., et al.: PointNet: deep learning on point sets for 3D classification and segmentation. In: Proceedings of the IEEE Conference on Computer Vision and Pattern Recognition, pp. 652–660 (2017)

21. Qi, C.R., et al.: PointNet++: deep hierarchical feature learning on point sets in a metric space. In: Advances in Neural Information Processing Systems, 30 (2017)

22. Liu, Z., et al.: Point-voxel CNN for efficient 3D deep learning. In: Advances in Neural Information Processing Systems, 32 (2019)

23. Vaswani, A., et al.: Attention is all you need. In: Advances in Neural Information Processing Systems, 30 (2017)

24. Hu, J., Shen, L., Sun, G.: Squeeze-and-excitation networks. In: Proceedings of the IEEE Conference on Computer Vision and Pattern Recognition, pp. 7132–7141 (2018)

25. Roy, A.G., Navab, N., Wachinger, C.: Concurrent spatial and channel squeeze and excitation in fully convolutional networks. In: Frangi, A.F., Schnabel, J.A., Davatzikos, C., Alberola-López, C., Fichtinger, G. (eds.) MICCAI 2018. LNCS, vol. 11070, pp. 421–429. Springer, Cham (2018). https://doi.org/10.1007/978-3-030-00928-1_48

26. Woo, S., Park, J., Lee, J.-Y., Kweon, I.S.: CBAM: convolutional block attention module. In: Ferrari, V., Hebert, M., Sminchisescu, C., Weiss, Y. (eds.) Computer Vision – ECCV 2018: 15th European Conference, Munich, Germany, September 8–14, 2018, Proceedings, Part VII, pp. 3–19. Springer International Publishing, Cham (2018). https://doi.org/10.1007/978-3-030-01234-2_1

27. Hou, Q., Zhou, D., Feng, J.: Coordinate attention for efficient mobile network design. In: Proceedings of the IEEE/CVF Conference on Computer Vision and Pattern Recognition, pp. 13713–13722 (2021)

Design and Experimental Study of An Intelligent Soft Crawling Robot for Environmental Interactions

Mengke Yang, Anqi Guo, Liantong Zhang, and Guoqing Jin[✉]

Robotics and Microsystem Research Centre, School of Mechanical and Electrical Engineering,
Suzhou University, Suzhou, China
gqjin@suda.edu.cn

Abstract. In the interaction process with complex environment, compared with rigid structure robot, soft crawling robot has the advantages of high degree of freedom, strong adaptability to complex environment, and high human-computer interaction security. Therefore, it is necessary to conduct in-depth research on intelligent soft crawling robot oriented to environment interaction. This paper designs and manufactures an intelligent soft crawling robot system for environmental interaction. The main research contents include: 1) design and manufacture of intelligent soft crawling robot; 2) mathematical modeling and fluid-structure coupling simulation of soft crawling robot; 3) design and research of the interaction module between the soft crawling robot and the environments; 4) build a software crawling robot drive control platform for environmental interaction experiments. In this paper, the body of soft crawling robot is designed to simulate the motion of earthworm. The combination of ontology, flexible bending sensor, infrared digital obstacle avoidance sensor and ORB-SLAM algorithm framework enables the soft crawling robot to intelligently pass through maze channels, complete the environment mapping function in a closed environment, obtain accurate map information, and complete the interaction with the environment.

Keywords: Soft crawling robot · Soft modeling and simulation · Flexible sensor · Environment interaction

1 Introduction

In the past decade, soft robots have attracted the attention of many scholars due to their inherent compliance, unprecedented agility, and infinite number of degrees of freedom [1, 2]. Compared with rigid robots, the body of soft robots is made of soft and scalable materials (e.g. silicone rubber, etc.) that have good elasticity to produce large deformations and can absorb most of the energy generated by collisions during motion [3–8]. On this basis, scholars at home and abroad have developed many impressive bionic soft-bodied robots inspired by mollusks such as octopus, looper, earthworm and jellyfish, including mimic deep-sea fish soft-bodied robots [9], soft-bodied octopus robots [10], mimic pelican eel soft-bodied robots [11], soft-bodied jellyfish robots [12], bionic soft-bodied hands [13], and mimic snorkel soft-bodied robots [14]. Among the bionic soft robots, there is an increasing interest in biologically inspired soft crawling robots, which can interact effectively with humans and uncertain environments and have the potential to accomplish various tasks, and therefore can be more widely used for exploration in complex environments, such as search and rescue [15], field exploration [16, 17], medical rehabilitation [18–20], human-robot interaction, etc. [21, 22].

In this paper, based on the in-depth study of domestic and foreign soft body crawling robots, we designed and manufactured a double-chambered flexible actuator for the torso of the soft body crawling robot based on the bionic principle to imitate the movement of natural earthworms [26] and looper [27], and an adhesion actuator for the head and tail parts to imitate the adsorption and stabilization form of octopus tentacles, and formed a soft body crawling robot through flexible structural connection. The body of the soft crawling robot is connected by a flexible structure. At the same time, the flexible bending sensor designed and manufactured by magnetic printing process is embedded inside the torso of the soft crawling robot to provide real-time feedback on the bending angle of the torso position. The infrared obstacle avoidance digital sensor and camera are arranged above the head of the soft body crawling robot, and linked with the control system to complete the function of identifying obstacles, avoiding obstacles, collecting environmental information and building a map of the complex environment to achieve the role of environmental exploration. This project provides new ideas and initiatives for the research of intelligent soft body crawling robots in the field of environmental interaction, and also has important significance and research value in the design and manufacturing, modeling and simulation, and intelligent perception of soft body crawling robots.

2   Design and Manufacturing of Soft Body Crawling Robots

For the intelligent soft crawling robot movement to complete straight-line walking and turning movements, this chapter designs a fiber-reinforced double-cavity flexible actuator and a positive-pressure anchored adsorption actuator.

2.1   Design and Fabrication of Soft Crawling Robot Torso Module

Design. The design of the dual-chamber flexible actuator is inspired by the earthworm, which has bristles on the surface of its body, and the head and tail bristles are used to fix it on the ground when it moves, while the circumferential longitudinal muscles of its body are extended or bent to produce displacement. The dual-chamber flexible actuator mimics the earthworm's annulus longitudinalis, and the Kevlar thread is embedded inside the actuator to limit its radial deformation and increase its stiffness, as shown in Fig. 1.

Manufacturing. The flexible double-cavity actuator is manufactured by the most common mold casting method. The manufacturing process is divided into the steps of mold printing and assembly, silicone preparation, casting and demolding, fiber wire winding, and post-processing, as shown in Fig. 2(a). The completed actuator is shown in Fig. 2(b). The actuator will bend in the opposite direction when the strain-limiting layer is bound by the fiber threads, and the actuator will elongate when the two chambers are inflated, so that the balloon effect will not occur even at higher atmospheric pressure.

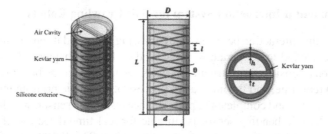

Fig. 1. Structural model of double-cavity flexible actuator.

2.2 Design and Fabrication of Head and Tail Modules for Soft Body Crawling Robots

Design. Inspired by octopus suction cups [28–30], the adsorption actuator consists of a double-layer structure with an embedded spiral pneumatic channel at the top, as shown in Fig. 2(c), which expands into a 3D dome structure after being driven by positive pressure, driving the substrate film to deform to form a negative pressure in the bottom cavity, and adsorbing and anchoring on a flat surface, as depicted in Fig. 2(d).

Manufacturing. The manufacturing process of mold printing and assembly, silicone preparation, pouring and demolding is the same as that of the two-cavity flexible actuator and will not be repeated here. After obtaining the funnel and acetabular structures separately, the upper and lower layers were directly bonded with Dow Corning 737, and then a small hole was opened to insert the rubber tubing. The actual object is shown in Fig. 3(b). The adhesion actuator mimicking the octopus suction cup shows good adsorption performance on the plastic plane, and the force on the adsorption plane increases with the increase of air pressure on the upper layer.

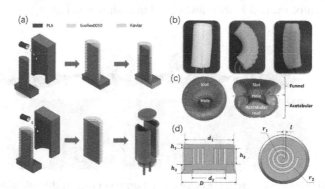

Fig. 2. (a) Dual-chamber flexible actuator manufacturing process; (b) Dual-chamber flexible actuator object; (c) Octopus suction cup structure schematic; (d) Structural model of soft adhesion actuator.

2.3 Environmental Interaction System for Soft Crawling Robots

To accomplish the interaction between a soft crawling robot and its environment, a series of sensors are needed to cooperate with each other. In this chapter, a flexible bending sensor based on a sensitive grid structure is designed to monitor the bending angle of the robot torso in real time, and the innovative process of magnetic printing method [31] is used to manufacture and complete the performance test of the sensor, which verifies that the designed flexible bending sensor is suitable for real-time detection of the bending angle of the torso of the feedback soft crawling robot. The W503-13 infrared digital obstacle avoidance sensor [32] is selected to cooperate with the flexible bending sensor to realize the robot's autonomous obstacle avoidance function, and the hardware platform [33] is built to calibrate the data of the sensor and fix the detection distance to detect the influence of the reflectivity of the target on the detection effect. The framework of feature point method ORB-SLAM [34, 35] is investigated, and the wireless monocular camera is calibrated using Zhengyou Zhang's checkerboard grid calibration method [36] to provide support for subsequent confined environment map building using SLAM. The interplay between sensors and cameras enables the soft robot to crawl through the sealed maze passage autonomously and reconstruct the environment map of the passage obtained.

2.4 Soft Body Crawling Robot Overall

As shown in Fig. 4, infrared obstacle avoidance digital sensors and wireless monocular cameras are placed in the cavities of the upper part of the skeleton connecting the head and torso actuators of the soft robot, which are used to interact with the environment while the robot is crawling. Due to the dual-cavity flexible actuator single-cavity inflatable bending and dual-cavity inflatable elongation, the adhesion actuator inflatable can be stably adsorbed on the surface, and the actuators cooperate with each other, the soft body crawling robot can easily complete the straight line and turning motion, the overall physical diagram of the soft body crawling robot is shown in Fig. 4.

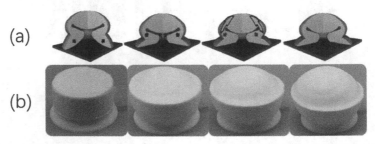

(a)

(b)

Fig. 3. Adsorption process diagram; (a) Octopus adsorption process; (b) Soft adhesion actuator adsorption process.

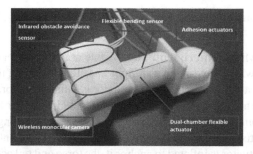

Fig. 4. The overall physical picture of the soft body crawling robot.

3 Environmental Interaction System for Soft Crawling Robots

3.1 Drive Control System Design of Intelligent Soft Crawling Robot

With the soft body crawling robot body designed and manufactured, the system is divided into two modules in the overall solution design, which are drive module and control module, considering the desired movement, control cost and control difficulty. The drive module includes the soft crawling robot body, solenoid valve, and air pump; the control module includes Arduino UNO development board, flexible bending sensor, infrared digital obstacle avoidance sensor, and relay. When the flexible crawling robot is in motion, the deformation of the bending sensor caused by the robot torso and the obstacle information detected by the infrared digital obstacle avoidance sensor will be fed back to the Arduino UNO development board through the circuit, and the development board will control the on/off of the relay module through the I/O interface according to the preset program, and the on/off of the relay will indirectly control the state of the solenoid valve. The air pump will charge and deflate the actuator of the soft crawling robot through the solenoid valve to provide power, and finally realize the autonomous crawling of the soft robot, while the movement can be monitored at all times to complete the obstacle avoidance action of interaction with the environment, and the environment map can be reconstructed after the movement is completed based on the video information taken by the monocular camera combined with the robot movement speed and the time of sensor information change (Fig. 5).

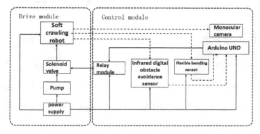

Fig. 5. Total solution for drive control system.

3.2   Experiments on the Interaction Between A Soft Crawling Robot and Its Environment

Straight-Line Crawling Experiment. The flexible crawling robot can both move forward and backward when crawling in a straight line. Take crawling forward as an example, see Fig. 6(a), firstly, the tail adhesion actuator is inflated and braked, and anchored in the plane of motion; then the two chambers of the dual-chamber flexible actuator are filled with equal amount of gas at the same time, and the actuator elongates and pushes the head adhesion actuator forward, producing a period of displacement; immediately after the head adhesion actuator is inflated to anchor it, the torso and tail actuators are deflated, and the tail actuator stops adsorption, and due to the Due to the super-elasticity of Ecoflex material, the torso actuator will quickly shrink back to its pre-actuation length, while dragging the tail actuator forward, and finally the soft body crawling robot produces displacement Δx.

Turn and Crawl Experiment. To mimic the movement of living creatures in nature, it is not enough for the robot to crawl in a straight line, but it also needs to be able to bend to avoid obstacles when it encounters them, and the movement schematic is shown in Fig. 6(b). Firstly, the tail adhesion actuator of the soft crawling robot is inflated and braked, and anchored on the motion plane; then the right chamber of the dual-chamber flexible actuator is filled with gas, and the actuator is bent to the left to produce a bending angle of the torso to the right and push the head adhesion actuator to rotate to a predetermined position; immediately after the head adhesion actuator is inflated and anchored, the torso and tail actuators are deflated, and the tail actuator stops adsorption. The torso actuator shrinks while dragging the tail actuator to rotate, and finally the soft crawling robot completes the left turn. The soft body crawling robot was placed on a plane with a right angle printed by 3D printing of PLA material, and the turning experiment was completed by several experiments, as shown in Fig. 9(b), and the crawling time was recorded, and it was found that the soft body crawling robot passed the 90° turning angle within 40s.

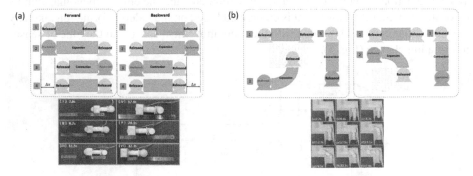

Fig. 6. (a) Straight line crawling; (b) Soft body crawling robot turning movement.

Weight Dragging Experiment. The designed soft crawling robot is experimentally demonstrated to have a certain load-bearing capacity on a smooth and dry surface by pneumatic control system driving the three actuators in turn, as shown in Fig. 7(a). The soft-body crawling robot propels itself forward by releasing the gas energy stored in its body during elongation in four consecutive steps within one motion cycle. Compared with the conventional soft body crawling robot, the soft body crawling robot proposed in this paper can withstand more load with the help of the adhesion actuator. The proposed soft crawler robot can withstand more load with the help of the adhesion actuator.

Climbing Experiment. In addition to the ability to move on a horizontal surface, the soft robot designed in this paper also demonstrates its ability to crawl on a plane with different tilt angles. The effect of climbing motion of the robot. It is known that the adsorption effect in the paper plane is the worst at the maximum atmospheric pressure of 70 kPa, and the shear adhesion force is 6.2 N. During the experiment, the inflation pressure of the fixed adhesion actuator is 70 kPa, which is equal to 0.69 standard atmospheric pressure, and it can be seen from Fig. 7(b) that the soft crawling robot can easily climb the platform with a bending angle of 60°.

Labyrinth Experiment. The flow chart of the control program of the soft crawling robot during operation is shown in Fig. 8. The infrared obstacle avoidance sensor is arranged above the head of the soft crawling robot. Considering the size of the sensor and the difficulty of controlling the robot when crawling, only one obstacle avoidance sensor is used in this paper, and the sequence of left and right steering is designed in the program to make up for the robot's inability to judge left or right to avoid obstacles at the same time.

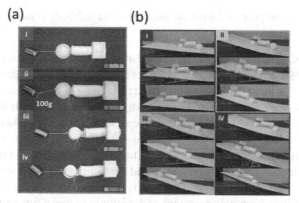

Fig. 7. Soft body crawling robot heavy dragging and climbing experiment; (a) Heavy dragging experiment; (b) Hill climbing experiment.

At the initial stage, the robot is in a straight crawling state, the infrared digital obstacle avoidance sensor continuously emits infrared signal to detect whether there is an obstacle within 5 cm, if there is an obstacle, the right cavity air pump of the double-cavity flexible actuator continues to work, the left cavity air pump stops working to deflate the robot torso to the left, at this time, the bending state is monitored in real time by the flexible bending sensor, when the bending angle reaches 80°–90°, the robot torso first maintains

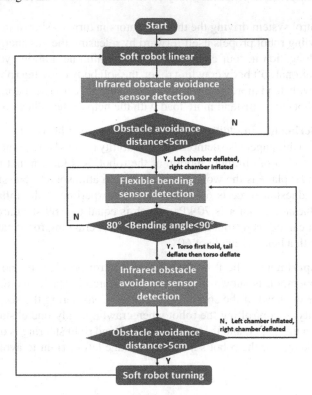

Fig. 8. Flow chart of the control program of the soft body crawling robot.

this state, the tail deflates after leaving the adsorption surface and the torso deflates to drive the robot as a whole to produce an offset angle. When the bending angle reaches 80°–90°, the robot's torso first keeps the state at this time, after the tail deflates and leaves the adsorption surface, the torso deflates and drives the robot as a whole to produce an offset angle, the infrared obstacle avoidance sensor detects whether there is an obstacle again, and if it is not detected, it proves that the soft body crawling robot turns correctly, if it is detected, it means that the robot should turn to the right to avoid obstacles, at this time the left cavity air pump starts working and the right cavity air pump stops working to deflate Make the robot torso bend to the right, reach the set bending angle to turn successfully and then keep going straight and continue to move forward.

In this paper, a maze model made of photosensitive resin material is designed to detect the obstacle avoidance effect of the soft crawling robot, as shown in Fig. 9(a). In order to facilitate the subsequent environmental mapping and improve the accuracy of mapping, marker points are made manually on the side walls of the maze, and the top cover is added on top of the maze model to form a closed channel which can greatly reduce the interference of the surrounding environment and improve the effect of maze channel mapping.

The soft body robot was put into the open maze channel and the crawling of the soft body robot was observed. After crawling in a straight line for 20 s, the robot encountered the first obstacle. According to the preset program, the robot firstly turned off the air pump on the left side, and the right side air pump continued to work to inflate and then made the robot body bend to the left, and when the bending angle reached 80°, the right side air pump was maintained, and after the front adhesion actuator was fixed, the other parts were deflated because the rebound elasticity of the material could make the torso square, and it was found in the experiment that a group of movement cycles the torso was not Therefore, in the program, when no obstacle is detected, i.e., when the direction of obstacle avoidance is correct, the torso of the soft crawling robot is set to move in a straight line after two sets of motion cycles. The soft body crawling robot took 38 s to avoid the first obstacle, and after 78 s of robot movement, it transported to the second obstacle, bent to the left first and still detected the obstacle, then bent to the right to complete the obstacle avoidance, and the robot took 44 s to avoid the second obstacle, and the soft body crawling robot took 147 s, about two minutes, to go through the maze tunnel as a whole, and showed excellent obstacle avoidance ability during the autonomous crawling process.

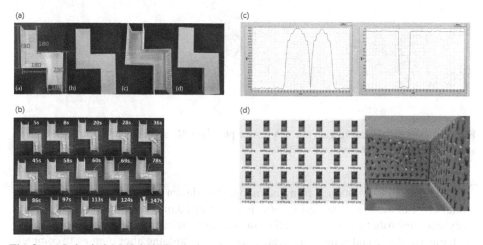

Fig. 9. (a) Labyrinth Model; (b) Environmental obstacle avoidance; (c) Labview Data Acquisition in Labyrinth Crawling Experiment; (d) Video Processing.

The robot is placed in the closed maze channel shown in Fig. 9(a) to crawl, and the Labview data acquisition platform is built to connect the output voltage of the flexible bending sensor and the infrared digital obstacle avoidance sensor in parallel with the NI data card, and the Labview programming is performed in the upper computer to reflect the sensor values in real time. As Fig. 9(c) shows the voltage data collected by the robot in the first minute while crawling in the confined channel. The environment in the channel is filmed by the self-contained camera while crawling, and the filmed video is imported into the linux system to build a map of the channel environment by ORB-SLAM2 algorithm.

Since the ORB-SLAM2 algorithm recognizes images as input, we need to split the video into numerous images. Open the terminal in the folder containing the video, enter python sep.py rgb command and python file.py command to save the images obtained after video segmentation in the rgb folder and get the timestamp corresponding to each image, and finally get a total of 2569 images. The ORB-SLAM2 algorithm is run to extract and match feature points for each image, and the location information of the extracted feature points is saved in mappoints.txt and exported to excel in Windows system for data processing.

The scatter3 function is used in matlab to present the data in excel in the form of a 3D scatter plot, and the results are shown in Fig. 10(a), and the rotated view is shown in Fig. 10(b). There are still many interference points in the environmental feature points collected by the algorithm, but the outline of the maze can be clearly seen from the rotated view of the scatter plot. Since the monocular camera cannot obtain specific depth information, it is necessary to combine the soft robot body length, the movement speed and the time information of the sensor signal change to determine the specific size of the maze.

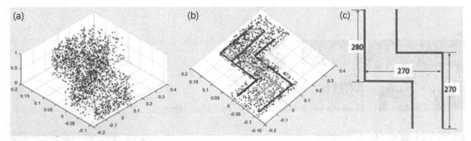

Fig. 10. Data processing to generate 3D scatter plots; (a) 3D scatter plot; (b) Rotated view of scatter plot; (c) Environment construction.

The maze model obtained from the mapping is shown in Fig. 10(c), and the dimensional error of the actual maze Fig. 9(a) is less than 10mm, which proves that the soft body crawling robot can both sense the surrounding environment obstacles to complete obstacle avoidance and achieve accurate environment building after running to complete the interaction with the environment.

4 Conclusion

This paper focuses on the intelligent soft crawling robot with the function of interacting with the environment, and designs a fiber-reinforced double-cavity flexible actuator as the robot's torso to realize the function of elongation and bending when moving, and a double-layer adhesion actuator driven by positive pressure as the robot's head and tail to adsorb on the moving surface when the robot is crawling, and completes the robot's linear crawling and The dual-cavity flexible actuator completes the robot's linear crawling and turning movements. The innovative magnetic printing method is used to design and manufacture a sensitive grid type flexible strain sensor, which is arranged in the strain limiting layer of the robot's flexible double-cavity actuator to monitor the bending angle of the robot's torso in real time. The infrared digital obstacle avoidance sensor is selected to realize the autonomous obstacle avoidance function of the robot, and the ORB-SLAM framework is studied to design a pneumatic control platform based on Arduino development board to combine the flexible bending sensor, infrared digital obstacle avoidance sensor and ORB-SLAM algorithm framework, so that the soft crawling robot can intelligently pass through the maze passage, complete the environment building map in the closed environment The function is to get accurate map information and complete the interaction with the environment to build the foundation for future applications in pipeline exploration and post-disaster rescue.

Acknowledgment. Research supported by Postgraduate Research and Innovation Project of Jiangsu Province (SJCX21_1339).

References

1. 曹玉君，尚建忠，梁科山，等. 软体机器人研究现状综述. 机械工程学报**48**(3), 25–33 (2012)
2. 王田苗，郝雨飞，杨兴帮，文力.软体机器人:结构、   驱动、   传感与控制. 机械工程学报**53**(13), 1–13 (2017)
3. Lu, M.Y., Chen, G.M., He, Q.S., et al.: Development of a hydraulic driven bionic soft gecko toe. J. Mech. Robot. (2021)
4. Pi, J., Liu, J., Zhou, K.H., et al.: An octopus-inspired bionic flexible gripper for apple grasping. Agriculture **11**(10) (2021)
5. Zhang, J.H., Wang, T., Wang, J., et al.: Dynamic modeling and simulation of inchworm movement towards bio-inspired soft robot design. Bioinspir. Biomim. **14**(6) (2019)
6. 陈尤旭，王德山，金国庆等. 面向软体机器人的3D打印硅胶软材料实验研究. 中国机械工程, **031**(005), 603–609, 629 (2020)
7. Tolley, M.T., Shepherd, R.F., Karpelson, M., et al.: An untethered jumping soft robot. IEEE (2014)
8. Bu, T.Z., Xiao, T.X., Yang, Z.W., et al.: Stretchable triboelectric-photonic smart skin for tactile and gesture sensing. Adv. Mater. (Deerfield Beach, Fla.) **30**(16) (2018)
9. Li, G., Chen, X., Zhou, F., et al.: Self-powered soft robot in the Mariana Trench. Nature **591**(7848) (2021)
10. Wehner, M., Truby, R.L., Fitzgerald, D.J., et al.: An integrated design and fabrication strategy for entirely soft, autonomous robots. Nature **536**(7617), 451–455 (2016)
11. Kim, W., Byun, J., Kim, J.K., et al.: Bioinspired dual-morphing stretchable origami. Sci. Robot. **4**(36), eaay3493 (2019)
12. Christianson, C., Bayag, C., Li, G., et al.: Jellyfish-inspired soft robot driven by fluid electrode dielectric organic robotic actuators. Front. Robot. AI **6**, 126 (2019)
13. Hughes, J.A.E., Maiolino, P., Iida, F.: An anthropomorphic soft skeleton hand exploiting conditional models for piano playing. Sci. Robot. **3**(25) (2018)
14. Wang, Y., Yang, X., Chen, Y., et al.: A biorobotic adhesive disc for underwater hitchhiking inspired by the remora suckerfish. Sci. Robot. **2**(10), eaan8072 (2017)
15. Ming, L., Tao, W., Chen, F., et al.: Design improvements and dynamic characterization on fluidic elastomer actuators for a soft robotic snake. In: IEEE International Conference on Technologies for Practical Robot Applications. IEEE (2014)
16. Tolley Michael, T., Shepherd Robert, F., Mosadegh, B., et al.: A resilient, untethered soft robot. Soft Robot. **1**(3), (2014)

17. Zarrouk, D., Mann, M., Degani, N., et al.: Single actuator wave-like robot (SAW): design, modeling, and experiments. Bioinspir. Biomim. **11**(4), 046004 (2016)
18. 袁鑫. 面向软体机器人的液态金属柔性传感器的研究. 苏州大学(2020)
19. Panagiotis, P., Zheng, W., Kevin, C., et al.: Soft robotic glove for combined assistance and at-home rehabilitation. Robot. Auton. Syst. **73** (2015)
20. Park, Y.-L., Chen, B., Pérez-Arancibia, N.O., et al.: Design and control of a bio-inspired soft wearable robotic device for ankle–foot rehabilitation. Bioinspir. Biomim. **9**(1), (2014)
21. 刘会聪,杨梦柯,金国庆等. 液态金属柔性感知的人机交互软体机械手. 中国机械工程**32**(12), 1470–1478 (2021)
22. Chang, L., Hai, J.S., Jonathon, C., Yu, S.: Design and fabrication of a soft robotic hand with embedded actuators and sensors. J. Mech. Robot. **7**(2) (2015)
23. Balaguer, C., Gimenez, A., Jardon, A.: Climbing robots' mobility for inspection and maintenance of 3D complex environments. Auton. Robots **18**, 157–169 (2005)
24. Shen, H., Magazine, N.: Beyond terminator: squishy Octobot heralds new era of soft robotics. Nat. News **545**(7655), 406–408 (2016)
25. 胡兵兵. 基于3D打印技术的软体机器人的设计与实验研究. 苏州大学(2019)
26. Goldoni, R., Ozkan-Aydin, Y., Kim, Y.S., et al.: Stretchable nanocomposite sensors, nanomembrane interconnectors, and wireless electronics toward feedback-loop control of a soft earthworm robot. ACS Appl. Mater. Interfaces (2020)
27. Shingo, M., Yusuke, H., Ryo, Y., Shuji, H.: Self-oscillating gel actuator for chemical robotics. Adv. Robot. **22**(12) (2018)
28. Drotman, D., Jadhav, S., Sharp, D., et al.: Electronics-free pneumatic circuits for controlling soft-legged robots. Sci. Robot. **6**(51) (2021)
29. Hawkes, E.W., Blumenschein, L.H., Okamura, A.M., et al.: A soft robot that navigates its environment through growth. Sci. Robot. **2**(8) (2017)
30. Rafsanjani, A., Zhang, Y., Liu, B., et al:. Kirigami skins make a simple soft actuator crawl. Sci. Robot. **3**(15), eaar7555 (2018)
31. Zhang, B., Fan, Y., Yang, P., et al.: Worm-like soft robot for complicated tubular environments. Soft Rob. **6**(3), 399–413 (2019)
32. Gu, G., Jiang, Z., Zhao, R., et al.: Soft wall-climbing robots. Sci. Robot. **3**(25), eaat2874 (2018)
33. Must, I., Sinibaldi, E., Mazzolai, B.: A variable-stiffness tendril-like soft robot based on reversible osmotic actuation. Nat. Commun. **10**(1) (2019)

Drogue Pose Estimation Based on Ultraviolet Camera and Asymmetric Markers

Bin Pu[1(✉)], Zhenguo Wu[1], Riming Lou[2], Jing Lu[2], Ze'an Liu[1], and Xuanyin Wang[1]

[1] State Key Laboratory of Fluid Power and Mechatronic Systems, Zhejiang University, Hangzhou 310027, China
binpu@zju.edu.cn
[2] Zhejiang Tianheng Wuwei Electronic Technology Co., Ltd., Hangzhou 311217, China

Abstract. Drogue pose estimation plays an important role in the docking process of aerial refueling. Many researchers have utilized vision-based methods, such as visible and infrared cameras. However, background signals like sunlight usually cause complex noise. Inspired by the fact that the atmosphere absorbs most Ultraviolet (UV) light around 254 nm, we propose a drogue pose estimation method based on a UV camera and asymmetric markers. Specifically, we place eight UV markers on the drogue and capture the scene image using a UV camera located at the root of the probe. To address the brightness variance of these markers, we propose a Region of Interest based adaptive threshold algorithm for UV images. By solving a Perspective-n-Points problem, our method can estimate the drogue pose. Simulated pose estimation and distance estimation experiments demonstrate that our methods are efficient and can run in real time. Overall, our approach offers an effective solution to drogue pose estimation in aerial refueling.

Keywords: Pose estimation · UV camera · Perspective-n-Point · Image threshold

1 Introduction

Pose estimation is a fundamental problem in machine vision that has various applications, such as human-robot interaction, mechanical component assembly, and aerial refueling. Aerial refueling is a crucial means to improve aircraft endurance, and it requires difficult piloting skills. Hose aerial refueling is a flexible scheme, mainly consisting of the drogue and the probe, as shown in Fig. 1. The receiving probe is a rigid tube that extends from the front of the aircraft, and the drogue is the refueling part with a funnel shape to catch the probe. Vision-based drogue pose estimation is an efficient method to guide the docking procedure, and cameras can be installed on the receiver aircraft. Due to the fixed

H. Yang et al. (Eds.): ICIRA 2023, LNAI 14267, pp. 387–398, 2023.
https://doi.org/10.1007/978-981-99-6483-3_33

connection between the camera and the probe, the pose of the drogue relative to the probe can be transformed into the pose to the camera. However, visual methods are often susceptible to interference from sunlight and lighting differences between day and night. For example, glare or shadows may affect the image quality significantly. Therefore, there are still many challenges to overcome in visual drogue pose estimation.

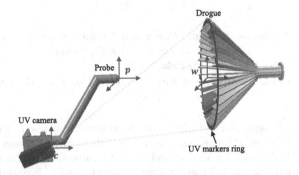

Fig. 1. Overview of vision-based aerial refueling. There mainly are a drogue, a fuel probe, and an ultraviolet camera. Markers can be installed on the drogue for guidance. Visual drogue pose estimation can assist the docking process.

Drogue pose estimation has attracted much attention from researchers in recent years. Some researchers detect the drogue with an RGB camera. Wang [1], for example, sets red double rings on the drogue and segments the drogue region through HSV color space feature extraction. Similarly, Sun [2] proposes using a bionic visual method and puts blue markers on a red paint drogue. The scene image is changed into four special channels to imitate an eagle eye. Ma [3] uses an arc feature to find the drogue and calculates its pose by photogrammetry. Different from RGB, Wilson [4] employs an Infra-Red (IR) vision system for drogue pose estimation and attaches 7 IR markers onto the drogue. Because of the background interference from the sun, there also are 5 more markers on the airplane to aid the detection. Three dimensional (3D) information provides a direct way to measure the distance of the drogue. Chen [5] proposes using a 3D Flash LiDAR to obtain the 3D data of aerial refueling scenes. After removing outliers and fitting a curve, it finds the drogue center. With technology developing, deep learning methods have also been applied in this area. Choi [6] utilizes both RGB and depth cameras. It feeds the RGB image into a YOLOv3 network to get the drogue position, then filters out the corresponding 3D point clouds. Overall, RGB and IR cameras are usually disturbed by sunlight and scene objects. Separating the drogue from a large number of 3D points causes a calculation burden for the depth camera.

Considering that aeronautical aircraft mainly work in the atmosphere, we use a specific Ultraviolet (UV) spectral camera for drogue pose estimation. While the solar spectrum covers a wide wavelength range, the atmosphere has a strong absorptive effect on UV light at 200–300 nm [7]. As a result, there is minimal UV light noise in this band within the atmosphere, and in such a way our built visual system can work both day and night. Specifically, we use a 254 nm UV light band. We place 8 UV lamps on the drogue at an asymmetric position and use a UV camera to capture scene images. We propose a UV image processing algorithm that matches the UV imaging spot with each UV lamp. By solving a Perspective-n-Points (PnP) problem, we obtain the transformation matrix of the drogue relative to the camera. We can then calculate the distance and the angle of the drogue relative to the camera.

Overall, the main contributions of this paper are:

1) We propose a drogue pose estimation method based on a UV camera and asymmetric markers. Our method can work in all weather conditions.
2) We propose a Region of Interest (ROI) based adaptive threshold algorithm to get the connected components of UV markers.
3) We have verified the accuracy of our system through robotic arm simulation experiments. Our method can run in real time with an error less than 100 mm and 3.0°C in pose estimation around 5 meters distance.

This paper is organized as follows. In Sect. 2, we introduce our scheme framework and the overall process of the image algorithm. Subsequently, the details of our method are discussed in Sect. 3, including camera calibration, our adaptive threshold algorithm, and asymmetric markers matching. We describe our testing experiments in Sect. 4 and report both the accuracy and speed. Finally, we summarize the conclusion and provide an outlook for our method in Sect. 5.

2   Methods Framework

The key step of aerial refueling is to dock the receiving probe on the drogue. In this process, pose estimation of the drogue can be beneficial. Due to the fixed position relationship between the camera and the receiving probe, the pose of the drogue relative to the probe can be transformed into the pose to the camera. Thus, our method focuses on achieving robust pose estimation of the probe relative to the camera through visual methods. There are mainly two parts: scheme design and algorithm design.

Scheme Design. In the scheme design part, we mainly use UV light in the 254 nm band. Because the atmosphere strongly absorbs ultraviolet light, components of the solar spectrum in this band are rare in the atmosphere. Therefore, applying it to drogue pose estimation can avoid interference from sunlight. We select an asymmetric location on the circumference of the drogue to install eight UV lamps. The UV camera located at the root of the probe captures the scene image. Due to the active light source, our method can work both day and night. According to the pinhole imaging model, the UV light circularly located on the

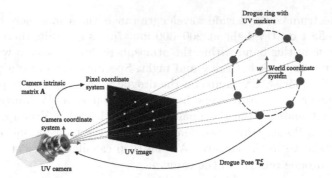

Fig. 2. Overview of our drogue pose estimation method. Circular distributed UV markers on the drogue appear as light spots in the image. Combining with the camera internal matrix $\mathbf{A}$, the transformation $\mathbf{T}_w^c$ between world coordinate system w and camera coordinate system c can be obtained.

drogue will appear as an ellipse in the camera image, as shown in Fig. 2. We establish the world coordinate system w on the drogue center, the pixel coordinate system s on the image's top left corner, and the camera coordinate system c on the camera's optical center. Using the corresponding relationship between Two dimensional (2D) points $\mathbf{p}_s = [u, v]^T$ on the imaging ellipse and 3D points $\mathbf{p}_w = [x_w, y_w, z_w]^T$ on the drogue ring, a Perspective-n-Point (PnP) problem can be conducted as,

$$
\begin{bmatrix} u \\ v \\ 1 \end{bmatrix} = \mathbf{A}\Pi^c \begin{bmatrix} x_c \\ y_c \\ z_c \\ 1 \end{bmatrix} = \mathbf{A}\Pi^c \mathbf{T}_w^c \begin{bmatrix} x_w \\ y_w \\ z_w \\ 1 \end{bmatrix},
\tag{1}
$$

where $\mathbf{A}$ is the camera intrinsic parameters matrix, and Π^c is the perspective projection model. By using OpenCV solvePnP API (regarded as ϕ), we can solve T_w^c as,

$$
\mathbf{T}_w^c = \begin{bmatrix} \mathbf{R} & \mathbf{T} \\ \mathbf{0} & 1 \end{bmatrix} = \phi(\mathbf{p}_s, \mathbf{p}_w).
\tag{2}
$$

After solving $\mathbf{T}_w^c$, we can get the rotation matrix $\mathbf{R}$ and the translation vector $\mathbf{T}$ of the world coordinate system relative to the camera coordinate system. In such a way, we obtain the drogue pose to the camera.

Image Algorithm. In the image algorithm part, our method mainly includes two steps: image preprocessing and pose solving, as shown in Fig. 3. In the preprocessing section, we continuously obtain images from the UV camera and place them in a First in First out (FIFO) image buffer queue to balance the image algorithm time and the image capture time. When the queue is full, adding new images to the queue will discard the earlier images to prevent the queue length from increasing. The UV markers appear as white spots in the UV image, and the halo of the highlight may vary under different viewing angles. The key operation of the preprocessing part is the image threshold. Due to the influence of halos, the connected regions of light spots obtained by traditional binary algorithms are prone to merge. When the number of connected domains is inconsistent with the number of markers, the PNP problem cannot be solved, which can lead to a failure of pose estimation. We propose a Region of Interest (ROI) based adaptive threshold algorithm that we will discuss in detail in Sect. 3.2. Our method can effectively segment the connected domains of different markers.

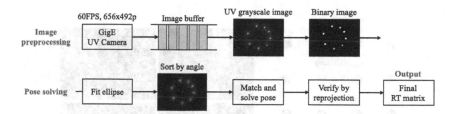

Fig. 3. The algorithm flow of our methods. Image threshold is the key section in the image preprocessing part. The pose solving part mainly includes ellipse regression, spots match, and pose solving.

In the pose solving section, the core step is the construction of the PnP problem, which involves three parts: 2D point attribute calculation, 2D and 3D point matching, and solving. We first calculate the centroid of the binary connected blobs by image moments. To improve solution accuracy, the centroid coordinates will undergo distortion correction. The 3D marker points located on the circumference of the drogue appear as an ellipse on the 2D image. To correspond 2D light spots with 3D markers, we use asymmetric 3D point position and search for the optimal match through a cyclic matching algorithm, which will be discussed in detail in Sect. 3.3. Then we input the 2D centroid data and 3D group table data into a solvePNP function to get the rotation matrix $\mathbf{R}$ and translation vector $\mathbf{T}$. We obtain the Euler angle information of the drogue relative to the UV camera by inversely solving the $\mathbf{R}$ matrix. From this, we get the pose information of the drogue relative to the camera.

3 Detail Designs

3.1 UV Camera Calibration

The drogue pose estimation algorithm employed in this study utilizes transformation from 3D markers to 2D images. The accuracy of the marker position directly impacts the accuracy of the drogue pose estimation. Therefore, we first perform camera calibration to determine the camera's internal parameters and distortion coefficients. Because UV cameras can only receive UV light for imaging, traditional visible cursor positioning methods cannot be used. Instead, we use ultraviolet lights arranged in an array for camera calibration, and the calibration board is shown in Fig. 4 (a). Based on the principle of pinhole imaging, we can obtain

$$\mathbf{A} = \begin{bmatrix} f_x & 0 & c_x & 0 \\ 0 & f_y & c_y & 0 \\ 0 & 0 & 1 & 0 \end{bmatrix}, \qquad (3)$$

where f_x, f_y are the normalized focal length on the x-axis and y-axis, and c_x, c_y is the image center. Following Zhang's method [8], we collect images from different angles to calibrate the camera. The calibration process is shown in Fig. 4 (b).

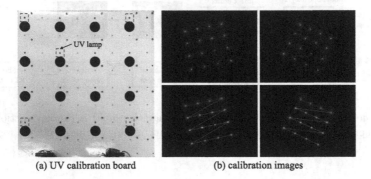

(a) UV calibration board   (b) calibration images

Fig. 4. The calibration board for the UV camera. There are 4×4 UV lamp arrays. By using Zhang's method [8] we can obtain the internal matrix of the UV camera.

3.2 ROI Based Adaptive Threshold Algorithm

The UV lamp appears as a bright spot in the UV camera, making image thresholding an effective operation for obtaining the imaging area of each UV marker. However, due to differences in the angle of lamps emitting light to the camera, as well as differences in the quality of each lamp, the overall imaging spot of each marker is similar but may vary. Using a global threshold in the traditional thresholding method can easily result in connected binary images, and the area size of each light varies greatly. Once connected, it becomes difficult to match the light spot with the markers, which can cause pose estimation failure.

To solve this problem, we propose an ROI based adaptive threshold algorithm, as shown in Algorithm 1. The algorithm based on global threshold employs the same value to segment the spots of all markers. The method based on local adaptive threshold has a high computational complexity and may introduce more noise in the background region. To integrate the characteristics of the two methods, our algorithm first uses a global threshold method to roughly locate the imaging area $\mathbf{S}$ of the drogue. Subsequently, in order to adapt to the imaging differences of each spot, we use an adaptive threshold algorithm based on Bernsen [9] in region $\mathbf{S}$. Both local contrast s_w and local mid gray $_w$ is considered in threshold. As shown in Fig. 5, compared with traditional global threshold,

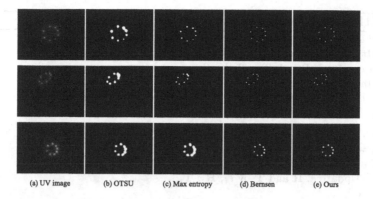

(a) UV image   (b) OTSU   (c) Max entropy   (d) Bernsen   (e) Ours

Fig. 5. Qualitative results of four image threshold algorithms. Our method could segment the spots well with high speed.

Algorithm 1: ROI based adaptive threshold algorithm

Data: Gray-scale UV image **P**, local window size w.
Result: Binary image **B**.
1 Calculate the OTSU threshold t_m and get the init threshold image $\mathbf{B}_s$;
2 Find the drogue region **S** in $\mathbf{B}_s$;
3 **for** *pixel p_i in* **S do**
4   Crop the local window **W** with size w;
5   Calculate the local contrast s_w and the mid gray value g_w;
6   **if** $p_i ¡ s_w$ **then**
7 | **B** pixel $b_i = (g_w \geq 128)?255 : 0$;
8   **else**
9 | **B** pixel $b_i = (p_i \geq g_w)?255 : 0$;
10   **end**
11 **end**

---

our method can better classify the regions to be detected without merging. Our results are similar to Bernsen [9], but we use 14.74 ms in threshold time cost compared to 256.71 ms in Bernsen's method. Our method is effective and can run at high speed.

3.3 Asymmetric Markers Match

In this study, we use the physical coordinates (x_w, y_w, z_w) of the eight markers on the drogue in the world coordinate system and the pixel coordinates (u, v) in the pixel coordinate system to perform a PnP solution to estimate the pose of the drogue. To identify the UV makers index, we use an asymmetric position design. UV lamps are installed on a ring, and they are not unify located. We put the UV markers on a counterclockwise angle array of 0, 30, 66, 106, 152, 202, 257, and 317. In such a method, we can identify the UV markers' relative position, so that we can estimate the roll angle of the drogue.

Algorithm 2: Asymmetric UV markers match algorithm

Data: 2D centroid vector $\mathbf{v}_s$, 3D markers coordinate vector $\mathbf{v}_w$.
Result: rotation matrix $\mathbf{R}$, translation vector $\mathbf{T}$.

1 Initial $e = 1000$, $\mathbf{R} = \mathbf{I}$, $\mathbf{T} = \mathbf{0}$, $K=8$;
2 **for** *i in range(K)* **do**
3   Get $\mathbf{v}_w^i$ by circularly shifting elements in $\mathbf{v}_w$ with i steps;
4     $\mathbf{R}_i, \mathbf{T}_i = \text{solvePNP}(\mathbf{v}_s, \mathbf{v}_w^i)$;
5   Reprojection 2D points $\mathbf{v}_s^i = \text{projectPoints}(\mathbf{v}_w^i, \mathbf{R}_i, \mathbf{T}_i)$;
6     $e_i = \|\mathbf{v}_s^i - \mathbf{v}_s\|_F^2$;
7   **if** $e_i < e$ **then**
8 | Update e, $\mathbf{R}$ and $\mathbf{T}$ by e_i, $\mathbf{R}_i$, $\mathbf{T}_i$;
9   **end**
10 **end**

Specifically, our asymmetric markers match algorithm is as following. After Sect. 3.2, we can calculate the centroid of each light spot after segmentation. Since they are located on an ellipse, we sort them counterclockwise and push them in a 2D vector $\mathbf{v}_s$. At the same time, UV markers in the world coordinate system can be pushed in a 3D vector $\mathbf{v}_w$ by angle. Then we get two vectors, but their match relationship is unknown. Since they are both counterclockwise indexing, there are only 8 solutions. So we use a traversal match method to infer its index. For each match, we solve the transformation matrix separately and compare the reprojection error. The algorithm details are shown as Algorithm 2. After the match, we can get a rotation $\mathbf{R}$ and translation $\mathbf{T}$ with minimal reprojection error. If this minimum reprojection error e meets the limit requirements, the corresponding $\mathbf{R}$ and $\mathbf{T}$ are the drogue poses we expect to obtain. If the requirements are not met, then we discard it and take a new image for processing.

4 Experiments

To verify the effectiveness of our method, we use a six Degree-of-Freedom (DoF) robotic arm to simulate the position and pose transformation of the drogue, and perform accuracy comparison tests using our method. By collecting robotic arm data, we can make comparisons with our method's output to evaluate accuracy. We put the UV camera on a tripod and fixed the drogue UV light ring at the end of the robotic arm. By changing the joint angle of the robotic arm, we simulate different positions of the drogue and capture the scene image. Our program runs on an Intel i7-11700k CPU with 32 G RAM. The UV camera we used is THUVCX2-1. The camera resolution is 656×492, and the field of view (FOV) is $60°C$. The model of the robotic arm we used is Chaifu SF6-C1400. In the experimental section, we first calibrate the experimental scene and then conduct accuracy testing for both pose estimation and distance estimation.

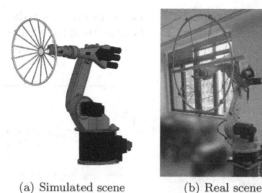

(a) Simulated scene   (b) Real scene

Fig. 6. The simulated scene and the real photo of the pose simulation experiment. A circular UV lamp ring is installed on a 6 DoF robotic arm. a UV camera on the tripod 5 meters away is used to capture images.

4.1 Hand-Eye Calibration

To evaluate the accuracy of pose estimation, we install the lamp ring at the end of a 6 DoF robotic arm, as shown in Fig. 6. The UV camera is mounted on a tripod and placed 5 meters away. The pose transformation of the robotic arm is controlled by a teaching pendant. The entire system has established four coordinate systems: the robot arm base coordinate system b, the robot arm end coordinate system g, the world coordinate system w on the drogue lamp ring, and the camera coordinate system c at the camera optical center. Together, they form a robotic vision system with eyes outside the hand. According to the relation between coordinate transformations, their transformation matrices satisfy the following equation,

$$\mathbf{T}_c^w * \mathbf{T}_b^c = \mathbf{T}_g^w * \mathbf{T}_b^g. \tag{4}$$

Among these, $\mathbf{T}_w^g$ can be calculated through the coordinate values displayed on the teaching pendant, and $\mathbf{T}_c^w$ can be obtained using our methods. There are two unknown variables in this equation, and we use an eye-out-hand calibration method to solve them. Specifically, we keep the tripod stationary, change the posture of the robotic arm, collect 15 images through the UV camera, and record the corresponding 6 DoF coordinate data of the robotic arm. The Shah method [10] is used to solve them through the OpenCV's calibration API.

4.2 Pose Estimation Experiment

To evaluate the accuracy of our system, we obtain extra data by changing the pose of the robotic arm and performing corresponding error calculations. Since there is no true value for the pose transformation $\mathbf{T}_w^c$ from the drogue to the camera, and according to Eq. 4, we have

$$\mathbf{T}_g^b = \mathbf{T}_c^b * \mathbf{T}_w^c * \mathbf{T}_g^w. \tag{5}$$

Therefore, we can use the left part $\mathbf{T}_g^b$ calculated from 6 DoF data as the ground truth, and we transform the output $\mathbf{T}_w^c$ of our method to calculate the right part $\mathbf{S}_g^b = \mathbf{T}_c^b * \mathbf{T}_w^c * \mathbf{T}_g^w$. The numerical comparison between $\mathbf{T}_g^b$ and $\mathbf{S}_g^b$ can serve as the error measure.

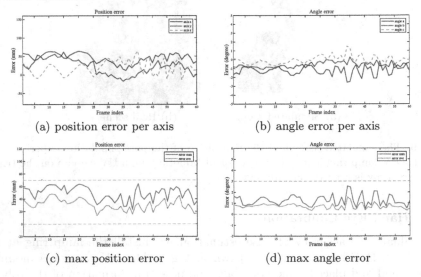

(a) position error per axis

(b) angle error per axis

(c) max position error

(d) max angle error

Fig. 7. The error plots of the pose estimation experiments.

For this purpose, we collected an additional 60 images with different arm angles, and these pose data have no intersection with calibration data. The error comparison results are shown in Fig. 7. Our single axis position estimation errors are 64.20 mm max, with a distance error 80.36 mm max. Our estimation error for the three rotational DoF is 2.48°C max. Thus, we can conclude that the position estimation accuracy of the system is less than 100 mm, and the angle estimation accuracy stands at 3.0°C in 5 meters distance. For a more comprehensive comparison, we list the accuracy situation among several methods in Table 1. These six methods except ours use RGB camera for visual pose estimation, such as PB [11] use point feature and CB [12] use circle feature. The OCL method [12] using 3L feature gets the highest accuracy with 8.13 ms time cost in i7 11700f. Our methods also acquire high accuracy with 20.56 ms time cost in i7 11700k. Even though there is still a little gap in performance compared with RGB cameras, our method can work even at night.

Table 1. Accuracy results of six drogue pose estimation methods.

Method	PB [11]	CB [12]	Ansar [13]	LDT [14]	OCL [15]	Ours
Mean Translation Error (mm)	102.78	53.34	13.17	17.76	6.08	28.94
Mean Angle Error (degree)	102.78	1.57	16.89	16.38	0.33	0.61
Time (ms)	0.25	0.14	69.09	59.66	8.13	20.56*

4.3   Distance Estimation Experiment

The above experiment represents the outcome of pose estimation using a fixed tripod. We do distance estimation experiments in a large range. We move the UV camera within 0–12 m, calculate the distance based on the output $\mathbf{T}_c^w$, and then manually measure the distance from the camera to the center of the drogue ring using a laser rangefinder. We compare them to evaluate the system's distance estimation accuracy, as shown in Fig. 8. According to the figure, the maximum distance error in 0–5 m is found to be 70.65 mm. With the distance increasing more than 5 m, the error rises quickly, since the drogue ring looks small in the image and the UV camera resolution is not enough. It should be noted that within the range of 0–2 m, the drogue ring is out of sight, resulting in an inability to solve for its position. However, this limitation has little effect in practical use since the receiving probe itself has a certain length and the camera is usually mounted at the bottom. When the distance is less than 2 m, the probe has almost docked on the drogue already.

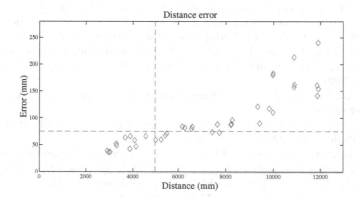

Fig. 8. The error plot of the distance estimation.

5   Conclusion

This paper proposes a drogue pose estimation method based on a UV camera and asymmetric markers. Compared with conventional vision methods that use visible light cameras and depth cameras, we extend the use of UV spectroscopy to aerial refueling. We install a set of asymmetrically arranged UV markers on the drogue, and a UV camera on the probe part. The 254 nm ultraviolet light we use has significantly less environmental noise. We propose an ROI-based adaptive threshold algorithm that can effectively segment UV light spots with different brightness levels. The unique arrangement of the markers allows for the estimation of the six degrees of freedom pose of the drogue by constructing a PnP problem. We conduct pose estimation and distance estimation experiments to demonstrate the performance and reliability of our methods. Our methods exhibit location errors of less than 100 mm and angle errors of less than 3.0°C at distances around 5 m. A higher resolution UV camera can be used in the future for an extension in the working distance.

References

1. Wang, X., Dong, X., Kong, X.: Feature recognition and tracking of aircraft tanker and refueling drogue for UAV aerial refueling. In: Chinese Control and Decision Conference (CCDC), pp. 2057–2062 (2013)
2. Sun, Y., et al.: Bionic visual close-range navigation control system for the docking stage of probe-and-drogue autonomous aerial refueling. Aerosp. Sci. Technol. **91**, 136–149 (2019)
3. Ma, Y., et al.: A novel autonomous aerial refueling drogue detection and pose estimation method based on monocular vision. Measurement **136**, 132–142 (2019)
4. Wilson, D., Goktogan, A., Sukkarieh, S.: Experimental validation of a drogue estimation algorithm for autonomous aerial refueling. In: IEEE International Conference on Robotics and Automation (ICRA), pp. 5318–5323 (2015)
5. Chen, C., et al.: Autonomous aerial refueling ground test demonstration-a sensor-in-the-loop non-tracking method. Sensors **15**(5), 10948–10972 (2015)
6. Choi, A., Yang, H., Han, J.: Study on robust aerial docking mechanism with deep learning based drogue detection and docking. Mech. Syst. Signal Process. **154**, 107579 (2021)
7. North, G., Pyle, J., Zhang, F.: Encyclopedia of Atmospheric Sciences, 2nd Edn. Elsevier (2013)
8. Zhang, Z.: A flexible new technique for camera calibration. IEEE Trans. Pattern Anal. Mach. Intell. **22**(11), 1330–1334 (2000)
9. Bernsen, J.: Dynamic thresholding of gray level image. In: Proceedings of International Conference on Pattern Recognition (ICPR), pp. 1251–1255 (1986)
10. Shah, M.: Solving the robot-world/hand-eye calibration problem using the Kronecker product. J. Mech. Robot. **5**(3), 031007 (2013)
11. Garcia, J., Younes, A.: Real-time navigation for drogue-type autonomous aerial refueling using vision-based deep learning detection. IEEE Trans. Aerosp. Electron. Syst. **57**(4), 2225–2246 (2021)
12. Sun, S., et al.: Robust landmark detection and position measurement based on monocular vision for autonomous aerial refueling of UAVs. IEEE Trans. Cybern. **49**(12), 4167–4179 (2018)
13. Ansar, A., Daniilidis, K.: Linear pose estimation from points or lines. IEEE Trans. Pattern Anal. Mach. Intell. **25**(5), 578–589 (2003)
14. Xu, C., et al.: Pose estimation from line correspondences: a complete analysis and a series of solutions. IEEE Trans. Pattern Anal. Mach. Intell. **39**(6), 1209–1222 (2016)
15. Zhao, K., et al.: Monocular visual pose estimation for flexible drogue by decoupling the deformation. IEEE Trans. Instrum. Meas. **71**, 1–11 (2022)

Vision Based Flame Detection Using Compressed Domain Motion Prediction and Multi-Feature Fusion

Jixiang Tang(✉), Jiangtao Chen, Xuanyin Wang, Bin Pu, and Ze'an Liu

State Key Laboratory of Fluid Power and Mechatronic Systems, Zhejiang University,
Hangzhou 310027, China
tangjx@zju.edu.cn

Abstract. Flame detection is an important capability for intelligent robot perception in unknown environments, which is essential for responding to devastating fire hazards in advance. This paper presents a vision based flame detection method using video compressed domain motion prediction and multi-feature pattern recognition. Firstly, the motion information in the macroblocks and motion vectors of H.264/AVC compressed domain data is fully utilized to extract the motion foreground. Secondly, the flame color conditions in the YCbCr color space are established to segment candidate flame regions. Then, the chromaticity, texture, and geometric features of a candidate flame region are extracted and combined into a multi-dimensional feature vector. Finally, the Support Vector Machine classifier is adopted to identify real flames or non-flames to improve sensitivity and stability. Experimental results of indoor and outdoor applications for flame and flameless scenes illustrate that the proposed method achieves superior performance with higher accuracy and lower false alarm rate.

Keywords: Flame detection · Video processing · Motion prediction · Multi-feature fusion

1 Introduction

Fire is one of the most severe natural disasters. It will cause heavy losses to human lives and property as well as cause massive damage to the ecological environment. An effective flame detection system discovering fire as soon as possible is particularly important to minimize losses. Robots are well suited to perform flame detection tasks and provide timely warnings to humans, thanks to their increasing computing performance and environmental sensing capabilities. Especially in dangerous and unknown environments, flame detection is an essential capability for robots to prevent damage to themselves and protect humans.

Although traditional fire detection systems have been widely used, they still have some limitations. Smoke detectors are not suitable for spacious indoor or

H. Yang et al. (Eds.): ICIRA 2023, LNAI 14267, pp. 399–410, 2023.
https://doi.org/10.1007/978-981-99-6483-3_34

outdoor scenes, while infrared detectors are difficult to be widely used limited by the high deployment costs. The vision cameras that have been widely equipped by robots can address these issues well. By employing computer vision technologies, fire can be detected and located efficiently based on video taken by the robot. Vision based fire detection methods have the advantages of low cost, high efficiency, and intuitive display of fire information [1].

Vision based fire detection methods have attracted much attention. The flame and smoke are the most important visual phenomena in a fire. Traditional fire detection algorithms generally focus on features such as the color and motion of the flame and take pattern recognition methods for further classification [2,3]. Some flame detection algorithms based on convolutional neural networks have also been proposed [4,5]. However, these methods rely on large datasets and computational resources, introducing instability and burden for fire detection in unknown environments. This paper is dedicated to proposing a stable and computation effective vision based flame detection method using traditional pattern recognition methods for robots.

The static characteristics like unique color, contour, and texture, as well as the dynamic characteristics such as the moving center, the changing shape, and the flicker of the flame region, are the main basis for vision based fire detection algorithms [6]. Chen et al. [7] proposed the classic RGB model-based chromatic analysis, combined with the dynamics of growth and disorder characteristics to extract fire pixels. Celik et al. [8] proposed a rule-based generic color model in YCbCr to separate the luminance for flame pixel classification. Besides, various flame color models in color spaces such as CIE L*a*b* [9] and HSI [10] are proposed. A probabilistic model for color-based fire detection is proposed in [11].

To distinguish objects with similar colors and motion characteristics to flames, region of interest (ROI) extraction, and pattern recognition are introduced [12,13]. Chi et al. [14] proposed a gradient motion history image based motion detection algorithm considering the flicker characteristics of flames. Rong et al. [15] calculated the probability of the flame by feeding BP neural network with multi-feature composed of light intensity, red component, flame area, and boundary roughness. Kong et al. [16] extracted the candidate fire region using background subtraction and color model in YCbCr color space, and then adopted logistic regression to classify the features of size, motion, and color information.

This paper proposes a vision based flame detection method using compressed domain motion prediction and multi-feature fusion. Firstly, a motion prediction method in H.264/AVC compressed domain is introduced to maximize the use of video information. Secondly, a color model is established in the YCbCr color space to segment candidate flame regions. Then, a multi-dimensional feature vector consisting of chromaticity, texture, and geometric features is extracted for each candidate flame region. Finally, the Support Vector Machine (SVM) is adopted for classification. Experimental results show that the proposed method achieves higher accuracy and lower false alarm rate than other methods.

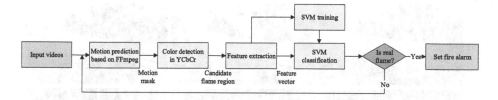

Fig. 1. The flow chart of the proposed flame detection method.

2 Methods

2.1 Framework

Figure 1 illustrates the flow chart of the proposed flame detection method, which mainly contains: motion prediction, candidate flame region extraction based on color conditions, and flame classification based on multi-feature extraction and pattern recognition. The motion mask is first generated by motion prediction. Then the candidate flame regions are extracted by superimposing the color conditions. Next is multi-feature extraction for training the SVM-based flame classifier. Finally, the system will issue a fire alarm if a flame is detected.

2.2 Motion Prediction

The videos transmitted and saved are all encoded for higher frame rates and lower storage space. H.264/AVC [17] is the mostly commonly used high-compression digital video codec standard. In H.264/AVC encoding process, information of the motion regions between frames is preserved [18]. The motion can be extracted directly from the compressed domain data in the decoding process [19].

The macroblock (MB), which contains a 16×16 pixel area, is the basic unit of processing while encoding and decoding video based on H.264/AVC. The MB will be further divided into 16×8, 8×16, 8×8, 8×4, 4×8, and 4×4 for regions with complex textures. During H.264/AVC encoding, the relative motion information between frames will be recorded in the motion vector (MV) of the MB. Therefore, the moving objects in the video can be efficiently predicted based on the positions of MBs and magnitudes of MVs in the compressed domain.

The FFmpeg codec (https://ffmpeg.org/) is utilized to perform compression domain motion detection during the video decoding process. After obtaining the MBs and MVs data, a motion map is constructed. The MBs with a size of 4×4 are regarded as motion regions because they are generally regions with strong motion. The motion of other pixels is calculated by the weighted summation of the MV of the MB to which it belongs. For convenience, they are all quantized to $[0, 255]$ as follows,

$$V(i, j) = \begin{cases} 255, & MB_{size} = 4 \times 4 \\ 255 \times Sat(\frac{|MV_x(k)| + |MV_y(k)|}{255}), & otherwise \end{cases} \quad (1)$$

Fig. 2. The motion detection results of sample frames. (a) shows original images of a flame scene, and (b) shows the corresponding masks of motion foreground.

where $Sat(x) = 1$ if $x > 1$, otherwise $Sat(x) = x$. $V(i, j)$ refers to the speed of the pixel located at the coordinate (i, j). $MV_x(k)$ and $MV_y(k)$ are the MVs in the x and y directions of the k_{th} MB corresponding to the pixel located at (i, j), respectively. Further, the motion speed map is binarized to the motion mask by a threshold, and it is depicted as,

$$F_{motion}(i, j) = \begin{cases} 255, & V(i, j) > V_{th} \\ 0, & otherwise \end{cases} \quad (2)$$

where $F_{motion}(i, j)$ indicates whether the pixel at (i,j) belongs to the motion foreground. V_{th} is the velocity threshold, which is automatically adapted by the OSTU threshold selection method. As demonstrated in Fig. 2, the moving flame and smoke are accurately extracted.

2.3   Color Detection Based on YCbCr Color Space

Color characteristics are one of the most important static characteristics of flames. Generally, the color of the natural flame is between yellow and red, with a yellow or white center and red edge [7,8]. RGB color space is the most commonly used color representation method for color images. However, the values of the three RGB channels will be affected by changes in chromaticity and brightness at the same time. To facilitate the extraction of flames based on chromaticity features, we converted the RGB image to the YCbCr color space. YCbCr comprises a luminance component Y, a blue chrominance component Cb, and a red chrominance component Cr.

Data analysis is performed on 119 annotated flame pictures from the BoW-Fire dataset [20] to get a more quantitative color distribution. 1000 flame pixels and 1000 non-flame pixels are randomly selected in each image based on the labeled flame mask. The final 119,000 flame pixels and 119,000 non-flame pixels are acquired. As can be seen in Fig. 3 (a), the Cr of the flame pixel is larger than

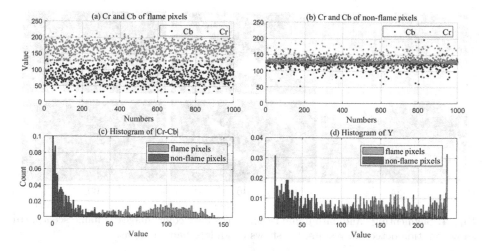

Fig. 3. Scatter plot and histogram for flame pixels and non-flame pixels.

Cb overall, and there is even a clear dividing line. In contrast, non-flame pixels have no apparent regulation, as shown in Fig. 3 (b).

For a more obvious comparison, Fig. 3 (c) and (d) show the normalized $|Cr - Cb|$ and Y distribution histogram of flame pixels and non-flame pixels. The results demonstrate a varying chroma difference distribution of flame pixels and non-flame pixels. The $|Cr - Cb|$ of flame pixels is distributed chiefly from 40 to 140, while non-flame pixels are mainly distributed in the vicinity from 0 to 40. The Y channel of YCbCr color space also has a similar distribution, where most flame pixels have a larger Y value than non-flame pixels. Therefore, thresholds of $|Cr - Cb|$ and Y can be set to extract the flame-colored regions. The color conditions to separate the flame foreground and non-flame background are established as,

$$F_{color}(i,j) = \begin{cases} 255, & C_i(i,j) - C_b(i,j) > C_{th} \& Y(i,j) > Y_{th} \\ 0, & otherwise \end{cases} \quad (3)$$

where C_{th} and Y_{th} are the thresholds of chroma difference and luminance, respectively. They are obtained from experiments, taken as 38 and 60, respectively. Then, the intersection of motion regions and flame-liked regions are extracted as "candidate flame regions", and it is expressed as,

$$F_{candidate}(i,j) = \begin{cases} 255, & F_{motion}(i,j) \& F_{color}(i,j) \\ 0, & otherwise \end{cases} \quad (4)$$

Figure 4 demonstrates the results of extracting candidate flame regions. The third column shows that the proposed color conditions have a strong response to the flame region. However, some moving flame-colored objects, such as red balloons and car taillights, may also meet the conditions of motion and color. Thus, further analysis is needed for the candidate flame regions.

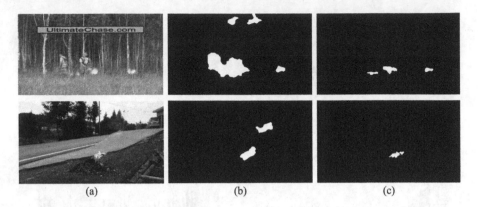

(a)   (b)   (c)

Fig. 4. Segmenting candidate flame region. (a) shows color images of flame scenes, (b) shows motion detection results, (c) shows candidate flame regions.

2.4   Multi-feature Extraction for Pattern Recognition

A flame feature descriptor is constructed to further distinguish misidentified objects in the candidate flame region. The flame feature descriptors consisting of chromaticity, texture, and contour features are introduced for further classification by pattern recognition.

Chromaticity Features. The center of the flame is generally white with higher brightness, and the surrounding area tends to be yellow or red. Although color conditions of individual pixels have been constrained, statistical analysis based on all pixels in the flame candidate region is also necessary. The $|Cr - Cb|$, Y, and S (saturation) channel of the candidate flame region pixels are selected to characterize the distribution. The common statistics, including mean, standard deviation, skewness, and kurtosis, are calculated to describe the pixel set data. Equation 5 shows their calculation formulas, which respectively measure the average level of the data distribution, the degree of dispersion, the asymmetry, and the steepness of the probability distribution.

$$\begin{cases} \mu = \frac{1}{N} \sum_{i=1}^{N} x_i, \\ \sigma = \sqrt{\frac{1}{N} \sum_{i=1}^{N} (x_i - \mu)^2}, \\ Sk = \frac{1}{N} \sum_{i=1}^{N} \left(\frac{x_i - \mu}{\sigma}\right)^3, \\ Ku = \frac{1}{N} \sum_{i=1}^{N} \left(\frac{x_i - \mu}{\sigma}\right)^4 \end{cases} \tag{5}$$

where x_i refers to the value of the i_{th} pixel; N represents the total number of pixels in the whole pixel set of the candidate flame region.

Texture Features. Local Binary Pattern (LBP) [21] is an operator based on structure and statistics to describe local texture features. Compared with the above statistical method, it considers the relative position information between pixels of different intensities to express complete texture information. The original LBP is given by,

$$LBP_{P,R} = \sum_{p=0}^{P-1} s(g_p - g_c) \times 2^p \tag{6}$$

where $s(x) = 1$ if $x \geq 0$, otherwise $s(x) = 0$. g_c and g_i are the gray value of the central pixel and its neighboring pixels, respectively. R is the radius, and P is the count of selected neighborhood pixels.

The original LBP operator traverses in clockwise order with the neighboring pixels relative to the center point $(0, R)$ coordinates as the starting point. Hence, it has no rotation invariance, and the number of LBP patterns will increase exponentially with P increases. To simplify LBP and make the realization of rotation invariance, Ojala et al. proposed the LBP representation of "uniform" as,

$$LBP_{P,R}^{riu2} = \begin{cases} \sum_{p=0}^{P-1} s(g_p - g_c), & U(LBP_{P,R} \leq 2) \\ P + 1, & otherwise \end{cases} \tag{7}$$

where,

$$U(LBP_{P,R}) = |s(g_{P-1} - g_c) - s(g_0 - g_c)| + \sum_{p=0}^{P-1} |s(g_p - g_c) - s(g_{p-1} - g_c)| \tag{8}$$

$U(LBP_{P,R})$ is the number of transitions from 1 to 0 or 0 to 1 when traversing the P neighborhood pixels in sequence. It is called a "uniform" pattern when U is not larger than 2, and the number of pixels in the neighborhood that has a greater gray value than the center pixel is used as the LBP operator. In comparison, it is collectively called a "nonuniform" pattern when U is larger than 2, with $P+1$ as the LBP operator. In this way, the LBP operator has only $P + 2$ output modes. In this paper, R is set to 1, and P is set to 8. Then the normalized histogram of the operator outputs of the entire candidate flame region will be computed. Finally, the occurrence frequency of $P + 2$ output modes from 0 to $P + 1$ are used as a part of the feature vector.

Geometric Features. Geometric features describe the contours of the flame regions. Although the shape of the flame region is irregular, it is generally round at the bottom, with many protruding sharp corners on the top and sides. This paper combines multiple geometric features of circularity, rectangularity, and aspect ratio to judge whether it is a real flame.

Circularity. Circularity describes how similar a shape is to a circle. The circularity of a circle is 1, and the greater the difference from the circle, the smaller the circularity, which is defined as,

$$C_k = \frac{4\pi A_k}{P_k^2} \tag{9}$$

where A_k and P_k are the area and circumference of the k_{th} candidate flame region.

Rectangularity. Rectangularity measures how similar a shape is to a rectangle. It reflects the fullness of a shape to its outer rectangle. The mathematical definition is as follows,

$$R_k = \frac{A_k}{A_{MER}} \tag{10}$$

where A_{MER} is the area of the smallest outer rectangle of the candidate flame region. For rectangular objects, R_k takes the maximum value of 1; for circular objects, R_k is $\frac{\pi}{4}$; for slender or curved objects, the value of R_k will be smaller, which is between 0 to 1.

Aspect ratio. Aspect ratio describes the shape of a region. It is defined by the ratio of the height to the width of the outer rectangle of one region as follows,

$$r_k = \frac{max(W_{MER}, H_{MER})}{min(W_{MER}, H_{MER})} \tag{11}$$

where W_{MER} and H_{MER} are the width and height of the outer rectangle of the k_{th} candidate flame region.

Combining all the above features, a 25-dimensional feature vector of the k_{th} candidate flame region can be represented by,

$$\begin{aligned}
\boldsymbol{x}_k &= [\mu_C, \sigma_C, Sk_C, Ku_C, \mu_Y, \sigma_Y, Sk_Y, Ku_Y, \mu_S, \sigma_S, Sk_S, Ku_S, U(LBP)_1, \\
&\quad \ldots, U(LBP)_{10}, C_k, R_k, r_k]^T \\
&= [x_1, x_2, \ldots, x_{25}]^T
\end{aligned} \tag{12}$$

Finally, a candidate flame region will be classified as either flame or non-flame by inputting the feature vector into the SVM.

3   Experiments and Results

3.1   Datasets and Implementation Details

The flame detection algorithm proposed in this paper has experimented on various flame and non-flame video datasets for comparison with other detection methods. The video dataset consists of 12 videos as demonstrated in Fig. 5, of which the first 8 videos are taken as test sets respectively from VisiFire, MIVIA, and https://media.xiph.org/video/derf/; the last 4 videos are self-collected for extracting features to train the SVM classifier. Table 1 describes the detailed information of test videos. These videos cover a variety of wild and roadside flames, various fire-like moving objects, etc. The resolution of these videos is not consistent due to varying sources, so all low-resolution videos are reconstructed to 1280 pixels width in advance by super-resolution based on linear interpolation.

There are 5 flame videos for detection accuracy testing and 3 non-flame videos for false alarm rate testing. The experimental results are compared with other 4 algorithms, i.e., proposed by Celik et al. [8] (Method 1), Borges et al. [11] (Method 2), Xuan et al. [22] (Method 3), and Chi et al. [14] (Method 4). The results of these four methods are obtained from [14].

Fig. 5. Sample frames from the video dataset.

Table 1. Details of the video dataset.

Video #	Spatial resolution	Total Frames	Fire or Not	Description
Video 1	1280 × 720	200	Yes	Forest fire
Video 2	1280 × 960	294	Yes	Christmas tree fire
Video 3	1280 × 960	1201	Yes	Fire in the backyard
Video 4	1280 × 720	208	Yes	Forest fire
Video 5	1280 × 720	260	Yes	Two man firing grass and trees
Video 6	1280 × 960	300	No	Two man walking through a hall
Video 7	1280 × 960	288	No	Car accident in the tunnel
Video 8	1280 × 960	150	No	Man in red playing table tennis

3.2 Comparison of Accuracy

The comparison results of flame detection accuracy on flame videos are shown in Table 2. The accuracy refers to the ratio of correctly detecting real flame frames to the total number of flame frames in the entire video. In video 1, too much fire in the forest results in inconspicuous movement characteristics of the flame region, resulting in low accuracy. In video 2, some white flames cause misjudgment when the fire is too large. Video 3 has many frames and the proposed algorithm performs very well. In video 4, the flame has prominent color, motion, and texture features, which are consistent with the proposed flame algorithm; thus, all flames are detected correctly. For video 5, the proposed method also achieves high

Table 2. Accuracy of flame videos.

Video #	Accuracy (%)				
	Method 1	Method 2	Method 3	Method 4	**Our Method**
Video 1	94.74	95.26	95.79	96.50	**98.99**
Video 2	96.00	96.00	96.00	96.00	**98.63**
Video 3	92.25	92.25	93.00	98.00	**99.67**
Video 4	94.50	94.50	95.00	98.08	**98.55**
Video 5	94.59	94.59	94.98	96.54	**98.84**
Average	94.42	94.52	94.95	97.02	**98.94**

Table 3. False alarm rate of non-flame videos.

Video #	False Alarm Rate (%)				
	Method 1	Method 2	Method 3	Method 4	**Our Method**
Video 6	0.00	0.00	0.00	**0.00**	**0.00**
Video 7	4.90	3.85	3.50	**0.00**	**0.00**
Video 8	4.46	3.57	1.79	**0.00**	**0.00**
Average	3.12	2.47	1.76	**0.00**	**0.00**

accuracy, with only some misrecognition in the early stage of the flame. Overall, the accuracy of the proposed flame detection algorithm is higher than 98% for each flame video for the experiment and even reached an average accuracy of nearly 99%, which is much higher than other algorithms.

3.3   Comparison of False Alarm Rate

Table 3 illustrates the false alarm rates on non-flame videos. In video 6, all methods achieve a 0% false alarm rate. In video 7, the moving car taillights are regarded as candidate flame regions. However, it is classified as non-flame by the proposed algorithm due to the difference in texture and contour characteristics from the flame and finally achieves a zero false alarm rate. For video 8, the zooming in the video brings difficulties to the motion detection method based on the H.264/AVC decoder, while the other conditions are still robust and thus avoid misclassification. Finally, the proposed flame detection algorithm and Method 4 achieve a false alarm rate of 0%.

4   Conclusions

Vision based flame detection methods are vital for intelligent robot perception in unknown environments. This paper proposes a flame detection algorithm based on the motion detection of H.264/AVC video compressed domain data and multi-feature pattern recognition. In the proposed algorithm, the motion information stored in the compressed domain is fully utilized to extract the moving flame foreground. According to the statistical analysis results, a flame color model in YCbCr color space is established to segment the candidate flame regions. Then the chromaticity, texture, and geometric characteristics are fused for further SVM-based pattern recognition, significantly reducing the false alarm rate. The experimental results demonstrate that the proposed method performs well in videos of various indoor and outdoor scenes, with an accuracy of 98.94% and a false alarm rate of 0.00%, which has higher sensitivity and stability than other methods.

References

1. Yang, Y., Wang, X.F., Pan, M.Y., Li, P., Tsai, Y.T.: Evaluation on algorithm reliability and efficiency for an image flame detection technology. J. Therm. Anal. Calorim. **148**, 5063–5070 (2023). https://doi.org/10.1007/s10973-023-12012-8
2. Emmy Prema, C., Vinsley, S.S., Suresh, S.: Efficient flame detection based on static and dynamic texture analysis in forest fire detection. Fire Technol. **54**, 255–288 (2018). https://doi.org/10.1007/s10694-017-0683-x
3. Kanwal, K., Liaquat, A., Mughal, M., Abbasi, A.R., Aamir, M.: Towards development of a low cost early fire detection system using wireless sensor network and machine vision. Wireless Pers. Commun. **95**, 475–489 (2017). https://doi.org/10.1007/s11277-016-3904-6
4. Muhammad, K., Khan, S., Elhoseny, M., Hassan Ahmed, S., Wook Baik, S.: Efficient fire detection for uncertain surveillance environment. IEEE Trans. Industr. Inf. **15**, 3113–3122 (2019). https://doi.org/10.1109/TII.2019.2897594
5. Wang, H., Pan, Z., Zhang, Z., Song, H., Zhang, S., Zhang, J.: Deep learning based fire detection system for surveillance videos. In: International Conference on Intelligent Robotics and Applications (ICIRA), pp. 318–328 (2019). https://doi.org/10.1007/978-3-030-27532-7_29
6. Gaur, A., Singh, A., Kumar, A., Kumar, A., Kapoor, K.: Video flame and smoke based fire detection algorithms: a literature review. Fire Technol. **56**, 1943–1980 (2020). https://doi.org/10.1007/s10694-020-00986-y
7. Chen, T.H., Wu, P.H., Chiou, Y.C.: An early fire-detection method based on image processing. In: International Conference on Image Processing (ICIP), vol. 3, pp. 1707–1710 (2004). https://doi.org/10.1109/ICIP.2004.1421401
8. Çelik, T., Demirel, H.: Fire detection in video sequences using a generic color model. Fire Saf. J. **44**, 147–158 (2009). https://doi.org/10.1016/j.firesaf.2008.05.005
9. Celik, T.: Fast and efficient method for fire detection using image processing. ETRI J. **32**, 881–890 (2010). https://doi.org/10.4218/etrij.10.0109.0695
10. Han, X.F., Jin, J.S., Wang, M.J., Jiang, W., Gao, L., Xiao, L.P.: Video fire detection based on Gaussian Mixture Model and multi-color features. SIViP **11**, 1419–1425 (2017). https://doi.org/10.1007/s11760-017-1102-y
11. Borges, P.V.K., Izquierdo, E.: A probabilistic approach for vision-based fire detection in videos. IEEE Trans. Circuits Syst. Video Technol. **20**, 721–731 (2010). https://doi.org/10.1109/TCSVT.2010.2045813
12. Yuan, F.: An integrated fire detection and suppression system based on widely available video surveillance. Mach. Vis. Appl. **21**, 941–948 (2010). https://doi.org/10.1007/s00138-010-0276-x

13. Hashemzadeh, M., Zademehdi, A.: Fire detection for video surveillance applications using ICA K-medoids-based color model and efficient Spatio-temporal visual features. Expert Syst. Appl. **130**, 60–78 (2019). https://doi.org/10.1016/j.eswa.2019.04.019

14. Chi, R., Lu, Z.M., Ji, Q.G.: Real-time multi-feature based fire flame detection in video. IET Image Proc. **11**, 31–37 (2017). https://doi.org/10.1049/iet-ipr.2016.0193

15. Rong, J., Zhou, D., Yao, W., Gao, W., Chen, J., Wang, J.: Fire flame detection based on GICA and target tracking. Opt. Laser Technol. **47**, 283–291 (2013). https://doi.org/10.1016/j.optlastec.2012.08.040

16. Kong, S.G., Jin, D., Li, S., Kim, H.: Fast fire flame detection in surveillance video using logistic regression and temporal smoothing. Fire Saf. J. **79**, 37–43 (2016). https://doi.org/10.1016/j.firesaf.2015.11.015

17. Wiegand, T., Sullivan, G., Bjontegaard, G., Luthra, A.: Overview of the H.264/AVC video coding standard. IEEE Trans. Circuits Syst. Video Technol. **13**, 560–576 (2003). https://doi.org/10.1109/TCSVT.2003.815165

18. Wang, S., Group, A., Lu, H., Deng, Z.: Fast object detection in compressed video. In: IEEE/CVF International Conference on Computer Vision (ICCV), pp. 7103–7112 (2019). https://doi.org/10.1109/ICCV.2019.00720

19. Kim, Y.K., Jeon, Y.G., Shin, S.H.: Real-time motion detection in H.264 compressed domain for surveillance application. J. Phys.: Conf. Ser. **1780**, 012032 (2021). https://doi.org/10.1088/1742-6596/1780/1/012032

20. Chino, D.Y.T., Avalhais, L.P.S., Rodrigues, J.F., Traina, A.J.M.: BoWFire: detection of fire in still images by integrating pixel color and texture analysis. In: SIBGRAPI Conference on Graphics, Patterns and Images (SIBGRAPI), pp. 95–102 (2015). https://doi.org/10.1109/SIBGRAPI.2015.19

21. Ojala, T., Pietikainen, M., Maenpaa, T.: Multiresolution gray-scale and rotation invariant texture classification with local binary patterns. IEEE Trans. Pattern Anal. Mach. Intell. **24**, 971–987 (2002). https://doi.org/10.1109/TPAMI.2002.1017623

22. Xuan Truong, T., Kim, J.M.: Fire flame detection in video sequences using multistage pattern recognition techniques. Eng. Appl. Artif. Intell. **25**, 1365–1372 (2012). https://doi.org/10.1016/j.engappai.2012.05.007

Vision-LiDAR-Inertial Localization and Mapping Dataset of a Mining Cave

Yang Zhou[1], Shiqiang Zhu[1], and Yuehua Li[2(✉)]

[1] Research Center for Intelligent Robotics, Research Institute of Interdisciplinary Innovation, Zhejiang Laboratory, Hangzhou 311100, China
{zhouyang,zhusq}@zhejianglab.com
[2] Beijing Research Institute of Zhejiang Laboratory, Beijing 100094, China
liyh@zhejianglab.com

Abstract. We present an abandoned mining cave dataset including vision, distance, inertial measurements. The vision measurements were captured by a stereoscopic camera system constituting of two industrial cameras. A LiDAR sensor provided the distance measurements in the form of point clouds, while an IMU provided the inertial data measured by accelerator and gyroscope. All above sensors were rigidly mounted on a mobile tracked vehicle that was capable of moving in the cave. Because the GPS signal cannot be detected in the cave, the position and attitude of the tracked vehicle were not available using high-precision GPS/INS integrated navigation system. Instead, we used a set of base stations to determine 6 Degrees of Freedom (DoF) ground truth poses for the tracked vehicle. The intrinsic and extrinsic of the sensors were calibrated. Time of sensors and processing units were well synchronized with a high-precision hardware to make our dataset more friendly for research of visual/lidar odometry, structure from motion, SLAM, etc. This paper describes the hardware-software platform and the data format in detail.

Keywords: Stereo vision · LiDAR · IMU · Sensors synchronization · Cave

1 Introduction

High-quality open source dataset is significant for robotics and related research, which saves a lot of efforts of researchers in setting up hardware, searching for appropriate scenarios and collecting data. As a result, software algorithm can be rapidly deployed and the performance is compared with related work in a transparent benchmark. Over past ten years, multiple well-known dataset were released and promoted in robotics and autonomous systems research, such as KITTI [6], NCLT [3], EuRoC MAV [1], TUM VI [8,14]. These datasets were generated using different mobile platforms (car, mobile robot, handheld and UAV) in different scenarios (indoors, outdoors and in/outdoors). Vision, distance and inertial measurements are included in above datasets. Additionally,

H. Yang et al. (Eds.): ICIRA 2023, LNAI 14267, pp. 411–422, 2023.
https://doi.org/10.1007/978-981-99-6483-3_35

some other datasets contains postprocessing features, for example Cityscapes [5] provides polygonal annotations of dense semantic segmentation in urban scene for the semantic analysis tasks.

In the outdoor scene, the 6 Degrees of Freedom (DoF) ground truth poses are usually obtained by GNSS/INS or more accurate RTK-GNSS/INS, which can provide up to centimeter-level positional accuracy and 0.03-degree-level attitude accuracy. However, GNSS/INS is not available in the indoor scene due to the GNSS signal is denied. Instead, motion capture system is widely used to obtain the 6 DoF ground truth poses with very high precision. However, its effective range is dozens of meters so this system is limited to small indoor facilities. In addition, motion capture devices are usually expensive and have poor portability. Therefore, motion capture system is more appropriate to a fixed laboratory environment.

Our purpose is to construct a high-quality cave dataset which provides not only the vision, distance, inertial measurements but also the high-precise 6 DoF ground truth poses. To balance the performance and convenience, the Lighthouse system [15] developed by Valve cooperation and made by HTC cooperation is selected to provide the ground truth. The Lighthouse system is a type of outside-in tracking system, which includes the base stations and tracked devices (headset and controller). The base stations emit IR signals which are detected by IR diodes on a tracked device. By measuring the time of flight at this device, the position and the orientation are estimated. The Lighthouse system achieves high translation and rotation tracking accuracy in the submillimeter and subdegree range [2].

In the selection of sensors, we use better-performance sensors for better data quality. The stereoscopic camera system comprises two FLIR industrial cameras with 5-megapixel resolutions The 3D LiDAR and IMU are Hesai Pandar40M and XSENS MTi-300, respectively. Sensors are fixed in a metal piece which is rigidly mounted on a mobile robot. The headset is fixed on the mobile robot as the tracked device in the Lighthouse system. The experimental environment is in a cave that is located at Huzhou city of Zhejiang province in eastern China. The structure of this cave is presented in Fig. 1 in the form of point clouds. Considering that the ground in the cave is very rough, the tracked vehicle is chosen as the mobile robot for its strong ability to overcome obstacles. The tracked vehicle moved in the cave controlled by a remote control, while sensor data and ground truth poses were recorded by an onboard computer kit.

The remainder of the paper is structured as follows: Sect. 2 reviews the related work on datasets. Section 3 presents the setup of the sensors. Section 4 describe the procedure of data collection, ground truth generation and sensor calibration in details. A experimental usage of our dataset is shown in Sect. 5, followed by the conclusion and future work of our work in Sect. 6.

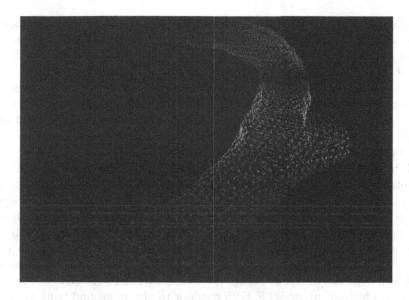

Fig. 1. Structure of cave we selected.

2 Related Work

According to the type of mobile platforms, datasets can be divided into car-based, mobile-robot-based, handheld-based and UAV-based.

Car-based datasets are always in a large-scale of scene and are widely applied to research of self driving. The MIT DARPA Urban Challenge dataset [7] is the first car-based dataset. It collected the dense point clouds and vision data of the urban environment during a 90 km traverse. The onboard GPS/INS integrated system provides high-precision ground truth poses. The KITTI dataset [6] is one of the most comprehensive self-driving dataset. The authors collected more than 6 h data of real traffic environment in urban, country and highway scenes, respectively. The dataset consists of corrected and synchronized images, LiDAR scans, high-precision GPS information, and IMU acceleration information. The 6 DoF ground truth trajectory is provided by RTK-GPS/INS with accuracy below 10 cm. The official site of KITTI also provides abundant benchmarks such as stereo, optical flow, depth, odometry, object detection/tracking, road/lane detection, semantic segmentation and so on. The Oxford RobotCar dataset [9] is the longest dataset, providing a total of about 1010 km km of driving data. It contains 100 repeated driving data of fixed driving routes in Oxford, UK within one year. The dataset captures many different combinations of weather, traffic, and pedestrian conditions, as well as long-term changes such as buildings and road construction. The Cityscapes dataset [5] focuses on semantic understanding of urban street scenes. It collected from 50 cities, including street scenes in spring, summer and autumn, and using binocular cameras to obtain stereoscopic video sequences. Pixel-level semantic and instance annotations are carried out on these images. The dataset only provides ego-motion data from vehicle odometry rather than RTK-GPS/INS. The Waymo Open Dataset (WOD) [17] is called largest multimodal sensor dataset for autonomous driving. Compare with above dataset, WOD used more high-performance sensors, including 5 3D LiDAR and 5 cameras. WOD contains 1000 autonomous driving paths, each path contains 20 s of uninterrupted video, equivalent to 200,000 frames of high-resolution images. Additionally, the vehicles, pedestrians, cyclists and traffic signs are annotated in LiDAR scans and images. As a result, WOD aims to solve 2D and 3D perception, scene understanding, behavior prediction tasks.

Mobile-robot-based datasets cover a smaller area compared with car-based datasets. The New College dataset [16] provides timestamped laser range data, stereo and omnidirectional imagery. The Segway wheeled robot is selected as the sensor platform that moves over 2.2 km on the grounds and garden areas. However, the ground truth is not provided in this dataset. The North Campus Long-Term (NCLT) dataset [3] also used Segway as platform to collect vision, distance and inertial data across a indoor and outdoor college campus. Compare with the New College dataset, NCLT used LiDAR scan matching indoor and high-accuracy RTK-GPS outdoor to obtain ground truth trajectory. Recently released Kimera-Multi-Data [18] is a large-scale multi-robot dataset for multi-robot SLAM. Each robot is equipped with a Realsense D455 camera, an Ouster/Velodyne 3D LiDAR and a Intel NUC, which is tele-operated by a human operator. Because both indoor and outdoor environments are contained in the dataset, the ground truth trajectory is generated using GPS and total-station assisted LiDAR SLAM based on LOCUS and LAMP.

Some datasets were collected in the handheld way for conveniences, such as PennCOSYVIO [11], TUM VI [8,14], and the Newer College Dataset [12]. In comparison, PennCOSYVIO has inertial and vision data but lacks LiDAR scans. It determined the ground truth by visual tags. Similar to PennCOSYVIO, TUM VI's device was not equipped with LiDAR sensor. The motion capture system was used to capture the 6 DoF ground truth. The Newer College Dataset has complete data of vision, inertial and distance. In particular, a unique method was applied to determine ground truth: registration of individual LiDAR scans with an accurate prior map, utilizing Iterative Closest Point (ICP), where the prior map is provided using a survey-grade 3D imaging laser scanner. Consequently, the ground truth has a approximately 3 cm accuracy.

For UAV application, UAV-based datasets were developed, such as EuRoC MAV [1] and Zurich Urban MAV [10]. Considering the limited payload of UAVs, LiDAR was not installed in above 2 datasets. Only inertial and vision data are provided. Because of the differences of experimental environments, ground truth is determined in different way. The ground truth of indoor EuRoC MAV is obtained by 6 DOF Vicon motion capture system, while the outdoor Zurich Urban MAV uses aerial photogrammetry.

The car-based platform is not appropriate for our work because a car cannot drive in the cave and scale of the cave is relatively smaller than abovementioned car-based datasets. In addition, the payloads of handheld-based and UAV-based platforms are not insufficient to carry a stereoscopic camera system, a 3D LiDAR, a IMU and other devices simultaneously. Therefore, a tracked vehicle, with a size of 100 cm × 78 cm × 40 cm, is selected as the platform, which is able to carry up to 70 kg devices and has stronger off-road capability. Taking into account the particularity of the cave environment, the low-cost Lighthouse system is used to determine ground truth. The base stations are deployed along the line of motion to track the 6 DoF poses of headset.

3   Sensor Setup

The sensor setup is shown in Fig. 2. The main sensors are set up on a rigid metal piece. Two cameras are fixed at the two ends of the metal piece with a baseline of about 30 cm. The IMU is set up in the middle of the metal piece and the LiDAR is mounted above the IMU. The metal piece with the sensors are mounted on the front of the tracked vehicle with a height of about 40 cm. In particular, the LiDAR is set up with a incline of 20°C to reduce dead zone in front of the tracked vehicle. The headset of Lighthouse system is fixed on the middle of the vehicle with a height of about 40 cm in order to ensure that it is not blocked relative to base stations.

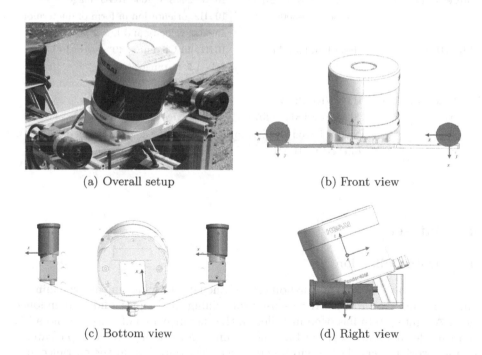

(a) Overall setup   (b) Front view

(c) Bottom view   (d) Right view

Fig. 2. Sensors setup from different views with corresponding coordinates.

To achieve high time precision, we use a Microcontroller Unit (MCU) as the system host clock, which outputs Pulse Per Second (PPS) signal to correct clocks in the master and LiDAR. MCU also outputs pulse width modulation (PWD) signal to trigger two cameras and IMU to sample data at the same time.

Nvidia Jetson AGX Orin developer kit, which takes on the task of driving the devices and recording sensor data, is selected as the master machine in our system due to its high performance and low power consumption. The other reason we select Jetson AGX Orin is that it is convenient to deploy Network Time Protocol (NTP) service. The clock in Jetson AGX Orin can synchronize with MCU using PPS signal. Intel NUC is selected as the slave machine to drive Lighthouse system because Lighthouse system cannot be deployed on a ARM framework machine like Jetson AGX Orin. Both master and slave are installed with Ubuntu 20.04 and ROS Noetic. The Precision Time Protocol (PTP) service is applied between master and slave using a local network. Combine with NTP between master and MCU, the whole system has been well time synchronized.

Details of the devices are presented in Table 1

Table 1. Details of our devices.

Device	Type	Descriptions
Stereoscopic camera	FLIR BFS-U3-51S5C-C	10 Hz, 2448 × 2048 RGB image
IMU	Xsense MTi-300	100 Hz, orientation in form of quaternion, angular velocity and linear acceleration
LiDAR	Hesai Pandar40M	10 Hz, 40 Channels, 40° vertical FOV, 0.3 - 120 m range @10%, return 1440000 3D points/second
Lighthouse system	HTC Vive Pro 2	Capturing gound truth poses
MCU	Alientek STM32F407ZG	Time service and triggering sensors
Master	Nvidia Jetson AGX Orin	Driving devices and recording data
Slave	Intel NUC11PAHi7	Driving Lighthouse system

4   Dataset

4.1   Data Collection

We select a cave located at Huzhou city of Zhejiang province in eastern China to carry out our experiment. It was used for mining in the past and is abandoned now. A light system has been installed in the entrance area of the cave and a few man-made goods are scattered on the ground. Considering stereoscopic camera cannot work in very dark environment, we collect data just in the entrance area of the cave, about 30 m in depth. The tracked vehicle is driven using a remote control to go into the cave from the origin and then come back to the origin. The trajectory is shown as Fig. 3, where each grid is 1 m × 1 m. The total length of the trajectory is about 60 m.

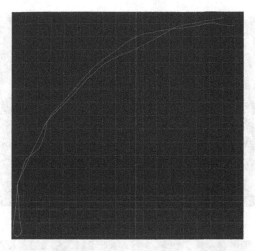

Fig. 3. Trajectory of our tracked vehicle.

All the data are recorded to a rosbag[1], including 2929 frames of stereo Image messages, 2929 frames of Pointcloud2 messages, 29292 frames of Imu messages and 15569 frames of 6 DoF ground truth poses in the form of Path messages. Figure 4 presents one frame stereo image and point cloud, respectively.

4.2   Ground Truth

The 6 DoF ground truth poses are provided by Lighthouse system. 4 base stations are evenly deployed along the trajectory and the tracked device, the headset, is mounted on the mobile platform. The driver of Lighthouse system is rewritten into a ROS framework, which is deployed on the Intel NUC, so that the ground truth poses can be advertised in the form of ROS messages with other sensor data.

4.3   Calibration

The open source calibration tool-box kalibr [13] is used to compute the intrinsic and extrinsic calibration of our stereoscopic camera system and spatial-temporal calibration of the IMU with respect to stereoscopic camera system along with IMU intrinsic parameters. A calibration target used in Camera-IMU calibration is shown as Fig. 5

For LiDAR-Camera extrinsic calibration, a special calibration target is applied shown in Fig. 6, where there are 4 round holes are distributed in the calibration target. The positions and sizes of round holes are known. The edges

---

[1] Our dataset is now available on this site: https://github.com/yang2333333/cave_dataset. It can be downloaded by the BaiduDisk or Onedrive link we provided. More net disks will be supported in the future.

(a) Stereo images

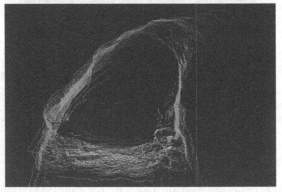

(b) LiDAR point clouds

Fig. 4. One frame stereo images and LiDAR point clouds.

of round holes are detected by LiDAR's point clouds as shown in Fig. 7, while they are detected by camera as well. As a result, a equation containing the LiDAR-Camera extrinsic calibration can be established. Solving the equation directly leads to the extrinsic.

5   Experimental Usage

This paper presents one experimental of our dataset by LiDAR odometry. An open source algorithm called Direct LiDAR Odometry (DLO) [4] is tested, which is lightweight and computationally-efficient frontend LiDAR odometry solution with consistent and accurate localization. By inputting the point clouds into DLO, a trajectory is estimated shown as Fig. 8, where any parameter is not modified. It is found that the estimated trajectory is nearly converged to the ground truth trajectory as shown in Fig. 3 but the local details are not satisfied.

Fig. 5. Calibration target for Camera-IMU calibration.

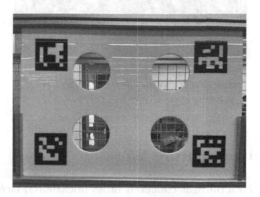

Fig. 6. Calibration target for LiDAR-Camera calibration.

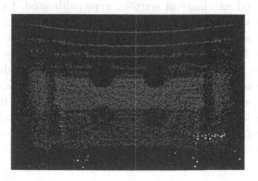

Fig. 7. LiDAR point clouds on calibration target.

For example, trajectory in the left-bottom area of Fig. 3 is smooth as well as that presents a jagged shape in Fig. 8.

Besides LiDAR odometry, our dataset can be applied to structure from motion, visual odometry and visual inertial odometry as well.

Fig. 8. Trajectory estimated by DLO.

6   Conclusion and Future Work

This paper presented a dataset collected in an unexplored cave. The vision, distance and inertial data were collected by a stereoscopic camera system, a 3D LiDAR and an IMU, respectively. The 6 DoF ground truth poses were provided by Lighthouse system. All devices were precisely time synchronized by hardware and the intrinsic and extrinsic of sensors were calibrated. Compared with previous datasets, this dataset has higher quality of sensor data, such as higher resolution of images and more precise time system. Our dataset is appropriate to research area of localization and mapping.

Current version of dataset only covers a about 60-meter-long motion due to the limitation of the coverage of Lighthouse. However, by adding base stations and patching trajectories, it is possible to provide longer distance of ground truth. Another work in the future is to add outdoor scenes. Instead of Lighthouse system, RTK-GPS/INS will be used to obtain the ground truth. Our aim is still the unexplored terrain, for example the desert.

Acknowledgement. The authors would like to thank the members of space robot group in Zhejiang lab, who helped with the development of sensor driver, hardware time synchronization, sensor calibration, etc.

This work is supported by National Natural Science Foundation of China (No. U21B6001), and Center-initialized Research Project of Zhejiang Lab (No. 2021NB0AL02).

References

1. Burri, M., et al.: The EuRoC micro aerial vehicle datasets. Int. J. Robot. Res. **35**(10), 1157–1163 (2016)
2. Kuhlmann de Canaviri, L., et al.: Static and dynamic accuracy and occlusion robustness of steamVR tracking 2.0 in multi-base station setups. Sensors **23**(2), 725 (2023)
3. Carlevaris-Bianco, N., Ushani, A.K., Eustice, R.M.: University of Michigan North Campus long-term vision and lidar dataset. Int. J. Robot. Res. **35**(9), 1023–1035 (2015)
4. Chen, K., Lopez, B.T., Agha-mohammadi, A.A., Mehta, A.: Direct lidar odometry: fast localization with dense point clouds. IEEE Robot. Autom. Lett. **7**(2), 2000–2007 (2022)
5. Cordts, M., et al.: The cityscapes dataset for semantic urban scene understanding. In: Proceedings of the IEEE Conference on Computer Vision and Pattern Recognition (CVPR), pp. 3213–3223 (2016)
6. Geiger, A., Lenz, P., Stiller, C., Urtasun, R.: Vision meets robotics: The KITTI dataset. Int. J. Robot. Res. **32**(1), 1231–1237 (2013)
7. Huang, A.S., et al.: A high-rate, heterogeneous data set from the DARPA urban challenge. Int. J. Robot. Res. **29**(13), 1595–1601 (2010)
8. Klenk, S., Chui, J., Demmel, N., Cremers, D.: TUM-VIE: the tum stereo visual-inertial event dataset. In: International Conference on Intelligent Robots and Systems (IROS), pp. 8601–8608 (2021)
9. Maddern, W., Pascoe, G., Linegar, C., Newman, P.: 1 year, 1000 km: the oxford RobotCar dataset. Int. J. Robot. Res. **36**(1), 3–15 (2017)
10. Majdik, A.L., Till, C., Scaramuzza, D.: The Zurich Urban micro aerial vehicle dataset. Int. J. Robot. Res. **36**(3), 269–273 (2017)
11. Pfrommer, B., Sanket, N., Daniilidis, K., Cleveland, J.: PennCOSYVIO: a challenging visual inertial odometry benchmark. In: 2017 IEEE International Conference on Robotics and Automation (ICRA), pp. 3847–3854. IEEE (2017)
12. Ramezani, M., Wang, Y., Camurri, M., Wisth, D., Mattamala, M., Fallon, M.: The newer college dataset: handheld lidar, inertial and vision with ground truth. In: 2020 IEEE/RSJ International Conference on Intelligent Robots and Systems (IROS), pp. 4353–4360. IEEE (2020)
13. Rehder, J., Nikolic, J., Schneider, T., Hinzmann, T., Siegwart, R.: Extending kalibr: Calibrating the extrinsics of multiple IMUs and of individual axes. In: 2016 IEEE International Conference on Robotics and Automation (ICRA), pp. 4304–4311. IEEE (2016)
14. Schubert, D., Goll, T., Demmel, N., Usenko, V., Stueckler, J., Cremers, D.: The TUM VI benchmark for evaluating visual-inertial odometry. In: International Conference on Intelligent Robots and Systems (IROS), pp. 1680–1687 (2018)

15. Sitole, S.P., LaPre, A.K., Sup, F.C.: Application and evaluation of lighthouse technology for precision motion capture. IEEE Sens. J. **20**(15), 8576–8585 (2020)
16. Smith, M., Baldwin, I., Churchill, W., Paul, R., Newman, P.: The new college vision and laser data set. Int. J. Robot. Res. **28**(5), 595–599 (2009)
17. Sun, P., et al.: Scalability in perception for autonomous driving: Waymo open dataset. In: Proceedings of the IEEE/CVF Conference on Computer Vision and Pattern Recognition, pp. 2446–2454 (2020)
18. Tian, Y., et al.: Resilient and distributed multi-robot visual SLAM: datasets, experiments, and lessons learned (2023)

Gesture Recognition Based on LightViT Network Against sEMG Electrode Shift

Tao Liu, Zheng Zhang, and Kairu Li[✉]

Shenyang University of Technology, Shenyang 110870, Liaoning, China
Kairu.Li@sut.edu.cn

Abstract. sEMG-based gesture recognition becomes popular in human-computer interaction due to its non-invasive nature and ease of signal acquisition. However, electrode-shift due to long-time use or re-wearing severely decreases the gesture recognition accuracy. In this paper, we apply a LightViT network to sEMG-based gesture recognition to improve the recognition accuracy under electrode-shift conditions with economical computational complexity. Firstly, an sEMG signals database is established to simulate conditions that the electrode-band in forearm shift between 0°–45°. Secondly, a short-time Fourier transform is used to transform sEMG signals into two-dimensional images, preserving the temporal dependency and correlation of the original time series. Then, the LightViT network is applied to feature extraction and classification of two-dimensional sEMG signals. A concept of feature alignment in transfer learning is introduced by applying Triplet Loss and Focal Loss as loss functions in the model to pay more attention to complex samples. Experiment results shows that the LightViT network achieves a gesture recognition accuracy of 91.9% within a range of 0°–45° electrode-shift compared with ResNet (85.7%) and mViT (89.3%) and demonstrates fewer methods parameters and floating-point operations.

Keywords: Gesture Recognition · sEMG · Electrode Shift · LightViT

1 Introduction

Gesture recognition enables natural human-robot interaction by interpreting hand movements. It is used for robot control, prosthetic control and improving quality of life [1]. Vision-based methods use cameras to capture hand motion images and recognise gestures by computer vision techniques. However, they are limited by environmental factors such as lighting and occlusion [2, 3]. In contrast, sEMG-based motion recognition techniques can directly capture electrical potential changes in arm muscles, which is less influenced by environmental factors and more suitable for intuitive prosthesis control [4]. However, electrode shift during long-term use causes sEMG variation [5–7] which severely decreases gesture recognition performance. Therefore, when users engage in long-term use or after repositioning the electrodes, signal characteristics change, lead to reduced accuracy and the inability to achieve precise control. Retraining is required, increasing the training burden on the users.

H. Yang et al. (Eds.): ICIRA 2023, LNAI 14267, pp. 423–432, 2023.
https://doi.org/10.1007/978-981-99-6483-3_36

To address the issue, Hargrove et al. [8] verified the impact of electrode shift on recognition accuracy and proposed a method by including all possible electrode-shift scenarios during training. Prahm et al. [9] proposed a recalibration scheme based on transfer learning (TL) for pattern recognition controllers. Ali Ameri et al. [10] introduced a supervised adaptation method using convolutional neural networks (CNN) and TL, requiring only short-term training for recalibration. High-density electrode arrays capture muscle activity over a larger area with higher resolution. He et al. [11] utilized a high-density surface electromyography (HD-sEMG) system and showed that multichannel configurations improve EMG recognition accuracy against electrode shift. Zhang et al. [12] proposed a deep fast neural network using spatio-temporal features of sEMG to mitigate electrode shift. Wu et al. [13] presented a shift-resistant CNN by replacing down-sampling layers with anti-aliasing filters and adaptive polyphase sampling modules. Díaz-Amador et al. [14] employed image processing techniques for gesture recognition with electrode shift in HD-EMG signals, enhancing gesture classification accuracy.

To ease users' training burden and increase sEMG-based gesture recognition accuracy with electrode shift, this paper proposes an sEMG-based gesture recognition method by applying a short-time Fourier transform to transform sEMG signals into a two-dimensional spectrogram and employing LightViT methods for feature extraction and gesture recognition. The remainder of this paper is organised as follows. Section 2 presents the data preprocessing of sEMG two-dimensional transformation Sect. 3 presents the LightViT network. Experiment setting and results analysis are detailed in Sect. 4, then concluding in Sect. 5.

2 sEMG Signals Transform Time-Frequency Diagram

Due to the random and non-stationary nature of raw sEMG signals, achieving both speed and accuracy in recognition is challenging. To leverage the temporal characteristics of sEMG signals, preprocessing is performed to highlight their features and transform them into spectrograms (see Fig. 1).

Fig. 1. Data preprocessing flow chart.

2.1 sEMG Signals Data Partitioning and Augmentation

The sliding window method is employed to segment continuous signals into overlapping windows, providing a valuable approach for managing complex and non-stationary signals like sEMG signals. This technique facilitates subsequent feature extraction and classification tasks by dividing the signal into multiple windows. In this study, the sliding window method is adopted to segment the acquired data for subsequent analysis.

Data augmentation is employed to increase the amount of data by transforming existing samples, enhancing the generalization ability and performance of the method. The dataset is three data augmentation techniques, namely scaling, amplitude distortion, and time distortion, are applied. These techniques generate synthetically augmented training data. The augmented data, combined with the original training data, are used to train the LightViT network. Subsequently, the performance of the trained LightViT network is evaluated using the initially separated test data.

2.2 sEMG Signals Denoising

The paper investigates noise in sEMG signals and proposes a method to mitigate it. To reduce noise, a second-order Butterworth bandpass filter is used. The squared magnitude response function of a Butterworth low-pass filter is defined as follows:

$$\left|H(j\omega)^2\right| = A\left(\omega^2\right) = \frac{1}{1 + \left(\frac{\omega}{\omega_c}\right)^{2N}} \tag{1}$$

According to the spectral characteristics of the signal, the cut-off frequency of the stopband is determined to be ω_{st} and the minimum attenuation in the stopband is δ_2, the cut-off frequency of the passband is ω and the maximum attenuation in the passband is δ_1. Then the order N and the cut-off frequency ω_c are obtained by (2) and (3).

$$N = \frac{\lg\left(\frac{10^{\delta_2/10}}{10^{\delta_1/10}-1}\right)}{\left[2\lg\left(\frac{\omega_{st}}{\omega_c}\right)\right]} \tag{2}$$

$$\omega_c = \frac{\omega_s}{\left(10^{\delta_2/10}-1\right)^{1/2N}} \tag{3}$$

To eliminate power-line interference, a notch filter corresponding to 50Hz is designed by selecting appropriate parameters according to the filter design standards.

2.3 Two-Dimensional sEMG Signals

Directly using the raw signal as input to the classifier may not adequately capture the temporal correlations. Therefore, in this study, we employ the short-time Fourier transform (STFT) to convert the one-dimensional EMG signals into a two-dimensional time-frequency representation, enhancing feature extraction and recognition accuracy.

The STFT is a method used for time-frequency analysis of signals. It divides the signal into multiple time segments and performs a Fourier transform on each segment to obtain the spectrum of each time segment. The formula for the STFT is as follows:

$$X(m, n) = \sum_{k=0}^{N-1} x(n+k)w(k)e^{-j2\pi mk/N} \tag{4}$$

Using the Hann window to window the part. The formula is (5).

$$w(k) = 0.5\left(1 - \cos\left(2\pi\frac{n}{N-1}\right)\right), 0 \leq n \leq N \tag{5}$$

The window overlap selects 50% overlap and limits the window length to 2 times the space size minus 1 to avoid the window length being too long.

Segment the signal and apply the window function to each segment, then perform the Fast Fourier Transform to convert the time-domain signal into the frequency-domain signal, generating a spectrogram of the EMG signals.

3 LightViT Network Structure

The Vision Transformer (ViT) has been successful in image processing tasks like image classification [15] and object detection [16]. To make ViT methods more lightweight, researchers have explored hybrid or heterogeneous approaches by incorporating CNN structures into ViT to develop various lightweight ViT methods. One such method is LightViT, proposed by Tao Huang et al. [17], as shown in Fig. 2. LightViT achieves lightweightization of ViT by modifying the self-attention mechanism and feed-forward network (FFN) design in the Transformer. Additionally, it introduces a novel optimization approach for information aggregation that replaces the commonly used hybrid convolution operation in traditional ViT methods.

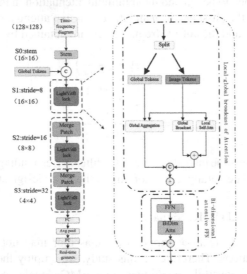

Fig. 2. LightViT architecture. © denotes concatenation in the token axis, ⊕ denotes element-wise addition

3.1 Local-Global Broadcast Mechanism in Self-attention

To reduce computational complexity, a common technique is to partition the feature map into multiple non-overlapping windows, followed by performing self-attention independently within each window. LightViT adopts local window self-attention as its fundamental module.

The local window self-attention divides the given input features, denoted as $X \in \mathbb{R}^{H \times W \times C}$, into non-overlapping windows of shape $(\frac{H}{S} \times \frac{W}{S}, S \times S, C)$. This approach is similar to the local window attention used in Swin [18] and Twins [19]. Subsequently, self-attention is performed within each local window. The computation formula for this process is as follows:

$$X_{local} = Attention(X_q, X_k, X_v) := SoftMax(X_q X_k^T) X_v \tag{6}$$

The computational complexity of self-attention $(H \times W)^2$ is reduced to $\left(\frac{H}{S} \times \frac{W}{S}\right) \times (S \times S)^2 = H \times W \times S \times S$.

At this stage, the input features X_{local} establish local dependencies through local window attention. However, local window attention exhibits clear limitations in terms of receptive field and long-range dependencies. To address this, the LightViT network aggregates global dependency relationships into a smaller feature space and then broadcasts them to the local features.

To gather global information from the input features X, a learnable embedding $G \in \mathbb{R}^{T \times C}$ is employed, which is computed alongside the image tokens in all LightViT blocks. This embedding, referred to as the global token G serves two purposes: global information aggregation and broadcasting. Firstly, it aggregates global representations across the entire image feature map. Then, it broadcasts the global information to the feature map. Specifically, while computing local self-attention, the input global token G (the query) and the image tokens X (the keys and values) are used to collect global representations. This process can be expressed as follows:

$$\hat{G} = Attention(G_q, X_k, X_v) \tag{7}$$

Then, in the global broadcasting, the output of the new token $\hat{G}$ is utilized and passed on to the next block for further processing.

The broadcasting of $\hat{G}$, computed through self-attention, to the local features is performed to compensate for the lack of global dependency information. The computational process can be expressed by the following formula:

$$X_{global} = Attention(X_q, \hat{G}_k, \hat{G}_v) \tag{8}$$

Then, the final output image tokens are calculated by element-wise addition of the local and global features. This can be expressed as:

$$X_{new} = X_{local} + X_{global} \tag{9}$$

3.2 Two-Dimensional Attention Mechanism of FFN

Inspired by attention mechanisms, LightViT incorporates a two-dimensional attention module to capture spatial and channel dependencies, refining the features. This module consists of two branches: the channel attention branch and the spatial attention branch. The channel attention branch first performs average pooling on the input features along the spatial dimension to aggregate global representations. Then, a linear transformation is applied to calculate channel attention. For spatial attention, the global representation is connected to each token feature (local representation) to methods pixel-level relationships. The employed two-dimensional attention module can serve as a plug-and-play module for existing variants of ViT. By slightly increasing the computational cost, it explicitly methods spatial and channel relationships, thereby enhancing the representation capability of the FFN.

4   Experiments and Results

4.1   Platform

This paper utilizes a commercial sEMG signals acquisition device for data collection. The device consists of a sEMG signals acquisition box, electrode sleeves, a Bluetooth adapter, and a data transmission cable (see Fig. 3). The acquisition device has a sampling frequency of 1 kHz and a 12-bit ADC resolution. The signal processing module of the device transmits the acquired sEMG signals data to a PC for further processing and analysis via a Bluetooth module.

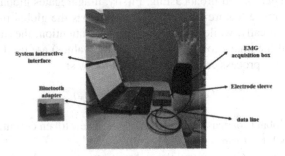

Fig. 3.   sEMG signal acquisition device.

This study utilizes a multi-channel sleeve-based mode of the sEMG signals acquisition device. The sEMG signals are captured by dry electrodes embedded in the sleeve, which is connected to the processor via a data transmission cable. The sleeve consists of 18 electrodes arranged in a zigzag pattern. Each electrode has a horizontal spacing of 30 mm, a diameter of 25 mm, and a vertical spacing of 16 mm. Out of the 18 electrodes, 16 channels are used for collecting sEMG signals data, excluding the reference electrode and the bias electrode.

4.2   Dataset

5 healthy subjects (all males) with a mean age of 25.0 ± 1.8 years were recruited for the study. Prior to the dataset, all participants signed informed consent forms. The study collected sEMG data for hand movements, including a rest (RE) and six hand gestures: hand open (HO), scissor hand (SH), OK hand (OH), hand closure (HC), wrist flexion (WF), and wrist extension (WE) (see Fig. 4). Each gesture was recorded for 10 s, starting

from a relaxed state and continuing until the motion was completed with a stable posture. There was a resting period of 5 s between each gesture test. To ensure data consistency, the electrodes on the sEMG signals acquisition sleeve were placed correctly on the corresponding muscle regions. However, electrode shift occurred due to the clockwise pulling required to secure the sleeve with electrodes. To examine the impact of electrode shift on the results, data were collected with different electrode shift angles ranging from 0° to 45°, including 0°, 9°, 18°, 27°, 36°, and 45°.

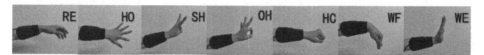

Fig. 4. Dataset gestures. RE: rest, HO: hand open, SH: scissor hand, OH: OK hand, HC: hand closure, WF: wrist flexion, WE: wrist extension.

4.3 Experiments

In the experiments, a dataset collected from fixed angles is used as the training set, while data collected from 0°–45° with random wear is used as the test set. Each person's dataset is separately used for training and testing the methods. Feature alignment and Triplet Loss and Focal Loss as loss functions are introduced to improve the accuracy of gesture classification. After completing the methods training, the gesture recognition methods are tested using the test set, and the average accuracy for each individual is calculated to validate the accuracy and reliability of the algorithm. Additionally, the ResNet and mViT methods are compared with the proposed LightViT methods. Through this experimental design, we can evaluate the performance of the LightViT methods in surface electromyography-based gesture recognition.

4.4 Results and Discussion

A line chart was constructed to compare the experimental results (see Fig. 5). Through the comparison, it can be observed that the LightViT network outperforms ResNet and mViT methods in terms of sEMG signals gesture recognition accuracy. HC and WE performed the best, while HO and SH, WF and OH had similar accuracy rates. Through analysis, it can be observed that HC and WE have significant signal fluctuations and clear features during signal acquisition, resulting in the highest accuracy. On the other hand, WE has smaller signal fluctuations, leading to the lowest accuracy. The main errors for OH occurred in HO, indicating a similarity in the exertion method, which caused a decrease in accuracy. RE, as the reference gesture, was not analyzed.

The LightViT network overcomes the limitations of traditional deep learning networks by effectively capturing both global and local information from the time-frequency representation of sEMG signals. It introduces a global self-attention mechanism and global broadcasting mechanism to extract important features. This leads to a significant improvement in the accuracy of sEMG signal gesture classification. The design of

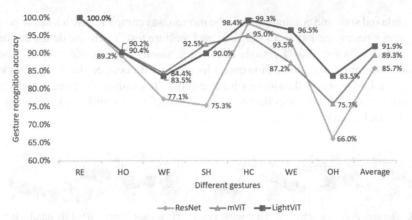

Fig. 5. Comparison histograms of the gestures' recognition accuracies of ResNet, LightViT and mViT. RE: rest, HO: hand open, SH: scissor hand, OH: OK hand, HC: hand closure, WF: wrist flexion, WE: wrist extension.

LightViT enables better understanding and utilization of the temporal characteristics of sEMG signals, resulting in more accurate gesture classification.

A comparative analysis of the parameters and floating-point operations (FLOPs) was conducted for the ResNet, mViT, and LightViT methods to validate the efficiency of the proposed method. Figure 6 presents the Params and FLOPs for each methods. The parameter count reflects the memory space occupied by the methods, with a smaller count indicating lower memory usage. On the other hand, FLOPs reflect the computational speed of the methods, with a smaller count indicating faster computations. From the graph, it can be observed that ResNet has a smaller parameter count but the highest FLOPs. Although mViT has a lower FLOPs, it has a relatively high parameter count. In comparison, LightViT has a slightly higher FLOPs than mViT, but the difference is not significant, and it has the lowest parameter count among the three methods.

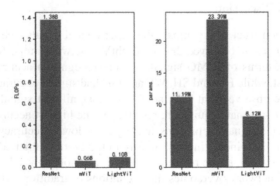

Fig. 6. The parameters and floating-point operations of the three networks.

Although the proposed method effectively addresses the impact of electrode shift on gesture recognition accuracy, it requires the collection of muscle signals from multiple angles, resulting in a lengthy data acquisition process. This study only focuses on the recognition of simple gestures, and it remains to be seen whether the high accuracy can be achieved for complex gestures under electrode shift. The next step involves collecting data for complex gestures to train the model and validate its performance. Real-time experimental validation of the model is also necessary to determine if it outperforms other models in real-time gesture recognition scenarios.

5 Summary

Compared to ResNet and mViT methods, the proposed sEMG gesture recognition methods based on the LightViT network demonstrates higher accuracy and a more lightweight structure. Within an electrode-shift range of $0°-45°$, the proposed LightViT methods only needs to be trained once, avoiding retraining before users wear sEMG device each time. Additionally, this study introduces the concept of feature alignment and further enhances the method's generalization ability and accuracy through the application of Triplet Loss and Focal Loss as loss functions. This makes the methods more user-friendly for elderly or disabled users who may have difficulty controlling their wearing habits, thus improving their experience in electromyography-based interaction systems.

Acknowledgments. We appreciate all the participants in the experiment. This work is supported by the National Natural Science Foundation of China (Grant No. 62003222), the Natural Science Foundation of Liaoning (Grant No. 2022-MS-267) and the Research Fund of Liaoning Provincial Department of Education (Grant No. LQGD2020018).

References

1. Song, S., Yang, L., Wu, M., Liu, Y., Yu, H.: Dynamic hand gesture recognition via electromyographic signal based on convolutional neural network. In: 2021 IEEE International Conference on Systems, Man, and Cybernetics (SMC), pp. 876–881 (2021)
2. Zhang, E., Xue, B., Cao, F., Duan, J., Lin, G., Lei, Y.: Fusion of 2D CNN and 3D DenseNet for dynamic gesture recognition. Electronics **8**, 1511 (2019)
3. Zhang, Y., Wang, C., Zheng, Y., Zhao, J., Li, Y., Xie, X.: Short-term temporal convolutional networks for dynamic hand gesture recognition (2019)
4. Cote Allard, U., et al.: A convolutional neural network for robotic arm guidance using sEMG based frequency-features. In: 2016 IEEE/RSJ International Conference on Intelligent Robots and Systems (IROS), Daejeon, South Korea, pp. 2464–2470. IEEE (2016)
5. Iqbal, N.V., Subramaniam, K., Shaniba Asmi, P.: A review on upper-limb myoelectric prosthetic control. IETE J. Res. **64**, 740–752 (2018)
6. Vidovic, M.M.-C., et al.: Covariate shift adaptation in EMG pattern recognition for prosthetic device control. In: 2014 36th Annual International Conference of the IEEE Engineering in Medicine and Biology Society, pp. 4370–4373 (2014)
7. Jain, S., Singhal, G., Smith, R.J., Kaliki, R., Thakor, N.: Improving long term myoelectric decoding, using an adaptive classifier with label correction. In: 2012 4th IEEE RAS & EMBS International Conference on Biomedical Robotics and Biomechatronics (BioRob), pp. 532–537 (2012)

8. Hargrove, L., Englehart, K., Hudgins, B.: A training strategy to reduce classification degradation due to electrode displacements in pattern recognition based myoelectric control. Biomed.
Signal Process. Control **3**, 175–180 (2008)

9. Prahm, C., Paassen, B., Schulz, A., Hammer, B., Aszmann, O.: Transfer learning for rapid recalibration of a myoelectric prosthesis after electrode shift. In: Ibáñez, J., González-Vargas,
J., Azorín, J., Akay, M., Pons, J. (eds.) Converging Clinical and Engineering Research on
Neurorehabilitation II. Biosystems & Biorobotics, vol. 15, pp. 153–157. Springer, Cham
(2017). https://doi.org/10.1007/978-3-319-46669-9_28

10. Ameri, A., Akhaee, M.A., Scheme, E., Englehart, K.: A deep transfer learning approach to
reducing the effect of electrode shift in EMG pattern recognition-based control. IEEE Trans.
Neural Syst. Rehabil. Eng. **28**, 370–379 (2020)

11. He, J., Sheng, X., Zhu, X., Jiang, N.: Electrode density affects the robustness of myoelectric
pattern recognition system with and without electrode shift. IEEE J. Biomed. Health Inform.
23, 156–163 (2019)

12. Zhang, H., Wang, C., Gou, W., Guo, L., Lin, C.: DFNN-based gesture recognition with the
shift and damage of the HD-sEMG electrodes. In: 2019 IEEE International Conference on
Robotics and Biomimetics (ROBIO), pp. 1275–1279 (2019)

13. Wu, L., Liu, A., Zhang, X., Chen, X., Chen, X.: Electrode shift robust CNN for high-density
myoelectric pattern recognition control. IEEE Trans. Instrum. Meas. **71**, 1–10 (2022)

14. Díaz-Amador, R., Mendoza-Reyes, M.A., Ferrer-Riesgo, C.A.: Improving myoelectric pattern
recognition robustness to electrode shift using image processing techniques and HD-EMG.
In: González Díaz, C., et al. (eds.) CLAIB 2019. IFMBE Proceedings, vol. 75, pp. 344–350.
Springer, Cham (2020). https://doi.org/10.1007/978-3-030-30648-9_45

15. Dosovitskiy, A., et al.: An image is worth 16x16 words: transformers for image recognition
at scale (2021)

16. Li, Y., Mao, H., Girshick, R., He, K.: Exploring plain vision transformer backbones for object
detection. In: Avidan, S., Brostow, G., Cissé, M., Farinella, G.M., Hassner, T. (eds.) ECCV
2022. LNCS, vol. 13669, pp. 280–296. Springer, Cham (2022). https://doi.org/10.1007/978-
3-031-20077-9_17

17. Huang, T., Huang, L., You, S., Wang, F., Qian, C., Xu, C.: LightViT: towards light-weight
convolution-free vision transformers (2022)

18. Liu, Z., et al.: Swin transformer: hierarchical vision transformer using shifted windows (2021)

19. Chu, X., et al.: Twins: revisiting the design of spatial attention in vision transformers (2021)

A Hybrid Scheme for Efficient Deformable Image Registration

Jinze Huo[1(✉)], Bangli Liu[1,2], and Qinggang Meng[1]

[1] Department of Computer Science, Loughborough University, Loughborough, UK
J.Huo@lboro.ac.uk
[2] De Montfort University, Leicester, UK

Abstract. Deformable image registration (DIR) is one of the important processing steps for image analysis in the compute vision field. Although various methods have been proposed to deal with the DIR problem, it is still challenging to achieve a good balance between the registration speed and accuracy. This paper introduces a novel hybrid registration model which is capable of fast and accurately warping a target image to a reference image. This achievement owns to a coarse-to-fine registration scheme, where an automatic thin plate splines-based (A-Tps) method is proposed for preliminary registration, then an improved inertia Demons (I Demons) algorithm is developed for fine warping the result of previous output. Experimental results demonstrate the outstanding performance of the proposed model in terms of registration speed and accuracy.

Keywords: Deformable image registration · Demons · Thin-plate splines · Hybrid model

1 Introduction

The target of image registration is to achieve the geometric alignment of two images by finding an optimal transformation function between them. It has a large range of applications, from medical imaging, remote sensing, to compute vision [1,3,5,6]. According to the transformation model used, image registration can be divided into two classes: linear and non-rigid transformation. The linear transformation is a global model that includes translating, rotation, scaling, and affine transforms, but it can not describe the local deformation information. Using this estimated global transformation to warp a target image to a reference image can only correct the differences globally rather than locally. However, in many applications, for example, image registration in the medical imaging field is applied to help diagnose some diseases which are sometimes represented by the local motion of tissues. In this case, estimating such local differences is essential.

The non-rigid transformation is capable of describing local deformation. Methods like B-spline [8], thin-plate splines [2], and Demons [7,10] are popularly used for non-rigid image registration. The Demons algorithm calculates the deformation force according to the local intensity difference of the target image

H. Yang et al. (Eds.): ICIRA 2023, LNAI 14267, pp. 433–441, 2023.
https://doi.org/10.1007/978-981-99-6483-3_37

to the reference image via an optical-flow model. Although Demons is outstanding in correcting local differences with high accuracy, it is quite time-consuming. Different from the Demons which deforms the target image only depends on the intensity information, the thin-plate splines method maps corresponding landmark points on the reference and target images and accomplishes the registration of non-landmark points via interpolation. Although it can improve the speed of registration compared to Demons, however, the registration accuracy (inadequate interpolation) might decrease due to the localization errors of landmark points.

Observing the above advantages and disadvantages of the thin-plate spline method and Demons algorithm, a hybrid image registration scheme combining their advantages is proposed in this paper. The scheme consists of two stages from coarse to fine registration. Specifically, an automatic thin-plate splines method is firstly used to correct the large deformation depending on the correspondence of landmark points on two images, then an advanced inertia Demons algorithm is applied for fine registration. The contributions of this paper can be summarized as follows: 1) an automatic thin-plate splines method with effective landmark points detection is developed to warp the image globally; 2) an advanced inertia Demons algorithm is applied to refine the warping; 3) the proposed coarse-to-fine hybrid scheme successfully improves the speed and accuracy of registration by combining each other's advantages.

The rest of this paper is organized as follows: Sect. 2 introduces the proposed hybrid image registration scheme. Section 3 presents experimental results as well as the comparison to the existing methods to demonstrate the effectiveness of the proposed scheme. Section 4 summarizes the work of this paper.

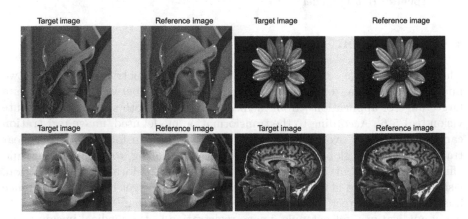

Fig. 1. Automatic landmark points detected on the target and reference images.

2   Proposed Method

A hybrid method is proposed for image registration, where a coarse-to-fine strategy is developed to achieve efficient image registration with low registration error and computational time. This method includes an automatic thin-plate spline (A-Tps) for coarse deformation correction and an advanced inertial Demons (I-Demons) algorithm for further tiny deformation correction.

2.1   Automatic Thin-Plate Spline-Based Registration

Thin-plate splines (Tps) is widely used for landmark-based image registration. Given an original image and a corresponding deformed image, with a set of N corresponding points (known as landmark points) in two images, the Tps aims to describe the warping function between two images using $2(N+3)$ parameters. The parameters could describe the global affine motion that depicts the overall shape of the splines, and correspondences of the landmark points which are described via a radial basis non-linear component. The correspondence away from the landmark points, Tps interpolates the displacement of each pixel of the image. Since this paper takes 2D images into account, two thin-plate spline functions will be used to model the coordinate changes in each dimension.

Landmark Points Detection. Observing that the majority of the existing points-based registration methods require manually marking the landmark points on two images before registration, this sometimes needs prior knowledge and limits the algorithms' application in practical scenarios. Therefore, this paper proposes to employ a harris corner detector [4] to automatically detect the points of interest through the reference image. Each point's local information is calculated to get its response value and the N points with a higher value are selected as landmark points q_i, for $i = 1, ..., N$. On the target image, the corresponding point of each landmark p_i ($i = 1, ..., N$) is searched via a matching algorithm. Figure 1 shows landmark points on different image pairs.

Thin-Plate Spline-Based Registration. With detected landmark points, Tps is utilized to calculate a mapping function $f(p)$ that effectively maps data points p_i to q_i with the following objective function:

$$\sum_{i=1}^{N} ||q_i - f(p_i)||^2 \tag{1}$$

Originally, Tps expresses the physical bending energy of a thin metal plate on point constraints. Therefore, to ensure the smoothness of the interpolation over the whole image area, a gradient-based regularization term is introduced to the objective function:

$$\sum_{i=1}^{N} ||q_i - f(p_i)||^2 + \lambda \int \int_{R^2} ((\frac{\delta^2 f}{\delta^2 x}) + 2(\frac{\delta^2 f}{\delta x \delta y}) + (\frac{\delta^2 f}{\delta^2 y})) dx dy \tag{2}$$

where x and y denote two dimensions of 2D images. This function has a unique minimizer which consists of affine and non-affine parts:

$$f(x,y) = a_1 + a_x x + a_y y + \sum_{i=1}^{N} w_i U(|p_i - (x,y)|) \tag{3}$$

here, $U(*)$ is radial basis functions and is often represented by

$$U(r) = r^2 * log(r^2) \tag{4}$$

2.2   Advanced Inertia Demons

The original Demons algorithm was proposed by Thirion in 1998 by improving the optical flow algorithm [9]. It warps a target image depending on the calculated deformation force between the target and reference images:

$$u = \frac{(F - M)\nabla F}{|\nabla F|^2 + (F - M)^2} \tag{5}$$

where u represents the update deformation field. F and M denote the reference image and the target image, respectively. ∇F is the gradient force of F.

Image registration can be regarded as a gas diffusion process in physics [12], where pixels' movement is driven by the deformation force. According to Newton's first law, all objects have inertia. Like moving objects, image pixels' moving also has such inertia characteristics, which means moving pixels will not immediately change the moving direction with the change of the deformation force. However, the deformation force calculated using Eq. 5 is only the optimal vector field of pixels at each time, which is a static consideration and ignores the inertial information. Therefore, the proposed I-Demons algorithm considers the effect of the deformation force in the previous stage as a kind of inertia to help update new deformation field at current stage (as shown in Fig. 2):

$$u_{(n)} = \alpha u_{(n-1)} + u_{(n)} \tag{6}$$

where $u_{(n)}$ and $u_{(n-1)}$ represent the update deformation field of time n and $n-1$, respectively. α $(0 < \alpha < 1)$ is a control coefficient to determine the weight of $u_{(n-1)}$. Here, we use the symmetric Demons algorithm [11] to update each time's static deformation field $u_{(n)}$.

$$u_{(n)} = \frac{2(M - F)(\nabla F + \nabla M)}{\|\nabla F + \nabla M\|^2 + \frac{(F-M)^2}{k^2}} \tag{7}$$

where k is a control coefficient. Compared to Eq. 5, this symmetric Demons further considers the gradient ∇M of the target image M to obtain the new deformation field, which can improve optimization speed. Thus, Eq. 6 is represented by:

$$u_{(n)} = \alpha u_{(n-1)} + \frac{2(M - F)(\nabla F + \nabla M)}{\|\nabla F + \nabla M\|^2 + \frac{(F-M)^2}{k^2}} \tag{8}$$

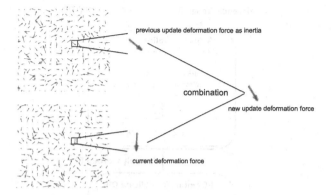

Fig. 2. Flowchart of the deformation field update with inertia information in the proposed I-Demons algorithm.

2.3 Hybrid Scheme

When processing images with large deformations, a Gaussian filtering K_{smooth} is applied for pre-processing the images. This can help relieve the impact of noise during image acquisition and improve the image deformation force calculation:

$$H \leftarrow K_{\text{smooth}} \star H \tag{9}$$

H represents the image to be processed.

The idea of the hybrid scheme is to use the proposed A-Tps method to automatically detect the landmark points and their corresponding points on two images, and then warp the target image according to the warping function between points. By doing this, a coarsely warped target image with large deformations corrected is obtained with a low computational cost. This speed achievement owes to the fast warping function calculation based on sparse points. Taking the coarsely warped image as the input, the improved I-Demons can delicately correct the minor difference between two images from the near stage to the reference image. This hybrid scheme elaborately makes each algorithm play its advantage (speed of A-Tps and accuracy of I-Demons). The flowchart of this coarse-to-fine process is described in Fig. 3.

3   Experiments

The experimental images were collected from different fields and each of them has unknown deformation compared to its reference image. Different image registration methods: B-spline [8], original Demons(O-Demons) [9], the proposed A-Tps, I-Demons, and the hybrid scheme are selected for the registration performance comparison.

To evaluate the registration performance of these methods, Table 1 lists the mean square error (MSE) between the reference image and the warped target

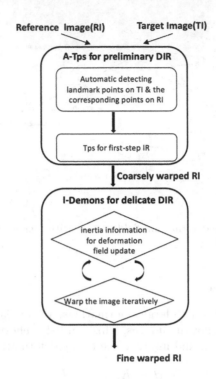

Fig. 3. Flowchart of the proposed hybrid image registration process.

Table 1. Comparison of MSE and Time on each image using the O-Demons, B-spline, and proposed method, respectively.

Images/Methods	-	O-Demons	B-spline	**Hybrid scheme**
lenag	MSE($*10^{-4}$)	3.746	3.862	2.419
	Time(s)	1.815	3.7	0.621
rose	MSE($*10^{-4}$)	49	35	25
	Time(s)	8.893	44.5	5.778
brainT1	MSE($*10^{-4}$)	0.217	0.755	0.62
	Time(s)	2.267	11.647	1.301
sunflower	MSE($*10^{-4}$)	0.361	0.8	0.434
	Time(s)	2.43	18.916	2.11
brainT2	MSE($*10^{-4}$)	0.194	0.651	0.114
	Time(s)	1.833	6.45	1.002

image as well as the time used. From the table, it can be found that the proposed hybrid scheme needs the lowest computational cost for completing registration on all image pairs. Although the proposed method depends on the Demons algorithm for the final fine registration, it is capable of obtaining comparable

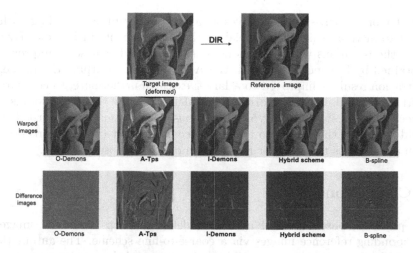

Fig. 4. Registration performance of different algorithms on the deformed 'lenag' image.

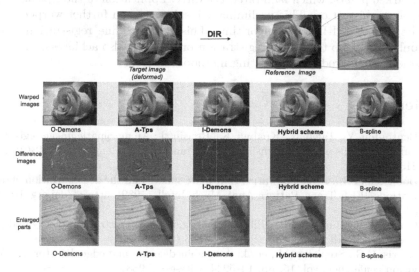

Fig. 5. Details comparison of different image registration algorithms on 'rose' images.

MSE in a shorter time compared to the O-Demons method. Moreover, the hybrid scheme achieves better registration results over the B-spline method in terms of MSE and speed.

In addition, Fig. 4 and Fig. 5 provides a more detailed comparison of the registration performance on the deformed 'lenag' and 'rose' image, including warped images and difference images (the difference between the reference and warped target images). From the image, it can be seen that the proposed hybrid method performs the best registration result with the smallest difference image. Although the performance of the proposed A-Tps is not outstanding compared to O-Demons and B-spline, it serves as a preliminary process dealing with the large deformation, which is beneficial for the improvement of I-Demons. By comparing the I-Demons with O-Demons, it can be found that some improvement is obtained by I-Demons, but with the A-Tps coarsely warping the image, the registration result is improved to a larger extent. Furthermore, to compare the registration details of each algorithm, an enlarged part of the image details (with red rectangles) is shown in Fig. 5. it is obvious that the small part warped by the hybrid scheme is the closest to the reference image part (with blue rectangles), which also reflects the superior registration of our proposed method.

4 Conclusions

This paper proposed a novel hybrid model that warps deformed images to corresponding reference images via a coarse-to-fine scheme. The automatically detected landmark points proposed in A-Tps removed the requirement of manually marked points, which facilitated the direct application of the Tps algorithm for global registration. This preliminary result was then further warped locally by the proposed I-Demons algorithm. This coarse-to-fine registration scheme not only speeds up the image registration process but also achieves outstanding accuracies compared to the existing methods.

References

1. Bentoutou, Y., Taleb, N., Kpalma, K., Ronsin, J.: An automatic image registration for applications in remote sensing. IEEE Trans. Geosci. Remote Sens. **43**(9), 2127–2137 (2005)
2. Bookstein, F.L.: Principal warps: thin-plate splines and the decomposition of deformations. IEEE Trans. Pattern Anal. Mach. Intell. (1989). https://doi.org/10.1109/34.24792
3. Crum, W.R., Hartkens, T., Hill, D.: Non-rigid image registration: theory and practice. Br. J. Radiol. **77**(suppl_2), S140–S153 (2004)
4. Harris, C.G., Stephens, M., et al.: A combined corner and edge detector. In: Alvey vision conference. vol. 15, pp. 10–5244. Citeseer (1988)
5. Lucas, B.D., Kanade, T., et al.: An iterative image registration technique with an application to stereo vision (1981)
6. Oh, S., Kim, S.: Deformable image registration in radiation therapy. Radiat. Oncol. J. **35**(2), 101 (2017)
7. Pennec, X., Cachier, P., Ayache, N.: Understanding the "Demon's Algorithm": 3D non-rigid registration by gradient descent. In: Taylor, C., Colchester, A. (eds.) MICCAI 1999. LNCS, vol. 1679, pp. 597–605. Springer, Heidelberg (1999). https://doi.org/10.1007/10704282_64
8. Rueckert, D., Sonoda, L.I., Hayes, C., Hill, D.L., Leach, M.O., Hawkes, D.J.: Non-rigid registration using free-form deformations: application to breast MR images. IEEE Trans. Med. Imaging **18**(8), 712–721 (1999)
9. Thirion, J.P.: Image matching as a diffusion process: an analogy with Maxwell's demons. Med. Image Anal. **2**(3), 243–260 (1998)

10. Vercauteren, T., Pennec, X., Malis, E., Perchant, A., Ayache, N.: Insight into efficient image registration techniques and the demons algorithm. In: Karssemeijer,
N., Lelieveldt, B. (eds.) IPMI 2007. LNCS, vol. 4584, pp. 495–506. Springer, Heidelberg (2007). https://doi.org/10.1007/978-3-540-73273-0_41
11. Vercauteren, T., Pennec, X., Perchant, A., Ayache, N.: Symmetric log-domain
diffeomorphic registration: a demons-based approach. In: Metaxas, D., Axel, L.,
Fichtinger, G., Székely, G. (eds.) MICCAI 2008. LNCS, vol. 5241, pp. 754–761.
Springer, Heidelberg (2008). https://doi.org/10.1007/978-3-540-85988-8_90
12. Wang, H., et al.: Validation of an accelerated 'demons' algorithm for deformable
image registration in radiation therapy. Phys. Med. Biol. 50(12), 2887 (2005)

A Trunk Map Construction Method for Long-Term Localization and Navigation for Orchard Robots

Enbo Liu, Jin Lou, Wei Tang$^{(\boxtimes)}$, Jiale Wu, and Xinli Liang

School of Automation, Northwestern Polytechnical University, Xi'an 710129, China
tangwei@nwpu.edu.cn

Abstract. Constructing a map for long-term localization and navigation poses significant challenges for orchard robots, especially as the orchard environment changes due to the growth cycle of fruit trees and seasonal changes. Considering the long-term static stability of fruit tree trunks in the orchard environment, it is well suited to markers for robot localization and navigation in the time-varying orchard environment. In this paper, we propose a novel method that combines camera and 3D LiDAR data to construct a static map for orchard robot navigation. Our approach involves aligning and fusing the sensor data, detecting tree trunks using a target detection algorithm, and mapping the results onto the 3D point cloud data. We further extract and segment the trunk point cloud using Euclidean clustering and the RANSAC algorithm. Finally, we register the trunk point cloud with the global point cloud map using the Simultaneous Localization and Mapping (SLAM) algorithm. Experimental results conducted in both simulated and real environments demonstrate that our method effectively constructs an accurate trunk point cloud map, which facilitates long-term localization and navigation for orchard robots.

Keywords: Orchard Robots · Camera · 3D LiDAR · Simultaneous Localization and Mapping (SLAM) · Trunk Map

1 Introduction

Orchard robots play a pivotal role in diverse agricultural operations, encompassing crucial tasks such as harvesting, spraying, fertilizing, and more. Within the realm of orchard management, the implementation of autonomous navigation technology offers a promising avenue for these robots, empowering them to navigate independently throughout orchards. An efficient autonomous navigation system comprises three fundamental components: perception, localization, and path planning. The perception component utilizes sensors to acquire data regarding the surrounding obstacles and generate a comprehensive orchard map. Precise mapping assumes a critical role in enabling the robot to accurately ascertain its position in relation to neighboring trees and other obstacles, which is essential for the robot to subsequently execute precise localization and navigation tasks.

SLAM technology has emerged as a prominent solution for providing robots with crucial localization and mapping capabilities in unfamiliar environments, finding widespread application across various industries. Notable SLAM frameworks include vision-based systems like ORB-SLAM3 [1] and VINS-Mono [2], 2D LiDAR-based approaches such as gmapping [3] and Cartographer [4], as well as 3D LiDAR-based methods like Lego-LOAM [5], LIO-SAM [6], and FAST-LIO [7], among others. However, a prevalent constraint observed in many SLAM algorithms is their reliance on the assumption of a static environment. In scenarios involving dynamic objects, these objects inevitably become integrated into the map as obstacles, thereby compromising the accuracy of localization and navigation. Moreover, substantial environmental changes can lead to a significant mismatch between the generated map and the actual surroundings. In such instances, the remapping process becomes imperative, introducing additional complexities to map management.

Orchards present unique challenges as semi-structured and dynamic environments. Unlike controlled indoor settings, orchards exhibit irregular ground surfaces and undergo continuous changes due to the growth cycles of trees and seasonal variations. This unique nature of orchards is vividly depicted in Fig. 1, showcasing a point cloud map of the same orchard location captured at different periods. Notably, the construction of the map exhibits significant variability across various seasons. Consequently, when the robot revisits the orchard environment, positioning errors may arise, necessitating constant updating of the environment map. This dynamic map updating process presents a substantial challenge for the application of SLAM technology in enabling autonomous navigation for orchard robots.

Fig. 1. Orchard point cloud map of the same place in different periods

To enhance the precision of priori maps for orchard robot localization and navigation, researchers have undertaken extensive investigations pertaining to orchard map construction. Earlier studies predominantly employed the fusion of global navigation satellite systems (GNSS) and LiDAR for this purpose within orchard settings. However, the considerable height and density of the orchard canopy frequently obstructed GNSS signals, leading to the generation of imprecise maps [8].

The camera has gained significant popularity among researchers owing to its cost-effectiveness and its ability to capture rich semantic information. In one study, a visual system combined with Support Vector Machines (SVMs) was employed to detect pear roots [9]. Furthermore, a 2D LiDAR sensor was utilized to capture distance information, while the EIF-SLAM algorithm facilitated the construction of a stem map. Chen et al. [10] explored the integration of eye-in-hand stereo vision with SLAM systems, developing a specialized dynamic stereoscopic matching algorithm tailored for complex fruit orchard environments. This innovative approach facilitated the construction of detailed and expansive 3D orchard maps. Additionally, Dong et al. [11] employed an RGB-D camera to detect fruit trees and fruits within the orchard environment, utilizing the ORB-SLAM2 framework for simultaneous localization and mapping of the robot.

In the orchard environment, LiDAR has gained extensive adoption due to its resilience against weather conditions and lighting variations, as well as its exceptional ranging accuracy. Underwood et al. [12] tackled point cloud data segmentation using a hidden Markov model, describing each tree with descriptors and correlating the results with maps derived from the hidden Markov model. Gao et al. [13] focused on optimizing the fruit tree map model by fusing data from LiDAR, inertial measurement unit (IMU), and GNSS sensors in the orchard environment. By incorporating additional factors into the factor map, they achieved a more accurate representation of the orchard. Additionally, a new 3D LiDAR scanning representation was introduced for unstructured and large-scale orchard environments [14]. A novel weighting strategy was employed to construct an attention score map, thereby enhancing the efficiency of loop closure detection.

Despite the considerable success achieved by the aforementioned methods in orchard map construction, they often overlook the influence of the dynamic nature of the orchard environment on the generation of fruit tree maps. In a recent study, a novel algorithm named GardenMap was introduced as a static point cloud mapping solution [15]. This algorithm leveraged semantic information to process point clouds and construct a static point cloud map from sequences of point clouds. Experimental results demonstrated the superior performance of GardenMap compared to state-of-the-art static point cloud mapping algorithms. While this method effectively accounted for moving objects in the orchard environment, such as pedestrians and vehicles, it did not fully address the impact of fruit trees themselves on map construction, specifically with regard to seasonal changes.

Given the pronounced variations in the canopy layer of fruit trees throughout different seasons, while the trunk remains relatively stable, we present a novel approach for the construction of a static trunk map in orchards. This map serves as a reliable resource for long-term localization and navigation purposes. The key contributions of this study can be summarized as follows:

- A method that utilizes the fusion of camera and 3D LiDAR data to extract trunk point clouds is proposed, which enables the achievement of precise point cloud segmentation through the utilization of Euclidean clustering and RANSAC fitting algorithms.
- A method for constructing a static point cloud map of an orchard that remains unaffected by seasonal changes. This map proves instrumental for subsequent long-term localization and navigation tasks.

The rest of this paper is organized as follows. Section 2 describes the architecture of the system. Section 3 describes the proposed method in this paper. Section 4 shows experiments in the simulated environment and our real dataset. Section 5 summarizes the work of this paper and provides some directions for future research.

2   System Framework

The overall framework of the system for constructing a static trunk map is visually depicted in Fig. 2. This framework comprises two fundamental components, namely the target point cloud extraction module and the SLAM mapping module.

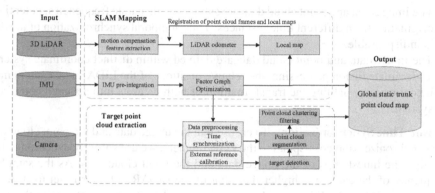

Fig. 2. Overall framework of the system for constructing a static trunk map

The target point cloud extraction module aligns image data and LiDAR data in the same moment and coordinates the system through spatiotemporal alignment. By employing a target detection algorithm, it effectively identifies tree trunks. And the corresponding LiDAR point cloud is extracted from the image detection frame using camera-LiDAR extrinsic parameters. Subsequently, the extracted point cloud undergoes clustering segmentation to eliminate noise and yield a refined point cloud specifically representing the tree trunks.

The SLAM mapping module capitalizes on data derived from the IMU and LiDAR sensors. By mitigating motion distortions and conducting feature extraction from the point cloud, it aligns the point cloud with the local map, consequently obtaining accurate LiDAR odometry. The results of IMU pre-integration are effectively integrated with laser odometry through factor graph optimization, ensuring precise robot localization. Subsequently, the localization obtained from the SLAM module is employed to register the trunk point cloud within the global point cloud map. This registration process facilitates the creation of a trunk point cloud map that exhibits minimal variations across different seasons, rendering it suitable for long-term localization and navigation purposes.

3   Method

The subsequent subsections comprehensively elucidate the sequential functional steps involved in both the target point cloud extraction and SLAM mapping modules. Each subsection provides detailed explanations of the respective processes and methodologies employed within these modules.

3.1   Target Point Cloud Extraction

Taking into consideration the inherent advantages of the semantic richness of the camera and the high range accuracy of LiDAR, we employ a fusion approach to combine image and point cloud data for tree trunk recognition and subsequent point cloud extraction. However, the fusion process necessitates addressing two critical issues:

1. The image data and point cloud data are sampled at disparate frequencies, potentially originating from different time instances. Thus, temporal synchronization of the data is indispensable.
2. The image data and point cloud data are defined within distinct coordinate systems. To facilitate fusion processing, the relative positions of the LiDAR and camera must be calibrated, enabling the transformation of both datasets into a shared coordinate system.

Sensor Time Synchronization.   To ensure that the image data and the point cloud data are synchronized and correspond to the same moment, we use software synchronization to align the timestamps of the image data and the point cloud data. As the sampling frequency of the camera is higher than that of the LiDAR, a buffer is set to store the image data. When the lidar completes a sampling, the image data closest to the point cloud data timestamp in the buffer is searched for matching.

Sensor Spatial Alignment.   The calibration of the relative position between the camera and the LiDAR involves the coordination of four different coordinate systems: the LiDAR coordinate system $O_L - X_L Y_L Z_L$, the camera coordinate system $O_C - X_C Y_C Z_C$, the pixel coordinate system $O - UV$, and the world coordinate system $O_W - X_W Y_W Z_W$. The interrelation between these coordinate systems is illustrated in Fig. 3.

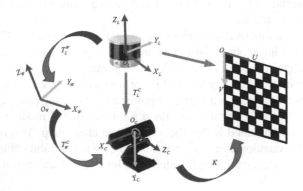

Fig. 3.   The relationship diagram of sensor coordinate systems

Let the coordinate of a point A in the defined space in the world coordinate system be (x_w, y_w, z_w), and the coordinates in the camera coordinate system be (x_c, y_c, z_c), The relationship between the two can be described as follows:

$$
\begin{bmatrix} x_c \\ y_c \\ z_c \end{bmatrix} = R_W^C \begin{bmatrix} x_w \\ y_w \\ z_w \end{bmatrix} + t_W^C = \begin{bmatrix} R_W^C & t_W^C \end{bmatrix} \begin{bmatrix} x_w \\ y_w \\ z_w \\ 1 \end{bmatrix}
\tag{1}
$$

where $R_W^C \in SO(3)$ and t_W^C are the rotation matrix and translation vector from the world coordinate system to the camera coordinate system, respectively. The coordinate of A in the pixel coordinate system is (u, v), and the coordinate in the camera coordinate system is (x_c, y_c, z_c). The relationship between the two can be described as follows:

$$
\begin{bmatrix} u \\ v \\ 1 \end{bmatrix} = \frac{1}{z_c} K \begin{bmatrix} x_c \\ y_c \\ z_c \end{bmatrix} = \frac{1}{z_c} \begin{bmatrix} f_x & 0 & c_x \\ 0 & f_y & c_y \\ 0 & 0 & 1 \end{bmatrix} \begin{bmatrix} x_c \\ y_c \\ z_c \end{bmatrix}
\tag{2}
$$

where K is the internal reference matrix of the camera; f_x and f_y are focal lengths; c_x and c_y are principal points. The coordinate of A in the LiDAR coordinate system is (x_l, y_l, z_l), and its relationship with the coordinates (x_c, y_c, z_c) in the camera coordinate system can be described as follows:

$$
\begin{bmatrix} x_c \\ y_c \\ z_c \end{bmatrix} = R_L^C \begin{bmatrix} x_l \\ y_l \\ z_l \end{bmatrix} + t_L^C = \begin{bmatrix} R_L^C & t_L^C \end{bmatrix} \begin{bmatrix} x_l \\ y_l \\ z_l \\ 1 \end{bmatrix}
\tag{3}
$$

where $R_L^C \in SO(3)$ and t_L^C are the rotation matrix and translation vector from the LiDAR coordinate system to the camera coordinate system, respectively. In conjunction with (1)–(3), the relationship between (x_l, y_l, z_l) and (u, v) can be obtained:

$$
\begin{bmatrix} u \\ v \\ 1 \end{bmatrix} = \frac{1}{z_c} \begin{bmatrix} f_x & 0 & c_x \\ 0 & f_y & c_y \\ 0 & 0 & 1 \end{bmatrix} \begin{bmatrix} R_L^C & t_L^C \end{bmatrix} \begin{bmatrix} x_l \\ y_l \\ z_l \\ 1 \end{bmatrix} = \frac{1}{z_c} K T_L^C \begin{bmatrix} x_l \\ y_l \\ z_l \\ 1 \end{bmatrix}
\tag{4}
$$

where $T_L^C = \begin{bmatrix} R_L^C & t_L^C \end{bmatrix}$ is the transformation matrix from the lidar coordinate system to the camera coordinate system. In this paper, the Calibration Toolkit module in the Autoware [16] is used to solve the above T_L^C and K.

Candidate Trunk Point Cloud Extraction. Given the considerable data volume contained in a single frame of point cloud data, a significant proportion of the data corresponds to ground points. However, including these ground points in subsequent point cloud processing significantly increases computational requirements. To mitigate this issue, we apply a filtering process to remove ground points based on the LiDAR installation height. Additionally, considering that LiDAR point clouds exhibit reduced ranging accuracy as the distance from the target increases, we implement a fusion pre-filtering step by excluding laser point cloud data beyond 50 m. Let $\mathcal{P} = \{P^1, P^2, \cdots P^j\}(j = 1, 2 \cdots M)$ be a frame of point cloud data after filtering, which $P^j = \left(p_x^j, p_y^j, p_z^j\right)$ represents the coordinates of the j-th point of the point cloud, and M is the number of points. Through Eq. (3), the corresponding pixel coordinates $U^j = \left(u^j, v^j\right)$ of the point P^j in the pixel coordinate system can be obtained.

To enable the accurate identification of tree trunks within the orchard, we employed the state-of-the-art object detection algorithm YOLOX [17] to train a custom dataset. Utilizing the trained model, we obtained detection boxes outlining the tree trunks in the captured images. The dimensions of these detection boxes are represented by (u_{max}^i, v_{max}^i) and $(u_{min}^i, v_{min}^i)(i = 1, 2 \cdots, N)$, where $u_{max}^i, v_{max}^i, u_{min}^i$ and v_{min}^i respectively represent the maximum and minimum coordinates of the u-axis and v-axis of the i-th detection box in the pixel coordinate system $O - UV$. To determine whether the point P^j belongs to the i-th detection box, the following condition is applied:

$$u_{max}^i < u^j < u_{min}^i \cap v_{max}^i < v^j < v_{max}^i \tag{5}$$

Through the above judgment, we can obtain the point cloud data $T^i = \{T_1^i, T_2^i, \cdots T_k^i\}(k = 1, 2 \cdots K)$ corresponding to the i-th detection box, where T_k^i is the k-th LiDAR point belonging to the i-th detection box, and K is the number of LiDAR points belonging to the i-th detection box. Let $T = \{T^1, T^2, \cdots, T^i\}(i = 1, 2 \cdots N)$ be a candidate trunk point cloud in the point cloud $\mathcal{P}$.

Point Cloud Clustering and Filtering. As the rectangular detection boxes generated by the YOLOX algorithm may not align perfectly with the actual shape of the tree trunk, and when mapping the 2D detection box to the three-dimensional space, it forms a visual cone, the candidate trunk point cloud may contain additional points representing other semantic information. Therefore, it becomes imperative to apply segmentation and filtering techniques to refine the candidate trunk point cloud T^i.

In this paper, the Euclidean clustering method based on KD-tree [18] is used to segment the candidate trunk point cloud T^i corresponding to each detection box. The processing flow of segmentation and screening is shown in Fig. 4. The candidate trunk point cloud T^i is used as the input point set, and the search domain radius R is given. The point q in the point set is selected. The Euclidean distance between two points in three-dimensional space is defined as:

$$d_e = \sqrt{(x_1 - x_2)^2 + (y_1 - y_2)^2 + (z_1 - z_2)^2} \tag{6}$$

a KD-Tree-based radius neighborhood search algorithm is used to search points in the neighborhood radius R of a point q, the points whose Euclidean distance d_e is less than the set threshold are accumulated into a group $\mathcal{Q}_i$. If the number of points in the group no longer increases, the group $\mathcal{Q}_i$ is output as a cluster family, and a new point q is selected for the remaining data set. Repeat the above process, and finally the target cluster set $\mathcal{Q} = \{\mathcal{Q}_1, \mathcal{Q}_2, \cdots, \mathcal{Q}_i\}(i = 1, 2, \cdots, M)$ can be obtained, where M is the number of clusters. The point cloud belonging to the trunk is clustered into one cluster. Therefore, it is necessary to further filter the trunk point cloud of fruit trees from the clustering data.

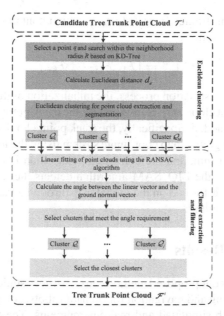

Fig. 4. The process of trunk point cloud clustering and filtering.

Considering the shape characteristics of the tree trunk, the Random Sample Consensus (RANSAC) algorithm [19] is used to fit a straight line to each class of point cloud $\mathcal{Q}_i$ after clustering, and the angle α between the direction vector $\boldsymbol{k}$ of the fitted line and the ground normal vector $\boldsymbol{n}$ is calculated.

$$\alpha - arccos\frac{\boldsymbol{k} \cdot \boldsymbol{n}}{|\boldsymbol{k}||\boldsymbol{n}|} \qquad (7)$$

where $|\boldsymbol{k}|$ and $|\boldsymbol{n}|$ are the modulus length of the vector $\boldsymbol{k}$ and the vector $\boldsymbol{n}$, respectively. If α is greater than the set threshold, the corresponding cluster is filtered as a noise point cloud. If multiple clusters meet the set conditions, the point cloud of the trunk is selected from the clusters with the nearest distance. Through the above method, we filter out the trunk point cloud $\mathcal{F}^i$ in the candidate trunk point cloud $\mathcal{T}^i$, so the trunk point cloud $\mathcal{F} = \{\mathcal{F}^1, \mathcal{F}^2, \cdots \mathcal{F}^i\}$ in the point cloud $\mathcal{P}$ is obtained.

3.2 SLAM Mapping

In the previous section, the fusion of camera and LiDAR data is introduced to obtain the trunk point cloud in a frame of point cloud data. Next, we will use the LIO_SAM algorithm [6] to construct a global tree trunk map, the idea of extracting keyframes in the LIO_SAM algorithm is used to avoid data redundancy. A series of methods from the previous section are used to extract the trunk point cloud from the key frame point cloud and register it into the global map. The global map represents the trunk geometric information contained in the historical environment. Let $\mathcal{M}_g^{cur}$ be the global trunk point cloud map built on scan frames from t_1 to t_{k-1}, which contains k frames of historical information, defined as follows:

$$\mathcal{M}_g^{cur} = \{\mathcal{F}_1, \mathcal{F}_2, \cdots, \mathcal{F}_{k-1}\} \tag{8}$$

In the global map construction process, the initialization of the global map is carried out using the trunk point cloud at t_1. Subsequently, the trunk point cloud $\mathcal{F}_k$ of the current frame at t_k needs to be added. Specifically, the trunk point cloud $\mathcal{F}_k$ of the current frame at t_k is converted to the global map coordinate system using the localization information of the LIO_SAM algorithm, and the converted point cloud is registered to the global point cloud map. When the LIO_SAM algorithm detects the loopback information, a global optimization is performed on the global map through a factor graph to ensure the accuracy of the map building.

4   Experimental Results

In order to evaluate that our proposed method can construct a static trunk point cloud map for long-term positioning and navigation for orchard robots, comprehensive evaluations were conducted in both simulated and real environments. The testing phase aimed to assess the accuracy of the mapping process by evaluating the error measurements.

4.1   Dataset

The dataset utilized in this paper mainly includes two parts. Firstly, a simulated robot was deployed within an open-source orchard simulated environment, as illustrated in Fig. 5. This simulated environment faithfully replicates real-world conditions, including potential potholes on the orchard ground. Equipped with a 32-line LiDAR, camera, and IMU, the simulated robot captures real-time environmental information, enabling comprehensive data collection.

Fig. 5. Orchard simulated environment and simulated robot

An additional segment of the dataset originates from our self-developed mobile robot, depicted in Fig. 6(a). This robot is equipped with a 32-line LiDAR, cameras, IMU, and various other sensors. To construct our proprietary dataset, we conducted data collection within the depicted scene in Fig. 6(b).

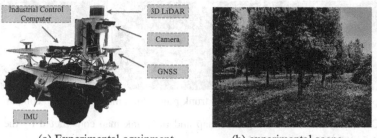

(a) Experimental equipment   (b) experimental scene

Fig. 6. Experimental equipment and experimental scene

4.2 Simulated Experiment

In the simulated environment, the robot acquires image and LiDAR data. The YOLOX algorithm is employed to detect the tree trunk, and the corresponding detection outcomes are illustrated in Fig. 7(a). By leveraging the spatial relationship between the camera and LiDAR, the detection results are projected onto the point cloud data. The extracted trunk point cloud is depicted as red points in Fig. 7(b).

(a) Detection results of trunks   (b) Extraction results of trunk point cloud

Fig. 7. Detection results in image and extraction results of the trunk point cloud in the simulated environment

We employed the LIO_SAM algorithm to generate the global map of the environment, which is represented as a white point cloud in Fig. 8(a). The environmental map created using the method proposed is depicted in Fig. 8(b). The combination of these point clouds is displayed in Fig. 8(c), where the blue point cloud represents the map constructed by our method. A clear comparison reveals that our proposed approach constructs a map that exclusively captures the characteristics of tree trunks, leading to a significant reduction in the resources consumed by the map. And the map excludes dynamic factors and remains well-suited for long-term robot navigation.

To assess the effectiveness of our approach, we utilize the Absolute Pose Error (APE) metric to analyze the trajectory error of the robot. We compute the absolute difference between the reference attitude and the estimated attitude. Figure 9(a) illustrates the time-varying APE along with its corresponding Root Mean Square (RMS) error, mean, median, and standard deviation. In order to visualize the distribution of APE within the

(a) Global point cloud map   (b) Global trunk point cloud map   (c) Map comparison

Fig. 8. Comparison between the global map and the trunk map constructed by the proposed method in a simulated environment

robot trajectories, Fig. 9(b) maps the error onto the trajectory using a color code. The specific localization error values are presented in Table 1.

Table 1. Localization error table.

Number of experiments	Max (m)	Min (m)	Mean (m)	RMSE (m)
1	0.27	0.02	0.11	0.10
2	0.23	0.03	0.12	0.13
3	0.28	0.05	0.13	0.17

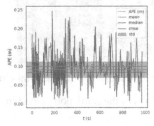 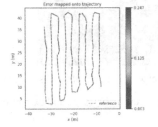

(a) Error curve diagram   (b) APE mapped onto the trajectory

Fig. 9. Robot trajectory error curve diagram in the simulated environment

4.3 Actual Experiment

The image data captured by the camera in the real environment reveals the detection results of tree trunks, as depicted in Fig. 10(a). Simultaneously, in Fig. 10(b), the corresponding LiDAR point cloud is represented by the color green. Notably, the number of extracted trunk point clouds is lower than the count of detection boxes observed in the image. This discrepancy can be attributed to our consideration of the sparsity of LiDAR point cloud data at varying distances. Specifically, we applied a filtering mechanism to exclude trunk information located far away from the robot, which enhances the overall accuracy and correlation of the results.

(a) Detection results of trunks   (b) Extraction results of trunk point cloud

Fig. 10. Detection results in image and extraction results of the trunk point cloud in the actual environment

Figure 11(a) presents the global map constructed in the real environment, showcasing the comprehensive representation of the surroundings. In Fig. 11(b), we observe the trunk point cloud map specifically constructed using our proposed method. To facilitate a direct comparison between the two, Fig. 11(c) juxtaposes them, with the trunk point cloud highlighted in blue. This visual examination underscores the distinctive characteristics and advantages of our proposed method in capturing and delineating tree trunks within the overall global map context.

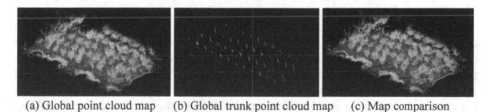

(a) Global point cloud map   (b) Global trunk point cloud map   (c) Map comparison

Fig. 11. Comparison between the global map and the trunk map constructed by the proposed method in the actual scene

Similarly, we obtained GNSS data during the robot movement as a reference for comparison, serving as the ground truth for the robot trajectory. The resulting error curve depicting the trajectory is depicted in Fig. 12, the average localization error of the robot is measured to be 0.64 m. It is worth highlighting that the error observed in the real environment surpasses that of the simulated environment, as observed during testing. Several potential factors contribute to this disparity, which include:

1. Occlusions within the orchard environment have the potential to impact the GNSS signal, leading to deviations from the accurate ground truth measurements.
2. Inherent noise is present in the actual IMU data, and there may be slight discrepancies in the position calibration between the LiDAR and IMU, which can influence the accuracy of mapping process.

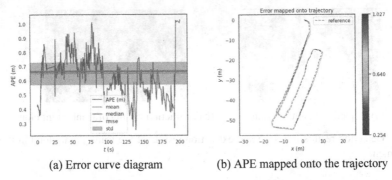

(a) Error curve diagram   (b) APE mapped onto the trajectory

Fig. 12. Robot trajectory error curve diagram in the actual experimental

5 Conclusion

A static map construction method for long-term positioning and navigation of orchard robots is proposed. The tree trunk is extracted by fusing the detection outcomes from the camera and LiDAR data Subsequently, the candidate point cloud undergoes segmentation and screening procedures employing Euclidean clustering and the RANSAC algorithm. The resulting trunk point cloud is then registered within the global map utilizing the SLAM algorithm, thereby generating the trunk point cloud map. And the trunk point cloud is registered into the global map by the SLAM algorithm to generate a trunk point cloud map. The map does not contain dynamic factors and can be used for long-term positioning and navigation of robots. We substantiate the efficacy of the proposed method through a series of experimental validations. In future investigations, we aim to employ the extracted trunk point cloud to further register it with the constructed map, enabling comprehensive exploration of the long-term localization and navigation capabilities for orchard robots.

Acknowledgments. This work is supported by Advanced Jet Propulsion Creativity Center, AEAC (No. HKCX2020-02-019), the China University Industry Research and Innovation Fund (No. 2021ZYA02014), the Natural Science Foundation of Shaanxi Province (No. 2021JM-072), and the Practice and Innovation Funds for Graduate Students of Northwestern Polytechnical University (No. PF2023106).

References

1. Campos, C., Elvira, R., Rodríguez, J.J.G., et al.: ORB-SLAM3: an accurate open-source library for visual, visual–inertial and multimap slam. IEEE Trans. Robot. **37**(6), 1874–1890 (2021)
2. Qin, T., Li, P., Shen, S.: VINS-Mono: a robust and versatile monocular visual-inertial state estimator. IEEE Trans. Robot. **34**(4), 1004–1020 (2018)
3. Grisetti, G., Stachniss, C., Burgard, W.: Improved techniques for grid mapping with rao-blackwellized particle filters. IEEE Trans. Robot. **23**(1), 34–46 (2007)

4. Hess, W., Kohler, D., Rapp, H., et al.: Real-time loop closure in 2D LIDAR SLAM. In: 2016 IEEE International Conference on Robotics and Automation (ICRA), pp. 1271–1278. IEEE (2016)
5. Shan, T., Englot, B.: LeGO-LOAM: lightweight and ground-optimized lidar odometry and mapping on variable terrain. In: 2018 IEEE/RSJ International Conference on Intelligent Robots and Systems (IROS), pp. 4758–4765. IEEE (2018)
6. Shan, T., Englot, B., Meyers, D., et al.: LIO-SAM: tightly-coupled lidar inertial odometry via smoothing and mapping. In: 2020 IEEE/RSJ International Conference on Intelligent Robots and Systems (IROS), pp. 5135–5142. IEEE (2020)
7. Xu, W., Zhang, F.: FAST-LIO: a fast, robust lidar-inertial odometry package by tightly-coupled iterated kalman filter. IEEE Robot. Autom. Lett. 6(2), 3317–3324 (2021)
8. Winterhalter, W., Fleckenstein, F., Dornhege, C., et al.: Localization for precision navigation in agricultural fields—beyond crop row following. J. Field Robot. 38(3), 429–451 (2021)
9. Cheein, F.A., Steiner, G., Paina, G.P., et al.: Optimized EIF-SLAM algorithm for precision agriculture mapping based on stems detection. Comput. Electron. Agric. 78(2), 195–207 (2011)
10. Chen, M., Tang, Y., Zou, X., et al.: 3D global mapping of large-scale unstructured orchard integrating eye-in-hand stereo vision and SLAM. Comput. Electron. Agric. 187, 106237 (2021)
11. Dong, W., Roy, P., Isler, V.: Semantic mapping for orchard environments by merging two-sides reconstructions of tree rows. J. Field Robot. 37(1), 97–121 (2020)
12. Underwood, J.P., Jagbrant, G., Nieto, J.I., et al.: Lidar-based tree recognition and platform localization in orchards. J. Field Robot. 32(8), 1056–1074 (2015)
13. Gao, P., Jiang, J., Song, J., et al.: Canopy volume measurement of fruit trees using robotic platform loaded LiDAR data. IEEE Access 9, 156246–156259 (2021)
14. Ou, F., Li, Y., Miao, Z.: Place recognition of large-scale unstructured orchards with attention score maps. IEEE Robot. Autom. Lett. 8(2), 958–965 (2023)
15. Han, B., Wei, J., Zhang, J., et al.: GardenMap: static point cloud mapping for Garden environment. Comput. Electron. Agric. 204, 107548–107559 (2023)
16. Autoware: the world's leading open-source software project for autonomous driving. https://github.com/autowarefoundation/autoware
17. Ge, Z., Liu, S., Wang, F., et al.: YOLOX: exceeding yolo series in 2021. arXiv preprint arXiv: 2107.08430 (2021)
18. Guo, Z., Liu, H., Shi, H., et al.: KD-tree-based euclidean clustering for tomographic SAR point cloud extraction and segmentation. IEEE Geosci. Remote Sens. Lett. 20, 400205–400210 (2023)
19. Han, J., Wang, F., Guo, Y., et al.: An improved RANSAC registration algorithm based on region covariance descriptor. In: 2015 Chinese Automation Congress (CAC), pp. 746–751. IEEE (2015)

Relational Alignment and Distance Optimization for Cross-Modality Person Re-identification

Feng Du[1] , Zhuorong Li[3] , Jiafa Mao[1] , Yanjing Lei[1] ,
and Sixian Chan[1,2]([⊠])

[1] College of Computer Science and Technology at Zhejiang University of Technology,
Hangzhou 310032, China
`sxchan@zjut.edu.cn`
[2] Hangzhou Xsuan Technology Co., LTD., Hangzhou, China
[3] School of Computer and Computing Science, Zhejiang University City College,
Hangzhou 310023, China

Abstract. Cross-modality person re-identification (VI-ReID) is a challenging pedestrian retrieval problem, where the two main challenges are intra-class differences and cross-modality differences between visible and infrared images. To address these issues, many state-of-the-art methods attempt to learn coarse image alignment or part-level person features, however, it is often limited by the effects of intra-identity variation and image alignment is not always good. In this paper, to overcome these two shortcomings, a relational alignment and distance optimization network (RADONet) is constructed. Firstly, we design a cross-modal relational alignment (CM-RA) that exploits the correspondence between cross-modal images to handle cross-modal differences at the pixel level. Secondly, we propose a cross-modal Wasserstein Distance (CM-WD) to mitigate the effects of intra-identity variation in modal alignment. In this way, our network is able to overcome the effects of identity variations by focusing on reducing inter-modal differences and performing more effective feature alignment. Extensive experiments show that our method outperforms state-of-the-art methods on two challenging datasets, with improvements of 3.39% and 2.06% on the SYSU-MM01 dataset for Rank-1 and mAP, respectively.

Keywords: Person re-identification · Cross-modality differences · Relational alignment · Distance optimization

1 Introduction

Person re-identification (ReID) [7] can be viewed as a single-modal image retrieval task. It has received a lot of attention [29,32] from researchers in the last few years due to its wide range of real-life applications such as video surveillance [19], intelligent security, etc. Visible cameras are capable of capturing clear

© The Author(s), under exclusive license to Springer Nature Singapore Pte Ltd. 2023
H. Yang et al. (Eds.): ICIRA 2023, LNAI 14267, pp. 456–470, 2023.
https://doi.org/10.1007/978-981-99-6483-3_39

images of pedestrians during the day, however, there are obvious shortcomings in visible cameras in poorly lit conditions (e.g. night time). Infrared cameras can capture the layout of a scene in dim conditions while ignoring the details of the scene. As a result, visible-infrared person re-identification(VI-ReID) [24] has recently attracted a great deal of interest from computer vision practitioners.

VI-ReID differs from ReID in that it is more challenging to retrieve a target image in the infrared gallery that matches the identity of the RGB images. There are two main challenges with VI-ReID, the first being intra-class differences caused by camera angle, pose, and background interference, etc. The second is the cross-modal difference caused by the different methods of image collection by visible and infrared cameras. To mitigate modal differences in VI-ReID many advanced approaches [4,6] use CNN to extract features and employ metric loss [11,13] to train the network to learn modality-sharing pedestrian representations. These methods focus on learning image-level or part-level image representations for coarse alignment of images. However, the presence of many misaligned features between RGB and IR images has a detrimental effect on the processing of cross-modal differences. At the same time, the presence of intra-identity differences may interfere with the optimization of cross-modal alignment. When inter-modal differences are reduced to a certain level, the model will tend to reduce intra-identity differences, preventing the network from concentrating on reducing cross-modal differences.

In this paper, we propose a cross-modal relational alignment(CM-RA) that exploits the correspondence between cross-modal images during network training. We establish cross-modal correspondence between the RGB and IR images in a probabilistic manner and use parameter-free masks to focus on the reconstruction of pedestrian areas while ignoring the reconstruction of background areas. We introduce identity consistency loss($\mathcal{L}_{ic}$) and use a dense triple loss($\mathcal{L}_{dt}$) of pixel association, which allows the network to learn more discriminative pedestrian features. We propose a cross-modal Wasserstein distance (CM-WD), which is able to select the best transmission strategy across modalities that assigns larger transmission weights to pairs with smaller identity changes, allowing the model to focus on reducing cross-modal variation rather than intra-class variation, resulting in more efficient modal alignment.

Our main contributions are as follows:

- We introduce cross-modal relational alignment (CM-RA), which exploits the correspondence between cross-modal images to effectively mitigate inter-modal differences, while further facilitating the network's ability to learn discriminative pedestrian features.
- We propose a cross-modal Wasserstein Distance (CM-WD) to mitigate the effects of intra-identity variation in modal alignment, allowing the network to focus on reducing modal variation rather than intra-class variation.
- Extensive experimental results have proven the superiority of our method over competing methods, and extensive ablation experiments have demonstrated the effectiveness of our proposed module.

2   Related Work

2.1   Feature Extraction-Based Methods

The feature extraction-based methods focus on the design of cross-modal feature extraction networks to extract modality-independent features and learn human discriminative features. Wu et al. [24] first proposed a cross-modal person re-identification task and contributed a visible-infrared dataset (SYSU-MM01). Chan et al. [1] proposed PFANet networks, where they added attentional mechanisms to single-stream networks to enhance the information interaction between channels and spaces, which led to a more focused network on human discriminative regions. Ye et al. [30] first introduced two-stream networks to handle the two modalities separately; they used parameter-independent shallow networks to extract modality-related features and deep networks with shared parameters to embed the two modalities into a common space. These methods design different feature extractors to extract global and part-level features. However, they ignore the joint use of global and local features for cross-modal alignment. Inspired by this, we design a framework to extract global and part-level features, which increases the richness of discriminative features.

2.2   Feature Alignment-Based Methods

The feature alignment methods are widely used in VI-ReID tasks. Mainly by aggregating cross-modal features to smooth out inter-modal differences in order to obtain modal-shared features [4,8,17]. Wang et al. [22] proposed an end-to-end aligned generative adversarial network for the cross-modal pedestrian re-identification task. Dai et al. [4] used a generative adversarial learning approach to design modal discriminators to learn discriminative features. Unlike converting images between two modalities, Li et al. [12], converted two-modal learning to three-modal learning by generating auxiliary X-modalities for modal alignment. In contrast to these feature alignment methods, we address cross-modal differences at the pixel level. To this end, we align semantically relevant regions by correspondence between cross-modal images, which not only suppresses modality-related features in the pedestrian representation but also facilitates the network to learn discriminative pedestrian features.

2.3   Metric-Based Learning Methods

Metric-based learning methods usually design reasonable metric functions to constrain the distribution of features and learn the embedding space by forcing two features with the same identity to approach each other. Triplet loss [11] is widely used for cross-modal pedestrian re-identification, which pulls together pedestrian representations with the same identity and pushes away pedestrian representations with different identities in the feature space. Liu et al. [13] proposed hetero-center triplet loss, which replaces the comparison of anchor samples with all other samples by comparing anchor sample centers with other sample centers. Ye *et al.* [31] proposed a bi-directional ranking loss that brings samples belonging to the same identity under different modalities closer together. The above methods can mitigate large inter-modal differences, but they ignore the fact that the presence of intra-identity variation may interfere with the optimization of cross-modal alignment. As a result, we propose the cross-modal Wasserstein Distance (CM-WD) to compute image features for both modalities. CM-WD enables the selection of the best transmission strategy across modalities, which assigns larger transmission weights to pairs with smaller identity changes, allowing the model to focus on reducing cross-modal variation rather than intra-class variation.

3   Method

3.1   Network Structure

We show the structure of the proposed VI-reID framework in Fig. 1, where we first extract global and local features from the training set for RGB and IR images respectively. For the global features (f_{rgb}, f_{ir}) we feed these features into the CM-RA module. It uses a probabilistic approach to establish cross-modal correspondence between the RGB image IR images and uses a parameter-free mask to focus on the reconstruction of pedestrian areas while ignoring the reconstruction of background areas. In the CM-RA module, we use the identity loss $\mathcal{L}_{id}^{g}$, identity consistency loss $\mathcal{L}_{ic}$, dense triplet loss $\mathcal{L}_{dt}$, and cross-modal Wasserstein Distance loss $\mathcal{L}_{CM-WD}^{g}$ for training respectively. For local features, we used horizontal slicing to obtain fine-grained features similar to PCB [20],

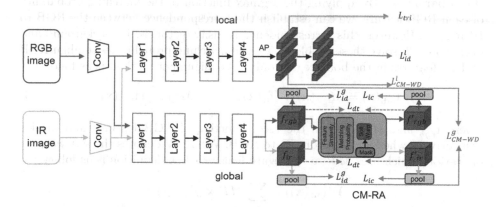

Fig. 1. The framework of the proposed method. We constructed a two-stream backbone network using ResNet-50 [10] to extract global features and local features respectively. For global features, we feed them into the designed CM-RA module for feature alignment and then calculate the $\mathcal{L}_{id}^{g}, \mathcal{L}_{dt}, \mathcal{L}_{ic}, \mathcal{L}_{CM-WD}^{g}$ losses for the corresponding features. We use horizontal slices to obtain local features and then calculate $\mathcal{L}_{tri}, \mathcal{L}_{id}^{l}$, and $\mathcal{L}_{CM-WD}^{l}$ losses for each slice.

and trained using $\mathcal{L}_{tri}$ loss, $\mathcal{L}_{id}^{l}$ loss, and $\mathcal{L}_{CM-WD}^{l}$ loss. We will describe these losses in Sects. 3.3 and 3.4. In the testing phase, we stitched together the local features after averaging pooling as a way to represent the final features of the pedestrian.

3.2   Cross-Modal Relational Alignment(CM-RA)

We propose cross-modal relational alignment (CM-RA), which establishes the cross-modal correspondence between RGB images and IR images in a probabilistic manner, bi-directionally aligning RGB and IR features. In the following, we describe RGB to IR alignment in detail, IR to RGB alignment is similar. For RGB to IR alignment, where the features of RGB image and IR image are denoted as $\mathbf{f}_{rgb} \in \mathbf{R}^{h \times w \times c}$ and $\mathbf{f}_{ir} \in \mathbf{R}^{h \times w \times c}$, respectively, we calculate the cosine similarity between RGB and IR features as follows:

$$CS(\mathbf{x}, \mathbf{y}) = \frac{\mathbf{f}_{\mathrm{rgb}}(\mathbf{x})^{\top} \mathbf{f}_{\mathrm{ir}}(\mathbf{y})}{\|\mathbf{f}_{\mathrm{rgb}}(\mathbf{x})\|_{2} \|\mathbf{f}_{\mathrm{ir}}(\mathbf{y})\|_{2}} \tag{1}$$

where, h, w, c denote the height, width, and number of channels, respectively. $\|\|_{2}$ denotes the L2 distance. $\mathbf{f}_{\mathrm{rgb}}(\mathbf{x})$ and $\mathbf{f}_{\mathrm{ir}}(\mathbf{y})$ denote the x-th position and y-th position of RGB features and IR features. Based on this similarity, we use the softmax function to calculate the probability of matching between RGB to IR features:

$$MP(\mathbf{x}, \mathbf{y}) = \frac{\exp(\beta \times CS(\mathbf{x}, \mathbf{y}))}{\sum_{\mathbf{y}'} \exp(\beta \times CS(\mathbf{x}, \mathbf{y}'))} \tag{2}$$

where, MP denotes the matching probability, which is of size $h \times w \times h \times w$. β is a parameter. By applying the argmax function to the matching probability of each RGB feature, we can establish the correspondence between the RGB to IR images. However, this correspondence is easily disturbed by background and occlusions. To solve these problems, we use matching probabilities to align RGB and IR features in the body region only. The alignment method is as follows:

$$\mathbf{f}_{\mathrm{rgb}}'(\mathbf{x}) = M_{\mathrm{rgb}}(\mathbf{x})\mathcal{W}(\mathbf{f}_{\mathrm{ir}}(\mathbf{x})) + (1 - M_{\mathrm{rgb}}(\mathbf{x}))\mathbf{f}_{\mathrm{rgb}}(\mathbf{x}) \tag{3}$$

where $\mathbf{f}_{rgb}'$ and M_{rgb} denote the reconstruction of RGB features and masks, respectively, when aligned from IR to RGB. Where $\mathcal{W}$ denotes the soft warping operation, which uses MP to aggregate features. The definition is as follows:

$$\mathcal{W}(\mathbf{f}_{\mathrm{ir}}(\mathbf{x})) = \sum_{y} MP(\mathbf{x}, \mathbf{y})\mathbf{f}_{\mathrm{ir}}(\mathbf{y}) \tag{4}$$

We use a mask to ensure that the features $\mathbf{f}_{rgb}'$ of the body region are reconstructed by aggregating the features of IR in a probabilistic manner, while the other features are the original features $\mathbf{f}_{rgb}$. To obtain the mask, we consider that the model is highly activated for features in its body region when learning features using ID labels, and we compute an activation map for the local feature vector using the L2 distance. The activation maps(AM) for these RGB features are represented as follows:

$$\mathbf{AM}_{\mathrm{rgb}}(\mathbf{x}) = \|\mathbf{f}_{\mathrm{rgb}}(\mathbf{x})\|_2 \tag{5}$$

where $AM_{rgb} \in \mathbf{R}^{h \times w}$,and we obtain the mask by:

$$M_{\mathrm{rgb}} = \tau\left(\mathbf{AM}_{\mathrm{rgb}}\right) \tag{6}$$

where τ denotes the calculation of the min-max normalization:

$$\tau(\mathbf{a}) = \frac{\mathbf{a} - min(\mathbf{a})}{max(\mathbf{a}) - min(\mathbf{a})} \tag{7}$$

3.3   Cross-Modal Wasserstein Distance(CM-WD)

To overcome the effect of intra-identity differences on cross-modal alignment, we propose to select pairs with smaller intra-class differences for modal alignment so that the model can focus on reducing the modal differences between the selected modal pairs. In our study, we find that WD [18] is a strategy to minimize the distance between two distributions. If different probability distributions are viewed as different sand piles, WD is the minimum total work required to convert one sand pile into another. Inspired by WD, we propose the CM-WD distance optimization strategy, which assigns larger transmission weights to pairs with smaller identity variations. Enabling the model to focus on reducing cross-modal variation rather than intra-class variation, resulting in more effective modal alignment (Fig. 2).

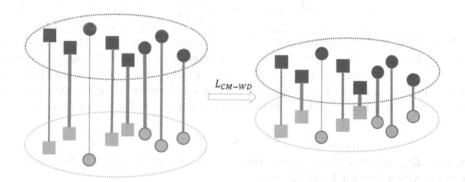

Fig. 2. Illustration of the proposed CM-WD, CM-WD assigns larger weights to pairs with less intra-identity variation, allowing the model to focus on reducing modal variation rather than intra-identity variation. Higher-weighted paired images are connected by thicker lines. Where shape represents identity and color represents modality, blue represents RGB modality, and yellow represents IR modality. (Color figure online)

In a mini-batch, we randomly select N^v visible and N^i infrared samples from C identities. We use $\mathbf{f}_{rgb}$ and $\mathbf{f}_{ir}$ to denote their features after model extraction respectively. We denote the feature distributions of RGB and IR images by $v \in P(\mathbf{f}_{rgb})$ and $i \in P(\mathbf{f}_{ir})$, and $\Pi(v,i)$ denotes the joint distribution $\rho(\mathbf{f}^v, \mathbf{f}^i)$, where $\mathbf{f}^v \in \mathbf{f}_{rgb}$, $\mathbf{f}^i \in \mathbf{f}_{ir}$. The CM-WD between two modalities can be defined as:

$$\mathcal{L}_{\text{CM-WD}}\left(\mathbf{f}_{rgb}, \mathbf{f}_{ir}\right) = \min_{\mathbf{S} \in \Pi(\mathbf{V}, \mathbf{I})} \sum_{h=1}^{N^v} \sum_{k=1}^{N^i} \mathbf{S}_{hk} \cdot CF\left(\mathbf{f}_h^v, \mathbf{f}_k^i\right), \tag{8}$$

where, $CF\left(\mathbf{f}^v, \mathbf{f}^i\right)$ is the cost function, calculated from the Euclidean distance between $\mathbf{f}^v$ and $\mathbf{f}^i$. Where $\mathbf{V} = \{v_h\}_{h=1}^{N^v}$, $\mathbf{I} = \{i_k\}_{k=1}^{N^i}$. v_h and i_k are the weights of the corresponding nodes. $\Pi(\mathbf{V}, \mathbf{I})$ indicates all transport options $\mathbf{S} \in R_+^{N^v \times N^i}$. S_{hk} denotes the weight transferred from v_h to i_k, which is:

$$S_{hk} \geq 0, \quad \sum_{k=1}^{N^i} S_{hk} = v_h, \quad \sum_{h=1}^{N^v} S_{hk} = i_k, \\ \forall h = 1, \dots, N^v, \quad \forall k = 1, \dots, N^i. \tag{9}$$

It is worth noting that we use $\mathcal{L}_{CM-WD}$ for both global and local level features in our network.

3.4   Loss Optimization

In this section, we provide a detailed description of the loss functions used in the model and explain how these loss functions assist in optimizing the network.

To prevent overfitting [15] of the model, we use a label-smoothed cross-entropy supervised network to learn identity information. The formula is as follows:

$$\mathcal{L}_{id} = \sum_{\omega=1}^{C} -q_\omega \log\left(p_\omega\right), q_\omega = \begin{cases} 1 - \frac{C-1}{C}\varepsilon & \omega = \eta \\ \varepsilon/C & \omega \neq \eta \end{cases} \tag{10}$$

where, C is the number of classes in the training set. η is the ID label of the pedestrian. p_ω is the ID prediction logits of class ω. ε is a small constant to prevent the model from being overfitted on the training set. Following the previous works [15], ε is set at 0.1. We calculate the label-smoothed cross-entropy loss separately for global and local features so that the total loss can be expressed as:

$$\mathcal{L}_{id}^{all} = \mathcal{L}_{id}^g + \mathcal{L}_{id}^l \tag{11}$$

where, $\mathcal{L}_{id}^g$ indicates the cross-entropy loss for global features. $\mathcal{L}_{id}^l$ indicates the cross-entropy loss for local features.

To bring the intra-class samples closer together and the inter-class samples further apart, we calculate a triplet loss [11] for local features($\mathbf{f}_{rgb}^l$ and $\mathbf{f}_{ir}^l$), which can be expressed as:

$$\mathcal{L}_{tri}^{(\mathbf{f}_{rgb}^l, \mathbf{f}_{ir}^l)} = \mathcal{L}_{tri}(\mathbf{f}_{rgb}^l, \mathbf{f}_{ir}^l) + \mathcal{L}_{tri}(\mathbf{f}_{ir}^l, \mathbf{f}_{rgb}^l) \tag{12}$$

where, $\mathcal{L}_{tri}(\mathbf{f}_{rgb}^l, \mathbf{f}_{ir}^l)$ indicates positive samples from the visible and infrared modalities and negative samples from the visible modalities, respectively. Similarly, $\mathcal{L}_{tri}(\mathbf{f}_{ir}^l, \mathbf{f}_{rgb}^l)$ denotes positive sample pairs from the infrared and visible modalities and negative sample pairs from the infrared modalities. For details refer to [11].

We reconstruct the body region $\mathbf{f}'_{rgb}$ of the RGB feature by aggregating the infrared feature $\mathbf{f}_{ir}$, so the identity of the reconstructed $\mathbf{f}'_{rgb}$ needs to remain the same as the original features $\mathbf{f}_{rgb}$ and $\mathbf{f}_{ir}$. To achieve this, we use identity consistency loss $\mathcal{L}_{ic}$. We use $\mathcal{L}_{id}$ to implement the above method, with the difference that its input is an image-level feature representation. We use $\phi(\mathbf{f}'_{rgb})$ and $\phi(\mathbf{f}'_{ir})$ to denote the image-level person representations of features $\mathbf{f}'_{rgb}$ and $\mathbf{f}'_{ir}$, respectively. $\mathcal{L}_{ic}$ loss keeps ID predictions consistent for pedestrians from the same identity but different modalities, which allows suppression of modality-related features in the pedestrian representations.

To solve the problem of suffering from object occluded or misaligned, we introduce dense triplet loss $\mathcal{L}_{dt}$. In order to compute $\mathcal{L}_{dt}$ loss only for the foreground regions of the RGB and IR images, we add a common attention map to highlight the human body regions in the RGB and IR images. Where the formula for defining the common attention map for RGB images is as follows:

$$A_{\mathrm{rgb}}(\mathbf{x}) = M_{\mathrm{rgb}}(\mathbf{x})\mathcal{W}\left(M_{\mathrm{ir}}(\mathbf{x})\right) \tag{13}$$

where, $A_{rgb} \in \mathbf{R}^{h \times w}$. The $\mathcal{W}\left(M_{\mathrm{ir}}(\mathbf{x})\right)$ is calculated similarly to Eq.(4), $M_{rgb}(\mathbf{x})$ is calculated similarly to Eq.(6). Calculating the common attention map for IR images is similar to Eq.(13). We use the superscripts a, p, and n to denote the features from the anchor, positive and negative images, respectively. For example, we use $\mathbf{f}'^{p}_{rgb}$ to denote a reconstructed RGB feature that uses an anchor $\mathbf{f}^{a}_{rgb}$ and a positive pair $\mathbf{f}^{p}_{ir}$ with the same identity as the anchor $\mathbf{f}^{a}_{rgb}$. Similarly, $\mathbf{f}'^{n}_{ir}$ is a reconstructed IR feature that uses an anchor $\mathbf{f}^{a}_{ir}$ and a negative pair $\mathbf{f}^{n}_{rgb}$ with a different identity than the anchor $\mathbf{f}^{a}_{ir}$.

The dense triplet loss($\mathcal{L}_{dt}$) is defined as follows:

$$\mathcal{L}_{\mathrm{dt}} = \sum_{\mu \in \{\mathrm{rgb,ir}\}} \sum_{\mathbf{x}} A_{\mu}(\mathbf{x}) \left[d^{+}_{\mu}(\mathbf{x}) - d^{-}_{\mu}(\mathbf{x}) + \alpha\right]_{+} \tag{14}$$

where, α is a margin. $[Z]_{+}$ indicates $max(0, Z)$. $d^{+}_{\mu}(x)$ and $d^{-}_{\mu}(x)$ calculate the local distances between the anchor features and the reconstructed features from the positive and negative images, and detail as follows:

$$d^{+}_{\mu}(\mathbf{x}) = \left\|\mathbf{f}^{a}_{\mu}(\mathbf{x}) - \mathbf{f}'^{p}_{\mu}(\mathbf{x})\right\|_{2}, d^{-}_{\mu}(\mathbf{x}) = \left\|\mathbf{f}^{a}_{\mu}(\mathbf{x}) - \mathbf{f}'^{n}_{\mu}(\mathbf{x})\right\|_{2} \tag{15}$$

The reconstructed $\mathbf{f}'^{p}_{\mu}$ and $\mathbf{f}'^{n}_{\mu}$ are aggregations of similar features, anchor $\mathbf{f}^{a}_{\mu}$ come from positive and negative images respectively.

We train the model in an end-to-end manner using the total loss $\mathcal{L}_{total}$, where $\mathcal{L}_{total}$ is defined as:

$$\mathcal{L}_{total} = \mathcal{L}^{all}_{id} + \mathcal{L}_{ic} + 0.5 \times \mathcal{L}_{dt} + \mathcal{L}^{(\mathbf{f}^{l}_{rgb}, \mathbf{f}^{l}_{ir})}_{tri} + \mathcal{L}^{l}_{CM-WD} + \mathcal{L}^{g}_{CM-WD} \tag{16}$$

Table 1. Results compared with state-of-the-art methods on SYSU-MM01 datasets(using single-shot mode).

Methods	SYSU-MM01							
	All Search				Indoor Search			
	R-1	R-10	R-20	mAP	R-1	R-10	R-20	mAP
Two-stream [24]	11.65	47.99	65.50	12.85	15.60	61.18	81.02	21.49
One-stream [24]	12.04	49.68	66.74	13.67	16.94	63.55	82.10	22.95
HCML [27]	14.3	53.2	69.2	16.2	24.5	73.3	86.7	30.1
ZERO-Padding [24]	14.8	54.1	71.3	15.9	20.6	68.4	85.8	26.9
BDTR [30]	17	55.4	72.0	19.7	–	–	–	–
HSME [9]	20.7	62.8	78.0	23.2	–	–	–	–
MHM [25]	35.9	73	86.1	38.0	–	–	–	–
MAC [26]	33.3	79.0	90.1	36.2	33.4	82.5	93.7	45.0
MSR [6]	37.4	83.4	93.3	38.1	39.6	89.3	97.7	50.9
expAT [6]	38.6	76.6	86.4	38.6	–	–	–	–
SSFT [14]	47.7	–	–	54.1	–	–	–	–
DFE [8]	48.71	88.86	95.27	48.59	52.25	89.86	95.85	59.68
DDAA [28]	54.8	90.4	95.8	53.0	61.0	94.1	98.4	68.0
NFS [2]	56.9	91.3	96.5	55.5	62.8	96.5	99.1	69.8
D2RL [23]	28.9	70.6	82.4	29.2	–	–	–	–
Hi-CMD [3]	34.9	77.6	–	35.9	–	–	–	–
JSIR-ReID [21]	38.1	80.7	89.9	36.9	43.8	86.2	94.2	52.9
AlignGAN [22]	42.4	85.0	93.7	40.7	45.9	87.6	94.4	54.3
X-Modality [12]	49.9	89.8	96.0	50.7	–	–	–	–
DG-VAE [17]	59.5	93.8	–	58.5	–	–	–	–
Ours	**67.88**	**94.51**	**97.96**	**64.43**	**72.89**	**97.15**	**99.46**	**76.83**

4 Experiment

4.1 Implementation Details

Dataset. We evaluate our method on RegDB [16] and SYSU-MM01 [24], respectively.

RegDB [16]: This dataset was captured by a dual camera system (visible and infrared) that overlap each other. It contains 412 identities, for each of which 10 visible and 10 infrared images are taken separately. We repeated the experiment ten times, following the previous evaluation protocol [27], and finally reported the average results of the ten experiments.

SYSU-MM01 [24]: This dataset contains 491 identities, taken by 4 visible and 2 infrared cameras that do not intersect. The training set contains 395

Table 2. Results compared with state-of-the-art methods on RegDB datasets.

Model	RegDB							
	Visible to Infrared				Infrared to Visible			
	R-1	R-10	R-20	mAP	R-1	R-10	R-20	mAP
Two-stream [24]	12.43	–	–	13.42	–	–	–	–
One-stream [24]	13.11	–	–	14.02	–	–	–	–
ZERO-Padding [24]	17.8	34.2	44.4	18.9	16.6	34.7	44.3	17.8
HCML [27]	24.4	47.5	56.8	20.8	21.7	45.0	55.6	22.2
MHM [25]	31.1	47.0	58.6	32.1	–	–	–	–
BDTR [30]	33.6	58.6	67.4	32.8	32.9	58.5	68.4	32.0
MAC [26]	36.4	62.4	71.6	37.0	–	–	–	–
MSR [6]	48.4	70.3	80.0	48.7	–	–	–	–
HSME [9]	50.9	73.4	81.7	47.0	50.2	72.4	81.1	46.2
SSFT [14]	65.4	–	–	65.6	63.8	–	–	64.2
expAT [6]	66.5	–	–	67.3	67.5	–	–	66.5
DDAA [28]	69.3	86.2	91.5	63.5	68.1	85.2	90.3	61.8
DFE [8]	70.2	–	–	69.2	68.0	–	–	66.7
NFS [2]	80.5	91.6	95.1	72.1	78.0	90.5	93.6	69.8
D2RL [23]	43.4	66.1	76.3	44.1	–	–	–	–
JSIR-ReID [21]	48.1	–	–	48.9	48.5	–	–	49.3
AlignGAN [22]	57.9	–	–	53.6	56.3	–	–	53.4
X-Modality [12]	62.2	83.1	91.7	60.2	–	–	–	–
Hi-CMD [3]	70.9	86.4	–	66.0	–	–	–	–
DG-VAE [17]	73.0	86.9	–	71.8	–	–	–	–
Ours	**89.60**	**96.80**	**98.38**	**80.51**	**84.83**	**94.48**	**96.86**	**76.75**

Table 3. Ablation study of different components on SYSU-MM01 dataset.

Methods	SYSU-MM01			
	R-1	R-10	R-20	mAP
B	64.49	92.34	97.06	62.37
B+CM-WD	65.50	92.95	97.27	63.10
B+CM-RA	66.82	93.97	97.82	63.52
B+CM-RA+CM-WD	**67.88**	**94.51**	**97.96**	**64.43**

identities, 19,659 visible images and 12,792 infrared images, and the test set contains 96 identities, 3803 infrared images as probes and 301 visible images as the gallery set. We used the previous evaluation protocol [24], using both all-search and indoor-search modes for testing.

Evaluation Protocol: We use the standard Cumulative Matching Characteristic (CMC) curve and the mean Average Precision (mAP) as performance evaluation metrics respectively.

Experimental Details: We implement our model through the PyTorch framework and train it on a single NVIDIA GeForce 3090 GPU. We use ResNet50 [10], pre-trained on the ImageNet [5] dataset, to construct a two-stream backbone network, where the first convolutional layer of the ResNet50 [10] network has independent parameters and the other layers are parameter shared. The model is trained for a total of 80 epochs, and all input images are adjusted to $3 \times 384 \times 192$, with random horizontal flipping and random erasing [33] used for data augmentation during the training phase. To make the training gradient smoother, we utilize a warm-up strategy [15]. The initial learning rate is set to 1×10^{-2} and then increases linearly to 1×10^{-1} every 10 epochs. Then, we reduce the learning rate to 1×10^{-2} at the 20-th epoch and further decay to 1×10^{-3} at the 60-th epoch. In each mini-batch, we randomly select 8 identities, where each identity is selected for training with 4 visible and 4 infrared images. We use the SGD optimizer for optimization and the momentum parameter was set to 0.9.

4.2   Comparison with Other Advanced Methods

In this section, we compare the proposed RADONet method with other state-of-the-art VI-ReID methods on SYSU-MM01 and RegDB, respectively, to highlight the effectiveness of our method. This includes the feature extraction-based method (Two-stream [24], One-stream [24], HCML [27] , ZERO-Padding [24], BDTR [30], HSME [9], MHM [25], MAC [26], MSR [6], expAT [6], SSFT [14], DFE [8], DDAA [28], NFS [2]) and the GAN-based method (D2RL [23], Hi-CMD [3], JSIR-ReID [21], AlignGAN [22], X-Modality [12], DG-VAE [17]). The results of our method on SYSU-MM01 and RegDB are presented in Table 1 and Table 2, respectively.

From Table 1 and Table 2, we can observe that our method significantly outperforms other competing methods. Our method achieves Rank-1 accuracy = (67.88%) and mAP = (64.43%) in all-search mode on the SYSUMM01 dataset, and Rank-1 accuracy = (89.60%) and mAP = (80.51%) in VIS to IR mode on the RegDB dataset. This result shows that the CM-RA and CM-WD methods in our model are effective in reducing modal differences and learning more discriminative features. All GAN-based methods use generative adversarial networks to generate new features or images to reduce the modal differences between VIS and IR. This method requires a large number of parameters for training. In contrast to GAN-based methods, we use the CM-RA module only during training. There are not any additional parameters introduced during testing.

4.3   Ablation Experiments

To further demonstrate the effectiveness of each module in the proposed method, we add modules to the baseline network for ablation experiments and evaluate them on the SYSU-MM01 dataset (using all-search mode). where B denotes our baseline network, consisting of the two-stream network and the PCB. As can be observed in Table 3, (1) the performance of the network is further improved when we use CM-WD loss for both global and local features. This suggests that CM-WD mitigates the effect of intra-identity variation in modal alignment to some extent. (2) We design the CM-RA module to be able to further reduce modal differences using the correspondence between cross-modal images, with an increase of 2.33% and 1.15% in Rank-1 and mAP, respectively, relative to the baseline network. By combining CM-WD and CM-RA, our model achieves the best results.

5 Conclusion

In this paper, we presented the RADONet for Cross-modality Person Re-Identification. Firstly, the cross-modal Relational Alignment (CM-RA) strategy is proposed to exploit the correspondence between cross-modal images for effectively mitigating inter-modal differences. Secondly, a cross-modal Wasserstein Distance (CM-WD) distance optimization is introduced to assign larger transmission weights to pairs with smaller identity variations and allow the model to focus on reducing cross-modal differences rather than intra-class differences, thus achieving more effective modal alignment. Extensive experiments have shown that our approach has a better performance compared to other state-of-the-art methods. In the future, the middle modal generated by Diffusion is the direction for us.

Acknowledgements. This work is partially supported by the National Natural Science Foundation of China (Grant No. 61906168, 62176237); Zhejiang Provincial Natural Science Foundation of China (Grant No. LY23F020023); Construction of Hubei Provincial Key Laboratory for Intelligent Visual Monitoring of Hydropower Projects (2022SDSJ01); the Hangzhou AI major scientific and technological innovation project (Grant No. 2022AIZD0061); Zhejiang Provincial Education Department Scientific Research Project (Y202249633);

References

1. Chan, S., Du, F., Lei, Y., Lai, Z., Mao, J., Li, C., et al.: Learning identity-consistent feature for cross-modality person re-identification via pixel and feature alignment. Mob. Inf. Syst. **2022**, 4131322 (2022)
2. Chen, Y., Wan, L., Li, Z., Jing, Q., Sun, Z.: Neural feature search for RGB-infrared person re-identification. In: Proceedings of the IEEE/CVF Conference on Computer Vision and Pattern Recognition, pp. 587–597 (2021). https://doi.org/10.1109/CVPR46437.2021.00065
3. Choi, S., Lee, S., Kim, Y., Kim, T., Kim, C.: Hi-CMD: hierarchical cross-modality disentanglement for visible-infrared person re-identification. In: Proceedings of the IEEE/CVF Conference on Computer Vision and Pattern Recognition, pp. 10257–10266 (2020). https://doi.org/10.1109/CVPR42600.2020.01027

4. Dai, P., Ji, R., Wang, H., Wu, Q., Huang, Y.: Cross-modality person re-identification with generative adversarial training. In: International Joint Conference on Artificial Intelligence (IJCAI 2018), pp. 677–683 (2018). https://doi.org/10.24963/ijcai.2018/94

5. Deng, J., et al.: ImageNet: a large-scale hierarchical image database. In: 2009 IEEE Conference on Computer Vision and Pattern Recognition, pp. 248–255. IEEE (2009). https://doi.org/10.1109/CVPR.2009.5206848

6. Feng, Z., Lai, J., Xie, X.: Learning modality-specific representations for visible-infrared person re-identification. IEEE Trans. Image Process. **29**, 579–590 (2020). https://doi.org/10.1109/TIP.2019.2928126

7. Gong, S., Cristani, M., Loy, C.C., Hospedales, T.M.: The re-identification challenge. In: Gong, S., Cristani, M., Yan, S., Loy, C.C. (eds.) Person Re-Identification. ACVPR, pp. 1–20. Springer, London (2014). https://doi.org/10.1007/978-1-4471-6296-4_1

8. Hao, Y., Wang, N., Gao, X., Li, J., Wang, X.: Dual-alignment feature embedding for cross-modality person re-identification. In: Proceedings of the 27th ACM International Conference on Multimedia, pp. 57–65. ACM (2019). https://doi.org/10.1145/3343031.3351006

9. Hao, Y., Wang, N., Li, J., Gao, X.: HSME: hypersphere manifold embedding for visible thermal person re-identification. In: Proceedings of the AAAI Conference on Artificial Intelligence. vol. 33, pp. 8385–8392. AAAI Press (2019). https://doi.org/10.1609/aaai.v33i01.33018385

10. He, K., Zhang, X., Ren, S., Sun, J.: Deep residual learning for image recognition. In: Proceedings of the IEEE Conference on Computer Vision and Pattern Recognition, pp. 770–778. IEEE Computer Society (2016). https://doi.org/10.1109/CVPR.2016.90

11. Hermans, A., Beyer, L., Leibe, B.: In defense of the triplet loss for person re-identification. CoRR abs/1703.07737 (2017). http://arxiv.org/abs/1703.07737

12. Li, D., Wei, X., Hong, X., Gong, Y.: Infrared-visible cross-modal person re-identification with an x modality. In: Proceedings of the AAAI Conference on Artificial Intelligence. vol. 34, pp. 4610–4617. AAAI Press (2020). https://ojs.aaai.org/index.php/AAAI/article/view/5891

13. Liu, H., Tan, X., Zhou, X.: Parameter sharing exploration and hetero-center triplet loss for visible-thermal person re-identification. IEEE Trans. Multim. **23**, 4414–4425 (2021). https://doi.org/10.1109/TMM.2020.3042080

14. Lu, Y., et al.: Cross-modality person re-identification with shared-specific feature transfer. In: Proceedings of the IEEE/CVF Conference on Computer Vision and Pattern Recognition, pp. 13379–13389 (2020). https://doi.org/10.1109/CVPR42600.2020.01339

15. Luo, H., Gu, Y., Liao, X., Lai, S., Jiang, W.: Bag of tricks and a strong baseline for deep person re-identification. In: Proceedings of the IEEE/CVF Conference on Computer Vision and Pattern Recognition Workshops, Computer Vision Foundation/IEEE (2019). https://doi.org/10.1109/CVPRW.2019.00190

16. Nguyen, D.T., Hong, H.G., Kim, K.W., Park, K.R.: Person recognition system based on a combination of body images from visible light and thermal cameras. Sensors **17**(3), 605 (2017). https://doi.org/10.3390/s17030605

17. Pu, N., Chen, W., Liu, Y., Bakker, E.M., Lew, M.S.: Dual gaussian-based variational subspace disentanglement for visible-infrared person re-identification. In: Proceedings of the 28th ACM International Conference on Multimedia, pp. 2149–2158. ACM (2020). https://doi.org/10.1145/3394171.3413673

18. Rubner, Y., Tomasi, C., Guibas, L.J.: A metric for distributions with applications to image databases. In: Sixth International Conference on Computer Vision (IEEE Cat. No. 98CH36271), pp. 59–66. IEEE Computer Society (1998). https://doi.org/10.1109/ICCV.1998.710701
19. Sreenu, G., Durai, M.A.S.: Intelligent video surveillance: a review through deep learning techniques for crowd analysis. J. Big Data **6**, 48 (2019). https://doi.org/10.1186/s40537-019-0212-5
20. Sun, Y., Zheng, L., Yang, Y., Tian, Q., Wang, S.: Beyond part models: person retrieval with refined part pooling (and A strong convolutional baseline). In: Ferrari, V., Hebert, M., Sminchisescu, C., Weiss, Y. (eds.) ECCV 2018. LNCS, vol. 11208, pp. 501–518. Springer, Cham (2018). https://doi.org/10.1007/978-3-030-01225-0_30
21. Wang, G.A., et al.: Cross-modality paired-images generation for RGB-infrared person re-identification. In: Proceedings of the AAAI Conference on Artificial Intelligence. vol. 34, pp. 12144–12151 (2020). https://doi.org/10.1016/j.neunet.2020.05.008
22. Wang, G., Zhang, T., Cheng, J., Liu, S., Yang, Y., Hou, Z.: RGB-infrared cross-modality person re-identification via joint pixel and feature alignment. In: Proceedings of the IEEE/CVF International Conference on Computer Vision, pp. 3623–3632. IEEE (2019). https://doi.org/10.1109/ICCV.2019.00372
23. Wang, Z., Wang, Z., Zheng, Y., Chuang, Y.Y., Satoh, S.: Learning to reduce dual-level discrepancy for infrared-visible person re-identification. In: Proceedings of the IEEE/CVF Conference on Computer Vision and Pattern Recognition, pp. 618–626. Computer Vision Foundation/IEEE (2019). https://doi.org/10.1109/CVPR.2019.00071
24. Wu, A., Zheng, W., Yu, H., Gong, S., Lai, J.: RGB-infrared cross-modality person re-identification. In: 2017 IEEE International Conference on Computer Vision (ICCV 2017), pp. 5390–5399. IEEE Computer Society (2017). https://doi.org/10.1109/ICCV.2017.575
25. Yang, F., Wang, Z., Xiao, J., Satoh, S.: Mining on heterogeneous manifolds for zero-shot cross-modal image retrieval. In: Proceedings of the AAAI Conference on Artificial Intelligence. vol. 34, pp. 12589–12596. AAAI Press (2020). https://ojs.aaai.org/index.php/AAAI/article/view/6949
26. Ye, M., Lan, X., Leng, Q., Shen, J.: Cross-modality person re-identification via modality-aware collaborative ensemble learning. IEEE Trans. Image Process. **29**, 9387–9399 (2020)
27. Ye, M., Lan, X., Li, J., Yuen, P.: Hierarchical discriminative learning for visible thermal person re-identification. In: Proceedings of the AAAI Conference on Artificial Intelligence. vol. 32. AAAI Press (2018). https://www.aaai.org/ocs/index.php/AAAI/AAAI18/paper/view/16734
28. Ye, M., Shen, J., J. Crandall, D., Shao, L., Luo, J.: Dynamic dual-attentive aggregation learning for visible-infrared person re-identification. In: Vedaldi, A., Bischof, H., Brox, T., Frahm, J.-M. (eds.) ECCV 2020. LNCS, vol. 12362, pp. 229–247. Springer, Cham (2020). https://doi.org/10.1007/978-3-030-58520-4_14
29. Ye, M., Shen, J., Lin, G., Xiang, T., Shao, L., Hoi, S.C.H.: Deep learning for person re-identification: a survey and outlook. IEEE Trans. **44**(6), 2872–2893 (2022). https://doi.org/10.1109/TPAMI.2021.3054775
30. Ye, M., Wang, Z., Lan, X., Yuen, P.C.: Visible thermal person re-identification via dual-constrained top-ranking. In: Proceedings of the Twenty-Seventh International Joint Conference on Artificial Intelligence (IJCAI). vol. 1, p. 2 (2018). https://doi.org/10.24963/ijcai.2018/152

31. Ye, M., Wang, Z., Lan, X., Yuen, P.C.: Visible thermal person re-identification via dual-constrained top-ranking. In: International Joint Conference on Artificial Intelligence (IJCAI). vol. 1, p. 2 (2018)
32. Zheng, L., Yang, Y., Hauptmann, A.G.: Person re-identification: Past, present and future. CoRR abs/1610.02984 (2016)
33. Zhong, Z., Zheng, L., Kang, G., Li, S., Yang, Y.: Random erasing data augmentation. In: Proceedings of the AAAI Conference on Artificial Intelligence. vol. 34, pp. 13001–13008. AAAI Press (2020). https://ojs.aaai.org/index.php/AAAI/article/view/7000

RGB-D Camera Based Map Building and Path Planning of Snake Robot

Yongjun Sun[(⊠)], Qiang Wang, Zhao Xue, Rongqiang Liu, and Hong Liu

State Key Laboratory of Robotics and System,
Harbin Institute of Technology, Harbin 150001, China
sunyongjun@hit.edu.cn

Abstract. Snake robot is a robot that can move freely in a small and complex space with super-redundant DOF and motion flexibility, and it has been proven to have a wide range of application prospects. RGB-D camera is a new type of visual sensor that can directly obtain color images and depth information. To enable the snake robot to work in some special task environments, we developed an orthogonal modular snake robot using RGB-D cameras, and conducted research on snake robot map building and path planning. An improved Batch Informed Tree (BIT*) algorithm is proposed. Finally, to verify the effectiveness of the proposed method, a corresponding experimental program is designed and related experimental analysis is carried out. The results show that our designed snake robot can complete the task of map building and path planning.

Keywords: Snake robot · Map building · Path planning

1 Introduction

Snake robots can play an important role in urban street fighting and battlefield reconnaissance, and can also be applied in some special situations, such as post-disaster ruin search and rescue, nuclear power plant radiation inspection, etc. [1]. Researchers at Tokyo Institute of Technology developed the first snake robot prototype ACM III [2]. Since then, the research on snake robots has continued to develop.

A key factor whether snake robot can be applied in a complex environment is snake robot navigation and obstacle avoidance technology [3]. Tanaka et al. developed a semi-autonomous snake robot [4], and they used Hector SLAM to obtain map data. Tian Y designed a snake robot with a 2D lidar on its head, and demonstrated the effect of using the Hector SLAM algorithm on the movement of a snake robot in a featureless environment [5]. The existing snake robot map building mostly uses two-dimensional lidar, but the lidar cannot obtain image information and has high power consumption, which limits the application of snake robots.

It is not enough to use only map information to realize robot navigation and obstacle avoidance, and efficient path planning technology is also required. The A* algorithm selects the block with the lowest current cost according to the expansion node and continues to search until it reaches the target position, and obtains the path with the

© The Author(s), under exclusive license to Springer Nature Singapore Pte Ltd. 2023
H. Yang et al. (Eds.): ICIRA 2023, LNAI 14267, pp. 471–483, 2023.
https://doi.org/10.1007/978-981-99-6483-3_40

lowest cost [6]. Artificial potential field methods are used on robotic arms [7]. The Q-learning algorithm is a reinforcement learning algorithm that enables mobile robots to use learning mechanisms to find collision-free paths [8]. The A* algorithm has a direct search path, but it has a large amount of calculation and low search efficiency. And most of these obstacle avoidance and path planning algorithms are aimed at wheeled robots, and further is needed for the application of wheel-less snake robots.

2   Design and Development of Snake Robot

2.1   Design and Development of Mechanical System

The modules of the snake robot are connected in an orthogonal configuration., and each module has a joint driven by an independent motor. The designed three-dimensional model and object of the snake robot are shown in Fig. 1.

Fig. 1. Porotype of the snake robot

The snake robot has a total of 10 joints. The directions of these joints differ by 90° in turn. The first joint is a yaw joint, and the last joint is a pitch joint. This structure enables the robot to complete 3D space movement. In line with the principle of light weight, simple structure and easy realization, all shells are made of 3D printing with resin materials. The key parameters of the snake robot are shown in Table 1.

Table 1. Related parameters of snake robot

Parameter	Value
Length (mm)	934
Weight (kg)	1.9
Joint limit (°)	±100
Maximum torque (Nm)	4
Power supply	Lithium battery (11.1 V)
Communication	USB/WIFI
Sensor	RGB-D

2.2 Design of Control System

The control system of the snake robot is mainly composed of computer, lower computer and bottom driver. The laptop is used as the upper computer, the Raspberry Pi 4B is used as the lower computer, and U2D2 is used as the underlying driver. The upper computer sends control commands to the lower computer, and the lower computer receives the instructions transmitted by the upper computer and the information returned by the sensor. After the data is processed, the underlying driver is used to drive the steering gear movement, and the Raspberry Pi will also provide feedback to the upper computer. The structure of the control system is shown in Fig. 2.

2.3 Design of Power Supply System

To reduce the constraints caused by the power cord, a lithium battery is used for power supply. The 11.1 V voltage is supplied to the U2D2 power hub, and the U2D2 power hub supplies power to the steering gear driver U2D2 and the steering gear. The 11.1 V voltage also has a parallel branch that passes through the 5V3 A step-down module to supply power to the Raspberry Pi, and the Raspberry Pi then supplies power to the RGB-D camera. The structure of the power supply system is shown in Fig. 3.

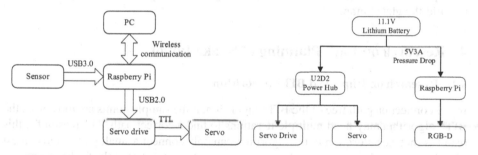

Fig. 2. The control system of snake robot   **Fig. 3.** Power supply system of snake robot

2.4 Sensor Selection

The most intuitive way to perceive the surrounding environment is image information, but ordinary RGB cameras can only obtain image information, which has great limitations on the extension of the snake robot's functions. Therefore, Intel RealSense D435i which is an RGB-D camera was chosen as the sensor of the robot.

3 Map Building Based on RGB-D Camera

RTAB-Map is an image-based SLAM method that can be implemented in the ROS system by using the ROS package called rtabmap. The node framework [9] of RTAB-Map is shown in Fig. 4. In the figure, WM is working memory, LTM is long-term memory, and STM is short-term memory. RTAB-Map continuously receives information from depth images, color double-sided images and odometry. It can synchronize this information and feed it into the graph-based SLAM algorithm. Finally, the octree map, point cloud information and odometry correction published on TF are generated.

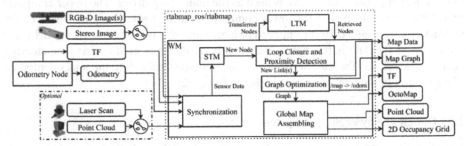

Fig. 4. Rtabmap ROS node framework

RTAB-Map can make the subsequent construction of the global map more flexible. When new nodes are added to the map, the global occupancy grid will be merged with the new local occupancy grid. When a closed loop is detected, the program will update all node poses to prevent some objects from being removed by mistake, and then continue to build the global map.

4　Research on Path Planning of Snake Robot

4.1　Research on Improved BIT* Algorithm

In the connection path tree of the BIT* algorithm, if the sample points are too dense, the BIT* algorithm may need multiple iterations to find a correct path. The reason for this result is that each iteration in the algorithm can only connect a small part of the nearest sample points, while ignoring those sample points that are slightly farther away but closer to the target point. This approach reduces the planning efficiency and performance of the BIT* algorithm [10]. Considering this problem, some improvements have been made to the node expansion module of the BIT* algorithm, which has improved the planning efficiency. The specific algorithm is shown in Table 2. In the table, the heuristic probability function used by the improved BIT* algorithm is shown in Eq. (1), and δ is any non-positive small amount.

$$P(x) = 1 - \exp\left(1 + \frac{1}{\tan\left[\left(\frac{\pi}{2} + \delta\right)\left(1 - \frac{r}{d}\right)\right]}\right), \ d = \|x - v\|_2 \tag{1}$$

The improved BIT* algorithm node expansion module is as follows: firstly, delete the optimal child node v from the node queue, and then calculate all points whose Euclidean distance to node v in the set $X_{samples}$ of sampling points is not greater than r. Then use the heuristic function $P(x)$ to accept or discard these points with probability. In this step, those points that are not helpful to improve the path are usually discarded. Denote the set of all accepted points as X_{near}. If any node in X_{near} satisfies the Formula (2), it means that the edge (v, x) can optimize the current path, and add it to the edge queue Q_E. If the optimal point is a new node in the tree, a rewiring operation is performed. In this step, ignore the sample points that are very close to the optimal point, and finally judge whether the nodes $w \in V$ satisfy the Formula (3) and Formula (4). If both are satisfied, the edge (v, w) will be added to the edge queue Q_E.

$$\hat{g}(v) + \hat{c}(v, x) + \hat{h}(x) < g_T(x_{goal}) \tag{2}$$

$$\hat{g}(v) + \hat{c}(v, w) + \hat{h}(w) < g_T(x_{goal}) \tag{3}$$

$$g_T(v) + \hat{c}(v, w) < g_T(w) \tag{4}$$

Compared with the original algorithm, the improved BIT* algorithm uses the introduced heuristic function $P(x)$ to screen the sample points before adding sample points to X_{near} and V_{near}. This can discard those sample points that are less helpful to reduce the path cost and improve the path. This method reduces the amount of calculation of the algorithm, and can converge to a certain precision solution faster in the case of large samples.

Table 2. Improved BIT* algorithm node expansion module

Input: queue of nodes Q_v	Output: *None*

1. $Q_v \xleftarrow{-} \{v\}$;
2. $X_{near} \leftarrow \{P(x) \mid x \in X_{samples}, \|x - v\|_2 \leq r\}$;
3. $Q_E \xleftarrow{+} \{(v, x) \in V \times X_{near} \mid \hat{g}(v) + \hat{c}(v, x) + \hat{h}(x) < g_T(x_{goal})\}$;
4. if $v \notin V_{old}$ then
5. $V_{near} \leftarrow \{P(w) \mid w \in V, \|w - v\|_2 \leq r\}$;
6. $Q_E \xleftarrow{+} \{(v, w) \in V \times V_{near} \mid (v, w) \notin E,$
7. $\hat{g}(v) + \hat{c}(v, w) + \hat{h}(w) < g_T(x_{goal}),$
8. $g_T(v) + \hat{c}(v, w) < g_T(w)\}$;

4.2 Simulation Experiment and Analysis

The experimental environment is composed of multiple static obstacles, and the environment is complex. Figure 5 shows the experimental results of the two algorithms, and their performance indicators are compared as shown in Table 3.

In Fig. 5, the green square represents the starting point. Black rectangular blocks represent static obstacles. The target point is represented by a red square. Cyan dots represent sample points. The blue solid line is the growth tree of the path. The elliptical area enclosed by the pink dotted line is the sampling range. The red solid line is the final planned path.

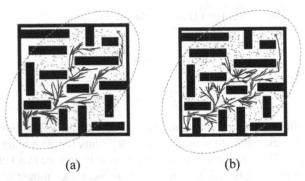

(a)   (b)

Fig. 5. (a) Path planned by BIT* algorithm (b) Path planned by improved BIT* algorithm

Table 3 shows that with the increase of the number of iterations, the search time of the BIT* algorithm and the improved BIT* algorithm is gradually increasing, and the optimal path length is also gradually decreasing. However, the improved BIT* algorithm always converges to the final solution faster than the original BIT* algorithm. When the number of iterations is 500, the search time is reduced by about 7.9%, when the number of iterations is 1000, the search time is reduced by about 15.4%, and when the number of iterations is 2000, the search time can be shortened by 15.0% compared with the original BIT* algorithm.

Table 3. The performance metrics of the two algorithms

		Iterations 500	Iterations 1000	Iterations 2000
Search time (s)	BIT*	16.37	20.39	28.47
	Improved BIT*	15.08	17.24	24.21
Path length (m)	BIT*	68.12	67.58	66.14
	Improved BIT*	68.83	67.54	66.11

5   Experiment and Analysis

5.1   Integration and Motion Experiment of Snake Robot

Module-to-Prototype Integration of Snake Robots. To realize the locomotion gait of snake robots, researchers have proposed different motion control methods. According to the principle of the control method, it can be divided into two categories: one is the method based on the motion control function, and the other is the method based on the trajectory curve [11]. In contrast, the method based on motion control functions has the advantages of simple control logic, low implementation difficulty, and high operating efficiency. Therefore, this paper chooses the motion control function method to control the motion of the snake robot. The most classic motion control function is the curvature equation of the serpentine curve proposed by Hirose [12]:

$$\kappa(s) = -\frac{2K_n\pi\alpha_0}{L}\sin\left(\frac{2K_n\pi}{L}s\right) \tag{5}$$

where K_n is the number of waveforms contained in the snake robot, α_0 is the initial angle (rad), L is the total body length and s is the arc length from a point on the curve to the starting point (m).

Use the DYNAMIXEL SDK to write the control code of the joints of the snake robot, and write the control function of the serpentine motion and the control function of the traveling wave motion to control the joints of the snake robot. The debugging of the snake robot's serpentine motion is shown in Fig. 6. The traveling wave motion debugging is shown in Fig. 7.

Fig. 6. Serpentine motion test for snake robot

Fig. 7. Traveling wave motion test of snake robot

Since the no-sideslip constraint condition is not met, the snake robot cannot advance in the form of meandering motion, so the snake robot in this paper adopts traveling wave motion for experiments. The integrated debugging of traveling wave motion for snake robot is shown in Fig. 8.

Fig. 8. Integrated debugging of traveling wave motion of snake robot

Motion Experiment of Snake Robot. Combined with the task requirements that the snake robot needs to face various complex environments when performing tasks, four task scenarios including rubber ground, concrete ground, wood plank ground and simulated grass are designed. The results show that the snake robot still has good motion performance in these four scenarios.

The snake robot has been tested on the rubber ground, and the results show that it can crawl flexibly. The motion test of the snake robot on the rubber ground is shown in Fig. 9. The camera was used to record the entire movement process. At the beginning, the joint angles of the snake robot were 0. As time went by, the joints of the snake robot moved repeatedly, and finally the snake robot realized forward motion.

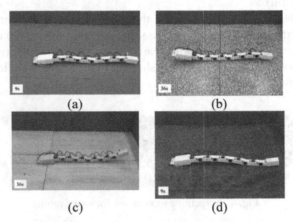

Fig. 9. Motion experiment of snake robot in various scenarios: (a) Rubber floor (b) Concrete floor (c) Wooden floor (d) Artificial grass

5.2 Map Building Experiments of Snake Robot

The experimental scene shown in Fig. 10 was built for the purpose of map building experiment. The experimental site is surrounded by square bricks with two holes made of EPP material. The size of each square brick with two holes is 15 mm × 15 mm × 30

Fig. 10. Experimental scene of snake robot map building

mm. The entire site is rectangular, and the rectangular range is 165 mm × 330 mm. The ground is a rubber ground, and two square bricks with two holes are placed in the field as obstacles and a spherical model as the task target.

Figure 11 shows the visualization picture observed from Rviz when the snake robot is constructing a map. It can be seen from the figure that as the snake robot moves to different locations in the environment, the obtained map information is more abundant, and the constructed map is gradually comprehensive. A two-dimensional grid map of the environment can be constructed by controlling the snake robot to cycle multiple times in the experimental field.

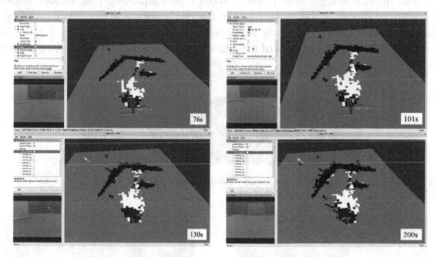

Fig. 11. Partial visualization of snake robot map building

The final result of the environment map is shown in Fig. 12. It can be seen that the established environment map is complete and clear. The black borders around the map are mainly fences. The black object inside the frame corresponds to two square bricks with two holes and a spherical model placed in the experimental site. The light gray area is a free passage area, where the snake robot can move freely.

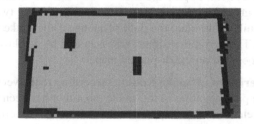

Fig. 12. The map of the site built by the snake robot

5.3 Path Planning Simulation and Experiment of Snake Robot

Path Planning Simulation of Snake Robot. ROS is an open-source robot operating system, which aims to improve the efficiency of research and development in the field of robotics [13]. In the path planning simulation of the snake robot under ROS, three parts need to be implemented: modeling the snake robot, creating a path planning simulation environment, and visual expression. URDF is an XML format description file in ROS. Rviz is a 3D visualization tool and integrates many interfaces. The structure of the snake robot is simplified by writing Xacro files, and visualized in Rviz, as shown in Fig. 13.

Gazebo is a robot dynamics simulation tool that can establish a simulation environment with quantifiable parameters and a robot model equipped with various sensors. The simplified model of the snake robot in Gazebo is shown in Fig. 14. According to the actual experimental scene of the snake robot for map building in Sect. 5.3, the path planning simulation environment of the snake robot is established in Gazebo, as shown in Fig. 15.

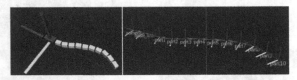

Fig. 13. Simplified model of snake robot in Rviz

Fig. 14. Simplified model of snake robot in Gazebo   **Fig. 15.** Simulation Environment for Path Planning of Snake Robot

In the Gazebo simulation, the snake robot is controlled to move from the origin of the world coordinate system, bypass the first obstacle and the second obstacle in turn, and finally reach the green ball, which is the target point. Use the two-dimensional grid map that has been built to simulate the path planning of the snake robot. The process is shown in Fig. 16. The two-dimensional grid map can be displayed in Rviz, and the target point can be specified on the displayed map.

Path Planning Experiment of Snake Robot. According to the verification of the simulation results of the path planning of the snake robot that has been carried out. On the basis of the known environment map, the snake robot can construct a path from the starting point to the target point.

In the actual experiment, the snake robot is consistent with the simulation and will move along the planned path. First, the snake robot performs a right sideways movement

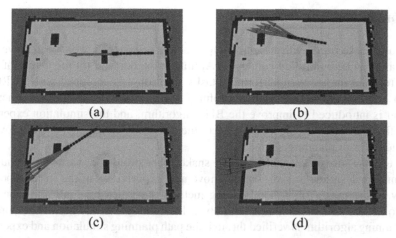

Fig. 16. Simulation process of path planning for snake robot: (a) go around the first obstacle (b) move in free space (c) go around the second obstacle (d) reach the target point

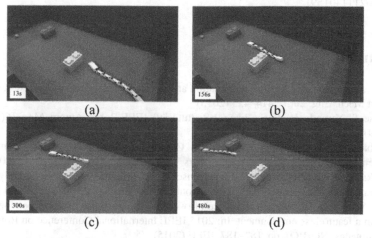

Fig. 17. Experimental process of path planning for snake robot: (a) go around the first obstacle (b) move in free space (c) go around the second obstacle (d) reach the target point

when facing the first obstacle. When the robot is no longer blocked by the first obstacle, the snake robot switches to the traveling wave forward state and moves straight forward. When approaching the second obstacle, the snake robot switches to a left-hand side-moving gait. When the second obstacle no longer blocks the snake robot, the snake robot will switch to the traveling wave forward state again until it reaches the target point. The experimental scene is shown in Fig. 17.

6 Conclusion

A modular snake robot with an orthogonal structure is designed, which can move in 3D space, and can be controlled wirelessly. Aiming at the demand for the ability of snake robots to build maps when performing tasks. The robot is equipped with an RGB-D camera and uses the RTAB-Map algorithm for map building. An improved heuristic function is introduced to improve the BIT* algorithm, and the simulation experiment proves that the improved algorithm reduces the amount of calculation and improves the efficiency of path planning.

To test the movement ability of the snake robot prototype, various ground environments are designed to carry out the movement experiments of the snake robot. The validity of the snake robot map building method is verified by controlling the snake robot to move in an environment with obstacles. Finally, the validity of the improved path planning algorithm is verified through the path planning simulation and experiment of the snake robot.

Acknowledgements. This work is supported by China Postdoctoral Science Foundation funded project (2021T140159).

References

1. Su, Z., Zhang, S., Li, X.: Present situation and development tendency of snake-like robots. China Mech. Eng. **26**(3), 414–425 (2015)
2. Hirose, S., Yamada, H.: Snake-like robots (tutorial). IEEE Robot. Autom. Mag. **16**(1), 88–98 (2009)
3. Liljebäck, P., Pettersen, K.Y., Stavdahl, Ø., Gravdahl, J.T.: A review on modelling, implementation, and control of snake robots. Robot. Auton. Syst. **60**(1), 29–40 (2012)
4. Tanaka, M., Kon, K., Tanaka, K.: Range-sensor-based semiautonomous whole-body collision avoidance of a snake robot. IEEE Trans. Control Syst. Technol. **23**(5), 1927–1934 (2015)
5. Tian, Y., Gomez, V., Ma, S.: Influence of two SLAM algorithms using serpentine locomotion in a featureless environment. In: 2015 IEEE International Conference on Robotics and Biomimetics (ROBIO), pp. 182–187. IEEE (2015)
6. Tang, G., Tang, C., Claramunt, C., Hu, X., Zhou, P.: Geometric a-star algorithm: an improved a-star algorithm for AGV path planning in a port environment. IEEE Access **9**, 59196–59210 (2021)
7. Khatib, O.: Real-time obstacle avoidance system for manipulators and mobile robots. In: Proceedings of the 1985 IEEE International Conference on Robotics and Automation, pp. 25–28. IEEE (1985)
8. Konar, A., Chakraborty, I.G., Singh, S.J., Jain, L.C., Nagar, A.K.: A deterministic improved Q-learning for path planning of a mobile robot. IEEE Trans. Syst. Man Cybern. Syst. **43**(5), 1141–1153 (2013)
9. Labbé, M., Michaud, F.: RTAB-map as an open-source lidar and visual simultaneous localization and mapping library for large-scale and long-term online operation. J. Field Robot. **36**(2), 416–446 (2019)
10. Zhang, B., Liu, J.: Research on robot path planning based on improved BIT*. Appl. Res. Comput. **39**(01), 59–63 (2022)

11. Enner, F., Rollinson, D., Choset, H.: Simplified motion modeling for snake robots. In: 2012 IEEE International Conference on Robotics and Automation, pp. 4216–4221 (2012)
12. Hirose, S.: Biologically inspired robots: snake-like locomotors and manipulators. Robotica **12**(3), 282 (1993)
13. Quigley, M., et al.: ROS: an open-source robot operating system. In: ICRA Workshop on Open Source Software, p. 5. IEEE (2009)

Map Smoothing Method for Map Distortion with Localization Error

Yang Zhou[1], Shiqiang Zhu[1], and Yuehua Li[2(✉)]

[1] Research Center for Intelligent Robotics, Research Institute of Interdisciplinary Innovation, Zhejiang Laboratory, Hangzhou 311100, China
{zhouyang,zhusq}@zhejianglab.com
[2] Beijing Research Institute of Zhejiang Laboratory, Beijing 100094, China
liyh@zhejianglab.com

Abstract. This paper presents a global map smoothing method to reduce the adverse impact of localization errors on the map. The errors along the direction of the ground normal vector will lead to map distortion, for example an undulating or stepped ground in the map. This type of error is difficult to be eliminated in visual or LiDAR odometry technically. The flat ground constraints are usually added to the odometry stage of SLAM to figure out above problem in structured scenes like urban road or indoor environments. However, it does not fit most of unstructured scenarios, such as the desert or the forest. Instead of solving this type of localization error, a global map smoothing method is proposed in our paper to improve the mapping accuracy. The matching method is applied between two a local map and the corresponding submap extracted from the global map. The pose correction is computed and then is applied to correct the local map. Finally, the corrected local map is fused into the global map. Demonstration is performed in our experimental environment and open source dataset, respectively.

Keywords: Matching · Map smoothing · Localization error

1 Introduction

Simultaneous localization and mapping (SLAM) [4], which obtains poses of a robot and construct a dense map of the surrounding environment simultaneously, is widely developed and applied in robotic application. Current main stream SLAM algorithm includes laser SLAM and visual or visual-inertial SLAM. Laser SLAM uses LiDAR point clouds to estimate poses of a robot, which has the characteristics of high reliability and mature technology, and the constructed is intuitive, high-precision, avoidance of cumulative error [3]. However, laser SLAM is limited by the effective detection range of LiDAR and the generated map only describes geometric information of the surrounding environment. Compared with laser SLAM, visual or visual-inertial SLAM is not limited by the effective range distance and richer information is supplied by camera [8]. But it is not stable and sensitive to the environment. In addition, its accuracy is lower than Laser SLAM in current stage.

© The Author(s), under exclusive license to Springer Nature Singapore Pte Ltd. 2023
H. Yang et al. (Eds.): ICIRA 2023, LNAI 14267, pp. 484–492, 2023.
https://doi.org/10.1007/978-981-99-6483-3_41

Datasets play a significant role in SLAM research because they allow the researcher to deploy and demonstrate the algorithms rapidly without constructing a hardware sensor platform. Well-known datasets, such as KITTI [7], Oxford RobotCar [9], NCLT [1], New College dataset [13], Cityscapes dataset [2], etc. Most of the datasets are generated in the human-made hard ground, of which obvious deformation of the ground will not occur. However, the situation is quite different in the nature environment. For example, if a mobile robot drives over a sand ground, the sand ground will have an obvious settlement. In fact, it means the mobile robot has a small displacement along the direction of the ground normal vector. Localization algorithm is not sensitive to this type of displacement technically so that the error will accumulate in the direction. As a result, a map distortion will occur in the form of the undulating or stepped ground. The originally flat ground will be identified as an obstacle, which will affect subsequent mission planning. To solve this problem, a map smoother is proposed in this paper. The grid map is selected as the base map in our work. To accelerate the mapping, an extension of elevation mapping [5,6] called GPU-accelerated elevation mapping [10,11] is applied for mapping. The local map is matched with the global map in order to find optimal match of a submap extracted from the global map. The pose correction is computed and then is applied to correct the local map. Finally, the corrected local map is fused into the global map. The method is demonstrated in our experimental environment and open source dataset, respectively.

The remainder of the paper is structured as follows: Sect. 2 introduces our method step by step. Section 3 gives the experimental results and corresponding analysis, followed by the conclusion and future work of our work in Sect. 4.

2   Method

The proposed method is described in this section step by step.

Before the execution of map smoother, the global map and local map are output by the elevation mapping module. Because the position each grid cell in the global map and local map is known, the overlapping area is easily obtained. The maximum matching map is then computed using a searching method. In details, Step1 is to initialize a searching position and searching length, where the initial searching position is limited in the overlapping area. Step2 is to judge whether 4 corners of the square, which is centered on the searching grid and has a size of initial length, is inside the overlapping area. If it is no, finish above operation and go to next Step3. If it is yes, increase length by 1 and continue above operation until obtaining a maximum length. Record the searching position and then go to Step3. Step3 is to change the searching position by one unit and then execute Step2 until all positions in the overlapping area are traversed. Step4 is to generate a maximum matching map by cropping the local map using the recorded position, length. The procedure is given as Fig. 1.

After obtaining the matching map, the map smoothing procedure is given as Fig. 2. Using the matching map to traverse the global map leads to map pairs

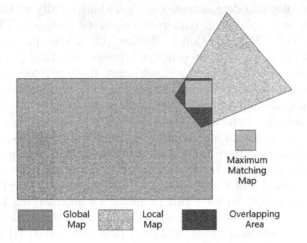

Fig. 1. Searching for maximum matching map.

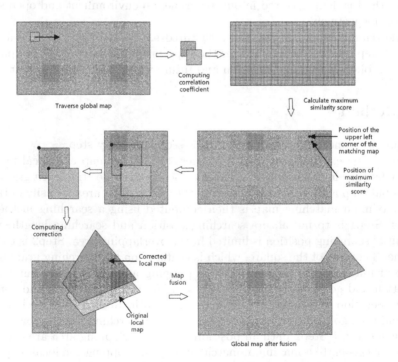

Fig. 2. Procedure of map smoother.

between the matching map and a submap of global map. Computing the correlation coefficient between the map pairs leads to a similarity score result. A submap, which corresponds to the maximum similarity score among the similarity score result, is extracted from the global map. The correction in horizontal direction is computed by comparing the positions of the matching map and the extracted submap, while the correction in the vertical direction is computed by averaging deviation the between the matching map and extracted submap. The two corrections are applied to modifying the original local map. Finally, the modified local is fused into the global map.

3   Experiments

To demonstrate that our method is valid to the problem of map distortion, it is tested in our experimental environment and open source dataset, respectively.

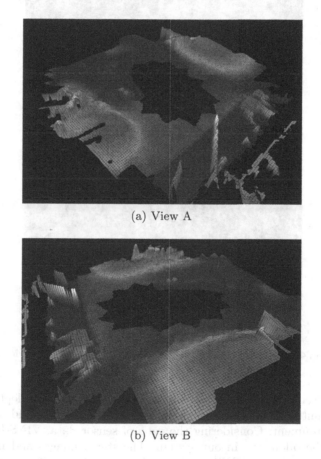

(a) View A

(b) View B

Fig. 3. Map results without map smoother from 2 different views.

3.1 Results in Our Experimental Environment

Our experimental environment is deployed indoor with a size of about 30 m in length, 8 m in width and 4 m in height. The ground is made of sand of about 10 cm, and there are more than a dozen of different scenes deployed on the sand ground such as sand dunes, sand traps, etc. The true pictures are not yet public due to some policy reasons at present.

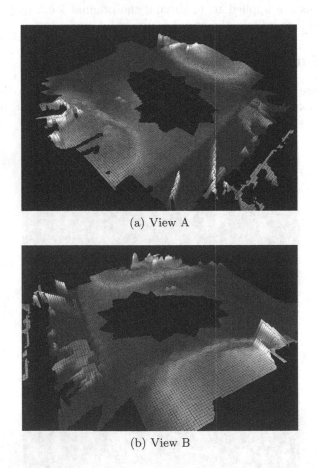

(a) View A

(b) View B

Fig. 4. Map results with map smoother from 2 different views.

Intel Realsense D455 is selected to collect stereo vision and depth data. The sensor is mounted on a mobile robot which moves on the ground of our experimental environment. Considering the type of sensor data, VINS-fusion [12] is selected as the odometry in our system. The stereo images and inertial measurements are input into VINS-fusion module set to be stereo camera odometry mode. Then, the 6° of freedom poses of the sensor platform with respect to a coordinate system fixed on the ground is provided by the odometry. After obtaining 6° of freedom poses, point clouds transformed from the depth data are used to construct using elevation map method with an updating rate of 1 Hz.

Figure 3 presents map results without map smoother from 2 different views. The mobile robot moves around center area so that the center of the map is empty due to the dead zone of point clouds. There are several obvious stepped grounds in the map, where the clearest one is in the left-top area in Fig. 3a, corresponding to the right-top area in Fig. 3b. In fact, it is the starting position of the mobile robot, meaning motion trajectory is loop-closed here. The error along the direction of the ground normal vector is accumulated and expressed in the map. In particular, the sand ground easily settles when the mobile robot moves over it. The change in the direction of the ground normal vector is hardly observed by the visual odometry so that the error accumulates.

Figure 4 presents the results with map smoother. Compared with results in Fig. 3, the phenomenon of stepped grounds is effectively eliminated, Especially the stepped ground in the left-top area in Fig. 3a, and the whole map is smoothed.

3.2 Results in KITTI

The method is tested in well-known KITTI dataset as well, where the sequence 2011_10_03_drive_0027 in residential data category is selected. The map is generated using the point clouds in the dataset, where 6° of freedom poses used for mapping is obtained from the ground truth of the dataset. Figure 5 presents the map of a crossroad in the dataset. It is considered as ground truth map because it is an accurate description of the true world.

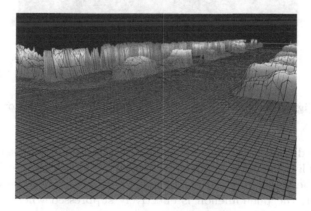

Fig. 5. A crossroad in ground truth map of KITTI.

Substituting poses estimated by VINS-fusion for ground truth poses leads to the results given in Fig. 6a. Unlike previous experiment, data in KITTI is collected in urban road that is not easy to settle. As shown in Fig. 6, the ground is not obviously deformed compared with that in Fig. 5. When the proposed map smoother is introduced, the generated map is given in Fig. 6b, which is almost the same with that in Fig. 6a.

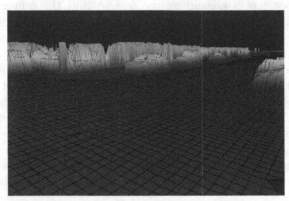

(a) Without map smoother

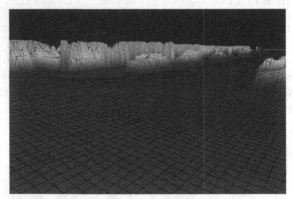

(b) With map smoother

Fig. 6. Map results using poses estimated by VINS-fusion.

In order to demonstrate our method under extreme conditions, the calibrated focal length of left camera is artificially changed to increase the localization error. As a results, the flat ground in Fig. 7a has a severe distortion to become a bumpy road. However, the phenomenon is effectively suppressed when using the map smoother as shown in Fig. 7b.

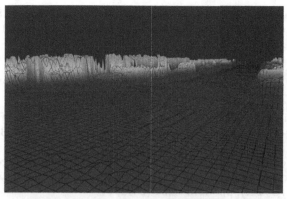

(a) Without map smoother

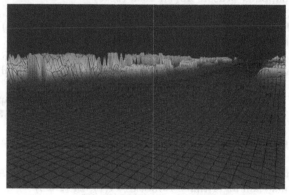

(b) With map smoother

Fig. 7. Map results using poses estimated by VINS-fusion with changed focal length of left camera.

4 Conclusion and Future Work

Most of the odometries are not sensitive to estimations along the direction of the ground normal vector technically, which easily leads to the map distortion. Based on a matching method, we proposed a map smoother to figure out the problem. The local map is matched with the global map in order to find optimal match of a submap extracted from the global map. The pose correction is computed and then is applied to correct the local map. Finally, the corrected local map is fused into the global map. The map smoother is applied to our experimental environment and KITTI dataset, respectively. The experimental results show the smoother effectively suppresses the adverse impact on the map and a consistent is generated. The smoother will be modified in the future considering multimodal information for example the semantic map will be combined to improve the matching accuracy.

Acknowledgements. This work is supported by National Natural Science Foundation of China (No. U21B6001), and Center-initialized Research Project of Zhejiang Lab (No. 2021NB0AL02).

References

1. Carlevaris-Bianco, N., Ushani, A.K., Eustice, R.M.: University of Michigan north campus long-term vision and lidar dataset. Int. J. Robot. Res. **35**(9), 1023–1035 (2015)
2. Cordts, M., et al.: The cityscapes dataset for semantic urban scene understanding. In: Proceedings of the IEEE Conference on Computer Vision and Pattern Recognition (CVPR), pp. 3213–3223 (2016)
3. Debeunne, C., Vivet, D.: A review of visual-lidar fusion based simultaneous localization and mapping. Sensors **20**(7), 2068 (2020)
4. Dissanayake, M.G., Newman, P., Clark, S., Durrant-Whyte, H.F., Csorba, M.: A solution to the simultaneous localization and map building (slam) problem. IEEE Trans. Robot. Autom. **17**(3), 229–241 (2001)
5. Fankhauser, P., Bloesch, M., Gehring, C., Hutter, M., Siegwart, R.: Robot-centric elevation mapping with uncertainty estimates. In: International Conference on Climbing and Walking Robots (CLAWAR) (2014)
6. Fankhauser, P., Bloesch, M., Hutter, M.: Probabilistic terrain mapping for mobile robots with uncertain localization. IEEE Robot. Autom. Lett. **3**(4), 3019–3026 (2018)
7. Geiger, A., Lenz, P., Stiller, C., Urtasun, R.: Vision meets robotics: the kitti dataset. Int. J. Robot. Res. **32**(1), 1231–1237 (2013)
8. Macario Barros, A., Michel, M., Moline, Y., Corre, G., Carrel, F.: A comprehensive survey of visual slam algorithms. Robotics **11**(1), 24 (2022)
9. Maddern, W., Pascoe, G., Linegar, C., Newman, P.: 1 year, 1000 km: the oxford RobotCar dataset. Int. J. Robot. Res. **36**(1), 3–15 (2017)
10. Pan, Y., Xu, X., Ding, X., Huang, S., Wang, Y., Xiong, R.: Gem: online globally consistent dense elevation mapping for unstructured terrain. IEEE Trans. Instrum. Meas. **70**, 1–13 (2021)
11. Pan, Y., Xu, X., Wang, Y., Ding, X., Xiong, R.: GPU accelerated real-time traversability mapping. In: 2019 IEEE International Conference on Robotics and Biomimetics (ROBIO), pp. 734–740. IEEE (2019)
12. Qin, T., Cao, S., Pan, J., Shen, S.: A general optimization-based framework for global pose estimation with multiple sensors. arxiv.org/abs/1901.03642 (2019)
13. Smith, M., Baldwin, I., Churchill, W., Paul, R., Newman, P.: The new college vision and laser data set. Int. J. Robot. Res. **28**(5), 595–599 (2009)

A Novel Line Approximation Approach for State Updates of Grid Maps

Jie Niu and Dong Zhang[✉]

Beijing University of Chemical Technology, Beijing 100029, China
zhang_dong@buct.edu.cn

Abstract. Straight-line approximation algorithms are often used in state update processes of grid maps. They are primarily designed for drawing and displaying. Due to limitations of per-step's single selection and sensors' noise, historical obstacles may not be eliminated clearly on grid maps. To ensure the accuracy of robots' environment modeling, we propose a cross-discrimination algorithm (CDA) for line approximation on grid maps. It introduces an optional extension to the single-selection strategy by considering the intersection coordinates of lines and grids. The incomplete removal problem is effectively addressed by incorporating these additional coordinate pairs for clearing, resulting in improved quality for downstream tasks. A series of experiments are conducted to assess the algorithm's universality and robustness. The results of the experiments confirm the effectiveness of our algorithm in grid map processing.

Keywords: Bresenham Algorithm · Grid Map · Environment Modeling

1 Introduction

Autonomous mobile robots is a research hotspot in recent years. Perception plays a crucial role in the motion planning and execution of robots. Grid-based methods have gained widespread acceptance for environmental modeling due to their simplicity, efficiency, and suitability for real-time perception and decision-making tasks. These methods facilitate path planning, navigation, and map updates. The accuracy of map updating determines the qualities of downstream tasks. Update procedures involve removing historical obstacles represented by approximate lines, from the robot's position to the obstacles' positions, and adding new obstacles. Line approximation algorithms were first proposed and gradually improved in computer graphics, to efficiently draw and display lines. In recent years, they have been widely used in the renewal of grid maps.

This work is supported by the China Postdoctoral Science Foundation (2021M690320), the Open Research Project of the State Key Laboratory of Industrial Control Technology, Zhejiang University, China (No. ICT2022B57), and Joint Project of BRC-BC (Biomedical Translational Engineering Research Center of BUCT-CJFH) (XK2022-06).

H. Yang et al. (Eds.): ICIRA 2023, LNAI 14267, pp. 493–502, 2023.
https://doi.org/10.1007/978-981-99-6483-3_42

Digital differential analyzer (DDA) algorithm, first proposed in 1950, is a linear scan conversion algorithm based on simple mathematical operations, which is suitable for digital devices, especially computer screens [1]. Although DDA algorithm is simple in calculating pixels on a straight path, it is more susceptible to round-off errors, leading to jagged lines [2]. Consequently, when used on high-resolution screens, DDA algorithm may produce unsmooth lines. To mitigate the issues arising from real number calculations and floating-point rounding errors, Huskey et al. proposed an integer representation of DDA algorithm [3]. Another algorithm, known as the Bresenham algorithm, was introduced in [4]. This algorithm calculates the pixel closest to the straight line path in each step by recursion and maintains an error term to determine whether a pixel should be drawn. The Bresenham algorithm is favored for its simplicity, high efficiency, and precision, making it widely used in various fields. Bresenham also presents the midpoint line algorithm(MPA) [5], which uses the midpoint for calculation. In addition, some work has been done on more in-depth research on anti-aliasing [6], improving computing speed [7,8], and plotting implementation [9], etc.

In the field of robotics, linear approximation algorithms, particularly the Bresenham algorithm, are commonly used in environment modeling, obstacle avoidance, path planning, and decision-making processes based on grid methods. These algorithms are favored for their simple calculations and fast execution. For instance, in literature [10], the Bresenham algorithm is employed to determine whether planned paths are occupied, enabling collision avoidance. Additionally, in paper [11], the Bresenham algorithm is utilized for low-level path planning. Together with the particle swarm optimization algorithm, the Bresenham algorithm was applied to realize the full coverage of the passable domain for distributed multi-UAVs paths [12]. This combination of algorithms enables efficient and comprehensive exploration of the environment. In the real-time simultaneous localization and mapping (SLAM) process of underwater exploration, Fairfield et al. used a 3D variant [13] of the classic 2D Bresenham line algorithm for performing ray tracing of ultrasonic sensors, adding obstacles on grid maps [14]. Similarly, in 2010, Steux and El Hamzaoui incorporated the Bresenham algorithm in a fast SLAM method for wheeled robots to update maps efficiently [15]. Droeschel et al. employed a beam-based inverse sensor model and a ray-casting method to update each cell representing the lidars' scan results in an aggregated map. The 3D Bresenham algorithm was also employed for each measurement value to refresh the occupancy information between the robot and the obstacles at a certain frequency [16]. The Bresenham algorithm detects boundaries and free spaces in article [17]. As for vision-based methods, Whelan et al. used the 3D Bresenham algorithm to mark and release obstacles on grid maps [18]. In work [19], Bresenham algorithm is employed for the representation of line features as the preprocessing for submap matching. Additionally, in recent remarkable implementations of robot autonomous navigation [20,21], the Bresenham algorithm has been extensively utilized as the underlying support for updating grid maps.

However, directly transferring line approximation algorithms from graph computing to environment modeling in robotics has revealed certain challenges. One of the major issues faced by autonomous robots is the incomplete clearance of historical obstacle information. This can be attributed to factors such as the low resolution of the robot sensor itself, the noise in the data collection, or the inaccurate map construction. In computer graphics, the approximation process of a straight line is operated on pixels at predetermined positions. Thus, the strategy of single selection is typically sufficient to meet the display requirement considering the efficiency of calculation. In the context of environment modeling for robots, low sensor resolution or the introduction of measurement errors will lead to positional uncertainty, leading to noise in the positions of the robot and obstacles. As shown in Fig. 1, this positional deviation results in the persistence of obstacles, which significantly hinders subsequent planning processes. To enhance the robustness of the linear approximation algorithms for robot environment modeling, CDA is proposed. By introducing the strategy of optional multi-selection, CDA increases the number of coordinate pairs for approximating the line and effectively clears historical obstacles. This reduces the likelihood of planning failures and improves the overall performance of the algorithm. Being able to adapt to different sensors and map setups enhanced the practicality of the algorithm for accurate updates of grid maps. By addressing the challenges associated with historical obstacle clearance, CDA contributes to improving the accuracy and reliability of environment modeling for autonomous robots.

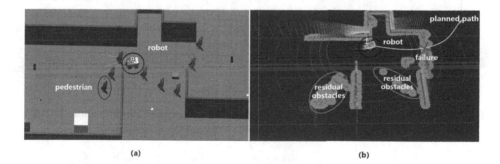

(a)   (b)

Fig. 1. (a) A robot navigates autonomously in a corridor with dynamic obstacles. (b) Residual obstacles of dynamic objects on a grid map prevent better planning due to the direct transfer of the linear approximation algorithms from computing graphics.

The paper is structured as follows. Sect. 2 discusses the limitations of previous algorithms in clearing historical obstacles and presents CDA along with its methodology. In Sect. 3, the experimental setup is described, including comparison experiments, transfer experiments, and result evaluation. Additionally, a visual example is provided to illustrate the experimental outcomes. Finally, Sect. 4 summarizes the main contributions of the paper and discusses potential future directions.

2   Framework

2.1   Historical Obstacles in Map State Updates

In summary, the grid map update process involves ray tracing from the robot to the obstacles using real-time point cloud data from sensors. Grids at the end of the line are marked as obstacles while other grids on the trace are considered unoccupied because the sensor signal is returned when it hits an obstacle. Therefore, based on each observation, the map update problem is transformed into a straight-line approximation problem.

A coordinate system, denoted as XOY, is established with the lower left corner of the grid map as the origin. The position of each grid is expressed by a two-tuple (x, y), where x and y are index values. The start and end points of the line to be approximated are represented as $(x0, y0)$, and $(x1, y1)$ respectively. The purpose of straight-line approximation is to generate a sequence of positions from $(x0, y0)$ to $(x1, y1)$ on a discrete grid map. When directly applying the Bresenham algorithm to map update processes, an issue arises where grids that should have been cleared are not selected, resulting in missing grids, as depicted in Fig. 2. This incomplete removal of historical obstacles hampers the accuracy of the map update process.

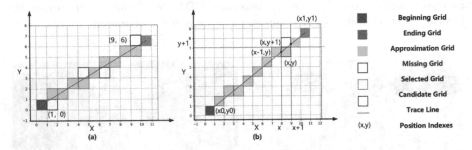

Fig. 2. (a) An illustrative example of the Bresenham algorithm's limitation in obstacle cleanup on a grid map. (b) The key principle of candidate grid selection.

For example, we consider the basic scenario of approximate straight line slope $0 < k < 1$. Under the configuration, the X-axis is the main axis. y is searched as the value x gradually increases by 1. Other cases can be transformed into basic cases through simple symmetry operations before processing. The slope k and line equation are calculated by:

$$\delta x = x1 - x0, \tag{1}$$

$$\delta y = y1 - y0, \tag{2}$$

$$k = \frac{\delta y}{\delta x}, \tag{3}$$

$$y = \frac{\delta y}{\delta x}(x - x0) + y0. \tag{4}$$

2.2 CDA for State Updates of Grid Maps

Similar to the Bresenham algorithm, selections of candidate grids are determined by the increments of x and y. Then, we calculate the intersection coordinates of lines and grids' boundaries, judging whether each candidate grid belongs to an approximate line. As shown in Fig. 2, grid $(x - 1, y)$ is selected in the previous step. Grids (x, y) and $(x, y + 1)$ should be chosen in subsequent steps according to the line-in-sight. In other words, all grids that a line passes through should be selected. Therefore, when selecting grids corresponding to coordinate x, it is only necessary to determine whether the two intersection points of the continuous line x and $x + 1$ are on both sides of the line $y + 1$ according to:

$$((x - x0)\delta y + (y0 - y - 1)\delta x)((x - x0 + 1)\delta y + (y0 - y - 1)\delta x) <= 0. \quad (5)$$

If (5) holds, grids (x, y) and $(x, y + 1)$ are selected, and x, y increment by 1; otherwise, (x, y) is selected, and x increment by 1. When grid $(x, y+1)$ is selected, we incrementally determine whether the intersection coordinates are on both sides of the straight line $y + 2$ until x reaches $x1$. Pseudocodes of the algorithm are shown in Algorithm 1.

Algorithm 1 CDA

```
 1: procedure CDA(int x0,y0,x1,y1;colorval color)
 2:     assert (x0¡ x1) and ((y1-y0)¡ (x1-x0))
 3:     δx ← x1 − x0
 4:     δy ← y1 − y0
 5:     x ← x0
 6:     y ← y0
 7:     while x < x1 do
 8:         x ← x + 1
 9:         y(x) ← (x − x0)δy + (y0 − y − 1)δx
10:         y(x+1) ← (x − x0 + 1)δy + (y0 − y − 1)δx
11:         if y(x)y(x+1) <= 0 then
12:             printpixel(x, y, color)
13:             y ← y + 1
14:         else
15:             printpixel(x, y, color)
16:         end if
17:     end while
18: end procedure
```

---

3 Experiments

3.1 Performance Assess: Globality and Robustness

Globality and robustness are key metrics for clearing algorithms. Globality refers to the effectiveness of large-scale obstacle removal, while robustness measures the algorithm's ability to handle noise. To assess the performance, we conducted two sets of experiments comparing our proposed CDA with the DDA, MPA, and Bresenham algorithms. Due to the lack of indicators of the effectiveness of historical obstacle removal in current map update studies, we present the evaluation index CL, which means the proportion of cleared obstacle grids in all obstacle grids. This index can quantitatively measure the algorithm's performance in removing historical obstacles.

$$CL = \frac{NOC}{NO} \times 100\%. \tag{6}$$

where NO and NOC denote the count of added obstacle grids and removed obstacle grids on the map, respectively. In the experiments, a general setup consists of four properties, e.g., P, M, R, and N. P is globality or robustness. M represents the number of grids for each axis of the map. A larger M means that each grid represents a smaller actual extent. R indicates how many equal parts the $360°$ detection range of the sensor is divided into. That is, the number of observation points in terms of angles is obtained in one measurement. As for N, it determines whether to add noise or not.

Same as conventional map settings, the robot is positioned at the center of the map. For a procedure of grid map update, obstacles randomly generated are added to the map at the first frame, and then the line approximation algorithm is used to clear obstacles according to the next observation. The generation of second-frame observations differs between the two sets of experiments, depending on the features being tested.

In open environments with dynamic obstacles, comprehensive obstacle clearance is required, meaning that all obstacle grids added before need to be cleared. In this case, all points in the point cloud of the second frame are set to be at a maximum distance of $M/2$ from the origin.

In fact, the observed data of two adjacent frames are usually similar. To test the robustness of our clearing strategy, we introduce random displacements to all points in the first frame as the acquisition data for the next frame. The range of random displacement scales with the size of the map. Especially, the range of random displacement in $[100, 100]$ grid map is $[-2, 2]$.

From Table 1, it can be observed that our method shows significant improvement in terms of globality and robustness compared to the other three algorithms. Additionally, as the map size increases, the CL value decreases consistently, but our method exhibits a smaller decrease. Even with a relatively low-resolution sensor (R), our approach performs well. Furthermore, when considering data noise, our method achieves a 10% better cleaning effect compared to other methods. Overall, our method demonstrates adaptability to different map settings, sensors, and data noise.

3.2   Clearing Algorithms: Instantiation and Visualization

In Fig. 3, the overall process of grid map update is shown. Free space is marked by the lines using the straight-line approximation algorithms. Then obstacles at the endings of the lines, together with the corresponding inflation layer are added

Table 1. Comparisons with other line approximation algorithms.

Configurations				Algorithms			
P	M	R	N	DDA	MPA	Bresenham	CDA
globality	[50, 50]	360	✗	97.90	98.60	98.26	**100.00**
	[50, 50]	180	✗	96.60	96.51	96.20	**100.00**
	[100, 100]	360	✗	96.93	97.52	97.49	**100.00**
	[100, 100]	180	✗	83.64	88.00	88.04	**95.81**
	[200, 200]	360	✗	83.73	88.23	88.25	**96.27**
	[200, 200]	180	✗	75.94	79.98	79.88	**92.74**
robustness	[50, 50]	360	✓	79.58	79.67	79.62	**84.92**
	[100, 100]	360	✓	64.04	64.29	64.36	**71.53**
	[200, 200]	360	✓	48.47	47.89	47.88	**55.57**
	[50, 50]	180	✓	67.37	67.89	67.82	**74.62**
	[100, 100]	180	✓	49.12	49.77	49.78	**57.40**
	[200, 200]	180	✓	34.20	34.61	34.59	**40.87**

to a grid map. Once the current update of the grid map is finished, real-time planning finds its way to the target.

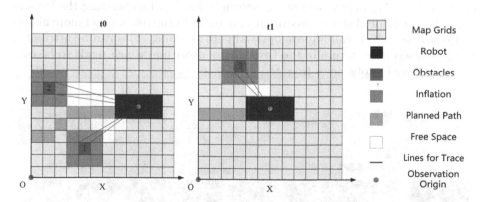

Fig. 3. Grid maps at different frames.

Here is a concrete example that visualizes the difference between our algorithm and the others while choosing grids to clear in Fig. 4. From point $(1, 0)$ to $(19, 15)$, the four algorithms draw approximate straight lines using grids on maps of size $[20, 20]$. Only in our algorithm, all the grids that the straight line passes through are patched. This is why it can completely remove historical obstacles on grid maps.

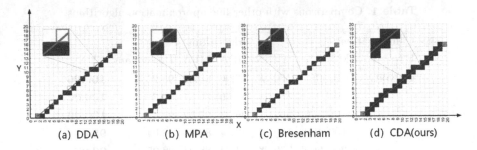

(a) DDA   (b) MPA   (c) Bresenham   (d) CDA(ours)

Fig. 4. Only CDA selects all grids which the line passes through, leading to obstacle clearance without omission.

3.3 Navigation Framework Migration: Enhancing Grid Map Updates with CDA

In a corridor environment with pedestrians, we have integrated CDA into the ROS Navigation framework, replacing the original Bresenham algorithm. The performance of the modified framework is compared with the previous implementation that utilizes the Bresenham algorithm.

The Bresenham algorithm and CDA are employed to update a robot-centric local map with dimensions of $5m \times 5m$, based on a pre-established global map. The local map is generated using point cloud data obtained from the robot's onboard lidar and depth camera. As shown in Fig. 5, when utilizing the Bresenham algorithm for obstacle removal, it may result in the retention of more historical obstacles, which can impede optimal path planning. This can be attributed to the conservative nature of the Bresenham algorithm, which tends to be cautious in removing obstacles from the local map.

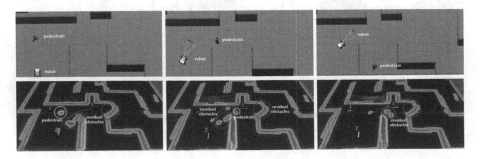

Fig. 5. Remnants of historical obstacles prevent optimal planning when using Bresenham's algorithm.

By incorporating our method into the navigation framework, we aim to leverage its advantages in clearing historical obstacles and improving the quality of

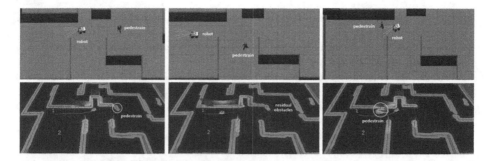

Fig. 6. CDA provides more accurate local maps with fewer obstacles remaining for later planning.

grid map updates. Figure 6 shows cleaner local maps when using CDA. By removing historical obstacles that are no longer relevant, it ensures that the local map accurately represents the current environment perceived by sensors. This approach eliminates potential obstacles that may have been mistakenly retained by the Bresenham algorithm, enabling the robot to plan paths that are more direct and efficient.

4   Conclusion and Future Work

Considering the actual needs of environment modeling for autonomous robots, we have introduced an innovative and straightforward line approximation method CDA for updating the state of grid maps. It can effectively removes obstacles from previous observations and constructs clear maps for subsequent planning. By incorporating a multi-selection strategy per step, the method enhances robustness against sensor noise and enables easier scalability for low-resolution sensors. Through simulations and real-world scenarios, our algorithm has demonstrated superior performance compared to other line approximation approaches adapted from computer graphics.

In future work, further research will be conducted to explore grid map updates in dynamic environments. By addressing transfer challenges, we aim to advance the capabilities of autonomous robots in accurately modeling their environments and enabling effective planning and decision-making processes.

References

1. Bartee, T.C., Lebow, I.L., Reed I. S.: Theory and design of digital machines. McGraw-Hill (1962)
2. Turtle, Q.C.: Incremental computer error analysis. IEEE Trans. Commun. Electron. **82**(4), 492–498 (1963)
3. Huskey, H.D., Korn, G.A., Balise, P.L.: Computer handbook. Phys. Today **15**(10), 64–66 (1962)

4. Bresenham, J.E.: Algorithm for computer control of a digital plotter. IBM Syst. J. **4**(1), 25–30 (1965)

5. Bresenham, J.: A linear algorithm for incremental digital display of circular arcs. Commun. ACM **20**(2), 100–106 (1977)

6. Wu, X.: An efficient antialiasing technique. ACM SIGGRAPH Comput. Graphics **25**(4), 143–152 (1991)

7. Angel, E., Morrison, D.: Speeding up Bresenham's algorithm. IEEE Comput. Graphics Appl. **11**(6), 16–17 (1991)

8. Wright, W.E.: Parallelization of Bresenham's line and circle algorithms. IEEE Comput. Graphics Appl. **10**(5), 60–67 (1990)

9. Cao, Z., Li, J., Zhang, D., Zhou, M., Abusorrah, A.: A multi-object tracking algorithm with center-based feature extraction and occlusion handling. IEEE Trans. Intell. Transp. Syst. **24**(2), 4464–4473 (2022)

10. Choi, S., Lee, J. Y., Yu, W.: Fast any-angle path planning on grid maps with non-collision pruning. In: 2010 IEEE International Conference on Robotics and Biomimetics(ICRB), pp. 1051–1056 (2010)

11. Rashid, A.T., Ali, A.A., Frasca, M., Fortuna, L.: Path planning with obstacle avoidance based on visibility binary tree algorithm. Robot. Auton. Syst. **61**(12), 1440–1449 (2013)

12. Ahmed, N., Pawase, C. J., Chang, K.: Distributed 3-D path planning for multi-UAVs with full area surveillance based on particle swarm optimization. Appl. Sci. **11**(8), 3417 (2021)

13. Amanatides, J., Woo, A.: A fast voxel traversal algorithm for ray tracing. Eurographics **87**(3), 3–10 (1987)

14. Fairfield, N., Kantor, G., Wettergreen, D.: Real-time SLAM with octree evidence grids for exploration in underwater tunnels. J. Field Rob. **24**(1–2), 03–21 (2007)

15. Steux, B., El Hamzaoui, O.: tinySLAM: a SLAM algorithm in less than 200 lines C-language program. In: 2010 11th International Conference on Control Automation Robotics & Vision(ICCAR), pp. 1975–1979 (2010)

16. Droeschel, D., Behnke, S.: Efficient continuous-time SLAM for 3D lidar-based online mapping. In: 2018 IEEE International Conference on Robotics and Automation (ICRA), pp. 5000–5007 (2018)

17. Li, M., et al.: High resolution radar-based occupancy grid mapping and free space detection. In: 4th International Conference on Vehicle Technology and Intelligent Transport Systems (VEHITS), pp. 70–81 (2018)

18. Whelan, T., Salas-Moreno, R.F., Glocker, B., Davison, A.J., Leutenegger, S.: ElasticFusion: real-time dense SLAM and light source estimation. Int. J. Robot. Res. **35**(14), 1697–1716 (2016)

19. Xie, H., et al.: Semi-direct multimap SLAM system for real-time sparse 3-D map reconstruction. IEEE Trans. Instrum. Meas. **72**, 1–13 (2023)

20. Marder-Eppstein, E., Berger, E., Foote, T., Gerkey, B., Konolige, K.: The office marathon: robust navigation in an indoor office environment. In: 2010 IEEE International Conference on Robotics and Automation (ICRA), pp. 300–307 (2010)

21. Macenski, S., Martn, F., White, R., Clavero, J. G.: The marathon 2: a navigation system. In: 2020 IEEE/RSJ International Conference on Intelligent Robots and Systems (IROS), pp. 2718–2725 (2020)

A Flexible and Highly Sensitive Ultrasonic Transducer for Accurate Three-Dimensional Positioning

Zhange Zhang[1,2], Zhongtan Zhang[2,3], Jiarui He[2], and Yancheng Wang[1,2,3]($\boxtimes$)

[1] State Key Lab of Fluid Power and Mechatronic Systems,
School of Mechanical Engineering, Zhejiang University, Hangzhou 310058, China
yanchwang@zju.edu.cn
[2] Zhejiang Province Key Laboratory of Advanced Manufacturing Technology,
School of Mechanical Engineering, Zhejiang University, Hangzhou 310058, China
[3] Donghai Laboratory, Zhoushan 316021, China

Abstract. Three-dimensional (3D) positioning enables the precise localization and processing of objects and has been regarded as a vital technology with diverse applications in numerous fields. This paper presents a novel ultrasonic transducer with high sensitivity and flexibility for detecting 3D positions of target objects. The proposed flexible transducer features a 1×3 array of 1–3 piezoelectric composites that exploits copper (Cu) for interconnection and is encapsulated by thin and flexible polyimide (PI) films. Thus, this design allows the transducer to be folded to confirm to intersecting surfaces. The 1–3 composite with high electromechanical coupling efficiency can convert electrical voltages into mechanical vibration to excite ultrasonic waves. A fabrication method using magnetron sputtering was developed to fabricate the flexible ultrasonic transducer. Experimental tests showed that the developed transducer exhibited a resonant frequency of approximately 4.79 MHz, good electromechanical coupling ($k_{eff} = 0.568$), wide bandwidth (34.7%), and a broad measuring range over 12 cm propagation distance with a diffusion angle of 28.08°. Three elements of ultrasonic transducer are covered onto an orthogonal plane to cross-locate the objects under water environment. The experimental results showed that the proposed ultrasonic transducer achieved over 94.14% accuracy for 3D positioning. Therefore, our developed ultrasonic transducer indicates the potential for the applications requires 3D positioning and positioning detection.

Keywords: Ultrasonic · Flexible · Transducer · Three-dimensional positioning

1 Introduction

The 3D positioning, as an integral aspect of observation technology, is commonly defined as the provision of precise positions of an object relative to a specific reference system [1]. It finds wide-ranging applications in various fields, including infrastructure monitoring [2], automated agriculture [3], intelligent manufacturing [4] and etc. With the

H. Yang et al. (Eds.): ICIRA 2023, LNAI 14267, pp. 503–514, 2023.
https://doi.org/10.1007/978-981-99-6483-3_43

development of refined operations in these fields, the significance of accurate close-range 3D positioning technology becomes more prominent. Notable examples encompass the precise positioning and assembly of minuscule components in precision engineering [5], and non-destructive harvesting in automated agriculture [6]. The close-range 3D positioning technology with high precision is key to enhancing operation efficiency and automation level. Therefore, it is crucial to develop a high-precision and dexterous close-range 3D positioning technology to meet the demands of modern society.

The close-range 3D positioning technology can be primarily classified into three categories: visual technology, visible light detection, and ultrasonic technology. Among them, visual technology provides high detection accuracy, while requires specific illumination conditions and an unobstructed field of view in the environment [7, 8]. Similarly, visible light detection also has these usage restrictions [9, 10]. Additionally, due to its high energy density and linear characteristics, visible light detection is often used for positioning in larger areas [11]. Ultrasonic technology has penetrating properties and high detection accuracy, and its ultrasonic transducer devices can be made small and thin for easy arrays [12, 13]. Thus, ultrasonic technology is considered the optimal option for close-range 3D positioning.

For 3D positioning, various types of ultrasonic transducers have been developed, such as the sphere and cylindrical ultrasonic arrays [14, 15]. However, the icosahedral transducers generally have a large volume for positioning detection, the high fabrication and installation cost will limit its real applications. In addition, due to the usage of traditional bulky and rigid shape design of most of these transducers restricts their ability to accurately identify the 3D positions of targets. Due to microelectromechanical system technologies, flexible ultrasonic transducers have emerged as an exciting solution for the miniaturization and lightweight of transducers, they can be used as conformal contact with intersecting surfaces. Thus, these flexible ultrasonic transducers would have the potential for object's 3D positioning [16, 17]. Generally, flexible ultrasonic transducers can be divided into two categories: using piezoelectric films or piezoelectric ceramics as transducers. The flexible piezoelectric films, such as using PVDF, can fit well with complex surfaces for installation. However, due to their poor electromechanical coupling efficiency and high dielectric losses, they may not suit for 3D positioning [18]. The piezoelectric ceramics possess high mechanical, electrical properties, and ease of processing. Combined with flexible polymer substrates, these ultrasonic transducers have been found applications in vascular monitoring [19], defect detection [20], and neuromodulation [21]. However, the used stretchable substrates, such as Polydimethylsiloxane and Ecoflex will reduce the electromechanical conversion efficiency of piezoelectric ceramics leading to weak output ultrasonic waves and hindering the improvement of measurement ranges of ultrasonic transducer. The polyimide (PI) is another commonly used flexible substrate for ultrasonic transducer, it has excellent thermal stability, dynamic tensile strength, superior dielectric, and structural stability. Anisotropic 1–3 piezoelectric composites have higher electromechanical coupling coefficients and lower acoustic impendence than that of isotropic piezoelectric ceramics [22]. Integration of the small and thin 1–3 piezoelectric composites with flexible PI substrate would be an effective way for fabricating flexible ultrasonic transducer with high sensitivity, and will be studied in this work.

In this study, we proposed an innovative flexible ultrasonic transducer with high sensitivity for accurate 3D positioning. The transducer has a 1×3 array of 1–3 piezoelectric composites and was encapsulated in flexible PI substrate. The implementation of PI substrate can enhance the electromechanical efficiency of the ultrasonic transducer. The Cu electrodes were fabricated on the PI substrate by magnetron sputtering to activate the 1–3 composites. The fabricated ultrasonic transducer was tested with a resonant frequency of 4.79 MHz, and has generally high electromechanical coupling coefficient ($k_{eff} = 0.568$), wide bandwidth of 34.7%, and a broad measuring range over 12 cm propagation distance with a diffusion angle of 28.08°. Then, the ultrasonic transducer was covered onto an orthogonal plane to cross-locate the objects under water. The experimental results demonstrate that the proposed ultrasonic transducer has over 94.14% accuracy for 3D positioning, which holds significant potential.

2 Design of Ultrasonic Transducer

2.1 Structural Design

The proposed flexible ultrasonic transducer presents a practical and versatile solution for accurately detecting the 3D positions of close-range objects. The device is designed as an L-shaped with 1–3 piezoelectric composites arranged in a 1×3 array, as shown in Fig. 1(a). The rigid 1–3 composites are interconnected by foldable Cu electrodes. PI with low elastic moduli is chosen as the encapsulation film, providing flexibility of the ultrasonic transducer for folding and twisting. Thus, the device can seamlessly adapt to orthogonal planes for 3D positioning.

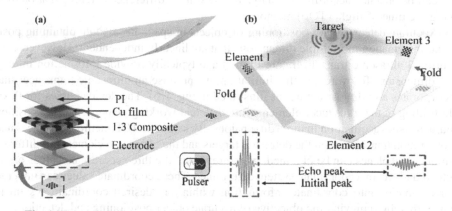

Fig. 1. Structural design (a) and working principle (b) of the ultrasonic transducer.

The middle of Fig. 1(a) shows the exploded view of one transducer element, which is composed of three layers, including the top electrode layer with one Cu electrode as public port, middle sensing layer, and bottom electrode layer. Both the top electrode layer and bottom electrode layer are 100 μm PI film sputtered with 250 nm Cu film. Compared with the stretchable polymer substrate, PI exhibits better acoustic coupling with the 1–3 composites, which can improve the electromechanical coupling efficiency of the ultrasonic transducer. The 1–3 composites as the middle sensing layer are sandwiched between the top and bottom electrode layers. The 1–3 composites are made by embedding the piezoelectric microrods in an epoxy matrix, the 15 μm Cu films on the upper and lower surfaces of the 1–3 composites are used to electrical connect each piezoelectric microrods. Benefiting from the unique structure, the 1–3 composites have a superior thickness-mode electromechanical coupling coefficient, which effectively suppresses the radial vibration and enhances the longitudinal waves entering the objects. In addition, the ultrasonic transducer frequency is inversely proportional to the thickness of 1–3 composite, while the intensity of the ultrasonic waves is directly proportional to both the frequency and the area of the 1–3 composite. Thus, the thickness of 1–3 composites is set at 300 μm with a resonant frequency of ~ 5 MHz, which is suitable for precise target positioning at close range. Furthermore, the 1–3 composites are determined as 5 × 5 mm², deeming adequate in the designated detection environment.

2.2 Working Principles

The 1–3 piezoelectric composite possesses a unique property of electromechanical transduction enabling the converting electrical voltage signals into mechanical vibration and vice versa, making it ideal for various ultrasonic applications. High-frequency vibrations excite ultrasonic waves that propagate forward, both transmission and reflection that take place at the interface of objects with different acoustic impedance. Large acoustic impedance difference results in higher reflection and lower transmission. When the ultrasonic waves encounter the target objects, they reflect back and affect the vibrations of 1–3 composites, thus generating a voltage difference. The target position characteristics can be obtained according to analyzing the voltage difference and propagation time using the time-of-flight (TOF) method.

Accurate detection and positioning of objects in space necessitate obtaining positional information in multiple dimensions that are linearly independent. However, conventional ultrasonic transducers are limited and typically provide information in only one dimension. To overcome this limitation, we propose an ultrasonic transducer that incorporates a folding structure, as illustrated in Fig. 1(b). The device allows for flexible folding of the transducer elements into different working planes, enabling position characteristics acquisition in three dimensions. By using the TOF method, distances and propagation times between the detection targets and the ultrasonic elements in different dimensional planes can be obtained, which represent the three coordinate values of the detected object in a coordinate system determined. These coordinate values can undergo transformation into coordinate information within any desired coordinate system in space, thereby achieving the objective of accurate object positioning and detection.

3 Experimental Setup and Procedure

3.1 Fabrication Process

For the developed ultrasonic transducer, a simple fabrication method using magnetron sputtering was adopted to fabricated the device. The fabrication process consists of three main steps, as shown in Fig. 2.

Step 1-Photoetching: A thin layer of photoresist was applied on the PI substrate and the UV light was used to photoetch the shape of the top and bottom Cu electrodes, as shown in Fig. 2(a-c); **Step 2-Magnetron Sputtering:** The 250 nm Cu electrodes were formed on the surface of the PI substrates through magnetron sputtering, as shown in Fig. 2(d); **Step 3-Assembling:** The top and bottom Cu electrodes were bonded to the arrayed 1–3 composites using a customized fixture mold by conductive paste, then gently pressed to fully contact with the electrodes. The whole device was cured in a heater at 80 °C for 2 h to solidify the conductive paste and ensure a solid adhesion between 1–3 composites and electrodes, as shown in Fig. 2(e-f).

The final fabricated ultrasonic transducer has an overall dimension of 136 mm × 136 mm × 1 mm. The transducer has three ultrasonic elements connected by Cu electrodes. The ends of the electrodes were connected with a 4-pin FPC connector for activating the transducers and recording the reflected echo signals.

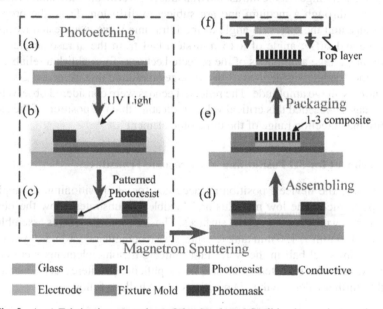

Fig. 2. (a-g) Fabrication procedure of the developed flexible ultrasonic transducer.

3.2 Characterization Tests

The sensing performance of the ultrasonic transducer needs to be characterized before further using. The impedance and phase angle of the ultrasonic transducer was tested by a precision impedance analyzer (TH2851, Changzhou Tonghui Electronics Co., Ltd.). An oscilloscope (2000X, Keysight Technology Co., Ltd.) was utilized to receive the reflected echoes, which were excited by a pulser-receiver (CTS8077PR, Guangdong Shantou Electronics Co., Ltd.), delivering a pulse excitation of −100 V.

High-performance ultrasonic transducer mainly has good efficiency of reversible conversion between mechanical and electrical energies, which is reflected by the electromechanical coupling coefficient. The electromechanical coupling coefficients k_t and k_{eff} for bare 1–3 composites and ultrasonic transducer can be calculated by

$$k_t = \sqrt{\frac{\pi}{2} \times \frac{f_r}{f_a} \times \tan(\frac{\pi}{2} \times \frac{f_a - f_r}{f_a})} \tag{1}$$

$$k_{eff} = \sqrt{1 - \frac{f_r^2}{f_a^2}} \tag{2}$$

where f_r is the resonance frequency, f_a is the anti-resonance frequency. They can be extracted from results of the impedance and phase angle spectra.

The detection ranges of the ultrasonic transducer are critical. Ultrasonic waves propagate linearly through a medium and are subject to diffusion. Thus, the propagation distance range and the diffusion angle of the ultrasonic wave were tested by adjusting the distance and offset angle of a 15 mm steel ball from the ultrasonic element and recording the voltage amplitudes of the reflected echoes. To establish a reliable threshold, the critical value was defined as the voltage amplitude that exceeded 20 times the ambient noise voltage amplitude. The reflected echoes were considered observable only if their voltages exceeded this critical value, indicating that the position of the steel ball was within the detection range of the ultrasonic element.

3.3   Experiment for 3D Positioning of Ultrasonic Transducer

To demonstrate the device's positioning accuracy for 3D positioning, an application test was performed. The low-modulus and flexible PI substrates allow the ultrasonic transducer to fit well with orthogonal surfaces. Thus, the transducer was assembled onto a 136 mm × 136 mm × 136 mm tank to establish a rectangular coordinate system. After fixing a 15 mm steel ball in the water tank, three ultrasonic elements were activated respectively, then the reflected three sets of amplified and filtered echo signals were recorded to further calculate the 3D positions of the ball, as follows.

$$L_i = \sqrt{(x_t - x_i)^2 + (y_t - y_i)^2 + (z_t - z_i)^2} \tag{3}$$

where (x_t, y_t, z_t) is the tested coordinates of the ball, $(x_i \ y_i \ z_i)$ is the coordinates of the ultrasonic element i ($i = 1, 2, 3$). And L_i is the distance between the ball and the ultrasonic element i, which can be obtained from the ultrasonic transducer.

Then, the spatial distance between the tested and real values of the ball was treated as an error, which can be calculate as

$$e = \sqrt{(x_t - x_r)^2 + (y_t - y_r)^2 + (z_t - z_r)^2} \tag{4}$$

where (x_r, y_r, z_r) is the real coordinates of the ball. The accuracy of the developed ultrasonic transducer is determined by calculating the ratio of the error to the distance between the rectangular coordinate origin and the ball.

4 Results and Discussion

4.1 Frequency Characterization Results

The impedance and phase angle of bare 1–3 composite and ultrasonic transducer were tested by the precision impedance analyzer, the results are shown in Fig. 3(a). Instinct peaks in the measured impedance were observed in the measuring impedance, which indicates the resonance frequency and the anti-resonance frequency. The bare 1–3 composite has a resonance frequency f_r of 4.82 MHz at the lowest peak, where it would obtain the strongest output vibration and penetration. On the opposite, the 1–3 composite would get the largest damping at the highest peak impedance, corresponding to the anti-resonance frequency f_a of 5.86 MHz. The resonance and the anti-resonance frequencies of the bare 1–3 composite transformed into 4.79 MHz and 5.82 MHz in the fabricated ultrasonic transducer with slight changes, demonstrating the reliability of the fabrication method. However, the impedance of the fabricated ultrasonic transducer rose significantly compared to bare 1–3 composite. This is mainly due to the inhomogeneity of the conductive paste connecting the 1–3 composites to the Cu electrodes. According to Eqs. (1) and (2), the k_t and k_{eff} are calculated as 0.608 and 0.568, which surpass a lot of existing ultrasonic transducers. The 6.58% decrease from k_t to k_{eff} may be due to the thickness of the device suppresses the vibration of 1–3 composite.

In addition, the phase angle of the developed ultrasonic transducer was over 75°, which was similar to the bare 1–3 composite, showing that most of the dipoles in the 1–3 composite align after poling. Figure 3(b) shows the impedance of the transducer when folding from 0° to 90°. The f_a and f_r remained unchanged, demonstrating that the mechanical folding has almost no effect on the frequency of the device. However, the impedances exhibited a gradual increase as the folding angle rose. This may be due to the conductive paste falling off the 1–3 composite after bending, resulting in reduced electrical conductivity.

The frequency response of the device was evaluated in an aqueous environment. As depicted in Fig. 3(c), the echo response of the transducer demonstrated three ultrasonic waves. The first wave corresponds to the initial peak generated by the input voltage signal, while the second and third waves indicate the front and back interfaces of the water reflecting from the test tank walls. Additionally, several waves of smaller amplitude were observed in the signal, which may be attributed to side echoes and other factors. The distance between the device and the water surface was set to 25 mm, resulting in a flight time of 32.25 μs. Therefore, the propagation speed of ultrasonic waves in water is ~ 1550 m/s, which is in good agreement with the empirical value of 1500 m/s. Figure 3(d) provides the echo signal analysis in both time and frequency domains, indicating a center frequency of 4.95 MHz and a narrow spatial pulse length of 1.5 μs. Due to the high-performance 1–3 composite, the device demonstrates an exceptional sensitivity of 34.7% at −6 dB bandwidth.

4.2 Detection Range Results

The propagation distance range and the diffusion angle of the ultrasonic transducer were tested and the results are shown in Fig. 4. For the diffusion angle of the ultrasonic waves,

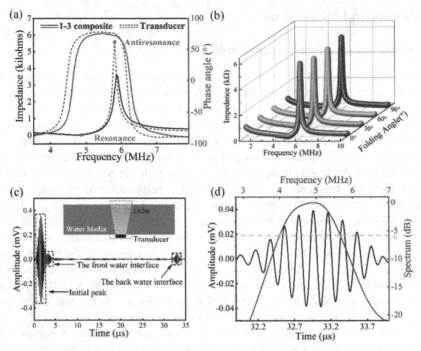

Fig. 3. Piezoelectric characterizations of the ultrasonic transducer. (a) impedance and phase angle of bare 1–3 composite and overall transducer, (b) the measured impedances under different folding angle, (c) the pulse-echo response and (d) frequency spectra of the ultrasonic transducer.

a steel ball was placed 6 cm away from the ultrasonic element, and subsequently moved in the vertical wave direction, as shown in Fig. 4(a). The experimental environmental noise amplitude was measured of ~ 0.002 mV. Thus, the voltage critical value of the observable ultrasonic waves is 0.04 mV. The diffusion angle results of the ultrasonic transducer are illustrated in Fig. 4(b). The voltage amplitudes reached the highest peak at an angle of 0° and decreased to the unmeasurable boundary at an angle of 14.04° with a distance of ~ 1.5cm from the center. Thus, the diffusion angle of the ultrasonic transducer is 28.08°, and increasing the area of the 1–3 composites can expand the diffusion angle.

For the propagation distance range of the ultrasonic waves, the steel ball continued to move away from the ultrasonic element in the direction of 0° diffusion angle, as shown in Fig. 4(c). As the penetration distance increased, the echo amplitudes decreased and eventually became indistinguishable from the surrounding environmental noise, as illustrated in Fig. 4(d). In addition, the propagation distance range of each piezoelectric element is determined by the diffusion angles of other two elements. When the penetration distance is higher than 12 cm, the steel ball cannot be detected because it exceeds the diffusion angle of the other two ultrasonic elements. Therefore, it was determined that the penetration distance range of the ultrasonic transducer should be limited to 0 ~ 12 cm. And the measured echo amplitudes within 0 ~ 12 cm was all above the specified boundary (0.04 mV).

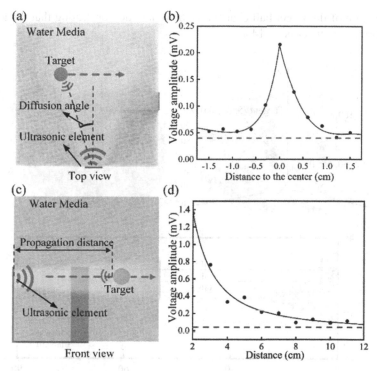

Fig. 4. The detection ranges of the ultrasonic transducer. (a-b) the diffusion angle test, (c-d) the propagation distance range test.

4.3 Three-Dimensional Positioning Results

The fabricated ultrasonic transducer was used to detect the 3D positions of a 15 mm steel ball under water. Firstly, the ultrasonic transducer was folded to fit the water tank, as shown in Fig. 5(a). Based on the rectangular coordinates system, the tested ball was placed at (75, 60, 70), and the coordinates of each ultrasonic element were set as (60, 0, 60), (60, 60, 0), (0, 60, 60). Three ultrasonic elements were activated respectively, and the reflected echoes were received by the pulser-receiver and were output to an oscilloscope.

As shown in Fig. 5(b), there are obvious echoes in the echo signals returned by each ultrasonic element, and the TOFs of the steel ball are 75.8 μs, 71.7 μs, and 80.6 μs, respectively. Thus, the distances between three elements and the ball are calculated as 58.99 mm, 55.81 mm, 62.71 mm. The possible positions of the ball for each element are a spherical surface with radius of the tested distances, and the steel ball position is on the intersection of the three spheres, as shown in Fig. 5(c). According to Eqs. (3) and (4), the ball coordinate is (62.48, 55.75, 58.75), with an error of 17.35 mm and an accuracy of 85.40%. The tested error may be attributed to the significant size of the target ball. Through compensation based on the radius of the 15 mm ball, the tested distance has been accurately determined to 66.49 mm, 63.31 mm, 70.21 mm and the resulting coordinate transformed to (70.01, 62.43, 65.82). Thus, the error between the real and

tested position of the target ball changed to 6.96 mm, demonstrating that the accuracy
of ultrasonic transducer is 94.14%.

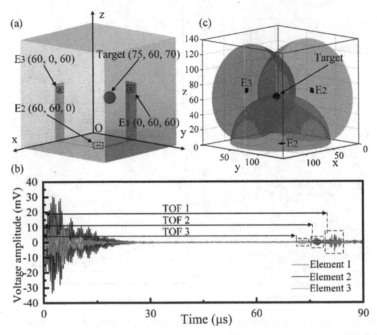

Fig. 5. Three-dimensional positioning of a steel ball using ultrasonic transducer. (a) the real
position of the target ball with the rectangular coordinates system, (b) the echoes of three elements,
(c) the tested position of the target ball.

5   Conclusion

In this work, we developed a flexible ultrasonic transducer with high sensivity for accurate 3D positioning. The proposed transducer with a 1 × 3 array of 1–3 piezoelectric
composites was encapsulated by thin and flexible PI substrates. A simple fabrication
method of the device was developed using magnetron sputtering. The overall dimensions
of the fabricated ultrasonic transducer are 136 mm × 136 mm × 1 mm. Characterization tests showed that the device has an effective electromechanical coupling capability
of $k_{eff} = 0.568$, wide bandwidth of 34.7%, and a broad detection range over 12 cm
propagation distance with a diffusion angle of 28.08°. Then, a position testing experiment was performed, and the result shows that the device has an accuracy of 94.14%,
demonstrating the potential of the developed ultrasonic transducer for 3D positioning.

Our future research will focus on equipping the ultrasonic transducer with adaptive
angle adjustment capabilities to further extend the detection range of the device and
dexterity.

Acknowledgments. This work was supported in part by the National Natural Science Foundation of China (Grant No. 52175522), Fundamental Research Funds for the Central Universities (Grant No. 2022FZZX01–06) and Science Foundation of Donghai Laboratory (Grant No. DH-2022KF01002).

References

1. Gao, W., Kim, S.W., Bosse, H., Haitjema, H.: Measurement technologies for precision positioning. CIRP Ann. Manuf. Technol. **64**(2), 773–796 (2015). https://doi.org/10.1016/j.cirp.2015.05.009
2. Spencer, B.F., Hoskere, V., Narazaki, Y.: Advances in computer vision-based civil infrastructure inspection and monitoring. Engineering **5**(2), 199–222 (2019). https://doi.org/10.1016/j.eng.2018.11.030
3. Wu, F.Y., Duan, J.L., Ai, P.Y., Chen, Z.Y.: Rachis detection and three-dimensional localization of cut off point for vision-based banana robot. Comput. Electron. Agric. **198**, 107079 (2022). https://doi.org/10.1016/j.compag.2022.107079
4. He, B., Bai, K.J.: Digital twin-based sustainable intelligent manufacturing: a review. Adv. Manufg **9**, 1–21 (2021). https://doi.org/10.1007/s40436-020-00302-5
5. Gao, W., Haitjema, H., Fang, F.Z.: On-machine and in-process surface metrology for precision manufacturing. CIRP Ann. Manuf. Technol. **68**(2), 843–866 (2019). https://doi.org/10.1016/j.cirp.2019.05.005
6. Gongal, A., Amatya, S., Karkee, M., Zhang, Q., Lewis, K.: Sensors and systems for fruit detection and localization: a review. Comput. Electron. Agric. **116**, 8–19 (2015). https://doi.org/10.1016/j.compag.2015.05.021
7. McCoy, J.T., Auret, L.: Machine learning applications in minerals processing: a review. Miner. Eng. **132**, 95–109 (2019). https://doi.org/10.1016/j.mineng.2018.12.004
8. Scime, L., Beuth, J.: Anomaly detection and classification in a laser powder bed additive manufacturing process using a trained computer vision algorithm. Addit. Manuf. **19**, 114–126 (2018). https://doi.org/10.1016/j.addma.2017.11.009
9. Zhuang, Y., Hua, L., Qi, L.: A survey of positioning systems using visible LED lights. IEEE Commun. Surv. Tutor. **20**(3), 1963–1988 (2018). https://doi.org/10.1109/COMST.2018.2806558
10. Armstrong, J., Sekercioglu, Y.A., Neild, A.: Visible light positioning: a roadmap for international standardization. IEEE Commun. Mag. **51**(12), 68–73 (2013). https://doi.org/10.1109/MCOM.2013.6685759
11. Kim, H.S., Kim, D.R., Yang, S.H., Son, Y.H., Han, S.K.: An indoor visible light communication positioning system using a RF carrier allocation technique. J. Light. Technol. **31**(1), 134–144 (2012). https://doi.org/10.1109/JLT.2012.2225826
12. Thrush, A., Hartshorne, T., Deane, C. R.: Vascular Ultrasound E-Book: How, why and when. Elsevier (2021).
13. Liu, W., Wu, D.: Low temperature adhesive bonding-based fabrication of an air-borne flexible piezoelectric micromachined ultrasonic transducer. Sensors **20**(11), 3333 (2020). https://doi.org/10.3390/s20113333
14. Chen, J., Zhao, J., Lin, L., Sun, X.: Quasi-spherical PVDF ultrasonic transducer with double-cylindrical PVDF structure. IEEE Sens. J. **20**(1), 113–120 (2019). https://doi.org/10.1109/JSEN.2019.2941980
15. Sadeghpour, S., Meyers, S., Kruth, J.P., Vleugels, J., Kraft, M., Puers, R.: Resonating shell: a spherical-omnidirectional ultrasound transducer for underwater sensor networks. Sensors. **19**(4), 757 (2019). https://doi.org/10.3390/s19040757

514   Z. Zhang et al.

16. La, T.G., Le, L.H.: Flexible and wearable ultrasound device for medical applications: a review on materials, structural designs, and current challenges. Adv. Mater. Technol. **7**(3), 2100798 (2022). https://doi.org/10.1002/admt.202100798

17. Liu, W., Zhu, C., Wu, D.: Flexible and stretchable ultrasonic transducer array conformed to complex surfaces. IEEE Electron Device Lett. **42**(2), 240–243 (2020). https://doi.org/10.1109/LED.2020.3045037

18. Qi, Y., Jafferis, N.T., Lyons, K., Jr., Lee, C.M., Ahmad, H., McAlpine, M.C.: Piezoelectric ribbons printed onto rubber for flexible energy conversion. Nano Lett. **10**(2), 524–528 (2010). https://doi.org/10.1021/nl903377u

19. Wang, C., et al.: Monitoring of the central blood pressure waveform via a conformal ultrasonic device. Nat. Biomed. Eng. **2**(9), 687–695 (2018). https://doi.org/10.1038/s41551-018-0287-x

20. Hongjie, Hu., et al.: Stretchable ultrasonic transducer arrays for three-dimensional imaging on complex surfaces. Sci. Adv. **4**(3), eaar3979 (2018). https://doi.org/10.1126/sciadv.aar3979

21. Liu, W., Chen, W., Zhu, C., Wu, D.: Design and micromachining of a stretchable two-dimensional ultrasonic array. Micro and Nano Engineering. **13**, 100096 (2021). https://doi.org/10.1016/j.mne.2021.100096

22. Gu, X., Yang, Y., Chen, J., Wang, Y.: Temperature-dependent properties of a 1–3 connectivity piezoelectric ceramic–polymer composite. Energy Harvesting Syst. **2**(3–4), 107–112 (2015). https://doi.org/10.1515/ehs-2014-0049

Grasp Compliant Control Using Adaptive Admittance Control Methods for Flexible Objects

Qirong Tang[✉], Hao Yang, Wenrui Wang, Min Yu, Lou Zhong, Baoping Ma, and Wenshuo Yue

Laboratory of Robotics and Multibody System, School of Mechanical Engineering, Tongji University, Shanghai 201804, China
qirong.tang@outlook.com

Abstract. In this paper, an admittance controller based on a gray prediction model is designed for end-effector gripping force. The gray prediction model is used to predict environmental parameters in real-time and dynamically adjusts the reference position to reduce the steady-state force error. In this way, the dynamic response capability of impedance control can be improved, and its steady-state force error is also reduced. To this end, the designed method can grasp soft objects with unknown characteristics. The algorithm is validated by simulation experiments, which provide a theoretical basis for flexible fruit grasping.

Keywords: Robotic grasp · Flexible objects · Admittance control · Compliant control

1 Introduction

Regarding the control of flexible deformable object gripping, with reference to the theories of gripping form closure and force closure, two aspects are usually

This work is supported by the projects of National Natural Science Foundation of China (No.61873192), the Innovative Projects (No. 2021-JCJQ-LB-010-11), the Shanghai 2021 "Science and Technology Innovation Action Plan" with Special Project of Biomedical Science and Technology Support (No.21S31902800), and the Key Pre-Research Project of the 14th-Five-Year-Plan on Common Technology. Meanwhile, this work is also partially supported by the Fundamental Research Funds for the Central Universities and the "National High Level Overseas Talent Plan" project, the "National Major Talent Plan" project (No. 2022-JCJQ-XXX-079), as well as one key project (No. XM2023CX4013). It is also partially sponsored by the fundamental research project (No. JCKY2022XXXC133), the Shanghai Industrial Collaborative Innovation Project (Industrial Development Category, No. HCXBCY-2022-051), Laboratory fund of Wuhan Digital Engineering Institute of CSSC, the project of Shanghai Key Laboratory of Spacecraft Mechanism (No. 18DZ2272200), as well as the project of Space Structure and Mechanism Technology Laboratory of China Aerospace Science and Technology Group Co. Ltd (No. YY-F805202210015). All these supports are highly appreciated.

H. Yang et al. (Eds.): ICIRA 2023, LNAI 14267, pp. 515–525, 2023.
https://doi.org/10.1007/978-981-99-6483-3_44

considered, deformation control and force control. The deformation control is responsible for controlling the deformation of the target object, while the force control takes the contact force between the end-effector and the target object as the control target to achieve stable contact with the target object. In recent years, numerous studies on flexible object grasping control have focused on these two aspects.

Force/position hybrid control, a method employed for flexible object manipulation, distinctively handles position and force control, ensuring compliance. It was first utilized for rigid object handling in multi-arm robots [1], extended to flexible items with dual-arm robots [2], and further refined through a genetic algorithm-optimized approach for force error corrections [3]. However, while dual-arm strategies streamline flexible object manipulation, they amplify cost and practicality concerns

The impedance control method is another commonly used control method to achieve compliant control by adjusting the dynamic relationship between the position of the end-effector and the contact force. It regulates the dynamic relationship between torque and displacement, subdivided into force-based and position-based strategies [4]. Alyahmadi et al. proposed a dual-arm grasping spring-connected flexible body based on impedance control [5], and Kaserer, et al. used a hybrid impedance control method to enable a dual-arm robot to carry a flexible beam successfully [6]. The impedance control grasping of flexible objects was first successfully applied on a dual-arm robot.

In robotic grasping, handling unpredictable environments with dynamic objects necessitates adaptive feedback controllers. Utilizing predictive control, researchers like Liu and Wang have introduced intelligent algorithms for end-effector force control [7,8], although limitations persist in comprehensively capturing environmental changes. Zhong and Zhang respectively proposed an adaptive impedance control method for different flexible target grasping in uncertain environments [9,10].

This paper introduces an end-effector gripping force impedance controller designed on a contact force model and analyzes its steady-state error. To counter the limited dynamic response and adaptability of fixed-parameter impedance control, a gray prediction model predicts real-time environmental parameters, adjusting the reference position dynamically. This allows compliant gripping force control even in the face of unknown target characteristics. The paper concludes with a simulation of admittance control and improved admittance control results.

2   Modeling of Contact Force

Firstly, an equivalent model of the gripping process of the end-effector is established, and the end-effector is equated to a second-order spring damping system [11]. Considering the gripping operation of soft deformable objects, the deformation of the environment is equated to a first-order variable stiffness spring model. Therefore, the established contact force model is shown in Fig. 1.

In this context, md, bd, and kd symbolize the inertia, damping, and stiffness coefficients of the end-effector impedance system, with ke being the environment stiffness coefficient. Figure 1(a) represents the actual scene of flexible object grasping. Figure 1(b), (c), (d) illustrate the end-effector's contact process with the environment. Figure 1(b) shows the non-contact phase as the manipulator approaches the target, with x and xe representing the end-effector's actual and initial contact positions, respectively. Figure 1(c) captures the initial contact point with zero contact force, and xr being the end-effector's set reference position. Figure 1(d) depicts stable contact achievement when the end-effector reaches the reference position, generating a contact force fe. The dynamic relation with position deviation is defined by a second-order differential equation as

$$m_d\left(\ddot{x}-\ddot{x}_r\right)+b_d\left(\dot{x}-\dot{x}_r\right)+k_d\left(x-x_r\right)=f_e. \tag{1}$$

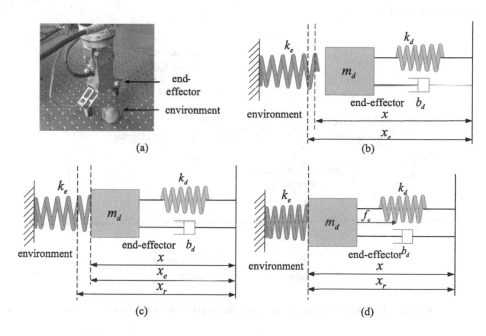

Fig. 1. End-effector and environment contact force model.

When the system is in a stable state, the finger is balanced at the reference position x_r and both acceleration and velocity converge to 0. The impedance coefficients m, b and k in the system are the characteristics of the impedance controller which need to be adjusted according to the application scenario.

For the grasping target, the force deformation is equated to a first-order system, and the relationship between its force and displacement can be expressed as

$$f_e=\begin{cases} k_e\left(x-x_e\right), x>x_e \\ 0, x<=x_e \end{cases}. \tag{2}$$

When the end-effector is in contact with the environment, the contact force will be generated, and the contact force is proportional to the deformation, which is equivalent to the spring model. Its stiffness may continuously change during contact with flexible deformable objects, and its contact model is equivalent to the first-order variable stiffness spring model.

3   Control System Design

This section will propose an admittance control system based on the gray prediction model to realize compliant grasp. It can predict the change of environmental stiffness k_e in real-time and dynamically adjust the reference position x_r. The block diagram of the improved admittance control system is shown in Fig. 2. Next, we will delve into the areas of admittance control system design and gray prediction model.

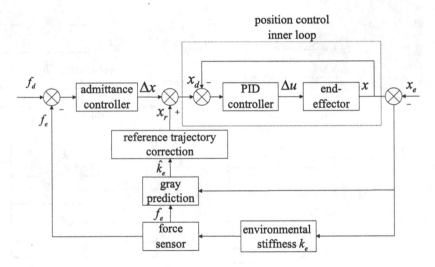

Fig. 2. Grey prediction-based grasp force admittance control system.

3.1   Gripping Force Admittance Control System Design

Considering the above model of contact force between the end-effector and the environment, set the gripping force f_d to grasp the object. In order to maintain the quality of the gripping, the desired force f_d needs to be set reasonably, and the goal is to make the contact force f_e as compliant and fast as possible consistent with the set force f_d during the gripping process. The deviation of the set force f_d from the actual contact force f_e is used as the input to the admittance controller, and the output is the correction Δx of the end-effector relative to the reference trajectory, and the admittance controller can be described as

$$m_d \left(\ddot{x} - \ddot{x}_r \right) + b_d \left(\dot{x} - \dot{x}_r \right) + k_d \left(x - x_r \right) = f_e - f_d. \tag{3}$$

After Laplace transform, the relationship between force deviation and position deviation in the frequency domain can be described as

$$x_f \left(s \right) = \frac{f \left(s \right)}{m_d s^2 + b_d s + k_d}. \tag{4}$$

Therefore, the admittance control system (4) can be considered as a second-order low-pass filter to filter the force deviation signal to obtain the position correction quantity relative to the reference trajectory, and then add it to the reference trajectory to obtain the ideal position x_d of the end-effector at that moment, which is shown in Fig. 2. The role of the position control inner loop is to make the end-effector track the given position quickly and accurately according to the position command obtained from the admittance control.

Combining (2) with controller (3), the steady contact force between the end-effector and the object is:

$$f_e = f_d - \Delta f = k_{eq} \left(\frac{f_d}{k_d} + x_r - x_e \right), \tag{5}$$

where k_{eq} is the equivalent stiffness of the end manipulator to the object

$$k_{eq} = \frac{k_e k_d}{k_e + k_d}. \tag{6}$$

Therefore, for the force deviation to be 0 under stable contact conditions, it can be obtained that the reference trajectory should satisfy

$$x_r = x_e + \frac{f_d}{k_e}. \tag{7}$$

3.2   Gray Prediction-Based Gripping Force Admittance Control Design

According to (5), To achieve accurate force tracking control when the environment is unknown or when gripping flexible objects, the existing impedance control must be improved to adapt to environmental changes and achieve the desired compliant gripping effect [12]. In this section, the gray prediction method will be used to build a prediction model, which can predict environmental stiffness in real-time [13].

The differential equation model of the gray theory is called the GM (Gray Model) model and $GM(1,1)$ is generally used for the prediction of a single variable, where the first 1 refers to the first order and the second 1 refers to one variable. For a known variable in the system, the data are represented as

$$x^{(0)} = \left\{ x^{(0)} \left(1 \right), x^{(0)} \left(2 \right), \cdots, x^{(0)} \left(n \right) \right\}, \tag{8}$$

where the superscript 0 indicates that the original data is accumulated 0 times, and n indicates the dimensionality of the data. The equation variables in gray theory are often expressed in the form of cumulative generation and note that $x^{(r)}$ is the generated series after r times of cumulative generation, denoted as

$$x^{(r)} = \left\{ x^{(r)}(1), x^{(r)}(2), \cdots, x^{(r)}(n) \right\}, \tag{9}$$

where $x^{(r)}(k) = \sum_{m=1}^{k} x^{(r-1)}(m)$.

The underlying differential model of the gray theory $GM(1,1)$ is expressed as

$$\frac{dx^{(1)}}{dt} + ax^{(1)} = u, \tag{10}$$

where a is the model development coefficient to be estimated and u is the gray system input. In order to maintain the independence of the model so that it contains only one variable, the input variable u is taken as the endogenous variable of the system so that the column of parameters to be identified in the system $\hat{a} = [a\ u]^T$. The differential equation can be transformed into

$$x^{(0)}(k+1) + af^{(1)}(k+1) = u, \tag{11}$$

where, $f^{(1)}(k+1) = 0.5x^{(1)}(k) + 0.5x^{(1)}(k+1)$ is the background values expression of differential $dx^{(1)}/dt$. According to (11), it is obtained that

$$\begin{cases} k = 1, x^{(0)}(2) = \left(-0.5\left(x^{(1)}(1) + x^{(1)}(2)\right)\right)a + u \\ k = 2, x^{(0)}(3) = \left(-0.5\left(x^{(1)}(2) + x^{(1)}(3)\right)\right)a + u \\ \cdots \\ k = n, x^{(0)}(n) = \left(-0.5\left(x^{(1)}(n-1) + x^{(1)}(n)\right)\right)a + u \end{cases}, \tag{12}$$

the above relationship can be expressed in matrix form as

$$\mathbf{X_n} = \mathbf{G}a + \mathbf{E}u. \tag{13}$$

Further combining $\mathbf{G}$ and $\mathbf{E}$, a and u, $\mathbf{X}_n$ can be expressed as $\mathbf{X}_n = \mathbf{B}\hat{a}$, where $\mathbf{B} = [\mathbf{G}|\mathbf{E}]$. By least squares, there is

$$\hat{a} = \left(\mathbf{B}^T\mathbf{B}\right)^{-1}\mathbf{B}^T\mathbf{X}_n. \tag{14}$$

Then $\hat{a}$ can be estimated from the above equations, and the values of the model development parameter a and the input u are obtained. And the analytical solution of the gray differential equation is that

$$\hat{x}^{(1)}(k+1) = \left(x^{(0)} - \frac{u}{a}\right)e^{-ak} + \frac{u}{a}. \tag{15}$$

The predicted values $\hat{x}^{(1)}(k+1), k = 1, ..., n$ are obtained by substituting the above equation. However, the data obtained at this point is the data accumulated once, and to obtain the predicted value of the original data, the data needs to be reduced, i.e.

$$\hat{x}^{(0)}(k+1) = \hat{x}^{(1)}(k+1) - \hat{x}^{(1)}(k). \tag{16}$$

Thus, the final data sequence containing the next predicted value, i.e., the data that can be used for prediction, is obtained

$$\hat{x}^{(0)} = \left\{ \hat{x}^{(0)}(1), \hat{x}^{(0)}(2), ..., \hat{x}^{(0)}(n), \hat{x}^{(0)}(n+1) \right\}. \tag{17}$$

The gray prediction module uses the contact force f_e measured by the force sensor in real-time and the position difference between the current position of the end-effector and the initial position x_e as inputs to build a gray prediction model to predict the value of the environmental stiffness $\hat{k}_e$, showing in Fig. 2. In the gray prediction model, the dimension of the data in (17) is 5, so the environmental stiffness values $\hat{k}_e(t+1)$ at the next moment can be predicted. The data series is built in a rolling queue, and the actual environmental stiffness at the current moment is calculated according to the spring model, that is

$$k_e = \frac{f_e}{x - x_e}. \tag{18}$$

4 Simulations Results

In this section, we compared the control effect of the admittance controller with the gray prediction-based admittance controller through simulation testing.

According to the mathematical model of the admittance controller presented in Sect. 3.1, a simulation model of the gripping force impedance control system is developed using SIMULINK [14]. The focus of the simulation is to verify the force tracking effect and stability of the admittance controller. The output position signals x_d is transmitted to the position control inner loop, and the PID control parameters are adjusted to make the end-effector track to the specified position x_d as quickly and accurately as possible. In the simulation environment, the manipulator end-effector can be described as a second-order system, using a transfer function as the mathematical model, expressed as

$$G(s) = \frac{6}{s^2 + 8s}. \tag{19}$$

In this paper, after continuous debugging in the simulation, the parameters of the gripping force admittance control system are set as shown in Table 1, taking into account the steady-state error, overshoot, response speed and other indicators of the system.

In order to simulate the gripping of the manipulator in an unknown environment, the environment stiffness k_e is set to be unknown for the controller. For soft objects such as fruits and vegetables, ingredients, dolls, etc., the environment stiffness changes with the grasping process. Therefore, the simulation in this section will test the force tracking effect of the improved grey prediction-based admittance control system when the environment stiffness k_e changes abruptly and according to the sinusoidal law. In addition, there is a certain measurement error in the contact force measurement by the force sensor, and a random signal with a mean value of 0 and a maximum value of 0.05 N is added to simulate the noise of the force sensor measurement in all simulations.

Table 1. Admittance control system parameters setting.

admittance control	m_d	1
	b_d	400
	k_d	2000
PID control	w_p	5.1
	w_i	6.1
	w_d	2.5

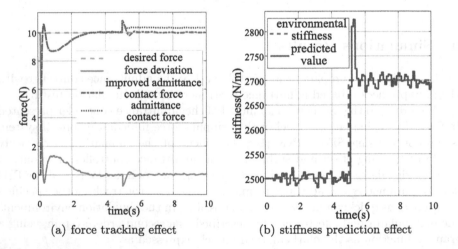

Fig. 3. Improved admittance control of constant force tracking effect during sudden changes in environmental stiffness.

First, consider the effect of constant force tracking. Also set the target contact force $f_d = 10$ N, the initial stiffness of the target $k_e = 2500$ N/m , the initial contact position $x_e = 5 \times 10^{-3}$m for stable grasping is calculated according to (7), and the sampling period set to 0.1 s. Set at the moment of 5 s, the environmental stiffness suddenly increases by 200 N/m. The grasping force tracking effect and the predicted value of the environmental stiffness by the gray model are shown in Fig. 3. On the other hand, the environmental stiffness k_e is set to vary sinusoidally with an amplitude of 100 N/m, and the force tracking effect and stiffness prediction effect in the simulation are shown in Fig. 4.

From Figs. 3 and 4, it can be seen that the improved admittance control has a smaller steady-state error and better force tracking under the change of environmental stiffness compared to the admittance control with fixed parameters. When the environmental stiffness changes abruptly, the prediction of the gray model for the environmental stiffness can converge to the exact environmental stiffness after a few sampling cycles of adjustment. The control signal can quickly return to the steady-state position of the desired force tracking so that the force tracking error tends to zero. When the environmental stiffness varies according to the sinusoidal law, the prediction of the gray model for the environmental stiffness is always maintained around the correct sinusoidal curve, and the improved admittance control is always maintained with a small steady-state error.

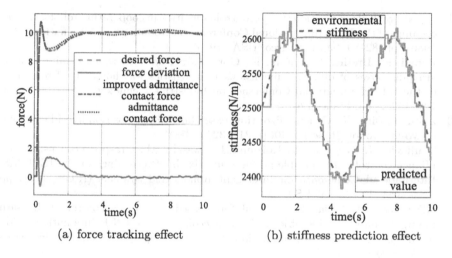

(a) force tracking effect   (b) stiffness prediction effect

Fig. 4. Improved admittance control of constant force tracking effect when environmental stiffness varies sinusoidally.

5   Conclusion

This paper focuses on the compliant gripping control method of the robotic end-effector for flexible objects and validates its effectiveness in the simulation environment. First, the contact force model between the end-effector and the flexible object is established. Then, an admittance control system based on the gray prediction model is proposed and the principle of the admittance controller is introduced in detail and the gripping force admittance control system is designed. The steady state of admittance control is derived and the error analysis is carried out. For the defects of the traditional admittance control, this paper proposes to predict the flexible object stiffness based on the gray prediction model and adjust the reference position in real time to reduce its tracking steady-state error in the dynamic environment. Multiple sets of simulation results show that the traditional gripping force admittance control is effective for constant force tracking, and also points out its insufficient dynamic response capability and difficulty in adapting to environmental changes. By contrast, the improved admittance control based on the gray prediction model can achieve fast tracking of the desired force, especially in the case of tracking the dynamic desired force as well as the environmental change. It can still maintain a small steady-state error with a certain degree of self-adaptability and can realize the compliant gripping of the flexible object.

References

1. Hayati, S.: Hybrid position/Force control of multi-arm cooperating robots. In: Proceedings of the IEEE International Conference on Robotics and Automation(ICRA 1986), pp. 82–89. San Francisco, USA (1986)
2. Benali, K., Brethé, J., Guérin, F., Gorka, M.: Dual arm robot manipulator for grasping boxes of different dimensions in a logistics warehouse. In: Proceedings of the IEEE International Conference on Industrial Technology (ICIT 2018), pp. 147–152. Lyon, France (2018)
3. Zhou, J., Ding, X.: Genetic algorithm-based fuzzy force/position hybrid control of a two-arm robot. Robotics **30**(4), 318–325 (2018)
4. Tsujiuchi, N., Ueyama, H., Koizumi, T., Iwasaki, M.: Grasp control using compliance control with variable stiffness matrix. In: Proceedings of the IEEE/RSJ International Conference on Intelligent Robots and Systems (IROS 2003), pp. 3294–3299. Las Vegas, USA (2003)
5. AlYahmadi, A., Hsia, T.: Internal force-based impedance control of dual-arm manipulation of flexible objects. In: Proceedings of the IEEE International Conference on Robotics and Automation(ICRA 2000), pp. 3296–3301. San Francisco, USA (2000)
6. Kaserer, D., Gattringer, H., Müller, A.: Time optimal motion planning and admittance control for cooperative grasping. IEEE Robot. Autom. Lett. **5**(2), 2216–2223 (2020)
7. Liu, H., Wang, L., Wang, F.: A hybrid force/position control method based on intelligent prediction. J. Northeast. Univ. **27**(12), 1365–1368 (2018)
8. Wang, G., Deng, Y., Zhou, H., Yue, X.: PD-adaptive variable impedance constant force control of macro-mini robot for compliant grinding and polishing. Int. J. Adv. Manufact. Technol. **124**(7), 2149–2170 (2023)
9. Zhong, Y., Wang, T., Pu, Y., Moreno, R.: An adaptive bilateral impedance control based on nonlinear disturbance observer for different flexible targets grasping. Comput. Electr. Eng. **103**(10), 83–88 (2022)
10. Zhang, Z., Zhou, J., Yi, B., Wang, K.: A flexible swallowing gripper for harvesting apples and its grasping force sensing model. Comput. Electron. Agric. **204**(2023), 107 (2023)

11. Bencak, P., Hercog, D., Lerher, T.: Simulation model for robotic pick-point evaluation for 2-F robotic gripper. Appl. Sci. **13**(4), 2599 (2023)
12. Zhuang, M., Li, G., Ding, K., Xu, G.: Research on the application of impedance control in flexible grasp of picking robot. Adv. Mech. Eng. **15**(4), 10–16 (2023)
13. Deng, J.: Gray Prediction and Decision Making. Huazhong University of Science and Technology Press, Wuhan (2002)
14. Wang, X., Xiao, Y., Bi, S., Fan, X., Rao, H.: Design and gripping force tracking impedance control of a flexible gripping test platform for robots. J. Agric. Eng. **31**(1), 58–63 (2018)

Vision-Based Human Robot Interaction and Application

Research on an Embedded System of Cotton Field Patrol Robot Based on AI Depth Camera

Wenxiong Wu, Jian Wu[✉], Ziyang Shen, Lei Yin, and Qikong Liu

School of Mechanical Engineering, Nanjing University of Science and Technology,
Nanjing 210094, China
895386202@qq.com

Abstract. In this paper, a low-latency, and high-performance and highly portable embedded vision system was proposed to meet the high real-time and high-performance requirements of the embedded vision system used in the cotton field patrol robot. The system utilized an AI depth camera "OAK" to achieve the function of video acquisition, object recognition and localization, providing real-time and high-performance capabilities. And the Robot Operating System 2 (ROS2) was utilized to solve the communication issues between modules, improving the versatility and portability of the system. Additionally, combined with SimAM attentional mechanism module, the YOLOv5s model was improved to enhance the ability of the system to recognize small objects. Experimental testing demonstrated that the system is capable of effectively completing object recognition and localization tasks, while also providing more computing resources for the main control module to handle other tasks.

Keywords: Embedded vision System · AI depth camera · Improved YOLOv5s

1 Introduction

Machine vision is a science and technology that enables robots to perceive the outside world and make decisions. With the rapid development of artificial intelligence technology, Machine vision has experienced unprecedented progress, which has made the ability of machine vision closer to human vision. In the field of agriculture, machine vision technology has been widely applied [1], including cotton planting, which is an important direction of application for computer vision technology. Cotton is one of the important economic crops in China, and its planting area and output rank first in the world. However, frequent field inspections are required during cotton planting, which incurs a significant amount of labor and time costs. Therefore, designing a robot that can independently complete tasks during field inspections is an urgent problem that needs to be solved.

However, research on the application of robots in cotton field patrols, especially those based on vision technology, is still relatively weak. The traditional architecture of machine vision systems consists of a camera and a PC, with the camera responsible for vision acquisition and the PC responsible for vision processing and decision execution.

H. Yang et al. (Eds.): ICIRA 2023, LNAI 14267, pp. 529–538, 2023.
https://doi.org/10.1007/978-981-99-6483-3_45

However, such vision systems rely heavily on the PC and the continuous transmission of images puts tremendous pressure on data communication. To address this, Li Jing et al. [2] proposed an embedded vision system based on ARM, which features small size, low cost, simple structure, and convenient functional expansion. To deploy more powerful but complex artificial neural network models on the embedded vision system, Yeh Kuanyu et al. [3] developed an embedded vision platform based on a multi-core heterogeneous processor, solving the problem of deploying neural network models on embedded platforms.

Considering the high-performance and low-latency demands of the cotton field patrol robot for the embedded vision system, a low-latency, high-performance and highly portable embedded vision system was proposed based on Artificial Intelligence (AI) depth camera [4] and Robot Operating System 2 (ROS2). And the performance of the system was tested using the hardware platform constructed with OAK camera and Jetson Xavier NX. Furthermore, in response to the complex operating environment and the presence of numerous small detection objects in cotton field, the attentional mechanism was introduced into the YOLOv5s model and the experimental comparison was conducted among various attentional mechanisms. Ultimately, the optimal model was deployed in the embedded visual system. The purpose of this paper is to provide an effective solution for the intelligent development of cotton planting and offer guidance and reference for the future intelligent development of agricultural production.

2   Design of System Hardware

2.1   Scheme of General Design

The workflow of the cotton field patrol robot includes the following steps: the master module enables the vision module, which completes video acquisition and implements object detection and location based on pre-deployed models, and transmits the processed video results and original video stream back to the master module; the master module utilizes the data information processed by the vision module to control external devices such as navigation, reseeding and other operations of the patrol robot, and outputs data processing results and video stream to the display module. In summary, the main tasks of an embedded visual system include: (1) video capture; (2) object detection and positioning; (3) result transmission.

Based on the above analysis, the hardware of an embedded visual system is mainly composed of four modules: the vision module, the master module, the display module, and the execution module. This paper mainly focuses on the hardware solutions for the vision module and master module in the embedded visual system, while the execution module can be selected or designed according to actual operation conditions of the patrol robot. The overall hardware design scheme of the system is shown in Fig. 1.

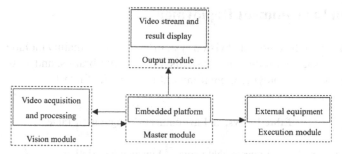

Fig. 1. General scheme of system hardware

2.2 Vision Module

The vision module is primarily responsible for data collection and processing. The system employed the AI depth camera "OAK-D-POE", developed by Luxonis, to complete the work of the vision module. The OAK camera is equipped with a BNO086 IMU, a binocular vision lens, and a high-pixel RGB lens. The rich sensor resources of the OAK camera provide the embedded system with strong environmental perception capabilities. In addition, the OAK camera has a high-performance Myriad X VPU processor with 4 Tops of neural network computing power. Therefore, the OAK camera can directly output high frame rates and high-precision depth maps. Meanwhile, the OAK camera supports the deployment of real-time AI algorithms, such as AlexNet, SSD series, and YOLO series, in its internal system. The OAK camera is powered by a gigabit Ethernet POE (Power Over Ethernet). Therefore, the OAK camera requires a POE switch to supply power to the device and connect it to the embedded platform.

2.3 Master Module

According to the system design scheme, the patrol robot needs to control several modules in real time, and the communication and control between each module will produce a large load of the master module. Therefore, the master module needs to have high performance. The Jetson Xavier NX, a multi-core heterogeneous processor developed by NVIDIA, was chosen as the master module for building the embedded development platform, based on a comparative analysis of existing embedded development devices. The Jetson platform runs the Linux operating system, and is equipped with a 64-bit 6-core NVIDIA Carmel ARM CPU and 48 384-core NVIDIA Volta™ GPUs, 16GB of LPDDR4 memory, 16GB of flash memory, and built-in Bluetooth and WiFi modules, as well as various external interfaces such as HDMI, USB, PCI-E, and M.2. However, due to the limited 16GB data storage on the Jetson platform, which is far from meeting the actual development needs, the system has extended the storage capacity with a 128GB solid-state drive through the M.2 interface of the Jetson platform, providing a basic condition for deploying development environments and related development tools on the development platform. Therefore, with up to 21 TOPS of computing power, the Jetson platform is suitable for the cotton field patrol robot.

3   System Environment Deployment

The deployment of the embedded vision system environment mainly includes the setup of operating systems, communication systems, third-party libraries, and visual processing model. The specific deployment environment is shown in Table 1.

Table 1. System Environment Configuration Table

Environment type	Environment name	Function description
Operating system	Ubuntu	Provide the basic development environment
Communication system	ROS2	Realize real-time communication between modules
Third-party libraries	DepthAI	Provides library functions required to use the OAK camera
	OpenCV	Provides libraries for image and video processing
Visual processing model	Improved YOLOv5s	Provides an object detection algorithm for the visual system

3.1   Operating System

The deployment of Ubuntu operating system was achieved by installing Jetpack package provided by NVIDIA company, which contains Ubuntu 20.04 system image, Cuda toolkit and other resources. Since Jetpack package is a $\times 86$ binary file that cannot run directly on Jetson, it needs to be completed by a host machine with Ubuntu operating system [5]. The construction of Jetson platform operating system was completed by installing SDK Manager tool provided by NVIDIA company on the host machine.

3.2   Communication System

The deployment of the communication system mainly considers the communication requirements between various modules and the universality of the embedded vision system. Therefore, the ROS2, a robot operating system, was adopted to complete the construction of the communication system [6]. There are some differences in data communication requirements among modules in embedded vision system. For example, the communication system is required to have strong logic when the master module sends enable instructions to the vision module, but the communication system is required to have periodicity and real-time performance when the vision module transmits data to the master module. Therefore, various communication mechanisms of ROS2 are sufficient to meet various communication requirements of the embedded vision systems. On the other hand, according to different operation requirements, the execution module can subscribe to different data information from the master module, which makes the development of each module independent from each other and does not interfere with each other, and guarantees the universality and portability of embedded vision system.

The Jetson platform has used Ubuntu20.04 as the operating system, so installed ROS2 foxy according to the ROS official advice. ROS2-foxy installation was completed by setting the encoding format on the Ubuntu terminal, starting the Universe repository, adding software sources, installing ROS2-foxy and configuring environment variables.

3.3 Third-Party Libraries

The installation of third-party libraries includes the DepthAI library and the OpenCV library. To use the OAK camera, the DepthAI library provided by the OAK official website needs to be called, and relevant functions in the DepthAI library can be used to control the OAK camera through the master module. In addition, the functions in the OpenCV library can be called to assist in video display and processing. The deployment of third-party libraries was completed by entering installation commands and configuring the system environment in the Ubuntu terminal.

3.4 Visual Processing Model

Visual processing mainly includes object recognition, localization and tracking. Since OAK cameras are equipped with functions such as 3D detection and feature tracking, you only need to provide configuration files and weight files of custom neural network models to use these functions. By converting the custom neural network model into a ".blob "format using OAK tools and deploying it into the OAK camera, object detection, location and tracking can be achieved on the OAK camera. Based on the above analysis, the main task of the vision module is to determine the object detection algorithm used. After determining the model, visual processing can be completed directly by calling the DepthAI library function.

Currently, the popular object detection algorithms based on deep learning can be divided into one-stage and two-stage object detection algorithms, and commonly used algorithms [7] are shown in Fig. 2. The one-stage object detection algorithm has the advantages of simple structure and high computational efficiency, which can meet the real-time detection requirement of the model. The two-stage object detection algorithm has higher recognition accuracy, but its recognition speed is lower than that of the one-stage object detection algorithm [8]. Considering both recognition speed and accuracy, the system deploys the YOLOv5s model to complete the object detection model. YOLOv5 [9] is one of the most advanced real-time detection models, which adopts the best optimization strategies in the field of CNN in recent years, and has different degrees of optimization in data processing, backbone network, network training, activation function, loss function, etc. YOLOv5s is a lightweight YOLOv5 model, which is characterized by simple structure and rapid detection, and can meet the application requirement of the cotton field patrol robots. In this paper, the collected cotton-related data set was used to complete the training of YOLOv5s model, and the model conversion was completed by OAK official tool.

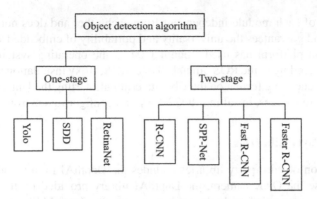

Fig. 2. Object detection algorithms based on deep learning

Considering the complexity of the field operating environment, the identification of cotton seeds and cotton holes may make it difficult for the YOLOv5s classifier to distinguish them due to their similar visual characteristics to other weeds. In order to improve the detection effect of the visual system on small objects, the attentional mechanism module was introduced into the yolov5s model. The YOLOv5s model combined with the attentional mechanism can further enhance the ability to correctly identify small objects in the complex field background, so as to meet the object recognition requirements of the cotton patrol robot. In light of the extensive research on attentional mechanisms, this research analyzed the performance differences among various attentional mechanisms. Three commonly used attentional mechanisms, namely SE [10], CBAM [11], and SimAM [12], were selected for experimental comparison. To ensure the reliability of the experiments, different attentional mechanism modules were placed at the same position within the network structure, while keeping the remaining parts of the network unchanged. Ultimately, based on the experimental results, the most optimal module in terms of performance would be deployed in the embedded system.

4   System Performance Test

4.1   Test Environment and Process

According to different working scenarios, the construction of the whole embedded system can be realized by connecting corresponding execution modules. The test environment is shown in Fig. 3. Jetson platform was connected to the power supply, OAK camera, mouse, keyboard, and displayer through the corresponding interface. The connection between Jetson platform and OAK camera was realized through the middleware POE switch. In addition, the trained YOLOv5s model was converted to ".blob "format and deployed into the AI depth camera. Thus, the whole test environment of embedded vision system was constructed.

System test process: 1) The master module issued the visual enable request through the service communication mechanism of ROS2; 2) The vision module received the request and starts OAK to complete video acquisition and data processing; 3) The vision

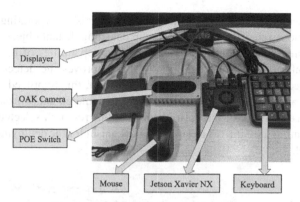

Fig. 3. Construction of test environment

module released the video stream and data processing results to the topic through the topic communication mechanism of ROS2; 4) The master module would output the video stream and data processing results to the display device by subscribing to the corresponding topics. In the experiment, multiple objects were tracked by the system, and the tracked objects were displayed on the displayer in real time, and the information of its three-dimensional coordinate was printed out in real time at the terminal.

4.2 Test Results and Analysis

Firstly, this research utilized the metrics of mAP (mean average precision), model size, and detection frame rate to evaluate the performance of the models. The training results are presented in Table 2. Compared to the original model, the improved models incorporating the SE, CBAM, and SimAM attentional mechanisms demonstrate respective mAP improvements of 4.1%, 4.9%, and 5.8%. However, the improved models exhibit slightly larger model sizes and lower detection frame rates compared to the original model.

Table 2. Comparative experiment of different attentional mechanism models

Model	mAP_0.5/%	Model size/MB	FPS
Origin	83.1	13.1	68.1
SE	87.2	14.0	62.5
CBAM	88.0	15.0	63.29
SimAM	88.9	14.0	64.2

The training and detection results of each model are compared and depicted in Figs. 4 and 5, respectively. Based on the analysis of Fig. 4, models incorporating the attentional mechanism exhibit superior training performance compared to the original model, with the SimAM attentional mechanism showing the best performance. Furthermore, Fig. 5 reveals that the original model fails to accurately recognize objects at far distances, leading to information loss, while models incorporating the attentional mechanism demonstrate improved accuracy in detecting distant objects.

Thus, the improved model possesses enhanced capabilities of the feature extraction, reduces information loss, and significantly improves the detection accuracy of small-sized objects in complex environment. However, this improved model increases the model size and decreases the detection rate to some extent. Through comprehensive performance analysis of the various models, this research selected the YOLOv5s model incorporating the SimAM attentional mechanism for the deployment of the visual detection model.

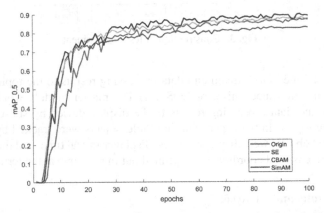

Fig. 4. Comparison of training results of different attentional mechanisms

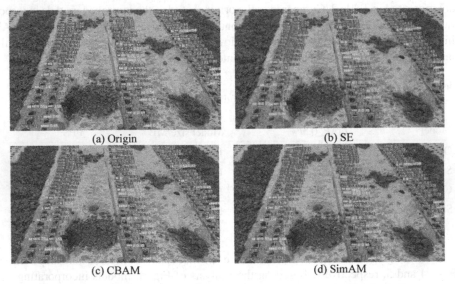

Fig. 5. Comparison of detection results of different attentional mechanisms

Secondly, the test results of the embedded system with the improved YOLOv5s model deployed are shown in Fig. 6. The system outputs the video stream of the tracking object in real time (in Fig. 6, the red box represents the cotton hole, and the pink box represents the cotton seed), and obtains the 3D coordinate information of the tracking object through the OAK camera. It can be seen from the results that the system can detect multiple objects in real time and output information of its three-dimensional coordinate of objects relative to the camera. During the test, the camera is moved, and the system does not lose objects tracked, which can meet the operation requirements of the cotton field patrol robot.

Fig. 6. Object tracking result

The memory footprint of the Jetson platform remained constant at around 30% during the beginning of objects tracking by the vision module. It can be seen that due to the OAK camera which is used to complete the image and analysis work, more computing resources are reserved for the main control module to deal with other tasks. Therefore, this system improves the overall performance of the cotton field patrol robot and enables the robot to adapt to complex outdoor operation scenes and complete various field patrol operations.

5   Conclusion

A high-performance embedded vision system was designed using OAK depth camera and Jetson platform, which can be applied to most embedded equipment based on machine vision, including the cotton field patrol robot. The embedded vision system can realize video acquisition and display. And it can obtain desired object information by deploying the vision processing algorithm and model, so as to provide technical support for the cotton field patrol robot. Compared with the traditional PC-based vision system, this system has the advantages of high performance, lightweight, miniaturization and strong portability. Compared with the depth camera based on ARM combination, this system solves the problem that it is difficult to deploy neural network models on ARM, due to the insufficient computational power of ARM. At the same time, the visual processing work completed by OAK camera enables the master module to have more computing resources to deal with other tasks, further improving the overall performance of the patrol robot and ensuring the real-time requirement of the vision module. Additionally, the SimAM attentional mechanism module was introduced into the deployed YOLOv5s model, which further enhanced the ability of cotton patrol robot to correctly identify small objects in the complex field environment. Therefore, the research of embedded vision system about cotton patrol robot has certain practical value and application space.

References

1. Chen, B.Q., Wu, Z.H., Li, H.Y., et al.: Research progress in agricultural application of machine vision technology. Sci. Technol. Rev. **36**(11), 54–65 (2018)
2. Li, J., Hao, W.D., Zhu, J.F.: Embedded vision system based on Linux. Comput. Syst. Appl. **20**(03), 121–124 (2011)
3. Yeh, K.Y., Cheng H.J., Ye, J., et al.: Constructing a GPU cluster platform based on multiple NVIDIA Jetson TX1. In: 2016 IEEE International Conference on Bioinformatics and Biomedicine (BIBM), pp. 917–922. IEEI, Shenzhen, China (2016)
4. Kim, T., Kang, C.H., Kim, Y.S., et al.: AI camera: Real-time license plate number recognition on device. In: 2022 IEEE International Conference on Consumer Electronics (ICCE). IEEI, Las Vegas, NV, USA (2022)
5. Meng, D.D., Hu, Y.X., Shi, T., Sun, R., Li, X.B.: Design and implementation of CUDA for airborne SAR real-time imaging processing based on NVIDIA GPU. J. Radars **04**, 481–491 (2013)
6. Zhang, Y.Z., Wang, J.Y., Han, Q.C.: ROS Robot Operating System Principle and Application. Science Press, Beijing (2022)
7. Fu, M.M., Deng, M.L., Zhang, D.X.: A review of image target detection algorithms based on deep neural networks. Comput. Syst. Appl. **31**(07), 35–45 (2022)
8. Gu, Y.L., Zong, X.X.: A review of object detection based on deep learning. Mod. Inform. Technol. **6**(11), 76–81 (2022)
9. Zhang, Z.H.: Intelligent image recognition detection based on YOLOv5. Inform. Technol. Inform. **275**(02), 200–203 (2023)
10. Hu, J., Shen, L., Sun, G., et al.: Squeeze-and-excitation networks. In: 31st IEEE/CVF Conference on Computer Vision and Pattern Recognition (CVPR), pp. 7132–7141. IEEE, Salt Lake City, UT (2018)
11. Hou, Q.B., Zhou, D.Q., Feng, J.S.: Coordinate attention for efficient mobile network design. In: 2021 IEEE/CVF Conference on Computer Vision and Pattern Recognition, pp. 13708–13717. IEEE Computer Society, Virtual, Online, United states (2021)
12. Yang, L.X., Zhang, R.Y., Li, L.D., Xie, X.H.: SimAM: a simple, parameter-free attention module for convolutional neural networks. In: 38th International Conference on Machine Learning. ICML 2021, pp. 11863–11874. ML Research Press, Virtual, Online (2021)

Hard Disk Posture Recognition and Grasping Based on Depth Vision

Chenyu Li[1], Cong Zhang[1](✉), Lun Shi[1], Renlei Zheng[2], and Qiongxia Shen[3]

[1] School of Mechanical and Electrical Engineering, Wuhan Institute of Technology, Wuhan 430073, China
Zhangcong94@foxmail.com
[2] Wuhan Fonsview Technologies Co., Ltd., Wuhan 430000, China
[3] Fiberhome Telecommunication Technologies Co., Ltd., Wuhan 430205, China

Abstract. The conventional operation and maintenance of 5G computer rooms is characterized by a low level of automation, which can result in untimely replacement of hard disks and potential data loss. In order to achieve efficient and timely replacement of hard disks in 5G computer rooms, this paper proposes a novel methodology for attitude recognition of such disks using an RGB-D depth camera and quintic polynomial interpolation algorithm. This method obtains two-dimensional position information of the hard disk through RGB images, and then combines depth images to obtain the coordinate system of the three-dimensional hard disk. The precise identification of the area to grasp a hard disk is achieved through the design of the grasping process, RGB-D image preprocessing, attitude estimation, and grasping trajectory planning. Additionally, by combining hard disk attitude estimation, the robot arm can be effectively controlled to complete the grasping process of the hard disk. The experiments carried out on the visual recognition method proposed in the article have shown that it achieves high accuracy in recognizing the grasping area of a hard disk. Moreover, the robot arm grasping system based on this method has been used to replace hard disks in 5G computer rooms automatically.

Keywords: RGB-D · Hard disk · Attitude estimation · Robot arm grasping trajectory planning

1 Introduction

As science and technology continues to advance, the automation and intelligence of the core backbone computer rooms in 5G carrier networks are continuously improving. This progress places a greater demand on the inspection of 5G base stations, as traditional inspection methods are slow, inefficient, and require significant resources and manpower [1]. Intelligent operation and maintenance of 5G computer rooms is becoming increasingly essential, as it is necessary for the efficient and reliable operation of the network [2].

With the rapid development of machine learning technology [3], the development of robots has taken a higher step and occupied a larger market. Robots can be seen in

H. Yang et al. (Eds.): ICIRA 2023, LNAI 14267, pp. 539–550, 2023.
https://doi.org/10.1007/978-981-99-6483-3_46

more and more industries. Robots can perceive the external environment through visual sensors [4], thus realizing interaction with the external environment. Sun et al. [5] have developed a novel approach to enhance the feature extraction capabilities of YOLO-V3 using a channel attention mechanism based on visual detection and grasping method of deep learning. Wan et al. [6] introduced a novel robotic visual grasping approach that combines deep learning and template matching algorithms. This combination resulted in an improved ability to accurately extract and capture target objects. Because the depth camera can acquire both color and depth images [7], the three-dimensional coordinate information of the object can be obtained. Shen et al. [8] proposed a visual attention model to detect target objects by creating projected arrows to guide the robotic arm's visual servo to grasp objects. Wu et al. [9] have proposed an innovative recognition and positioning method that utilizes the visual fusion of monocular cameras and depth cameras. By exploiting the three-dimensional features of objects, this approach object positions and leverages two-dimensional image fusion to enhance recognition and positioning accuracy. Gong et al. [10] have proposed an innovative method for addressing the challenges associated with tracking and grasping objects that are in constant motion. The proposed approach involves the development of a position-based visual servo that integrates a particle filter framework for object tracking and grasping. Zhang et al. [11] have proposed a novel robot grasping strategy that leverages YOLO-V3 for object detection and positioning, while also integrating visual information to execute grasping tasks. Matak et al. [12] employed a vision-guided robot to initiate motion towards an object without making contact, thus creating an accurate model while avoiding actual grasping. Once contact with the object has been established, the model corrected using tactile sensors, resulting in a flexible and precise multi-finger grasp.

At present, the research on the task of visual manipulator grasping mainly focuses on simple moving desktop object recognition and grasping, but the research on object recognition and grasping under complex working conditions is relatively less. To address the issue of replacing hard disks in intelligent 5G computer rooms, this study proposes a method that utilizes an RGB-D depth camera to identify the posture of hard disks and a quintic polynomial interpolation algorithm to capture them with precision. Through accurate visual identification and positioning, the number of coordinate conversion is reduced, and the calculation efficiency is improved.

2   Composition of the Whole System and Its Working Principle

The target recognition and grasping system for visual manipulation, based on RGB-D technology, comprises three crucial functional units: the machine vision unit, robotic control unit, and computer control unit [13]. The machine vision unit captures images of the hard disk by controlling the depth camera sensor, while the robotic arm control unit ensures precise motion control for each joint via a servo driver. The computer control unit is responsible for performing essential functions, such as image detection and position calibration. Figure 1 displays the overall system composition and working principle of this system.

To achieve hard disk grasping, the first step is to determine the position of the hard disk in the robotic arm coordinate system. Directly obtain the image containing the hard disk

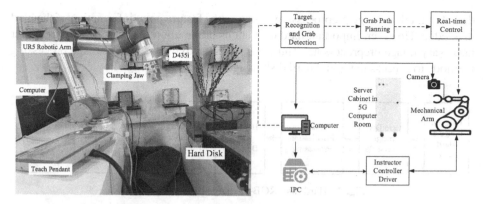

Fig. 1. Overall system composition and working principle

through a depth camera, and use image recognition and detection algorithms to obtain the coordinates of the hard disk in the pixel coordinate system. Transform the pose of the hard disk from the pixel coordinate system to the robotic arm coordinate system through calibration. The calibration of the visual system includes camera calibration and hand eye calibration [14]. The transformation relationship from pixel coordinate system to camera coordinate system is established through camera calibration, and the transformation relationship from camera coordinate system to robotic arm coordinate system is established through hand eye calibration.

On the basis of completing coordinate conversion, in order for the robotic arm to complete hard disk grasping, it is necessary to obtain the coordinates of each joint of the robotic arm. By calibrating, the pose of the object in the robotic arm coordinate system is obtained. Based on the shape of the hard disk and the structure of the robotic arm end clamp, coordinate transformation is performed to obtain the required pose of the robotic arm end clamp for grasping the hard disk. According to the kinematics model of the manipulator, the corresponding joint angle of the manipulator is obtained by calculating the inverse solution of kinematics, and each joint of the manipulator is driven to the designated coordinates to implement the grasping task.

3 Hard Disk Posture Recognition

The Intel RealSense Depth Camera D435i is mainly composed of a vision processor and a depth module. The depth module obtains the depth information of an object through the Structured light principle and 3D ranging and converts it into a depth image. The vision processor module obtains RGB images through a color camera. However, depth images are susceptible to external factors, resulting in loss of depth information and voids. In summary, targeted preprocessing of RGB-D images is required to improve image quality before hard disk pose estimation, point cloud generation, and point cloud registration.

For the inspection of the 5G computer room, two critical steps are identifying the hard disk image and extracting the feature points information of the hard disk edge. For this purpose, a depth camera can be utilized to obtain the original image of the hard disk, but it takes image preprocessing to obtain the feature point information of the hard disk edge. However, important hard disk status information can only be acquired after necessary image preprocessing. Thus, it is essential to use advanced image processing methods to process the initial hard disk image, as depicted in Fig. 2.

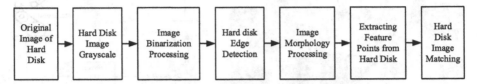

Fig. 2. Hard disk RGB-D image processing process

3.1 Hard Disk RGB Image Processing

In a visual robotic arm grasping system, the camera captures color images initially. To reduce the amount of image data, color images undergo grayscale processing. Edge detection technology has the capability to efficiently safeguard the critical information of interest within the image while simultaneously enhancing the proficiency of computer processing. For exploring hard disk edge detection within this research, the Scharr operator [15] has been employed, leading to the successful extraction of the edge image information of the hard disk, as illustrated in Fig. 3.

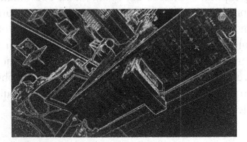

Fig. 3. Hard disk edge

3.2 Depth Image Preprocessing

Depth images represent distance information between objects and cameras, and can be used to recognize and track objects, establish 3D models and obtain pose information of objects. The conversion of depth data into point cloud data, facilitated through the camera calibration principle, plays a crucial role in ensuring high-quality point clouds. In cases where the depth image's hard disk edge appears blurred due to background interference, it results in deformities during the conversion of such images into three-dimensional spatial coordinates. This outcome adversely affects the accuracy of robotic arm grasping. Consequently, when filtering deep images, it is imperative to prioritize edge and detail information retention while simultaneously eliminating image noise.

The Bilateral filter is a notable improvement over traditional Gaussian filters because it effectively preserves image edges. This algorithm builds upon the strengths of both mean filtering and Gaussian filtering, while incorporating two critical parameters that influence its outcome: the spatial domain Gaussian kernel function W, and the range Gaussian kernel function H. The filter expression is as follows:

$$\begin{cases} W(s, t) = e^{-\frac{(s-x)^2+(t-y)^2}{2\sigma_W^2}} \\ H(s, t) = e^{-\frac{\|f(s,t)-f(x,y)\|^2}{2\sigma_H^2}} \end{cases} \tag{1}$$

wherein, (x, y) is the central coordinate point of the template window, (s, t) is the other pixel coordinate points of the template window, σ_W is the standard deviation of the Gaussian function, $f(s, t)$ represents the pixel value of the image at (s, t), and $f(x, y)$ represents the pixel value corresponding to the central coordinate. Multiply the spatial domain Gaussian kernel function W and the range domain Gaussian kernel function H to obtain the template weight of Bilateral filter, as shown in Eq. (2):

$$G(s, t) = e^{-\frac{(s-x)^2+(t-y)^2}{2\sigma_W^2} - \frac{\|f(s,t)-f(x,y)\|^2}{2\sigma_H^2}} \tag{2}$$

The Gaussian kernel function $W(s, t)$ in the spatial domain is used to measure the proximity of the space, with the weight decreasing as the distance increases; The range Gaussian kernel function $H(s, t)$ is used to measure the similarity of pixel values, and the more similar the value, the greater the weight. In the flat area of the image, the difference between the pixel values is small, and the spatial weight plays a major role, which is similar to Gaussian blur; In the edge area of the image, if the pixel value difference is large and the corresponding range weight approaches 0, the current pixel will be less affected and the edge preservation effect will be better.

3.3 RGB-D Image Alignment

RGB-D image alignment is a crucial step due to the differences in viewpoints and imaging methods used by RGB and depth cameras. This alignment process involves spatially transforming both the RGB and depth images to ensure that their perspectives, positions, and sizes are completely consistent for 3D reconstruction purposes [16]. The algorithm for RGB image alignment typically involves two steps: mapping depth image coordinates to RGB image coordinates, followed by RGB image and depth image registration. The initial step involves converting the coordinates of the depth image from the camera coordinate system to the RGB image coordinate. The cv:: undortPoints function in the OpenCV library can be utilized to correct the distortion of depth image coordinates and convert them to the camera coordinate system using the camera matrix and transformation matrix. Then, the points in the camera coordinate system can be multiplied by the transformation matrix to obtain their corresponding RGB image coordinates. The OpenCV functions cv:: SIFT and cv:: SURF can extract and match RGB and depth images, following which the cv:: findHomography function estimates the transformation matrix required to align the RGB image to the depth image. Figure 4 displays an image captured by the camera sensor.

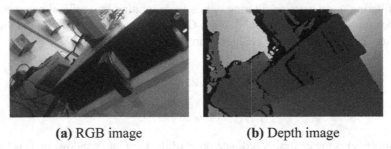

(a) RGB image   (b) Depth image

Fig. 4. Image captured by Realsense D435i

3.4   Point Cloud Computing

The point cloud data is transformed from the camera internal parameter matrix and depth data obtained from camera calibration experiments, and the imaging principle of the camera is shown in the Fig. 5.

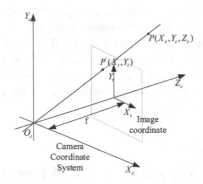

Fig. 5. Schematic diagram of camera imaging principle

The camera coordinate system is defined as the coordinate system of attitude detection of hard disk. The inherent parameters of the camera, such as the focal length f and the projection coordinate (u_0, v_0) of the center of light in the image coordinate system, are obtained by camera calibration experiments. The pixels $p(i, j)$ in the depth image are transformed into the depth camera coordinate system by formula (3) (4) and the corresponding point cloud coordinates $P(X, Y, Z)$ can be obtained by combining the depth value Z of each pixel.

$$X = \frac{i - u_0}{f_x} Z \tag{3}$$

$$Y = \frac{j - v_0}{f_y} Z \tag{4}$$

By calculating a series of points in depth camera coordinate system, the scene of three-dimensional grasping space can be restored, and then the RGB value of each pixel in depth image, that is, the RGB value of each point in three-dimensional space, can be obtained by combining the RGB image aligned with the depth image. By projecting the (X, Y, Z, R, G, B) information of each point P in the depth image into the three-dimensional space, the texture point cloud of the target scene is formed.

4 Analysis of Trajectory Planning Algorithm for Robotic Arm Grasping Hard Disk

The trajectory planning of a robotic arm is the foundation for executing tasks. Trajectory planning refers to calculating the change of the position and pose of the manipulator with time under the constraint conditions such as the kinematics equation of the manipulator, joint driving conditions and given motion path [17].

Figure 6 depicts the key points and process of the robotic arm in grasping a hard disk. The first step, denoted as P1, is to position the arm by identifying the starting point. The hard disk is installed within the server, and each disk corresponds to a switch button. Second step, P2, involves pressing this button to activate the hard disk handle to pop out. By performing point cloud calculations on depth images, the coordinates of the point cloud at the hook of the hard disk handle are obtained, and then matched to an RGB image to obtain the posture of the hard disk handle. The robotic arm then returns to the starting point in step P3. Step P4 involves the clamping jaws at the end of the robotic arm grasping the hard disk handle and initiating a circular motion. Subsequently, in step P5, the robotic arm handle is turned into a horizontal direction. In step P6, the hard disk handle is pulled for linear motion, resulting in the removal of the hard disk from the server by 10 cm. Finally, in step P7, the clamping jaw holds the hard disk in a straight line and maintains its position until the hard disk, denoted as P8, is removed. It can be inferred from the aforementioned process that the path followed by the robotic arm while grasping the hard disk is complex. In this paper, the kinematics of the robotic arm is analyzed, and a segmented trajectory planning design scheme is proposed to address the challenge posed by the complex and variable trajectory of the robotic arm when grasping a hard disk.

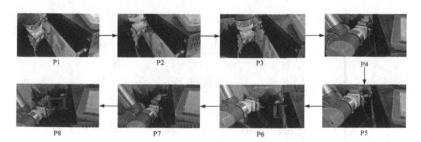

Fig. 6. Schematic diagram of grasping process

4.1 Cubic Polynomial Interpolation

Cubic polynomial interpolation must satisfy at least four constraints. The joint angles corresponding to the starting and ending points of the arm are respectively $\varphi(t_0)$ and $\varphi(t_k)$. In order to maintain the continuity of the motion speed of the arm and follow the planned trajectory, the speed of the arm at the starting and ending points is set to 0. It can be seen that the four constraints are:

$$\begin{cases} \varphi(t_0) = \varphi_0; \ \varphi(t_k) = \varphi_k \\ \dot{\varphi}(t_0) = 0; \ \dot{\varphi}(t_k) = 0 \end{cases} \tag{5}$$

The cubic polynomial interpolation function can be uniquely determined by the four constraints in Eq. (5):

$$\varphi(t) = g_0 + g_1 t + g_2 t^2 + g_3 t^3 \tag{6}$$

In Eq. (6), g is the interpolation coefficient of the robotic arm joint.

4.2 Quintic Polynomial Interpolation

In the realm of motion trajectories, stricter requirements and a greater number of constraints must be satisfied. The limitations of cubic polynomial interpolation render it inadequate, necessitating the use of higher-order polynomial interpolation methods for planning motion trajectories. Quintic polynomial interpolation is a superior approach to cubic polynomial interpolation due to its greater number of acceleration constraints for the starting and ending points. The six undetermined coefficients in quintic polynomial interpolation correspond to the starting and ending point angles, angular velocities, angular acceleration, and the first and second derivative functions. These six constraints are:

$$\begin{cases} \varphi(t_0) = \varphi_0; \ \varphi(t_k) = \varphi_k \\ \dot{\varphi}(t_0) = \dot{\varphi}_0; \ \dot{\varphi}(t_k) = \dot{\varphi}_k \\ \ddot{\varphi}(t_0) = \ddot{\varphi}_0; \ \ddot{\varphi}(t_k) = \ddot{\varphi}_k \end{cases} \tag{7}$$

The unique quintic polynomial interpolation function can be obtained from Eq. (7):

$$\varphi(t) = g_0 + g_1 t + g_2 t^2 + g_3 t^3 + g_4 t^4 + g_5 t^5 \tag{8}$$

By taking the derivative of Eq. (8) and connecting (7), it can be obtained that:

$$\begin{cases} g_0 = \varphi_0; \ g_1 = \dot{\varphi}_0; \ g_2 = \dfrac{\ddot{\varphi}_0}{2} \\ g_3 = \dfrac{10}{t_k^3}(\varphi_k - \varphi_0) - \dfrac{4\dot{\varphi}_k + 6\dot{\varphi}_0}{t_k^2} + \dfrac{\ddot{\varphi}_k - 3\ddot{\varphi}_0}{2t_k} \\ g_4 = \dfrac{15}{t_k^4}(\varphi_0 - \varphi_k) + \dfrac{7\dot{\varphi}_k + 8\dot{\varphi}_0}{t_k^3} + \dfrac{3\ddot{\varphi}_0 - 2\ddot{\varphi}_k}{2t_k^2} \\ g_5 = \dfrac{6}{t_k^5}(\varphi_k - \varphi_0) - \dfrac{3}{t_k^4}(\dot{\varphi}_k + \dot{\varphi}_0) - \dfrac{1}{2t_k^3}(\ddot{\varphi}_0 - \ddot{\varphi}_k) \end{cases} \tag{9}$$

4.3 Simulation Experiment and Result Analysis

In order to verify the influence of this design scheme on smoothness, running speed, working efficiency and economy of the manipulator during operation, the cubic and quintic polynomial interpolation algorithms are simulated and analyzed with MATLAB. The parameter designs are shown in Table 1, in which the starting joint angle φ_0, the termination angle φ_k, the starting time t_0, the termination time t_k, the starting speed v_0, the termination speed v_k, the starting acceleration a_0 and the termination acceleration a_k.

Table 1. Polynomial interpolation simulation parameters

polynomial	$\varphi_0/°$	$\varphi_k/°$	t_0/s	t_k/s	$v_0/(°/s)$	$v_k/(°/s)$	a_0 $/(°/s^2)$	a_k $/(°/s^2)$
Cubic (A)	0	50	0	6	0	0		
Cubic (B)	0	50	0	6	−3	−7		
quintic (A)	0	50	0	6	0	0	0	0
quintic (B)	0	50	0	6	−3	−7	0	0

Figure 7 shows a comparison of the trajectories of cubic polynomials and quintic polynomials. Where Fig. 7(a) corresponds to the cubic and quintic polynomials (i) in Table 1 and Fig. 7(b) corresponds to the cubic and quintic polynomials (ii). As shown in Fig. 7, the cubic polynomial interpolation algorithm can ensure smooth and continuous joint angular displacement and angular velocity curve, but the angular acceleration curve changes linearly, which can't reach the boundary condition of acceleration; The quintic polynomial interpolation algorithm can satisfy the smooth and continuous curves of joint angular displacement, angular velocity and angular acceleration.

In order to verify whether the quintic polynomial interpolation algorithm is also reasonable and effective in practical grasp application, simulation experiments are required to verify it. Set the starting point A coordinate (0, −192.65,0) and the ending point B coordinate (444.64, 200.41, −303.67) of the six-axis robot arm. By Matlab calculation, the corresponding joint coordinates between the two points are: A (0, 0, 0, 0, 0, 0), B (190.02, −66.72, 128.65, −175.28, −82.54, 99.95). Time t = 6S from point A to point B, with speed and acceleration set to 0.

Using the quintic polynomial interpolation algorithm, a space trajectory is planned between the starting point (A) and the ending point (B), and then the robot is allowed to move along the trajectory. The angle, angular velocity and angular acceleration of the 6 joints during motion are collected and plotted as curves, as shown in Fig. 8.

As can be seen in Fig. 8, when the robot travels along the space trajectory planned in this paper, the curves of angle, angular velocity and angular acceleration are very smooth and have high continuity, and the differences of angle, angular velocity and angular acceleration between each joint are small. It can be concluded that the space trajectory of the six-axle robot arm planned by the method in this paper can ensure that

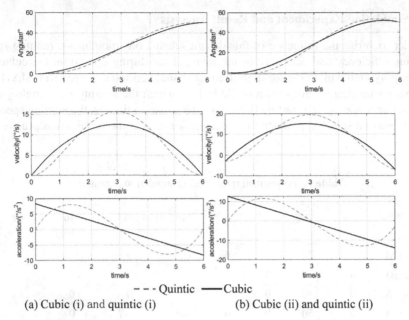

- - - Quintic ——Cubic

(a) Cubic (i) and quintic (i)   (b) Cubic (ii) and quintic (ii)

Fig. 7. Comparison of polynomials of the third and fifth degree

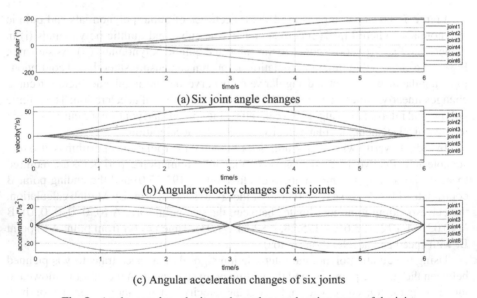

(a) Six joint angle changes

(b) Angular velocity changes of six joints

(c) Angular acceleration changes of six joints

Fig. 8. Angle, angular velocity and angular acceleration curve of the joint

the robot travels smoothly from the starting point to the end point in accordance with the desired route without major fluctuations and vibrations.

5   Conclusion

This paper presents a method for 5G UAV room robot to identify and replace hard disk. First, the method can independently identify the working state and posture of the hard disk in the computer room, calculate the position and posture of the hard disk relative to the end of the mechanical arm through the results of hand-eye calibration, and calculate the angle of each joint by inverse kinematics. Then MATLAB is used to carry out simulation analysis of cubic polynomial and quintic polynomial. It is obvious that the result of quintic polynomial is better. Finally, the quintic polynomial algorithm is used to grasp the hard disk trajectory planning. The experimental results show that the method is accurate and reliable, and the grasping process is not affected by the position of the camera. The proposed method for replacing the hard disk can meet the actual requirements. Future work will study the replacement of mobile arm in 5G computer room for other parts which are fragile and need to be replaced in time. If smaller parts are replaced, there is still room for improvement of grasping accuracy.

Acknowledgements. This research is supported by National Natural Science Foundation of China (Grant nos. 52205536). Wuhan Science and Technology Program (Grant nos. 2022012202015069). Gusu Innovation and Entrepreneurship Leading Talent Plan (Grant nos. ZXL2022518). Provincial Service Industry Development Guided Funds Plan of Wuhan in 2022 (Grant nos. Wufa Reform Service [2023] NO.120). Fourteenth Graduate Education Innovation Fund of Wuhan Institute of Technology (Grant nos. CX2022076).

References

1. Wang, J.X.: Application of 5G technology in intelligent patrol inspection of power plant rooms. Lamps Light. **164**(2), 107–109 (2022)
2. Ma, M., Liu, W.T., Wu, X.X., et al.: Research and application exploration on intelligent operation and maintenance of 4G/5G wireless network. Telecom Eng. Techn. Standard. **35**(8), 44–50 (2022). https://doi.org/10.13992/j.cnki.tetas.2022.08.008
3. Sun, S., Cao, Z., Zhu, H., Zhao, J.: A survey of optimization methods from a machine learning perspective. IEEE T. Cybern. **50**, 3668–3681 (2020). https://doi.org/10.1109/TCYB.2019.2950779
4. Zhu, W., Cheng, X.: Indoor localization method of mobile educational robot based on visual sensor. J. Internet Technol. **24**(1), 205–215 (2023). https://doi.org/10.53106/160792642023012401019
5. Sun, X.T., Cheng, W., Chen, W.J., et al.: A visual detection and grasping method based on deep learning. J. Beijing Univ. Aeron. Astronaut. 1–13 (2023). https://doi.org/10.13700/j.bh.1001-5965.2022.0130
6. Wan, G., Wang, G., Xing, K., Fan, Y., Yi, T.: Robot visual measurement and grasping strategy for rough castings. Int. J. Adv. Robot. Syst. **18**(2), 1729881421999937 (2021). https://doi.org/10.1177/1729881421999937
7. Gao, M., Yu, M., Guo, H., Xu, Y.: Mobile robot indoor positioning based on a combination of visual and inertial sensors. Sensors. **19**, 1773 (2019). https://doi.org/10.3390/s19081773
8. Shen, J., Gans, N.: Robot-to-human feedback and automatic object grasping using an RGB-D camera-projector system. Robotica **36**(2), 241–260 (2018). https://doi.org/10.1017/S0263574717000339

9. Wu, Q.Y., Xie, F., Huang, L., et al.: Chess positioning and playing strategy of robot based on integrated depth/mono vision and reinforcement learning. Control Dec. **36**(2), 1–20 (2019). https://doi.org/10.13195/j.kzyjc.2021.0756

10. ZeYu, G., ChunRong, Q., Bo, T., HaiSheng, B., ZhouPing, Y., Han, D.: Tracking and grasping of moving target based on accelerated geometric particle filter on colored image. Sci. China-Technol. Sci. **64**, 755–766 (2021). https://doi.org/10.1007/s11431-020-1688-2

11. Zhang, L., Zhang, H., Yang, H., Bian, G.-B., Wu, W.: Multi-target detection and grasping control for humanoid robot NAO. Int. J. Adapt. Control Signal Process. **33**, 1225–1237 (2019). https://doi.org/10.1002/acs.3031

12. Matak, M., Hermans, T.: Planning visual-tactile precision grasps via complementary use of vision and touch. IEEE Robot. Autom. Lett. **8**(2), 768–775 (2023). https://doi.org/10.1109/LRA.2022.3231520

13. Qin, Z.M., Gao, Z.Q., Gao, B.L., et al.: Exploring target recognition and grasping technology and developing vision manipulator system. Mech. Sci. Technol. Aerospace Eng. **41**(7), 1018–1022 (2022). https://doi.org/10.13433/j.cnki.1003-8728.20200385

14. Lu, Y., Guo, X.J., Guo, B., et al.: Research on visual positioning based on hand-eye system. China Measure. Test. **44**(12), 117–121 (2018)

15. Zhang, X., Feng, X., Wang, W., Xue, W.: Edge strength similarity for image quality assessment. IEEE Signal Process. Lett. **20**, 319–322 (2013). https://doi.org/10.1109/LSP.2013.2244081

16. Gomes, L., Silva, L., Pereira Bellon, O.R.: Exploring RGB-D cameras for 3D reconstruction of cultural heritage: a new approach applied to brazilian baroque sculptures. ACM J. Comput. Cult. Herit. **11**, 21 (2018). https://doi.org/10.1145/3230674

17. Han, Y., Zhao, K., Chu, Z., Zhou, Y.: Grasping control method of manipulator based on binocular vision combining target detection and trajectory planning. IEEE Access **7**, 167973–167981 (2019). https://doi.org/10.1109/ACCESS.2019.2954339

Design of a Visual Guidance Robotic Assembly System for Flexible Satellite Equipment Unit Assembly

Yixiao Feng[✉], Xiangyu Tian, Tiemin Li, and Yao Jiang

Department of Mechanical Engineering, Tsinghua University, Beijing 100084, China
fengyx17@mails.tsinghua.edu.cn

Abstract. The growing demand for small satellite manufacturing has stimulated the need for automated assembly of satellite equipment units. The assembly process requires flexibility, characteristic of space assembly while also demanding high levels of automation. However, existing space assembly solutions struggle to balance the automation and flexibility requirements. This paper proposes a flexible assembly scheme for equipment units, utilizing a local feature measurement scheme that integrates cameras and laser displacement sensors (LDS). Two measurement modules are installed on the outside of two fingers to achieve flexible assembly and measurement. By designing a calibration scheme for multiple sensor extrinsic, the finger motion error and sensor extrinsic can be calibrated simultaneously. This scheme eliminates the need to install auxiliary tools on the assembly object, and only requires a one-time extrinsic calibration. It greatly improves assembly efficiency while preserving flexibility. A flexible assembly system for equipment units is designed and tested in simulated assembly scenarios. The experimental results show a high level of assembly accuracy in a short assembly time.

Keywords: Aerospace Assembly · Multi-sensor Calibration · Flexible Measurement · Flexible Assembly

1 Introduction

Low-orbit satellite constellation projects have been proposed and developed globally to meet the growing demand for services, such as satellite-based internet and intelligent automobile navigation. Examples of such projects include the next-generation Iridium and SpaceX's Starlink [1]. The ground coverage of low-orbit satellite constellations requires the deployment of multiple satellites on orbit [2]. This calls for the large-scale production of satellites. Satellites are designed by combining multiple cuboid equipment units, which are bolted to the cabin panel [3]. The relatively heavy weight of an equipment unit and the lack of proper handles make manual assembly challenging, increasing the chances of accidental damage due to falling [4]. Furthermore, the large size of the cabin panel makes it difficult to maintain a comfortable posture while assembling manually, which is not suitable for long-term work. Manual assembly is highly inefficient under these circumstances, necessitating the automation of unit assembly using a manipulator.

Robotic assembly has been utilized in aerospace manufacturing for several years due to the high flexibility of assembly and the small batch size of spacecraft manufacturing, which makes automation of assembly challenging. The assembly process consists of two steps: manually moving the parts near the installation position and obtaining the accurate installation pose through vision measurement, aligning the feature sets of both the parts [5, 6]. Due to the small batch size of spacecraft assembly, the primary focus is on the accuracy and flexibility of the assembly process, with limited consideration for efficiency. Some researchers have utilized motion capture systems and designed probes to measure the 3D position of the holes on the two parts, match two point sets to obtain the assembly pose, and control the manipulator to complete the assembly action [7]. Although manually measuring all assembly features with probes yields maximum flexibility, human involvement drastically reduces assembly efficiency. Researchers have designed visual measurement modules that measure local features, using a combination of multiple modules to achieve flexible measurement of different types of large parts, followed by assembly [8]. This approach requires installation of measurement modules on parts before each measurement, and calibration of the installation pose of the modules. After assembly completion, manual removal of the measurement modules is mandatory. There are techniques using auxiliary visual features added to parts to achieve high-precision measurement, in addition to direct measurement of assembly features [9]. These techniques mandate the arrangement of auxiliary positioning features on the parts, which must be removed after assembly, and still require human involvement.

Equipment unit assembly differs from traditional aerospace assembly due to a higher number of equipment units and the need for greater efficiency and automation. In scenarios such as automobile and 3C assembly, robots are utilized in large numbers, with high levels of automation. Researchers have employed a stereo camera equipped at the end of a manipulator for 3D positioning, achieving the automatic assembly of mobile phone backs [10]. However, equipment unit assembly scenarios retain aerospace assembly's flexibility characteristics, with significant variations in equipment unit sizes. The creation of an end effector for each type of equipment unit is prohibitively expensive. A flexible gripping and measuring end effector, along with a flexible equipment unit assembly system, is essential for these assembly scenarios.

The main aim of this article is to focus on the automation of equipment unit assembly and designing flexible equipment unit assembly systems. Here, we will introduce the assembly task analysis and assembly system design, as well as the calibration of the sensor system on the end effector, equipment positioning process, and equipment unit assembly experiments, which will be conducted to validate the effectiveness of the system.

2 Designing of Equipment Unit Assembly System

Conventional measurement and assembly methods are limited and require a system designed for the unique requirements of the assembly task. This section analyzes these requirements and designs a gripping and sensor system to form a prototype platform for assembly.

2.1 Analysis of Task Requirements

In the automated assembly line of equipment units illustrated in Fig. 1(a), the cabin panel is transported by a conveyor belt to the manipulator, while an automated guided vehicle (AGV) is responsible for carrying the equipment unit and placing it next to the manipulator. The manipulator then picks up the equipment unit from the AGV and positions it onto the installation position on the cabin panel in such a way that the through-holes at the bottom of the unit correspond to the threaded holes on the panel. However, there is a margin of deviation in the actual positions of the equipment unit and cabin panel. To negate this issue, a measurement system is used at the end effector to measure the grip pose of the equipment unit on the AGV as well as the placement pose of the equipment unit on the cabin panel.

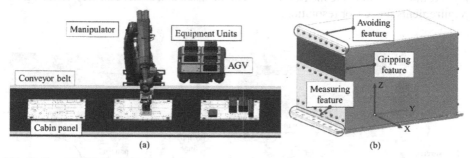

(a)   (b)

Fig. 1. Automatic assembly scene of equipment unit: (a) automated assembly line of equipment unit; (b) simplified model of equipment units.

For flexible assembly, the gripping end effector must be adjustable to allow for different sizes of equipment units, while considering avoidance in the design and measurement process at the end. The cuboid shape of the equipment unit includes through-holes used for bolt installation located at the bottom of both sides, corresponding to two rows of threaded holes on the cabin panel, as the measurement feature for installation. A typical equipment unit, shown in Fig. 1(b), was designed for combination with various equipment units arranged closely along the X-axis direction. The gripping features of the equipment unit are designed on the two side surfaces in the Y-axis direction, while certain features must be avoided on these two faces. There are two dimensions related to gripping: the distance between the two side surfaces along the Y-axis direction ranges between 100 mm and 400 mm, and the distance between the bottom of the contact area and the top of the equipment unit ranges from 40 mm to 150 mm. Therefore, the gripping end effector must be adaptable to the dimensions of equipment units during gripping, gripping pose measurement, and mounting pose measurement. The following subsection will describe the design of the equipment unit gripping end effector for this purpose.

2.2 Designing of End Effector

In this paper, a two-finger gripper mechanism with independent drives is used for flexible gripping of equipment units, as illustrated in Fig. 2(a). The gripper has two fingers that are driven by servo motors and move on linear guides via ball screw mechanisms. The position of the fingers is indirectly measured using motor encoders, which are then converted through the ball screw reduction ratio. The distance between the two fingers can be adjusted between 100 mm to 415 mm.

When designing the sensor system, the choice between overall and local measurement must be considered. The cabin panel have threaded holes on both sides, making it possible to employ a wide-range sensor for overall measurement or two sets of sensors for local measurement. The overall measurement scheme has the advantage of being able to measure all features at once theoretically, but the equipment unit's height can overshadow the holes and make it challenging to measure all the features on both sides. The local measurement scheme, on the other hand, can measure the two rows of holes on both sides of the equipment unit without any issues related to equipment unit shading. At the same time, the measurements can be taken at a closer distance, reducing the requirements for sensor resolution.

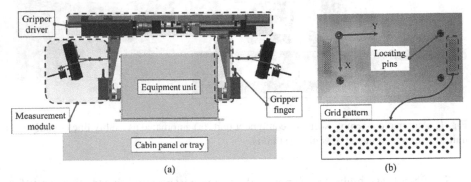

(a)   (b)

Fig. 2. Measurement system of assembly system: (a) Design of end effector (b) Design of tray

To adapt the sensor to the different distances between the two rows of threaded holes, the sensor needs to move accordingly. Using the two fingers of the gripper as a reference point for sensor installation will ensure flexible measurement of the equipment unit. To achieve 3D position measurement of the threaded holes, the study selects a combination of a camera and LDSs. Four LDSs positioned on both sides of the gripper are employed to measure the tray and cabin panel surface planes, and the hole position in the camera coordinate system is combined with the plane equation to obtain the 3D coordinates.

Since the through hole's plane on the equipment unit is not coincidence to the tray's plane, it is necessary to design a locating pattern on the tray to assist in measuring the equipment unit's position. To aid in the location of the equipment unit and the tray, the tray is equipped with locating pins that use the through holes on both sides of the equipment unit as reference points. As illustrated in Fig. 2(b), each equipment unit is positioned using four locating pins. Two sets of locating patterns were created on each side of the tray using a milling cutter to facilitate the measurement of the tray by the camera. This study employs a circle grid pattern that is easy to process and recognize as the locating pattern, as illustrated in Fig. 2(b). The circle grid patterns on both sides of the tray are oriented in the same direction and are not symmetrical to distinguish the direction of the equipment unit.

2.3 Prototype Platform Introduction

The assembly system for the equipment unit comprises a gripping end effector for the unit, a manipulator alongside its controller, a comprehensive control cabinet, and a tray devised to hold the equipment unit. The gripper is linked to the manipulator through ATI's automatic quick-change system. The manipulator boasts KUKA's KR210-R2700-2, and the KR-C4 serves as its controller. The comprehensive control cabinet connects and communicates with the gripper end effector and the manipulator controller, provides a power supply for the end effector, and manages the compressed air control for the quick-change system.

The sensor system incorporates a pair of 12MP industrial cameras with 6mm focal length wide-angle distortion-free lenses to provide a wider shooting range, and a bar-shaped LED light source is installed on each finger. Four LDSs equipped with a 60 mm to 160 mm measurement range are installed on each side of the fingertips. These models are recognized as LDS-S2-100-D0. A data acquisition board collects data from the sensors, converts it to the EtherCAT protocol with an RS485-EtherCAT coupling module, and transmits the data to the comprehensive control cabinet.

3 Calibration of the Gripping End Sensor

The end effector comprises a total of eight sensors, which are two cameras, four LDSs, and two gripper motor encoders. The frames of the sensors are displayed in Fig. 3. We define O_{tool} as the origin of the manipulator's tool coordinate system, O_{f1} and O_{f2} as the origins of the coordinate systems of the two gripper fingers, O_{cam1} and O_{cam2} as the origins of the coordinate systems of the two cameras, and O_{LDS1}, O_{LDS2}, O_{LDS3}, and O_{LDS4} as the origins of the coordinate systems of the four LDSs. The following subsections describe the calibration of camera intrinsic and extrinsic parameters, the calibration of camera extrinsic and finger positions, and the calibration of LDS positions.

3.1 Calibration of Camera Intrinsic and Extrinsic Parameters

Camera calibration consists of two steps, namely calibration of the camera's intrinsic parameters and calibration of the camera's extrinsic parameters. Due to the limited measurement range of the cameras when capturing images, it is difficult to capture the same calibration board using both cameras by reducing the distance between the cameras. Therefore, the intrinsic and extrinsic calibration should be performed separately using different schemes.

The camera's intrinsic parameter calibration method is mature [11], and MATLAB's camera calibration toolbox can be used to obtain the camera's intrinsic matrix and distortion parameters by taking 10 to 20 pictures of the 14×13 chessboard with a square size of 6 mm at different distances and poses. In this project, each camera takes 15 pictures for calibration.

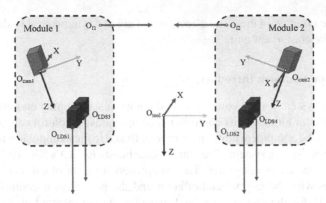

Fig. 3. Coordinate system of the sensors on the end effector

The camera's extrinsic calibration is to obtain the position and orientation relationship between O_{cam1}, O_{cam2}, and O_{tool}. The end effector is controlled to rotate along the X, Y, and Z axes of the tool coordinate system to capture the calibration board. To ensure that the cameras can still locate the calibration board when the end moves over a wide range in orientation, a ChArUco calibration board [12] is used for the calibration of the two cameras simultaneously. The calibration board used in this project has a grid size of 40x28 squares with a square size of 10 mm. The end is moved in the ±0.2rad range along the X, Y, and Z axes at intervals of 0.05rad above the calibration board at a height of 105 mm. Each set of data contains the tool poses and calibration board images captured by the two cameras.

The parameters calibrated are the position and orientation relationship of the camera and calibration board in the tool coordinate system. Let X_{c1} be the parameters of camera 1, corresponding to the homogeneous transformation matrix ${}^{t}T_{c1}$; X_{c2} be the parameters of camera 2, corresponding to the homogeneous transformation matrix ${}^{t}T_{c2}$; X_b be the pose parameters of the calibration board, corresponding to the homogeneous transformation matrix ${}^{t0}T_b$. Each pair of captured images corresponds to the homogeneous transformation matrices ${}^{c1}T_{bi}$ and ${}^{c2}T_{bi}$, respectively, which can obtain the pose of the calibration board using OpenCV. With $\Delta^r T_{ti}$ as the tool movement of each time, the following is obtained:

$$\begin{cases} {}^{t0}T_b = \Delta^r T_{ti}{}^{t}T_{c1}{}^{c1}T_{bi} \\ {}^{t0}T_b = \Delta^r T_{ti}{}^{t}T_{c2}{}^{c2}T_{bi} \end{cases} \tag{1}$$

The GSL library's nonlinear least squares fitting function is used for calibration to make the left and right sides of Eq. (1) as close as possible.

3.2 Camera Extrinsic Calibration and Finger Position Calibration

The gripper's two fingers are controlled by separate motors and rail sharing is not feasible. As a result, finger position calibration is necessary with the motor displacement. The finger spacing is set to 150 mm, 200 mm, and 250 mm, respectively, and experiments mentioned in Sect. 3.1 were conducted. The calibration parameters consist of the camera pose, the calibration board's pose, and the finger's initial coordinates and direction vectors for finger movement. For fingers 1 and 2 motor displacements l_{1i} and l_{2i}, respectively, the following is obtained:

$$
\begin{cases}
{}^{t}\boldsymbol{T}_{f1i} = \begin{bmatrix} 1 & 0 & 0 & t_{xf1} + l_{1i}v_{xf1} \\ 0 & 1 & 0 & t_{yf1} + l_{1i}\sqrt{1 - v_{xf1}^2 - v_{zf1}^2} \\ 0 & 0 & 1 & t_{zf1} + l_{1i}v_{zf1} \\ 0 & 0 & 0 & 1 \end{bmatrix} \\
{}^{t}\boldsymbol{T}_{f2i} = \begin{bmatrix} 1 & 0 & 0 & t_{xf2} + l_{2i}v_{xf2} \\ 0 & 1 & 0 & t_{yf2} - l_{2i}\sqrt{1 - v_{xf2}^2 - v_{zf2}^2} \\ 0 & 0 & 1 & t_{zf2} + l_{2i}v_{zf2} \\ 0 & 0 & 0 & 1 \end{bmatrix}
\end{cases}
\tag{2}
$$

The representation of the calibration board pose in the camera coordinate system and the pose change between the initial pose of the tool during each measurement aligns with the previous section and can be obtained via homogeneous transformation.

$$
\begin{cases}
{}^{t0}\boldsymbol{T}_{b} = \wedge^{r}\boldsymbol{T}_{ti}{}^{t}\boldsymbol{T}_{f1i}{}^{f1}\boldsymbol{T}_{c1}{}^{c1}\boldsymbol{T}_{bi} \\
{}^{t0}\boldsymbol{T}_{b} = \Delta^{r}\boldsymbol{T}_{ti}{}^{t}\boldsymbol{T}_{f2i}{}^{f2}\boldsymbol{T}_{c2}{}^{c2}\boldsymbol{T}_{bi}
\end{cases}
\tag{3}
$$

Hence, the calibration employs the non-linear least squares fitting method in the GSL library to minimize the difference between the left and right sides of Eq. (3). The objective function processing method and fitting algorithm are identical to the previous subsection.

3.3   Calibration of LDS

The calibration of the LDSs requires the assistance of the camera and should be conducted after the extrinsic parameter calibration of the camera and fingers. The end effector moves on the same calibration board along the X, Y, and Z axes at 0.05 rad intervals within the range of ±0.15 rad and at heights of 85 mm, 95 mm, 105 mm, and 115 mm above the calibration board. Each dataset includes data from four LDSs, the end effector pose, and two camera-captured images of the calibration board.

The calibration parameters consist of the positions of the LDSs in the end effector coordinate system. For example, X_{L1} represents the parameters of LDS 1, and LDSs 2 to 4 have similar parameters. The displacements of the four LDSs are denoted by l_{1i}, l_{2i}, l_{3i}, and l_{4i}, and the following equation holds:

$$
\begin{cases}
\boldsymbol{p}_{1i} = [x_{l1} \; y_{l1} \; z_{l1} + l_{1i}] \\
\boldsymbol{p}_{2i} = [x_{l2} \; y_{l2} \; z_{l2} + l_{2i}] \\
\boldsymbol{p}_{3i} = [x_{l3} \; y_{l3} \; z_{l3} + l_{3i}] \\
\boldsymbol{p}_{4i} = [x_{l4} \; y_{l4} \; z_{l4} + l_{4i}]
\end{cases}
\tag{4}
$$

For each measurement, two pose of the calibration board can be obtained from each camera images and the plane equation can be derived. The plane equation can be expressed as $p \cdot v = 1$, where v is the plane vector that aligns with the plane normal direction. The distance between p_{1i}, p_{2i}, p_{3i}, and p_{4i} and the plane can be determined from the plane equation. The calibration process utilizes the nonlinear least squares fitting method in the GSL library to minimize the root mean square error in the distance between the measurement points of the LDS and the plane. The fitting algorithm used is the same as the previous one.

4   Pose Measurement Process

The equipment unit is first placed on a tray and positioned with locating pins. Prior to grabbing, the manipulator assesses the tray's pattern to determine the gripping pose of the equipment unit. The gripper's center is aligned with the equipment unit's center to ensure the end effector's relative pose after grabbing. To install the equipment unit on the cabin panel, the threaded holes on the cabin panel require measurement to obtain the mounting pose of the equipment unit. This section delineates the measurement methods utilized by the manipulator to grasp the equipment unit, as well as the methodology utilized to establish the equipment unit's mounting pose.

4.1   Gripping Pose Measurement Method

The equipment positioning process before grabbing involves three stages: pattern recognition and localization, tray plane fitting, and pattern pose correction. Figure 4 illustrates the pattern recognition process, consisting of three steps: obtaining two camera images through Ethernet, enhancing the pattern contrast, recognize the pattern in the image and determine its center pose.

Fig. 4. Pattern recognition process

Due to the restriction of the tray's size, the pattern size is relatively small, leading to considerable error on the pattern plane. Hence, the measurement precision is enhanced by installing four LDSs on the outer side of the gripper fingers for measuring the tray plane. Thus, the surface equation is adjusted to yield more precise measurement outcomes for the pattern. Four point coordinates, p_i, on the plane are determined via the LDSs. The surface equation is expressed as $p_i \cdot v = 1$, with v representing the plane's normal vector. The plane vector is derivable using the least-squares method for the system of equations of the four points.

After obtaining the plane vector v, the position p_b and orientation R_b of locating pattern from the camera can be corrected. This correction aims to reposition the origin of the pattern coordinate system along the Z-axis of the end coordinate system to the plane.

Moreover, the Z-axis of the pattern coordinate system should be parallel to the plane vector. The correction process consists of three steps. Firstly, estimate the Z-component from the plane equation: $\tilde{p}_{bz} = (1 - p_{bx}v_x - p_{by}v_y)/v_z$ to adjust the Z-component of the modified end coordinate system. Secondly, determine the rotation direction by calculating $\boldsymbol{R}_{bz} \times \boldsymbol{v}$ and the rotation angle using $\cos^{-1}(\boldsymbol{R}_{bz} \cdot \boldsymbol{v}/|\boldsymbol{v}|)$ Finally, obtain the rotation transformation $\Delta\boldsymbol{R}$ to adjust the axis direction followed by the final corrected coordinate system direction $\tilde{\boldsymbol{R}}_b = \Delta\boldsymbol{R} \cdot \boldsymbol{R}_b$.

4.2 Mounting Pose Measurement Method

The measurement process has been divided into four steps. The first involves identifying and locating the threaded holes on the cabin panel. As shown in Fig. 5, the cabin image is then matched with the threaded hole image to get a matching map. The local image containing the threaded hole was denoised by the median filtering and Gaussian filtering. The HoughCircles function in OpenCV was used to extract the 2D coordinates of the threaded hole center. The second step involves fitting the cabin panel plane, by using the LDS to measure the cabin panel. The third step involves obtaining the 3D coordinates of the threaded holes by solving the equation of intersection between the camera's internal parameter and the panel plane. Finally, calculate of the mounting pose of the equipment unit. It is divided into two sub-steps: projecting the ideal threaded hole position onto the actual measured plane, optimizing the 2D pose transformation in the plane, and the pose transformation is obtained using the steepest descent method.

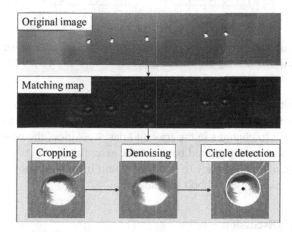

Fig. 5. Threaded hole localization process

5 Equipment unit Assembly Experiment

We conducted a continuous assembly experiment of two equipment units with a flexible assembly system to verify its assembly capability. We tested both assembly processes to compare the effects of the order of equipment unit grasping and mounting pose measurement on assembly and compared the efficiency and effectiveness of assembly. The equipment unit assembly experiment will be described below, and the test results will be analyzed.

5.1 Equipment unit Assembly Experiment Process

Prior to conducting the experiment, equipment unit 1 and equipment unit 2 were positioned on a tray. Their grasping and mounting locations were manually determined ensuring that the marker patterns and threaded holes were within the end camera and LDS measuring range. An assembly program was generated by the program in which the end position and gripper finger position were calculated based on the measured grasping and mounting positions of the equipment units. Figure 6 depicts the two types of assembly programs. The experiment was conducted with two groups: group A, which grasped the equipment unit first and then measured the mounting position, and group B, which measured the mounting position first and then grasped the equipment unit.

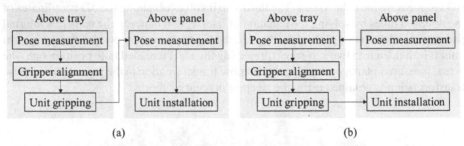

(a)   (b)

Fig. 6. Equipment unit assembly process: (a) Grasping the equipment unit before measuring the mounting position; (b) Measuring the mounting position before grasping the equipment unit.

Upon initiation of the experiment, the assembly program was sent to the control cabinet of the assembly system via the computer. To demonstrate the assembly system's stability in response to changes in the tray and panel position, the positions of the tray and panel were intentionally altered between the assembly of the two equipment units. After the experiment, the accuracy of equipment unit installation position was assessed using both visual inspection and bolt installation.

5.2 Results and Discussion

Table 1 shows the assembly time of equipment units. It can be observed that by eliminating the step of moving between the tray and the panel, equipment unit assembly time of group A is shorter than that of group B by 12–15 s.

Visual observation revealed that there were significant errors in the installation pose of equipment units in group A as depicted in Fig. 7. Unit 1 had an offset due to the incorrect identification of a row of threaded hole through holes on the equipment unit, resulting in a displacement of the final installation pose. Unit 2 was affected by its own

Table 1. Assembly time of equipment units

	Group A	Group B
Equipment unit 1	168s	180s
Equipment unit 2	170s	185s

Fig. 7. Installation result of group A

shadow in the camera shooting process, causing misalignment of the hole positions that were roughly aligned. The misalignment was insufficient for bolt installation.

Figure 8 shows the assembly results of group B. Despite unit 1 having a deviation in the X direction on its left side, it still met the conditions for bolt installation because all its holes are slotted holes. All threaded holes on the right side of unit 1 are placed at the center of the slotted holes, meeting subsequent bolt installation requirements. Unit 2 is comparable to unit 1, where all through holes, despite minor deviations in through holes and threaded holes, facilitated bolt installation.

Fig. 8. Installation result of group B

In summary, it is apparent that while group A reduced the manipulator's motion, it caused a significant decrease in the installation pose measurement accuracy. Consequently, group B's approach was adopted for the final system implementation. This approach involved the measurement of the mounting pose first before grasping the equipment unit for assembly.

6 Conclusion

This paper suggests a visual measurement-based system for achieving flexible equipment unit assembly. It incorporates a tray to assist in positioning and combining data from two cameras and four LDSs. It can obtain the installation pose of the equipment units after hole matching for achieving flexible installation. The sensor system eliminates the requirement for manual involvement in mounting auxiliary measurement tools, thereby enhancing assembly efficiency. The sensor modules move with the gripper fingers to allow for flexible measurement. The system tested successfully in simulated scenarios and achieved one-to-one alignment of through holes and threaded holes of the cabin panel in approximately 180 s. It can install multiple satellite equipment units and can be used in the automation assembly process of satellites.

While the system has the potential to install various sizes of equipment units successfully, it can be affected by deformations of the gripper fingers and self-occlusion. These affect its measurement accuracy, necessitating the pre-measuring of threaded holes before grabbing the equipment unit, which can result in efficiency loss. Recognizing the significance of this issue, future designs will optimize the stiffness of the gripper fingers, and the installation position of the sensor to diminish the impact of deformation and occlusion on measurement accuracy. This will reduce the movement of the manipulator and ensure that further assembly efficiency is attained.

References

1. Lalbakhsh, A., Pitcairn, A., Mandal, K., et al.: Darkening low-earth orbit satellite constellations: a review. IEEE Access **10**, 24383–24394 (2022)
2. Mcdowell, J.C.: The low earth orbit satellite population and impacts of the SpaceX starlink constellation. Astrophys. J. Let. **892** (2020)
3. Xu, Y., Zheng, J., Wang, T., et al.: Module design of micro-nano satellite assembled in space station. Spacecraft Eng. **31**, 48–55 (2022)
4. He, Z., Qiu, Z., Shen, Q., et al.: Typical cases and enlightenments of assembly safety improvement for small satellite. Spacecraft Eng. **30**, 171–176 (2021)
5. Wang, J., Xie, Y., Song, T., et al.: A precise robot control technology for satellite assembly based on force interaction control. Mach. Design Res. **35**, 47–52 (2019)
6. Guo, T., Hu, R.Q., Xiao, Z.Y. et al.: Research to Assembly Scheme for Satellite Deck Based on Robot Flexibility Control Principle. Kuala Lumpur, MALAYSIA (2017)
7. Hu, R.-Q., Long, C.-Y., Zhang, L.-J.: Robotic assembly technology for satellite components based on visual and force information. Opt. Precis. Eng. (China) **26**, 2504–2515 (2018)
8. Chen, S.Q., Li, T.M., Jiang, Y.: Pose measurement and assembly of spacecraft components based on assembly features and a consistent coordinate system. Int. J. Adv. Manuf. Technol. **120**, 2429–2442 (2022)
9. Ji, X., Wang, J., Zhao, J., et al.: Intelligent robotic assembly method of spaceborne equipment based on visual guidance. J. Mech. Eng. **54**, 63–72 (2018)
10. Chang, W.C.: Robotic assembly of smartphone back shells with eye-in-hand visual servoing. Robot. Comput. Integrat. Manufac. **50**, 102–113 (2018)
11. Zhang, Z.Y.: A flexible new technique for camera calibration. IEEE Trans. Pattern Anal. Mach. Intell. **22**, 1330–1334 (2000)
12. An, G.H., Lee, S., Seo, M.W., et al.: Charuco board-based omnidirectional camera calibration method. Electronics **7** (2018)

Full Resolution Repetition Counting

Jianing Li[1,2], Bowen Chen[1,2], Zhiyong Wang[1,2(✉)], and Honghai Liu[1,2]

[1] School of Mechanical Engineering and Automation, Harbin Institute of Technology,
Shenzhen, China
yzwang_sjtu@sjtu.edu.cn
[2] State Key Laboratory of Robotics and System, Harbin Institute of Technology,
Harbin, China

Abstract. Given an untrimmed video, repetitive actions counting aims
to estimate the number of repetitions of class-agnostic actions. To handle the various length of videos and repetitive actions, also optimization
challenges in end-to-end video model training, down-sampling is commonly utilized in recent state-of-the-art methods, leading to ignorance
of several repetitive samples. In this paper, we attempt to understand
repetitive actions from a full temporal resolution view, by combining
offline feature extraction and temporal convolution networks. The former step enables us to train repetition counting network without down-
sampling while preserving all repetitions regardless of the video length
and action frequency, and the later network models all frames in a flexible and dynamically expanding temporal receptive field to retrieve all
repetitions with a global aspect. Besides, temporal self-similarity matrix
is used in our model to represent the correlation of action, which contains
much cycle information in time series. We experimentally demonstrate
that our method achieves better or comparable performance in three
public datasets, i.e., TransRAC, UCFRep and QUVA. We expect this
work will encourage our community to think about the importance of
full temporal resolution.

Keywords: Repetition counting · Full temporal resolution · Temporal
convolution networks · Temporal self-similarity matrix

1 Introduction

Repetition counting, aiming to count the repetitions of class-agnostic actions,
is a fundamental problem in computer vision. It has great importance for analyzing human activities which are commonly involves repetitive actions, such as
physical exercise movements. This task is challenging since following challenges
(see Fig. 1): (a) various duration of actions within the video; (b) breaks exiting
in actions; (c)incomplete actions being counted; (d) noise in the datasets such
as changes in view point, multiple people in videos and so on. These challenges
make most of models with down-sampling not perform very well. In terms of
down-sampling, earlier works for repetition counting can be grouped into two

© The Author(s), under exclusive license to Springer Nature Singapore Pte Ltd. 2023
H. Yang et al. (Eds.): ICIRA 2023, LNAI 14267, pp. 563–574, 2023.
https://doi.org/10.1007/978-981-99-6483-3_48

Fig. 1. Several challenging examples in RepCount dataset: (a) The duration of actions within the video is different; (b) There is a break between actions. (c) There are incomplete actions in the videos, which may be mistaken for a repetitive action by the models; (d) There are two people in the video, which may affect the predicted count.

categories: sliding window [4] and down-sampling to fixed frames [4,9,18,19]. For sliding window, It's hard to choose one optimal fixed window size and it is unable to handle various duration, also leading to context loss. As for down-sampling to fixed frames, too few selected frames may ignore some repetitions, while too much frames will cause computational burden. The state-of-the-art method [7] relies on multi-scale temporal correlation encoder to make up for missing information caused by down-sampling. Despite the success of the multi-scale model, these approaches operate on low temporal resolution of a few frames per second.

In this paper, we introduce a new model which combines offline feature extraction and temporal convolutional networks. In contrast to previous approaches, the proposed model operates on the full temporal resolution and brings performance improvements compared with recent state-of-the-art methods. **First,** we utilize the full temporal resolution and offline feature extraction [10] for the inputs, which can offer more fine-grained information. **Second,** how to extract high-level features for long videos is of great importance. Inspired by action segmentation [5,8], we use Temporal convolutional networks(TCNs) as the encoder of the model, which consists of several layers of dilated 1D convolution. The use of dilated convolution enables the model to have a huge temporal receptive field, which can deal well with various duration of actions whether in inter-videos or intra-videos. To the best of our knowledge, we are the first to introduce full temporal resolution into the repetition counting filed.

In a nutshell, our **contributions** are three-fold:

1) We first adopt two-phase strategy to understand repetition actions based on offline frame-wise feature extraction. It enables the model to explore extensive temporal context and extract complete motion patterns, which is important for retrieving all repetitions in videos.
2) Temporal convolutional networks is designed to extract high-level features and explore similar patterns from a global view. We utilize dilated 1D convolution to obtain a huge temporal receptive field, which can capture long-range dependencies as well as inconsistent action periods.
3) Extensive experimental results demonstrate that our method achieves better or comparable performance on three public datasets.

2 Related Works

2.1 Repetition Counting

Crowd counting and objects counting in images are active fields in computer vision, while repetitive actions counting did not receive much attention. In terms of methods, earlier works is focusing on how to convert the motion field into one-dimensional signals, where peak detection [14], Fourier analysis [1–3,12,15] can be used. However, they are only suitable for stationary situations. Then some methods pay attention on estimation of action periods. Levy et al. [9] uses CNNs to classify cycle lengths within a fixed number of frames, while it does not take complex situations into account, such as variations in video length. Recent approaches [4,18] propose some novel frameworks for repetition counting. Zhang et al. [18] propose a context-aware and scale-insensitive framework, which can estimate and adjust the cycle lengths in a coarse-to-fine manner, integrating with a context-aware network. However, it predicts the number of repetitions for down-sampled inputs, and then estimates the count for the entire videos, which does not consider the interruptions or inconsistent action cycles existing in some videos. RepNet [4] focuses on repetition counting and periodicity detection, which converts the repetition counting task into a per-frame binary classification problem. However, the input of model is consecutive non-overlapping windows of fixed-length frames, which is easy to lose context information if the action cycles are too long. Moreover, there is an upper limit to the predicted period lengths, whose applications are limited. Recently, [19] utilizes the sound for the first time and achieves cross-modal temporal interaction. Though this method also down-samples the videos, it adds a temporal stride decision module to select the best temporal stride for each video. TransRAC [7] proposes a multi-scale model, which can compensate for the loss of information caused by down-sampling. Whether high and low-frequency actions nor long and short videos, multi-scale fusion can all perform well. The latest method is PoseRAC [17] which is the first pose-level model and outperforms all existing video-level methods.

2.2 Temporal Convolutional Networks

Temporal Convolutional Networks(TCNs) is a class of time-series models, which contains a set of convolutional filters. Lea et al. [8] introduces two types of TCNs which are Encoder-Decoder TCN and Dilated TCN, whose input and output share the same length. They both use a hierarchy of temporal convolutional filters. ED-TCN consists of a series of long convolutional filters, pooling and upsampling, while Dialted TCN uses a deep stack of dilated convolution with dilated factor. Due to their huge receptive field, they can perform fine-grained action detection and capture action cycles with long-range dependencies.

2.3 Temporal Self-Similarity Matrix

In the counting task, the most important is to explore similar patterns between instances, thus it is crucial to introduce temporal self-similarity matrix into repetition counting task, which is the representation of the similarity between frames and contains periodic information in time series. The most common method to calculate similarity matrix is dot product. Of course, cosine similarity can also be used. RepNet [4] uses the negative of squared euclidean distance as the similarity between frames, and TransRAC [7] utilizes the attention mechanism [16] to calculate the similarity, where the attention function can be described as mapping a query and a set of key-value pairs to an output, which can focus on important information in long sequences with less parameters and fast speed.

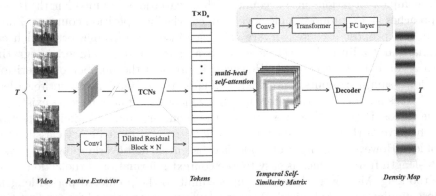

Fig. 2. Overview of our proposed model. For an input video, we use the encoder to extract high-level features. Then calculate the similarity between frames and apply the decoder on the temporal self-similarity matrix, which outputs the predicted density map.

3 Methodology

Given a video that contains class-agnostic repetitive actions, our goal is to estimate the number of repetitions. To achieve this, we propose a model based
on the full temporal resolution. An overview of our model is depicted in
Fig. 2. The model is composed of three modules: (1)an encoder which consists of video feature extractor and temporal convolution networks(TCNs),
(2)temporal self-similarity matrix which represents the similarity between
frames, (3)a decoder which outputs the predicted density map. In the following
sections, we present the details of each component.

3.1 Encoder

Our encoder is composed of two main components: video feature extractor
and TCNs. Assume that the given video has T frames $F = [f_1, f_2, ..., f_t]$.
We extract the features and feed them into the TCNs to produce embeddings
$X = [X_1, X_2, ..., X_t]$.

Video Feature Extractor. Processing long videos in both spatial and temporal dimensions is challenging. There are many existing methods such as C3D,
SlowFast and I3D which can be used to extract features. Specially, we use a video
swin transformer backbone to extract features. Video swin transformer [10] has
several stages which consist of video swin transformer block and patch merging.
It performs well in both effect and efficiency. RGB frames are fed as an input
clip to the video swin transformer network and the output is of size $7 \times 7 \times D_0$.
We apply a layer of global average pooling to get the final tokens $1 \times D_0$. All
the tokens (outputs of video swin transformer) are stacked along the temporal
dimension and thus form a $T \times D_0$ video token representation, which is the input
of TCNs.

Temporal Convolution Networks. TCNs uses a deep stack of dilated convolutions to capture long-range dependencies. Compared with vanilla convolution,
dilated convolution has a dilation rate parameter, which indicates the size of the
expansion. Without increasing the number of parameters, dilated convolution
has a huge receptive field.

TCNs consists of a 1×1 convolution layer which can adjust the dimension
of tokens, and $\times N$ dilated residual blocks (see Fig. 3). Each block has the same
structure, which contains a dilated convolution layer, ReLU activation and 1×1
convolution layer. As the number of blocks N increases, the dilation factor is
doubled. However, there are also some problems with the dilated convolution,
such as gridding problem, which may lead to some tokens that are underutilized.
Despite larger receptive field to capture long-range temporal patterns, some long-
distance information that are completely uncorrelated with current frame will
affect the consistency of the data, which is detrimental to shorter action cycles.
Thus we further add skip connections, which not only effectively reduces the

problems of gradient vanishing and network degradation, but also ensures the re-usability of features. The output of each block is added to the output of the previous block as the input of the next block.

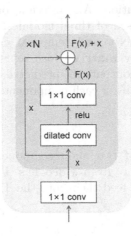

Fig. 3. Overview of the TCNs. TCNs is composed of one 1×1 convolution layer and several dilated residual blocks.

3.2   Temporal Self-Similarity Matrix

Temporal self-similarity matrix is used to represent the similarity between frames, from which the cycle information in time series can be found. We use multi-head attention [16] to generate temporal self-similarity matrix. The input contains queries(Q) and keys(K) of dimension D_k, and values(V) of dimension D_v. Specially, queries, keys and values are the same in our model, which are the output of TCNs. Then we compute the dot product of the queries with all keys and divide each by $\sqrt{D_k}$ with a softmax function to get the attention scores, which form the temporal self-similarity matrix whose size is $T \times T \times h$. The similarity matrix can roughly present the distribution of repetitive actions. The set of operations can be formally described as follows:

$$score = softmax(\frac{QK^T}{\sqrt{D_k}}) \tag{1}$$

3.3   Decoder

We apply a 2D convolution and a fully connected layer on similarity matrix. After that, similarity matrix needs to be flattened into the sequence whose size is $T \times D$. Following this, the sequence with position embeddings is fed as an input into the transformer [16]. Finally, the output passes through the fully connected layer to get the predicted density map D, which is of size $T \times 1$.

The ground-truth density map D^{gt} is generated by Gaussian functions, where each repetitive action corresponds to a Gaussian distribution and the mean of the Gaussian function is in the mid-frame. The density map indicates contribution of each frame to the complete action. Thus the count is the sum of the density map:

$$c = \sum_{i=1}^{T} D_i \tag{2}$$

where D_i is the predicted value of each frame.

We use the Euclidean distance between the predicted density map D and ground truth D^{gt} as the loss function, which is defined as follows:

$$L = \|D - D^{gt}\|_2^2 \tag{3}$$

4   Experiment

4.1   Experiment Setup

Datasets. Our experiments are conducted on three datasets: RepCount [7], QUVA [4], UCFRep [18]. The **RepCount** dataset provides fine-grained annotations in the form of start and end of actions, while two other datasets only provide the start or end of actions. In RepCount dataset, there are 758 videos used for training, 132 videos for validation and 151 videos for testing. RepCount dataset covers a large number of video length variations and contains anomaly cases, thus is more challenging than other datasets. The **QUVA** dataset is composed of 100 videos for testing with a wide range of repetitions, where each video contains 12.5 action cycles in average. It includes action videos in realistic scenarios with occlusion, changes in view point, and inconsistency in action cycles. The **UCFRep** dataset contains 526 repetitive action videos, which are collected from the dataset UCF101 [13]. The original UCF101 is an action recognition dataset collected from YouTube, which can be classified into 101 action categories. The details about datasets is shown in Table 1.

Table 1. Dataset statistic of RepCount, UCFRep and QUVA.

	RepCount	UCFRep	QUVA
Num. of Videos	1041	526	100
Duration Avg. $\pm$ Std	30.67 $\pm$ 17.54	8.15 $\pm$ 4.29	17.6 $\pm$ 13.3
Duration Min. $\pm$ Max	4.0/88.0	2.08/33.84	2.5/64.2
Count Avg. $\pm$ Std	14.99 $\pm$ 17.54	6.66	12.5 $\pm$ 10.4
Count Min. $\pm$ Max	1/141	3/54	4/63

Evaluation Metric. Following the previous work, we use Mean Absolute Error(MAE) and Off-By-One(OBO) count errors to evaluate the proposed method. MAE and OBO are defined as follows:

$$OBO = \frac{1}{N} \sum_{i=1}^{N} [|\widetilde{c}_i - c_i| \leq 1] \tag{4}$$

$$MAE = \frac{1}{N} \sum_{i=1}^{N} \frac{|\widetilde{c}_i - c_i|}{\widetilde{c}_i} \tag{5}$$

where $\widetilde{c}$ is the ground truth repetition count and c is the predicted count. N is the number of given videos.

Implementation Details. In the proposed network, we use the output features of video swin transformer (after global average pool) as the inputs of TCNs, and thus $D_0 = 768$. Taking the computational cost and performance into account, the frame rate is set to 5. Due to various length of videos, we need to pad feature vectors to the same length. In TCNs, the number of dilated residual blocks N is set to 6. In the process of calculating the similarity matrix, the dimension of queries, keys and values is 512. Our model is implemented in PyTorch and trained on two NVIDIA GeForce RTX 3090 GPUs. We train the model for 200 epochs with a learning rate of 8×10^{-6} with Adam optimizer and batch size of 48 videos. Testing is conducted on the same machine.

4.2 Evaluation and Comparison

We compare our model with existing video-level methods on RepCount, UCFRep and QUVA datasets. The greatest difference between our method and previous methods is the use of full temporal resolution and TCNs. We introduce full temporal resolution into repetitive counting field and try to preserve all repetitions by using offline feature extraction, while previous methods down-sample the inputs and strive to understand repetition counting from a low temporal resolution view. Additionally, TCNs in our model is used to extract high-level features from a global view and get information about correlation of actions. Table 2 shows that our methods outperforms previous methods on RepCount dataset, achieving OBO metric of 0.3267 and MAE metric of 0.4103 compared to the 0.29 and 0.4431 of TransRAC, demonstrating the effectiveness of our proposed method. On UCFRep and QUVA datasets, our model also performs well without any fine-tuning, which indicates the good generalization of our model.

In Fig. 4, we give the visualization of predicted results. As can be seen from the failure cases, our model still have some problems. The left in (b) indicates that interference such as other people in the background affects the model's predictions. The right in (b) shows that the duration of actions within the video varies greatly, while our model cannot capture inconsistent action cycles in some extreme cases, which is left to future work.

Table 2. Performance of different methods on RepCount test, UCFRep and QUVA when trained on RepCount dataset. The best results are in **bold** and the second best results are underlined.

Method	RepCount		UCFRep		QUVA	
	MAE↓	OBO↑	MAE↓	OBO↑	MAE↓	OBO↑
RepNet [4]	0.995	0.0134	0.9985	0.009	**0.104**	0.17
X3D [6]	0.911	0.106	0.982	0.331	–	–
VideoSwinTransformer [10]	0.576	0.132	1.122	0.033	–	–
TANet [11]	0.662	0.099	0.892	0.129	–	–
Zhang et al. [18]	0.8786	0.1554	0.762	**0.412**	–	–
TransRAC [7]	<u>0.4431</u>	<u>0.2913</u>	<u>0.6401</u>	0.324	–	
Ours	**0.4103**	**0.3267**	**0.4608**	<u>0.3333</u>	0.4952	**0.25**

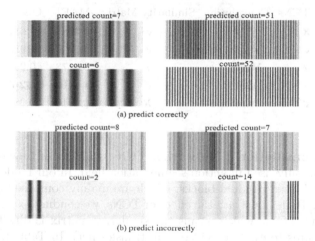

Fig. 4. Visualization of prediction results. The results in (a) is the samples that are predicted correctly. The left in (b) indicates that there is interference in the background. The right in (b) shows various duration of actions.

4.3 Ablation Study

We perform several ablations to justify the decisions made while designing the model.

Frame Rate. In our paper, we are the first to introduce full temporal resolution into repetition counting field, which can provide rich information for network. However, considering the maximum duration of the video, in order to reduce the computational burden, we sample input videos with different frame rates. In Table 3, we compare the performance of different frame rate. Too small frame rate results in redundancy of information, while too large frame rate will lead to ignorance of some repetitions. With the consideration of performance and efficiency, we set the frame rate to 5.

Table 3. Ablation study of different frame rate on the RepCount dataset.

frame rate	MAE↓	OBO↑
1	0.4366	0.3
2	0.6455	0.2667
3	0.5231	0.3067
4	0.4343	0.32
5 (ours)	**0.4103**	**0.3267**
6	0.4131	0.3133

Table 4. Ablation study of the full temporal resolution, TCNs and similarity matrix on RepCount dataset. The number behind the convolution indicates the kernel size. ✗ indicates we remove the TCNs, convolution or similarity matrix.

TCNs	Convolution	Similarity Matrix	MAE↓	OBO↑
✗	✗	✓	0.4683	0.2667
✓	Vanilla/1	✓	0.578	0.1933
✓	Vanilla/3	✓	0.4573	0.24
✓	Dilated/3	✓	**0.4103**	**0.3267**
✓	Dilated/3	✗	0.4715	0.28

Temporal Convolutional Networks. TCNs is a class of time-series models, which is commonly used in action segmentation field. In our model, TCNs contains several dilated residual blocks, which are mainly composed of 1D dilated convolutions. To demonstrate the effect of TCNs, we conduct experiment on the model without TCNs, which means the similarity matrix is directly generated by video features (outputs of video swin transformer). In Table 4, we find that vanilla convolution does not bring great improvement in performance, on the contrary, it may cause a decrease in performance. The reason for this may be the limited receptive field of vanilla convolution, which could not get information from a global view. Besides, the use of dilated convolution can obtain improvements on MAE by 12.39% and OBO by 24.50% compared to the model without convolution, which is because dilated convolution has a larger receptive field and can capture similar patterns in long videos.

In Table 5, we further perform ablations on the number of dilated residual blocks. This observation shows that it is the most appropriate to set the number of blocks to 6. The number of blocks means the depth of the network. More blocks mean that we can get higher-level features, but the blocks are not the more the better, too many blocks are not necessary, which may cause a decrease in performance.

Temporal Self-Similarity Matrix. Temporal self-similarity matrix contains much information about the relevance and irrelevance of actions, and also pro-

Table 5. Performance of different number of dilated residual blocks on the RepCount dataset. When there are six residual blocks, both OBO and MAE can achieve the best results.

nums of blocks	MAE↓	OBO↑
4	0.4126	0.3
6	**0.4103**	**0.3267**
8	0.4333	0.2667
10	0.486	0.2867
12	0.4172	0.26
14	0.4327	0.2667
16	0.4612	0.2733

vides interpretation for model's predictions. In Table 4, we perform ablations on the similarity matrix. The results demonstrate that similarity matrix is an important part of the model, which can bring improvement on MAE by 12.98% and OBO by 16.68%.

5   Conclusion

In this paper, considering the problems of existing methods in dealing with long videos, we propose a model based on full temporal resolution together with temporal convolutional networks for repetition counting. Our model makes the first attempt to introduce the full temporal resolution into the repetition field. Using dilated convolution can have a huge receptive filed and make it possible to get fined-grained information as well as capturing long-range dependencies. Experimental results show that our model performs better than other video-level models on RepCount dataset and generalizes well on multiple datasets.

Acknowledgements. This work is supported in part by the National Natural Science Foundation of China under Grant 62261160652; in part by the National Natural Science Foundation of China under Grant 61733011; in part by the National Natural Science Foundation of China under Grant 62206075; in part by the National Natural Science Foundation of China under Grant 52275013; in part by the Guang-Dong Basic and Applied Basic Research Foundation under Grant 2021A1515110438; in part by the Guangdong Basic and Applied Basic Research Foundation under Grant 2020B1515120064; in part by the Shenzhen Science and Technology Program under Grant JCYJ20210324120214040; in part by the National Key Research and Development Program of China under Grant 2022YFC3601700.

References

1. Azy, O., Ahuja, N.: Segmentation of periodically moving objects. In: 2008 19th International Conference on Pattern Recognition, pp. 1–4. IEEE (2008)
2. Briassouli, A., Ahuja, N.: Extraction and analysis of multiple periodic motions in video sequences. IEEE Trans. Pattern Anal. Mach. Intell. **29**(7), 1244–1261 (2007)
3. Cutler, R., Davis, L.S.: Robust real-time periodic motion detection, analysis, and applications. IEEE Trans. Pattern Anal. Mach. Intell. **22**(8), 781–796 (2000)
4. Dwibedi, D., Aytar, Y., Tompson, J., Sermanet, P., Zisserman, A.: Counting out time: class agnostic video repetition counting in the wild. In: Proceedings of the IEEE/CVF Conference on Computer Vision and Pattern Recognition, pp. 10387–10396 (2020)
5. Farha, Y.A., Gall, J.: MS-TCN: multi-stage temporal convolutional network for action segmentation. In: Proceedings of the IEEE/CVF Conference on Computer Vision and Pattern Recognition, pp. 3575–3584 (2019)
6. Feichtenhofer, C.: X3D: expanding architectures for efficient video recognition. In: Proceedings of the IEEE/CVF Conference on Computer Vision and Pattern Recognition, pp. 203–213 (2020)
7. Hu, H., Dong, S., Zhao, Y., Lian, D., Li, Z., Gao, S.: TransRAC: encoding multi-scale temporal correlation with transformers for repetitive action counting. In: Proceedings of the IEEE/CVF Conference on Computer Vision and Pattern Recognition, pp. 19013–19022 (2022)
8. Lea, C., Flynn, M.D., Vidal, R., Reiter, A., Hager, G.D.: Temporal convolutional networks for action segmentation and detection. In: Proceedings of the IEEE Conference on Computer Vision and Pattern Recognition, pp. 156–165 (2017)
9. Levy, O., Wolf, L.: Live repetition counting. In: Proceedings of the IEEE International Conference on Computer Vision, pp. 3020–3028 (2015)
10. Liu, Z., et al.: Video Swin transformer. In: Proceedings of the IEEE/CVF Conference on Computer Vision and Pattern Recognition, pp. 3202–3211 (2022)
11. Liu, Z., Wang, L., Wu, W., Qian, C., Lu, T.: Tam: temporal adaptive module for video recognition. In: Proceedings of the IEEE/CVF International Conference on Computer Vision, pp. 13708–13718 (2021)
12. Pogalin, E., Smeulders, A.W., Thean, A.H.: Visual quasi-periodicity. In: 2008 IEEE Conference on Computer Vision and Pattern Recognition, pp. 1–8. IEEE (2008)
13. Soomro, K., Zamir, A.R., Shah, M.: UCF101: a dataset of 101 human actions classes from videos in the wild. arXiv preprint arXiv:1212.0402 (2012)
14. Thangali, A., Sclaroff, S.: Periodic motion detection and estimation via space-time sampling. In: 2005 Seventh IEEE Workshops on Applications of Computer Vision (WACV/MOTION 2005)-Volume 1, vol. 2, pp. 176–182. IEEE (2005)
15. Tsai, P.S., Shah, M., Keiter, K., Kasparis, T.: Cyclic motion detection for motion based recognition. Pattern Recogn. **27**(12), 1591–1603 (1994)
16. Vaswani, A., et al.: Attention is all you need. In: Advances in Neural Information Processing Systems, vol. 30 (2017)
17. Yao, Z., Cheng, X., Zou, Y.: PoseRAC: pose saliency transformer for repetitive action counting. arXiv preprint arXiv:2303.08450 (2023)
18. Zhang, H., Xu, X., Han, G., He, S.: Context-aware and scale-insensitive temporal repetition counting. In: Proceedings of the IEEE/CVF Conference on Computer Vision and Pattern Recognition, pp. 670–678 (2020)
19. Zhang, Y., Shao, L., Snoek, C.G.: Repetitive activity counting by sight and sound. In: Proceedings of the IEEE/CVF Conference on Computer Vision and Pattern Recognition, pp. 14070–14079 (2021)

Human-Robot Interactive Operating System for Underwater Manipulators Based on Hand Gesture Recognition

Yufei Zhang, Zheyu Hu, Dawei Tu$^{(\boxtimes)}$, and Xu Zhang

School of Mechatronic Engineering and Automation, Shanghai University, Shanghai, China
tdw@shu.edu.cn

Abstract. Manipulators are the primary tool for robotic operations, and human-robot interaction for manipulators is an effective way in complex environments or dealing with complex operational tasks. This paper focuses on developing a human-robot interactive operating system for underwater ECA ARM 5E-Micro manipulator based on hand gesture recognition. The system used an RGB-D camera to acquire the operator's hand gestures and a hand image segmentation method was proposed based on color images combined with depth information. A convex hull algorithm and image moments were used to extract hand contour features, and then hand gesture was recognized by using Hu invariant moment features and KNN classification algorithm. The experiment results showed that the human-robot interactive operating system for underwater manipulators based on hand gesture recognition has a good hand gesture recognition rate and interaction effectiveness. This study provides a solution for implementing human-robot interaction for underwater robots.

Keywords: Hand gesture recognition · Human-robot interaction · Image segmentation · Feature extraction

1 Introduction

Human-robot interactive operation for manipulators is an effective way in complex environments or dealing with complex operational tasks [1], by using the operator's (human) hand gestures to issue the control commands to the manipulator. The key to this method is hand gesture recognition based on data gloves or vision sensors [2]. Vision sensors are widely used in human-robot interaction because of their natural, non-contact and low-cost characteristics [3]. In general, hand gesture recognition based on vision sensor includes hand image segmentation, hand contour extraction, gesture classification recognition and so on. Therefore, they will be discussed correspondingly in this paper including: RGB-D camera was used as the vision sensor; hand image segmentation was performed by fusing depth information with color images of the hand; hand contour features were extracted using convex hull algorithm and image moments; hand gesture recognition was achieved through Hu invariant moment features and KNN classification

H. Yang et al. (Eds.): ICIRA 2023, LNAI 14267, pp. 575–586, 2023.
https://doi.org/10.1007/978-981-99-6483-3_49

algorithm. The proposed system was experimentally verified to have an excellent hand gesture recognition rate and interaction effectiveness. This research provides a practical implementation solution for the human-robot interaction of underwater manipulators.

2 Human-Robot Interactive Operating System for Underwater Manipulator

Human-robot interactive operating system for underwater robots is shown in Fig. 1. An operator, an RGB-D camera, a computer and an underwater manipulator comprise the system. The RGB-D camera captures the hand gestures representing the operator's operational intentions. The computer recognizes the hand gestures and transforms them to the underwater manipulator. At the same time, the operator observes the feedback information of manipulator motion and the underwater environment through the human-robot interaction screen, and adjusts the interactive intentions until the task is completed. The operator's hand gestures to the robot command process include hand image segmentation, hand contour detection, hand gesture recognition and other modules.

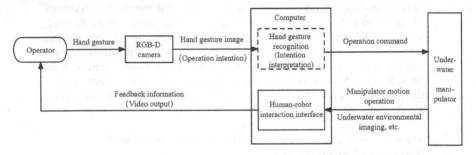

Fig. 1. Human-robot interactive operating system

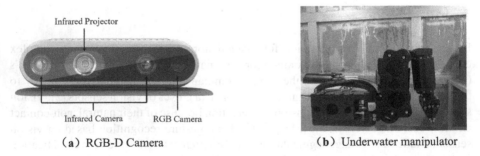

(a) RGB-D Camera   (b) Underwater manipulator

Fig. 2. Main devices of the interactive operating system

The computer used for the system is an Intel Core i7-4700MQ with 16GB RAM and an Nvidia GTX765M graphics card. All programs were developed and ran under Microsoft Windows 10 64-bit with Visual Studio 2017 as the development tool. The chosen RGB-D camera—Intel Realsense D435, is shown in Fig. 2(a). The underwater manipulator is a 5-function lightweight underwater manipulator called ECA ARM 5E-Micro developed by ECA Hytec, France, as shown in Fig. 2(b).

3 Hand Image Segmentation Method Based on Color Image Segmentation Combined with Depth Information

The Intel Realsense D435 provided the RGB color image and the depth image of the hand. The skin color ellipse model [4] in YCbCr space with luminance channel separation was selected to perform the initial segmentation for the acquired hand image. If (Cb, Cr) of the pixel point is inside the ellipse, the pixel is a skin color pixel and its gray value is set to 1 and vice versa, Fig. 3 shows the skin color ellipse model. However, using only color images for hand segmentation will interfere with the segmentation when there are skin color-like environmental colors (such as the color of the carton in Fig. 4(a)), leading to poor hand image segmentation (as shown in Fig. 4b)).

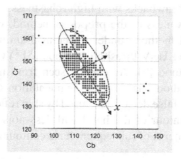

Fig. 3. Skin color ellipse model

The pixel's gray value in the depth map indicates the distance from the point in space to the camera. Hand image segmentation by setting the gray value to 255 for pixels within the depth threshold and 0 for pixels outside is independent of illumination, color, and others. Although using only depth information reduce the impact of skin-like areas and complex backgrounds when acquiring hand image, more details are missing from the hand, as shown in Fig. 4(c). And it is hard to perform proper segmentation when the hand is close to other items.

Therefore, we proposed a hand image segmentation method based on color image segmentation combined with depth information, which relies on the pixels' depth values corresponding to the segmentation results of the skin color ellipse model for further filtering. Combination is defined as follows:

$$M_{out}(i,j) = \begin{cases} M_h(i,j) \wedge M_d(i,j) & N > 0.2N_h \\ M_h(i,j) & else \end{cases} \tag{1}$$

where M_h and N_h are the hand binary image matrix and the number of pixels with a gray value of 255 based on the ellipse model. M_d and N_d are the hand depth image matrix and

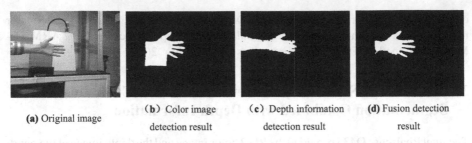

(a) Original image

(b) Color image
detection result

(c) Depth information
detection result

(d) Fusion detection
result

Fig. 4. Detection results

the number of pixels with a gray value of 255. M_{out} represents the output image matrix. N denotes the number of pixels with differences after comparing the corresponding pixels in M_d and M_h. i and j denote the number of rows and columns of the image matrix.

Applying the combination to segment the hand image in Fig. 4(a), a more accurate hand image was obtained, as shown in Fig. 4(d). The proposed method maintains the respective advantages of segmentation based on color image and depth information alone while circumventing both drawbacks with high robustness.

To evaluate the effectiveness of the proposed method, we compared the proposed method with other typical methods under different illumination and the presence of interfering pixels, including HSV threshold method [5], YCbCr threshold method [6] and skin color model method [7]. As can be seen from the experimental results in Table 1, the proposed method has the best segmentation effect except under strong illumination because of the false detection caused by skin reflections, but it still retaining the details of the outer contour of the hand with less noise. Therefore, the proposed method fulfills the requirements of subsequent hand contour feature extraction and hand gesture recognition.

4   Hand Contour Feature Extraction

The accuracy in extracting hand contour feature directly affects the results of hand gesture recognition because the hand contour features have significant representational invariance for the same hand gestures and distinguishability for the different. However, the exposed arm part is inevitably introduced into the picture during the interaction. Even if the operator makes the same type of hand gesture, the length and posture of the arm in the segmented hand image may change (as shown in the original image for the four cases in Table 1), which will affect the subsequent feature extraction. We extracted the hand contours using a convex hull algorithm and then used image moments to remove the arm.

In a two-dimensional image, convex hull can be briefly described as the smallest convex polygon that contains all the points of the stored point set, which effectively in describing features like the shapes of objects [8]. In Fig. 5, the outer contour is the convex hull and the inner contour is the hand contour; the space between the convex hull and the hand contour represents the convexity defect, as shown in regions A to F. The convexity defect comprises a start point, an end point and a far point. The start and end

Table 1. Results of hand image segmentation comparison experiments

	Normal illumination	Weak illumination	Strong illumination	Mass interfering pixels
Original image				
HSV threshold method				
YCbCr threshold method				
Skin color ellipse method				
Proposed method				

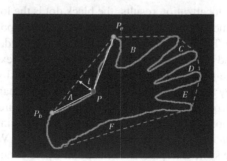

Fig. 5. Convex hull of hand contour and the information it contains

points are defined as the two intersections Pb, Pe of the hand contour and the convex hull's edge in the clockwise direction. The point P is the far point, whose distance to the corresponding edge of the convex hull is the farthest distance l, as illustrated by Fig. 5.

For the hand contour shown in Fig. 5, a screening condition was set to locate the concave point (the far point of the convexity defect B in Fig. 5) based on the information contained in each convexity defect. The concave point is located between the thumb and forefinger with properties such as ease of detection and translational invariance [9]. The screening condition is defined as:

$$
\begin{cases}
10\text{pixel} \le l \\
0.2 \le \frac{P_b P}{P_e P} \le 0.7 \\
30° \le \angle P_b P P_e \le 120°
\end{cases}
\tag{2}
$$

where PbP and PeP are the lengths of the line segments PbP and PeP. $\angle PbPPe$ is the angle between the line segments PbP and PeP. The size of l is specified to eliminate the impact of tiny convex hulls.

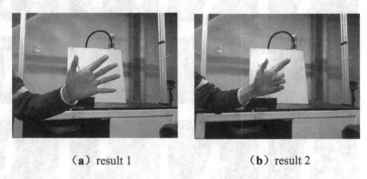

(a) result 1   (b) result 2

Fig. 6. Concave point positioning results

Figure 6 shows the localization results, the black dot is the localized concave point, and the black line segment is the line connecting the concave point with the tips of the thumb and index finger. The proposed screening condition provides accurate localization to the concave point and is adaptable to multiple hand gestures except for fist clenching.

Image moments are features related to the probability density function for the gray value of an image. They are widely applied to understanding images due to their numerical simplicity and interpretability, which can describe a picture's geometric features, e.g., centroid, orientation and area [10]. A hand image coordinate system was established to obtain the hand contour features, as shown in Fig. 7. We set the y-axis of the hand image coordinate system to pass over the point C, the centroid of the image, with the direction pointing in the direction of the hand image. The $p+q$ order moment of the digital image $V(i, j)$ is given as follows:

$$
m_{pq} = \sum_i \sum_j i^p j^q V(i, j)
\tag{3}
$$

The first and second-order moments characterize the centroid $(\bar{x}, \bar{y})$ and direction θ of the image respectively. They are computed as follows:

$$(\bar{x}, \bar{y}) = \left(\frac{m_{10}}{m_{00}}, \frac{m_{01}}{m_{00}} \right) \tag{4}$$

$$\tan 2\theta = \frac{2b}{a - c} \tag{5}$$

where $a = m_{20}/m_{00} - \bar{x}^2$, $b = m_{11}/m_{00} - \overline{xy}$, $c = m_{02}/m_{00} - \bar{y}^2$.

The x-axis of the hand image coordinate system is perpendicular to the y-axis and passes through the concave point P. The origin of the hand image coordinate system Oh is the intersection of the x-axis and the y-axis. θ represents the angle of the y-axis tilt and uOv is the pixel coordinate system of the whole image. To get the hand contour features, we made a dashed line parallel to the x-axis at a distance of L along the opposite direction of the y-axis. Then the gray value of the pixels in the region y less than or equal to -L will be set to 0, while the rest unchanged.

We set $L = 0.6PA$. Compared with Fig. 8(a), the arm is well removed and exactly represents the hand gesture in Fig. 8(b), so the accuracy of the proposed method is verified. In addition, L can be fine-tuned according to the operator's hand to ensure the precision of hand contour feature extraction.

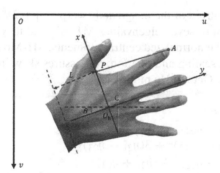

Fig. 7. Hand image coordinate system

5 Hand Gesture Recognition Based on Hu-Invariant Moments and KNN Classification Algorithm

For each particular hand gesture, Hu moments [11] give a specific set of values that can be used to perform hand gesture recognition and classification. Employing they to describe hand image contours addressed the issues posed by transformations such as gesture rotation, scaling and translation during hand gesture recognition.

For a digital image $f(x, y)$, to construct translational invariance, the $p + q$ order central moments are introduced; to construct scale invariance, the central moments are

(**a**) Hand-arm contoure image   (**b**) Hand contour image

Fig. 8. Contour features extract information

normalized to obtain normalized central moments. The $p + q$ order central moments and normalized central moments are defined as follows:

$$\mu_{pq} = \sum_{x=1}^{M} \sum_{y=1}^{N} (x - x_0)^p (y - y_0)^q f(x, y) \tag{6}$$

$$\eta_{pq} = \frac{\mu_{pq}}{\mu_{00}^r} \tag{7}$$

where (x0,y0) is the centroid of the image and r = (p + q + 2)/ 2.

Hu moments consist of seven eigenvalues M1-M7, and they are obtained by mathematically combining the normalized central moments. M1-M6 make the hand contour invariant to translation, scaling and rotation; M7 assures skew invariance to distinguish between mirror images. Get the Hu moments:

$$\begin{cases} M_1 = \eta_{20} + \eta_{02} \\ M_2 = (\eta_{20} - \eta_{02})^2 + 4\eta_{11}^2 \\ M_3 = (\eta_{20} - 3\eta_{12})^2 + 3(\eta_{21} - \eta_{03})^2 \\ M_4 = (\eta_{30} + \eta_{12})^2 + (\eta_{21} + \eta_{03})^2 \\ M_5 = (\eta_{30} + 3\eta_{12})(\eta_{30} + \eta_{12})\left[(\eta_{30} + \eta_{12})^2 - 3(\eta_{21} + \eta_{03})^2\right] \\ \quad + (3\eta_{21} - \eta_{03})(\eta_{21} + \eta_{03})\left[3(\eta_{30} + \eta_{12})^2 - (\eta_{21} + \eta_{03})^2\right] \\ M_6 = (\eta_{20} - \eta_{02})^2\left[(\eta_{30} + \eta_{12})^2 - (\eta_{21} + \eta_{03})^2\right] \\ \quad + 4\eta_{11}(\eta_{30} + \eta_{12})(\eta_{21} + \eta_{03}) \\ M_7 = (3\eta_{21} - \eta_{03})(\eta_{30} + \eta_{12})\left[(\eta_{30} + \eta_{12})^2 - 3(\eta_{21} + \eta_{03})^2\right] \\ \quad + (3\eta_{12} - \eta_{30})(\eta_{21} + \eta_{03})\left[3(\eta_{30} + \eta_{12})^2 - (\eta_{21} + \eta_{03})^2\right] \end{cases} \tag{8}$$

The K-Nearest Neighbors (KNN) classification algorithm is simple and does not require training, so it was adopted after extracting the Hu moments of the hand contours. KNN achieves hand gesture recognition by calculating and comparing the similarity of the hand contours between the hand gesture to be measured and the template gesture. Its core idea is to construct a dataset with different categories of samples, where the sample being-tested is most similar to the K samples in the dataset (i.e., the K most adjacent samples). Whichever category has the most samples among the K most adjacent samples, the sample to be tested also belongs to that category.

We defined the Hu moment similarity D(A,B) between hand contour A and B because the Hu moments of hand contours are the primary basis for the classification of KNN during hand gesture recognition. D(A,B) is calculated as follows:

$$D(A, B) = \sum_{i=1}^{7} \left| \frac{1}{m_i^A} - \frac{1}{m_i^B} \right| \qquad (9)$$

M1 and M7 are not comparable due to the extensive order of magnitude difference, so the Hu moments are log-transformed to be within the same range for comparison, as follows:

$$\begin{cases} m_i^A = sign(M_i^A) \cdot \log(M_i^A) \\ m_i^B = sign(M_i^B) \cdot \log(M_i^B) \end{cases} \qquad (10)$$

where Mi denotes the Hu moment of the gesture contour and mi is the log-transformed Hu moment.

Three hand gestures (as shown in Fig. 10) were selected to complete the motion control of the underwater manipulator, each gesture corresponding to a control command. $0^{\#}$ hand gesture (any direction movement within the visual field of this hand gesture) controls any direction movement of the manipulator; $1^{\#}$ hand gesture indicates opening the gripper; $3^{\#}$ hand gesture indicates closing the gripper.

We built a hand gesture template library and then conducted hand gesture recognition experiments to verify hand gesture recognition accuracy. By acquiring and segmenting the three hand gesture images shown in Fig. 10, a sample set of hand gesture images was developed, which is composed of 30 hand gesture images and 10 for each hand gesture as illustrated by Fig. 9.

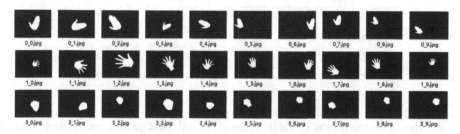

Fig. 9. Sample set of hand gesture images

The hand gesture template library was constructed by calculating and saving the contour's Hu moments of each image within the sample set, Table 2 shows the Hu moments for one sample of each hand gesture contour. Then, we collected 100 hand gesture images of each type, a total of 300 images. Based on the constructed template library, the 300 hand gesture images were recognized using the KNN algorithm according to the similarity D(A,B), and the parameter value K was chosen as 5.

Table 2. Hu moments for each hand gesture contour

Hand gesture	M_1	M_2	M_3	M_4	M_5	M_6	M_7
$0^\#$	0.218510	0.013333	0.00191	0.00024	4.8160e$-$08	1.7289e$-$05	1.6014e$-$07
$1^\#$	0.233947	0.010848	0.00063	0.00012	$-$1.4921e$-$08	1.2000e$-$05	$-$2.9707e$-$08
$3^\#$	0.164818	0.001001	0.00016	1.6170e-06	1.9315e$-$11	2.7139e$-$08	$-$1.7363e$-$11

Figure 10 demonstrates the partial results of the hand gesture recognition, the binary image in the top left corner is the sample with the highest similarity recognized; the black number in the top right corner indicates the kind of hand gesture currently recognized.

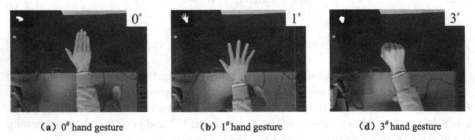

(a) $0^\#$ hand gesture   (b) $1^\#$ hand gesture   (d) $3^\#$ hand gesture

Fig. 10. Partial results for hand gesture recognition

Table 3. Hand gesture recognition rate

Hand gesture	Number of hand gesture images	Number of correct recognition	Recognition rate
$0^\#$	100	92	92%
$1^\#$	100	85	85%
$3^\#$	100	98	98%
Total	300	275	91.67%

As shown by the results in Table 3, the proposed hand gesture recognition method achieves an average accuracy by 91.67%, which satisfies the recognition rate requirement and human-robot interaction needs. However, the recognition rate of $1^\#$ hand gesture is relatively low, which is due to $1^\#$ hand gesture requiring all fingers to be fully opened. But parts of the 100 $1^\#$ hand gesture images collected where the fingers were not fully opened, resulting in too small or no finger gaps and thus making their contours somewhat differ from the $1^\#$ hand gesture contours. Ultimately, they had been misclassified as $0^\#$ or $3^\#$ hand gestures.

6   Experiment and Analysis of Human-Robot Interaction Operations

A further human-robot interaction experiment was carried out to verify the effectiveness of the proposed system by using hand gestures for controlling the manipulator to grasp the target object (rectangular foam) and hold it back to its initial position. According to the experimental process with a total of 4 stages in Fig. 11, the hand gesture processed as $0^{\#}$ hand gesture (moves to the left and forward), $1^{\#}$ hand gesture, $3^{\#}$ hand gesture and $0^{\#}$ hand gesture (moves to the right and backward). In Fig. 11(a), the $0^{\#}$ hand gesture controls the leftward and forward movement of the manipulator, bringing the object within the effective grasping range of the gripper. In Fig. 11(b), the $1^{\#}$ hand gesture opens the gripper to prepare for subsequent grasping of the object. In Fig. 11(c), the $3^{\#}$ hand gesture closes the gripper enabling effective gripping of the target object. In Fig. 11(d), the $0^{\#}$ hand gesture controls the gripper moving rightward and backward thus returning to the initial position. Finally, Fig. 11(a) and (d) jointly show that within the visual field of the $0^{\#}$ hand gesture, the gripper can follow the $0^{\#}$ hand gesture from side to side with excellent spatial position following performance.

The results of the human-robot interaction experiment identify that the manipulator can accurately recognize the operator's hand gestures to achieve the specified function, hence accomplishing the goal of gripping and moving the object, and finally completing the human-robot interaction. The proposed system's interaction effectiveness was proven.

(a) The stage where the manipulator moves to the left and forward

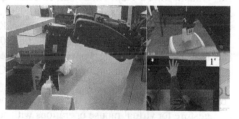

(b) The stage where the manipulator gripper opens

(c) The stage where the manipulator gripper closes

(d) The stage where the manipulator clips the object and returns

Fig. 11. Human-robot interaction experiment for underwater manipulator

7 Conclusion

This paper implements a human-robot interaction operation system based on hand gesture recognition for underwater manipulator. The system used an RGB-D camera to acquire the operator's hand gestures and achieved hand image segmentation by using color images combined with depth information. The hand contour features were extracted using a convex hull algorithm and image moments. Hand gesture recognition through Hu invariant moment with the KNN classification algorithm was achieved. The experimental results showed that the average accuracy of hand gesture recognition is 91.67% and has good human-robot interaction effectiveness. This research provides a solution for implementing human-robot interaction for underwater manipulators.

Acknowledgements. This research was supported by the National Natural Science Foundation of China (Nos. 62176149 and 61673252).

References

1. Chandrasekaran, B., Conrad, J.M.: Human-robot collaboration: a survey. In: SoutheastCon 2015, pp. 1–8. IEEE, Fort Lauderdale (2015)
2. Uwineza, J., Ma, H., Li, B., et al.: Static hand gesture recognition for human robot interaction. In: 2019 Intelligent Robotics and Applications (ICIRA). vol. 11741, pp. 417–430. Springer, Cham (2019)
3. Oudah, M., Al-Naji, A., Chahl, J.: Hand gesture recognition based on Computer Vision: a review of techniques. J. Imag. **6**, 73 (2020)
4. Hsu, R.-L., Abdel-Mottaleb, M., Jain, A.K.: Face detection in color images. IEEE Trans. Pattern Anal. Mach. Intell. **24**, 696–706 (2002)
5. Pan, H., Zhu, Q., Tang, R., et al.: Accurate hand detection method for noisy environments. In: 2018 Cloud Computing and Security (ICCCS). vol. 11068, pp. 360–368. Springer, Cham (2018)
6. Ozturk, O., Aksac, A., Ozyer, T., et al.: Boosting real-time recognition of hand posture and gesture for virtual mouse operations with segmentation. Appl. Intell. **43**, 786–801 (2015)
7. Tang, H.-K., Feng, Z.-Q.: Hand's skin detection based on ellipse clustering. In: 2008 International Symposium on Computer Science and Computational Technology, pp. 758–761. IEEE, Shanghai (2008)
8. Shukla, J., Dwivedi, A.: A method for hand gesture recognition. In: 2014 Fourth International Conference on Communication Systems and Network Technologies, pp. 919–923. IEEE, Bhopal (2014)
9. Mesbahi, S.C., Mahraz, M.A., Riffi, J., et al.: Hand gesture recognition based on convexity approach and background subtraction. In: 2018 International Conference on Intelligent Systems and Computer Vision (ISCV), pp. 1–5. IEEE, Fez (2018)
10. Martín H.J.A., Santos, M., de Lope, J.: Orthogonal variant moments features in image analysis. Inform. Sci. **180**, 846–860 (2010)
11. Ming-Kuei, H.: Visual pattern recognition by moment invariants. IEEE Trans. Inf. Theory **8**, 179–187 (1962)

Registration of Structured Light Camera Point Cloud Data with CT Images

Wencong Chen[1], Juqing Song[1], Shuai Wang[1], and Qinghua Zhang[2,3]([✉])

[1] Department of Mechanical Engineering, Dongguan University of Technology,
Dongguan 523808, China
[2] Department of Neurosurgery, Huazhong University of Science and Technology Union
Shenzhen Hospital, Shenzhen 518052, China
doctorzhanghua@163.com
[3] The 6th Affiliated Hospital of Shenzhen University Health Science Center, Shenzhen
518000, China

Abstract. With the advancement of structured-light cameras, surgical robots equipped with such cameras have been utilized for lesion localization during surgeries. Achieving precise registration between CT images and point cloud data remains a challenge. This study proposes a registration method for CT images and point cloud data. Firstly, the CT images are converted into a point cloud representation, and Feature Histograms (FPFH) are computed based on the point cloud's normal vectors. Subsequently, the Fast Global Registration (FGR) algorithm is employed to perform coarse registration of the point cloud. Finally, the Iterative Closest Point (ICP) algorithm is utilized for fine registration of the point cloud data. Experimental evaluation is conducted using CT images of a human brain model and point cloud data obtained from a structured-light camera. The results demonstrate a favorable registration performance. The coarse registration facilitated by the FGR algorithm serves as an effective initialization for the ICP algorithm, thereby enhancing the convergence speed and accuracy of the fine registration process.

Keywords: Point cloud registration · Surgical robots · Structured-light cameras

1 Introduction

In recent years, the rapid advancement of medical robot technology has brought about revolutionary changes in modern medicine. Among the various domains of medical robotics, surgical robots are widely recognized as one of the most important areas, and significant progress has been made in terms of technological research and product development. With the development of structured light cameras, surgical robots equipped with structured cameras are now capable of precisely locating the site of lesions during surgeries for patients. As shown in Fig. 1, the surgical robot utilizes a structured light camera to determine the exact location where the patient requires craniotomy.

In order to achieve accurate localization of lesions, precise registration between CT images and point cloud data is necessary. Therefore, the first step involves converting CT

H. Yang et al. (Eds.): ICIRA 2023, LNAI 14267, pp. 587–594, 2023.
https://doi.org/10.1007/978-981-99-6483-3_50

images into point cloud data, thereby transforming the problem into an accurate registration between two point clouds. Numerous experts and scholars have proposed various registration approaches. For instance, Chen et al. proposed a coordinate transformation method based on the minimum distance between points and corresponding point tangential planes [1]. This method achieves point cloud registration by computing the minimum distance between each point in the point cloud and its corresponding point's tangential plane. By considering the local shape characteristics of the point cloud, this method enables more accurate registration. Additionally, Guskov extracted local shape descriptors from the point cloud and performed registration through approximated transformations [2]. This method segments the point cloud into subsets and extracts local shape descriptors for each subset, enabling point cloud registration by comparing descriptors among different subsets. Furthermore, H. Alt et al. proposed a geometric structural shape registration method based on Hausdorff distance and Fréchet distance [3]. This method achieves point cloud registration by comparing the geometric structural shape features between two point clouds. Hausdorff distance and Fréchet distance are metrics used to measure shape similarity between two point clouds, and optimizing these metrics enables point cloud registration. Compared to traditional ICP methods, the use of statistical models can provide better results by effectively eliminating outliers, improving convergence, and achieving more accurate geometric matching. The realization of these advantages can be better explained theoretically [4–6]. Zhao et al. have improved the ICP algorithm to enhance registration accuracy [7–9], In addition to the above traditional methods, there are other registration methods using neural networks, such as PointNet++, PointNetLK, etc.[10, 11], but these algorithms have longer registration times and certain hardware requirements.

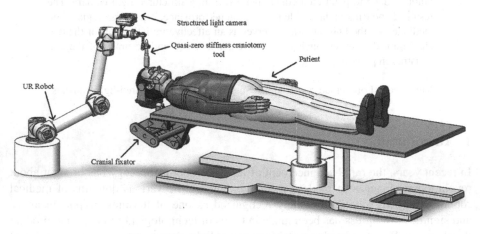

Fig. 1. Surgical robots performing craniotomy

To address the aforementioned challenges, this paper proposes a registration method for CT images and point cloud data. Firstly, the CT images are transformed into a point cloud data representation, and Feature Histograms (FPFH) are computed based on the point cloud's normal vectors. Subsequently, the Fast Global Registration (FGR) algorithm is employed for coarse registration of the point cloud. Finally, the Iterative Closest Point (ICP) algorithm is utilized for fine registration of the point cloud data. Experimental evaluation is conducted using CT images of a human brain model and point cloud data captured by a structured-light camera. The results demonstrate excellent registration performance in both the coarse and fine registration stages. The coarse registration provided by the FGR algorithm serves as a beneficial initialization for the ICP algorithm, significantly improving the convergence speed and accuracy of the fine registration process. This study provides new insights and directions for the development of medical navigation and surgical robots.

2 Point Cloud Preprocessing

Due to the large volume of point cloud data, performing coarse registration using the raw point cloud data would be time-consuming and yield suboptimal results. Therefore, preprocessing of the point cloud data is required prior to coarse registration.

Firstly, a Voxel Down sample technique is applied to down sample the point cloud data. The basic principle of Voxel Down sample is to divide the point cloud space into a series of equally sized voxels and treat each voxel as a single point. Then, a representative point for each voxel is selected. The selection method can involve choosing the point nearest to the voxel's center or the point farthest from the voxel's center. Finally, the resulting point cloud, consisting of all the representative points, serves as the down sampled result.

Next, the Fast Point Feature Histograms (FPFH) are computed. FPFH has advantages such as fast computation speed, insensitivity to noise and varying sampling density, as well as good rotational invariance and repeatability compared to other point cloud feature descriptors. The following steps outline the calculation process.

- Within the neighborhood of a feature point p_q, search for k points and form point pairs by pairing each point with p_k. Calculate the normal vectors of the points n_i and n_j within each point pair and establish coordinate systems between the point pairs.

$$u = n_i \tag{1}$$

$$v = (p_j - p_i) \times u \tag{2}$$

$$w = v \times u \tag{3}$$

- Calculate the angular features between points and construct a feature vector called SFPH (Spin Image Feature Histogram).

$$\alpha = v \cdot n_j \tag{4}$$

$$\phi = (u \cdot (p_j - p_i)) / \|p_j - p_i\| \tag{5}$$

$$\theta = \arctan(w \cdot n_j, \, u \cdot n_j) \tag{6}$$

- Compute the FPFH (Fast Point Feature Histogram) based on the calculated SFPH (Spin Image Feature Histogram).

$$FPFH(p) = SPF(p) + \frac{1}{k} \sum_{i=1}^{1} \frac{1}{w_k} \cdot SPF(p_k) \tag{7}$$

Here, w_k represents the distance between the feature point p_q and its neighboring point p_k.

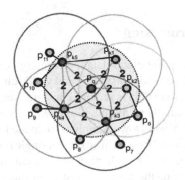

Fig. 2. K-domain computational schematic diagram of FPFH

3   Rough Registration

Fast Global Registration is a feature-based matching algorithm. Firstly, it computes the FPFH (Fast Point Feature Histogram) features for the points p in point cloud P and q in point cloud Q that require registration.

$$F(P) = \{F(p) : p \in P\} \tag{8}$$

$$F(Q) = \{F(q) : q \in Q\} \tag{9}$$

For each F(p) in F(P), the closest F(q) in F(Q) needs to be found. Similarly, for each F(q) in F(Q), the closest F(p) in F(P) needs to be found. These corresponding pairs of points, p and q, are collected into a set K_1, forming the initial correspondence set $K_1 = \{(p_1, q_1), (p_2, q_2), \cdots, (p_n, q_n)\}$. However, in practical scenarios, if K_1 contains a significant number of outliers, it can adversely affect the final computation results. Therefore, the following two rules are applied to filter the point pairs in K_1.

Reciprocity test: For all point pairs (p, q) in K_1, a point pair (p, q) is included in set K_2 if and only if F(p) is the closest point to F(q) in F(P) and F(q) is the closest point to F(p) in F(Q). This test is applied to all point pairs, and the point pairs that satisfy this condition are added to set K_2.

Tuple test: Selecting three point pairs $(p_1, q_1), (p_2, q_2), (p_3, q_3)$ from the set, form two new point pairs (p_1, p_2, p_3) and (q_1, q_2, q_3). Check if these two point pairs satisfy the following conditions. Here, with $\tau = 0.9$, if the above conditions are satisfied, the three point pairs are added to set K_3. If the conditions are not met, the three point pairs are removed.

$$\forall i \neq j, \quad \tau < \frac{\|p_i - p_j\|}{\|q_i - q_j\|} < 1/\tau \tag{10}$$

After completing the aforementioned feature matching, the transformation matrix T is solved based on the following equation.

$$E(\mathbf{T}, \mathbb{L}) = \sum_{(\mathbf{p},\mathbf{q}) \in K_3} l_{\mathbf{p},\mathbf{q}} \left\| \mathbf{p} - \mathbf{Tq}^2 \right\| + \sum_{(\mathbf{p},\mathbf{q}) \in K_3} \Psi(l_{\mathbf{p},\mathbf{q}}) \tag{11}$$

Here, $\Psi(l_{\mathbf{p},\mathbf{q}}) = \mu(\sqrt{l_{p,q}} - 1)^2$, $l_{p,q} = (\frac{\mu}{\mu + \|\mathbf{p} - \mathbf{Tq}\|^2})^2$

The main advantage of defining the objective function in this way is that it allows for improved computational efficiency by alternately optimizing T and L. The optimization process employs a block coordinate descent method, where T is fixed while optimizing L, and L is fixed while optimizing T. Both steps optimize the objective function, ensuring convergence of the objective function.

4 Precise Registration Based on ICP

After the coarse registration, the initial transformation matrix T between the two point clouds is computed. However, the accuracy of the coarse registration is limited, and there may exist deviations between the two point clouds. Therefore, the ICP algorithm is employed for fine registration of the point clouds. The process involves selecting a point p_i from point cloud P and finding the closest point q_i in point cloud Q based on the Euclidean distance to p_i. Then, using the point pair (p_i, q_i), an initial transformation matrix is computed. However, after the coarse registration, this step can be skipped, and the result of the coarse registration is directly used as the initial matrix for fine registration. To improve the computational efficiency during registration, the point cloud data is stored using a k-d tree, which is a binary-tree-like data structure that enhances data retrieval efficiency. By iteratively minimizing the following loss function through multiple iterations, the result of fine registration can be obtained.

$$E(\mathbf{T}) = \sum_{i=1}^{n} \left\| \mathbf{p}_i - \mathbf{Tq}_i \right\|^2 \tag{12}$$

5 Experiment and Analysis

To evaluate the effectiveness and registration performance of the proposed algorithm, a comparative simulation experiment was conducted using a brain model. The point cloud data used in the experiment was acquired using the Zivid2 structured light camera and CT scanning. The improved algorithm proposed in this paper was compared with the classical ICP algorithm. The hardware platform used was a computer with a Core(TM) i7-10870H CPU, 16GB of memory, and Windows 10 64-bit operating system. The CT images were processed using 3D Slicer software, and the point cloud data was processed using PCL 1.11.1. As per the experimental requirements, the CT images were imported into 3D Slicer for 3D reconstruction, and then the point cloud data was exported as shown in Fig. 2.

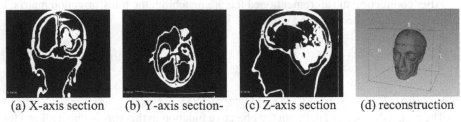

(a) X-axis section   (b) Y-axis section-   (c) Z-axis section   (d) reconstruction

Fig. 3. CT image and reconstructed model.

The point cloud data was preprocessed by cropping the regions of interest and down-sampling the point cloud together. The results are shown in Fig. 3. The facial region was selected for registration in this experiment.

(a) CT point cloud   (b) point cloud   (c) initial status

Fig. 4. The CT image point cloud data and Zivid2 point cloud data.

The FPFH features were computed for both point cloud sets using their respective normal vectors. Subsequently, the Fast Global Registration (FGR) algorithm was applied for coarse alignment of the point clouds. Finally, the Iterative Closest Point (ICP) algorithm was employed for fine registration of the point cloud data. The results are depicted in Fig. 4(a). Figure 4(b) shows the results obtained by directly applying the ICP algorithm (Fig. 5).

By comparing the first two images, it can be observed that the proposed method achieves better registration results. This is because the initial transformation matrix has a significant impact on the performance of the ICP algorithm. If the initial transformation matrix is not appropriate, the algorithm may converge to a local optimum. Performing coarse registration on the point cloud data provides a better initial matrix for the ICP algorithm, resulting in improved registration results. Additionally, it reduces the number of iterations and thus decreases the computation time. The combination of FGR and ICP can obtain better registration results and require less time than other coarse registration algorithms. The computation times for these algorithms are presented in Table 1.

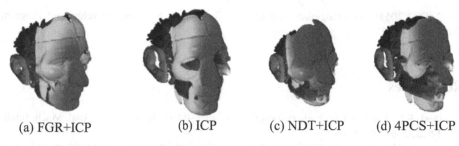

    (a) FGR+ICP   (b) ICP   (c) NDT+ICP   (d) 4PCS+ICP

Fig. 5. The results of point cloud registration.

Table 1. Experimental Results

	Time/s	RMSE/mm
ICP algorithm	3.11	2.043
FGR + ICP	0.258	0.655
NDT + ICP	0.683	1.257
4PCS + ICP	0.821	1.493

6 Conclusion

This paper proposes a registration method for aligning CT images and point cloud data. Firstly, the CT images are converted into point cloud representations, and feature histograms (FPFH) are computed based on the point cloud's normal vectors. Then, the Fast Global Registration (FGR) algorithm is employed for coarse registration of the point cloud. Finally, the Iterative Closest Point (ICP) algorithm is used for fine registration of the point cloud data. Experimental results on CT images of a human brain model and point cloud data captured by a structured light camera demonstrate the effectiveness of the proposed method in achieving accurate registration. Through the comparison between the standalone use of the ICP algorithm and the combination of other coarse registration algorithms with the ICP algorithm, it was found that the FGR+ICP combination can achieve better registration results in this application scenario.

Acknowledgments. This research was Supported by the Joint Funds of Guangdong Basic and Applied Basic Research Foundation (2019A1515110261), National Natural Science Foundation of China (Grant No. 52105009), Shenzhen Science and Technology Plan Project (Grant No. KCXFZ20201221173202007), the Key Scientific Research Platforms and Projects of Guangdong Regular Institutions of Higher Education, China, under Grant 2022KCXTD033, the Scientific Research Capacity Improvement Project of Key Developing Disciplines in Guangdong Province, China, under Grant 2021ZDJS084, the Guangdong Natural Science Foundation, China, under Grant 2023A1515012103, the Key Laboratory of Robotics and Intelligent Equipment of Guangdong Regular Institutions of Higher Education, China, under Grant 2017KSYS009, the Innovation Center of Robotics and Intelligent Equipment, China, under Grant KCYCXPT2017006, the Special Projects in Key Fields from the Department of Education of Guangdong Province

(2022ZDZX2059), the Dongguan Science and Technology of Social Development Program (20221800905072).

References

1. Besl, P.J.: A method for registration of 3-D shapes. IEEE Trans. Pattern Anal. Mach. Intell. **14**(2), 239–256 (2016)
2. Jie, D.: Multi-label classification feature selection algorithm based on neighborhood rough sets. Comput. Res. Develop. **52**(1), 56–65 (2015)
3. Lei, Z.: Constrained improved ICP point cloud registration method. Comput. Eng. Appl. **18**, 197–200 (2012)
4. Tamaki, T.: Softassign and EM-ICP on GPU. IEEE Int. Conf. Network. Comput. **2**(3), 179–183 (2010)
5. Myronenko, A.: Point set registration: coherent point drift. IEEE Trans. Pattern Anal. Mach. Intell. **32**(12), 2262–2275 (2010)
6. Wang, Q.: Point cloud registration algorithm based on NDT and ICP. Comput. Eng. Appl. **56**(07), 88–95 (2020)
7. Li, X.: 2020 Point cloud registration based on neighborhood feature point extraction and matching. Acta Photonica Sinica **49**(04), 255–265 (2020)
8. Zhao, M.: Point cloud registration method integrating sampling consistency and iterative nearest point algorithm. J. Laser Appl. **40**(10), 45–50 (2019)
9. Huang, J.: Point cloud registration algorithm base on ICP algorithm and 3D-NDT algorithm. Int. J. Wireless Mobile Comput. **22**(2), 125–130 (2022)
10. Zhang, Z.: An automatic extraction method on medical feature points based on PointNet++ for robot-assisted knee arthroplasty. Int. J. Med. Robot. Comput. Assist. Surg. **19**(1), 26–38 (2023)
11. Wang, H.: Deep-Learning-Based multiview RGBD sensor system for 3-D face point cloud registration. IEEE Sensor Let. **7**(5), 1–4 (2023)

Automatic Loading and Unloading System with Workpiece Identification Based on YOLOv5

Nianfeng Wang[✉], Junhao Lin, and Xianmin Zhang

Guangdong Key Laboratory of Precision Equipment and Manufacturing Technology,
School of Mechanical and Automotive Engineering, South China University
of Technology, Guangzhou 510641, China
menfwang@scut.edu.cn

Abstract. In the production process, the workpiece must be mounted
and fixed on the machine tool before the machine tool performs various processes on the part's surface. After the process, the workpiece is
removed and placed in the corresponding area. In this paper, a robotic,
automatic loading and unloading system for small workpieces is designed
for machine tools' automatic loading and unloading. In order to find
workpieces in the system, a YOLO-based workpiece object detection
algorithm is used to obtain information about the type and location
of workpieces in the automatic loading and unloading process. For the
problems arising from the experiments, the α-IOU loss function is used
to replace the GIOU loss function in the original network. The experimental results show that α-IOU significantly improves object detection
accuracy compared to GIOU.

Keywords: Workpiece identification · Object detection · Industrial
robot

1 Introduction

In the process of processing the workpieces, not only the machine tool is required
to process the surface of the parts, but it also needs various ways to install and
fix the workpiece to the machine tool. After the machining, the workpiece is
removed and placed in the corresponding area. At present, in the processing
of the loading and unloading process, the quality of the workpiece varies from
hundreds of grams to hundreds of kilograms. Most manufacturing enterprises still
use manual handling for loading and unloading. In the process of processing, the
workforce handling speed is slow. After the handling is completed, the workers
need to select the processing instruction according to the processing workpiece,
which often leads to a long waiting time for the machine to be empty, thus
reducing production efficiency. At the same time, if the workpiece is heavy, it is
difficult and dangerous for workers to carry it. Long-term continuous work can
be harmful to their health. During work, there is often a lack of protection for
workers and workpieces. Once a workpiece drops, it can result in wear or damage
to the surface of the workpiece, more seriously, injury to the worker.

H. Yang et al. (Eds.): ICIRA 2023, LNAI 14267, pp. 595–606, 2023.
https://doi.org/10.1007/978-981-99-6483-3_51

2   Related Work

Most of the research on the automatic loading and unloading of robots can be divided into the following two categories:

Make sure that the position of the workpiece is fixed by the fixture of the feed table each time it is clamped. Then the workpiece is clamped by teaching. Through teaching, put the workpiece into the machine tool, and the three-jaw chuck of the machine tool is automatically clamped by motor control. When the parts are clamped, the feed table rises a certain distance to ensure that the next part is still in the same position waiting to be clamped. In recent years, when designing this clamping system, researchers often use the digital twin system to speed up the debugging process of robot loading and unloading and to verify and optimize the overall system. The teaching method can only passively perform loading and unloading according to the teaching path and position. This method has low technical difficulty and is suitable for large quantities and a few kinds of workpiece processing.

With the improvement of vision sensors, more and more scholars use vision technology to assist the robot in clipping the workpiece. In 1963, Roberts [1] first proposed 3D feature extraction of the workpiece based on the 2D image. In 1975, Tsuji and Nakamura [2]proposed the concept of vision application in industry. Rohrdanz [3] proposed a model-based automatic grasp planning system for robots. Lihui Wang [4] et al. proposed an automatic assembly system that uses three-dimensional visual information to guide robots for assembly. Zhang et al. [5], in many complex workpiece placement scenarios, based on the visual collection workpiece coordinate, using the edge template matching method, complete the workpiece positioning, and according to the hand-eye classify artifacts, can be through the fixed template to identify artifacts.

The development of object detection algorithms can be divided into two stages: based on the traditional vision period and based on the deep neural network period. In recent years, the accuracy and speed of deep learning-based algorithms have greatly surpassed traditional algorithms. Figure 1 shows the development roadmap of the object detection algorithm in the field of object detection from 2001 to 2021.

In the one-stage method, the object detection is completed in one step by the backbone network, and the prediction box is generated to give the category and location information of the object in the image. One-stage has a faster detection speed, but because it does not learn the candidate region, the accuracy of the one-stage algorithm is slightly lower compared to the two-stage object detection network algorithm. Typical one-stage object detection networks include YOLO [6], SSD [7], etc.

The two-stage object detection network can be divided into two parts: The first step is to train the candidate prediction network by using the details in the image. The candidate region prediction network is used to predict the position of the object in the image so that fewer windows with higher accuracy can be generated before the subsequent convolution. The second step is to train the object region detection network. The accuracy of the network is higher, but the

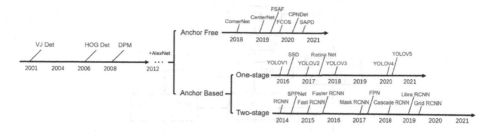

Fig. 1. Target detection development Roadmap.

speed is slower than in the one-stage method. Typical two-stage networks are Fast-RCNN [8], SPPNet [9], R-FCN [10], etc.

Intelligent manufacturing is more emphasis on the processing of a customized variety of workpieces. The number of individual types is small. Therefore, this paper designed a flexible machine tool loading and unloading robot system through the visual camera information, identifying the type of workpiece and locating the workpieces through the clamping module to grasp and install the workpiece so as to achieve the function of processing various types of workpiece loading and unloading.

3 Artifact Object Detection Network

3.1 Construction of Automatic Loading and Unloading System Based on Vision

Robot automatic loading and unloading system consists of the vision system, computer control system, robot, machine tool, and loading-unloading system five parts. The vision system uses the camera to collect workpiece images. It uses LED lamps to illuminate the feeding table so that the camera can collect high-quality images at night or in dim light. The electromagnetic chuck is selected as the actuator of the automatic loading and unloading robot. According to the quality of the workpiece to be clamped, the electromagnetic chuck with different specifications is selected to clamp it. The ball screw lift is selected as the auxiliary mechanism of the loading and unloading platform. After the robot picks up a workpiece, the lift moves up a certain distance so that the next workpiece reaches where the previous workpiece was picked up. The actual operation is shown in Fig. 2, and the overall schematic of the system is shown in Fig. 3.

3.2 Algorithm for Recognizing Workpieces

In this paper, the YOLOv5 object detection algorithm is selected to realize the detection and recognition of the workpiece. The network has the advantages of fast convergence speed, small model size, fast operation speed, and perfect deployment ecology. YOLOv5 uses a typical one-stage structure, and the whole

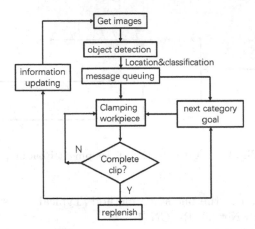

Fig. 2. Automatic loading and unloading system flow chart.

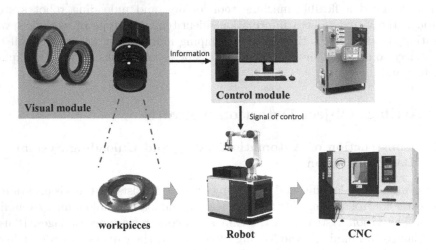

Fig. 3. Automatic loading and unloading system.

model can be divided into four parts: input layer, backbone network, neck, and prediction layer [6]. Figure 4 shows the network structure of YOLOv5 (taking YOLOv5s as an example).

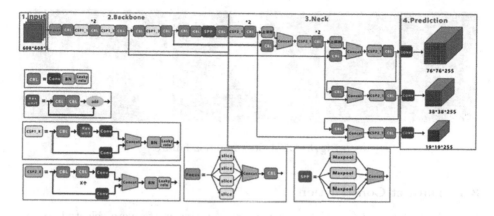

Fig. 4. YOLOv5s Network Structure Diagram.

3.3 Improvement of the YOLO Network

YOLO's DIOU, GIOU, and CIOU can hardly handle the situation where the prediction box is inside the target box, and the center distance is the same. Figure 5 shows the DIOU failure in object detection.

Therefore, an improved loss function is considered to replace the GIOU loss function of the original YOLO.

Even after many improvements, GIOU still has the potential for improvement. Reference proposes the idea of α-IoU, whose formula is shown in Eq. 1, where α is the formula transformation parameter, and IoU is a different type of IoU loss: [11]

$$L_{\alpha-IOU} = \frac{(1 - IOU^{\alpha})}{\alpha} \tag{1}$$

It has the following three essential features:

(1) Order preservation: The α-IOU transform preserves the key performance indices of the original IOU.
(2) Loss revaluation: The property shows that when $0 < \alpha < l$ and $\alpha > 1$, α-IoU adaptively reduces and increases the relative loss of all objects according to the loss of all objects. (2) Loss revaluation: The property shows that when $0 < \alpha < l$ and $\alpha > 1$, α-IoU will adaptively reduce and increase the relative loss of all objects according to the loss of all objects.
(3) Relative gradient weight changes: when $\alpha > 1$, the weight coefficient w ∇ r increases monotonically with the increase of the number of losses, and when $0 < \alpha < 1$, it decreases monotonically with the increase of the IOU value.

Fig. 5. DIOU loss function failure.

3.4   Dataset Construction

Considering the actual needs, seven representative parts were selected to construct the workpiece data set. The following seven parts are called: T-valve, Y-valve, large flange, small flange, blue valve, bolt, and nut. The components are shown in Fig. 6.

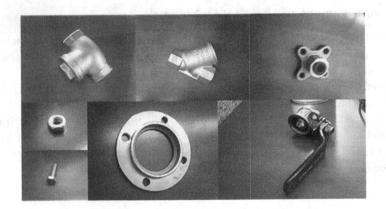

Fig. 6. Pictures of seven workpieces for identification.

According to the observation and analysis of VOC, COCO, ImageNet, and other data sets [7–9], the workpiece data set should have the following requirements:

(1) Include all kinds of workpieces, and the number of samples of each kind of workpiece should be approximately equal to avoid the imbalance of the proportion of different kinds of samples.
(2) The background should include simple background and complex background to ensure that the network can discriminate the detection object in the complex background.
(3) Include images of workpieces under various lighting conditions to simulate the light changes in the system's field of view caused by strong sunlight or dim light in practical applications.

(4) Include multi-perspective images of the workpiece to ensure that the workpiece does not affect the recognition effect when it is placed in different positions during actual recognition.
(5) Include some objects similar in shape and color to the object, which can interfere with the object detection to make the network have better discrimination ability and reduce the probability of misidentification.

According to the size of the object detection data set in the relevant literature [12] et al., the number of images in the training set and validation set is preliminarily determined to be 3000, and the number of images in the test set is 500. In the training set and validation set, the original image is recorded and amplified by image data enhancement. In the original and enhanced images, a certain number of pump and valve images similar to the detected part are added as interferences. In the test set image, the workpiece is retaken, and a certain number of interference images are also added.

According to the dim light and complex background that may occur in practical application, the workpiece image is collected in the complex background and dark light, respectively. In order to train the ability of the network to discriminate different artifacts, a variety of artifacts are mixed and placed, and images with multiple samples in a part of the field of view are taken to improve the ability of the network to recognize objects (Fig. 7).

Fig. 7. Capture the original image and video screenshots.

3.5 Data Amplification

Since collecting original data by the camera is time-consuming and the diversity of sample data collected needs to be improved, data enhancement technology is used to amplify the collected original images. To achieve the purpose of increasing the data volume and enriching the data diversity [13].

The data amplification techniques used in this paper include random flip in single sample enhancement, random angle rotation, random distance translation, random change of image contrast, blur, and other methods.

After the enhancement is completed, the obtained images are manually screened to remove the samples that are unusable due to too vague, missing targets and other factors. After the above enhancement and supplementation, the number of different images in the dataset is shown in Fig. 8 below. According to the statistics, the proportion of samples in the training set is relatively balanced.

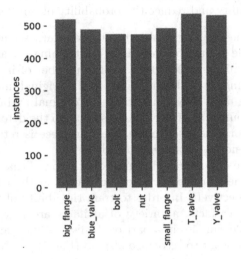

Fig. 8. Sample size statistics.

4   Experiments

In this experiment, the operating system uses Windows10, the programming software is Pycharm, the hardware part uses Intel Core i7-10700CPU@2.9GHz × 12 processor and the parallel computing graphics part uses NVIDIA GEFORCE RTX 3060 graphics card, 16G memory.

The YOLOv5 model is from the open-source Pytorch release published by the authors on GitHub. According to the author's suggestions, RTX3060 requirements for the cuda version, finally Python3.8 version, pytorch1.10.1, cuda11.3 was chosen.

The weight data of YOLOv5s and YOLOv5l trained on the COCO dataset were downloaded for the subsequent pre-training experiment.

During the training experiment, the hyperparameters of the network are set: according to the experience of YOLOv5's author, the frozen feature extraction network is canceled. Two data input methods are used to compare the effects of different input methods in subsequent experiments. The two input methods are 540 × 540 batch size = 16, 928 × 928 batch size = 8, and the optimizer is the Adam function.

4.1   Experimental Design

Two models, YOLOv5s and YOLOv5l, were used in the experiment. GIOU and
α-IOU loss were used in the loss function. The data were loaded in the form of
540 × 540 resolution, batch size = 16, and 928 × 928 resolution, batch size =
8. According to the different model, loss function and loading form, it is divided
into eight groups of experiments. Each experimental group is trained uniformly
for 100 epochs. After training, the model's weight is stored and tested on the test
set. The model's recall, accuracy, mAP@0.5, and mAP@0.5 are counted as four
evaluation indexes, according to the evaluation indexes, to analyze the effect of
model training.

4.2   Results and Analysis

Firstly, the YOLOv5l model is used, and the parameters are selected: the input
resolution ratio is 928 × 928, batch-size = 8, and the loss function is the default
loss function GIOU-loss. The evaluation indexes of various samples are observed
after training for 100 epochs. Table 1 shows the evaluation index values of the
seven types of samples.

Table 1. Each evaluation index value of the seven types of samples.

	P	R	mAP@0.5	mAP@0.5:0.95
big flange	0.994	0.933	0.986	0.953
blue valve	0.961	0.967	0.981	0.917
bolt	0.986	0.981	0.993	0.889
nut	0,98	0.984	0.987	0.70
small flange	0.994	0.987	0.994	0.939
valve	0.99	0.929	0.99	0.956
Y valve	0.977	0.944	0.975	0.933

First, the YOLOv5l model is used, and the parameters are selected: the input
resolution ratio is 928 × 928, batch size = 8, and the loss function is the standard
loss function GIOU-loss. The evaluation indices of different samples are observed
after training for 100 epochs. Table 1 shows the evaluation index values of the
seven types of samples.

Among the seven kinds of workpieces, the accuracy, recall, and mAP@0.5
values of all workpieces are within the acceptable range, but the mAP@0.5:0.95
value of the blue valve, bolt, and nut are low, which means that the identification
and positioning accuracy of the blue valve, bolt, and nut in the identification process is low. Therefore, mAP@0.5:0.95 is the primary focus index in the following
optimization.

On this basis, two models: YOLOv5s and YOLOv5l, are used, and the loss
function is GIOU and α-IOU (α = 2) loss. The data is read from the 540 ×

540 resolution batch size = 16 and the 928 × 928 resolution, batch size = 8. According to the different models, the loss function and reading from it are divided into eight experimental groups to compare and observe the evaluation index of the blue valve, bolt, and nut samples.

The evaluation index of each experimental combination of the blue valve, bolt, and nut is shown in the table below. In the table, when mAP@0.5:0.95 is increased after the use of α-loss, bold words are used to indicate the following (Tables 2,3 and 4):

Table 2. Blue valve experimental combination training results.

Model	Loss function	Batch-size	P	R	mAP@0.5:0.95
YOLOv5l	GIOU	16	0.961	0.967	0.917
YOLOv5l	αIOU	16	0.988	0.922	**0.919**
YOLOv5l	GIOU	8	0.988	0.942	0.916
YOLOv5l	αIOU	8	0.996	0.989	**0.938**
YOLOv5s	GIOU	16	0.987	0.878	0.819
YOLOv5s	αIOU	16	0.965	0.922	**0.849**
YOLOv5s	GIOU	8	0.988	0.922	0.817
YOLOv5s	αIOU	8	0.987	0.867	0.814

Table 3. Bolt experimental combination training results.

Model	Loss function	Batch-size	P	R	mAP@0.5:0.95
YOLOv5l	GIOU	16	0.986	0.981	0.889
YOLOv5l	αIOU	16	0.995	0.959	**0.874**
YOLOv5l	GIOU	8	0.968	0.959	0.842
YOLOv5l	αIOU	8	0.985	0.916	**0.867**
YOLOv5s	GIOU	16	0.954	0.945	0.847
YOLOv5s	αIOU	16	0.991	0.973	**0.867**
YOLOv5s	GIOU	8	0.959	0.973	0.809
YOLOv5s	αIOU	8	0.933	0.949	**0.835**

The following conclusions can be drawn from the above experimental results:

(1) When the batch size, input image size, training epoch, and loss function are the same, the training result of the YOLOv5l model is better than that of YOLOv5s, but YOLOv5l will spend more time on object detection.

(2) When all other things are equal, the experiments using the α-loss function can improve the detected mAP@0.5:0.95 value in most cases compared with the original GIOU loss function.

Table 4. Training results of each nut experiment combination.

Model	Loss function	Batch-size	P	R	mAP@0.5:0.95
YOLOv5l	GIOU	16	0.98	0.984	0.79
YOLOv5l	αIOU	16	0.985	0.951	0.784
YOLOv5l	GIOU	8	0.997	0.984	0.797
YOLOv5l	αIOU	8	1	1	**0.809**
YOLOv5s	GIOU	16	0.983	0.943	0.78
YOLOv5s	αIOU	16	0.978	0.984	**0.792**
YOLOv5s	GIOU	8	0.964	0.951	0.778
YOLOv5s	αIOU	8	0.967	0.976	**0.801**

(3) The use of the α-loss function may slightly decrease the accuracy and recall of some objects in a few cases, but the recall and accuracy are still above 95% after the decrease, which meets the requirements of practical use.

5 Conclusions

This paper takes automatic workpiece loading and unloading as the research object, collects the image of the workpiece, and constructs the workpiece recognition dataset through video interception, network crawling, image enhancement, etc., uses the object detection neural network based on YOLO to realize the workpiece object detection, and improves its IOU loss function. Experiments show that the neural network has a good recognition effect on the workpiece in various scenes. The automatic workpiece loading and unloading system is designed and constructed on this basis.

Acknowledgment. The authors would like to gratefully acknowledge the reviewers comments. This work is supported by National Natural Science Foundation of China (Grant No. 52075180), and the Fundamental Research Funds for the Central Universities.

References

1. Roberts, L.G.: Machine perception of three-dimensional solids, Ph. D. dissertation, Massachusetts Institute of Technology (1963)
2. Tsuji, S., Nakamura, A.: Recognition of an object in a stack of industrial parts. In IJCAI, pp. 811–818 (1975)
3. Röhrdanz, F.: Modellbasierte automatisierte Greifplanung, Ph. D. dissertation (1997)
4. Wang, L., Mohammed, A., Onori, M.: Remote robotic assembly guided by 3D models linking to a real robot. CIRP Ann. **63**(1), 1–4 (2014)

5. Wang, Z., Jia, L., Zhang, L., Zhuang, C.: Pose estimation with mismatching region detection in robot bin picking. In: Huang, Y.A., Wu, H., Liu, H., Yin, Z. (eds.) ICIRA 2017. LNCS (LNAI), vol. 10463, pp. 36–47. Springer, Cham (2017). https://doi.org/10.1007/978-3-319-65292-4_4

6. Bochkovskiy, A., Wang, C-Y., Liao, H.Y.M.: YOLOv4: optimal speed and accuracy of object detection. arXiv preprint arXiv:2004.10934 (2020)

7. Liu, W., et al.: SSD: single shot multibox detector. In: Leibe, B., Matas, J., Sebe, N., Welling, M. (eds.) ECCV 2016. LNCS, vol. 9905, pp. 21–37. Springer, Cham (2016). https://doi.org/10.1007/978-3-319-46448-0_2

8. Girshick, R.: Fast R-CNN. In: Proceedings of the IEEE International Conference on Computer Vision, pp. 1440–1448 (2015)

9. Purkait, P., Zhao, C., Zach, C.: SPP-Net: deep absolute pose regression with synthetic views. arXiv preprint arXiv:1712.03452 (2017)

10. Dai, J., Li, Y., He, K., Sun, J.: R-FCN: object detection via region-based fully convolutional networks. In: Advances in Neural Information Processing Systems, vol. 29 (2016)

11. He, J., Erfani, S., Ma, X., Bailey, J., Chi, Y., Hua, X-S.: Alpha-IoU: a family of power intersection over union losses for bounding box regression. In: Advances in Neural Information Processing Systems, vol. 34, pp. 20230–20242 (2021)

12. Li, L., Fu, M., Zhang, T., Wu, H.Y.: Research on workpiece location algorithm based on improved SSD. Ind. Robot Int. J. Rob. Res. Appl. 49(1), 108–119 (2021)

13. Wang, J., Sun, Z., Guo, P., Zhang, L.: Improved leukocyte detection algorithm of YOLOv5. Comput. Eng. Appl. 58, 134–142 (2022)

Author Index

© The Editor(s) (if applicable) and The Author(s), under exclusive license
to Springer Nature Singapore Pte Ltd. 2023
H. Yang et al. (Eds.): ICIRA 2023, LNAI 14267, pp. 607–609, 2023.
https://doi.org/10.1007/978-981-99-6483-3

Printed in the United States
by Baker & Taylor Publisher Services